A SYSTEMS FRAMEWORK OF THE MARINE FOODS INDUSTRY IN INDIA

A SYSTEMS FRAMEWORK OF THE MARINE FOODS INDUSTRY IN INDIA

Edited by
G.R. KULKARNI
U.K. SRIVASTAVA
PROFESSORS, IIMA

M. Visvesvaraya Industrial Research and Development Centre
BOMBAY
Jointly with
Indian Institute of Management
AHMEDABAD

CONCEPT PUBLISHING COMPANY, NEW DELHI

First Published 1985

Published by

Naurang Rai
Concept Publishing Company
H-13, Bali Nagar
NEW DELHI-110 015 (India)

Printed in India by

Ajit Singh, Printco India
Maujpur, Delhi-110 053

FOREWORD

MARINE fisheries form an important sector of the Indian economy. Not only does it happen to be a major source of livelihood for several thousands of traditional fishermen and others, but it also provides an immensely rich source of protein for the entire Indian population. Added to these are the tremendous prospects for marketing, both domestic and overseas, and the exciting potential that the Exclusive Economic Zone (EEZ) holds for development in future.

Realizing this significant role of the Indian marine fisheries sector, M. Visvesvaraya Industrial Research and Development (MVIRD) Centre, Bombay, organized and conducted an exhaustive scientific research study of this sector. The approach adopted was that of the application of the systems concept for providing an integrated framework for the marine foods industry in India. It is unique in the sense that the industry has never been considered in its entirety so far. The MVIRD Centre takes pride in presenting the findings and results of this study to the readers.

The MVIRD Centre is indebted to Professor G.R. Kulkarni of the Indian Institute of Management (IIM), Ahmedabad, who has throughout been the Advisor to the Centre in planning its strategy for its research activities and for initiating and implementing this research study. The Centre is also thankful to Professor U.K. Srivastava of IIM, Ahmedabad, who in collaboration with Prof. Kulkarni ably edited the various research reports and prepared the manuscript copy. Dr. S.V. Gokhale has rendered valuable assistance to the Centre in co-ordinating and implementing the research work and the Centre is grateful to him.

Finally, the Centre would like to express its sincere thanks to the Indian Institute of Management, Ahmedabad, for extending its co-operation in bringing out this study as a joint publication. It is hoped that the publication will be of considerable use to all those involved in the many sided development of the Indian marine fisheries sector.

President
MVIRD Centre
Bombay.

S.K. WANKHEDE

20 December 1984

PREFACE

M. VISVESVARAYA Industrial Research and Development (MVIRD) Centre, Bombay, has great pleasure in presenting the findings and results of its research study titled *A Systems Study of Marine Foods Industry in India.* As this is the first publication of the MVIRD Centre, it would not be out of place to indicate the research activities of the MVIRD Centre, and the manner in which they are being presently pursued.

The main object of the MVIRD Centre, which is a company set up on June 26, 1970, under Section 25 of the Indian Companies Act, is to promote scientific research in any way or by any means whatsoever and in any area or field. With a view to the attainment of the main object, the Centre provided as the ancillary object, development of a World Trade Centre in Bombay, as an activity of general public utility not carried out for profit.

The Council of Management of the MVIRD Centre constituted a Research Committee consisting of eminent industrialists under the Chairmanship of Shri S.L. Kirloskar with a view to initiating and organizing the Centre's R & D efforts. Since the retirement of Shri S.L. Kirloskar, Shri Pranlal J. Patel is the Chairman of the Research Committee.

While the scope for research activity of the Centre is very wide, the Committee decided that the Centre's effort should be principally directed towards increasing the export potential of the country by application of research in solving problems faced by Indian industry, agriculture and trade and so increasing their productivity and competitiveness, especially in foreign markets. As a World Trade Centre helps considerably the development of international trade in various ways, the Centre pursued the establishment of a World Trade Centre in Bombay consisting of Trade Centre, Commerce

Centre, Exhibition Centre, and so on, on the large piece of land leased by the Government of Maharashtra on very concessional terms in the reclamation area in South Bombay. Such a Centre will be visited by a number of visitors from abroad and up-country. It will serve as a laboratory to the research department in deciding upon the subjects which should be chosen orf research in the interest of its members and the public at large.

Professor G.R. Kulkarni, a faculty member of the Indian Institute of Management (IIM), Ahmedabad, and an eminent expert in international trade, business policy and management kindly agreed to assist the Centre in conducting its research activities. Professor Kulkarni submitted to the Centre a report on "A Research Strategy for MVIRD Centre" outlining in detail the approach and methodology for the Centre's research activities. The salient features of the suggested research strategy are as follows :

1. MVIRD Centre's research activity and the World Trade Centre activity should be complementary and interactive to each other.
2. MVIRD Centre's research efforts should be distinct from those carried out by other institutions and as far as possible duplication of research activity should be avoided.
3. The principal objective of the Centre's research activity should be to gain a scientific understanding of the various factors which affect India's foreign trade flows, so as to assist :

   (i) industry and trade in developing competitive strategies at the aggregate industry and trade levels ;

   (ii) individual exporters and importers in their strategic and operational planning for product development, identification of new products, new technologies, R & D, cost savings, market development, technology and marketing tie-ups, joint ventures, and so on ;

(iii) government, in more realistic planning of production and export targets, framing appropriate policies and controls in the area of foreign trade; and consequently in the areas of economic and technological co-operation and to a limited extent in the area of foreign trade promotion as an instrument of technological modernisation and economic development ; and

(iv) government and industry in negotiating and bargaining for better terms at bilateral and international levels.

4. Accordingly, the Centre's research efforts would basically be of a multi disciplinary nature and outside, especially technical, expertise would require to be utilized wherever necessary and desirable. Such research will be undertaken by the Centre on the basis of its own findings and will not be specifically on behalf of any specific industry or organization. The studies will be made available to the public.

Based on the recommendations of the strategy report submitted by Professor Kulkarni which were fully adopted, the MVIRD Centre set up a nucleus of its Research Department in 1977 and later appointed Shri S.M. Lad (since deceased), formerly Additional Director of Industries, Government of Maharashtra, as Director of Research and Information. In developing its research and other activities, the Centre has a major limitation of finance as it has largely depended upon its own internal resources which are bound to be limited in the early years of development.

MVIRD Centre initiated its research efforts by starting a four-monthly research-oriented journal titled *Visvesvaraya Centre World Trade Review*. As the title indicates the *Review* contains qualitative and quantitative information about the various aspects of international trade with special reference to India and identifies and analyses in the brief editorial the researchable issues and developments having practical and immediate significance. Over a period of time, the *Review* has formed a valuable source material not only for well-documented information about international trade but also for significant developments requiring further in-depth research to be undertaken by the MVIRD Centre itself or elsewhere in the country. The *Review* assists the exporters and entrepreneurs in decision-making and identifying new business opportunities, the government in policy making and planning, and the research institutions and individuals in exploring new directions for research.

The main idea of the systems study emerged from the *Review* and during the discussions the MVIRD Centre's research staff had from time to time with various visitors to and members of the Centre, the government officials, the representatives of financial institutions and the industrial experts. Representatives of the Food and Agricultural Organization (FAO) of the United Nations during their visit to the Centre expressed the view that the Indian marine fisheries sector offers a tremendous growth potential while the European Economic Community (EEC) Buyers' Mission and other foreign visitors evinced keen interest in importing Indian marine products on a large scale as well as in setting up joint ventures. Whereas Indian seafood exporters and banks who are the members of MVIRD Centre indicated problems in promotion of exports and financing the fishing industry, the government officials explained the constraints in policy formulation on sound and scientific basis, especially lack of data.

With a view to eliciting reactions and views of all those involved in the Indian marine fisheries sector with regard to the systems study proposal, the Centre organized, during 1980, a meeting of the representatives from the industry, government and financial institutions to discuss the proposed study. The meeting came to the conclusion that there was a strong need for such a comprehensive research study and the application of the systems approach towards the marine fisheries sector as suggested was, in a sense, unique. The meeting unanimously endorsed the study proposal, and recommended that the MVIRD Centre should go ahead with implementing the study as proposed without any hesitation.

The proposal was approved by the Centre on the recommendations of the Research Committee which was authorized to initiate further steps.

As a first step towards implementation of the systems study, the Centre set up an Advisory Committee under the chairmanship of Shri R.D. Pusalkar (since deceased), past President of the Association of Indian Fishery Industries, to generally guide and supervise the research work and entrusted the responsibility of co-ordinating and directing the research work to Dr. S.V. Gokhale, presently with Konkan Fisheries of Chowgule Group of Industries. The following was the composition of the Advisory Committee :

1. **Late Shri R.D. Pusalkar** —*Chairman*
2. **Dr. T.A. Mammen** —*Member*
   Joint Commissioner (Fisheries)
   Ministry of Agriculture
   Government of India
   New Delhi.
3. **Shri M.A Chidambaram** —*Member*
   Managing Director
   Agricultural Refinance and
   Development Corporation
   Bombay.
   (ARDC—Presently NABARD)
4. **Shri Ghulam Ghouse** —*Member*
   Managing Director
   Agricultural Finance
   Corporation
   Bombay.
5. **Prof. G.R. Kulkarni** —*Member*
   Indian Institute of Management
   Ahmedabad.
6. **Dr. S.V. Gokhale** —*Member and Project Co-ordinator*
7. **Shri D.R. Joshi** —*Member*
   Executive Director
   MVIRD Centre
   Bombay.

8. **Late Shri S.M. Lad** —*Member-Secretary*
Director of Research
MVIRD Centre
Bombay.
9. **Chief Officer** —*Co-opted Member*
SI and SB
State Bank of India
Bombay.
10. **General Manager** —*Co-opted Member*
Maharashtra State
Co-operative Bank
Bombay.

As per the recommendations of the Advisory Committee, the Centre entrusted the assignments relating to carrying out the detailed research work under various sub-systems already identified to the experts in these disciplines.

As the research study is of a comprehensive nature, it was expected to take quite some time for submission of individual reports, their scrutiny and co-ordination with the total scheme finally to be rounded up by the systems study of marine foods industry, which has now been edited and presented by Professors Kulkarni and Srivastava.

The Centre expresses its sincere thanks to the members of the Advisory Committee, the experts associated with the study and the Indian Institute of Management (IIM), Ahmedabad for bringing out this publication and particularly to Professors Kulkarni and Srivastava without whose valuable assistance and guidance it would not have been possible to undertake and publish this study.

MVIRD Centre
Bombay

D.R. JOSHI
Executive Director

ACKNOWLEDGEMENTS

M. VISVESVARAYA Industrial Research and Development (MVIRD) Centre, Bombay, is grateful to the Indian Institute of Management (IIM), Ahmedabad, for extending full co-operation in bringing out "A Systems Study of Marine Foods Industry in India" as a joint publication.

MVIRD Centre is deeply indebted to Professor G.R. Kulkarni of the IIM, Ahmedabad, who has been closely associated with the Centre's research activities and the systems study research project was envisaged and implemented under his valuable guidance. The Centre would like to express its gratitude to Professors Kulkarni and U.K. Srivastava also of IIM, Ahmedabad, for carrying out the difficult task of editing various reports prepared under the systems study and bringing out this publication as well as contributing a chapter on the systems perspective.

The Centre gratefully acknowledges the co-operation extended by the members of the Project Advisory Committee for their valuable guidance in implementing the research project. Particular mention should be made of Shri R.D. Pusalkar, Chairman (since deceased), Dr. S.V. Gokhale, Project Co-ordinator and Shri S.M. Lad (since deceased), Director of Research of MVIRD Centre who made significant contributions to the implementation of the research study.

The list of the members of the Committee is given below:

1. Shri R.D. Pusalkar	Chairman (since deceased)
2. Prof. G.R. Kulkarni	Member
3. Dr. S.V. Gokhale	"
4. Shri Sant Dass	"
5. Shri Ghulam Ghouse	"
6. Shri V. Srinivasan	"

7. Dr. D.B. Kadam Member
8. Dr. T.A. Mammen "
9. Shri S.M. Lad Member-Secretary (since deceased)

The Centre is indebted to the following experts in various disciplines of the Indian marine fisheries, who have contributed papers to this study:

1. Shri K.M. Joseph
2. Shri K. Chidambaram
3. Shri H.P.C. Shetty
4. Shri Anant G. Kalawar
5. Dr. B.S. Saxena
6. Dr. R.G. Dandekar
7. Dr. N.K. Thingalaya
8. Dr. T.A. Mammen
9. Shri T.R. Menon
10. Shri N.P. Bhakta
11. Dr. Prakash C. Raje
12. Prof. G.R. Kulkarni
13. Dr. S.V. Gokhale
14. Mrs. Kamla Suri
15. Dr. U.K. Srivastava
16 Prof. V.K. Gupta

Finally, the Centre thanks various research and other organizations involved in the Indian marine fisheries sector which have extended assistance by making available their information and publications for completion of the study. These include the Central Marine Fisheries Research Institute (CMFRI), the Marine Product Export Development Authority (MPEDA), the Directorates of Fisheries in various states, and the Central Institute of Fisheries Education (CIFE).

PRANLAL J. PATEL

EDITORS' NOTE

THE development of fishing and allied industries has received a special emphasis in the developmental plans because: (i) this sector is eminently suited to assist a large mass of backward and economically weaker sections of the rural community, (ii) it can provide a high quality protein subsidiary food at reasonable prices, and (iii) it has a large export potential. Initially, when the planning began in 1950-51 the total fish production was 7.52 lakh tonnes of which 71 per cent was contributed by the marine sector and the remaining 29 per cent by the inland sector. The production has gone up to 25 lakh tonnes in 1983 with the share of the marine sector being 60.8 per cent. Despite the emphasis on deep sea exploitation from the Second Five Year Plan itself, this increase is far too small as compared with the potential. Marine fish production has been stagnant at nearly 1.5 million tonnes from 1975 onwards.

Initially, the entire production in the marine fisheries sector was mainly by non-mechanized fishing craft and gears which operated within 16 km from the coast. Since the very beginning of the Plans it was recognized that mechanization of fishing craft and improvement of fishing methods were essential for increasing marine fish production. Accordingly, special emphasis has been laid on this aspect since the Second Five Year Plan. As a result of these developmental activities, India has 16,000 small mechanized vessels operating on the coast. The impetus for mechanization mainly came from the export market for prawns and lobsters. As a result, India's marine product exports increased from a mere 17,000 tonnes valued at Rs. 4.13 crore (1960-61) to 85,000 tonnes valued at Rs. 370 crore (1983-84). Exports largely consist of prawns and lobsters. Only to a small extent exports consist of products like dried fish, fish maws, shark fins, fish oil, and so on.

Despite the declaration of the Exclusive Economic Zone (EEZ), the exploitation of offshore fishery resources beyond 50 metres depth has not been very intense in the country. Therefore, both Sixth and Seventh Plans have emphasized strategies for exploitation of deep sea fisheries. They have also emphasized the development of brackish water fisheries for augmentation of prawn production.

These aspects have implications for the complexity of the systems and sub-systems of the marine fishery industry. For example, when most of the boats were non-mechanized (a) they required only beach landings; (b) only non-mechanized boats were in operation hence, no conflicts were observed between various buyers of boat owners; (c) in terms of use flow there was very little use of fish other than in fresh farms; (d) crafts and gears were made by local craftsmen and these required only hereditary skills on the part of fishermen to operate; and (e) the markets were mainly contained to local areas.

The introduction of small trawlers, gill-netters, purse-seines, and so on has resulted in increased marine fish production and has also made the marine fishery system more complex as described below:

(a) The new craft requires landing and berthing facilities.
(b) The construction of craft requires more facilities like boat building yards.
(c) Supply of fishery prerequisites like diesel oil, ice and so on.
(d) Operating of these craft requires skilled persons.
(e) The craft are capital intensive; therefore credit facilities and subsidies have to be arranged.
(f) Along with the introduction of high value export varieties, the phenomenon of low value fish as a predominant part of catch has also to be dealt with.
(g) High value export varieties need processing facilities as fish is exported in fresh, frozen, dried as well as in other forms of byproduct. As per the statistics, about 36,000 tonnes of cold storage capacity, nearly

2,000 tonnes of ice-making capacity and 1,500 tonnes of freezing capacity per day are available in the country. Ten fish meal plants with capacity of 374 tonnes per day and 46 fish pulverisors with capacity of 231 tonnes per day are also operating in the country.*

(h) Use flows of fish catch expanded considerably. Of about 75 per cent of the total fish landing going to domestic market, 31 per cent are sold in dry form, about 14 per cent goes for fish meal extraction, and 11 per cent goes for export markets.

(i) Conflict between the traditional fishermen and mechanized boat owners has emerged and has become severe at various places.

With the intensification of efforts to exploit deep sea fishery resources the sub systems of the marine fishery industry have become even more complex. Some of these are mentioned below:

(i) The fishery resources and variety compositions are not known with certainty.

(ii) Prawn fishery resources are not known to exist in large proportion in the deep sea waters and the varieties known to be available do not have ready market in the domestic sector as yet.

(iii) Lack of knowledge on the part of entrepreneurs regarding the type of vessel required by them is a major constraint in using indigenous vessels, which in turn creates lack of aggressive marketing by indigenous shipyards.

(iv) The indigenous capacity of fishing craft of 20 m and above is extremely limited or almost non-existent. The craft of this type can be acquired either under charter from foreign countries or under joint ventures or imported as owned vessel.

(v) Repair and maintenance of these vessels is very capital intensive as well as time consuming.

*V.K. Gupta, *et al.*, *Marine Fish Marketing in India*, Vol. IV, (New Delhi: Concept Publishing Company), 1983, pp. 328-333.

(vi) If the craft are taken under charter, domestic supplies do not get augmented and gains to the country from the deep sea exploitations are minimal. But this has the advantage of taking care of marketing problems in the export markets.

(vii) In the case of joint venture, vessels can be imported and operated in India and marketing problems can be taken care of by the foreign party under joint venture.

(viii) In the case of owned vessels, the marketing of fish catch in the foreign markets is a very limiting factor, making the economics of these vessels very uncertain.

(ix) The craft are extremely capital intensive and require landing, berthing and processing facilities which are limited at the moment.

(x) As these vessels are highly capital intensive, they require liberal credit arrangements on long-term basis on concessional terms particularly in view of uncertain economics.

(xi) The operation of these vessels requires highly skilled manpower and systems to locate fishery resources which are scarce at the moment. They also require sophisticated managerial resources of the type which are presently available only with large business houses.

(xii) No deep sea fisheries development can take place without the development of a domestic marketing base. This aspect requires development of fishery products from low value and unconventional species. This task requires entrepreneurial skills and has a long gestation period.

(xiii) Along with the technical development the financial requirements of the fishermen have also increased. They have to look for financial support to outside sources which have directed them to organize themselves in a group from where finance could be readily available. As a result the organizations like fishery co-operatives and fishery corporations have come into existence.

(xiv) So far the emphasis has been given mainly on the involvement of fishermen community, but with introduction of the deep sea, non-fishermen would enter the fishing operations.

Similarly, the development of brackish water resources is also a complex task because of the following factors:

1. The commercial side of intensive brackish water culture is highly dependent on seed availability and the seed supply is in a very primitive stage.
2. The technology for prawn seed production and layout of production farm is not fully developed in the country to the level which can facilitate this task. Therefore, in the initial years this technology may have to be imported and adopted.
3. Brackish water culture is highly capital intensive which requires provision for long-term finance on a large scale.
4. The operations require sophisticated managerial skills and trained manpower.
5. Transfer of scientific technology to the farmer in the manner he understands is difficult.
6. The foremost constraint is that almost all the developmental attempts in this field have been experimental in nature and are yet to be adopted at actual farms.
7. Since the payback period of the investment is large, the development of brackish water resources requires several policy support measures, particularly long-term lease of government land.

All the above mentioned complexities of the marine fishery system necessitate a more comprehensive understanding on the part of all the functionaries involved in various sub-components of the sector and also the policy makers at various levels. This book is designed to generate an understanding of the linkages between sub-components of the system and the role of central variables in achieving the goals set for production, export and domestic supply of marine fish.

This book is divided in two parts. Part-I deals with the concept of system and complexity of the marine fishery system. Part-II contains various invited papers by the experts in different fields of marine fishery industry.

LIST OF CONTRIBUTORS

BHAKTA, N.P.
Director
Central Institute of Coastal
Engineering for Fishery
64, Palace Road
Bangalore-560 052

CHIDAMBARAM, K.
Chairman and Managing Director
Matsyasagar Consultancy Services Pvt. Ltd.
32, Mowbrays Road
Madras-600 018

DANDEKAR, R.G.
Dy General Manager (Technical)
National Bank for Agriculture and Rural Development
Sriniketan, III Floor
Dr. Annie Besant Road, Worli
Bombay-400 018

GUPTA, V.K.
Professor
Indian Institute of Management
Ahmedabad-380 015

JOSEPH, K.M.
Exploratory Fisheries Project
Botawala Chambers
Sir P.M. Road, Fort
Bombay-400 001

KALAWAR ANANT, G.
7, Kasturba Bandra Reclamation
Bandra (West)
Bombay-400 050

KULKARNI, G.R.
Professor
Indian Institute of Management
Ahmedabad-380 015

KAMLA SURI (MRS)
E.T.R.B.
Bombay-400 001

LAXMAN, B.
Syndicate Bank H.O.
P. O. Box No. 1
Manipal-576 119

MAMMEN, T.A.
Tropical Fisheries Consultancy Services
C-12, Vivek Vihar
Delhi-110 032

MENON, M.R.
Chief Instructor (Craft and Gear)
CIFNET, Dewans Road
Cochin-682 016

MEHTA, RAJESWAR
Indian Institute of Management
Ahmedabad-380 015

RAJE, PRAKASH C.
Marine Biological Research Station
Konkan Krishi Vidyapeeth
Ratnagiri-514 612

RAMA RAO, P.G.P.
Syndicate Bank H.O.
P. O. Box No. 1
Manipal-576 119

SAXENA, B.S.
Professor
Central Institute of Fisheries Education
Versova
Bombay-400 061

SHETTY, H.P.C.
Director of Instruction
College of Fisheries
Mangalore-575 002

SINGH, AMAR JEET
Dy Manager
Marketing and Purchase
Bhavnagar Vegetable Products Unit
Old Bunder Road
Bhavnagar-380001

SRIVASTAVA, U.K.
Professor
Indian Institute of Management
Ahmedabad-380 015

THINGALAYA, N.K.
Syndicate Bank H.O.
P. O. Box No. 1
Manipal-576 119

CONTENTS

LIST OF TABLES

LIST OF FIGURES

PART ONE

THE MARINE FOODS INDUSTRY : A SYSTEMS FRAMEWORK

1

SYSTEMS APPROACH TO MARINE FOODS INDUSTRY

U.K. SRIVASTAVA
AND
G.R. KULKARNI

SYSTEM'S FRAMEWORK

SYSTEM is a commonly used term that eludes definition in the context of management. "A system may be defined as a regularly interacting or interdependent group of items forming a unified whole".[1]

System has also been defined "as an integrated assembly of interacting elements, to carry out co-operatively a predetermined function".[2] Here the idea is almost the same as in the previous definition with only some changes in words. The term 'system' conjures up the picture of a group of individual entities, each of which has a peculiar part to play, but each of which is entirely dependent for its effectiveness on the other entities. In other words, it is composed of a hierarchy of subsystems. The parts that form the major system may themselves be systems and their parts may be a part of other systems, and so on.

Yet another definition on similar lines is that 'a system is a set of parts co-ordinated to accomplish a set of goals'.[3] The systems concept does not provide a set of rules for solving the problems but it is a useful device for viewing many phenomena. It is, therefore, necessary that a system should be understood as such, so that it could be designed to accomplish its overall purpose. In addition to this, it emphasizes the relationships between the parts and how these relationships affect the performance of the overall system. To understand the idea of a system, we have to consider five basic concepts listed below :

1. The total system objectives, and more specifically the performance measures of the whole system.
2. The system's environment : the fixed constraints.
3. The resources of the system.
4. The components of the system, their activities, goals and measures of performance.
5. The management of the system.

System's objectives

If the objectives of the total system are not well thought of all subsequent steps are futile. In the system's approach, the statements of purpose should be dependent on the performance of the system to be called an objective.

Environment

The system's environment is recognized when it affects the system, but is not under its control.

Resources

Here we have to take into account the resources which exist within the system. These may be of any kind but can be used by the system to meet its own objectives. As this is a decision area, a strong data base is essential.

Components

To enable the specific actions for the system to be effective and operational, the component (sub-systems) needs to be identified so that the action plan can be translated for each sub-system. Once the sub-system is identified, then its performance should be in consonance with the system's objective.

Management

Management is quite crucial and the most operational level of dimensions in system's approach. It involves the generation of a plan for the system which is not an easy job. Planning means outlining a course of action that can be adhered to reach the desired objectives.

MARINE FISHERY SYSTEM

All produce from the sea, whether raw or processed, and used as food are termed marine foods and the industries dealing with marine foods at whatever stage directly or indirectly are covered under the marine foods industry.

In any such industry where various organizations are involved, some amount of confusion and uncertainty in understanding the inter-relationships among their roles is likely to occur. The situation is the same in marine foods industry too. All the member groups involved in the marine foods industry at various stages experience a sense of frustration because of the lack of proper knowledge and interlinkage between them.

The systems approach is a general method by which individual components of a system are analysed as part of a total integrated system with full consideration given to many complex system interactions and inter-relationships. The systems approach has to face various difficulties because of the segmentation of the fishing industry. It comprise many different interests and activities each with its own problems, management objectives, and needs for solution. It is also expected that each facet of the industry attempts to solve its own problems and to reach operational efficiency according to its own standards.

The introduction of mechanized boats which has brought about a substantial increase in production has also brought into focus the need to develop a more complex infrastructure. Permitting foreign vessels to operate in the Indian ocean either as joint venture or chartered vessels has, along with some advantages, brought about conflicts with the traditional fishermen. The increasing export market on the other hand has caused neglect of the domestic markets resulting in shortages and rapid increases in fish price.

In these circumstances, a systems study of the marine foods industry will provide a base for bringing about a balanced growth. The study will be helpful in many ways : (a) to identify the various sub-systems of the whole industry; (b) to understand the manner in which various sub-systems function; and (c) to identify the solution for the conflicts within and among sub-systems so as to optimize proper working of the whole system. Our aims are :

1. To ensure an increase in the production of marine foods —the assessed potential;
2. To devise measures for the protection of interests of traditional fishermen and those depending upon them (crew members) ; and
3. To locate surpluses for export and follow-up measures for maximizing foreign exchange earnings from this source.

OBJECTIVE OF FISHERIES DEVELOPMENT

From the beginning of the development plans, the prime objective for development of the fisheries sector has been to increase fish production, and thereby to bridge the gap between its demand and supply. However, despite the developmental efforts, the objective of increased domestic supplies of fish at reasonable prices has not been achieved. The potential and resources of fish are enough to cater to the need, but the exploitation of the resources is hardly 50 per cent. In recent years, the development of fisheries has been considered to be a prime activity because it is a powerful income and employment generator as it stimulates the growth of a number of subsidiary industries like boat building yards, manufacture of fishing gears, synthetic twine, winches, outer board sinkers, floats, diesel engines, refrigerated cabinets, insulated boxes, establishment of service stations for repairs, ice factories, cold storages, processing plants, and allied infrastructure facilities.

Even in the Seventh Plan which is under preparation, the

prime objective for development of the fishing industry envisages to raise the fish production from 2.5 million tonnes to 4.15 million tonnes by the end of the plan period (1989-90). The target for marine fish production is fixed at 2.5 million tonnes. It has also been decided to achieve the goal of increased marine fish production through : (a) improving efficiency of country craft ; (b) selective operations of mechanized craft ; (c) use of diversified fishing methods ; and (d) deep sea exploitation.

Normally, the efforts are judged by the number of fishing boats being added in the country fleet, but in spite of addition of fishing fleet, year by year, the production has virtually remained stagnant at 1.5 million tonnes during the last five years. The demand for the same has, however, been increasing day by day with the increase in population and per capita incomes. As per the current estimates the gap between demand and supply of marine fish is to the tune of one million tonnes in India. According to the IIMA study[4] the gap between the supply and demand of marine fish in the domestic markets in 1985 will be of the order of 0.94 million tonnes as per liberal estimates and about 1.34 milion tonnes as per conservative estimates. Likewise, the demand for industrial use and exports is expected to increase which will add to the overall gap between supply and demand. It has been estimated that by 1985, these two sectors will need 0.54 million tonnes and 0.39 million tonnes of marine fish respectively. Thus, the total demand for 1985 is expected to be of the order of about 2.3 million tonnes as against the estimated production of 1.55 million tonnes. The National Commission on Agriculture (NCA) has estimated that the marine fish demand will be between 3.59 million tonnes (low estimates) and 5.53 million tonnes (high estimates) by A.D. 2000. The supply would be about 3.5 million tonnes leaving wide gap between the supply and demand (See chapter 13 of this book).

This gap can be filled either by increasing the annual growth rate of fish production to 16 per cent (as against the existing 3.5 per cent) or could be corrected by market forces such as price increase, substitution of other food items for marine fish. Increasing fish prices would not be appropriate because as such, fish prices have increased almost six times in the last ten years which is much higher as compared to increases in the price of other food items (see chapter 12 of this book). Finding the substitution for marine fish will be difficult because developing consumer taste for the substitutes will take time. Hence, the only solution is to increase the production through a rapid development of the fishing industry as we have a substantial potential is lying untapped in deeper waters. This development requires a thorough knowledge and understanding of each of its sub-systems.

The Indian marine fishing industry consists of three distinct sub-sectors.

(i) *Traditional Sector* : Involving inshore water fishing with non-mechanized craft and gears which operate within 16 km. from the coast.

(ii) *Modern Sector* : Consisting of small mechanized boats.

(iii) *Ultramodern Sector*: Consisting of large vessels designed to operate in high seas beyond the areas of operation of traditional and small mechanized craft.

The traditional sector, which forms the base of the Indian fishery industry, accounts for over 67 per cent of the current marine fish production of 1.5 million tonnes. This is followed by the modern and ultra-modern sectors with a share of 32 per cent and 1 per cent respectively. These sub-systems are linked with other sub-systems like input processing, sub-system and marketing sub-system. All of these have interlinkages with each other. Unless all the sub-systems are developed properly, nothing can be achieved because they all are interdependent. The linkages of the major sub-systems industry are presented in Figure 1.1 and resource-wise linkages are given in Figures 1.2, 1.3 and 1.4.

RESOURCES SUB-SYSTEM

The resource sub-system defines the limits of growth and where actual fishing operations take place. India occupies the third

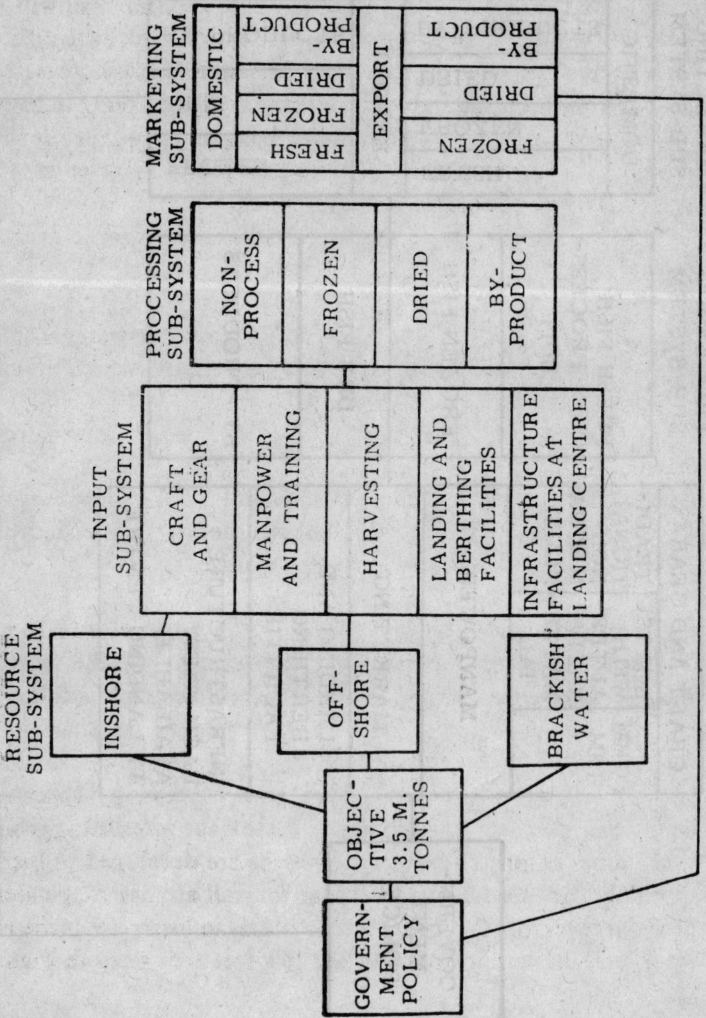

FIG. 1.1 : *Systems chart for marine fisheries*

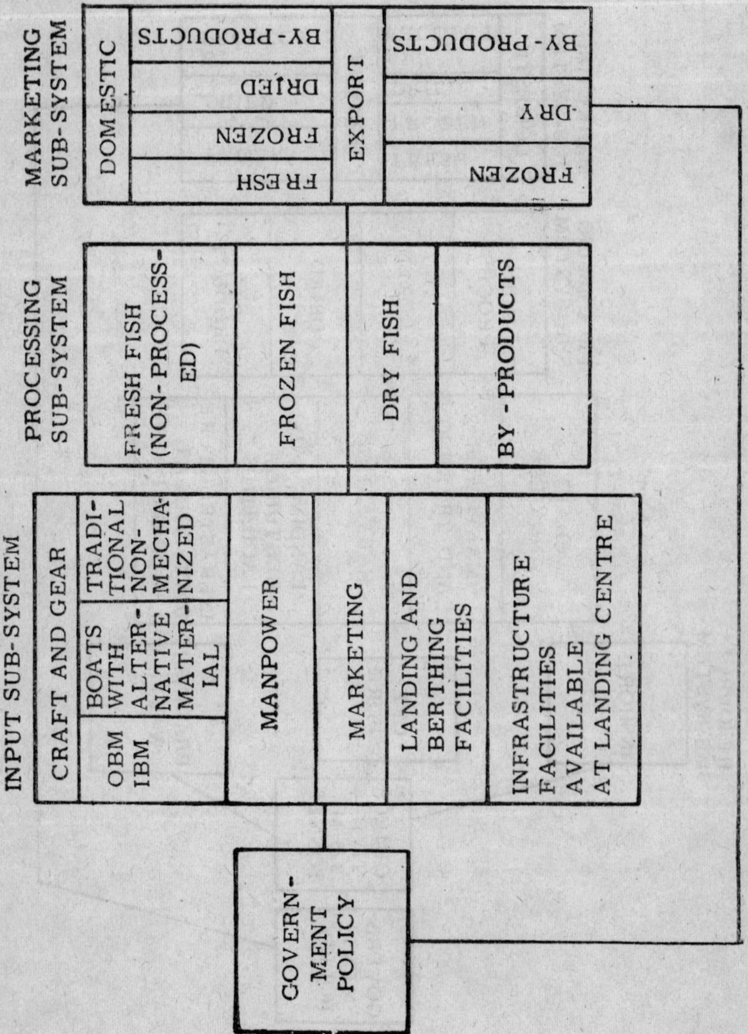

FIG. 1.2 : *Systems chart for inshore resources*

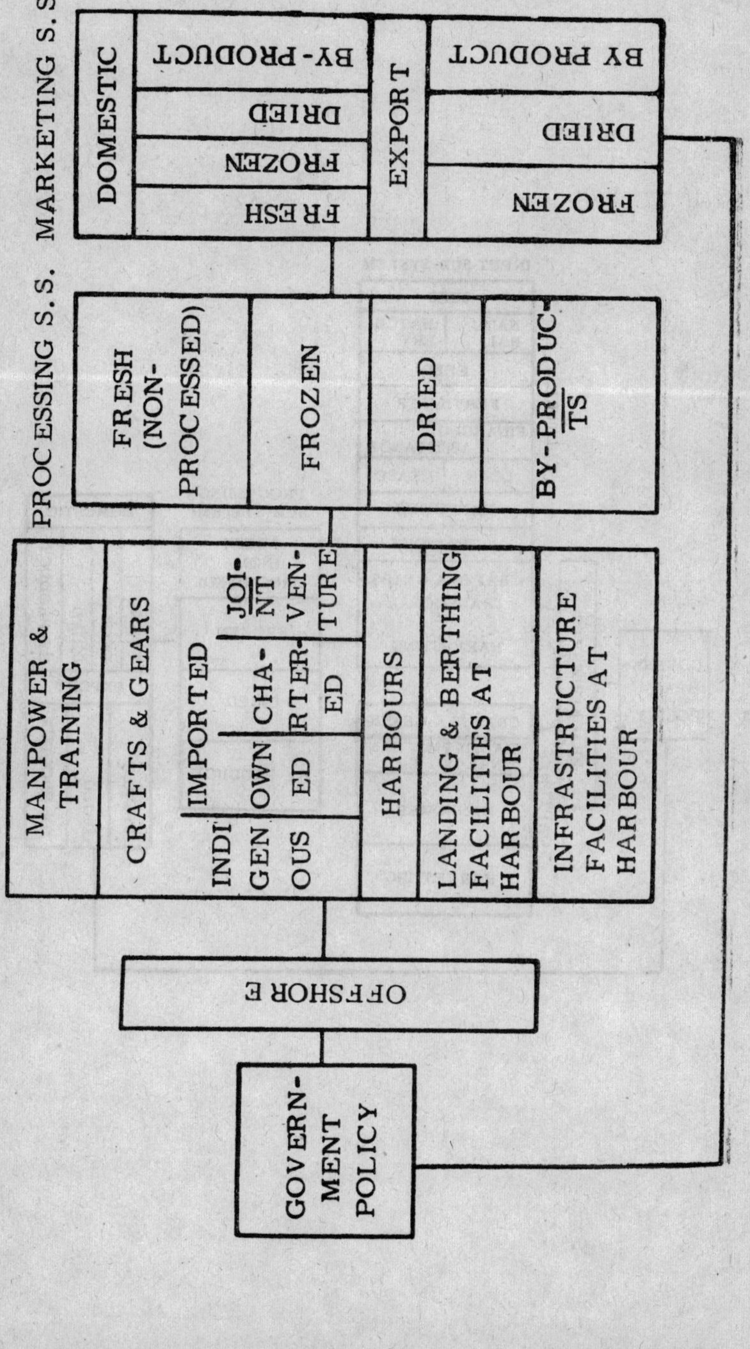

FIG. 1.3 : *Systems chart of offshore fisheries*

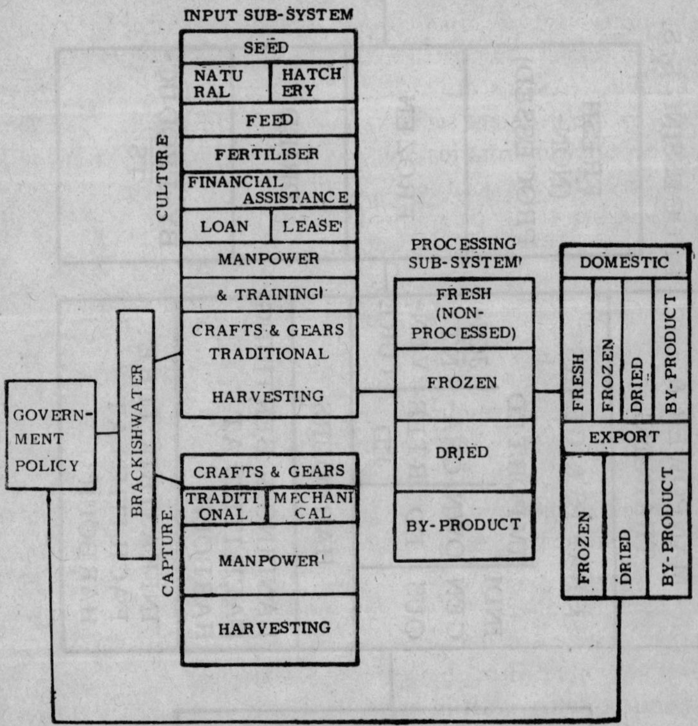

FIG. 1.4 : *Systems chart for brackish water fisheries*

position in the Indo-Pacific region with 2.7 million hectares of water area. India with a coast line of 6,100 kms. has very rich marine fish potential, and EEZ of 2.02 million sq. km. The yield from the Exclusive Economic Zone (EEZ) alone can be about 4.5 million tonnes, if these areas are properly developed.

The National Commision on Agriculture (NCA) in 1976 has estimated a potential of 3.15 million tonnes as a quantity harvestable from Indian waters. Subsequently, in 1977, George and others[5] have estimated the annual potential to be 4.47 million tonnes. The catch figures reveal that hardly 50 per cent of Indian resources are exploited. Moreover, the catch composition by the different sectors reveals that more than 67 per cent of the catch is from inshore regions within 16 km. Hence, we can say that majority of the resources in the waters beyond 16 kms. are lying unexploited. If proper measures are taken to exploit them, they can yield a rapid growth.

The resources can be broadly classified into three categories. They are :

(a) Inshore resources,
(b) Offshore resources, and
(c) Brackish water resources.

Inshore resources

The continental shelf area could be divided broadly into two regions, that is inshore region and offshore region. The inshore region is the area extending up to 50 metres depth range. These are the areas highly exploited and sometimes over exploited also, because the majority of the fishermen operate country craft in areas very near to the sea. However, it is known that the inshore regions are more productive than the offshore region. The possibility of increasing our marine fish catch is much more, if we increase our efforts in inshore areas since tapping our deep sea resources can be very costly.

Marine fish resources can be broadly classified into, (i) west coast resources and (ii) east coast resources.

West coast resources

The length of the west coast is about 3,100 km. and the total area is about 2.05 lakh sq. km. (about 75 per cent of the continental shelf is along the west coast). Marine fishery in this region is developed considerably more than it is along the east coast. At present, more than 70 per cent of the marine fish landings come from the west coast. Of the total 16,000 mechanized boats in operation, 12,000 operate only in the west coast which shows the development of the west coast compared to that of the east coast. The major reason for its development is the west coast accounts for the largest share of high value fish like crustaceans, promfrets, and so on which are mainly exported.

The fish potential of the west coast is estimated to be 2.3 million tonnes comprising 1.5 million tonnes of pelagic and 0.8 million tonnes of demersal fish. Whereas the current average production is only 0.9 million tonnes.[6] If this area is exploited extensively, it can yield at least more than double the current production (see Chapter 3 of this book).

East coast

The length of the east coast is about 2,600 km. and the total area of continental shelf is about 11,780 sq. km. As per the estimates, around 50 per cent of the exclusive economic zone (EEZ) lies in the east coast which implies the importance of its development. Its contribution to fish landings is only about 30 per cent. However, it is found that all the present landings from the east coast are mainly from 23 km. depth. Much resources have remained untapped beyond that depth. The major reason for low development of this east coast could be the narrowness of the continental shelf along the east coast.

Only 25 per cent of the total mechanized boats operate in the east coast. The majority of fishing fleet comprises non-mechanized country craft which operate very near shore areas. The catch comprises different species but it is found that the upper east coast is rich in peneoid prawns.

The potential yield on the basis of exploratory fishing and current landings is estimated to be 4.2 lakh tonnes from the lower east coast and about 6.4 lakh tonnes from the upper east coast. Various studies have estimated the fish potential of the east coast which varies from 10 to 14 lakh tonnes whereas the current production is to the tune of 3.5 lakh tonnes only.

Offshore resources

The declaration of EEZ has opened up new potentials for fisheries development. The deep sea zone (beyond 50 metres depth) contains 38.3 per cent of the total marine potential, while 11.1 per cent of the total potential is in the depth beyond 200 metres. In other words, half of the potential yield is in the inshore zone or in nine per cent of the EEZ.

The importance of deep sea fishing was realized 20 years ago at policy making level. It is estimated that our deep sea resources are capable of producing about 4.5 million tonnes of fish if developed and exploited properly. However, the contribution of the deep sea resources to present catch is hardly one per cent.

Deep sea fishing is highly capital intensive. It requires sophisticated crafts and equipments, and highly skilled personnel too. Owing to the following limitations, development of deep sea fishing is delayed :

(1) Lack of the data on fishery resources of the deeper areas.
(2) Suitability of type of vessel and gear is unknown.
(3) Lack of infrastructure.
(4) Requirement of high investment with high degree of risk as returns are not known.
(5) Non-availability of trained personnel.
(6) Low consumer preference for the majority of deep sea varieties.
(7) Deep sea fishing is mainly export-oriented. High value fish is exported, but there is no developed domestic market for the remaining low value fish.
(8) Lack of suitable harbours and adequate infrastructure facilities constitute the biggest hinderance to the deep sea fishing programme.

As these operations are high by capital intensive, only large business houses can take the risk of investment as the varieties which will be caught are unknown. To encourage small fishermen co-operatives and business houses to enter the deep sea fishing, the government started giving permission to import the foreign vessels either on charter or joint venture or as their own vessels.

So far, the fish potential either in inshore or offshore areas is estimated only on the basis of weight. Not one estimate has been made on the type of species available in certain fishing grounds. If catch compositions are not known, the economic viability of fishing operation cannot be made out. Fishing is basically an economic activity and mainly based on rate of return on capital invested. A fisherman cannot be just expected to exploit certain resources only because a certain quantity of fish (which may be low value fish) is available in the ground. Fishermen have been always selective in their operation. They never go for low value fish which fetch very low prices. The operational expenditure for catching high value fish or low value fish remains almost the same, whereas in the case of returns it always differs with catch composition. The catch of promfret will bring a fisherman around Rs. 20/kg. whereas low value fish will fetch only Re. 1/kg. One may argue that he can make up in quantity what he loses in quality, but the major constraint is that his hold capacity is always limited. Moreover, if he brings more catch of low value fish, then their price declines due to excess quantity in the market.

The reason for fishermen fishing near the coast is obvious. Farther the fishing ground, the operation becomes costlier as it requires more fuel and more powerful vessels. And with the increasing fuel prices, all the fishermen cannot afford to go for deep sea operations. Moreover it takes longer duration also. For deep sea, the craft should be of a different type which will again require more capital investment.

According to the IIMA study[7] the capital/output ratio of a deep sea vessel will be 2 to 3 times that of a traditional craft or a small mechanized boat. Hence, we cannot expect fishermen to go for deep sea fishing unless they are assured of reasonable returns. To some extent this can be assured by assessing the potential of fishing grounds. This is achieved by conducting actual fishing operations on such grounds and calculating yields per unit effort of fishing. However, the results of such experimental fishing cruises are also not indicative of the presence of particular fish as fish is a dynamic population and hence, always migrating. That is the main reason why in all developed nations such surveys are a continuous process and results are made available periodically to the industry.

Brackish water resources

The importance of brackish water culture lies in its capacity to supply exportable prawns. Of the total 182,000 tonnes of prawn production in India in 1980, the share of brackish water was about 30 per cent. Prawns have a place of importance in the export market. Prawn from about 70 per cent of the fish exports in quantity and about 85 per cent in value and India is the largest exporter of prawns.

The need to develop brackish water areas was not felt in the past, as enough catch was available from coastal resources. However, export demand has been increasing and the possibility of increasing prawn catch from the coastal areas is ruled out owing to heavy exploitation of these areas in recent past. In fact in certain areas exploitation crossed the level of sustainable yield and production has started declining. Hence, brackish water areas are the only source for enhancing prawn production.

Information available on the brackish water area and production level does not appear to be reliable. Estimates of the area range from 0.9 million to 2.7 million hectares. According to the IIMA study[8] the estimated area of brackish water in India is about 0.95 million hectares. The area utilization during 1980-81 was only 2.91 per cent of the potential which accounted for a production of about 10,000 tonnes.[9] The estimates of area under utilization by Central Marine Fisheries Research Institute (CMFRI) and IIMA studies are presented in Table-1.1. Only three states namly West Bengal, Kerala and Karnataka have some significant aquaculture programmes for brackish water resource development. In other states the utilization of brackish water area for fish production is negligible. Large areas suitable for brackish water fish farming still remain unutilized primarily due to lack of huge capital investment required for brackish water aquaculture. The main constraint for the potential brackish water areas remaining unutilized could be the lack of facilities like approach roads, protective embankments and feeder canals Table 1.1.

TABLE 1.1. **Estimates of brackish water area potential and area under exploitation in India**

Area potential in '000 ha.
Area utilized in ha.

State	Area potential with sources of data						area utilize as per	
	CMFRI *		NCA (1976)	IIMA (1983)†	Hand-book** of fishery statistics (1981)		CMFRI (1978)‡	IIMA (1983)†
Andhra Pradesh	200	566.5	200	121	150	123	NA	—
Gujarat	376	189.0	376	375	376	187	88	—
Karnataka	8	109.2	180	7	9.5	85	4800	2520
Kerala	243	339.9	200	203	242.8	142	5117	7100
Tamil Nadu	80	145.7	80	47	46.7	72	NA	—
West Bengal	405	817.5	400	404	404.7	210	20000	12530
Maharashtra	81	121.4	80	—	—	70	NA	—
Orissa	299	412.8	8	8	306	8	NA	—
Others	20	—	—	—	0.9	5	NA	—
Total	1712	2702	1424	1165	1536.6	902	3005	22150

Note : *Dr. Silas in *Fourth Conference of Agricultural Research Statisticians*, June 1979.

**U.K. Srivastava, *et al.*, *Inland Fish Marketing in India*, Vol. VI, (New Delhi : Concept Publishing Company, 1984).

†U.K. Srivastava and A.J. Singh, 'Brackish Water Culture : Some Policy Issues', Chapter 5 of this book.

‡Dr. Vedavyasa Rao in *Proceedings of the National Symposium on Shrimp Culture*, MPEDA, August, 1978.

INPUT SUB-SYSTEM

The importance of the input sub-system lies in the involvement of its interlinked sub-systems in increasing the production. It covers the components from actual fishing to fish landing. Only if all the components of this sub-system are well developed, the objective of increased production can be achieved.

CRAFT AND GEARS, CREDIT FACILITIES, SEED AND FEED REQUIREMENTS

Craft and gears are the basic components for the capture of fish. A wide variety of fishing craft and gears is put to use in the coastal waters. In inshore areas non-mechanized (traditional) and small mechanized boats (small trawlers up to 48') have been operating. In the deep sea, big vessels like large trawlers of 17 metres and above in length have been used.

Commercial fishing is carried out by more than two lakh traditional craft, over 16,000 small mechanized boats, and nearly 200 medium and large fishing vessels. The former two types of craft have been operating into inshore region and the last in the deeper zone.

Inshore resource

As mentioned before, over two lakh traditional fishing crafts and more than 16,000 mechanized crafts have been operating in our inshore areas. The details of the various types of traditional crafts and gears operating in coastal areas are presented in a paper by T.R. Menon (See chapter 6). Mainly the small mechanized boats ranging from 9 to 12 metres operate in the sea waters near the coast. The majority of them are Out Board Motors (OBM) or In Board Engine (IBE) type. However, the operation of these mechanized boats is becoming non-viable due to the hike in fuel price and cost of its spare parts as well as the cost of wood itself. The catch and its value have remained almost the same whereas the cost of production has increased 2 to 3 times because of the increase in cost of inputs. (See chapter 17). To overcome the problem of increased cost of wood, at present, boats have to be constructed from materials like FRP/ ferro-cement which are cheaper in cost compared to wood and better in strength.

At present, there are 112 wooden boat building yards in the country with a capacity to construct about 2000 boats a year. In addition to this, there are 17 boat building yards for construction of steel vessels with capacity of 29 vessels per year of various sizes (from 14 to 18 metres). (See chapter 8).

It has been estimated that introduction of 3,500 improved traditional fishing craft in FRP with outboard drives and 5,000 mechanized boats in FRP/ferro-cement for fishing in different regions of the country would be needed for exploitation of our marine resources in the coming decade.

Since normally the operators of the country craft belong to economically weaker classes the government has to provide credit facilities for purchasing either new type of boats (constructed from alternative material) or engine for old non-mechanized boats. Another problem is fuel. The hike in fuel price has prevented the fishermen from going in for deeper waters.

Offshore resources

The development of offshore resources has been the prime objective for fisheries development in the Seventh Plan under preparation. However, there has been no significant development in deep sea fishing in India for the last two decades.

Offshore resources are exploited by big mechanized vessels (mainly trawlers). In India technology development in fishing vessel is quite poor compared to other countries. Our mechanized boats have no onboard freezing facility, hence they cannot go for long voyages.

The indigenous capacity of shipyards building is 122 trawlers a year. However, the capacity in underutilized because of the following:

— Lack of demand
— Lack of the knowledge of entrepreneurs regarding type of trawlers required by them for exploiting deep sea resources.
— Lack of aggressive marketing by indigenous shipyards.

The major reason for lack of demand has been mainly trawler size. The indigenous capacity is restricted to making trawlers of 15 metre length whereas the preference has been normally for 17 metres and above. This has directed the entrepreneurs to import fishing vessels. The preference is found either for charter or joint venture, because in both the cases the investment of the host party has been very less and export marketing has been also taken care of by the foreign party. (See chapters 10 and 11).

In the case of owned vessels, the investment and degree of risk are high. The returns to the investment are not known as the varieties which will be caught are not known. The varieties likely to be caught have no ready domestic market at present because consumer preference is very low. In addition to this, there is no guarantee for export market. Details of the manpower requirements for operating these vessels are given elsewhere.

Credit an important input in case of the offshore exploitations. Till 1975, the only source of fund for acquisition of deep sea fishing vessels is the term loans extended by commercial banks. At present, the Industrial Development Bank of India (IDBI) and NABARD are also extending refinancing facilities for acquisition of deep sea vessels. Moreover, the Shipping Development Fund Committee (SDFC) has been established to extend long term assistance to the National Shipping Industry (NSI) to purchase new as well as second hand deep sea fishing vessels. Shipping Development Fund Committee soft loans are also available for purchase of deep sea vessels at low interest rate. As per the current policy large industrial houses cannot avail soft loans from SFDC.

The number of commercial deep sea vessels (1983-84) operating in Indian sea waters will reveal the picture of preference of big houses for fishing vessels. It is as follows:

Chartered	110
Imported	73
Indigenous	21
	204

All these vessels have been predominently concentrating on shrimps as they have a high export value. In some of the fishing grounds, heavy mechanized fishing has caused over exploitation of shrimps and resulted in a decline of shrimp catch. Another drawback of these vessels is that the low value fish caught by these vessels are thrown back to the sea dead or injured. There is need for a proper policy and infrastructure facilities on the shore for using low value fish.

The catch composition of fish changes as the vessel and the fishing ground change. But the capacity of the vessel is almost same in the case of same type of vessel. The estimates of catch by different type of vessels is given in Table 1.2. It has been found that an efficiently designed small size vessel could perform the functions of large size vessel. If such designs are standardized, boat construction can make rapid progress.

Deep sea exploitation can succeed only if economic from the point of view of investors. Extensive exploitation will require additional fleet. The estimates of fishing boats required by 1990 are given in Table 1.3.

Brackish water resources

Brackish water resources are mainly exploited by two methods: Capture (filtration) and culture. Culture fishing can be broadly classified into intensive culture and semi-intensive culture. Filtration is still done by traditional methods. However, culture practices have been improving.

Development of brackish water farms for fish/prawn culture is highly capital intensive. Brackish water culture is a risky business. Large production fluctuations do not give a guarantee for high returns.

Prawn seed is the most critical input for brackish water culture development. Seed supply is very much in its primitive stage. One should not rely on natural seed sources for supporting intensive brackish water culture. Even in the case of seed collection and rearing, technology is in its infancy. Skills for efficient natural seed collection are yet to be developed. Technology in India is restricted to research level as no commercial hatcheries are operating. Fertilizer feed is another important input in the case of both intensive and

TABLE 1.2 : **Estimated annual landings by different types of boats**

(*Qty : tonnes*)

Vessels	Inshore areas	Offshore areas
Large trawlers over 30 metres	924	660
Medium trawlers of 22 to 30 metres length	462	330
Small wooden boats up to 13 metres	72	—
Lager Purse-seiners	1000	800
Small wooden purse-seiners	65	—

Note : Compiled from various sources.

TABLE 1.3 : **Statewise break-up of additional boats required by 1990 for exploitation of Indian sea resources (Nos.)**

State	Non-mechanized	Mechanized	Deep sea vessels	
			Trawlers	Purse-seiners
Gujarat	4280 (3371)	5829 (2368)	107	—
Maharashtra and Goa	12298 (3349)	3981 (1521)	290	66
Karnataka	3686 (8140)	944 (1183)	35	20
Kerala	15693 (27559)	1268 (2629)	46	36
Tamil Nadu & Pondicherry	964 (44002)	1410 (2363)	40	—
Andhra Pradesh	— (24000)	438 (809)	27	—
Orissa and West Bengal	47931 (10079)	3420 (641)	75	—

Note : Figures in parentheses indicate the existing number of boats in 1980.

Source : V.K. Gupta, *et al.*, *Marine Fish Marketing in India*, Vol. IV (New Delhi : Concept Publishing Company, 1984).

semi-intensive culture. The intensive culture of prawns requires knowledge of their nutrient requirements in order to provide adequate food for its growth and survival. Inadequacy of knowledge of proper feed and mass availability of feed at culture centre is one of the constraint in the successful culture operation.

Most brackish water areas suitable for fish/prawn culture are owned by state governments. Such lands can be economically utilized if a pragmatic policy is adopted to develop them. At present, the lands have been leased for 3 to 5 years for fish/prawn culture. Looking at the high investment and the risk involved in the business, the fish farmer is not sure of good returns because of the short lease. Moreover, short-term lease discourages creating any permanent development over the pond. It is, therefore, advisable to give these lands on long term lease. Long term lease would also be helpful in obtaining credit from financial institutions.

Finance is one of the major constraints for fishermen other way. Support will be fruitful in (*a*) increasing production which will bring better export earnings, and (*b*) uplifting the condition of fishermen. Nationalized banks and other financial institutions have started financing prawn farm schemes in Kerala and West Bengal. NABARD is releasing funds through land development Banks. The Marine Products Export Development Authority (MPEDA) has also taken some measures to promote brackish water prawn culture as an industry for export.

INFRASTRUCTURE FOR LANDING AND BERTHING

Fishing harbours or fish landing centres are an important link between freshness fishing operations and delivery of fishes to consumer. Establishment of fishery harbours with facilities like landing quay, berthing jetties, fuel, ice, water, and so on are essential. Boat and net repair facilities are the prime requirements at fishing harbour. A plan for a model fishery harbour is presented in Figures 1.1 and 1.2 of the paper by N.P. Bhakta. (See chapter 7). In the absence of such prerequisites, increased production cannot bring about an increase in domestic supply because of high rate of wastage.

Till the forties, fishing was mainly done by non-mechanized, sailing craft which required only beach landings. No extra infrastructure was needed because the quantity of the catch was quite low and the fish were sold immediately. With the introduction of mechanized crafts in 1949, the necessity for landing and berthing facilities has been recognized.

At present, the number of mechanized fishing crafts operating in the Indian ocean is estimated to be around 16,000 which includes 204 deep sea fishing vessels. The number of harbour/landing centres catering is about 86 which are designed to cater about 8,640 small mechanized boats and 200 deep sea vessels. It is proposed to develop 54 more harbours/landing centres during the Seventh Plan which will cater 110 deep sea vessels and 6,360 small mechanized boats. However, the progress of construction of landing and berthing facilities for fishing vessels has been found to be very slow. Moreover, landing and berthing facilities at majority of the minor ports have been very poor. Further, management and maintenance of harbours has not received adequate attention after its construction.

Not only landing and berthing facilities but also facilities like cold storages, approach road, and transportation should be made available. At every fishing port, auction and packing hall should be provided and sufficient land for the processors should be earmarked. In the absence of such infrastructure facilities quite a large quantity of fish is wasted on the shore itself. Now it is time to think for constructing better harbours with inbuilt facilities. Fishery harbours (small and big) should be established at suitable places to ensure proper distribution of mechanized boats and proper exploitation of different zones. Jetties may also be constructed.

MANPOWER, TRAINING AND EDUCATION

In developing the marine foods industry, education and training have major roles to play. In the past when all the craft and gears were non-mechanized and locally made, it required only hereditory skills to operate them. Fishing operations were conducted mostly in the areas close to the coast. Hence, skilled personnel were not much in demand.

When deep sea and brackish water resources are to be exploited, the need for training and education for the complex operations has become more intensive. Training needed for both sectors is entirely different. In the case of deep sea operations, the education of fishery grounds and fishery sciences are needed along with the training of operations of deep sea craft and gears, whereas in case of brackish water culture the system is totally different. Prawn culture in brackish water fields has emerged as a multidisciplinary science, which involves many aspects from fishery biology to engineering.

Getting trained manpower and technical assistance have been equally important for brackish water prawn culture. At present, there is a dearth of trained hands for prawn culture. The people engaged in the traditional system of prawn culture will also need training towards scientific prawn farming. Even in the case of prawn culture technology, we are far behind the world. Compared to other countries, our prawn production rate is very low. In Taiwan, as much as 7,500 kg/ha/year prawn production has been reported. Even if we introduce this technology to produce 1000 kg/ha/year in our fields currently under traditional culture, our brackish water production can go up to 30,000 to 45,000 tonnes per year which is hardly 10,000 tonnes at present. Adoption of suitable technology borrowed from developed countries would be helpful in enhancing brackish water prawn production.

Even in the case of inshore operations, training in operating mechanized craft and advanced gears improves the efficiency of the fishermen.

The aim of training is to have both the industrial and traditional sectors of fisheries developed. Skill formation through more sophisticated educational and training programmes assume major significance in manpower planning, as the country attempts to improve its production and utilization process.

The Karnataka University of Agricultural Sciences was the first to establish professional fisheries education and training facilities at university level through the College of Fisheries at Mangalore which was established in 1969. At present, there are many institutes in India connected with fisheries education and training like CIFNET, CMFRI, CIFT, CIFRI, CIFE, and so on. They include basic courses like fishery science, fundamental of marine fisheries, fisheries technology, fishing methods, fishery biology, aquaculture, processing technology, and so on. (See chapter 8 for details of various courses).

Training is needed not only for exploitation but also for processing. The new varieties which are likely to be caught from the deep sea have no market at present. Hence, these varieties need to be processed such a way that they can be acceptable to consumers. The age old processing methods will not help and new processing methods need to be deployed.

So far, nearly 15,000 fishermen have been trained by various fishery institutions. Still there is a gap between demand and availability of trained personnel. The development programme of the deep sea areas for fishing will call for a large number of trained personnel because of the complex nature of fishing grounds and fishing operations. According to one estimate, the country presently requires about 125 fishery graduates and post-graduates every year for the government sector alone. The requirements of the private sector are yet to be assessed but estimates shows that it would be around 250. (See chapter 10).

It is desirable if separate fisheries universities are established in different regions to meet the country's need at different levels. This would ensure the uniformity in educational and training pattern and establish same standard at different professional level in all the institutions. It will also avoid overlapping of the courses.

K. Chidambaram estimated that additional requirement of of trained personnel in the marine fisheries sector in the coming ten years will be to the tune of 1.82 lakh. (See chapter 9). The break-up could be as follows:

	(in '000 numbers)
Capture fisheries	54.5
Culture fisheries	112.4
Utilization and marketing	15.2
	182.1

PROCESSING SUB-SYSTEM

Fish is highly perishable, nature, the fresh fish cannot be stored overnight in normal temperature. At present we do not have onboard processing facilities in our fishing vessels. Hence, fish has to be either kept in ice or chilled store to keep it fresh until it is processed on land.

At present, icing is a widely used method for preserving fish. Two types of ice are used for fish preservation: (a) block ice, and (b) snow ice. However, the use of snow ice is very limited in India as it melts much faster than block ice. Actually, ice is used at different stages of the operation, such as after catching, before processing, during processing, and so on. Storing the fish in cold storages is another way of extending the shelf life of fish. The majority of cold storages in India are used for various purposes. At present, we do not have many cold storages for fish alone.

About 2,000 tonnes of ice making capacity, nearly 36,000 tonnes of cold storage capacity, and about 1,500 tonnes of freezing capacity are available in India. Of these, about one-third of capacity exists in Kerala, another one-third in Maharashtra, and Tamil Nadu, and the remaining in all other maritime states.[10] Such facilities are not available in the interior. Cold and frozen storages should be planned and constructed in the interior also. Each district headquarter should be linked with a cold chain system for further distribution of fish.

Curing is the oldest preservative technique practised by the fishing industry. In spite of the impact of the modern techniques of preservation like freezing, canning, and so on, fish curing continues to occupy an important position in fish preservation.

The share of domestic fresh fish consumption was 43 per cent of the total catch in 1978-79 followed by 31.5 per cent dry edible ; 14.7 per cent fish meal and 10.8 per cent exportable.[11] The majority of the fish is exported in frozen form.

Fish is processed in many ways to make several byproducts. Fishery byproducts means a subsidiary product produced incidently while manufacturing some other major products, or a product made from some part of the fish or out of the waste material resulting from the manufacture of a major product. Some times the entire fish is utilized for the production of byproducts such as fish meal, fish oil, fish manure, and so on. The general idea behind making various byproducts is to utilize the low value fish which have poor demand (due to their small size and poor taste) for augmenting the fish supplies for higher value uses, including the edible uses.

As per the estimates about 25 per cent of the landings consist of 'low value fish'. Previously, a lot of this fish was going for either sun drying, or fish meal, or fish manure, but now with current advancement in technology, new methods have developed to make this fish available for human consumption. Apart from the possibilities of processing or preserving those fish by the age-old traditional method, now it is possible to prepare a variety of palatable products for human consumption.

A large number of fish byproducts have been developed in different forms. (See chapter 15). Unfortunately very few of these products are being produced on commercial scale.

It is estimated that the Integrated Fisheries Project (IFP) is handling about 400 tonnes of low value fish every year making them into finished products. The results of marketing these products are very encouraging.

Till now, we were only bothered for processing the low value varieties which were caught incidentally while catching shrimps. But now the time has come to think of product development. The thrust on development of deep sea resources in the coming years calls for product development as majority of the species which are likely to be caught are not known.

Earlier the returns on investments were known as prawn catch ensured very good price and the price realized for low value fishes was a bonus to the fishermen. The picture is totally different. Nobody has any guarantee of getting enough returns on the huge investment as varieties which are likely to be caught are not known, hence there is no ready market here or abroad. Unless taste for these new varieties is created in the consumers of domestic as well as export markets, deep sea operations cannot be made economically viable. However, there is an urgent need for product development, out of those new varieties, which should aim at—

1. Increasing the shelf life of fish,
2. Making the convenient food available for direct human consumption,
3. Converting low value fish into higher value products.

If this is done then the preference for chartered vessels or owned imported vessels will be more. If catches of deep sea are converted into good high value products, this can help in three ways: (1) in making the fishing operations viable, (2) to add to the country's availability of protein rich food to the consumer, and (3) to boost the export earnings.

The existing technology of product development by various research institutions can possibly utilize these catches and make high value products out of them. Now it is high time to commercialize these technologies in the form of new products.

MARKETING SUB-SYSTEM

Fish marketing can be broadly divided into two categories: (a) domestic market, and (b) export market.

Domestic market

As per the estimates about 45 per cent of the total fish catch is available for domestic market at present. The share of domestic fresh fish consumption to the total availability has declined from 71.2 per cent (1966) to 43.8 per cent (1978-79). (See chapter 12). As a result, the net availability of fresh fish virtually has remained static inspite of increase in the gross availability of fish. The decline in the share of domestic fresh fish can be mainly attributed to lack of proper marketing infrastructure. Another reason for short supply can be the composition of catch by mechanized fleet which were mainly concentrating on shrimps. Low value fish brought along with this just by chance had very low consumer preference, hence, it was mainly going for drying, adding very little to the supplies of table fish to the domestic fresh fish market. As a result, the share of dry edible and fish meal almost doubled whereas the share of domestic fresh fish almost decreased by half. The picture will be very clear if one looks at the useflow pattern of marine fish in 1966 and 1978-79.

Pattern	*1966*	*1978-79*
Fresh	71.2	43.0
Dry edible	17.8	31.5
Fish meal	7.2	14.7
Exportable	3.1	10.8

However, the utilization pattern varies between states depending on the variety composition, consumer taste, and so on. The major constraint in the case of fish marketing is inadequacy of fish markets in India. Even where fish markets exist, very limited infrastructure facilities are available. The majority of markets have very little running water facilities. Quite a large number of markets are highly unhygienic and almost nowhere proper infrastructure facilities for fish preservation is available. As a result, substantial losses in terms of spoilage are noted. Moreover, the existing markets have been unable to accommodate the existing retailers. Almost everywhere the number of retailers has been much more than the capacity. The estimates of the IIMA study[12] reveals that 135 small and 70 medium markets are required to accommodate the existing excess retailers. Moreover, the increased supply will again call for new retailers joining the business which will require 175 small and 247 medium markets. The cost of constructing these additional markets is estimated to be

Rs. 18.54 million for the former, and Rs. 43.72 million for the latter.

In the initial stages, not much importance was given to infrastructure for the development of the industry. But now it is found that resource development alone cannot develop the industry; along with that sufficient infrastructure should also be available. Transportation of fish is very inefficient in India. Due to inadequate transportation, no fresh fish is available in potential markets located 500 miles from the landing centres, whereas the surplus fish at ports is being sent to fish meal plants. If the transport facilities are properly made available, this constraint could be overcome.

Fresh fish consumption in producing centres and nearby places has been nearly 50 per cent of the production. About 45 per cent of the fish has been flowing to the locations within a distance of 200 km. from the producing centres. Hardly 5 per cent goes to the places located beyond 200 km. from the coast. The consumption of fish in metropolitan cities has been around 23 per cent, followed by 31 per cent in urban areas and 46 per cent in rural areas. (See chapter 12). Most of the interstate flows have been around the coast line.

It has been found that more than 50 per cent of fish flows by road transport. A common mode of road transport is open truck. Fish is packed in baskets with ice in 1 : 1 ratio. This can be used only for short distances because of the hot climate of our country. Long distance transport is done by refrigerated rail vans. To coastal areas fish is transported by sea. Among all the modes, sea transport is the cheapest, followed by rail transport (about 2 times of sea transport), and truck transport (2.5 times of sea transport).

Recently use of insulated vans for fresh fish transport has been started but due to its high cost, its usages are limited.

It has been observed that the catches of certain varieties like sardines and mackerels are landed in large quantity in fishing season which results in price crash at producing centres. Moreover, proper exploitation plan will further bring larger quantity of marine fish in the coming years. To add to the shelf life of these catches, it is important to develop a system of cold chain from the producing centre to consuming centre. As per the current estimates as explained earlier, at least 50 per cent of the production will require handling and storing for the domestic markets. The experiments of the Karnataka Fisheries Development Corporation (KFDC) in this aspect has been very encouraging. The IIMA study has suggested a model of cold chain covering the producing and consuming states. This model needs to be considered by the policy makers for implementation in the Seventh Plan.

There are six major types of market intermediaries with different functions in the marine fish trade namely auctioneers, commission agents (purchase); wholesalers, commission agents (sales), retailers and vendors. A few of these intermediaries undertake multiple functions. The processor is an additional intermediary in the case of processed fish.

The share of the fishermen in consumer rupee depends on the number of intermediaries and the distance between landing and consuming centre. The major constraint of the present marketing system is lack of standardization in quality and weighing which has left both fishermen and consumer at the mercy of traders. Financial risks of the intermediaries in the transactions have been more or less coverd by high profit margins and relatively low prices to fishermen. It is necessary that the fishermen are properly rewarded for their strenuous efforts which in turn will encourage them to bring more catch and the way production get accelerated.

In spite of our efforts of encouraging co-operative marketing for the last 25 years, we have not made much headway. Hardly ten per cent of fish is marketed through co-operatives. In fact, it was considered to be a suitable organization for not only increasing fishermen's share in consumer rupee but also for looking after his daily needs. However, co-operatives have more or less failed to either replace the traders or at least give them competition because they did not provide an integrated service covering the input supplies, working capital requirements and marketing as the traders have been doing. In the case of fishery corporations also, the picture has been almost the same as co-operatives. The poor performance of the corporations is because :

(a) unclear objectives,
(b) non-professional management,
(c) unsuitable organizational structure, and
(d) disproportionate financial allocations.

In general, developmental and commercial activities have been mixed up with one another. To make the better working of both co-operatives and corporations, the corporations should confine themselves to developmental activities and co-operatives to make the commercial activities which will make the operations of both viable.

There is an urgent need for establishment of a National Fisheries Development Board for effective policy making and planning on one hand and initiating and co-ordinating national level activities on the other. This will be very helpful in collecting data on national level and developing information system for better policy decisions and planning. The contribution of the National Federation of Fisheries Co-operatives in the marketing of fish in metropolitan cities has also been emphasized in Seventh Five Year Plan.[13]

Export markets

India has acquired an important place in the international fish market. The industry earns foreign exchange worth more than Rs. 300 crore a year. Marine products export from India between 1952-53 and 1982-83 have increased more than three times in terms of quantity and hundred times in terms of value. However, India's share in the world trade of fisheries has been very small in terms of value, which was 2.2 per cent in 1977 and 1.9 per cent in 1980.[14]

Till the end of 1960, marine dried fish constituted the largest component of the export though shipments of frozen items commenced as early as 1953. However, the position has changed after 1960. While the exports of dried items were showing downward trend, the frozen items were making a steady progress.

Before 1960, the markets for Indian marine products were largely confined to developing countries. But as soon as the frozen and canned items figured in our exports, developed and sophisticated markets like USA, Japan, UK started taking interest in our marine products and have become major buyers.

At present India is the single largest supplier of frozen shrimp. Of the 30 items exported from India, frozen shrimps account for nearly 88 per cent in terms of value, and 70 per cent in terms of quantity. (See chapter 14).

As shrimp is the most demanded variety in export markets, fishing efforts have been mainly concentrated on this single item. No efforts have been made by the fishermen community to increase the landings of other varieties of fish as other varieties fetch unremunerative price compared to shrimps. This has affected our exports in two ways :

1. Deep sea resources are not being exploited; as a result no new product figures in exports in significant quantity.
2. The existing inshore shrimp resources have been over-exploited, leading to stagnation or even decline in shrimp catch over the years.

This has directed the industry to develop some other sources for shrimp catch. As a result the development of brackish water shrimp culture has, acquired on extremely commercial necessity.

To overcome the shortage of shrimp supply for exports, one has to think of product development for the non-conventional varieties which are likely to be caught from the deep sea resources. So far no ready export market has been available for such varieties. These have been processed and developed into some tasty products, to increase our exports.

Till 1964, the United States of America was almost the sole buyer of our frozen shrimp. From 1964 onwards Japan started purchasing our marine products and very soon became a major competitor to USA. During 1982, Japan's share formed about 53.6 per cent of the total exports in quantity and 71.5 per cent in terms of value.

There has been a steep fall of dried fish exports since 1978. The trade has definitely received a setback. Its share in the total export is less than one per cent now. At present Sri Lanka is the major buyer of dried fish.

There has been a consistent increase in the unit value realization of our marine products export in recent years. It was as low as Rs. 2.39 per kg. in 1961 and has spurted to Rs. 43.5 per kg. in 1983.

The marine products export target for the Sixth Plan was set at Rs. 555 crores. Though we have touched Rs. 370 crores mark in 1983-84, we are still behind the plan target. The Seventh Plan target has been fixed at around Rs. 700 crore. If we want to achieve this target we have to overcome our certain drawbacks and diversify our export of fishery products, including the products developed out of unconventional varieties.

In order to sustain our exports on a long term basis, there arises an immediate need to diversify our export production and also export markets. Apart from shrimps, there are many other items which hold high export potenial but have not been exploited for export purposes. So far no concerted effort has been made for the export potential of the new items. Our extensive deep sea programme will bring some new species which may be demanded in foreign markets in the coming years. If they are developed properly, it can boost our exports.

As mentioned in earlier paragraphs inshore areas have been overexploited and as a result shrimp production has become stagnant and in some cases even declining, whereas much potential has been lying untouched in deep waters. However, the much demanded shrimps are not available in those waters, but some other species which have very poor consumer demand. If these varieties are developed, it may cross the shrimp demand in export markets. Efforts should be made to develop some new products from those low value species and export them. This will help in two ways :

(a) it will lessen the excess demand for shrimps, and
(b) encourage the fishermen to go for deep sea operations.

The other major constraints for the development of our

export trade are as follows :

1. High freight rates and infrequent sailing.
2. Inadequate processing technology for handling special products for export.
3. Absence of specialized equipment and machinery for preparing and packing special products.
4. Insufficient market information on the varieties other than shrimps.
5. Unwillingness on the part of exporters to take risk.
6. Inadequate and irregular supply of raw material in bulk for export processing.

In spite of the recorded phenomenal growth of our marine food export, we have not reached the stage of catering to the actual consumer market abroad. We just supply in bulk which are re-processed and repacked as per local demands in these countries. The consumers abroad hardly know that the product is from India because our product is just used as raw material, which are reprocessed and repacked according to the consumer needs there. To develop our export trade, now we should think about the required international standards of processing and packing and put our marine foods with Indian brands in foreign markets.

However, introducing new varieties in foreign markets from India needs extraordinary marketing skills. We have to think of comprehensive marketing plan, aggressive promotional efforts if we really want to market our products on our name and enhance the export marketing of our marine foods.

ROLE OF GOVERNMENT POLICY INTERVENTION IN VARIOUS ELEMENTS OF MARINE FISHERY SYSTEM

The government policy support is crucial in the development of all the three types of marine fishery resources : (a) inshore, (b) offshore, and (c) brackish water. (See chapter 2). Again, the role of government policy is crucial for the functioning at various sub-systems of each of the resources : (a) input subsystems, (b) processing, and (c) marketing sub-system. Important policy support measures for strengthening each of the sub-system are briefly indicated in figures 1.5, 1.6 and 1.7. It

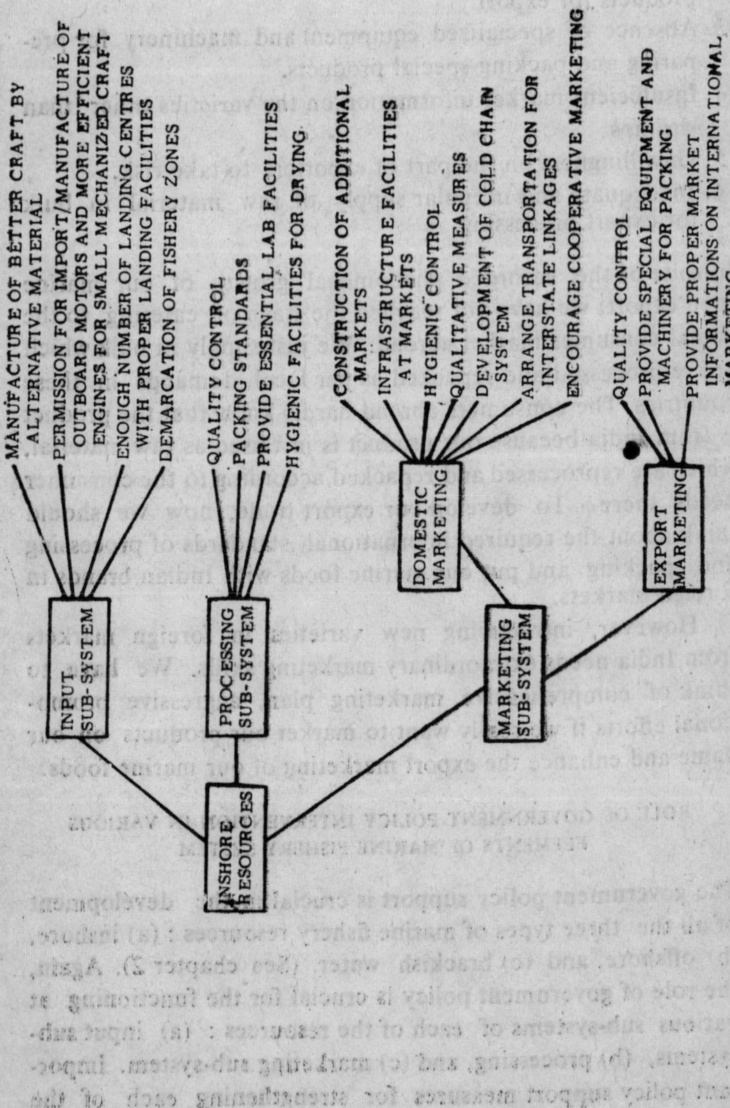

FIG. 1.5 : ***Role of government policy intervention in a systems framework (inshare resources)***

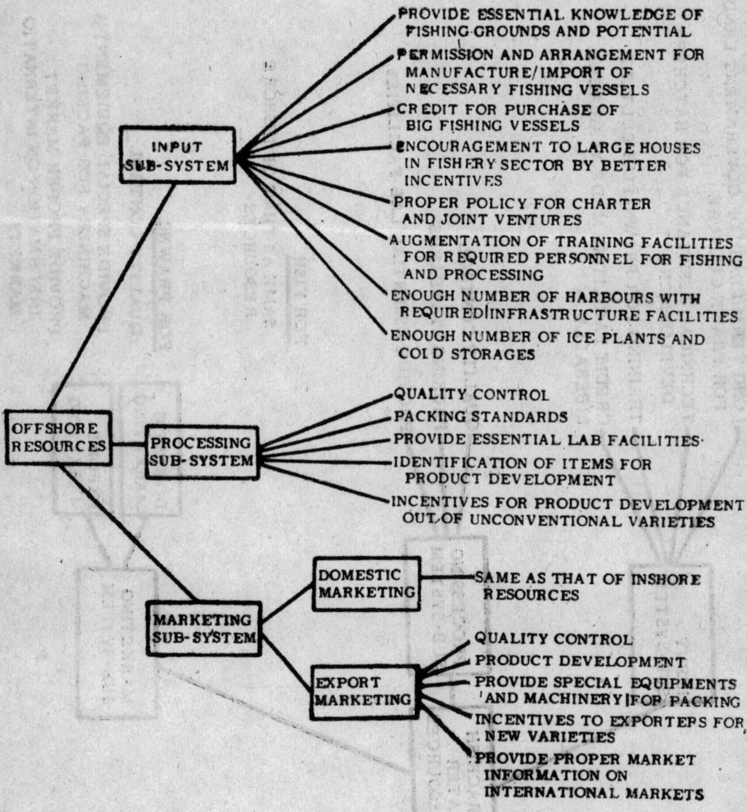

FIG. 1.6 : *Role of government policy intervention in a systems framework (offshore resources)*

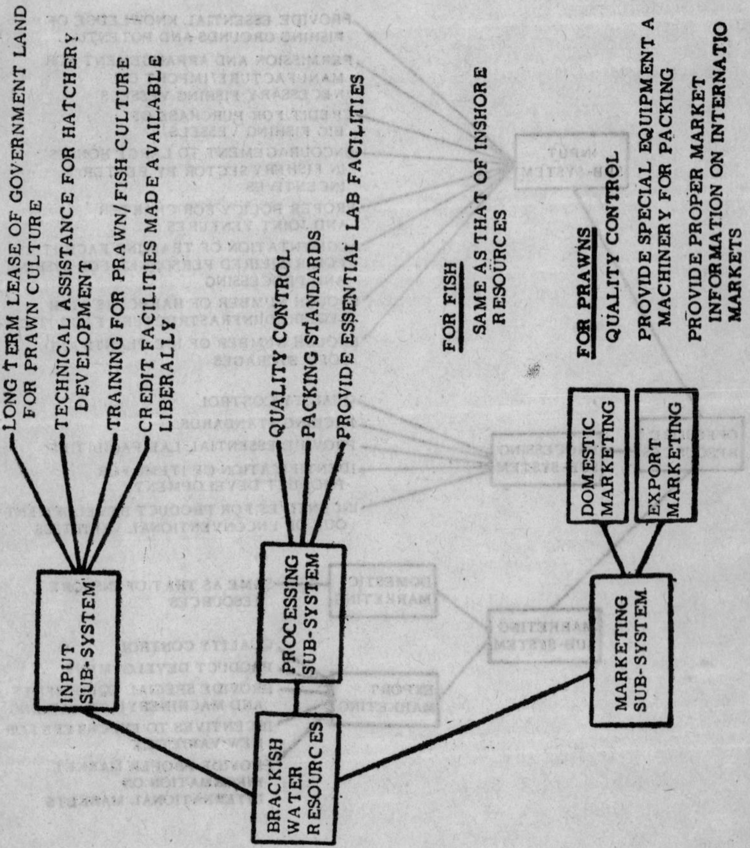

FIG. 1.7 : *Role of government policy intervention in a systems framework (Brakish water resources)*

may be seen from these figures that in the development of both inshore and offshore resources, government policy support measures are extremely crucial in the hitherto neglected area of the marketing sub-system. This is the area which, therefore, requires to be given crucial importance in the Seventh Plan.

In the case of brackish water resources, it is the input sub-system which is most crucial. The upgradation of technology and adoption of practices by the fishermen for prawn culture in these resources considerably depend on the availability of credit, policy with respect to long term lease of government land and liberalization of import of technology. Since, this is a new area, the development of inland fishery resources for augmenting prawn production will require an integrated view as indicated in Figure 1.7.

It can be seen that various policy support measures have to be implemented in a cohesive fashion. In this context it is necessary to emphasize the need for co-ordination and integration of the tasks handled by various ministries if the marine fishery system is to record the required rate of growth.

REFERENCES

1. D.I. Cleland and W.R. King. *Management : A Systems Approach*, (New York : McGrow Hill), 1972.
2. D.I. Cleland and W.R. King, *Systems, Organizations, Analysis, Management : A Book of Reading* (New York : McGraw Hill Book Co. 1969), p. 64.
3. Churchman, C. West, *The Systems Approach* (New York : Delacorte Press, 1968), p. 29.
4. V.K. Gupta, *et al.*, *Marine Fish Marketing in India*, Vol. I, (New Delhi : Concept Publishing Company, 1985).
5. P.C. George, *et al.*, "Fishery Resources of the Indian Economic Zone", in the Souvenir Silver Jubilee Celebration of the Integrated Fisheries Project, Cochin, October 1977.
6. George, *et al.*, *Ibid.*
7. V.K. Gupta, *et al.*, *Marine Fish Marketing in India*, Vol. VII (New Delhi : Concept Publishing Company, 1983)

8. U.K. Srivastava, *et al.*, *Inland Fish Marketing in India*, Vol. VI, (New Delhi : Concept Publishing Company, 1985).
9. *Ibid.*
10. V.K. Gupta, *et al.*, *Marine Fish Marketing in India*, Vol. IV, (New Delhi : Concept Publishing Company, 1983).
11. Amar Jeet Singh and V.K. Gupta, 'Marketing of Marine Fish : Some Policy Issues' in U.K. Srivastava and M.D. Reddy (eds), *Fisheries Development in India* (New Delhi : Concept Publishing Co. 1983).
12. V.K. Gupta, *et al.*, *Marine Fish Marketing in India*, Vol. VII, (New Delhi : Concept Publishing Company, 1983).
13. Report of the Working Group on Fisheries for Formulation of Seventh Five Year Plan (1985-90).
14. S.N. Rao, 'Product Development for Export' in U.K. Srivastava and M.D. Reddy (ed.), *Fisheries Development in India* (New Delhi : Concept Publishing Company, 1983).

PART TWO

INVITED PAPERS

2

ROLE OF GOVERNMENT POLICY IN INDIAN MARINE FISHERIES SECTOR

A.G. KALAWAR

INTRODUCTION

THE marine food industry is primarily based on the natural resources of the sea. Natural resources like marine fishery resources are gifts of nature, men can only accept them if offered, they cannot 'demand', it nor complain about it. The tropical waters, as compared to temperate waters, are not so well endowed with fish. So, if the fishery resources of India are not so rich as those of Norway or Iceland, the only remedy is to get the maximum benefit out of what exists. Moreover, this being a living resource is liable to die a natural death if not harvested. Such a resource has to face the risk of depletion if it is overexploited. As the marine foods industry almost entirely depends on the marine fishery resources the central objective of development of this industry could be 'optimum' utilization of the marine fishery resources.

DEVELOPMENT PLAN AS THE BASIS FOR STUDYING GOVERNMENT POLICY

Planning the economic development of the country is the primary responsibility of government. Efforts were made in this country to bring about economic development through five year plans, and annual plans. The development plans have been taken as the basis for studying the Government policy as invariably the governments frame proper strategies and policies for effective implementation of the development plan in order to achieve the stipulated objectives.

First Five Year Plan (1950-51 to 1955-56)

The First Plan was a very modest one with the main object of restoring the pre-war level conditions regarding availability of consumer goods. Against the total plan outlay of Rs. 2,013 crore, the share of the fisheries sector was Rs. 5.14 crore and actual expenditure was only Rs. 2.8 crore. The First Five Year Plan for fisheries was more or less a compendium of the existing development schemes which were production oriented. The principal objectives of the fisheries plan were :

(1) Increase marine fish production by increasing the number of mechanized fishing boats.

(2) Ameliorate the socio-economic conditions of the fishermen who were the prime producers of raw meterial by giving them necessary financial and technical assistance.

Second Five Year Plan (1956-61)

More emphasis was given in the Second Plan on industrial development and expansion of employment opportunities. As against a provision of Rs. 4,800 crore, the share of fisheries was only Rs. 10.73 crore. Actual expenditure was, however, only Rs. 9 crore. The objectives for the fisheries plan were the same as those of the First Plan, but the efforts were proposed to be intensified.

Achievements during the first two Five Year Plans

1. Investigations were undertaken by the Central Fisheries Technological Research Institute at Cochin for improvement in the designs of fishing crafts and fishing gear.
2. Exploratory fishing activity was intensified by establishing more stations at Cochin, Tuticorin, and Vishakhapatnam.

3. Fishing boat building yards were established in Gujarat, Maharashtra, Karnataka, Kerala, Tamil Nadu and Andhra Pradesh.
4. About 1,800 mechanized boats were introduced.
5. Production of fish increased from seven lakh tonnes to 10 lakh tonnes by the end of the First Plan and to 14 lakh tonnes by the end of the Second Plan.

Third Five Year Plan

Out of the plan outlay of Rs. 7,500 crore the share of the fisheries sector was only Rs. 29.00 crore. Many schemes were formulated with the main objective of increasing fish production so that protein diet became available to the population. Due consideration was given towards effecting improvements in the condition of fishermen. Emphasis was also placed on the development of export trade.

Formation and running of fisheries co-operatives was an important aspect of fisheries development during this plan period. At the end of the Second Plan there were about 2100 fisheries co-operatives with a total membership of about 2,20,000 mainly located in Andhra Pradesh, Maharashtra, Gujarat, Kerala and Tamil Nadu. They were functioning with varying degree of success and only about 800 of them could be considered to have satisfactory performance.

In order to increase fish production it was proposed to introduce about 4000 new mechanized crafts. Four more new stations for exploratory survey work at Veraval, Mangalore, Paradeep and Port Blair were proposed to be established. It was also proposed to operate 35 large vessels and to provide landing and berthing facilities at 16 ports. It was proposed to establish 72 ice and cold storage plants in different states. It was expected that fish production would increase from 14 lakh tonnes to 18 lakh tonnes. Exports may go up from Rs. 6 crore to Rs. 12 crore.

Research activity at the Central Marine Fisheries Research Institute, Central Inland Fisheries Research Institute, and Central Institute of Fisheries Technology would be itensified. An institute for training fisheries operatives would be started at Cochin.

Annual plans (1966-69)

These three annual plans were really meant for consolidating the achievements made in the last three plans rather than for further development. Outlay provided for each sector was in respect of continuing schemes with the object of bringing them to a stage of giving anticipated results. In view of this, it would be worthwhile taking a review to see if the important targets fixed for the Third Five Year Plan were achieved by 1969 through the third plan ended in 1966. The three years were a grace period to make up shortfalls in the Third Five Year Plan.

Target	*Achievements*	*Shortfall*
1. Introduction of 400 mechanized boats	5,700	Nil
2. Increase fish production to 18 lakh tonnes	15 lakh tonnes (Revised to 17.69 in May 1970)	No shortfall
3. Increase in the value of exports Rs. 12 crore	18 crore	Nil
4. Introduction of 35 large fishing boats	Nil	100%
5. Provision of landing and berthing facilities at 16 ports	Work taken up at 30 ports	Works in progress

Fourth Five Year Plan (1969-74)

In the Fourth Plan, fisheries development had three main objectives: Increase in fish production to meet protein requirements, development of export potential, and improvement in the economy of the fishermen. It was contemplated that the demand for fish would grow at the rate of six per cent per annum. However, keeping in view the various constraints the target for fish production in the final year of the Fourth Plan was fixed at 1.97 million tonnes as against the base level of 1.50 million tonnes in 1968-69. It was proposed to introduce 5,500 mechanized boats during the plan period.

Offshore and deep sea fishing failed to receive adequate attention due to non-availability of requisite number of fishing trawlers, lack of infrastructure, and lack of information on fishing grounds. It was proposed to introduce 300 large fishing trawlers. The Internal Bank for Reconstruction and Development (IBRD) had agreed to finance the indigenous trawlers and provision was made in the plan for providing suitable subsidy. Investigations connected with deep sea fishing with special reference to fishing methods, fishing craft and charting of fishing grounds would continue by the Deep Sea Fishing Station, Indo-Norwegian Project, Central Inland Fisheries Research Institute (CIFT) and Central Marine Fisheries Research Institute (CMFRI). A survey was also to be undertaken by United Nations Development Programme (UNDP) assistance on deep sea fishery resources. It was proposed to provide landing and berthing facilities for larger vessels at major and minor ports and for small boats at 48 minor ports.

Marketing of fish was proposed to be properly organized by strengthening the Central, State Fisheries Corporations and Co-operative Federations. It was also intended to set up 10 composite plants and 73 ice factories and cold storage plants. Availing assistance from financing agencies such as National Bank for Agriculture and Rural Development (NABARD) and Internal Bank for Reconstruction and Development (IBRD) was a new aspect.

As regards research activities the main strategy was to organize co-ordinated multidisciplinary research projects for effective utilization of available resources. Three central research institutes would continue to conduct industry oriented applied research on different aspects of fisheries.

Review of the progress in the fourth plan

Target	*Achievement*	*Shortfall*
1. Fish production Level : —Original target 1.97 million tonnes —Revised target 2.41 million tonnes	2.27 million tonnes	0.24 million tonnes

Target	Achievement	Shortfall
2. Introduction of 5,500 mechanised boats	2,300	3,200
3. Introduction of 300 large trawlers	76	224
4. Procurement of 25 survey boats	8	17
5. Fishing harbours at 9 major ports—provision Rs. 13.50 crore	Expenditure Rs. 2 crore	Slow progress
6. Facilities at minor ports —provision Rs. 6 crore	Expenditure Rs. 5 crore	Slight setback
7. 10 composite refrigeration plants	10	Nil
8. 73 ice plants and cold storages	73	Nil
20 refrigerated rail vans	10	10
8. Seven co-ordinated research projects	7	Nil

Fifth Five Year Plan

Out of the total outlay of Rs. 37,382 crore the share of fisheries sector was only Rs. 160.51 crore. It was recognized that, as a source of protein rich food fisheries have been inadequately exploited and, therefore, there was need and scope for increase in fish production. It was considered necessary to develop this industry from the point of view of improving the economic conditions of fishermen and increase foreign exchange earnings by export.

The Fifth Plan target, of fish production were as under:

	Base-level *1973-74*	*Target* *1978-79*
Inland (lakh tonnes)	7.84	10.55
Marine (lakh tonnes)	14.85	20.25
Total	22.69	30.80

Fifth plan target of fisheries programme

	Base level 1973-74	*Target 1978-79*
Mechanized boats	9,300	13,300
Large fishing boats	100	300
Refrigerated insulated rail vans	12	53

As against the plan target of 20.25 lakh metric tonnes of marine fish which was revised to 19.7 lakh metric tonnes. the actual achievement was only 16.00 lakh metric tonnes. This was largely due to shortfall in the introduction of both coastal and deep sea fishing vessels. During the plan, out of a targeted introduction of 4,000 mechanized fishing vessels only about 2,700 vessels could be introduced. Introduction of mechanized vessels was slow in the upper east coast areas especially in West Bengal, Orissa, and Andhra Pradesh. Although 300 large deep sea fishing vessels were proposed to be in operation only about 52 vessels were actually operated in the commercial sector.

Out of the total outlay of Rs. 69,380 crore proposed allocation for fisheries sector was Rs. 400 crore which works out to 0.58 per cent of the total outlay.

Sixth Five Year Plan (1980-81 to 1984-85)

Planning Commission later decided not to finalise the draft Five Year Plan 1978-83 but to formulate the Sixth Five Year Plan (1980-85) taking the base year as 1979-80.

The Sixth Five Year Plan has been formulated taking into account the achievements and failures of the previous plans. It envisages a significant augmentation in the rate of growth of the economy with an annual growth of over five per cent. Reduction in the incidence of poverty and unemployment are the major objectives of the Sixth Plan. High priorities has been given to agriculture and rural development and also to allied agricultural activities like animal husbandry, dairying, fisheries, and so on.

The total investment (gross capital formation) envisaged is Rs. 1,58,710 crore for the plan period (1980-85) at 1979-80 prices. Of this Rs. 748 crore (0.47%) has been allocated to the fisheries sector.

In the marine fisheries sector, the major attention has been given to organizing a National Fishery Survey in the areas covered by the Exclusive Economic Zone. To encourage the mechanization of fishing fleet has been given prior attention with which the major objective of increasing production could be achieved. Targets and achievements of fish production and selected inputs are as follows:

Programme	*Unit*	*(Revised) Target (1984-85)*	*Achievement*
Fish production	lakh tonnes	29.50	28.50
— Inland	—do—	12.05	11.00
— Marine	—do—	17.45	17.50
Machanized boats	Nos.	19,000	19,000
Large deep sea fishing vessels	Nos.	258	75
Harbour/landing centres	Cumulative Nos.	Not fixed	80

NATIONAL COMMISSION ON AGRICULTURE

Recommendations on policy and strategy

National Commission on Agriculture (1976) in its report—Part-II—Policy and Strategy—has made the following recommendations on Marine Fisheries (paragraphs 7.3.20 to 7.3.23, pages 74 and 75).

(i) Marine fishery policy should be recast in the light of an exclusive fishery zone adjoining the coast. The accent on distant water fishing fleet should be replaced by more concentrated effort for the exploitation of the seas within 320 km. of the Indian coast with emphasis on small and medium size trawlers. The inshore fisheries areas and coastal creeks should be developed for higher yields through mariculture of prawns, molluscs and suitable coastal fish. In marine fisheries also, the small fishermen should be given preferential facilities in terms of fishing boats and gears and landing facilities. It will be essential to take necessary measures for delimitation of fishing zones through legislation in order to avoid conflicts among the non-mechanized crafts and mechanized boats and larger fishing vessels and between the fishermen of adjoining states. Uptodate information about marine fish stocks should be built up through comprehensive research. Oceanographic research will have to be intensified so as to develop fully the strategy to utilize the extended resources of pelagic fisheries beyond the traditional zone of exploitation of coastal regions particularly in the west.

(ii) Fishery development should invariably be accompanied by arrangements for storage so that fishermen are not required to dispose of the catch at throw away prices. In marine fisheries, infrastructural facilities like fishery harbours should be developed to support marine fishery development. In order to utilize fully the resources in the deep waters, it would be necessary to create infrastructural facilities in the public sector which could then give the lead to the industry as a whole. A policy of developing specialisation in fishing boat building by a few yards should be fostered.

(iii) Special attention should be paid to crustacean fisheries, which have great export potential by comprehensive survey of the resources, regular monitoring of the status of the fisheries and diversification of (a) production and processing centres, (b) export products, (c) export markets. In this sector small entrepreneurs as well as large business houses need to be encouraged as scope exists for both.

(iv) All aspects of fisheries activities and ancillary industries based on them need to be brought under uniform control. The Indian Fisheries Act of 1897 being outdated, it is necessary to enact a new fisheries Act to cover all these aspects on an all-India basis to confer enabling powers to the State Governments particularly in respect of prawn fisheries and others showing signs of depletion.

Comments

There are the broad policy directives suggested by the National Commission on Agriculture on marine fisheries development. They are being very much generalised, there is no possibility of difference of opinion on the general guidelines suggested. As regards marine fishery policy it is presumed that Government of India had given accent on distant water fishing at one time. It is not known when such an approach was adopted at any time when fishing effort was barely touching the fringe of the offshore fishing zone which is considered to lie between 10 fathom line and 40 fathom line. There is hardly any commercial fishing done, even now, beyond 40 fathom line which is considered to be the deep sea area. As will be seen in the chapter relating to fisheries resources the experts have estimated the fish production potential in the region from 0 to 50 metres depth (1,92,000 sq. kms.) at 2.5 million metric tonnes whereas the actual fish production in this area is about 1.5 million metric tonnes. Similarly, in the region from 50 m to 200 m (4,22,000 sq. kms.) the fish production potential is estimated at 1.5 million metric tonnes from where the actual fish production is almost negligible. As compared to this, fish production potential in the area beyond 200 m depth upto 320 kms. (about 16,00,000 sq. kms.) is estimated at only 0.5 million metric tonnes. This shows that the fish stocks are more widely distributed in the zone beyond 200 m depth, that is beyond continental shelf. This situation would naturally tempt the planners to fix priorities in the pattern of marine fisheries exploitation by giving top most priority for exploitation of the remaining resources in the 50 m depth line and extend it upto the continental shelf where the resources are richer as compared to the area beyond 200 m line. Fishing effort will have to be extended beyond the continental shelf with due caution. Other recommendations with regard to transport, preservation and marketing of fish, and provision of infrastructural facilities and so on are very appropriate. Lastly, it has been suggested to enact a new fisheries Act to cover all the aspects of fisheries development on an all India basis so that the fisheries activities would be brought under uniform control. It is true that the Indian Fisheries Act of 1897 deals with only the conservation aspect of both marine and inland fisheries. The fishing industry during the course of its development particularly in the post-independence era has brought several other aspects of the industry into prominence which require regulatory measures. The Indian Fisheries Act, 1897, being applicable only up to the territorial waters and 'Fisheries' being a state subject under the Indian Constitution several State Legislatures have passed separate State Fisheries Acts applicable upto territorial waters depending upon the local conditions in the states. Some of the states, however, have not passed any separate legislation and continue to operate the Indian Fisheries Act taking recourse to the provision enabling them to make rules to suit the local conditions. Some of the states have recently passed Marine Fishing Regulations Act as the Indian Fisheries Act or the State Fisheries Act do not provide for taking measures to regulate fishing other than for coservation. Registration of fishing boats is done under different Acts in different States. It is, therefore, high time to consider whether a new fisheries Act can be enacted to cover all aspects of the fisheries activities. It would be desirable to constitute a study group of experts to examine the entire issue and to recommend a model fisheries Act to cover all aspects of registration of boats, fishing regulation, processing, marketing and even export.

PRINCIPAL OBJECTIVES OF FISHERIES DEVELOPMENT UNDER FIVE YEAR PLANS

Taking into consideration the principal objectives for economic development under the Five Year Plans as indicated by the Planning Commission from time to time objectives for fisheries were formulated. The principal objectives are :

(i) Optimum utilization of marine living resources to increase marine fish production by judicious increase in the strength of fishing fleet of small mechanized boats and large fishing vessels,

(ii) To support introduction of large fishing vessels by intensified surveys for assessment of resources,

(iii) To assist the traditional fishing sector to improve the quality and quantity of fish and to improve their economic condition by providing the necessary infrastructural facilities,

(iv) To improve the systems of processing and marketing of fish to ensure reasonable return to the producer and fair price to the consumers,

(v) To generate additional employment and enhanced income to the weaker section of the community, and

(vi) Promotion of exports of marine products in order to earn foreign exchange.

BASIC POLICY ADOPTED IN THE DEVELOPMENT OF FISHERIES

The most important objective was to increase fish production and to improve the economic condition of fishermen who are the primary producers in this industry. In order to achieve this Government's policy was to associate as far as possible the fishermen in the development activity so that the benefit of development will go to them directly or indirectly. First step taken in this direction was to provide fishermen with better tools so that they can improve their efficiency in fish production. They were, therefore, assisted financially to procure suitable mechanized boats, improved type of gear. In order to improve their skill, facilities were provided for their training. Fishermen were organized into Fisheries Co-operative Societies so that these co-operative institutions can take care of the economic interests of fishermen such as fish preservation, transport and marketing. It was only those activities which the fishermen or their co-operatives are not in a position to handle were entrusted to other agencies. This policy is also applicable to all other related activities such as net making by machines. The policy clearly indicates that while setting up of net making plants care should be taken to see that the cottage industry of hand-made nets should not suffer on account of operation of machines for net making. Though Government of India has not issued any policy resolution like the Scientific Policy Resolutlon of 4th March, 1958, this has been the basic policy adopted with regard to fisheries development in India.

SUGGESTIONS FOR A BROAD POLICY FRAMEWORK

Marine fisheries resources—Survey

The government realized the importance of surveying of marine fisheries resources. An organization called Deep Sea Fishing Station, which is now designated as the Exploratory Fishery Project, was established as early as in 1946. This organization has surveyed the resources up to about 40 fathoms. The area of continental shelf reckoned at 100 fathoms depth is about 4.5 lakh sq. km. The area of shelf within 40 fathoms depth is about 2.8 lakh sq. km. and of this an area of about 2 lakh sq. km. has so far been surveyed by bottom trawling. This area represents about 45 per cent of the total continental shelf area of the country. This performance, however, cannot be considered impressive. Important reasons for not being able to undertake survey of deeper waters beyond 40 fathoms were absence of suitable large vessels and delays in procurement of such vessels under foreign aid. Now with the declaration of the Exclusive Economic Zone (EEZ) an area of about 20.2 lakh sq. km. has come under national jurisdiction. A more dynamic approach and policy is necessary in completing the survey of this vast area to identify productive fishing areas.

The fishing industry is interested in knowing the concentration of fish population in the sea from the point of view of exploitation of fisheries on commercial lines. The industry would also like to have a consolidated picture from one agency rather than approaching different agencies for the purpose. This will be possible if an attempt is made to co-ordinate and integrate fishery survey activities undertaken by the Exploratory Fisheries Project (EFP), Integrated Fisheries Project (IFP), Central Marine Fisheries Research Institute (CMFRI), National Institute of Oceanography (NIO), Zoological Survey of India (ZSI), Naval Hydrographic Office (NHO), Central Institute of Fisheries Technology (CIFT), Department of Science and Technology, training institutions, and so on.

The industry is also interested in receiving day-to-day information on fish stocks immediately available for exploitation. There is provision for forecasting the information on AIR, but the required unit for data collection and analysis has to be built up.

A rapid industrial type of fishery survey beyond the 30 fathom line conducted by the Government of India in collaboration with the Government of Poland was a step in the right direction. Unfortunately, detailed reports on economics of such experiments have not so far been published though the survey was completed long back. Data available from the provisional reports indicate that there is dearth of high value marketable species in deeper waters. During a quick survey of this type, there can be some gaps which may have to be filled by repeating the survey. Such surveys take quite a long time and hence the feasibility of issuing licences to foreign vessels may be considered on the condition that they would supply the information about the fish catches and other data. This arrangement may help in obtaining the resource data so far as deep sea areas are concerned.

The policy on survey of fisheries resources should be as follows :

(a) A time-bound programme of completing the survey work of the entire EEZ within a period of ten years including the time required for procurement of suitable and sufficient number of survey boats should be undertaken,

(b) Assessment of fish stocks and preparation of fishery maps indicating productive fishing grounds should be done,

(c) On the basis of information collected as at (b) specifications for fishing boats and gear for commercial exploitation of fisheries resources should be prescribed,

(d) Fishery information should be forecasted regularly,

(e) Measures for conservation of fishery resources wherever necessary should be suggested,

(f) Areas should be demarcated in the EEZ where foreign fishing vessels should be prohibited from fishing.

Manpower

One of the most important objectives of the overall economic development is to provide gainful employment. So far as fishing is concerned nearly 25 lakh active fishermen are engaged in fishing whether gainfully or otherwise. Development of coastal fishery will be labour intensive and will contribute towards raising the earnings above subsistance level. Development of capital intensive fishery for offshore and deep sea exploitation will contribute towards upgrading of labour skills, technical expertise and managerial manpower, creating job/opportunities, and higher wage level for the fishermen. This would mean that the training policy should be comprehensive to cover all types of operatives taking into consideration not only what is expected from them but also the capacity to absorb the skills.

The Government of India and the state governments have taken the responsibility of affording training facilities for all types of operatives in the marine fishing industry. Institutes of the Indian Council of Agricultural Research and some universities are assisted in conducting *ad hoc* training and refresher courses for the operatives. They are also providing facilities for undergraduate and post-graduate courses. The Government of India has established the Central Institute of Fisheries Nautical and Engineering Training (CIFNET) at Cochin and Madras to train candidates as skippers, bosuns, engine drivers, engineers, and so on. In spite of turning out several trained men in this field there were complaints from the large trawler owners about the paucity of skippers and engineers to man their trawlers. On the other hand, there were several men trained by these institutes who were unemployed. When this question was examined carefully it was found that many candidates who were trained by these institutes did not have prescribed 'sea time' and, therefore, could not appear for the skipper's or engineer's examinations held by Mercantile Marine Department. As these persons did not have the prescribed certificate from the Mercantile Marine Department, they could not be employed on the large fishing boats. Efforts are being made now by the Government of India to incorporate sea time as part of the training which will lengthen the duration of training. State governments have been running training centres for fishermen where theoretical and practical instructions are given in operating machanized boats, handling and undertaking simple repairs of marine diesel engines, and operation of improved types of gear such as trawl nets. Though there is no separate institute for training in preservation and processing of fish, courses are conducted by the Central Institute of Fisheries Technology (CIFT), Cochin, and CIFE, Bombay, some others conduct training courses in mariculture. Central Institute of Fisheries Education (CIFE), Bombay provides comprehensive training in both marine as well as inland fisheries to graduate candidates to groom them as techno-administrators to take up fisheries development work in the various states.

With so many institutes engaged in giving training to operatives in the various fields and levels it is necessary that there is some kind of co-ordination and communication among the institutes in order to avoid duplication, contradiction, and also improve the quality of instruction by mutual exchange of views. Training programmes have also to be so designed that they will not only meet the immediate requirements of trained operatives but also consider the long range requirements especially with regard to operatives like skippers who require a period of six to seven years of training and experience.

Capital and equipment

Till recent years the government was the only agency to provide capital to the fishing industry as investment in it was considered very risky by the financing agencies. In some states, the banks started giving medium term loans to fishermen and non-fishermen with refinance facilities provided by the National Bank for Agriculture and Rural Development (NABARD) for which, in some cases, the state governments gave guarantee for repayment of loan and interest. In some states, however, the banks and the state financial corporations have advanced loans for fishing boats where the returns are more secure due to prawn fishing. Still, more than 90 per cent of advances is made by the government directly or through banks by way of guarantees The same has been the case with regard to introduction of large fishing boats. Till 1978, the Government of India financed to the extent of Rs. 12.30 crore through the Shipping Development Fund Committee for purchase of large fishing vessels. This arrangement was terminated in 1978 and the government is considering alternate system of financing through the NABARD.

Money has no value if the material and equipment required to be purchased are not available. Here too, the government has played an important role. When the programme of mechanization of fishing boats was intensified in the early fifties the government allowed import of marine diesel engines and nylon for fishing nets liberally. Simultaneously, efforts were made to produce engines and nylon in the country in a phased manner. At the moment, the essential requirements of marine diesel engines and nylon are completely met by indigenous manufacturers. Other equipments such as winches, wire-ropes, gallows, and shackles are also manufactured such as echo-sounders and fish finders, which are not required in large number are not manufactured in the country.

Credit

Short term loans or production loans are entirely advanced by the financing agencies. These are short term credits which are required every year before the fishing starts for keeping the boat and gear ready for the next season and also to meet operational expenses. These loans are returned within 11 months so that the operator can borrow fresh loan for the next year. Here too, because the vageries of fishing seasons, it is not always possible to repay loan in time. In such cases, some banks have a system of converting the short term loan during the slack season into a medium term loan so that the loanees will not be considered as defaulters and they can be advanced fresh loans during next year. The lending agencies should have a flexible system of financing to suit the peculiar conditions of the fishing industry. This should be applicable not only to fishing but also cover activities like processing, marketing and even export as these activities almost entirely depend on the quality and quantity of fish landed.

Marine fisheries exploitation

Though the principal objective is the optimum utilization of marine fisheries resources, the planning has not been systematic and on scientific lines because it has not been possible to estimate the fisheries resources with a reasonable degree of accuracy. The result has been introduction of mechanized boats almost indiscriminately without any regard to the size of fish stock. There is concentration of fishing activity in inshore waters (within 10 fathom depth) in certain areas, leading to what may be termed as 'over fishing'. Catch per unit effort has been reducing in such areas and the time is not too far when fishing in those areas may prove to be uneconomic. Sometimes when the fishing trawlers follows the migrating prawn, fishing is concentrated where the prawns are found resulting in conflicts between the local sail boat owners of the migrating trawlers. In the name of deep sea fishing, the government has allowed large shrimp trawlers which also operate in shallow waters. On account of unregulated fishing activities all over there has been more confusion, the stronger section trying to claim their right to fish anywhere and weaker section asking the government for protection.

Though there is some difficulty in formulating a clear policy because of lack of knowledge about fishery resources itself, the policy may outline the following issues:

(a) As one of the objectives of development is to improve the economic condition of the fishermen, protection should be given to the traditional fishermen who operate sail boats and beach sienes in the coastal region. The next vulnerable group is of the fishermen who operate small mechanized boats whose operational range and endurance of the sea conditions are limited. This group also required protection from encroachment by large deep sea trawlers. Hence delimitation of fishing zones should be introduced wherever necessary taking into consideration the local conditions. It will not be practicable to enforce regulations in the open sea as it is difficult to demarcate the sea area and it is equally difficult to obtain evidence for or against the default. It is true that enforcement of any regulation in the sea is more difficult but not impracticable. When once the need for enforcement of regulations is established ways can be found out for enforcement as is done in some of the developed countries like Japan and Norway. The Committee on Delimitation of Fishing Zones appointed by the Government of India had studied the problem in detail and suggested a model Marine Fishing Regulation Bill to be adopted by the maritime states with suitable modifications considering the local conditions.

(b) With the declaration of the EEZ up to 200 nautical miles the area exclusively available for exploitation has been extended much beyond the 100 fathom line or the continental shelf area. According to the present trend of the Law of the Sea Conference, if the resources of the littoral states remain unutilized other nations can enter into the area to harvest the fish. This being the position it would be necessary for this country to utilize this resources without loss of time. A law has been passed by Parliament in 1981 to regulate fishing in the EEZ beyond territorial waters by foreign fishing vessels. Due to heavy capital investment and uncertainty of economic returns small entrepreneurs and fishing co-operatives hesitate to undertake deep sea fishing projects. The Government of India has declared their policy of encouraging deep sea fishing the EEZ and provided facilities for import of trawlers, credit permitting collaboration arrangements with foreign companies, grant of rebate on excise duty on diesel oil used by deep sea fishing boats, and so on. Guidelines have also been issued for charter of foreign fishing vessels. But, these promotional efforts have not yielded the desired results because of several reservations and so-called safeguards to prevent misuse of facilities. Firstly, the deep sea fishing vessels allowed to be imported were not given a clear understanding that they should operate only in deep sea fishing areas. Hence when the government expressed their intention at a later stage to restrict their operation to deeper waters the parties expressed their displeasure. Though deep sea fishing requires heavy investment and returns are uncertain, the government's intention was to assist one and all without ascertaining the capacity of the party to sustain shocks of uncertainty. Hence many weak parties withdrew at the last moment. Knowing the nature of activity and the risks involved it would have been prudent to assist such parties who could bear the financial risks. On the other hand, the government tried to exclude large business houses from deep sea fishing. Similarly, the schemes of giving facilities such as rebate on excise duty were so full of safeguards that availing of the facility became an ordeal. Collaborations in joint ventures were permitted but the terms and conditions were not conducive to smooth working. The terms will have to be liberal enough to attract foreign collaborators. It would, therefore, be necessary to take clear policy decision as follows:

1. In the absence of response from small entrepreneurs and co-operatives any party including large business houses may be permitted to undertake deep sea fishing projects.
2. In order to ensure proper and steady flow of knowhow it is necessary that government policies for joint ventures/ foreign collaborations including charters/purchase of vessels and engagement of foreign technicians take a pragmatic view in the following matters:

   (a) An opportunity should be provided to the Indian investor to negotiate terms with minimum financial risk, and allow for payment of charter and other charges on catch sharing basis. The policy in this respect should be a clear that the Indian party can make firm commitments with the foreign collaborator within the framework prescribed by the government,
   (b) Collaborations should be allowed for a reasonable period of ten years so that suitability of boats and equipments can be established and transfer of knowhow and training in various skills can be completed satisfactorily,
   (c) Investors should be given freedom in the choice of boats and settle commercial terms for the transaction.
   (d) Main objectives for permitting charter arrangements should be to—

(i) establish the suitability of particular type and size of boats, fishing gear and other equipment,

(ii) transfer of fishing technology by training Indian counterpart personnel,

(iii) study the economic viability of the operation.

The charter arrangements should, therefore, be basically in the nature of pilot projects and should be viewed as such. These objectives should be kept in mind while approving the charter arrangements.

(e) Policy and procedures relating to duty free imports of fishing boats, fishing gear and essential equipment on board, and spare parts need to be spelt out in clear and unambiguous terms and made known to the customs personnel at the ports. The normal 'appeal' procedure being cumbersome and time consuming a simple procedure should be evolved. A certification from the DGTD should be accepted as is done in the case of the engineering industry.

(f) Policy and procedures regarding engagement of foreign technicians, their replacement or substitution in emergencies at short notice, and matters pertaining to their remuneration need to be clearly defined on realistic basis and the procedure should be simple and expeditious.

(g) Policy and procedures pertaining to sanction and disbursement of loans for the purchase of trawlers need to be streamlined and made simple and expeditious. Sanctioning and disbursing the loan directly by the Ministry of Agriculture may be considered.

(h) The procedure for grant of exemption from excise duty on diesel oil also needs to be streamlined. The present procedure is so cumbersome and time consuming that in actual practice operators are sometimes forced to forgo this benefit.

(i) Regulations prescribed by the Mercantile Marine Department need a thorough review to suit the requirements of the fishing industry.

(j) Rules pertaining to wireless cummunication need modifications considering the peculiar problems of the fishing industry.

(k) Fish being highly perishable commodity suitable procedure relating to handling and marketing should be evolved specially in the context of customs rules. The feasibility of issuing customs passes to fishing trawlers may be examined.

(l) Adequate infrastructure in terms of fishing harbours capable of handling large deep sea fishing vessels should be created on priority basis. Till then facilities should be made available at the existing commercial ports on a priority basis.

3. Exploration work and collection of resource data by government agencies should be intensified and given a commercial bias. Efforts should be madc to provide data to commercial operators for planning long term investments and for planning day-to-day fishing operations.

At the same time private operators should also be encouraged to take up exploratory surveys side by side with commercial exploitation and some subsidy may be given.

4. The huge investments involved in deep sea fishing projects requires that managerial inputs are highly professionalized so that the operations are well controlled and the investments protected. The investment requires is beyond the capacity of even large business houses. As such, soft loans should be extended to all without discrimination and the policy should be clear and unambiguous in opening this field to all sectors and business houses.

5. Though the Ministry of Agriculture is the sponsoring authority, ten other departments in different Ministries are to be consulted before approval is given to a project with foreign collaboration. On account of this, decisions are unreasonably delayed. It is worthwhile considering creation of a separate cell for processing such proposals so that final approval can be given in consultation with and on behalf of different ministries.

It would be desirable to create a separate Ministry of Fishery Development to ensure proper planning and healthy growth of the industry.

6. A policy once formulated should not be amended to the disadvantage of entrepreneurs at least for a period of ten years so that investors can plan their strategy with some confidence and assurance of continuity.
7. It is necessary to have a regular channel of consultation between the government and the industry so that all major policy issues are discussed before decisions are taken. Decisions thus taken will be more practical and since the industry is associated with them, implementation will be more effective. Two suggestions are offered :

   (i) Establishment of a Development Council for the fishing industry under the Industries Development and Regulations Act.

   (ii) Giving representation to apex co-operatives of fishermen and associations of the fishery industry on committees appointed by the government which have a bearing on the industry.

8. Adequate arrangements should be made to train the required technicians to reduce the dependability on foreign technicians.
9. After the profitability of deep sea fishing projects is known co-operative societies can be motivated to take up the project.
10. It would be desirable to implement pilot projects at two selected centres on each coast (east and west) to ascertain the profitability by operating deep sea vessels on purely commercial lines. This can be entrusted to the state fisheries corporations. Export-oriented deep sea fishing projects for tuna can be considered particularly on the southern coast.
11. Tax concessions on profits made in deep sea fishing projects and permitting investment of profits in the expansion of project will give a boost to the industry. Unless a liberal and hold policy is implemented, the hopes and aspirations regarding deep sea fishing and utilization of EEZ may remain only on paper.

Infrastructure

Being a highly perishable commodity, fish should quickly landed either for processing, preservation, and storage, or for further distribution. Creation of such facilities for both small mechanized or non-mechanized boats and large deep sea fishing fleet has been the joint responsibility of the central and state governments. There are about 15,000 mechanized boats and about 120 large fishing vessels requiring proper landing facilities. In the absence of these facilities mechanized boats have been operating from the sheltered river mouths and bays and large vessels are operating from commercial harbours where facilities like supply of ice and auction hall are not available. Moreover, the charges levied by commercial harbours are very high. Realizing the necessity of having separate facilities for fish landing, the Government of India has sanctioned minimum landing and berthing facilities at 80 centres and self-contained fishing harbours at about 15 centres. Most of the minor landing and berthing facilities are completed. Work in respect of self-contained fishing harbours is in progress. However, facilities so far created can accommodate about 3,600 small mechanized boats and about 650 medium fishing boats up to 18 m size. Considering the present fleet of mechanized boats, the facilities are very inadequate.

Preservation, transport and marketing

Facilities for preservation and storage of fish at important landing centres are a must. Producers co-operatives should be given preference while establishing such units by providing them land, water, power, and so on for operating such plants. All the fish produced cannot be taken care of by the co-operatives, and, therefore, agencies rendering this service to the industry should also be assisted. Fresh fish consumption in India has considerably increased during the last 30 years on account of availability of facilities for chilling fish, approach roads to fishing centres, improvements in the fish transport system, and so on.

Use flow of fish

Category	*Percentage (1977)*
Fresh fish	51.32
Frozen fish	8.19
Cured fish	27.86
Canned fish	0.47
Reduction	0.87
Others	4.29

Substantial quality of fish is even now cured by the conventional methods where there is much scope for improvement. Though, freezing is a best known method for preservation, its introduction on a large scale will require establishment of well planned cold chain facilities in the hinterland. Diversification of processing has still to take root. With increase in the number of deep sea fishing vessels there is possibility of landing large quantities of less popular varieties of fish which can be converted into fish meal. Though there is considerable interest in undertaking processing and export of marine products there is not significant progress in domestic marketing. This is so because the government's policy on marketing fish in the country is not very clear. While the government's intention is to organize marketing through the co-operative sector, the co-operative structure is strong enough and sufficiently organized so that it has not been able to create any impact on marketing. Hence, the age-old system of handling this activity by the merchant community still continues. With increase in fish production there is urgent need to organize integrated fish marketing in the country so that reasonable returns to the producers and fair price to the consumers are ensured. A pre-requisite for organized marketing is a systematic marketing survey. In the meantime, whether the system adopted of regulated markets for agricultural products can be extended to fish can be examined at certain selected centres to minimize the malpractices prevailing in the fish marketing system.

Marine products export policy

Foreign exchange earnings on account of export of marine products rose to about Rs. 200 crore in 1979 from about

Rs. 2.46 crore in 1951. This phenomenal increase is mainly due to change from export of low unit value items like dry fish and salt cured products to export of high unit value items like frozen prawns, lobster tails, and so on. It was also on account of the policy of government to promote exports by giving facilities and incentives. To meet the needs of the marine products export industry, a Marine Products Export Development Council (MPEDC) was set up in 1961 in the Ministry of Commerce. This council was reconstituted in 1972 as Marine Products Export Development Authority (MPEDA) under an Act. This over enthusiastic Act tried to cover almost all activities of marine fisheries development including measures for conservation and management of offshore and deep sea fishing, registration of fishing boats, and processing plants. Naturally, without adequate machinery for implementation, the Authority could do much. It would have been better to leave these aspects to the government so that the Authority could concentrate more on promotional aspects of marine products export. The Authority has, no doubt, done commendable work in promoting exports and protecting the interest of the export industry by trying to mould the attitude of the government and representing the case of the export industry to the authorities in the importing countries. Efforts are also made to improve the image of the Indian products in foreign countries by constructive propoganda.

Though the overall policy is to promote the marine products export industry sometimes priorities are given to meet the domestic demand by fixing a quota for export. It must be remembered that apart from earning foreign exchange exports were singularly responsible for increasing the earnings of the fishermen. At present the economics of operation of trawlers almost entirely depends on the price the producer gets for prawns which, in turn, depends on the international market. Though such complete dependence on the foreign market is not desirable, it is inevitable till the products obtain an equally high local price from domestic consumption which means improvement in the paying capacity of the domestic consumer. Owning to high capital and operating costs, there can be two ways of facing the problem : (i) allow exports so that the producer gets better price to balance his expenditure and (ii) subsidizing the unit. The first alternative appears to be advantageous.

Investment policy on development of fisheries

The size of investment in marine fisheries has been so modest that it can be said to be insignificant as compared to other sectors. In all the Five year and annual plans the share of the fishery sectors has not exceeded 0.50 per cent on an average. With the declaration of the EEZ the area available for fishing exploitation will be equal to two-thirds of the land area of the country. Therefore, investment on development of fisheries should be stepped up to at least 1 per cent of the plan outlay.

Policy on research and extension

The Central Marine Fisheries Research Institute, established by the Government of India in 1947, has now developed into a foremost Indian centre for marine fisheries research. With headquarters in Cochin, it has one regional centre, nine sub-stations, three research units, and 26 survey units. The Institute is engaged in : (a) estimating marine fish production on all-India basis, (b) biological studies of commercial species of fishes, (c) environment studies in relation to fisheries, (d) interpretation of survey data collected by the Exploratory Fisheries Project, and (e) mariculture. The Institute could intensify the research programme after it was transferred to the ICAR in 1967. The other institute which undertakes research on technological aspects is the Central Institute of Fisheries Technology (CIFT) which was established in 1957. The research programme includes investigations on craft and gear technology and processing technology. This institute was also transferred to the ICAR in 1967. These institutes have done very valuable work and conduct training courses for state fisheries departments and operatives from the private sector. Experiences has, however, been that many of the research findings remain within the four walls of the laboratory and do not reach the field. In order to remove this gap the government has decided to strengthen the extension machinery in the states and initiated the research institutes to conduct training of the extension staff so that some of the findings which can be immediately passed on to the field can reach the operatives. Field demonstrations are also arranged under the laboratory-to-land programme. Its impact is still to be evaluated.

In the context of the present stage of the industry reorientation of research to contribute towards rural development is of immediate necessity. The value of research in a developing economy is gauged on the basis of its utility to the industry in improving the economic benefits. It is, therefore, necessary to lay stress on industry oriented research. The research institutions can play an important role in developing suitable technology for utilizing brackish water areas which will greatly help in integrated rural development.

Fisheries development through co-operative sector

One of the important objectives of fisheries developnent has been improvement of economic condition of fishermen who are the prime producers. It was considered that the best way to bring about economic development of this section was to organize them into co-operative societies which would look after their economic interests. Thus, about 5,251 primary fisheries co-operative societies were formed by 1977-78 with a membership of about 5,75,000 and a total share capital of about Rs. 3.6 crore including government contribution. Though the number appears to be impressive, when their performance is seen in the table below :

State	No. of primary societies	Running on profit	Running in loss	Without profit or loss
Gujarat	137	41	43	63
Karnataka	154	64	54	36
Kerala	748	24	716	8
Maharashtra	530	247	212	71
Orissa	190	63	52	75
Tamil Nadu	500	87	409	4
West Bengal	714	226	256	232
Andaman & Nicobar	10	2	3	5
Goa, Daman & Diu	13	2	3	8
Lakshadweep	2	1	1	—
Pondicherry	37	7	30	—

The position in Kerala and Tamil Nadu which are the major marine states is really alarming, where the percentages of societies running in losses are 96 and 82 respectively. The general position remains almost the same even today.

Why does such a position exist when government has given so much importance and priority to the co-operative sector in all its development plans ? Analysis of the working of the various societies will reveal the following important facts :

1. Attention has been more on increasing the number of fisheries co-operative societies for wider coverage than on ensuring efficient working of the co-operatives.
2. Economic viability has not been given due importance at the time of registration of societies.
3. Politically motivated co-operatives have come to grief as they were unable to solve economic problems.
4. The Rajwade Working Group had estimated as early as 1962 that a primary fisheries cooperative society should have a turnover of at least Rs. 3 lakh to make it viable. Considering the present price level, the turnover should be at least Rs. 10 lakh. A share capital base of at least Rs. 1 lakh will be required for such a turnover. The average business turnover per society, however, does not exceed Rs. 1 lakh in any maritime state. Hence the share capital base of the primary societies is very inadequate.
5. Many societies are formed mainly to avail of the various facilities offered by government. Societies are registered with all the enthusiasm of the leaders but when once the facilities are availed of the enthusiasm fades away and the leaders almost abandon the society.
6. There is dearth of good leadership in the fishing community. Wherever there is good leadership the societies have not only prospered but they have been able to considerably assist the fishermen in obtaining fishery requisites and marketing fish.
7. Many of the co-operative societies have come into trouble because of lack of loyalty of the members towards the society. This resulted in categorizing the societies as defaulters.

8. There is much scope for improving the management of the co-operatives. Many of the societies do not have efficient trained staff.
9. The co-operative federations are not able to play an effective role owing to lack of co-ordination at different levels. At times, there is duplication of functions resulting in undue competition among the co-operative institutions.

Some measures for improving their performance are given below :

1. Steps should be taken for improving the working of the existing co-operative societies and less priority be given for registering new co-operative societies.
2. A critical review should be taken to identify the weak societies and to categorise them as :

   (a) societies which cannot be made economically viable at all, and
   (b) societies which can be made economically viable after revitalization and reorganization.

3. Those societies which cannot be made viable should be liquidated forthwith.
4. Speedy steps should be taken to revitalize and reorganize those societies which can be made economically viable by giving financial and managerial support. This programme should be time-bound.
5. A co-operative institution should primarily have economic considerations before it, and politics should be kept away from these institutions.
6. Selection of a leader with integrity is the responsibility of senior social leaders in the area. The selected leaders should be given training in co-operation and fisheries and should play a major role in inculcating loyalty, discipline, and co-operative spirit among the members.
7. Economically feasible integrated fisheries co-operative projects should be prepared by experts and allowed to be implemented by really capable co-operative institutions.

Managerial expertise and technical & financial assistance should be provided by government. Institutions such as the NABARD and the National Co-operatives Development Corporation are always anxious to provide finance for economically viable projects effecting the weaker sections of the community. If a few such projects become successful, they will serve as demonstration centres and provide the necessary motivation for other institutions in taking up development projects. While doing this, care must be taken to formulàte proper projects and select the most appropriate co-operative institutions disregarding the political and other extraneous considerations.

Mariculture and brackish water farming

Marine fish production is subjected to great fluctuations. In recent years the rate of increase in production has been very marginal in spite of increasing the fishing effort by introducing more mechanized fishing boats every year. In some areas the catch per unit effort has been going down. This shows that the fishing effort in such areas has increased beyond the capacity of the fishery resource to sustain. It would, therefore, be prudent not to increase the fishing effort particularly in such areas and to pay more attention to mariculture including coastal aquaculture along the edge of the sea and brackish water farming.

The country has about 1.4 million hectares of the brackish water area mostly belonging to government. Inshore area of the sea also belongs to government. Hence development of brackish water farming and mariculture will very much depend upon the government's policy. Though government policy has all along been to provide more gainful employment and protection to the weaker sections of the community, considering the problems involved in this activity it would be better to associate this weaker section at later stage when the important problems are overcome.

On the lines of encouragement given for deep sea fishing, big industrial houses, particularly those engaged in shrimp processing, could lease brackish water areas. The lease period has to be sufficiently long as initial investment is heavy. Simultaneously, government through public sector undertakings may develop some selected brackish water areas into small but economically viable units and lease out to small-scale operators. Arrangement will have to be made by that undertaking for supply of fish and prawn seed.

Those co-operative institutions which are willing to take up this activity may be granted lease of the area for a period of 15 years. In the initial stages, subsidy to the extent of 20 per cent of the capital cost of the farm and equipment may be given as an incentive for taking up this new activity.

Marine pollution

Pollution of the sea by industrial and other wastes has created a hazard to local fishery. Waters in some of the creeks and rivers are excessively polluted resulting in complete destruction of fisheries in those areas. In spite of efforts to prevent pollution it will take many years to rehabilitate fish life there. Fortunately, the adverse effects have not so far been evident in the open sea. Top most priority has to be given for preventing pollution and for protection of marine fisheries resources by taking timely steps to see that pollution does not spread to the open sea.

The Central Government has passed a Prevention of Water Pollution Bill in 1974 and most of the states have also passed similar state legislations. There is an impression that pollution has not abated to the desired extent in spite of legislation and creation of law enforcing authority. What is required is effective implementation of pollution prevention law.

Central board of fisheries—Advisory body on government policy

The Government of India have constituted an advisory body, the Central Board of Fisheries, to advise on policy matters with regard to fisheries. The cabinet minister of the Ministry of Agriculture and Irrigation is the chairman of the Board and State ministers in charge of fisheries and a few fisheries experts. Recommendations made by the Board are accepted by the Government of India.

Need for statutory restrictions on destructive methods of exploitation of fish, for example prawns, lobsters, sardines and Bombay duck

There cannot be two opinions about the need for enforcing restrictions if and when any particular fish stock is indiscriminately exploited by destructive methods. Destruction of fish by dynamites or other explosive substances and poison is prohibited. Government can make rules to prohibit or regulate dimension, size of mesh, and kind of nets to be used and the manner of using them. Rules to prohibit or regulate methods of catching fish and to prescribe periods when fishing should be completely prohibited can be framed. In some States Marine Fishing Regulation Acts have been passed to regulate fishing activities. However, it has not been possible to enforce the regulations because the problems involved are quite complex. For example, though in certain areas prawn catch per unit of effort has gone down enforcement of mesh regulations by prescribing a bigger mesh has not been possible because in case the larger mesh is prescribed the smaller varieties of prawns would not be caught at all. If they are not caught it will be a waste of natural resources as such prawns do not grow to bigger sizes at all. The same is the case with Bombay duck which is caught by dol nets. The Marine Biological Research Station at Ratnagiri has been conducting investigations to evolve a proper mesh size for trawl net by studying the escapement of fishes and prawns. Similar investigations are taken up by the Research Unit of the Central Marine Fisheries Research Institute regarding Bombay duck caught in dol net. When the question of regulating fishing in specified areas arises will have to be based on scientific investigations about the resources and fishing effort.

The need is to identify problems and communicate them to research institutions.

Incentive support

Any developing industry needs incentives for its healthy growth and development. It is particularly so with the marine fishing industry with its heavy investment requirements and inherent risks involved on account of economic uncertainties. The fishing industry has been given the required incentives in almost all countries—developing or developed. They may be indirect incentives in the form of provision of infrastructural facilities, preferential loans on long term basis or direct incentives in the form of soft loans and subsidies. The form and the quantum of incentive depends upon the conditions prevailing in the country or the region and the type of beneficiaries.

There is often a demand that fisheries should be treated on par with agriculture and all the facilities given to agriculture should be made available to fisheries. When some concessions were announced for small scale industries there was a demand that fisheries should be treated as a small scale industry and the facilities extended to it. Incentives are given to enable the industry to take improved equipments and methods for increasing the efficiency in production and improve the quality of the produce. They are required till the initial resistance to take to new things is overcome and the new methods are proved to be more economical and increase the profitability. The type and quantum of incentive to be given will depend upon the type of project, its investment, likely profitability, probability of risk involved and the type of beneficiaries.

Important incentives are indicated below. The quantum will very much depend upon the special conditions prevailing in the different regions and the cost factor.

Direct incentives

Production phase

1. Subsidy on the capital cost of fishing boats.
2. Subsidy on recurring cost of nylon, HSD oil, LSD oil, lubricating oil, fishing hooks, cotton twine, and hemp twine (in certain areas).
3. Long term loan up to 12 years with a provision for non-payment for three months of the non-fishing period.
4. Short term loans up to one year as working capital.
5. Preferential loans for import and indigenous construction of large fishing vessels at concessional rate of interest.
6. Freedom to import large fishing vessels according to the choice of users.

Manpower. Training of fishermen and operatives at the cost of government. Training under collaboration arrangements.

Transport, preservation and marketing of fish

1. Medium term loan with subsidy to meet the capital cost of trucks, launches, and so on.
2. Long term loan with subsidy to meet the capital cost for setting up of ice factories, freezing plants, cold storage and other processing plants.
3. Organizing marketing of fish in the country through the co-operative or corporate sector by providing necessary funds.
4. Encouraging export of marine products by giving incentives such as cash subsidies, import entitlement on the basis of exports, and credit.

Indirect incentives

1. Location of rich fishing grounds by fishery surveys.
2. Provision for fish landing and berthing of fishing vessels at important fish landing centres.
3. Construction of fish markets by local bodies.
4. Reduction in taxes and duties levied on the manufacture of equipments such as marine diesel engines, nylon twine, cotton twine, winches, and so on.
5. Research on problems connected with the fishing industry.

SUMMARY OF SUGGESTIONS FOR FRAMING NATIONAL POLICY ON MARINE FISHERIES DEVELOPMENT

Objectives

Marine fisheries resource is a gift of nature and it is obligatory on the part of the country to utilize this resource to the optimum level for the benefit of the people. This becomes more necessary when the major population of the country suffers from malnutrition and deficiency of protein in their diet and the product extracted from the resource is protein rich food. Principal objectives of marine fisheries development should be:

(i) Optimum utilization of marine fisheries resources including brackish water,

(ii) Improvement in the socio-economic condition of fishermen who are the primary producers in the fishing industry,

(iii) Judicious utilization of the marine products extracted from the sea by adopting proper preservation, storage, processing and distribution arrangements,

(iv) Making available the [protein rich food in the form of fish and fish products to the population to make deficiencies in the diet,

(v) Provide gainful employment by developing the fishing and fish based industries specially to the rural population,

(vi) Export of marine products to earn foreign exchange.

Summary of suggestions

Government of India may like to decide upon a national policy on development of marine fisheries or marine foods industry so that different constituents of the industry can draw their future plan of action with more confidence. On the basis of discussion made earlier on the various aspects of the industry the suggestions for formulation of government policy on national basis are summarised as under:

(i) Fishermen being the primary producers of raw material in this age-old industry they should be associated as closely as possible with the development activities so that benefit of development will go to them. They should be assisted in procuring improved mechanized fishing boats by providing incentives in the form of subsidies and soft loans whenever necessary. Necessary training facilities to improve their skills and required input should be provided,

(ii) Weaker section of the fishing community which depends upon the traditional methods of fishing by non-mechanized boats should be given necessary assistance and protection for fishing in coastal inshore areas,

(iii) Whenever necessary, measures for delimitation of fishing zones through legislation should be taken to avoid conflicts among non-mechanized crafts and mechanized boats and larger fishing vessels and between fishermen of adjoining states,

(iv) Exploratory survey of fishing grounds in the EEZ should be intensified by increasing the fleet of survey boats and by strengthening the Exploratory Survey Project organization so as to complete the work within a period of about ten years. Fisheries resource data collected should be such that it should be helpful in assessing the economic viability of operating fishing vessels in the areas surveyed. Efforts should also be made to ascertain the commercial feasibility of deep sea fishing in suitable areas by undertaking pilot projects. Feasibility of issuing licences to the foreign fishing vessels for fishing in the EEZ may be examined so that resources data based on fish catch can be obtained from these vessels. Fishery maps should be prepared to indicate productive fishing grounds and efforts should be made to forecast fishery information to the extent possible,

(v) Measures for conservation of fisheries such as close season, mesh regulations should be enforced where there is evidence of over-fishing,

(vi) Necessary regulatory measures on the fishing activities should be taken wherever necessary by introducing licensing system for fishing boats,

(vii) Deep sea fishing in the EEZ should be encouraged by allowing import of large fishing vessels and technical knowhow. Arrangements for providing necessary long term finance with concessional rate of interest should be made for purchase of deep sea fishing vessels. As advanced credit through NABARD is beset with usual problems pertaining to banks it would be more convenient if the Ministry of Agriculture advance loans directly. A condition that such vessels should operate only in prescribed sea area be, however, insisted upon. Proposals of deep sea fishing projects under foreign collaboration should also be encouraged. While private entrepreneurs and business houses can avail of these facilities, co-operative institutions of fishermen, and state government corporations may be given preference. Suitable tax concessions may also be considered if necessary during the initial period. Terms and conditions for collaboration should be liberal enough to attract foreign collaborators,

(viii) Adequate training facilities should be provided to the operators in different fields of the industry so as to improve their skills. The training programmes may be designed to meet the immediate requirements and also the long term needs. Collaboration arrangements with foreign firms may also include an item of training of Indian personnel,

(ix) Adequate arrangements should be made to provide capital on long term basis for purchase of assets either directly or through the institutional financing agencies on terms suited to the fishing industry. Efforts should also be made to make available the material and equipment either by import or by arranging manufacture of items in the country,

(x) Fisheries are considered as on par with agriculture and the production credit should be arranged on the same terms as is available to agriculture through the institutional financing agencies. Adequate incentive support should be given taking into consideration the peculiar conditions prevailing in the industry,

(xi) Important requirements of the fishing industry are infrastructural facilities such as landing and berthing facilities at the fishing centres, self-contained fishing harbours for large deep sea fishing vessels and small mechanized boats, ice factories and cold storage plants and processing plants. Government should make arrangements to provide landing and berthing facilities and fishing harbours at suitable places at its cost. Till such time the full-fledged fishing harbours are constructed fish landing and harbour facilities should be provided at the existing minor and major harbours. The port charges and dry docking charges should be commensurate with the paying capacity of the fishing industry. Necessary finance in the form of loan and subsidies to the fisheries co-operative societies for setting up ice plants, cold storage plants, freezing plants and other processing plants are to be provided. Privatesector entrepreneurs can obtain finance from the nationalised banks who will be availing refinance facilities from the NABARD.

(xii) The feasibility of organizing regulated markets for fish on the lines of those established for some of the agriculture products should be examined and such regulations enforced at some selected centres in the initial stages,

(xiii) Intensive efforts should be made to promote export of marine products by diversification of products and markets. Considering that only very small quantity is exported, restrictions on exports in the form of fixing quota etc., should be removed,

(xiv) Marine Products Export Development Authority (MPEDA) should concentrate more on export promotion activities leaving development of offshore, deep sea fishing and such other general development activities of the industry to Government of India and State governments. Export promotion activities should be intensified by this Authority both in this country and in foreign countries,

(xv) Having regard to the urgency of developing the fishing industry in a real big way of account of the extended EEZ covering an area equal to two-third of the land area of the country, investment on development of fisheries in the future plans should be enhanced to at least one per cent of the total plan outlay,

(xvi) Due importance should be given to fisheries research as it is the base for technological innovations. Industry-oriented or adaptive research should be given more stress so that the findings can be applied in the industry to derive more economic benefit. Arrangements should also be made to transfer the technology developed in the research institutions to the field by adopting proper extension methods,

(xvii) Many of the developed countries have taken up utilization of brackish water areas for growing fish and prawns. Some of the inshore areas are utilized for culture of clams and so on rafts. Encouragement should be given for undertaking such farming by grant of lease of the area. Finance facilities should be given to fishermen, landless labour and fisheries co-operatives for undertaking such farming either directly by government or through institutional financing agencies. Private sector undertakings should also be given lease of the area for sufficiently long period and finance can be availed of by them from the banks,

(xviii) It is the responsibility of government to ensure that necessary equipment is made available to the fishing industry either by importing or by arranging manufacture locally. The taxation policy with regard to indigenous equipment and spare parts should be to give protection to the industry. However, it should be seen that the manufacturing units will not overcharge the users by inflating the cost,

(xix) Utmost importance should be given for improving the working of existing co-operative societies rather than increasing their number,

(xx) Top-most priority should be given for protection of marine fishery resources by taking timely steps to see that the pollution in some of the creeks and rivers does not spread in the sea. Law for prevention of pollution of water should be effectively enforced.

ANNEXURE—I

GOVERNMENT OF INDIA NOTIFICATION REGARDING DEEP SEA FISHING

DEEP SEA FISHING INDUSTRY

Government of India have recently declared an EEZ upto a distance of 200 miles from the outer limits of the territorial waters, in order to increase the utilization of the marine resources in the zone for national benefit. In this context, it has been decided to encourage Indian enterprises to invest in deep sea fishing and thereby step up fishing supplies for internal consumption as well as exports. To start with, acquisition of 100 nos. of deep sea fishing vessels of 20 m overall length and above have been promoted in 1977-78. In addition to this, suitable proposals of charters have also been considered.

Import of deep sea fishing vessel

Import of 60 nos. of deep sea fishing vessels of 20m overall length and above, new or second-hand in 1977-78 from reputed foreign shipyards have been considered. Second-hand vessels should, however, normally be not more than five years old and covered by a certificate of sea-worthiness by a recognized agency.

Joint ventures

Foreign collaboration in the field of deep sea fishing have been entertained from Indian enterprises for joint ventures with reputed foreign fishing companies, involving sale or charter of deep sea fishing vessels, new or second-hand.

Financing facilities

Financing facilities for the acquisition of deep sea fishing vessels are available from the Shipping Development Fund. The Shipping Development Fund Committee (SDFC) would consider granting loans to the extent of 90 per cent of the cost of vessels.

ANNEXURE—II

GUIDELINES FOR THE CHARTER OF FISHING VESSELS

1. The vessels to be charted shall be in a good condition for operation, and certified by such a competent agency.
2. The vessels shall operate beyond the zone of operation of mechanized and non-mechanized fishing vessels.
3. The vessels may fly the flags of their countries of registration, till such time as they are acquired by the Indian companies.
4. The company shall furnish full details of the machinery and equipment including electronic equipment and all inventory items on the vessels.
5. The Customs Clearance Permit (CCP) shall be obtained from the Chief Controller of Imports & Exports and Customs clearances and other clearances of the Government before the vessels are operated.
6. The foreign technicians shall be employed only after necessary clearance is obtained from the government.
7. No customs duty is payable on the vessels and their permanent fitments.
8. The company shall make arrangements for the training of counterpart personnel under the foreign technicians who should be replaced in a period as approved by the government.
9. The company shall furnish periodical reports, once in a quarter on the details of the operation and the catches and the exports to the government.
10. The processing will be permitted on board the vessels in addition to processing onshore.
11. The company shall export all their products from Indian ports.
12. Government will have the right to inspect the vessels at any time without notice and post their representative on the vessels to check and operations, if and when necessary.
13. Such other conditions, as the Government may impose.

ANNEXURE—III

REGULATION OF FISHING

1. The State governments may have power to regulate, restrict or prohibit certain fishing activities within specified area.
2. Prohibition of use of fishing vessels which are not permitted in certain area like, wherever tradition crafts are used, scientific fishing should be prohibited. Big vessels should be prohibited in certain area to prevent damage to any fishing nets or tackles used by traditional fishermen.
3. Every fisherman should have the licence for using specified fishing vessel in specified area. The Licensing Officer has the full authority to grant or refuse the licence to the owner provided that he shall give a reasonable cause for refusing. The licence be valid for a period of 3 years which may be renewed from time to time.
   No fishing vessel without licence shall be permitted for fishing.
4. The holder of the licence without any reasonable cause fail to comply with the conditions subject to which the licence has been granted, the Licensing Officer may suspend or cancel the licence after giving the reasonable cause for the same.
5. Registration of fishing vessel may be done as and when the holder of the vessel intend to use it for fishing purpose. Without registration no fishing vessel shall be given the licence for fishing. Every registered vessel should carry a registration mark assigned to it by the Registration Officer.
6. For getting the fishing vessel registered, the holder shall declare his base port from which he shall operate. The base port shall not be changed without getting the permission from the Registration Officer.
7. Every owner of registered fishing vessel shall furnish to the Registration Officer at the prescribed time and in the prescribed manner such returns as may be prescribed.

The Registration Officer has the right to verify the accuracy of any return made by the owner.

8. Any person aggrieved by the order of Licensing Officer refusing to grant licence or so, may appeal to the Appellate Authority, that is the Chief Ports Officer of the State Port Organization. Every order passed by the Appellate Authority shall be final.
9. Any Enforcement Officer may impound the vessel and seize the fish found in it if the vessel is used in contravention of any of the above regulations.
10. The caught fishing vessel shall be impounded by the Enforcement Officer in such place and manner as may be prescribed. And in absence of suitable storage facilities, the seized fish may be disposed and the amount shall be deposited in the prescribed manner in the office of the Adjudicating Officer.
11. If any fishing vessel has been found in contravention of the rules, the Enforcement Officer shall report to the Adjudicating Officer who shall hold an enquiry into the matter and do the needful.
12. If the Adjudicating Officer find some person using any fishing vessel in contravention of any of the provisions of this Act, he may impose penalty of Rs. 5,000 (in case of the catch value less than Rs. 1,000) or five times of the value of fish (in case of catch value more than Rs. 1,000). In addition to this, the Adjudicating Officer may cancel, revoke or suspend the licence for sometime.
13. In each district, the District Magistrate shall constitute the Appellate Board for the whole district who has to hear the appeal of the person aggrieved by Adjudicating Officer. No appeal shall be entertained by the Appellate Board unless the appellant has deposited the aforesaid penalty.
14. The Appellate Board may call for an examination of the records of any order passed by an Adjudicating Officer and against which no appeal has been preferred and give the opportunity to the person affected of being heard in the matter.

15. The Adjudicating Officer and the Appellate Board shall have all the powers of a civil court under the code of civil procedure, 1908 for summoning, enforcing the witness, receiving evidence on affidavits and so on.
16. Whoever contravenes any of the provisions of this Act or any rule made thereunder shall without any prejudice be punished with fine which may extend to Rs. 1,000 and with further fine which may extend to Rs. 50 per day, on which such contravention continues after the first conviction.
17. When an offence has been committed by a company, every person who is involved in the offence, shall be punished accordingly.
18. The exemption is given to the vessels belonging to the States or Central Governments or any public undertakings from the above rules and regulations.
19. Protection shall be given to such action which is taken in good faith.
20. The state government has power to make certain rules consistent with the original Act and shall be subject to the condition of previous publication. Every rule made under this Act shall be passed only if both houses agree on it. Nothing in this Act shall apply to fishing and fisheries beyond territorial waters.

3

MARINE FISHERY RESOURCES OF INDIA

K.M. JOSEPH

PART I : RESOURCES ON THE WEST COAST

BACKGROUND

THE Arabian Sea, particularly the continental shelf along the west coast is of considerable significance to the development of the Indian Sea Food Industry. Firstly, more than 70 per cent of the present marine fish landing of approximately 14 lakh tonnes is accounted by the west coast. Secondly, about 75 per cent of the continental shelf, that is an area within 200 m depth, is along the west coast. This aspect is particularly significant when we consider the fact that demersal and coastal pelagic species account for about 96 per cent of the world sea fish production and about 99 per cent of India's marine fish production. Thirdly, the south west coast is one of the important areas of upwelling in the Indian ocean, yielding productive pelagic fisheries particularly sardine and mackerel. Fourthly, the west coast accounts for the largest share of the high value and export-oriented species of crustaceans, cephalopods and fishes like pomfrets and perch. Further the west coast has been surveyed more extensively than the east coast for fisheries resources. It may also be mentioned that marine fisheries is relatively more developed along the west coast than along the east coast.

The length of the west coast is about 3100 km. and the total area of tbe shelf is about 2,05,000 sq. km. as detailed below (Joseph, 1973; Joseph, *et al.*, 1975) :

	Approximate length of coastal line (km)	Approximate area of continental shelf (sq. km)
Gujarat	1600	108,761
Maharashtra	600)	
Goa	100)	115,970
Sub-total of north west coast :	2300	224,731
Karanataka	250	27,014
Kerala	500	39,723
Tamil Nadu	50	12,763
Sub-total of south west coast :	800	79,500
	3100	304,231

The maximum width of the shelf is about 340 km. and is north of Bombay at about lat. 20°N. The shelf narrows down to a width of about 75 km. along the Kerala coast and even in certain sections of the Gujarat coast. The shelf is generally flat and muddy or soft up to a depth of about 60 m along the entire coast. It is generally strewn with rocky and coral out-crops between the depth belts 60 to 100 m. The area beyond 100 m is generally hard and uneven. The continental slope is generally steep and starts from 200 to 230 m depth. In some areas, particularly off Quilon, a second shelf having a depth of about 250 to 450 m has been found. Off Gujarat, the shelf slopes down from 200 m to 250 m and then abruptly to over 600 m.

An effort has been made to evaluate the fisheries resources of the coast of India within 200 m depth, both exploited and exploitable. The deep sea and oceanic fish resources are dealt with seperately.

EXPLOITED RESOURCES

Average annual landing from west coast

The Table 3.1 indicates the contribution of the east and the west coasts to total sea fish landing during the five-year period from 1975. It may be seen that about 72 per cent of our average marine fish production of about 13.56 lakh tonnes comes from the Arabian Sea/west coast. This does not include the catch landed in the Tamil Nadu territory along the west coast which is about 20,000 tonnes per annum.

TABLE 3.1 : **Average fish landing from the west and east coast**

('000 tonnes)

	West coast	East coast	Total	Percentage Contribution of west coast
1975	990.82	431.84	1422.67	69.54
1976	928.76	424.10	1342.86	68.65
1977	923.22	335.56	1259.78	73.28
1978	1042.26	361.35	1403.61	74.25
1979	951.74	398.84	1341.58	70.94
Average :	967.36	388.88	1356.10	71.32

State-wise landing

Table 3.2 gives state-wise break-up of the landing for the same period, that is 1975-79. Kerala State with an annual average

TABLE 3.2 : **State-wise marine fish landing**

('000 tonnes)

	1975	1976	1977	1978	1979	Average
Gujarat	193.78	171.29	189.64	201.93	174.80	186.20
Maharashtra	256.62	293.60	264.45	284.24	293.21	278.42
Goa	29.17	34.97	24.73	27.11	25.29	28.25
Karnataka	87.49	95.28	97.15	152.86	124.14	111.38
Kerala	420.84	331.05	345.04	373.34	330.45	360.14
Lakshadweep	2.93	2.57	2.21	2.78	3.85	2.87
	990.83	928.76	923.22	1042.26	951.74	967.36

landing of about 3,60,000 tonnes contributes to about 36 per cent of the total landing from the west coast. Karanataka accounts for the lowest average annual catch.

Production on regional basis

Table 3.3 gives the average fish landing from the north-west and south-west coasts. The average annual landing from the north-west coast comprising Gujarat, Maharashtra, and Goa (lat. 15°N and 24°N) is about 4,93,000 tonnes while that from the south-west coast (lat. 7°N and 15°N) comprising Karnataka, Kerala, and the Lakshadweep is about 4,74,000 tonnes. From the table it may be seen that the north-west coast contributes to about 55 per cent of the total landing from the west coast.

TABLE 3.3 : **Average fish landings from North-west and South-west coasts**

('000 *tonnes*)

	1975	1976	1977	1978	1979	Average
North-west Coast	479.57	499.86	478.82	513.28	493.30	492.97
South-west Coast	511.26	428.90	444.40	528.98	458.44	474.40
	990.83	928.76	923.22	1042.26	951.74	967.36

Species composition of pelagic fish landing

The composition of the pelagic fish catches is given in Table 3.4 on the basis of the last five years' average landing. From the table it may be seen that about 33 per cent of the pelagic fish catch consists of oil sardine while Bombay duck accounts for about 21 per cent. The only other species that contributes to more than 10 per cent of the pelagic fish catch is mackerel. Thus, sardines, Bombay duck, and mackerel together account for about 71 per cent of the pelagic fish landing along the west coast. The other important varieties in the pelagic fish catches are species of ribbon fish, carangids, tuna and tuna-like fishes anchovies, seer fish, Chirocentrus, Thrissocles, Hilsa, and so on. It is significant to note that Clupeoids including oil sardine and lesser sardines

TABLE 3.4 : **Average landings of principal varieties of fishes—1979**

('000 tonnes)

	Gujarat	Maharashtra	Goa	Karnataka	Kerala	Lakshadweep	Total	Percentage contribution
Oil Sardine	—	837	829	40709	115078	—	159455	32.51
Lesser sardine	—	1577	5430	1690	23190	—	31799	6.48
Bombay duck	44570	56073	22	4	4	—	100675	20.52
Mackerel	7	1384	5730	30150	19879	—	57151	11.65
Ribbon fish	7768	9442	592	535	16039	—	34376	7.01
Tuna	495	952	235	729	9512	1812	13734	2.80
Carangids	1121	2221	1302	867	10913	68	16491	3.36
Anchoviella	126	347	9	479	11856	—	12817	2.59
Seer fish	2352	2826	546	1411	4583	—	11718	2.39
Chirocentrus	2297	2552	64	364	876	52	6205	1.27
Thrissocles	351	1707	585	691	1941	—	5275	1.08
Hilsa	5389	1367	4	60	69	—	6889	1.40
Other Clupeoids	10295	18036	526	1190	866	—	30913	6.30
Other Pelagic fishes	1087	615	118	161	942	119	3042	0.62
	75759	99939	17902	79041	215748	2050	490438	

contributes to about 49 per cent of the pelagic fish catch from the west coast. While Kerala accounts for about 70 per cent of sardine catch, Karnataka contributes to about 80 per cent of mackerel catch. Gujarat and Maharashtra together account for nearly 100 per cent of Bombay duck catch.

Species composition of pelagic fish on regional basis

Table 3.5 indicates the composition of the pelagic fish catch for the north-west and south-west coasts. The south-west coast accounts for about 61 per cent of the pelagic fish landing from the west coast. About 98 per cent of oil sardines, 88 per cent of tuna, and 88 per cent of the mackerel, 78 per cent of lesser sardines, and 97 per cent of anchovies are accounted for by the south-west coast while 100 per cent of Bombay duck, 52 per cent of ribbon fish, 79 per cent of Chirocentrus, 98 per cent of Hilsa, and 50 per cent of Thrissocles are contributed by the north-west coast. The mainstay of the pelagic fishery of the south-west coast is sardines and mackerel in contrast with Bombay duck, ribbon fish, Chirocentrus, and Hilsa which support the pelagic fishery of the north-west coast.

Species composition of demersal fish

Table 3.6 gives the state-wise composition of the demersal fish. For the purposes of this analysis prawns, lobsters, and Cephalopods are also included in the demersal group. Panaeid prawns accounted for about 21 per cent of the landing of the demersal species while scienids contributed to about 15 per cent of the demersal catch. In all crustaceans including lobster contributed to about 36 per cent of the demersal fish landings. Other groups which contributed 5 per cent or more are elasmobranchs, cat fish, pomfrets, and perches.

In the case of penaeid prawns nearly 50 per cent of the catch is accounted for by Kerala and about 30 per cent by Maharashtra while nearly 95 per cent of the non-penaeid prawn landings comes from Maharashtra. About 40 per cent of the sciaenids and 30 per cent of the elasmobranchs catches are taken from Gujarat waters. About 60 per cent of the perches and 40 per cent of the cat fish landings are from

TABLE 3.5 : **Species-wise composition of pelagic fishes**

('000 tonnes)

Species	North-west coast		South-west coast		Total quantity	Percentage contri-bution
	Quantity	Percen-tage	Quantity	Percen-tage		
Oil sardine	3668	2.30	155787	97.70	159455	32.51
Lesser sardine	6919	21.75	24880	78.75	31799	6.48
Bombay duck	100665	99.99	10	0.01	100675	20.52
Mackerel	7121	12.46	50029	87.54	57151	11.65
Ribbon fishes	17802	51.79	16574	48.21	34376	7.01
Tuna	1682	12.24	12053	87.76	13734	2.80
Carangids	4644	28.16	11848	71.84	16491	3.36
Anchoviella	382	3.00	12335	97.00	12717	2.59
Seer fish	5724	48.85	5994	51.15	11718	2.39
Chirocentrus	4913	79.18	1292	20.82	6205	1.27
Thrissocles	2643	50.10	2632	49.90	5275	1.08
Hilsa	6760	28.12	129	1.87	6889	1.40
Other Clupeoids	28857	93.35	2056	6.65	30913	6.30
Other Pelagic fishes	1820	59.83	1222	40.17	3042	0.62
	193600	39.47	296839	60.53	490440	100.00

TABLE 3.6 : **Species-wise composition of demersal fish**

('000 tonnes)

Species	Gujarat	Maharashtra	Goa	Karnataka	Kerala	Lakshadweep	Total	Percentage contri-bution
Elasmobranchs	10665	9100	875	2210	7923	307	31081	6.51
Cat fish	4571	9514	1058	5064	14729	—	34936	7.32
Sciaenids	35206	19198	2643	2376	10802	—	70225	14.72
Polynemids	3273	2025	13	2	72	—	5385	1.12
Perches	2844	3418	368	604	15421	191	22845	4.79
Mullets	294	395	15	45	628	35	1412	0.30
Lizard fish	839	1326	160	180	5627	—	8131	1.70
Cephalopods	2304	2416	140	1124	3719	23	9726	2.04
Eel	3727	3707	31	19	15	—	7499	1.57
Silver bellies	182	335	709	2571	4456	—	8251	1.73
Pomfrets	8149	14323	200	623	1809	—	25105	5.26
Soles	1469	1453	360	925	5610	—	9817	2.06
Lactarius	4909	517	326	288	812	—	6852	1.43
Penaeid prawns	9842	35766	2216	4476	45278	—	97579	20.45
Non-penaeid prawns	3497	60031	119	5	289	—	63940	13.40
Lobsters	911	513	173	16	36	—	1649	0.34
Other crustaceans	807	200	474	1286	3519	—	6285	1.31
Miscellaneous	17308	14250	472	10533	23646	267	66203	13.88
	110527	178487	10352	32345	144396	819	476926	

Kerala. Maharashtra contributes to about 60 per cent of pomfret while Gujarat accounts for about 30 per cent of the same.

Species composition of demersal fish region-wise

Table 3.7 furnishes the composition of the demersal fish catches separately for the north and south-west coasts. The north-west coast accounts for about 63 per cent of the demersal fish catch from the west coast. Quantitatively sciaenids, elasmobranchs, lactarius, eel, and so on are important while qualitatively, the noteworthy groups are polynemids, pomfrets, eel, lobster, penaeid prawns, and cephalopods. Along the south-west coast quantitatively, the notable species are silver bellies, soles, cat fish, lizard fish, mullets, and so on, whereas qualitatively the important groups are penaeid prawns, perches, and cephalopods. One of the noteworthy features of the demersal fishery of the south-west coast is the preponderance of low value and miscellaneous species of fish in the catches. On the whole about 14 per cent of the demersal catch consists of miscellaneous varieties as against less than 1 per cent in the case of pelagic fish.

EXPLOITABLE RESOURCES

Available estimates

The exploitable yield from the Indian continental shelf has been worked out by various authors (Prasad, *et al.* 1970; Jones and Banerji 1973; Antony Raja 1974) on the basis of primary production, average landing per unit area and so on. These estimates range from 13 lakh to 26 lakh tonnes. George, *et al.* (1977) estimated additional yield of about 40 lakh tonnes fish from the continental shelf. Of this, the share of the west coast is about 23 lakh tonnes comprising 15 lakh tonnes of pelagic fish and 8 lakh tonnes of demersal fish. Mention has already been made that the current average production is about 9 lakh tonnes. Joseph (1974) and Joseph, *et al* (1975) indicated an additional yield of about 5 lakh tonnes of demersal fish from within 70m (40 fm) depth on the basis the exploratory fishing data available from 1950 to 1974. Joseph (1980) estimated the

TABLE 3.7 : **Species-wise composition of demersal fishes**

('000 tonnes)

Species	North-west coast		South-west coast		Total quantity	Percentage contribution
	Quantity	Percentage	Quantity	Percentage		
Elasmobranchs	20640	66.41	10440	33.59	31081	6.51
Cat fishes	15143	43.34	19793	56.36	34936	7.32
Sciaenids	57047	81.23	13178	18.77	70225	14.72
Polynemids	5311	98.63	74	1.37	5385	1.12
Perches	6630	29.02	16216	70.98	22845	4.79
Mullets	704	49.86	708	50.14	1412	0.30
Lizard fish	2325	28.59	5807	71.41	8132	1.70
Cephalopods	4860	49.97	4866	50.03	9726	2.04
Eel	7465	99.55	34	0.45	7499	1.57
Silver bellies	1226	14.86	7027	85.14	8253	1.73
Pomfrets	22672	90.31	2432	9.69	25104	5.26
Soles	3282	33.43	6535	66.57	9817	2.06
Lactarius	5752	83.95	1100	16.05	6852	1.43
Penaeid prawns	47824	49.01	49754	50.99	97578	20.45
Non-penaeid prawns	63652	99.55	289	0.45	63941	13.40
Lobsters	1597	96.85	52	3.15	1649	0.34
Other crustaceans	1481	23.56	4805	76.44	6286	1.31
Miscellaneous fishes	31760	47.97	34446	52.03	66206	13.88
	299366	62.77	177560	37.23	476926	

potential yield of demersal fish from within 70m (40 fm) depth along the west coast at about 11 lakh tonnes including the current demersal production of about 5 lakh tonnes.

Methodology

As far as demersal fish resources are concerned, there appears to be rather reliable data for computation of the potential yield up to 70 m depth. There is also certain amount of information available about some deep water resources including deep sea lobster, deep sea prawns, and so on found beyond 200 m depth particularly along the south-west coast. However, very little information is available about the pelagic fish resources on the basis of actual exploratory fishing. Some information is available for the south-west coast on the basis of an acoustic survey conducted by the erstwhile Pelagic Fisheries Project. In the case of the north-west coast some information is available on the basis of acoustic observations and exploratory mid-water trawling conducted by the chartered polish vessels *Murena*, *Matsya Nireekshani*, and *Matsya Varshini* of the Exploratory Fisheries Project.

An attempt is made to provide three alternative methods of potential yield calculations. The first method is based on the current landing per unit area in respect of both demersal and pelagic fish resources. In an attempt to refine this method further, in the second method the potential yield is worked out separately for pelagic and demersal resources on the basis of current landing. In the third method the potential yield of demersal fish resources is worked out exclusively on the basis of the result of exploratory fishing whereas in the case of pelagic fish resources the potential is worked out on the basis of average current landing/unit area and the results of available exploratory surveys. In the case of the north-west coast the data of the exploratory surveys are used for the computation of pelagic fish resources. Since similar data are not available in the case of the south-west coast, the projection made by the erstwhile Pelagic Fisheries Project on the basis of the acoustic survey is used.

Assumptions and limitations of the study

This study deals with resources of the continental shelf as defined on geographical basis that is upto a depth of 200 m (100 fm). Firstly, the important reasons for limiting the scope of this study to 200 m is that the continental shelf rarely exceeds this limit. Secondly, we have very little data available about the resources in areas beyond this depth range. Thirdly, the immediate purpose of this study is to identify resources that could be exploited by the small sector within about 100 m depth. However, a separate section deals with the resources, of which we have some knowledge, of the continental slope and oceanic waters.

One of the most important and basic assumptions underlying the potential yield estimates contained in this paper is that the present landing of about 9.7 lakh tonnes of marine fish from the west coast is taken entirely from within 45 m (25 fm) depth. It may be recalled in this context that a study conducted by the Government of India (Anon, 1981) on the basis of 1978 marine fish landing had shown that about 62 per cent of India's marine fish landing was contributed by the traditional or non-mechanized sector and about 99 per cent of the remaining 38 per cent was landed by mechanized fishing vessels. Contribution of deep sea fishing vessels was placed at about less than 1 per cent of the 38 per cent of landings by mechanized vessels. Having regard to the fact that most of the mechanized boats are of 9 m to 11 m length and a sizeable number are catamarans and canoes fitted with outboard engines, it may be concluded that the assumption that the present landings of mechanized vessels are by and large from within 45 m depth is reasonable. To be very realistic no further increase in production is assumed from within 45 m depth for the purpose of this study although some increase is possible in the case of demersal species. Since the major quantity of the additional harvestable resources are expected to be contributed by stocks presently exploited, the potential yield also includes the current production in most cases. Other assumptions specific to each method are discussed separately.

Potential yield on the basis of current production

Appendix I provides the estimated potential yield from both pelagic and demersal fish resources from within 200 m depth along the west coast on the basis of the first method. It is assumed that the average yield per sq. km. area between 45—70 m depth and 70—200 m depth are likely to be 60 per cent and 40 per cent respectively of the current landings from within 45 m depth. On this basis the potential yield including current production from within 200 m depth is about 18.7 lakh tonnes. This indicates additional harvestable resources of about 9 lakh tonnes.

Potential yield on the basis of current landing of demersal and pelagic fish taken separately

On the basis of the second method it may be seen from Appendices II and III that the potential yield from pelagic fish resources within 200 m depth is about 8.2 lakh tonnes whereas from demersal fish resources, it is about 8.6 lakh tonnes. Thus the combined potential yield is 16.8 lakh tonnes, that is about 2 lakh tonnes less than that worked on the basis of the first method. The only difference in the assumptions between the first and second methods is that in the latter case, it is assumed that the average yield of pelagic fish from within 45—70 m depth and 70—200 m depth are likely to be 50 and 25 per cent respectively instead of the uniform rate of 60 and 40 per cent employed in the first method. However, the percentage production in the case of demersal fish resources remains the same.

Potential yield on the basis of exploratory fishing and current landing

From Appendix IV it may be seen that on the basis of exploratory fishing, the potential yield for the demersal fish from within 200 m depth is worked out to about 13.6 lakh tonnes. As already discussed else-where, the potential yield from within 70 m depth worked out on the basis of results obtained by the 17.5 m trawlers operated from six bases along the west coast during the period from 1970 to 1980 (Joseph 1980) is about 10.7 lakh tonnes. As far as the area from 70 to

200 m depth is concerned, on the basis of recent exploratory fishing, it is assumed that the rate of production is likely to be about 40 per cent of that obtained from within 70 m. Thus the potential yield of demersal fish stock from the west coast is about 13.6 lakh tonnes. Including the potential yield from the pelagic fish calculated on the basis of current production, the total potential yield of fish along the west coast on the basis of this approach is likely to be 21.9 lakh tonnes.

Potential yield exclusively on the basis of exploratory survey

Table 3.8 gives the potential yield estimates on the basis of the exploratory survey. On the basis of preliminary information it is seen that in the case of pelagic resources of the north-west coast, the average yield per sq. km. from 70 to 200 m depth is likely to be more than that from within 45 to 70 m depth. On the basis of the information available, it is assumed that about 2 lakh tonnes of pelagic fish is likely to be obtained from within 45 to 200 m depth. Thus, the potential yield of pelagic fish from the north-west coast is likely to be about 3.9 lakh tonnes. As regards the south-west coast it has already been mentioned that very little information is available on the basis of exploratory fishing and only information which can be used is the potential yield estimates made by the erstwhile Pelagic Fisheries Project which is about 8 lakh tonnes including the present production of about 3 lakh tonnes. The

TABLE 3.8 : **Estimated potential yield of marine fishes from the west coast**

	North-west coast			South-west coast			West coast Total	
	Potential yield	Current yield	Addl. exploitable yield	Petential yield	Current yield	Addl. exploitable yield	Potential yield	Addl. exploitable yield
Pelagic	394	194	200	797	297	500	1190	700
Demersal	928	299	628	438	178	260	1366	888
	1322	493	828	1235	475	760	2556	1588

potential yield from demersal stocks has already been discussed. Thus the combined potential yield of pelagic and demersal fish stocks calculated mainly on the basis of the exploratory survey is about 25.56 lakh tonnes.

Comparative evaluation of the potential yield estimates

Table 3.9 gives the potential yield worked out on the basis of the three methods. It may be seen that the potential yield worked out on the basis of the present average production is about 18.6 lakh tonnes as against about 25.6 lakh tonnes worked out on the basis of exploratory fishing. It may be seen that on the basis of exploratory fishing, the potential yield estimate is about a third more than that is estimated on the basis of average current landing. The additional exploitable resources on the basis of this from within the 200 m depth along the west coast is likely to be about 16 lakh tonnes of consisting of about 7 lakh tonnes of pelagic fish and 9 lakh tonnes of demersal fish, in contrast with about 23 lakh tonnes estimated by George, *et al.* (1977). They have projected an additional harvestable yield of 12 lakh tonnes from within 50 m depth and this accounts for the major difference.

TABLE 3.9 : **Comparative study of potential yield estimates—west coast of India**

(*Quantity in lakh tonnes*)

Method of study	Potential yield 66			Additional exploitable yield		
	Pelagic	Demersal	Total	Pelagic	Demersal	Total
Based on current production	—	—	18.69	—	—	9.02
Based on current production	8.25	8.59	16.84	3.34	3.83	7.17
Based on current production (pelagic) and exploratory survey (demersal)	8.25	13.66	21.91	3.34	8.88	12.22
Based on exploratory Survey	11.90	13.66	25.56	7.00	8.88	15.88

POTENTIAL YIELD—VARIETY-WISE

Pelagic group

The anticipated additional exploitable yields from important groups of pelagic fishes are furnished in Table 3.10.

Ribbon fishes

The results of the recent survey conducted along the north-west coast and the acoustic surveys carried out by the erstwhile Pelagic Fisheries Project indicates that Ribbon fish is likely to be one of the most promising pelagic fish resources particularly from the offshore waters of the west coast. Thirty-six per cent of *M.T. Murena's* catch from 70 to 200 m consisted of ribbon fish. George, *et al.* (1977) estimated a potential of about 200,000 tonnes of ribbon fish from the west coast as against the present production of about 35,000 tonnes. The fact that ribbon fish constituted about 40 per cent of the catch of the recently confiscated Taiwanese trawlers, from the north-west coast lends further support to the view that ribbon fish is a very promising offshore pelagic fishery resource. An additional catch of about 180,000 tonnes appears to be a reasonable estimate and a sizeable portion of it is expected from the north-west coast.

Anchovies

Species of Stolephorus, Thryssa, Setipinna, and Coilia contribute the anchovy fisheries of the west coast. Of these the first mentioned species popularly known as white bait is the most predominant species. Mainly on the basis of the acoustic survey, the erstwhile Pelagic Fisheries Project has estimated the standing stock of anchovies along the south-west coast as 376,000 tonnes (Anon, 1977), while George, *et al.* (1977) placed the potential yield of anchovies at 250,000 tonnes the bulk of which is to come from the south-west coast. The present landing along the west coast is about 12,000 tonnes only. It is reasonable to place the potential yield at about 50 per cent of the standing stock mentioned above which works out to about 180,000 tonnes. Giving allowance for the present production and the share of the

TABLE 3.10 : **Estimated additional yield from important pelagic fishes**

('000 tonnes)

Pelagic group	North-west coast			South-west coast			Total west coast		
	Potential yield	Current yield	Addl. exploitable yield	Potential yield	Current yield	Addl. exploitable yield	Potential yield	Current yield	Addl. exploitable yield
Oil sardine	8	3	5	241	156	85	249	159	90
Mackerel	19	7	12	118	50	68	137	57	80
Anchovies	1	—	1	111	12	99	112	12	100
Ribbon fishes	125	18	107	90	17	73	215	35	180
Carangids	59	5	54	48	12	36	107	17	90
Tuna and Tuna-like fishes	6	2	4	98	12	86	104	14	90
Other Clupeoids	44	36	8	16	6	10	60	42	18
Pelagic shark	8	—	8	32	—	32	40	—	40
Bombay duck	101	101	—	—	—	—	101	101	—
Other Pelagic fishes	23	22	1	43	32	11	66	54	12
	394	194	200	797	297	500	1191	491	700

Gulf of Mannar which was included in the standing stock assessment, the additional harvestable yield from the west coast may be placed at about 100,000 tonnes which is less than half of the estimates of the authors cited above. About 90 per cent of the catch is to be obtained from the area between Ratnagiri and Cape Comorin.

Carangids

Carangids consisting mainly of species of Megalaspis is likely to form another potential resource in the offshore waters. The bulk of this resource is to be exploited probably by purse-seining or midwater/pelagic trawling. Although the present landing of this group is only about 17,000 tonnes, it is reasonable to conclude that the additional yield is likely to be in the region of 90,000 tonnes. It may be recalled here that George, *et al.* (1977) estimated a potential yield of 110,000 tonnes from the north-west coast for carangids.

Tuna-like fishes

Recent surveys indicate that there is considerable potential to develop a fishery based on tune-like fishes consisting mainly of frigate mackerel, little tuna and bonito along the west coast of India. George *et al.* (1977) worked out the potential at about 60,000 tonnes from the south-west coast alone. Having regard to the subsequent findings of the Exploratory Fisheries Project vessels, it is expected that the additional potential from the west coast is likely to be about 90,000 tonnes of which about two-thirds will be from the south-west coast. Catches up to 20 tonnes/haul were taken during 1969-71 by the *Tuna* of the Indo-Norwegian project by purse-seining. Recent observations have indicated presence of all the species including bonito in shoals of sizeable quantities. Upto 4 tonnes/haul was taken. This resource is seasonal, with peak availability between September and January. Oceanic and skip jack tuna resources are dealt with separately.

Oil Sardines

There are divergent views about the potentiality of sardines, particularly of oil sardines, the catch of which has been fluctuating from 1,25,000 to 3,00,000 tonnes between 1965 and 1979. The average landing of oil sardine during the last five years is about 1,59,000 tonnes. On the basis of three decades of research, it is reported that the average standing stock of oil sardines is about 4,00,000 tonnes. Having regard to the fact that the total mortality of oil sardine is about 80 per cent at the fishing ground, the potential yield can safely be estimated anything between 50 and 75 per cent of the standing stock. Assuming that 60 per cent of the estimated stock will be available for harvest, the potential will be about 2,40,000 tonnes. Since the stock is under heavy pressure and the present landing is about 1,50,000 tonnes, it is likely that the additional potential will be about 90,000 tonnes as against 2,00,000 tonnes estimated by George *et al.* (1977). Other sardines are ignored for the purpose of this study.

Mackerel

As in the case of oil sardine, the mackerel fishery has been subject to wide fluctuations from year to year and its landings have ranged between 25,000 and 2,00,000 tonnes during the last 15 years. One author has placed the average stock of the mackerel at about 2,80,000 tonnes. Large shoals of mackerels are found unexploited be ween 40 and 72 m depth. George *et al.* placed the additional yield at about 1,00,000 tonnes. It is pertinent to note that in spite of the recent introduction of about 300 small and medium size purse-seiners along the south-west coast, there has been no apprecia-ble increase in its annual landing from the west coast. How-ever, since the mackerel fishery is also supported by yearlings and under-yearlings, it is safe to conclude that the potential is about 50 per cent of the estimated standing stock stated above. Thus the additional yield from this resource is likely to be about 80,000 tonnes which may have to come mainly from areas beyond 45 m depth.

Pelagic shark

According to Gulland (1971), pelagic shark is one of the most potentially rich fish resources of the Indian Ocean. The tuna longline fishing conducted by the Exploratory

Fisheries Project from its Cochin base during 1962-67 has shown hooking rate up to 7 in the case of shark from relatively shallow waters (Joseph 1972). Surveys conducted by the Maharashtra Government and the Gujarat Fisheries Department during the sixties also indicated good scope for shark fishery. It is perhaps one of the least exploited of large sized pelagic fishes. Although no precise estimates are possible owing to lack of inadequate data, it is reasonable to assume a potential yield of about 40,000 tonnes from the west coast. The magnitude of the resources will be much more outside of 200 m depth and in the oceanic waters which will be discussed separately.

Clupeoids

The present landing of other clupeoids consisting mainly of species of Chirocentrus, Thrissocles, Pellona, and so on is about 42,000 tonnes from the west coast. There is good scope for increasing the present catch by at least 50 per cent. An additional yield of about 18,000 tonnes is projected from this group of fish, particularly from the north-west coast.

Demersal fish resources

Table 3.11 gives the estimated additional yield from important groups of demersal fish.

Cat fish

Surveys conducted by the Exploratory Fisheries Project indicate that cat fish is perhaps one of the most promising resources in the deeper water. Catches of the trawlers of the Exploratory Fisheries Project consisted of 18—37 per cent of cat fish from various regions along the west coast (Joseph 1980). The recent surveys by larger vessels of the Exploratory Fisheries Project have also shown the existence of cat fish in sizeable quantities in waters up to 100 m depth. Cat fishes are also being taken by small purse-seiners along the south-west coast. George *et al.* projected a potential yield of about 210,000 tonnes of cat fist as against the present production of about 35,000 tonnes. It is, therefore, reasonable to anticipate an additional catch of about 1,50,000 tonnes. Mention may be

TABLE 3.11 : **Estimated additional yield from important demersal fishes**

Demersal fishes	North-west coast			South-west coast			Total west coast		
	Poten-tial yield	Current yield	Addl. exploi-table yield	Poten-tial yield	Current yield	Addl. exploi-table yield	Poten-tial yield	Current yield	Add. exploi-table yield
Elasmobranchs other than pelagic shark	83	21	62	28	10	18	111	31	80
Cat fish	90	15	75	95	20	75	185	35	150
Sciaenids	136	57	79	24	13	11	160	70	90
Perches	67	7	60	81	16	65	148	23	125
Nemipterus spp.	92	21	71	47	18	29	139	39	100
Eel	32	7	25	—	—	—	32	7	25
Silver bellies	1	1	—	18	7	11	19	8	11
Cephalopods	55	5	50	25	5	20	80	10	70
Penaeid prawns	60	48	12	55	50	5	115	98	17
Pomfrets	73	23	50	5	2	3	78	25	53
Perch like fishes	50	—	50	—	—	—	50	—	50
Other fishes	188	94	94	60	37	23	248	131	117
	927	299	628	438	178	260	1365	477	888

made of the fact that the cat fish has a relatively wider distribution by both depth and distance.

Elasmobranchs

The present catch of elasmobranchs is about 31,000 tonnes. The surveys have shown a catch rate of about 20 per cent of elasmobranchs consisting mainly of rays and skates. M.T. Murena has recorded about 7 per cent catch rate. George *et al.* estimated a potential of about 80,000 tonnes of elasmobranchs from the west coast. Since the bottom condition is rather hard beyond 70 m depth, it is unlikely that the demersal species of elasmobranchs will be more than the estimate given here.

Perches

The exploratory surveys conducted along the south-west coa st by the erstwhile Indo-Norwegian Project and by the Exploratory Fisheries Project on the north-west coast show that there is considerable scope for increased harvesting of this group of fish not only by trawling but also by hand line fishing, trap fishing, and so on. There appears to be a good resource of perches along the entire west coast between 60 –100 m depth belt which is characterized as rocky and coral out crops (Menon and Joseph 1969, Silas 1969). About 20 per cent of the trawal catches from the Wadge Bank also consists of perches. It is, therefore, anticipated that an additional catch of about 1,25,000 tonnes of perches is possible from the west coast. George, *et al.* projected an additional potential of 1,50,000 tonnes.

Thread fin breams

This is perhaps one of the demersal fish resources which has a wider distribution than the cat fishes along the west coast of India. It is well known that the species of Nemipterus forms about 25 per cent of the trawal catches along the south-west coast. Recent surveys have shown the existence of this resource up to 200 metres depth along the north-west coast. Catch rates up to 150 m was recorded from 200 m depth. In fact thread fin breams have been identified as one of the predominant groups of fish along the north-west coast in areas deeper than 70 m. It is, therefore, reasonable to believe that thread fin breams will yield an additional catch of about 1,00,000 tonnes from the west coast. The present landing is about 29,000 tonnes.

Perch-like fishes

Recent surveys have indicated the existence of certain species of perch-like fishes popularly known as Sweet lips belonging to the genus Gaterin. This fish looks like perches and its average weight/fish is about 300 gm. It grows to 25 – 30 cm in length. An average catch rate of 14 kg was obtained from 100—200 m depth. This together with thread fin bream, forms the bulk of the catches along the north-west coast. The potential yield of this new found resource is estimated at about 50,000 tonnes which appears to be very modest.

Sciaenids

Sciaenids constitute about 70,000 tonnes of the present demersal catch of the west coast. George, *et al.* estimated an additional potential of about 90,000 tonnes of sciaenids from the west coast. Having regard to the fact that the distribution of sciaenids is rather sparse in deeper waters, the above estimate is considered reasonable.

Cephalopods

There is considerable potential for the development of squid and cuttle fish fishery in waters deeper than 50 m. The highest catch rate of 200 kg/hr was obtained from the depth range 70—120 m. However, the exploitation of this resource is to be done either by midwater or pelagic trawl and squid jigging. It is estimated that the potential yield of cephalopods is likely to be about 70,000 tonnes as against the present production of about 10,000 tonnes. The bulk of this catch is to come from the north-west coast.

Other important species

Eel, silver bellies, and pomfret are expected to produce additional catches of about 25,000, 11,000 and 53,000 tonnes respectively. The bulk of the eel and pomfret catches are expected from the north-west coast. The exploratory midwater pelagic trawling has shown very encouraging results in the case of pomfrets. As far as penaeid prawns are concerned, a marginal increase of about 17,000 tonnes is considered possible. Other species such as lizard fish, polynemids, mullets, soles, lactarius, non-penaeid prawns, and so on, are expected to contribute to an additional catch of about 1,20,000 tonnes.

PART II : RESOURCES OF THE EAST COAST

The fact that a little more than 50 per cent of the Exclusive Economic Zone (EEZ) of India lies in the Bay of Bengal brings to the focus the relative importance of the Bay of Bengal in the context of the marine fisheries development of the country. It is also significant to note that more than 50 per cent of the EEZ area of the Bay of Bengal belongs to the Andaman and Nicobar group of Islands. The shelf area of the east cost in general and of the lower east coast and Andaman and Nicobar group of Islands in particular is rather narrow and steep. It is also well known that the Bay of Bengal is more influenced by the north-east monsoon than by the south-west monsoon.

The marine fishery of the east coast consists of perhaps more species than that of the west coast. It is also remarkable that unlike in the case of the west coast where the bulk of the fish landing is accounted by a few dominant species such as oil sardine, mackerel and Bombay duck, the east coast has no such prolific fishery. Another significant factor is the emergence of the upper east coast as a potentially rich penaeid prawn ground.

Other features of the east coast

The length of the east coast is about 2600 km. and the total area of the shelf is approximately 1,11,780 sq. km. as detailed below (Joseph *et al.*, 1976). The shelf area of the Andaman and Nicobar group of Islands is estimated at 16,056 sq. km. (Jones and Banerji, 1973).

For convenience the whole east coast has been divided into two regions: lower east coast (lat. 8° N and 15° n) comprising

Tamil Nadu, Union Territory of Pondicherry, and part of Andhra Pradesh, and upper east coast (lat. 16°N and 21° N) which consists of a major part of Andhra Pradesh, Orissa and West Bengal. The extent of the shelf area of these two regions are given below:

Lower east coast	:	44,180 sq. km.
Upper east coast	:	67,600 sq. km.
		1,11,780 sq. km.

	Approximate length of the coast (km.)	Approximate area of coast shelf (sq. km.)
Tamil Nadu Pondicherry	950	38,400
Andhra Pradesh	970	24,670
Orissa and West Bengal	680	48,710
Total:	2,600	1,11,780
Andaman and Nicobar Islands	—	16,056

The continental shelf along the east coast is relatively narrow and its width varies from a maximum of 80 km. off Point Calimore in the lower east coast to about 180 km. off Balasore in the upper east coast. The average width may be placed at about 40 km. as against about 75 km. along the west coast. Except for the estuarine areas and some areas off West Bengal and Orissa, the shelf is generally hard and uneven. As in the case of the West coast there appears to be a rocky/coral ridge right along the coast of about 90 m (50 fm) depth. The slope of the shelf is rather steep in most of the places. The average value of the salinity ranges between 30 and 35 per cent while the surface temperature varies between 27°C and 29°C. The thermocline is usually below 55 m and at times goes down to 100-125 m level. The shelf water is generally isothermal. Although upwelling is reported as a seasonal phenomenon, nutrients in high concentrations are absent in the surface water (Panikkar and Jayaraman, 1966).

EXPLOITED RESOURCES

Average annual landing from east coast

Table 3.12 furnishes the contribution of the east coast and the Andaman and Nicobar islands to the total sea fish landing during the five-year period 1975-79 (1980 figures are furnished in Appendices V & VI). From the table it will be seen that about 29 per cent of the average marine fish production or approximately 3.9 lakh tonnes is landed along the east coast. It may further be seen from the table that the catch has been fluctuating between 3.36 lakh and 4.31 lakh tonnes during the period 1975-79.

TABLE 3.12 : **Average fish landing from the east coast**

Fish landing period	East coast	West coast	Total	Percentage contribution to total catch
1975	431.87	990.82	1422.69	30.36
1976	424.08	928.77	1352.85	31.35
1977	336.56	923.22	1259.78	26.72
1978	361.35	1042.26	1403.61	25.75
1979	398.14	990.24	1388.38	28.68
Average:	390.73	975.07	1379.13	28.39

State-wise landings

Table 3.13 indicates the state-wise break up for the same period, that is 1975-79. From the table it may be seen that Tamil Nadu with an average landing of about 2.2 lakh tonnes contributed to about 56 per cent of the landing from the east coast. Andhra Pradesh with an average annual landing of about 1.12 lakh tonnes ranks second among the maritime states of the east coast. The average landing from West Bengal and Orissa works out to only 16,000 and 31,000 tonnes respectively although about 50 per cent of the continental shelf of the east coast forms part of these two maritime states. The average contribution of the Andaman islands is about 2,500 tonnes.

TABLE 3.13 : **State-wise landings from the east coast**

('000 tonnes)

State-wise landing	1975	1976	1977	1978	1979	Average
Tamil Nadu	221.22	226.08	206.05	212.90	234.88	220.04
Pondicherry	8.15	10.12	6.46	6.83	10.07	8.33
Andhra Pradesh	155.64	131.32	100.76	82.12	91.18	112.20
Orissa }	45.76 }	29.82	15.07	39.67	41.37	31.48
West Bengal }		25.41	6.69	12.75	18.99	15.96
Andamans	1.10	1.33	1.53	7.07	1.72	2.55
TOTAL :	431.87	424.08	336.56	361.35	398.14	390.73

Production on regional basis

Table 3.14 furnishes the average landing from the lower east coast and the upper east coast. The average landing from the lower east coast comprising mainly Tamil Nadu which includes its west coast is about 2.3 lakh tonnes or approximately 58 per cent of the total landing from the east coast. The upper east coast comprising a major portion of Andhra Pradesh and the entire West Bengal and Orissa coasts contributes to about 41 per cent of the catch.

Species composition of pelagic fish landing

The composition of the pelagic fish landing along the east coast is given in Table 3.15 on the basis of the landing during 1975-79. It may be seen that about 27 per cent of the pelagic fish catch consists of lesser sardines while ribbon fish accounts for about 16 per cent and anchovies 11 per cent. Thus sardines, ribbon fish, and anchovies account for a little over 50 per cent of the pelagic fish catch from the east coast, as against 71 per cent accounted by oil sardine, Bombay duck, and mackerel along the west coast. Other species which contribute more than 5 per cent of the landing are carangids, Hilsa Spp., seer fish, and mackerel. It is noteworthy that clupeoids form about 50 per cent of the total pelagic fish landed from the east coast as in the case of west coast.

Tamil Nadu accounts for about 60 per cent of the sardine and ribbon fish, while the bulk of the remaining catch is landed in Andhra Pradesh. About 50 per cent of the anchovies catch also is landed in Tamil Nadu, whereas about 50 per cent of the Hilsa Spp. is landed in Orissa.

Species composition of the pelagic fish on regional basis

Table 3.16 furnishes the composition of the pelagic fish separately for the upper east coast and lower east coast. The lower east coast accounts for about 58 per cent of the pelagic fish. It also contributes to more than 60 per cent of the landing of lesser sardines, ribbon fish, thrissocles, tuna, carangids, and mackerel, while the upper east coast for nearly 100 per cent of Bombay duck, 71 per cent of Hilsa Spp., 57 per cent of

TABLE 3.14 : Average fish landings from lower and upper east coast 1975-1979

('000 tonne)

Lower and upper east coast	1975	1976	1977	1978	1979	Average
Lower east coast	229.37	236.20	212.51	219.74	244.89	228.54
Upper east coast	201.40	186.55	122.52	134.54	151.54	159.64
Andaman and Nicobar Islands	1.10	1.33	1.53	7.07	1.72	2.55
	431.87	424.08	336.56	361.35	398.15	390.73

TABLE 3.15 : Landings of principal varieties of pelagic fishes

('000 *tonnes*)

Pelagic fish varieties	Tamil Nadu	Pondicherry	Andhra Pradesh	Orissa	West Bengal	Andamans	Total	% age contribution
Oil sardine	352	—	49	—	—	—	401	0.22
Lesser sardine	28383	1445	16210	1964	4	93	48099	26.95
Bombay duck	3	—	670	171	1472	—	2316	1.30
Anchovies	10128	401	8198	624	12	102	19465	10.91
Ribbon fishes	18227	231	8906	250	495	—	28109	15.75
Thrissoeles	4951	399	2039	183	702	—	8274	4.64
Tuna & Tuna-like fishes	2467	1	442	190	—	35	3135	1.76
Hilsa Spp.	3378	118	1462	6961	449	28	12396	6.95
Carangids	7212	485	4244	696	57	127	12821	7.19
Mackerel	5392	972	1972	274	—	100	8710	4.88
Seer fish	4847	46	4019	1271	176	112	10471	5.87
Chirocentrus	1984	91	1642	978	246	38	4979	2.79
Other Clupeoids	6103	135	4524	1046	1297	14	13119	7.36
Other Pel. fishes	4719	385	818	27	—	230	6179	3.46
	98147	4708	55196	14634	4911	879	178475	

TABLE 3.16 : **Species-wise composition of pelagic fishes region-wise**

Species	Lower east coast		Upper east coast		Andamans		Total	
	Qnty.	Percentage	Qnty.	Percentage	Qnty.	Percentage	Qnty.	Percentage
Oil sardine	352	87.78	49	12.21	—	—	401	0.22
Lesser sardine	29828	62.01	18178	37.79	93	0.19	48099	26.95
Bombay duck	3	0.13	2313	99.87	—	—	2316	1.30
Anchovies	10529	54.09	8834	45.38	102	0.53	19465	10.91
Ribbon fishes	18458	65.67	9651	34.33	—	—	28109	15.75
Thrissoeles	5350	64.66	2924	35.34	—	—	8274	4.64
Tuna	2468	78.72	632	20.16	35	1.12	3135	1.76
Hilsa Spp.	3496	28.20	8872	71.57	28	0.23	12396	6.95
Carangids	7697	60.03	4997	38.98	127	0.99	12821	7.19
Mackerel	6364	73.07	2246	25.78	100	1.15	8710	4.88
Seer fish	4893	46.73	5466	52.20	112	1.07	10471	5.87
Chirocentrus	2075	41.68	2866	57.56	38	0.76	4979	2.79
Other Clupeoids	6238	47.55	6867	52.34	14	0.11	13119	7.36
Other Pel. fishes	5104	82.60	845	13.68	230	3.72	6179	3.46
	102855	57.63	74741	41.88	879	0.49	178475	

Chirocentrus, and 52 per cent of seer fish. The main pelagic fish caught from Andaman waters are mackerel, carangids, seer fish, anchovies, and lesser sardines, basides tuna.

Species composition of demersal fish

Table 3.17 illustrates the composition of demersal fish landing on state-wise basis. Penaeid prawns accounted for 10 per cent of the total landings of the demersal species. The contributions of silver bellies, sciaenids and elasmobranchs were respectively 16, 13 and 13 per cent. Other species which contributed more than 5 per cent are cat fish (7.19 per cent), perches (5.24 per cent), pomfrets (6.5 per cent) and other crustaceans (5.8 per cent).

About 50 per cent of the total penaeid prawn landing is accounted for by Tamil Nadu, while 80 per cent of the remaining is landed in Andhra Pradesh. Similarly, about 60 per cent of the elasmobranchs, 50 per cent of the sciaenids, 70 per cent of silver bellies, 50 per cent of cat fish, and 70 per cent of perches are also landed in Tamil Nadu. About 50 per cent of the pomfret is taken from Orissa and of the remaining about 80 per cent is accounted by West Bengal and Andhra Pradesh.

Species composition of demersal fish region-wise

From Table 3.18 it may be seen about 59 per cent of the demersal fish are landed in the lower east coast and the major constituents are silver bellies, sciaenids, elasmobranchs, panaeid prawns and perches, besides other crustaceans. The major constituents to the landings from ths upper east coast are pomfret, eel, polynemids, lactarius, sciaenids, and cat fish, besides prawns. The main groups landed from the Andaman waters are silver bellies, panaeid prawns, perches, cat fish, elasmobranchs and pomfrets. The demersal fish landing is approximately twice the quantity of pelagic fish landing in the Andaman islands. It may also be seen that about 93 per cent of the pomfret caught along the east coast is landed in the upper east coast.

TABLE 3.17 : **Average state-wise landings of demersal fishes**

('000 *tonnes*)

Species	Tamil Nadu	Pondicherry	Andhra Pradesh	Orissa	West Bengal	Andaman	Total	Percentage
Elasmobranchs	17092	213	7761	2964	230	77	28337	13.36
Cat fish	7715	95	5734	1378	302	30	15254	7.19
Sciaenids	13519	317	9435	1579	1893	—	26743	12.60
Polynemids	1187	17	1367	693	88	—	3352	1.58
Perches	7304	608	2881	81	56	194	11124	5.24
R. Mullets	1287	104	470	1	—	—	1862	0.88
Lizard fish	1004	129	744	15	—	—	1892	0.89
Eel	281	21	761	1	—	—	1064	0.50
Silver bellies	28148	486	5361	491	157	92	34735	16.38
Pomfrets	884	39	5366	6861	2560	26	13736	6.48
Soles	1312	146	400	52	6	—	1916	0.90
Lactarius	1100	67	1398	8	—	—	2573	1.21
Cephalopods	1745	83	324	11	8	—	2171	1.02
P. Prawns	10414	207	7778	1219	939	88	2645	9.73
N.P. Prawns	477	29	3111	40	950	—	4607	2.17
Lobsters	373	17	46	—	—	—	436	0.21
Crabs and other crustaceans	11300	313	634	10	—	—	12257	5.78
Misc. fish	16749	726	5435	1447	3861	1167	29385	13.86
	121889	3618	57006	16850	11050	1674	212089	

TABLE 3.18 : **Species-wise catch composition**

('000 tonnes)

Species	Lower east coast		Upper east coast		Andaman		Total	
	Qnty.	Percentage	Qnty.	Percentage	Qnty.	Percentage	Qnty.	Percentage
Elasmobranchs	17305	61.07	10955	38.66	77	0.27	28337	13.36
Cat fish	7810	51.20	7414	48.60	30	0.20	15254	7.19
Sciaenids	13836	51.74	12907	48.26	—	—	26743	12.60
Polynemids	1204	35.92	2148	64.08	—	—	3352	1.58
Perches	7912	71.13	3018	27.13	194	1.74	11124	5.24
R. Mullets	1391	74.70	471	26.30	—	—	1862	0.88
Lizard fish	1133	59.88	759	40.12	—	—	1892	0.89
Eel	302	28.38	762	71.62	—	—	1064	0.50
Silver bellies	28634	82.44	6009	17.30	92	0.26	34735	16.38
Pomfrets	923	6.72	12787	93.09	26	0.19	13736	6.48
Soles	1458	76.10	458	23.90	—	—	1916	0.90
Lactarius	1167	45.36	1406	54.64	—	—	2573	1.21
Cephalopods	1828	84.20	343	15.80	—	—	2171	1.02
P. Prawns	10621	51.45	9936	48.12	88	0.43	20645	9.73
N.P. Prawns	506	12.63	4101	87.37	—	—	4607	2.17
Lobsters	390	89.45	46	10.55	—	—	436	0.21
Other Crustaceans	11613	94.75	644	5.25	—	—	12257	5.78
Misc. fish	17475	59.47	10743	36.56	1167	3.97	29385	13.86
	125507	59.18	84906	40.03	1674	0.79	212089	

EXPLOITABLE RESOURCES

Available estimate

Estimates common to both west and east coasts have already been given earlier. George *et al.* (1977) have placed the potential yield from the east coast at about 14 lakh tonnes. Antony Raja (1980) in a review has placed the sustainable yield from the east coast between 10 and 10.5 lakh tonnes of fish. Joseph (1980) on the basis of exploratory demersal trawling has placed the potential yield of demersal fish from within 40 fm (70 m) depth at about six lakh tonnes.

Methodology

As in the case of west coast as far as demersal fish resources are concerned there appears to be rather dependable data for computation of potential yield up to 70 m depth. There is also some amount of information available on the existence of resources which is available in deeper waters, especially in the case of the Gulf of Mannar and areas between Point Calimere and Madras. The survey by the Project vessel *Matsya Nireekshani* during the last quarter of 1981 has also thrown open some interesting information about the demersal fish resources of the Wadge Bank upto a depth of 100 fm (Anon, 1982). However, very little information is available about the pelagic fish resources on the basis of actual exploratory fishing as in the case of the west coast except for the scanty information available from the midwater trawl/purse seining operation conducted very recently by the project vessels *Matsya Darshini* and *Matsya Shikari* operating from Visakhapatnam (Anon, 1980, 1981). The methodology adopted for estimating potential yield is, therefore, almost identical to that has been employed in the case of the west coast. The results of the recent surveys by the large vessels have also been taken into account for the computation of demersal and pelagic fish resources.

Assumptions and limitations of the study

Here also, we will estimate the resources of the continental shelf as defined on geographical basis, that is up to 180 m depth. The reasons for limiting the scope of the study to 180 m depth has been given earlier. One of the most important assumptions underlying the potential yield estimate is, that the present landing of 3.9 lakh tonnes of marine fish from the east coast is taken mainly from 40 m depth. The main exception to this will be the catch landed by about 50 out rigger shrimp trawlers operated from Visakhapatnam. However, the contribution of these vessels, the catch of which comprises mainly panaeied prawn, appears to be insignificant to the total landing. Nevertheless, having regard to the relatively poor level of exploitation of marine fisheries along the east coast, particularly along the upper east coast in comparison with the west coast, even the resources within 40 m are not fully exploited especially in the case of pelagic fish. Fishing in both inshore and offshore areas, particularly off the Orissa and West Bengal coasts appears to be insignificant when viewed from the number of mechanized boats operating there. The total number of fishing vessels including 18280 mechanized boats available along the Orissa and West Bengal coasts during 1982-83 were 607 and 178 respectively as against 3100 in Kerala. The significance of this observation will be clear from the fact that Orissa and West Bengal have a continental shelf area of about 49,000 sq. km. as against 39,000 sq. km. in the case of Kerala.

Potential yield estimates on the basis of current production

Appendix VII gives the estimated potential yield of both demersal and pelagic resources up to 180 m depth on the basis of the average current yield. The average current production per sq. km. is 9.37 tonnes and 7.70 tonnes for the lower east coast and Andhra Pradesh respectively while it is only 1.57 tonnes in the case of Orissa and West Bengal. On the assumption that the average yield per sq. km. from within 45—70 m (25—40 fm) and 70—180 m (40—100 fm) are likely to be 60 per cent and 40 per cent respectively of the current production from within the 45 m (25 fm) depth it is estimated that the potential yield including the present production from the east coast will be about five lakh tonnes. This gives an additional harvestable yield of about 1.2 lakh tonnes. Obviously the reason for this low estimate is the narrowness of the continental shelf along the east coast as compared to the west coast, besides the low current harvest from the Orissa-West Bengal coast.

By separately computing the potential yield on the basis of average current production of demersal fish and pelagic fish a slightly lower figure of 4.96 lakh tonnes is obtained (Appendices VIII and IX). The assumption regarding the average yield from 45 to 70 m and 70 to 180 m remains the same as in the case of the west coast. It appears that estimates based on current production may not be very valid for the east coast. The relatively poor development of marine fisheries along the east coast and in particular along the upper east coast has also been discussed elsewhere. The average current yield per sq. km. from Orissa and West Bengal is only 1.57 tonnes. About 80 per cent of the continental shelf area falls within 70 m depth which is generally believed to be the most productive area. In the case of the west coast, on the other hand, the area within 70 m depth is approximately 60 per cent of the shelf area of 3.4 lakh sq. km. It is also significant to note that on the basis exploratory fishing a potential yield of demersal fish from within 70 m depth is placed at about 6 lakh tonnes.

Potential yield on the basis of the exploratory fishing and current landing

From Appendix X it may be seen that the potential yield of demersal fish from within 180 m depth is about 6.59 lakh tonnes comprising about 6 lakh tonnes from within 70 m depth and 58,000 tonnes from 70—180 m depth. The present landing of demersal stock is estimated at 2.1 lakh tonnes which would mean that an additional harvestable yield of about 4.49 lakh tonnes.

There is very little data to make such estimates for the pelagic fish stock on the basis of exploratory fishing. Based on current production and exploratory surveys the potential yield of the pelagic fish resources within 180 m is estimated to be about 4 lakh tonnes (Appendix XI). The additional harvestable yield is likely to be about 75 per cent of the present production from the lower east coast and 100 per cent from the upper east coast. These assumptions are mainly on the basis of existence of sizeable quantities of mackerel, carangids, ribbon fish, other clupeoids, and so on, in areas outside 40 m limit along the upper east coast of anchovies in the lower east coast, besides the relatively poor pressure of fishing in the upper east coast. The additional harvestable yield of pelagic resources from within 180 m depth is thus likely to be about 2.2 lakh tonnes as against the current production of 1.7 lakh tonnes.

The total potential yield from the lower east coast is estimated at about 4.2 lakh tonnes as against 6.4 lakh tonnes from the upper east coast. The additional harvestable yield from the lower east coast is about 1.95 lakh tonnes which is little less than the present production from the lower east coast. The additional harvestable yield from the upper east coast on the other hand is 4.3 lakh tonnes which is about 3 times the present production from that area.

POTENTIAL YIELD VARIETY-WISE

Pelagic group

The anticipated additional exploitable yield from important groups of pelagic fishes projected on the basis of the information available is given in Table 3.19. Out of the 14 species of fish which contribute to about 93 per cent of the present pelagic fish landing on the east coast, lesser sardines, anchovies and ribbon fish account for more than 50 per cent of the landing. It is expected that mackerel, carangids, other clupeodis, pelagic, shark, lesser sardines, anchovies, and ribbon fish, will contribute to the bulk of additional harvestable yield of pelagic fish from the east coast. The total additional harvestable yield estimate is about 2.2 lakh tonnes as against 4.5 lakh tonnes estimated by George *et al.* One of the major differences between the present estimate and that of George *et al.* is that the present estimate envisages that a suitable portion of the additional harvestable yield should come from resources such as mackerel, carangids and pelagic shark. The recent purse seine and midwater tawl surveys conducted by the project vessels have indicated potentially rich resources of mackerel, carangids, and ribbon fish, and their percentages in the catches were respectively 17, 10, and 5.

TABLE 3.19 : **Estimated additional yield of important pelagic fishes from east coast**

('000 tonnes)

Pelagic fishes east coast	Lower east coast			Upper east coast			Total east coast		
	Total pot. yield	Current production	Addl. harvestable yield	Total pot. yield	Current production	Addl. harvestable yield	Total pot. yield	Current production	Addl. harvestable yield
Lesser sardine	38403	29828	8575	29548	18178	11370	67951	48006	19945
Anchovies	26004	10529	15475	14519	8834	5685	40523	19363	21160
Ribbon fishes	32733	18458	14275	29102	9652	19450	61835	28110	33725
Tuna & Tuna like Fishes	6793	2468	4325	4832	632	4200	11625	3100	8525
Mackerel	10314	6364	3950	42616	2246	40370	52930	8610	44320
Carangids	17672	7697	9975	28937	4997	23940	46609	12694	33915
Seer Fish	7293	4893	2400	7861	5466	2395	15154	10359	4795
Other clupeoids	22840	14015	8825	30676	12706	17970	53516	26721	26795
Hilsa Spp.	3496	3496	—	10667	8872	1795	14163	12368	1795
Pelagic shark	7000	—	7000	13500	—	13500	20500	—	20500
Other pelagic fishes	7457	5107	2350	11965	3158	8807	19422	8265	11157
TOTAL	180005	102855	77150	224223	74741	149482	404228	177596	226632

The potential yield of pelagic fish from east coast is estimated at about 4.1 lakh tonnes consisting of about 1.8 lakh tonnes of the present production and about 2.3 lakh tonnes of the additional anticipated yield. The present estimate is very conservative as compared to the estimates made by George *et al.* which is about 8 lakh tonnes. This is partly because of inadequate information available on the basis of actual exploratory fishing. Table 3.20 furnishes a comparison of the estimates by this author and George *et al.*

TABLE 3.20 : **Comparison of additional harvestable yield estimates from the east coast**

(Qnty. '000 tonnes)

Species	Current Production	Estimate by George *et al.* (1977)	Estimate of present study
Elasmobranchs	28	75	67
Cat fishes	15	100	51
Perches	11	90	37
Sciaenids	27	120	60
Leognathids	35	85	29
Pomfrets	14	55	33
Pen. Prawns	21	55	19
Other crustaceans	17	40	12
Cephalopods	2	120	49
Nemipterids	12	—	25
Lesser sardine	48	85	20
Mackerel	9	15	44
Anchovies	19	80	21
Ribbon fish	29	70	34
Carangids	13	85	34
Other Clupeoids	27	85	27
Pelagic sharks	—	—	21
Tuna	3	30	9
Other fishes	60	240	83
	390	1420	675

Demersal fish

Table 3.21 furnishes the additional harvestable yield and potential yield estimates of the important varieties of demersal

TABLE 3.21 : **Estimated additional yield of important demersal fishes**

(in tonnes)

Species	Lower east coast			Upper east coast			Total east coast		
	Total pot. yield	Current production	Addl. harvestable yield	Total pot. yield	Current production	Addl. harvestable yield	Total pot yield	Current production	Addl. harvestable yield
Elasmobranchs	36055	17305	18750	59290	10955	48335	95345	28260	67085
Cat fishes	14440	7810	6630	52090	7415	44675	66530	15225	51305
Perches	31542	7912	23630	16708	3018	13690	48250	10930	37320
Sciaenids	24476	13836	10640	62612	12907	49705	87088	26743	60345
Nemipterids	15775	7500	8275	20749	4184	16565	36524	11684	24840
Leiognathids	51089	28634	22455	12199	6009	6190	63288	34643	28645
Eel	1482	302	1180	4076	761	3315	5558	1063	4495
Pomfret	3443	923	2520	42832	12787	30045	46275	13710	32565
Cephalopods	16578	1828	14750	35043	343	34700	51621	2171	49450
Pen. Prawns	10621	10621	—	29361	9936	19425	39982	20557	19425
Other crustaceans	14009	12509	1500	14891	4791	10100	28900	17300	11600
Other fishes	23787	16327	7460	66106	11800	54306	89893	28127	61766
	243297	125507	117790	415957	84906	331051	659254	210413	448841

fish including caphalopods and crustaceans. The varieties which are likely to contribute considerably to the additional harvestable yield are elasmobranchs, sciaenids, cat fish, perches, cephalopods, pomfrets, leiognathids, and nemipterus. The total estimated additional harvestable yield is about 4.5 lakh tonnes as against the estimate of 9.5 lakhs by George *et al.* From Table 3.9 it may be seen that in almost all the cases except in the case of nemipterus and pelagic shark the present estimates are underestimates as compared to the estimates made by George *et al.* On the basis of exploratory surveys it is estimated that the nemipterus is likely to emerge as a potentially rich resources as in the case of the west coast. Silas (1976) and Krishnamoorthy (1973) have also placed nemipterus as an important emerging fishery which is likely to be found up to 180m depth. Gulland (1971) has indicated that pelagic shark resources from the Indian ocean are likely to be very high.

Potential yield estimates from Andaman and Nicobar waters

Only scanty information is available about the resources on the Andaman and Nicobar water on the basis of exploratory surveys. Although, exploratory fishing by trawling is done from 1971, extensive surveying in the area has not been possible due to a variety of reasons. The present landing of fish in the Andaman and Nicobar waters is estimated at about 2,500 tonnes. George *et al.* have estimated an harvestable yield of 1.6 lakh tonnes from within 180 m depth of which about one lakh tonnes is tuna and tuna-like fishes. Antony Raja (1980) has estimated the potential yield at about one lakh tonnes. Sudarshan (1977) has estimated a standing stock of about 45,000 tonnes in the case of demersal fish, which is perhaps the only estimate available on the basis of the exploratory fisheries survey.

Table 3.22 indicates the potential yield from important varieties of fish resources from the Andaman and Nicobar waters. The estimated potential of the pelagic fish resoures is about 50,000 tonnes as against 20,000 tonnes in the case of demersal fishes. The potential yield is placed at about 70,000 tonnes from within 180 m which is less than 50 per cent of that is estimated by George *et al.* The important species which are likely to contribute to the fishery are tuna and tuna-like fishes, pelagic shark carangids, leiognathids, perches, anchovies, mackerel, sciaenids, and so on.

TABLE 3.22 : Estimated potential yield of important varieties of marine fishes

Varieties	Current landings	Harvestable yield from pelagic fishes	Addl. Harvestable yield from demersal fishes	Total pot. yield
Elasmobranchs	77	—	1,000**	1,077
Perches	194	—	4,220	4,394
Leiognathids	92	—	4,000	4,092
Sciaenids	—*	—	1,000	1,000
Upenoids	—*	—	800	800
Other fishes	1,733	2,500	9,000	13,233
Tuna and Tuna-like fishes	35	25,000	—	25,035
Pelagic shark	—*	10,000	—	10,000
Mackerel	100	1,000	—	1,100
Anchovies	102	2,000	—	2,102
Lesser sardines	93	1,500	—	1,593
Carangids	127	8,000	—	8,127
	2,553	50,000	20,000	72,533

*Separate landing figures not available.

**Excluding Pelagic shark.

APPENDIX-I

ESTIMATED POTENTIAL YIELD OF MARINE FISHES FROM WEST COAST OF INDIA BASED ON CURRENT PRODUCTION

	Current produc-tion	Current yield/ sq. km	Addl. harvestable yield			Potential yield
			45—70 m	70—200 m	Total	
Gujarat	186286	2.86	24216	33774	57990	244,276
Maharashtra	278426	10.84	120921	261233	382154	660,580
Goa	28254	8.23	11876	18072	29948	963,058
Sub-Total North-west coast	492966		157013	313079	470092	58,058
Karnataka	111386	12.43	66857	45182	112039	223,425
Kerala	360144	2.42	216088	99888	315976	676,120
Lakshadweep	2869	1.43	1290	2434	3724	6,593
Sub-Total South-west coast	474399		284235	147504	431739	906,138
	967365		441248	460583	901831	1,869,196

APPENDIX-II

ESTIMATED POTENTIAL YIELD OF PELAGIC FISHES FROM THE WEST COAST OF INDIA BASED ON CURRENT PRODUCTION

(*tonnes*)

	Current production	Current yield/ sq. km	Addl. harvestable yield 45—70 m	70—2000 m	Total	Potential yield
Gujarat	75759	1.16	8166	8592	16758	92,517
Maharashtra	99939	3.89	36576	58386	94962	194,901
Goa	17902	5.21	6274	7141	13415	31,317
Sub-Total North-west coast	193600		50016	74119	125135	318,735
Karnataka	79041	8.82	39522	20091	59613	138,654
Kerala	215748	14.63	107970	37420	145390	361,138
Lakshadweep	2869	1.43	1290	2434	3724	6,593
Sub-Total South-west coast	297658		148782	59945	208727	506,385
	491258		199798	134064	333862	825,120

APPENDIX-III

ESTIMATED POTENTIAL YIELD OF DEMERSAL FISHES FROM THE WEST COAST OF INDIA BASED ON CURRENT PRODUCTION

	Current production	Current yield/ sq.km.	Addl. harvestable yield			Potential yield
			45—70 m	70—200 m	Total	
Gujarat	110527	1.70	14360	20146	34506	145,033
Maharashtra	178487	6.95	78217	100520	178737	357,224
Goa	10352	3.01	4351	6592	10943	21,295
Sub-Total North-west coast	299366		96928	127258	224186	523,555
Karnataka	32345	3.61	19448	13091	32539	64,884
Kerala	144396	9.79	86583	40078	126661	271,057
Sub-Total South-west coast	176741		106031	53169	159200	335,941
	476107		202959	180427	383386	859,493

APPENDIX-IV

ESTIMATED POTENTIAL YIELD OF MARINE FISHES FROM WEST COAST OF INDIA BASED ON CURRENT PRODUCTION (PELAGIC FISHES) AND EXPLORATORY SURVEY (DEMERSAL FISHES)

(tonnes)

	PELAGIC					DEMERSAL					TOTAL				
	Current production	Addl. exploitable yield			Potential yield	Current production	Addl. exploitable yield			Potential yield	Current production	Addl. exploitable yield			Potential yield
		45—70 m	70—200 m	Total			40—70 m	70—200 m	Total			40—70 m	70—200 m	Total	
Gujarat	75759	8166	8592	16758	92517	110527	259127	59539	314666	425193	186286	267293	64131	33141	517710
Maharashtra	99939	36576	58386	94962	194901	178487	120608	161938	282546	461033	278426	157184	220324	377508	655934
Goa	17902	6274	7141	13415	31317	10352	19674	11385	31059	41411	28254	25948	18526	64148	92402
Sub-total North-west coast	193600	61016	74119	125135	318735	299366	399409	228862	628271	927637	492966	450425	302981	773080	1266046

APPENDIX-IV (Contd.)

Karnataka	79041	39522	20091	59613	138654	32345	67355	20293	87648	119993	111386	106877	40384	147261	258647
Kerala	215748	107970	37420	145390	361138	144396	116004	36006	152010	296406	360144	223974	73426	297400	657544
Lakshadweep/ Wadge Bank	2869	1290	2434	3724	6593	—	16725	4860	21585	21585	2869	18015	7294	25309	208178
Sub-Total South-west coast	297658	148782	59945	208727	506385	176741	200084	61159	261243	437984	474399	343866	121104	469970	944369
	491258	199798	134064	333862	825120	476107	599493	290021	889514	1365621	967365	799291	424085	1223376	2190741

APPENDIX-V

ESTIMATED MARINE FISH LANDINGS OF EAST COAST OF INDIA DURING 1980

State/varieties	Tamil Nadu	Pondi-cherry	Andhra Pradesh	Orissa	West Bengal	Andaman & Nicobar Islands	Total east coast
Oil sardine	320	—	—	—	—	—	320
Lesser sardine	29940	2736	13930	1891	—	243	48740
Bombay duck	6	—	611	378	419	—	1414
Anchovies	13126	287	6182	270	—	99	19964
Ribbon fishes	7862	179	15646	928	142	—	24757
Thrissocles	5048	387	7326	333	194	—	13288
Tuna & Tuna-like fishes	4233	—	419	34	—	55	4741
Hilsa Spp.	3121	78	1363	5137	664	25	10388
Carangids	6883	483	6791	1174	130	147	15608
Mackerel	7229	445	6203	265	—	183	14325
Seer fish	7179	85	2970	1542	234	117	12127
Chirocentrus	2695	98	1123	1460	276	25	5677
Other clupeoids	1833	273	5486	2576	674	29	10871
Other pelagic fishes	3364	133	255	72	—	225	4049
Sub-Total pelagic	92839	5184	68305	16060	2733	1148	186269

APPENDIX-V (Contd.)

Elasmobranchs	15442	435	4842	3772	114	56	24661
Cat fish	4047	78	2338	2198	723	32	9416
Sciaenids	19547	320	9496	2864	358	—	32585
Polynemids	629	6	1448	1126	186	—	3395
Perches	6886	666	4639	341	13	302	12847
R. Mullets	1079	150	349	296	—	—	1874
Lizard fish	1123	160	931	189	—	—	2403
Eel	85	8	289	—	—	—	382
Silver bellies	38153	681	3775	704	34	102	43449
Pomfrets	1306	188	2201	9072	921	15	13703
Soles	2094	151	573	69	3	—	2890
Lactarius	938	29	940	65	—	—	1972
Cephalopods	1472	40	470	98	4	—	2084
Pen. Prawns*	9082	485	5660	1074	152	54	16507
N.P. Prawns	946	42	4346	30	48	—	5412
Lobsters	90	4	10	—	—	—	104
Other crustaceans	6174	172	1413	359	20	—	8138
Other Fishes**	15462	591	3988	1058	788	94	21981
Sub-Total demersal	124555	4206	47708	23315	3364	655	203803
Total :	217394	9390	116013	39375	6097	1803	390072

* 32 tonnes by private trawlers

** 2212 tonnes by private trawlers

APPENDIX-VI

ESTIMATED MARINE FISH LANDINGS OF WEST COAST OF INDIA DURING 1980

State/varieties	Gujarat	Maharashtra	Goa	Karnataka	Kerala	Lakshadweep	Total west coast
Oil sardine	—	663	2367	42727	69667	—	115424
Lesser sardine	—	1363	1798	4135	11017	—	18313
Bombay duck	36671	57393	12	15	—	—	94091
Anchovies	—	78	249	5621	7772	—	13720
Ribbon fishes	10858	11550	1089	1499	12937	—	37933
Thrissocles	913	1271	779	850	2241	—	6054
Tuna and Tuna-like fishes	277	1674	356	952	10611	1760	15630
Hilsa Spp.	4021	1624	22	33	35	—	5735
Carangids	1483	2061	955	4806	4741	80	14126
Mackerel	112	288	2446	19634	18474	—	40954
Seer fish	4180	3219	735	1941	3763	21	13859
Chirocentrus	3792	2039	124	171	1002	—	7128
Other clupeoids	8538	16897	302	1088	574	—	27399
Other pelagic fishes	1797	258	190	358	842	142	3587
Sub-Total pelagic	72642	100378	11424	83830	143676	2003	413953

APPENDIX-VI (Contd.)

Elasmobranchs	14558	7752	894	2910	6803	284	33201
Cat fish	5235	8653	1151	5354	13936	—	34329
Sciaenids	31625	13956	1530	3500	6164	—	56775
Polynemids	667	1976	10	—	8	—	2661
Perches	2454	3712	269	1069	17814	376	25694
R. Mullets	—	461	15	38	1	27	542
Lizard fish	85	1057	199	508	7080	—	8929
Eel	8403	3154	6	131	6	—	11700
Silver bellies	—	406	1727	4671	4147	—	10951
Pomfrets	12587	10081	257	696	907	—	24528
Soles	2459	1797	1311	782	4394	—	10743
Lactarius	2520	450	614	998	861	—	5443
Cephalopods	3471	1191	210	122	4244	13	9251
Pen. prawns	14481	23433	1853	3098	52633	—	95498
N.P. prawns	4109	47309	—	128	1742	—	53288
Lobsters	204	225	18	110	18	—	575
Other crustaceans	4967	297	1933	2765	7286	—	17248
Other fishes	23027	5475	1069	4612	7823	206	42212
Sub-Total demersal	130852	131385	13066	31492	135867	906	443568
Total :	203494	231763	24490	115322	279543	2909	857521

APPENDIX-VII

ESTIMATED POTENTIAL YIELD OF MARINE FISHES FROM EAST COAST AND ANDAMAN SEAS BASED ON CURRENT PRODUCTION

(*tonnes*)

	Current production	Current yield/sq. km	Additional harvestable yield			Potential yield
			45—70 m	70—200 m	Total	
Tamil Nadu and	2,20,036	9.37	37,850	18,319	56,169	2,34,531
Pondicherry	8,326					
Andhra Pradesh	1,12,203	7.70	30,071	18,588	48,659	1,60,862
Orissa and	31,484	1.57	6,944	7,015	13,959	61,406
West Bengal	15,963					
Total east coast	3,88,012	—	74,865	43,922	1,18,787	5,06,799
Andamans	2,554	0.21	390	84	474	3,028
	3,90,566		75,255	44,006	1,19,261	5,09,827

APPENDIX-VIII

ESTIMATED POTENTIAL YIELD OF PELAGIC FISHES FROM EAST COAST AND ANDAMAN SEAS BASED ON CURRENT PRODUCTION

(*tonnes*)

	Current production	Current yield/sq. km	Additional harvestable yield			Potential yield
			45—70 m	70—200 m	Total	
Tamil Nadu &	98,147					
Pondicherry	4,708	4.22	14,186	5,178	19,364	1,22,219
Andhra Pradesh	55,196	3.79	12,367	5,733	18,100	73,296
Orissa and	14,634					
West Bengal	4,911	0.65	2,412	1,782	4,194	23,739
Total east coast	1,77,596	—	28,965	12,693	41,658	2,19,254
Andamans	879	0.07	120	21	141	1,020
	1,78,475		29,085	12,714	41,799	2,20,274

APPENDIX-IX

ESTIMATED POTENTIAL YIELD OF DEMERSAL FISHES FROM EAST COAST OF INDIA BASED ON CURRENT PRODUCTION

(*tonnes*)

	Current production	Current yield/ sq. km	Additional harvestable yield			Potential yield
			45—70 m	70—200 m	Total	
Tamil Nadu &	1,21,889	5.15	20,774	10,063	30,837	1,56,344
Pondicherry	3,618					
Andhra Pradesh	57,006	3.91	15,296	9,415	24,711	81,717
Orissa &	16,850	0.92	4,020	4,120	8,140	36,040
West Bengal	11,050					
Total east coast	2,10,413	—	40,090	23,598	63,688	2,74,101
Andamans	1,674	0.14	240	63	303	1,977
	2,12,087		40,330	23,661	63,991	2,76,078

ESTIMATED POTENTIAL YIELD OF MARINE FISHES FROM EAST COAST OF INDIA BASED ON CURRENT PRODUCTION (PELAGIC FISHES) AND EXPLORATORY SURVEY (DEMERSAL FISHES)

(tonnes)

	PELAGIC					DEMERSAL					TOTAL				
	Cur. Production	Addl. Harv. Yield 40—70 m	Addl. Harv. Yield 70—200 m	Addl. Harv. Yield Total	Potential yield	Cur. Production	Addl. Harv. Yield 40—70 m	Addl. Harv. Yield 70—200 m	Addl. Harv. Yield Total	Potential yield	Cur. Production	Addl. Harv. Yield 40—70 m	Addl. Harv. Yield 70—200 m	Addl. Harv. Yield Total	Potential yield
Tamil Nadu & Pondicherry	98147 4708	14186	5178	19364	122219	121889 3618	103428	14362	117790	243297	220036 8326	117614	19540	137154	365516
S.T. Lower east coast	102855	14186	5178	19364	122219	125507	103428	14362	117790	243297	228362	117614	19540	137154	365516
Andhra Pradesh	55196	12367	5733	18100	73296	57006	11935	7906	19847	76847	112202	24302	13639	37941	150143
Orissa & West Bengal	14634 4911	2412	1782	4194	23739	16850 11050	275244	35966	311210	339110	31484 15961	277656	37748	315404	362849
S.T. Upper east coast	74741	14779	7515	22294	97035	84906	287179	43872	331051	415957	159957	301958	51387	353345	512992
	177596	28965	12693	41658	219254	210413	390607	58234	448841	659254	388009	419572	70927	496499	878508

APPENDIX-XI

ESTIMATED POTENTIAL YIELD OF MARINE FISHES FROM EAST OF INDIA BASED ON EXPLORATORY SURVEY

(tonnes)

	PELAGIC					DEMERSAL					TOTAL				
	Cur. Produc-tion	Addl. Harv. Yield			Penten-tial yield	Cur. Produc-tion	Addl. Harv. Yield			Poten-tial yield	Cur. Produc-tion	Addl. Harv. Yield			Poten-tial yield
		40—70 m	70—200 m	Total			40—70 m	70—200 m	Total			40—70 m	70—200 m	Total	
Lower east coast	102855	54000	23150	77150	180005	125507	103428	14362	117790	243297	228362	157428	375122	194940	423302
Upper east coast	74741	89690	59792	149482	224223	84906	287179	43872	331051	415957	159647	376869	103664	480533	640180
	177596	143690	82942	226632	404228	210413	390607	58234	448841	659254	388009	534297	141176	675473	1063482

REFERENCES

Anon, Report of the technical team on development of fisheries in Andaman and Nicobar Islands, 1976.

Anon, Indian Fisheries 1947—77. Fisheries Research 7-21. CMFRI Cochin, 1977.

Anon, Report of Acoustic Survey along the south-west coast of India. November 1976 UNDP/FAO Pelagic Fisheries Project on the south-west coast of India, Phase II—*Progress Report No. 1, 1977.*

Anon, Summary report on the cruise of *M.T. Murena* in the north-west coast of India (*M.S.*) 1978.

Anon, Marine Fisheries Information Services. *CMFRI Mar. Fish Infor. Serv. T. & E Ser. No. 03/1978.*

Anon, Marine Fisheries Information Service, *CMFRI Mar. Fish Infor. Serv. T & E Ser. No. 9-1979.*

Anon, Annual Report. *Exploratory Fisheries Project 1979-80.*

Anon, Annual Report. *Exploratory Fisheries Project 1980-81.*

Anon, Sixth Plan proposal for fisheries development, Ministry of Agri., Govt. of India, 1981.

Anon, Results of Exploratory survey of fisheries resources of Wadge Bank—*Progress Report No. 1, 1982.*

Alverson, D.L. Field surveys and the survey and charting of resources. IOFC/DEV/71/6.0.22, 1971.

Antony Raja, B.T., Our Pelagic fishery resources. Present and potential harvest. *Sea Food Exp. Jon.* vol. 6 (1) 79-85, 1974.

Antony Raja, B.T., Current knowledge of fisheries resources in the shelf area of the Bay of Bengal. BOBP/W.P./8. PAO/SIDA., 1980.

Banerji, S.K., Report of the FAD/Norway workshop on the fishery resources of the North Arabian Sea. Karachi, Pakistan 16-28. January 1978 Vol. I proceedings (Report and country statements). IOFC/DEV/78/43.1.53. p., 1978.

Banerji, S.K., Report of the FAO/Norway workshop on the fishery resources of the north Arabian Sea Karachi, Pakistan 16-28. January 1978 Vol. II Papers IOFC/DEV/78/43.2:204 p., 1978.

Cushing, D.A., Survey of the resources in the Indian ocean and Indonesian area IOFC/DEV/71/2 p. 123, 1971.

Dwivedi, S.N., N. Radhakrishnan, and K.P. Philip Preliminary report of the first cruise of *M.T. Murena* (8th to 10th January 1977) and supporting vessels Report No. 1, Exploratory Fisheries Project, Bombay, 1977.

Dwivedi, S.N., N. Radhakrishnan, and M.K.R. Nair, Preliminary report of the second cruise of the *M.T. Murena* and supporting vessels from 19th February to 12th April, 1977. Report No. 2, Exploratory Fisheries Project, Bombay, 1977.

Dwivedi, S.N., Radhakrishnan, N., P. Sulochanan, M.K.R. Nair and Antony Joseph, Preliminary report of the third cruise of *M.T. Murena* and supporting vessels for the period from 21st April to 21st

May, 1977. Report No. 3, Exploratory Fisheries Project, Bombay, 1977.

George, P.C. B.T. Antony Raja and K.C. George, Fishery Resources of the Indian Economic Zone. Sovu. Integrated Fisheries Project, Silver Jubilee Celebrations 79-120 p., 1977.

Gulland, J.A., The fish resources of the ocean. Fishing News (Books) Ltd., England, 255 p. 1971.

Hayasi, S. Stock assessment—IOFC/DEV/71/3.34 p. 1971.

Jones, S. and S.K. Banerji, A review of the living resources of the Central Indian Ocean. *Proc. Symp. on living resources of the seas around India*, Spl. publication: CMFRI 1-17 p., 1973.

Joseph, K.M., A study of the deep sea prawn resources of the south west coast of India. *Sea Food Export Journ.* 1 (8) 77-33 p. 1970.

Joseph, K.M., Crustacean Fisheries of the west coast of India IOFC/DEV/71/21-23 p. 1971.

Joseph, K.M., Some observations on the exploitation of the Indian Ocean Tuna Resources. *Sea Food Export Jour.* 14 (8): 11-18, 1972.

Joseph, K.M., A profile of the deep sea fishery resources of the south-west coast of India. *Sea Food Export. Jour.* 4 (1), 1974.

Joseph, K.M., Demersal fishery resources of the north-west coast of India. *Bull. Expl. Fish. Proj.* No. 1, 1-45 p., 1979.

Joseph, K.M., Radhakrishnan, N. and K.P. Philip, Demersal Fisheries Resources of the south west-coast of India. *Bull. Expl. Fish. Proj.* No. 3, 1975.

Joseph, K.M., Radhakrishnan, N., Antony Joseph and K.P. Philip, Results of demersal fisheries resources survey along east coast of India. *Bull. Expl. Fish Project.* No. 5, 1975.

Joseph, K.M., Comparative study of the Demersal fishery reasources of the Indian Waters as assessed by 17.5 m trawlers, *Bull. Expl. Fish. Proj.* No. 10, 1980.

Krishnamurthy, B., An assessment on Nemipterus fishery of Andhra-Orissa Coasts based on Exploratory Fishing. *Proc.: Symp. on living resources of seas around India Spl.* publ. CMFRI 495-575. 1973.

Kumaran, M., The fishery potential of Andaman and Nicobar Islands, Ibid. p. 387-389. 1973.

Mar. J.C. *et al.* A plan for fishery development in the Indian ocean IOFC/DEV/71/1 78 p., 1971.

Mendis, A.S., Resources of wadge and pedro bank. *Bulletin of Fisheries Research Station*, Sri Lanka 18 (2). 47-51, 1965.

Menon, M.D. & K.M. Joseph, Development of Kalava (rock cod) fishery of south-west coast of India—A prospectus. *Sea Food Export Journal*, 1 (2) 7-28, 1969.

Panickar, N.K. and R. Jayaraman, Biological and Oceanographic difference between the Arabian Sea and the Bay of Bengal as observed from the Indian region. *Proc. Indian Acad. Sci.* 64 (5) p. 231-240. 1966.

Prasad, R. Raghu, S.K. Banerji and P.V.R. Nair, A quantitative estimate of the potential fishery resources of Indian ocean and adjacent seas. *Indian Jou. Anim. Sci*, 40 (1) : 73-98, 1970.

Silas, E.G., Exploratory trawl fishing by R.V. Varuna, *Bull. Cent. Mar. Fish Res.* Inst. No. 12 86-p, 1969.

Silas, E.G., S.K. Dharmaraja & K Rangarajan, Exploited marine fishery resources of India. *Bull. of Cen. Mar. Fish. Res. Inst.* No. 27., 1976.

Swaminathan, M., N. Radhakrishnan, M.K.R. Nair and Antony Joseph, Preliminary report of the fourth cruise of *M.T. Murena* for the period from 15th June to 22nd August 1977. Report No. 3 Exploratory Fisheries Project, 1977.

Swaminathan, M., N. Radhakrishnan, Mohammed Roshan Aktar, M.K.R. Nair and Antony Joseph, Preliminary report of the fifth cruise of *M.T. Murena* and supporting vessels for the period from 7th September to 14th October, 1977. Report No. 5 Exploratory Fisheries Project, Bombay, 1977.

Swaminathan, M., D. Sudarsan, N. Radhakrishnan, M.K.R. Nair and Antony Joseph, Preliminary report of the sixth cruise of *M.T. Murena* and supporting vessels for the period from 28th October to 14th December, 1977. Report No. 6 Exploratory Fisheries Project, Bombay, 1978.

Sudarsan, D., Results of Exploratory survey around Andaman Islands *Bull. Expl. Fish. Proj.* No. 7, 1978.

West, W.O.B., Fishery resources of the Upper Bay of Bengal, IOFC/DEV/72/28-44 p. 1973.

Yamanika, Y., Nishigawa and J. Moita, Summary report on the cruise of the *R/V Shoyomaru* in the Northern Arabian Sea 2. Oct. 75—14 January 1976. IOP/TECH/76/11, 44-p. 1976.

4

MARICULTURE*

AQUATECH ENTERPRISE

INTRODUCTION

THE term 'Mariculture' was coined by Winston Menzel to distinguish aquaculture (cultivation or culture or aquatic organisms) in marine environment as against that carried out in fresh water environment. In its simplest expression, mariculture means growing of marine plants and animals with some degree of control with the aim of harvesting and marketing the resulting crop. It, sometimes, needs to be clarified that mariculture is not a technology; it is, like agriculture, a terminology used for several types of operations which differ in operational details but largely follow a uniform logical chain of functional principles.

Mariculture, or activities which can now be classified as mariculture, has ancient history. Written records of brackish water fish, culture, are available from fifth century B.C. Oyster cultivation by Greeks was mentioned by Aristotle and Pliny gives an account of oyster farming by Romans from 100 B.C. Milkfish (*Chanos chanos*) cultivation presently flourishing in south-east Asia, is believed to have developed in the A.D. 15th Century. Although authentic records are not available, brackish water farming, albeit employing a low grade cultivation technology, has been practised for centuries in India.

*Prepared by Acquatech Enterprises, Ratnagiri.

The present day seafood industry consists of procurement, processing, and marketing of products derived from marine plants and animals. The industry depends almost entirely on natural marine living resources which are harvested by using fishing technology. In the light of scientific knowledge regarding the potential of marine living resources, clear limits to procurement are becoming increasingly apparent. While such limits may not have been reached presently it is obvious that they will be eventually reached. It is necessary that additional, if not alternative, sources of raw material procurement be developed. Mariculture holds the strongest possibility for such development.

Mariculture can contribute directly towards this goal by producing plants and animals as is done presently by maricapture. However, mariculture has a distinct advantage over maricapture in that its production can be market-oriented. For example, in the world seafood market the penaeid shrimps are the top-priced commodity. It is not entirely possible even with a high degree of technological sophistication to conduct selective fishing for shrimps whereas with mariculture every possibility exists of intentional production of penaeid shrimps of desired variety, quality, and quantity.

Why then, in spite of such long history and advantages, mariculture is yet to make its impact on societies in general and the seafood industry in particular ? It is obvious that over the centuries maricapture gained industrial proportions but, apart from a few exceptions, mariculture never grew beyond the subsistence level. Bardach *et al.* (1972) have put up an interesting explanation for this situation. They state that :

> Since man is a land dweller it is logical that he applied scientific and engineering skill to land animal production first and foremost, especially since he could, and still can, gather, rather than grow and tend, fish from sea and inland waters. In part, this is (also) the reason why animal husbandry in water is far less developed than the corresponding branch of agriculture on land.

With context to shrimp farming Raje and Ranade (1978)

ask: "Why has not shrimp farming developed as an industry so far? Like any other business venture the reason could be either that this project has not been given sufficient thought or that the project has been sufficiently thought over and shelved as unappealing. We are of the opinion that while the industry was appraised of the benefits of shrimp farming the specific details of the technology and the financial implications have never been provided. Of the two directions... (available, that is shrimp catching and shrimp farming) . . . . for increase in shrimp production the industry possibly felt that the second was uncertain and resorted to the first where the technology was already or at least allegedly, known."

Development of mariculture on industrial proportions thus appears to have been hampered owing to complex reasons, social, psychological, biotechnological, biochemical reasons.

MARICULTURE AS A SYSTEM

We propose to begin our task by presenting mariculture as a system. A 'system' is defined as "...... a set of parts co-ordinated to accomplish set of goals" (Churchman, 1968). Mariculture as a system will be better understood if the following five considerations are taken into account :

(a) The objective of mariculture and their performance measures.
(b) Environment of mariculture.
(c) Resources of mariculture.
(d) Components and sub-systems of mariculture, their objectives, goals and performance measures.
(e) Management of mariculture.

For the present we propose to adopt a simple, generalized, and perhaps less refined objective for the mariculture system as "production of seafood by employing the principles of cultivation". In view of the competition imposed by the system's nearest rival, mariculture, the system must produce seafood comparable on par with or better than the produced in mari-capture with respect to the quantity, quality, and cost of production.

The performance measure of the system's overall objective will therefore be known by applying the following tests :

(i) Does it add to seafood production, and
(ii) Is this additional comparably on par or superior to that being produced by maricapture with respect to quantity, quality, and production cost?

The *environment* of mariculture comprises fixed constraints which matter relatively to the objective but are beyond the control of the system operator. Five such limits within which the system has to function can be identified. These are: (i) Geographical limits, (ii) Hydrographical limits, (iii) Topographical limits, (iv) Market limits, and (v) Legal limits.

Geographical limits

Geographical limits of mariculture are three dimensional. The vertical limit is 2 metres above sea-level to 10 metres below sea-level. Although mariculture can be extended beyond these limits, such aspects are, and will be in near future, largely experimental. The horizontal limit along the shore axis will be governed by the extent of the +2 metre contour inland and 10 metre contour seawards at any given point on the coast. The horizontal limit along the coastal axis is directly proportional to the length of the coastline. The first estimate of the maximum possible area available for mariculture (A^1) will thus be : $A^1 = (B^1 \times L)$ sq. metres where L is the running coastal length in metres, Area A^1, however, is the theoretical maximum extent within the vertical limit AB (Fig. 4.1) and is subject to further limitations mentioned below.

Hydrographical limits

To understand hydrographical limits it is essential to define the scope of the word 'marine' in the definition of mariculture. The 'marine environment' of mariculture is not restrictive to oceanic waters but also inclued brackishwater which are formed by admixture of fresh water and oceanic water. In chemical terms such waters are denoted by "parts per thousand salinity" (p.p.t.). Maricultural technologies have been successfully employed in hydrographic environment of 0.8 p.p.t. to 40.0 p.p.t. salinities. This range of salinity can, therefore, be considered as the hydrographic limits of mariculture. Any given water body in the area AL will be suitable for the system only if the water is within these hydrographical limits.

Topographical limits

Topographical limits of mariculture arise from the engineering requirements for providing containments, empoundments, enclosures, and so on in which cultivation is to be undertaken. Cultivation technologies require dug-out or bunded, net or pen enclosures, stakes, cages, and rafts in or upon which the candidate species of plants or animals are cultivated. Such cultivation units have specific topographical requirements for their construction and operation. For example, shrimp farming requires either bunded or dug-out earthen ponds; the bunded ponds require protection from turbulent sea and, therefore, can only be constructed in protective places like estuaries or creeks. On the other hand, raft farming of oysters requires good depth of water which is invariably not available in creeks and, therefore, the rafts need to be operated in bays. Site selection for various types of cultivation has rigorous specifications in mariculture. Any given area of water must have topographic suitability.

Legal limits

Legal limits upon mariculture environment are imposed by the legal activities of other enterprises or industries in the prospective water body or area. These include urban development, navigational rights, fishing rights, and so on. For example, the vast low-lying areas in New Bombay (Maharashtra) can be developed for mariculture by creating excavated ponds had it not been for the development plans of New Bombay. Similarly, every major creek, estuary, or bay has an established navigational route leading to a port, harbour, jetty, or anchorage. By law the maricultural activities must yield a portion of its prospective area howsoever suitable it may be for its own purpose, to such 'right-of-the-way'. Such factors collectively contribute towards imposing legal limits on the system environment.

Market limits

Market limits arise from the selective demand for sea-food.

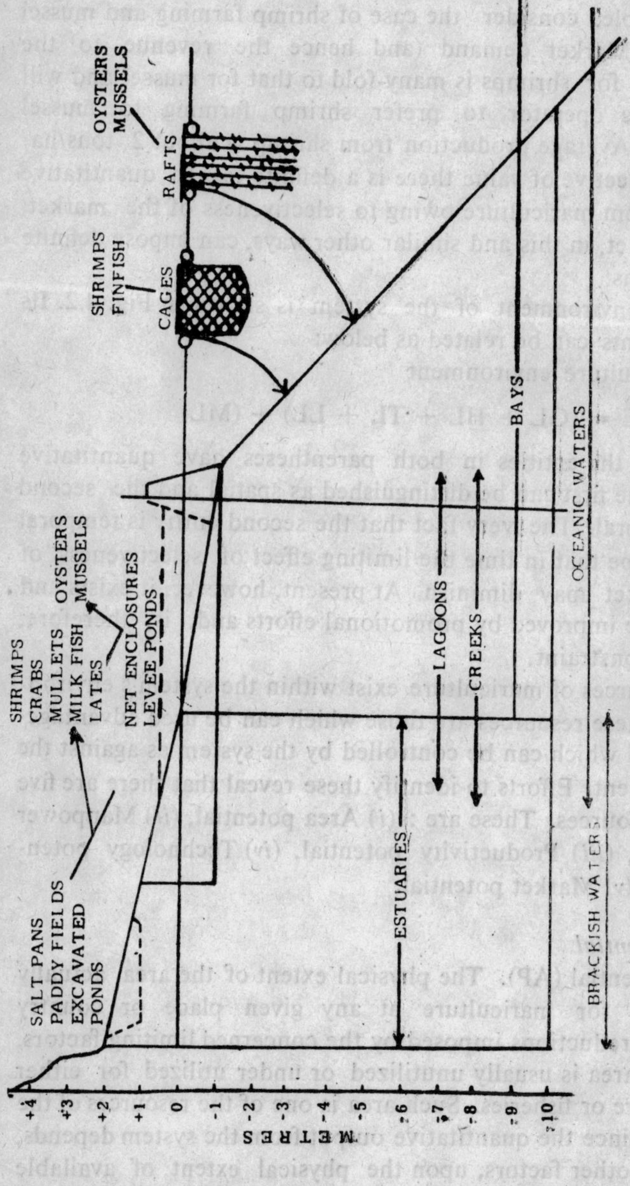

FIG. 4.1 *Coastal cross section (Theoretical) physical extent of present day moriculture*

Restriction imposed by the market is qualitative in nature but its effect on the system objective can be quantitative. To site an example, consider the case of shrimp farming and mussel farming. Market demand (and hence the revenue to the operator) for shrimps is many-fold to that for mussel and will induce the operator to prefer shrimp farming to mussel farming. Average production from shrimp is about 2 tons/ha/yr. Irrespective of value there is a definite loss in quantitative output from mariculture owing to selectiveness of the market. The market, in this and similar other ways, can impose definite restrictions.

The environment of the system is shown in Fig. 4.2. Its components can be related as below:

Mariculture environment

$$E = (GL + HL + TL + LL) + (ML)$$

Although the entities in both parentheses have quantitative effects, the first can be distinguished as spatial and the second as temporal. The very fact that the second entity is temporal yields hope that in time the limiting effect of selectiveness of the market may diminish. At present, however, it exists and cannot be improved by promotional efforts and, is, therefore, a fixed constraint.

Resources of mariculture exist within the system's environment. These resources are those which can be used advantageously and which can be controlled by the system as against the environment. Efforts to identify these reveal that there are five major resources. These are : (*i*) Area potential, (*ii*) Manpower potential, (*iii*) Productivity potential, (*iv*) Technology potential, and (*v*) Market potential.

Area potential

Area Potential (AP). The physical extent of the area actually available for mariculture at any given place or country after the reductions imposed by the concerned limiting factors. Such an area is usually unutilized or under utilized for either agriculture or fisheries. Such area is one of the resources of the system. Since the quantitative output from the system depends, amongst other factors, upon the physical extent of available area its magnitude is a definite asset.

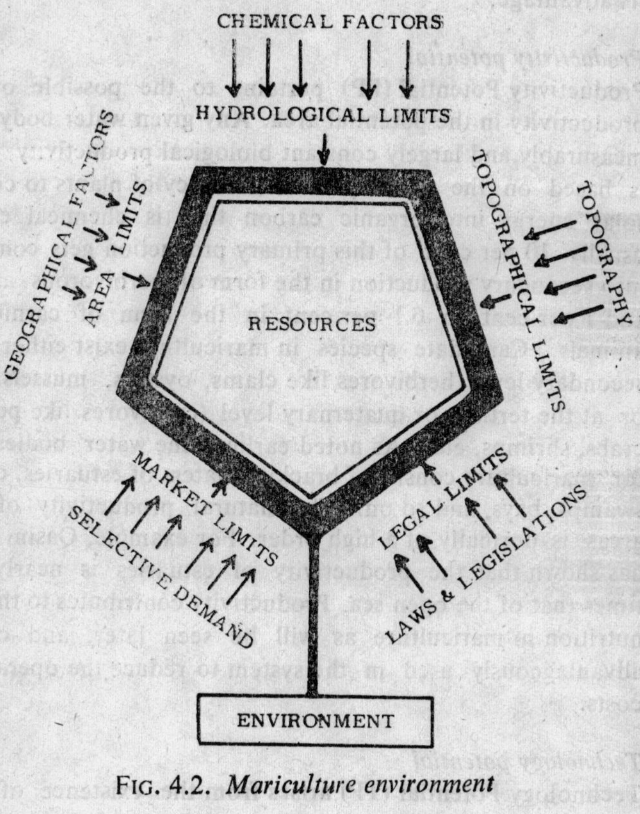

FIG. 4.2. *Mariculture environment*

Manpower potential

Manpower Potential (MP) can be a major resource, particularly in developing countries. Owing to socio-economic factors a wealth of manpower, usually unemployed or underemployed, exists within the system environment. A labour-intensive industry like mariculture can exploit this potential resource to its advantage.

Productivity potential

Productivity Potential (PP) pertains to the possible organic productivity in the potential area. Any given water body has a measurably and largely constant biological productivity which is based on the primary level efficiency of plants to convert solar energy into organic carbon that is chemical energy; usually 10 per cent of this primary production gets converted into secondary production in the form of herbivorous animals and 1 per cent to 0.1 per cent in the form of carnivorous animals. Candidate species in mariculture exist either at the secondary level (herbivores like clams, oysters, mussels, etc.) or at the tertiary or quaternary level (carnivores like perches, crabs, shrimps, etc.) As noted earlier, the water bodies used for mariculture consist of brackish waters of estuaries, creeks, swamps, bays, and so on. The natural productivity of such areas is normally of a high order. For example, Qasim (1972) has shown that the productivity of estuaries is nearly four times that of the open sea. Productivity contributes to the crop nutrition in mariculture as will be seen later, and can be advantageously used in the system to reduce the operational costs.

Technology potential

Technology Potential (TP) arises from the existence of cultivation technologies, their level of sophistication, and adaptability within the environment. This is a contribution of the R & D institutions. Commercial cultivation is a result of research cultivation and follows a laborious process of sequential events and achievements. It will be seen later than the operational efficiency of the system, and, therefore, the quantitative output, depends upon the prevailing level of technological sophistication. Improvement in the level of sophistication is possible with vigorous R & D efforts, provided that the cultivation technology exists. Thus the very existence of technology is a part of the resource of the system.

Market potential

Market Potential (MP) is not to be confused with market limits. Market potential arises from the existence and proximity of the marketing outlets for the products of mariculture. These could be in the form of the wholesale purchasing units or the local market. Since the products of mariculture are supposed to be market-oriented and as the entire revenue is to be derived from the market-returns, the existence and proximity of the best available marketing outlet is an advantage to the system.

A generalized picture of the resources of mariculture contained within the environment is shown in Fig. 4.3 alongwith the possible contributing or exploiting forces.

SUB-SYSTEMS AND COMPONENTS

While the above classification gives a generalized picture regarding the environment and resources of the system, definite sub-systems and components can be identified at the operational level. Such operational parameters can be classified into three major sub-systems : (i) Cultivation sub-system, (ii) Seed sub-system, and (iii) Nutrition sub-system.

Commensurate with the technological sophistication each sub-system performs with a corresponding output efficiency. We aim to demonstrate that while technological advancement brings refinement and elevates the degree of productivity in each sub-system, it also increases the inputs in the form of labour, finance, overheads, and so on.

Cultivation sub-system

Cultivation sub-system performs the basic operation of product output. This sub-system can be identified as operating at one of the following five levels : (a) Subsistence level, (b) Semi-

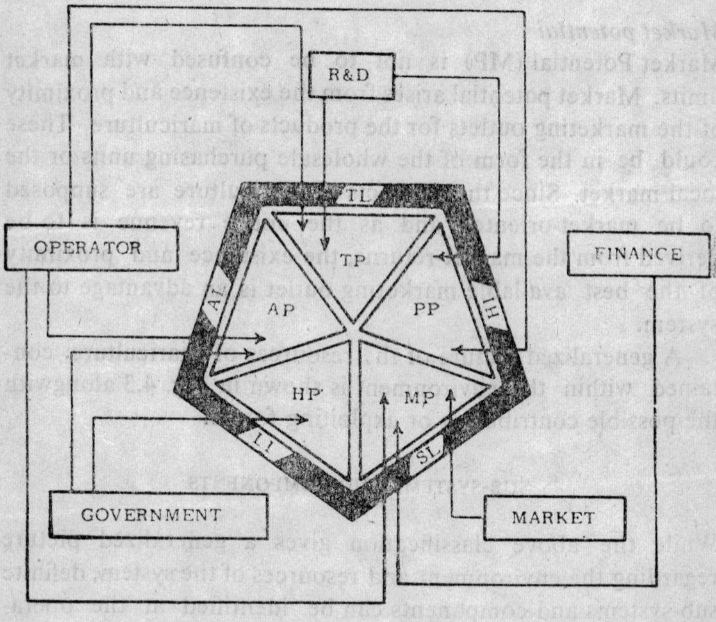

TP = TECHNOLOGICAL POTENTIAL

AP = AREA POTENTIAL

HP = MANPOWER POTENTIAL

MP = MARKET POTENTIAL

PP = PRODUCTIVITY POTENTIAL

FIG. 4.3. *Resources of mariculture and contributing/exploiting agents*

extensive level, (c) Extensive level, (d) Semi-intensive level, and (e) Intensive level.

A flow chart of the sub-system operating at above five levels is shown in Fig. 4.4. Each box represents an estimate of cost arising from the requirement of the particular component. Matrix for cultivation sub-system is given in Table 4.1.

TABLE 4.1: **Matrix for cultivation sub-system**

Sl. No.	Measure of performance	Level of operation A	B	C	D	E
1.	Production of desired species	1	1	5	5	5
2.	Control of physical environment	1	2	4	4	4
3.	Crop nutrition	1	1	2	4	5
4.	Control of biological environment	1	1	2	3	4
5.	High yield/unit area	1	1	2	4	5
6.	High market price	2	2	4	5	5
	Matrix total (out of 30)	7	8	19	25	28

Code : Yes = 5, No = 1 ; A = Subsistence level
B = Semi-extensive level
C = Extensive level
D = Semi-intensive level
E = Intensive level

Subsistence level

At Subsistence level (Fig. 4.4-A) the operation of the sub-system can be best described as harvest of a crop of organisms naturally trapped and grown in natural empoundments. Apart from harvesting, the operator requires no other inputs. Mariculture can be only barely distinguished from maricapture at this level and although the inputs are of low order the output is also at lower level. This is mainly because the operator has no control over the variety of organisms nor does he exert efforts to enhance its survival and growth. Harvest of a variety of animals in coastal paddy fields during off-season and salt pans are typical examples.

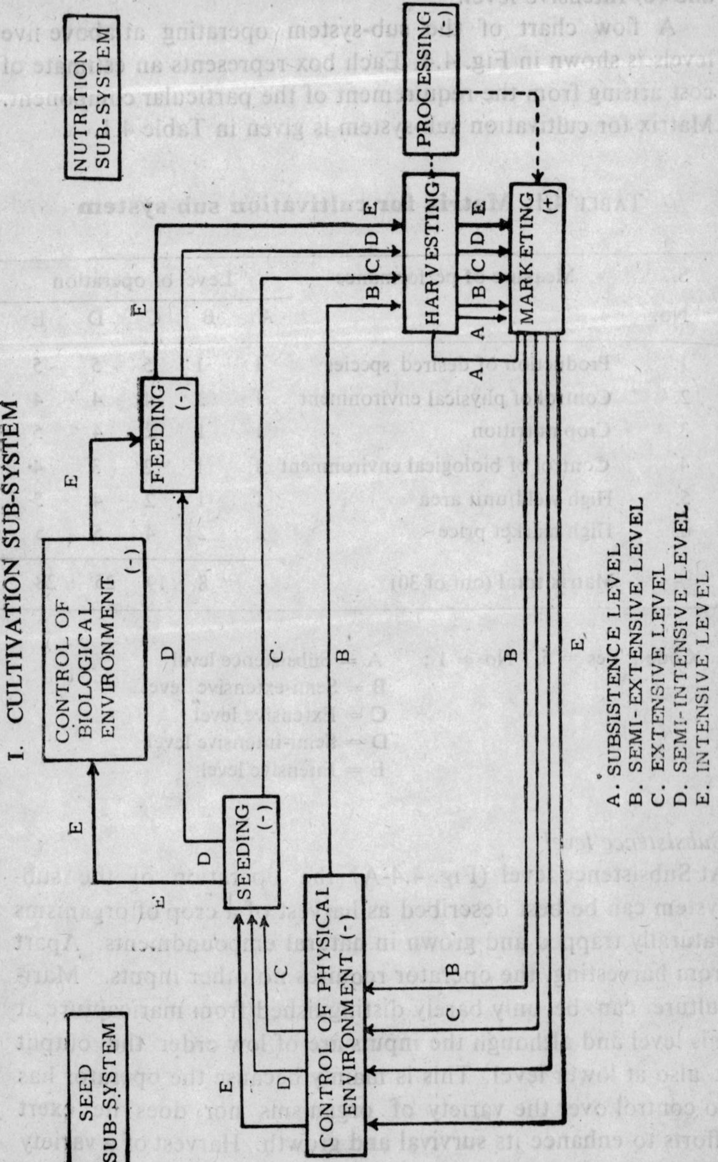

FIG. 4.4 : *Mariculture sub-systems and components*

Semi-extensive level

At semi-extensive level (Fig. 4.4-B) the operator is required to exert control over the physical environment by way of creating empounding structures in which the marine animals gets trapped. Such empoundments could be either permanent structures (*e.g.* bunded or excavated ponds) or semi-permanent constructions (*e.g.* temporary bunds or screens). No control over biological environment is exerted. Variety and quantity of marine animals getting trapped in the empoundments is beyond the *complete* control of the operator. Input requirements at this level are the expenses on preparing the empoundments, harvesting, and minimal overheads arising from amortization of capital facilities. Production and returns are better than those at subsistence level but still at a low level. The paddy-cum-prawn filtration operations traditionally carried out along the coastal belt of Kerala and elsewhere in south-east Asia is typical.

Extensive level

At Extensive level of operations (Fig. 4.4-C) the operator is required to stock the empoundment with the seed of the desired variety of animal. *Dependence on the seed sub-system* is inavoidable from this level onwards. The operator is required to spend on empounding structures and seed of the candidate species of aquatic animal. He, however, does not control the biological environment nor provide supplementary feed for the cultivated but depends upon the natural productivity of the empounded area to produce food naturally for the cultivated animal. Output from this operation is much better than those from the previous two levels but is still much short of the maximum potential yield. Lack of adequate control over the biological environment is one of the main reasons. Since the operator is dependent upon naturally available feed this becomes the limiting factor for the resultant yield. As the operator cannot increase the yield per unit area, he is prone to increase the production by increasing the cultivated area.

Semi-intensive level

At semi-intensive level of operation (Fig. 4.4-D) the operator is required to give supplementary feed for the cultivated animal in addition to providing empoundments, seed of the candidate species, and harvesting expenditure. The feed, as stated, is supplementary and may consist of scrap fish, fish meal, algae or grain waste like rice bran. This provision brings in additional expenditure not encountered earlier. The overheads are also of a higher order. The output is usually of a higher order as the maximum yield potential is normally reached. Japanese shrimp farming is the best example of this level of operation.

Intensive level

At Intensive level of cultivation operation (Fig. 4.4-E) the operator derives the maximum production per unit area. To achieve this he is required to control the biological environment and use a refined *nutition sub-system* in addition to control over the physical environment, seed sub-system, and harvesting. To control the biological environment the operator needs to employ crop protection measures (e.g. preventive and curative treatment for diseases, removal of predators and competitors etc.). While the production per unit area is quite high the cost per unit of area is also of a higher order. Cage culture of the finfish yellow tail (seriola sp.) is a good example of this type of operation.

A possibility of *super-intensive level* of operation in the cultivation sub-system may arise in near future. At this level the cultivation unit is separated from the natural water bodies and complete control over the physical and biological environment is achieved by monitoring the physiochemical parameters of the rearing medium. A highly refined nutritional sub-system is employed wherein an artificial pelletized feed, optimizing the total nutritional requirements of candidate species and yielding maximum 'feed-to-flesh' conversion is used. While such close systems are under active experimentation, particularly in Japan and USA, their commercial utility is yet to be demonstrated.

Seed sub-system

The seed sub-system is the second important sub-system involved in operational mariculture. Since it is a matter of common sense that to grow a crop one must have seed this sub-system holds the key position in mariculture. 'Seed' is in the form of post-larval stages or juveniles of candidate species. Extent of mariculture is limited by the timely availability in quantity and quality of seed of the candidate species of aquatic animal. To achieve this measure of performance the operator of this sub-system is required to control various parameters of the reproduction of candidate species (see Table 4.2). As in the previous sub-system each measure of control and the degree thereof makes a positive contribution towards better performance and at the same time brings in a proportionate increase in cost owing to overheads and operational expenditure. Major operations of this sub-system are: (i) Seed procurement, (ii) Seed storage, (iii) Seed transportation, and (iv) Seed marketing. By employing technological refinements one can operate this sub-system at one of the four levels shown in Fig. 4.5. The operator of this sub-system need not necessarily be the one who operates the cultivation sub-system; usually he is not marketing outlet, since the sub-system is restricted to the cultivation sub-system from extensive level onwards.

TABLE 4.2: **Matrix for seed sub-system**

Sl. No.	Measure of performance	Level of operation			
		A	B	C	D
1.	Seed of desired species	3	5	5	5
2.	Continuous seed production	1	2	4	5
3.	Quantitative seed production	2	4	5	5
4.	Seed of superior strain	1	1	4	5
5.	Cheap cost	4	3	2	1
	Matrix total (out of 25)	11	15	20	21

Code: Yes=5, No=1.
For A, B, C, D refer to Fig. 5.

II. SEED-SYSTEM

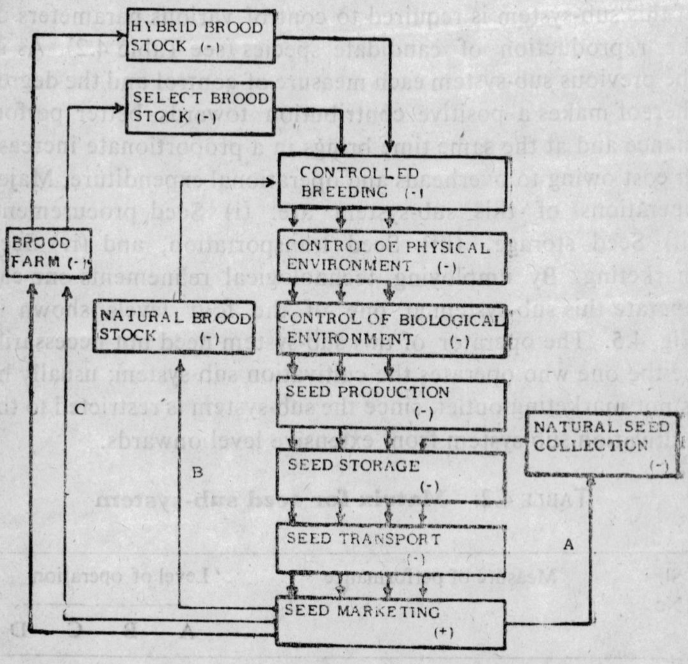

FIG. 4.5 : *Mariculture sub-systems*

Procurement of seed can be made from two sources. The first source is from the natural seed stock seasonally available in creeks, estuaries, and back-waters. The sub-system at this level (Fig. 4.5-A) is in its simplest form and the operator is required to incur minimum expenditure on seed procurement. While inputs are low, the output (i.e. revenue from marketing) is characteristically low. The main reason for this is that the seed is seldom produced in large quantities and, owing to seasonal nature of operation, without control over the time of procurement. Thus, while the operator of this sub-system may succeed in producing seed of desired quality, he fails to produce it in desired quantity or at desired time for the benefit of the cultivation operator.

The second source for seed procurement is controlled breeding. This brings in hatchery operations which require operator's complete control of the physical environment (physico-chemical parameters of breeding/rearing medium) and the biological environment (larval nutrition and health management). The main items of cost are shown in Fig. 4.5. Provision of hatchery facility naturally contributes to the overheads in this sub-system. For seed production the sub-system can operate at one of the three levels shown in Figs. 4.5-B, C, D. The sub-system at level B utilizes the naturally occurring breed stock. This is usually collected during the breeding season of the candidate species.

While seed procurement from this source can be quite significant, production is limited to the availability and breeding season of the candidate species. To obviate this dependence upon the uncontrollable variables, the operator can make provisions for his own brood stock. This necessitates a brood farm and its management which adds to the overheads and operational expenditure. With this brood stock at his disposal the operator cannot only produce seed of desired quantity and quality but at desired time as well. As shown in the flow diagram the operator can now elevate the level of the sub-system with the technology of selective breeding (Fig. 4.5-C) or hybridization (Fig. 4.5-D) and thereby producing seed of superior quality.

From whichever source the seed may be procured, the operator of the seed sub-system is required to make provisions for its storage or temporary holding till marketing and thereafter for transporting to the market that is the cultivation site. Depending upon the quantity and nature of the seed, expenditure on these two items will vary. For instance at level of the holding time may be few hours whereas for the other three levels it could be weeks till the stock builds up or seed grows to marketable size. The cost of the seed sub-system operating at these four levels is shown in the flow diagram. Although seed production can be a separate industry its relevance for the present purpose arises from its contribution to mariculture. It is obvious that seed produced through controlled breeding will be more benefiting for the cultivation sub-system than that collected from natural sources. In view of the net economic negatives in the seed sub-system operating at levels B, C and D, seed from this source will also be more costly. This higher cost may be discounted by better crop yield resulting from possibilities of adequate seed stocking and superior strains of candidate species.

The nutrition sub-system

The nutrition sub-system aims to provide food for growth of the candidate species selected for cultivation. Performance measured expected from sub-system is that this food (i) should satisfy the total nutritional requirements of the candidate species, (ii) should not be detrimental to its survival, (iii) should evince rapid growth, and (iv) should ensure the food-to-flesh conversion ratio close to unity. Depending upon the type of method employed the feed can be basically of two types: (a) Live feed, and (b) Dead feed.

Live feed

Live feed developed in this sub-system makes use of the trophic chain of natural productivity at either primary or secondary level. Input requirements are either mineral fertilizers (nitrates, phosphates, silicates) or organic fertilizers (chicken manure, cow dung, bone meal, and so on). Output at primary level is of autotraph like planktonic unicellular algae

TABLE 4.3: **Matrix for nutrition sub-system**

Sl. No.	Measure of Performance	Live feed	Fresh feed	Dry feed	Processed feed
1.	Raw material availability	5	3	3	4
2.	Can be stored	5	1	5	5
3.	Nutritionally ideal	4	3	3	5
4.	Produces good survival rate	5	4	4	5
5.	Produces fast growth rate	3	4	4	5
6.	Ideal conversion ratio	2	3	2	5
7.	Cheap cost	5	4	3	2
	Matrix total	29	22	24	31

Code: Yes=5, No=1

or submerged multicellular filamentous algae. Output at secondary level is of zooplanktors like copepods, astracods, and so on. Nutritional efficiency of the sub-system at this level is restricted by the feeding behaviour of the candidate species. For example, the live feed produced at primary level can be consumed by only a select few aquatic animals for example the filter feeders like bivalve molluscs (oysters, mussels and clams) or herbivorous finfish (milkfish, mullets, and so on). Similarly, the food produced at secondary level can be consumed by only those candidate species which are plankton feeders.

Although it is believed that the live feed produced in this manner satisfies the nutritional requirement of the candidate species *in toto*, the very fact that supplementary feed produces increased yield suggests that this may not be so. However, employment of the nutrition sub-system at this level is of distinct advantage in mariculture for two reasons. The first and the most important reason is that the inputs are restricted to fertilizers and their storage and the energy for actual feed production is derived from the natural ecological phenomenon, thereby effecting a considerable reduction in cost. The second reason is that when the candidate species is a filter feeder or a herbivore or a plankton feeder the operator has little option to employ any other level of the sub-system.

Dead feed

The second type of food is dead feed. For this type of food the sub-system operates at one of the three levels: (b-1) Fresh feed. (b-2) Dry feed, and (b-3) Processed feed.

Fresh feed is usually in the form of chopped fish but many times this can be substituted or supplemented by slaughter house waste, kitchen waste, and so on. Storage of this type of feed is usually not possible. While this reduces the cost, it necessitates recurrent procurement and transportation both of which ultimately add to the cost. The advantage at this level of operation is that it provides animal protein to the candidate species and may come close to approximating the total nutritional requirement. The disadvantage is that nutritional performance is limited to availability of raw material on regular basis in required quantity and the nutritional value thereof.

Dry feeds used in mariculture are usually the various derivates of fresh feed: rice bran, oil-seed cake, dried fish, fish meal and so on. Advantages and disadvantages of the subsystem at this level are similar to those mentioned for fresh feed but a distinct advantage is that the raw material can be stored so that very frequent procurement is not necessary.

Processed feed is formulated according to the nutritional requirements of candidate species and is, therefore, the best amongst the various feed mentioned so far. Production of this type of feed is by itself a separate sub-system, usually operated separately. It requires, first, the knowledge of the complete nutritional requirement of the candidate species, secondly the raw material to provide the proper constituents and machinery to produce pelletized feed.

5

BRACKISH WATER CULTURE: SOME POLICY ISSUES*

U.K. SRIVASTAVA AND AMAR JEET SINGH

INTRODUCTION

DURING 1980, the world prawn production was about 1.7 million tonnes; of this, about 10 per cent came from brackish water culture. In India, of the total 182 thousand tonnes of prawn production, brackish water culture contributed about 30 per cent (5,533 tonnes). In some of the other countries the share of prawn from culture fisheries is quite significant. For example in 1982, 70 per cent of Philippines prawn exports came from brackish water culture[1].

For India, the importance of prawn lies in its high export demand. Signs of stagnation are visible in prawn supply from the marine sector and in certain pockets, exploitation having crossed the level of sustainable yield. Therefore, to sustain its high share in world prawn exports, India has to optimize utilization of brackish water culture resources.

The data available on brackish water culture generally include the estuarine and brackish water culture details. Under such a situation, based on various assumptions, India's brackish water culture potential is estimated to be about 9 lakh

* The Paper is taken from U.K. Srivastava and Vathsala (eds), *Strategy for Development of Inland Fishery Resources in India*, Concept Publishing Company, New Delhi, 1984, pp. 357-87. The has been reprinted here with the permission of authors and editors.

ha. Against this, the present utilization of brackish water culture is a meagre 2.91 per cent. The total area under use is about 26,270 ha. ; the concentration is mainly in West Bengal (47.7%), Kerala (27.3%) and Karnataka (9.6%) (Exhibit 22.1). Andhra Pradesh follows mostly capture through basket trap, which to an extent, resembles the estuarine system.

At full use of the potential area, the brackish water culture can yield more than 9 lakh tonnes of prawns. As against this, in 1981-82 the production of prawn and fish was only 10,080 tonnes (1.06%). The value of current production was Rs. 21.00 crore (0.53%) of the potential value ; this was also partly due to lower realization of price.

The low utilization of potential area, low productivity, and low realization of price, all point to the importance of increasing coverage, productivity, and species mix.

Objectives

The objectives of this paper is to identify bottlenecks and to develop a strategy for brackish water culture development by,

(a) Reviewing the levels of available technology and gaps in its adoption;

(b) Comparing economics at farm level across existing systems;

(c) Reviewing the market flows and economics of marketing;

(d) Analysing through systems approach the adaptability of latest technology available in India, and the experiences of other countries, and

(e) Presenting some preliminary estimated investment needs.

The first three aspects are covered in Part I of this paper, and the last two are focussed in Part II.

Data

The primary data for this study were collected through survey of 127 farmers. Secondary data were collected as available with all coastal states, fisheries institutes, Marine Products Export Development Authority (MPEDA) and fisheries corporations. Brackish water lakes (Chilka and Vembanad) were covered as case studies. The marketing aspects were covered as systems study through qualitative indepth survey of selected intermediaries.

PART I

ANALYSIS OF CURRENT SYSTEM OF PRODUCTION AND MARKETING

PRODUCTION SYSTEMS

Based on method of operations, the current brackish water culture system could be classified broadly into two categories : (a) paddy and fish culture, and (b) paddy-cum-fish culture.

Paddy and fish culture

In this system, paddy is grown in the fields for one season, and for the remaining period fisheries are undertaken. Here, two common methods are followed : (i) filtration which involves trapping fish and the prawn coming with tides, and (ii) stocking and feeding which includes stocking of prawn seeds feeding them during fisheries season.

Paddy-cum-fish culture

Under this system, fish culture and paddy growing are undertaken simultaneously. The design of field and water management practices take care of the needs of both. A systematic programme of both the activities is shown in Fig 5.1. This also involves two methods: (i) stocking only and raising seed to marketable size; and (ii) stocking and feeding during the growth during the growth periods.

Filtration in paddy and fish culture is a common practice in Kerala, and is the only practice in Karnataka. Stocking and feeding under paddy and fish culture is undertaken only in Kerala. Paddy-cum-fish culture is in practice in West Bengal where major area (87.47%) is covered under the system of stocking only and the remaining area (12.53%) is covered under stocking and feeding.

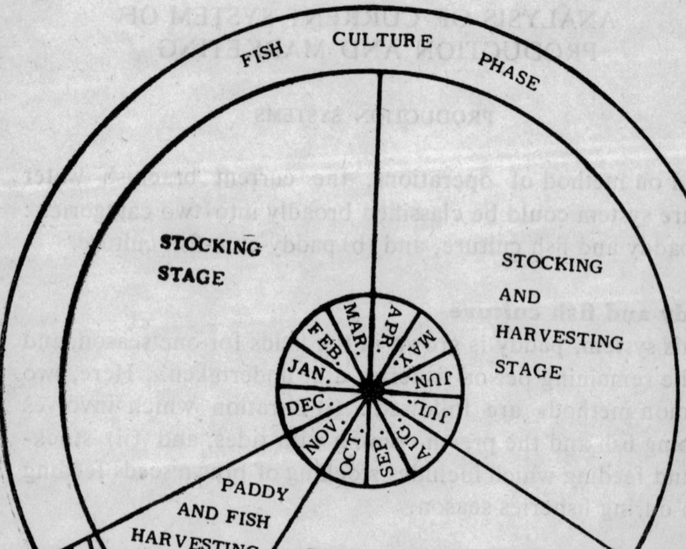

FIG. 5.1 : *Culture cycle : Paddy-cum-fish culture*

During 1981-82, out of the total area under culture 42.12 per cent (22,150 ha.) was under filtration, 1.31 per cent under stocking and feeding in paddy and fish culture. In paddy-cum-fish culture about 49.48 per cent of the total area was under stocking only, and the remaining 7.09 per cent was covered by stocking and feeding (5.2).

Level of lab-technology

The level of technology at lab was analysed based on the results of field experiments carried out by Central Inland Fisheries Research Institute (CIFRI) between 1977-78 and 1980-81 period. Varied varieties were used and experiments lacked in rapetitiveness. The total number of experiments conducted being 102 constituted rather a small sample. Of these, 67 were monoculture and the remaining 45 were polyculture experiments.

The average production of prawn monoculture experiments was only 264 kg./ha., and about 15 per cent of the experiments had a productivity of less than 100 kg./ha. Fish monoculture production averaged at 527 kg./ha., and majority of the experiments (65%) had production ranging from 251 to 1,000 kg. (5.3).

Polyculture experiments though fewer in number showed better productivity than monoculture. The prawn mix production was 485 kg./ha. and fish mix was 1,063 kg./ha. In fish and prawn mix the average production was 844 kg./ha. of which about 25 per cent were prawn (5.3).

Constraints

The development of brackish water culture has several constraints. These are grouped under ten major heads.[2] Intensity and type of constraints varied across the States (5.4).

Seed shortage is an important constraint. Prawn seed hatchery technology on commercial scale is well developed in many countries while in India there are no commercial hatcheries.

Tidal amplitude constraint, whether high or low, can be overcome by appropriate investments and aquaculture engineering skills. This, however, reflects on economics of production.

High salinity and high temperature if unchecked in time can result in prawn mortality. This makes the prawn culture risky but is controllable.

Sandy soil areas drain very quickly, and, therefore, are both risky and capital intensive to control. The crab interference and prawn diseases are identifiable and controllable, Pollution, of course, is man-made and controllable.

Economics of production

Each of production system has different functional characteristics. The profitability of paddy and fish culture is not comparable with paddy-cum-fish culture. The former is a seasonal activity while the latter is a year round activity. Under controlled systems, where stocking was undertaken, large size prawns and fishes were harvested and, therefore, price realization was better. The land ownership for brackish water culture was vested with paddy farmers. Many paddy farms jointly made a brackish water culture farm depending on topography. By and large, the fish farmers were different entrepreneurs than paddy growers. One to three year lease system was prevalent in paddy-cum-fish culture; both fish and paddy were grown consecutively, yet this never resulted in conflicts of interests.

Filtration farms in Kerala showed the maximum total productivity (566 kg./ha.) while filtration in Karnataka showed the lowest productivity (339 kg./ha.). The prawn productivity was the best in stocking and feeding farms of Kerala (463 kg./ha.), where only prawn were reared. The fish productivity was the best in paddy-cum-fish culture (5.5).

The farm value of production was a factor of species groups, sizes and marketing practices. The highest turnover was achieved by stocking and feeding farms in Kerala (Rs. 15,031/ha.) where prawns were harvested after full maturity. The turnover was also quite high under paddy-cum-fish culture (Rs. 9,604/ha. stocking and feeding, and Rs. 8,657/ha. stocking only). The turnover was the lowest form filtration at Karnataka (Rs. 2,893/ha.) followed by Kerala (Rs. 5,901/ha.).

By value, prawns were the most important group in production. Share of prawn value in total value was above 80 per cent in paddy-cum-fish culture, in filtration 99 per cent in Kerala and 96 per cent in Karnataka (Exhibit 5.5). Under controlled systems where stocking was undertaken, the large size prawn and fishes were harvested, and therefore, price realization was better.

The net profit per hectare for stocking and feeding farms in Kerala was the highest (Rs. 7,291). It was followed by stocking and feeding under paddy-cum-fish culture (Rs. 4,131/ha). The profitability was the lowest under filtration in Karnataka (Rs. 1,327/ha.) followed by filteration in Kerala (Rs. 2,404/ha.) (Exhibit 5.5).

In paddy and fish culture, the filtration farmers in Kerala, with 160 per cent return on investment were better off than others. Stocking and feeding farmers in Kerala realized a Return on Investment (ROI) of 147 per cent. In paddy-cum-fish culture ROI of stocking and feeding farmers was higher (162%) than that of stocking only (119%) (Exhibit 5.5).

Marketing flows

Marketing comprised of use, channel, physical, finance, and information flows.

Use flows

Use flows varied across systems and practices. The total production from surveyed area was 9,690 tonnes during 1980-81. Of this 57.09 per cent went for exports, 38.61 per cent for domestic market, and 4.30 per cent was dried for edible purpose.

In filtration, out of the total production (3,649 tonnes), 66 per cent went for exports, 24 per cent was domestic fresh fish and the balance 10 per cent was dried for edible use. On the other had, in stocking and feeding under paddy and fish culture, 93 per cent of the total production of 130 tonnes, was used for exports. The paddy-cum-fish culture production was 5,911 tonnes, of which 51 per cent was exported, 48 per cent was domestic fresh, and only one per cent was dried for edible use (Exhibit 5.6).

The paddy-cum-fish culture, which amounted to 61 per cent of total production, contributed 54 per cent of exportable supply, and 76 per cent of domestic fresh supply. Share of filtration in total production was 38 per cent and it contributed 43 per cent of exports, 24 per cent of domestic fresh, and feeding in Kerala was only 1 per cent of total production, and 2 per cent of exportables (Exhibit 5.6).

Channel flows

The brackish water production is sold as domestic fresh exportable and dry edible. The markets and their systems of all the three products vary due to the nature of product.

The importance of brackish water culture lies in exportables due to its high demand. Domestic fresh fish was usually a subsidiary product; however, it was important in West Bengal. The share of dry edible production was low, and as such, it was sold at a low price. Therefore, channel flows for exportable and domestic fresh only were worked out.

Exportables

The exportables, mainly prawns, passed from nil to four hands (Fig 5.2). The farmer sold about 17 per cent directly to processing factories. The farmers sold 42 per cent of their production through commission agent (sales-cum-auctioneers, 18 per cent directly to wholesalers, and another 12 per cent to peeling shed owners who worked as wholesalers). The commission agents (purchase) bought 8 per cent of production on behalf of wholesalers. The processors also bought 10 per cent through auction. There were, however, marked variations from state to state.

About 42 per cent of production was sold in auction, 17 per cent directly to processors on fixed prices, and the remaining 41 per cent to wholesalers through bilateral bargaining. The sale through wholesalers reflected the extent of bonding.

Peeling and beheading of prawns before processing increased its shelf life. The job of semi-processing (peeling and/or beheading) was undertaken at various levels. During 1980-81 the states surveyed produced 5,532 tonnes of prawns, wholesalers semi-processed 34 per cent (1,900 tonnes) of the

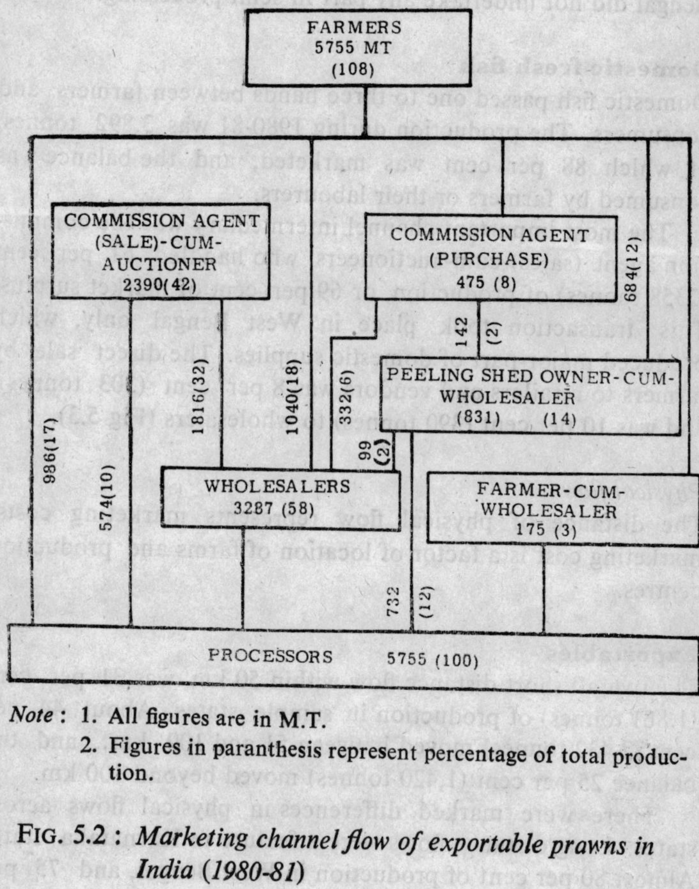

Note : 1. All figures are in M.T.
2. Figures in paranthesis represent percentage of total production.

FIG. 5.2 : *Marketing channel flow of exportable prawns in India (1980-81)*

total, followed by 22 per cent (1191 tonnes) by farmers themselves. Peeling shed owner-cum-wholesalers peeled 20 per cent (1,113 tonnes) and processors peeled 17 per cent (955 tonnes) (Exhibit 5.7). The market intermediary, the commission agent (sale)-cum-auctioneer who operated only in West Bengal did not undertake any part in semi-processing.

Domestic fresh fish

Domestic fish passed one to three hands between farmers and consumers. The production during 1980-81 was 3,892 tonnes, of which 88 per cent was marketed, and the balance was consumed by farmers or their labourers.

The most important channel intermediary was the commission agent (sales)-cum-auctioneers who handled 61 per cent (2358 tonnes) of production, or 69 per cent of market surplus. This transaction took place in West Bengal only, which produced major part of domestic supplies. The direct sale by farmers to retailers and vendors was 8 per cent (303 tonnes), and was 10 per cent (390 tonnes) to wholesalers (Fig 5.3).

Physical flows

The distance of physical flow represents marketing costs; marketing cost is a factor of location of farms and production centres.

Exportables

The overall short distance flow within 50 km. was 31 per cent (1,861 tonnes) of production in sample states. About 44 per cent (2,432 tonnes) moved between 51 and 100 km., and the balance 25 per cent (1,420 tonnes) moved beyond 100 km.

There were marked differences in physical flows across states. Long distance flows were a feature in Karnataka state. Almost 80 per cent of production in West Bengal, and 75 per cent in Kerala moved to processing factories located at less than 100 km. (Exhibit 5.8).

Domestic fresh fish

The domestic fresh fish did not move to longer distances. About 12 per cent (471 tonnes) was consumed by producers

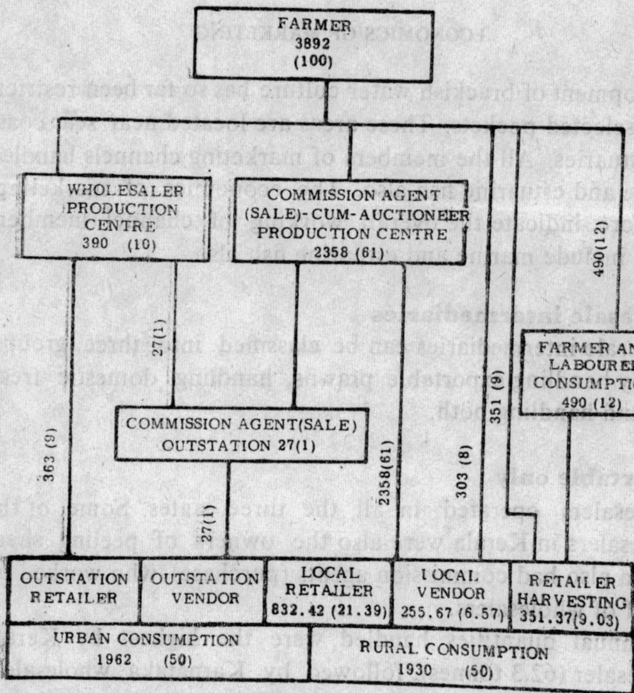

Note : 1. All figures are in M.T.
2. Figures in paranthesis represent percentage of total production.

FIG. 5.3 : *Marketing channel flow of domestic fresh fish in India (1980-81)*

and their labourers, and 37 per cent (1, 397 tonnes) was sold around producing centres itself, less than 2 per cent (55 tonnes) moved beyond 100 km. However, only in Kerala where wholesalers themselves accompanied the fish for sale (Exhibit 5.9) ice was used in transporting fish to long distances.

ECONOMICS OF MARKETING

Development of brackish water culture has so far been restricted to selected pockets. These areas are located near sea coast and estuaries. All the members of marketing channels handled marine and estuarine fish also. The economics of marketing, therefore, indicate the overall working of channel members which include marine and estuarine fish also.

Wholesale intermediaries

Wholesale intermediaries can be classified into three groups, namely handling exportable prawns, handling domestic fresh fish, and handling both.

Exportable only

Wholesalers operated in all the three states. Some of the wholesalers in Kerala were also the owners of peeling shed. Kerala also had commission agents (purchase) who worked on behalf of wholesalers.

Annual quantities handled were the highest by Kerala wholesaler (62.3 tonnes), followed by Karnataka wholesalers (41.6 tonnes). It was low around 22 tonnes for wholesalers in West Bengal, and commission agents (purchase) in Kerala (Exhibt 5.10).

Fresh fish only

In domestic fresh fish, wholesalers operated only in Kerala and Karnataka, and all their sales represented outstation flows. Karnataka wholesalers handled an average of 29.3 tonnes during 1980-81, while wholesalers in Kerala handled an average of 14.3 tonnes. Their capital investments and net profits also showed similar features. However, the net profit percentage of Karnataka wholesalers was the largest (10%)

than that of Kerala wholesalers (7%). But, return on investment (ROI) of Kerala wholesalers was higher (117%) than of Karnataka wholesalers (60%) (Exhibit 5.10). This was so because the Kerala wholesalers themselves accompanied fish for sale, and could rotate their capital more times. The Karnataka wholesalers despatched fish to consuming centres for sale through commission agents (sale).

Investment in working capital was accordingly the highest for Kerala wholesalers (Rs. 1.25 lakh). West Bengal wholesalers also invested a large sum (Rs. 0.63 lakh). The commission agents (purchase) mostly operated on wholesalers' capital and invested only Rs. 2,500 of their own (Exhibit 5.10).

Net profit percentage was quite high for West Bengal wholesalers (6%) and peeling shed owner wholesalers in Kerala (5%). Other wholesalers operated only at 3 per cent while commission agent (purchase) had 2 per cent net profit only (Exhibit 5.10).

The ROI was the best for commission agents (purchase) at 204 per cent mainly because their own investment was very low. The peeling shed owner wholesalers also had a good ROI (101%). Amongst other wholesalers, West Bengal wholesalers had a ROI of 70 per cent, Karnataka 45 per cent, and Kerala 42 per cent (Exhibit 5.10).

Domestic and exportable

Only commission agents (sale)-cum-auctioneers in West Bengal handled domestic fresh fish as well as exportables. Auction system was prevalent only in this state. They handled 56.5 tonnes of fish and prawn, operated at 3 per cent profit, and earned ROI at 46 per cent on their capital of Rs. 0.22 lakh (Exhibit 5.10).

Retail intermediaries

Retailers operated in all the three states. West Bengal retailers sold larger quantity (11.4 tonnes/annum) than Karnataka (7.2 tonnes/annum) and Kerala (7.3 tonnes/annum). The profit was the highest at 10 per cent for Karnataka retailers, followed by 8 per cent for Kerala, and 7 per cent for West Bengal retailers (Exhibit 5.11).

The trunover of retailers was small and their main concern daily operating profit. This was the highest for West Bengal retailers (Rs. 23.57) followed by Kerala (Rs. 13.00), and Karnataka retailers (Rs. 11.00). In all cases retailing was an economically viable activity (Exhibit 5.11). Vendors operated only in Kerala and handled 8.1 tonnes during 1980-81 which was more than handled by retailers, but in view of their increased quantities the daily profit was higher at Rs. 13.66 than that of retailers at Rs. 13.00 (Exhibit 5.11).

PART II

INTEGRATED PROJECT APPROACH : A STRATEGY FOR DEVELOPMENT OF BRACKISH WATER CULTURE

Brackish water culture, as it exists, is a risky business. There are large yearly production fluctuations, even at research level. Lack of easy availability of prawn seed has so far restricted its growth to selected pockets in the country. The skills for natural seed collection have developed in private sector, only in West Bengal. New areas under culture, specially in high tide and low tidal effect zones, requires large capital which is beyond the reach of existing producers. The demand for prawns in international markets is large, and there are no market demand risks.

To overcome risks in brackish water culture, and to make it all attractive to entrepreneurs an integrated project approach is essential. Philippines could increase its brackish water culture production from 1,700 tonnes in 1975 to 4,200 tonnes in 1979 by adopting an integrated approach.[3] A schematic outline of integration and agencies involved is given in Fig. 5.4. The area approach concept has to be followed by an intensive effort in selected pockets. Details of integration are explained below.

EXTENSION AND RESEARCH

Extension and the research are the first and ongoing needs of brackish water culture fishery development. The extension

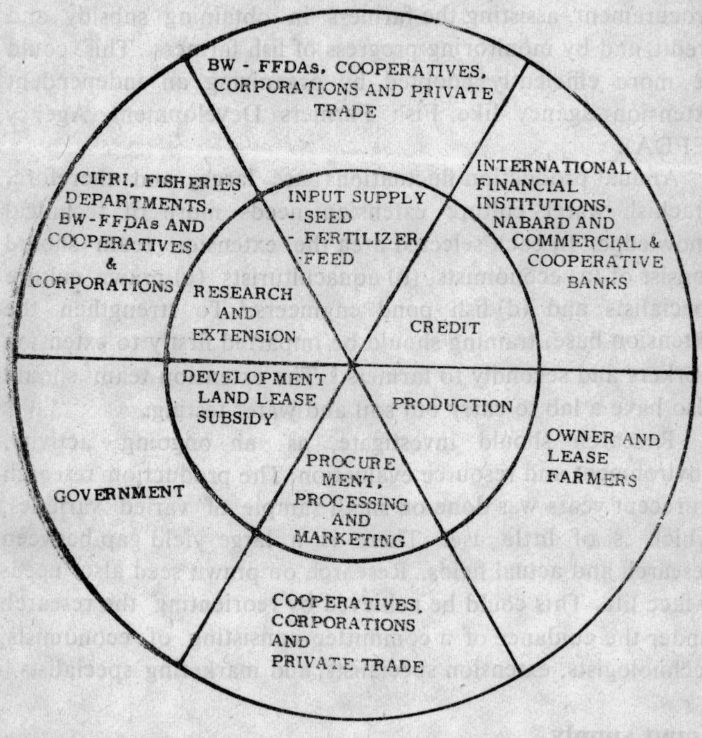

FIG. 5.4 :: *An integrated project approach system chart for development of brackishwater fish culture in India*

should aim at improving level of production in existing farms, increasing area, and production intensity under brackish water culture. Research should support this by undertaking environmental and resource evaluation, and by carrying out aquaculture investigations.

The extension system can achieve its objectives by undertaking techno-economic advisory services, assisting in input procurement, assisting the farmers in obtaining subsidy and credit, and by monitoring progress of fish farmers. This could be more efficiently adopted by organizing an independent extension agency like Fish Farmers Development Agency (FFDA).

Annual production fluctuations are large, and therefore, brackish water culture extension needs more of technical knowledge. In each selected area the extension team should consist of (a) economists (b) aquaculturists (c) prawn culture specialists and (d) fish pond engineers.[4] To strengthen the extension base, training should be imparted firstly to extension workers and secondly to farmers.[5] The extension team should also have a lab to carry out soil and water testing.

Research should investigate, as an ongoing activity, environment and resource evaluation. The production research in recent years was done on small sample of varied varieties, which is of little use. There is a large yield gap between research and actual fields. Research on prawn seed also needs a face lift. This could be achieved by reorienting the research under the guidance of a committee consisting of economists, technologists, extension specialists, and marketing specialists.

Input supply

In the absence of assured inputs, specially seed, all the efforts of extension can go waste. Therefore, it is essential to develop input supply simultaneously. Inputs should include fish and prawn seed, fertilizer feed and pesticides.

Prawn seed is the most critical input for brackish water culture development. The present level of technology in India is restricted to research level as no commercial hatcheries are seen operating. In other countries like philippines and Taiwan the prawn seed hatcheries are well developed. In Philippines seed was earlier being produced from wild spawners. The last step in the development of P. monodon seed supply is the hatchery production of fry from tennals matured in captivity.[6] It would therefore, be essential not only to undertake large scale commissioning of commercial hatcheries but also to develop technology. The technology can be borrowed from already developed countries, and also by sending seed specialists to such countries. Seed also needs to be standardized for the purpose. In other countries, prawn seed technology has advanced considerably.[7]

The prawn hatcheries and feed supply can be developed by establishing separate brackish water culture FFDA, or in co-operatives or in the public sector. Private trade to own and mange hatcheries should be encouraged.

Credit

Brackish water culture, at farm level, is capital intensive. Even the larke business houses may find it difficult to raise enough resources for developing high tide and low tidal effect areas.

The United Commercial Bank in financing brackish watar culture farmers in West Bengal had some good experience. However, once a large scale development is sought in under developed areas, massive institutional credit support would be essential. The norms for brackish water culture fishery have not been developed so for. Separate norms for existing farm development and new pond development need to be worked out and standardized. Long term credit at low interest rates would be needed for pond construction while short term credit would also be needed to meet expenses on seed, other inputs, labour, pond maintenance and so on.

The funding agencies at farm level could be co-operatives ; commercial banks, in turn would need policy and credit support from agencies like National Bank for Agriculture and Rural Development (NABARD). The project areas, as such, will need large amounts, and to meet this, assistance from international financial institutions can be sought.

Production

Producers and their farms are the kingpin of brackish water culture development. At pond, many of the activities which need close supervision and extension, research input supply and credit support are : (i) levelling and clearing of pond bottom, (ii) making, repair and maintenance of dykes, (iii) installation and management of efficient water control structures like canals, gates. pipes, and pumps, (iv) systematic pond arrangement, and (v) stocking, feeding, weeding and disease control, watch and ward and so on.

The current level of on-farm adopted technology is poor as mostly one to three year lease system is prevalent, and also the system is paddy and/cum fish culture. Two to three crops are possible. The complete system will need an overhaul.

The land near the coast is mostly owned by various departments of goverment. To attract new entrepreneurs, it would be essential to generate his long term interest. The pay back period will be long. Therefore, a long lease of least 25 years duration would be essential. It would also be necessary for banks to treat long lease as good as ownership for financing.

Procurement, processing and marketing

The existing system of procurement, processing and marketing is in private hands. Due to its nearness to seashore, the existing infrastructure system has developed mainly for marine sector, while brackish water culture is currently a secondary source of supply.

Once large development projects are undertaken, infrastructure and marketing practices will need a face lift. Wherever there are lacunae, development investments and policies shall have to be geared up in advance. Its management could be in the hands of private trade, co-operative or corporations. The brackish water culture offers a more stable and timely supply. Farmers can schedule their harvesting debts based on market conditions.

Policy support

Government, as key development agency has to play the instrumental role in integrated project development. Various incentive schemes like subsidy could assist in achieving the developmental objectives. The land, mostly belonging to government, is an essential input. The credit institutions respond well to a clear out policy support. Research and extension, of course, are the responsibilities of government. Foreign exchange, in any case, is needed to keep balance of payments. The processing industry will not respond unless they are convinced of long term benefits. Therefore, government should support in the following ways :

(i) by providing its land to farmers on long lease of at least 25 years ;
(ii) by partially meeting the cost of pond making and renovation through subsidy ;
(iii) by extending subsidy on input supply, at least during first five years of each pond ;
(iv) by providing free soil and water testing facilities ;
(v) by developing suitable extension agency ;
(vi) by arranging for funds ;
(vii) by gearing up the training and research activity ; and
(viii) by monitoring the progress.

Prawn exports earn foreign exchange. Areas with high and low tidal effects need larger investments. The fixed costs in high tide areas run into lakhs of rupees, while per ha. cost is more than Rs. 30,000. It is unlikely that small or medium farmers or entrepreneur will be able to mobilize resources for this. The payback period is also long and risky. Under such circumstances, government should have a relook at its policies and encourage entry of large business houses. It should facilitate entry by providing soft loans and subsidies.

Preliminary estimate of investment needs

It has been stated earlier that potential area for brackish water culture is about 9 lakh ha., this however, seems to be an over estimate. As of 1980-81 only 12,820 ha. of brackish water culture area were stocked with prawn seed mostly collected from riverine source. The future possibilities of area increase will depend on assured seed supply position.

Seed supply and coverage

Estuaries are natural hatcheries for prawn breeding. Only Hooghly estuary was exploited for seed harvesting. Quantitative estimates of sustainable seed supply capacity from Hooghly and other estuaries are not available. However, it is assumed that Hooghly can supply about 50 per cent more seed and estuarine area in other state has similar seed supply capacity on per ha. basis.

Given the above assumptions of estuary seed supply and stocking rates, it is possible to bring an additional area of 14,600 ha. under brackish water culture. Of this, West Bengal alone will account for 43 per cent (6,260 ha.). The share of other important states would be 16 per cent (2,320 ha.) for Andhra Pradesh, 15 per cent (2,270 ha.) for Kerala, and 13 per cent (1,920 ha.) for Gujarat. Other states have less of estuarine area and less patential. This area can give an annual production of 6,570 tonnes (Exhibit 5.12).

A second source of seed supply is through hatcheries. There are presently no commercial hatcheries in India. The experience of philippines in this connection is noteworthy. During 1982, the prawn fry stocking in Philippines brackish water culture was 55 million, of which 73 per cent (40 million) came from hatcheries. Philippines has 50 hatcheries. The breed stock harvesting from sea is gradually being reduced due to on farm stock breeding achievements.[8] Not only hatcheries but the hatchery technology will also need a face lift.

To bring additional 12,750 ha. under brackish water culture, India will need hatcheries with a capacity to handle 65 million post-larve seeds. These hatcheries have to be spread across states depending on potential and intended development. Maximum would, however, be in West Bengal which has the largest potential.

Investment needs

The area which could be covered for brackish water culture development includes suitable area[9], swampy area, high tide effect area, and area with low tidal effect.[10] The capital investment needs and water management costs vary according to the type of area and developmental need. It is possible to bring an addition 27,350 ha. under culture in five years. About 14,600 ha. (53%) will get seed harvested from estuaries, and the remaining 12.750 ha. (47%) shall have to be supplied seed from hatcheries. Based on the experience of Kerala stocking and feeding, and Henry Island farm development by West Bengal Corporation, various cost and return estimates have been worked out (Exhibit 5.13).

The development of brackish water culture has beed considered on 26 years project cycle. The capital cost for 27,350 ha. and hatcheries needed would be Rs. 66.68 crore. Operating costs and value of production during 25 years, based on 1980-81 prices, could be Rs. 403.74 crore and Rs. 855.75 crore respectively. The project would give a gross benefit of Rs. 385.32 cror overe 25 years project cycle which will be equivalent to Rs. 39.29 crore based on 18 per cent discount rates (Exhibit 5.13).

The Internal Rate of Return (IRR) is a measure of investment profitability. The IRR for development with natural seed supply is better, obviously because there is very little capital cost in seed supply. However, the possibility of any development beyond 14.800 ha. with natural seed supply is ruled out. Therefore, the development of hatcheries is essential in spite of low IRR.

In all situations, projects are worthy of investment. Appropriate project reports need to be prepared and international financial institutions like World Bank may be approached for funding. The approximate fund requirement would be more Rs. 73 crore. The priorities to be followed based on IRRs than should be as under :

	IRR in percentage
I. With natural seed supply	
Swamp areas	127
Suitable	126
High tide areas	28
Areas with low tidal effect	39
II. With hatchery seed supply	
high tide areas	23
Areas with low tidal effect	27

EXHIBIT—5.1

Estimated statewise brackish water culture potential area and its utilization (1981-82)

(Unit : Area in '000 ha.)

State	Total brackish water culture and estuarine potential area*	Estimated brackish water culture area potential	Area under culture	Percentage under utilization
Andhra Pradesh	150	124	4.03*	7.28
Gujarat	376	187	0.09	0.05
Karnataka	95	85	2.52	2.96
Kerala	242	142	7.10	5.00
Maharashtra	80**	70	Neg.	Neg.
Orissa	8**	8	Neg.	Neg.
Tamil Nadu	80**	72	Neg.	Neg.
West Bengal	405	210	12.53	5.97
Others (Goa and Pondicherry)	20	5	Neg.	Neg.
TOTAL	1456	902	26.27	2.91

Source : Handbook on Fisheries Statistics, 1981, Department of Agriculture and Co-operation, Ministry of Agriculture, Government of India, New Delhi-1.

*Area includes swamps where capture of fish and prawns was being undertaken.

**Report of the National Commission on Agriculture, 1976, Part-VIII (Fisheries), Ministry of Agriculture and Irrigation, Government of India, New Delhi-1.

Assumptions :

1. The figures of total brackish water culture and estuarine area do not include brackish water estuarine lakes.
2. A statistics provided by the Government of India 1981 does not give statistics for Maharashtra, therefore, NCA data has been used.

3. Government of India, 1981 statistics for Maharashtra and Tamil Nadu seems to be on much higher side based on our field estimates: therefore, NCA data has been used.
4. For calculating brackish water culture potential area, estuarine area has been reduced from total, and also authors' judgements have been used.

EXHIBIT—5.2

Statewise utilization pattern of existing brackish water culture fishery area (1981-82) in the states surveyed

(Unit : tonnes)

State	Filtration	Paddy and fish culture (stocking and feeding)	Paddy-cum-fish culture		Total
			Stocking only	Stocking and feeding	
Karnataka	2.52 (100)	—	—	—	2.52
Kerala	6.81 (95.92)	0.29 (4.08)			7.10
West Bengal	—	—	10.96 (87.47)	1.57 (12.53)	12.53
Grand Total	9.53 (42.12)	0.29 (1.31)	10.96 (49.48)	1.57 (7.09)	22.15

Note : Figures in parentheses represent percentage in total area.

EXHIBIT—5.3

Frequency of experiments and production levels attained during CIFRI experiments (1977-81)

Level of production (kg./ha.)	Monoculture			Polyculture	
	Prawn	Fish	Prawn mix	Fish mix	Fish and prawn mix
I. Frequency of experiments					
100 or less	6	2	—	—	—
101 to 250	17	5	—	2	—
251 to 500	14	6	7	1	1
501 to 1000	2	11	3	—	12
1001 and more	2	2	—	4	5
Total experiments	41	26	10	7	18
II. Average production (kg./ha.)					
Fish	—	527	—	1063	636
Prawn	264	—	485	—	208
Total average	264	527	485	1063	844

EXHIBIT—5.4

Constraints for brackish water forming

Sl. No.	Constraints	States where mostly applicable
1.	Cyclone and flood	Orissa, Andhra Pradesh
2.	Seed availability	All Costal States
3.	Low tidal amplitude	Tamil Nadu
4.	High tidal amplitude	Gujarat, Andhra Pradesh, Maharashtra, Orissa
5.	High salinity	Tamil Nadu, Andhra Pradesh, Kerala, West Bengal
6.	High temperature	Gujarat, Andhra Pradesh, Tamil Nadu
7.	Sandy soil	Tamil Nadu
8.	Crab population	Andhra Pradesh, West Bengal, Kerala, Karnataka
9.	Diseases	Tamil Nadu, West Bengal, Kerala, Karnataka
10.	Pollution	Kerala, West Bengal

Source : U. K Srivastava, Amar Jeet Singh, and J. Santhakumar Martin "Economics of Brackish Water Culture Fisheries in India : Some preliminary evidence" in U. K. Srivastava and M. Dharma Reddy, *Fisheries Development in India : Some Aspects of Policy Management* (New Delhi: Concept Publishing Company) 1983.

EXHIBIT—5.5

Per hectare working of brackish water culture farms by states and practices

(Unit : production in Kg.) (Amount in rupees)

Particulars	Paddy and fish culture			Paddy-cum-fish culture West Bengal	
	Kerala	Karnataka			
	Filtration	Stocking and feeding	Filtration	Stocking only	Stocking and feeding
1. Production					
Prawn	552	463	293	243	260
Fish	14	—	46	210	219
Total	566	463	339	453	479
2. Capital investment	1,501	4,944	1,221	2,721	2,547
3. Turnover	5,838	15,031	2,782	7,129	7,781
Prawn	(99)	(100)	(96)	(82)	(81)
Fish	63	—	111	1,528	1,823
	(1)		(4)	(18)	(19)
Total	5,901	15,031	2,893	8,657	9,604
	(100)	(100)	(100)	(100)	(100)
4. Direct costs	873	7,109	723	2,641	2,906
	(15)	(47)	(25)	(31)	(30)
5. Operating income	5,028	7,922	2,170	6,016	6,698
	(85)	(53)	(75)	(69)	(70)
6. Rent*	2,624	631	843	2,774	2,567
	(44)	(4)	(29)	(32)	(27)
7. Net profit	2,404	7,291	1,327	3,242	4,131
	(41)	(49)	(46)	(37)	(43)
8. Return on investment (%)	160	147	109	119	162

Note : Figures in parentheses represent percentage of total turnover.
* In case of ownership farms annual lease value of land is considered.

EXHIBIT—5.6

Production system and utilization pattern of brackish water culture production (1980-81)

(Unit : quantity in tonnes)

Particulars	Exporters		Domestic fresh		Dry edible		Total	
	Quantity	%	Quantity	%	Quantity	%	Quantity	%
I. Paddy and fish culture	2,079 (68)	37	758 (25)	20	212 (7)	51	3,049 (100)	32
(a) Filtration								
Kerala	324	63	132	4	144	35	600	6
Karnataka	(54)		(22)		(24)		(100)	
Sub total	2,403 (66)	43	890 (24)	24	356 (10)	86	3,649 (100)	38
(b) Stocking and feeding								
Kerala	121 (93)	2	9 (7)	Neg.	—	—	130 (100)	1
Total (Paddy and fish	2,524 (67)	45	899 (24)	24	356 (9)	86	3,779 (100)	39
II. Paddy-cum-fish culture West Bengal								
(a) Stocking only	2,688 (51)	49	2,482 (48)	66	55 (1)	13	5,225 (100)	54
(b) Stocking and feeding	320 (47)	6	360 (52)	10	6 (1)	1	686 (100)	7
Total (Paddy-cum-fish culture)	3,008 (51)	55	2,842 (48)	76	61 (1)	14	5,911 (100)	61
Grand Total	5,532 (57)	100	3,741 (39)	100	417 (4)	100	9,690 (100)	100

EXHIBIT—5.7

Peeling and be-heading undertaken by different members (1980-81)

(Unit : tonnes)

Intermediaries	Karnataka		Kerala		West Bengal		Total	
	Qty.	%	Qty	%	Qty.	%	Qty.	%
Farmers	—	—	889	40	302	10	1,191	22
Commission agent (Purchase)	—	—	198	9	—	—	198	4
Peeling shed owners-cum-wholesalers	—	—	1,113	51	—	—	1,113	20
Wholesalers	149	46	—	—	1,751	58	1,900	34
Farmer-cum-wholesaler	175	54	—	—	—	—	175	3
Processors	—	—	—	—	955	32	955	17
Total	324	100	2,200	100	3,008	100	5,532	100

EXHIBIT—5.8

Physical flow of exportable prawns from brackish water culture fields to processing factories (1980-81)

(Unit : tonnes)

State	Flow within 25 km.	Flow within 26.50 km.	Flow within 51-100 km.	Flow more than 100 km.	Total
Kerala	230 (11)	533 (24)	883 (40)	554 (25)	2,200 (100)
Karnataka	—	—	67 (21)	257 (79)	324 (100)
West Bengal	310 (10)	608 (20)	1,482 (50)	609 (20)	3,009 (100)
Total	540 (10)	114 (21)	2,432 (44)	1,420 (25)	5,533 (100)

Note : Figures in par entheses represent percentage to total state production.

EXHIBIT—5.9

Physical flow of domestic fresh fish (1980-81)

(*Unit : tonnes*)

State	Consumption by producers & labourers	Sale at local market	Outstation less than 100 kms.	Flow more than 100 kms.	Total
Kerala	206	225	281	55	767
	(27)	(29)	(37)	(7)	(100)
Karnataka	25	66	41	—	132
	(19)	(50)	(31)		(100)
West Bengal	240	1,106	1,496	=	2,842
	(8)	(39)	(53)		(100)
Grand total	471	1,397	1,818	55	3,741
	(12)	(37)	(49)	(2)	(100)

Note : Figures in parentheses represent percentages to state totals.

EXHIBIT—5.10

Annual working of wholesale market intermediaries in brackish water culture production

(Uuit : in '000 rupees)

Intermediary	State	Quantity handled (t)	Working capital	Turnover	Gross margin	Operat-ing costs	Net profit value (%)	Return on invest-ment (%)
(1)	(2)	(3)	(4)	(5)	(6)	(7)	(8)	(9)
1. Demestic fresh								
(a) Wholesalers	Kerala	14.3	7.0	115.4	15.6	7.4	8.2(7)	177
	Karnataka	29.3	27.0	202.2	38.6	20.6	18.0(10)	66
II. Exportables								
(a) Wholesalers	Kerala	62.3	125.0	1,619.8	133.6	61.6	51.9(3)	42
	Karnataka	61.6	72.0	940.2	66.6	34.0	32.7(3)	45
	West Bengal	22.0	63.0	879.0	70.2	25.9	44.3(5)	70
(b) Wholesaler-cum-peeling shed owners	Kerala	38.8	40.0	853.6	73.9	33.5	40.4(5)	101
(c) Commission agents (purchase)	Kerala	22.4	2.5	511.3	12.6	4.0	8.6(2)	204

EXHIBIT—5.10 : (Contd.)

(1)	(2)	(3)	(4)	(5)	(6)	(7)	(8)	(9)
III. Domestic fresh and exportable								
(a) Commission agents (sale) -cum-auctioneers	West Bengal	56.5	22.0	1,017.5	40.7	8.3	32.4(3)	46

Note : Figures in parentheses represent percentages of sale value.

EXHIBIT—5.11

Working of retail/vending market intermediaries in fresh domestic fish (1980-81)

Intermediary	Annual Operations (Rs. in '000s)						
	Quantity handled(t)	Sale value	Gross margin	Operating cost	Net profit	Operating days (Nos)	Daily profit (Rs.)
I. Retailers							
Kerala	7.3	46.6	4.5	0.6	3.9(8)	300	13.00
Karnataka	7.2	35.3	4.5	1.0	3.5(10)	310	11.33
West Bengal	11.4	81.9	6.5	1.1	5.4(7)	222	23.57
II. Vendors							
Kerala	8.1	52.6	4.6	0.4	4.2(8)	310	13.66

Note : **Figures in parentheses represent percentages of sale value.**

EXHIBIT—5.12

Statewise brackish water culture area potential, area under stocking (1980-81) and possible area to be brought under stocking and expected production in five years

State	Potential area (000 ha.)	Area under stocking (1980-81) (ha.)	Additional possible area and production in five years					
			With capture seed supply		With hatchery development		Total area (ha.)	Production(t)
			Area (ha.)	Production(t)	Area (ha.)	Production(t)		
Andhra Pradesh	123	—	2,320	1,044	340	153	2,660	1,197
Gujarat	187	—	1,920	864	960	432	2,880	1,296
Karnataka	85	—	250	113	130	59	380	172
Kerala	142	290	2,270	1,021	1,270	571	3,540	1,592
Maharashtra	70	—	250	113	130	59	380	172
Orissa	8	—	200	90	100	45	300	135
Tamil Nadu	72	—	810	364	400	180	1,210	544
West Bengal	210	12,530	6,260	2,817	9,300	4,185	15,560	7,002
Others	5	—	320	144	120	54	440	198
Total	902	12,820	14,600	6,570	12,750	5,738	27,350	12,308

Note : Annual production in tonnes.

EXHIBIT 5.13

Area development project costs, production, net benefits and internal rate ofreturn over 25 years project cycle through development of various project areas of brackish water culture

Particulars of development	Area covered (ha.)	Expected annual production (t)	Coasts			Gross value of production	Gross benefit	Net present benefit at 18%	International rate of return (%)
			Capital	Operating	Gross				
I. With natural seed collection									
(a) Swamp area	1,640	738	164	2,426	2,590	5,162	2,572	443	127
(b) Suitable area	6,360	2,862	291	9,481	9,772	19,842	10,070	1,771	126
(c) High tide area	5,380	2,421	1,614	7,931	9,545	16,874	7,329	581	28
(d) Area with low tidal effect	1,220	549	305	1,816	2,121	3,863	1,742	196	39
II With hatchery seed supply									
(a) High tide area	8,990	4,046	3,155	13,197	16,352	28,080	11,723	528	23
(b) Area with low tidal effect	3,760	1,692	1,139	5,524	5,663	11,754	5,091	389	27
Total	27,350	12,308	6,668	40,375	47,043	85,575	38,532	3,929	—

Note : Rupees in lakh.

REFERENCES

1. J. H. Primavera, "Breedstock technology and the prawn industry", paper presented at the First Annual Convention of the Philippines, Federation of Agriculturists Inc., Manila Garden Hotel, April 8-9, 1983.
2. U. K. Srivastava, Amar Jeet Singh, and Santhakumar, J. Martin in "Economics of Brackish Water Culture Fisheries in India: Some Preliminary Evidence" in U. K. Srivastava and M. Dharma Reddy (eds.) *Fisheries Development in India: Some Aspects of Policy Management* (New Delhi: Concept Publishing Company), 1983.
3. J. H. Primavera, *op.cit*.
4. For details of recent innovations in pond designs see H. R. Rabanal "Recent Trends in Aquaculture", Paper contributed to the Seminar/workshop for Fishery Schools' Administrators (Philippines: Bureau of Fisheries and Aquatic Resources, Manila) October 24-28, 1977.
5. Also see "National Training Programmes" (Philippines SEAFDC Aquaculture Department) 1983.
6. J. H. Primavera, Breedstock of sugpo in Agriculture Extension Manual No. 7, Tigbaual, Iioilo, Philippines, Agriculture Department, South East Asian Fisheries Development Centre, February 1982.
7. See P. Pascual Felicitas, "Recent Advances in the Nutrition and Feed Development of Penacus Monodon in the Philippines" (Paper read at the 4th Fishery term BFAR, Manila) October 12, 1982.
8. J. H. Primavera, *op.cit*.
9. Suitable areas are those areas where natural tidal flow of water meets the needs for brackish water culture. Mostly these areas are near estuary mouth and present development in West Bengal has been only in these areas.
10. This classification is different than the tidal wave height at sea-shore. For example, tidal wave height in West Bengal is high, but present culture is being done in suitable areas located away from sea.

6

TRADITIONAL CRAFTS AND GEARS

T.R. MENON

INTRODUCTION

FISHING gear forms the actual tool/implement to catch fish, and craft is the floating platform for operating the gear to catch fish. Craft and gear form the basic components for the capture of fish. There are a few fishing gear and methods which do not require a craft, as they are shore based. Certain gear can be operated by fishermen in shallow waters without a craft. In many cases, the craft is used only to transport the fishermen and gear to the fishing ground and to bring them back to shore with the catch. In certain cases, the craft is also a functional part of the fishing operations, without which the gear cannot be operated. However, in modern fishing, both craft and gear are the essential for capture of fish.

CRAFTS

A wide variety and type of fishing craft have been used in India for capture of fish from time immemorial, each type having been evolved through generations on trial and error methods and possibly through "influence from neighbouring countries" as a result of trade relations, but most suited to local conditions and requirements. Each region has own characteristics of weather, climate, and coast formation and hence its own boat types.

No exhaustive or through study has been conducted by any agency on the existing fishing craft types in India, in relation to fishing gear and methods used by them. The only information available is from the FAO report to the Government of India on fishing boats, and also from the small descriptions of the crafts and craft types given by the different maritime states of the country.

The background information available regarding different coastal crafts and craft types used in India are from the studies conducted by James Hornell and recorded in 1920. He observed certain correlation of designs with regions of the coast line, which are characterized by clearly marked physical features. Eventhough, the variety and type of fishing craft used along the coast of India are very wide with different regional designations, all these types can be grouped into a few basic types. However, only the important types and their salient features are dealt with here.

Kattumaram

The word "Kattumaram" seems to have been originated from the Tamil word "Kattu maram" which literally means "logs tied together". In Malayalam the word carried the same meaning and is also known as "Chalathadi". in Andhra Pradesh, the kattumaran is known as "theppa" or "theppalu". In Orissa coast these crafts are called "theppa". Kattumarams are surf-landing/beach landing craft and are well suited for heavy surf-conditions. The English word "Catamaran" used to refer to beach landing craft appears to have its origin from the Indian word "Kattumaram" and is now widely used to refer all types of beach landing craft. But in India, kattumaram is used only to refer to craft made of logs lashed together either in a boat or raft form.

Possibly, these types of craft would have been the first floating platform used by the coastal inhabitants much before the first built up boat was used. The kattumaram was used by man for various purposes, especially for fishing. These are still being used by fishermen in many parts of the world as an efficient craft, especially in areas where normal displacement craft cannot be used.

The kattumaram is the most important and predominant traditional fishing craft used for fishing, all along the east coast of India, where the maximum stretch of coast line is sandy and surf beaten, with very few harbours or protected areas. They can also be seen along the west coast of India from Trivandrum towards south and the south-east coast upto Mukkur in Ramanad District.

The type of kattumaram seen in the area between Trivendrum and to Mukkur is the boat type, made by lashing together 3 to 4 shaped logs, with the centre log/logs placed keel-wise at a lower level than the side logs, so as to form a canoe/boat shape. They are hence classified as "boat kattumarams". These craft use sails for propulsion (very large sails in comparison to the size of the craft) and use centre-boards (leeboards) for stability. Rowing or paddling (which is rarely done) is done by split bamboo cars. These craft range in size from 4.5 m to 9 m OAL, with width ranging from 60 cm to 1.8 m.

Raft kattumarams are found all along the Coromandel coast from Point Calimere to Nellore in Andhra Pradesh bordering Tamil Nadu. The raft kattumaram is formed by lashing together 3 to 8 or even 9 shaped logs in a raft form, slightly curved and not absolutely flat. These crafts are much more elegant in their proportion and lines than the boat types of the south-west and south-east coasts.

These are wider in beam towards raft, and use sails for propulsion. Craft having beam up to 2.8 m are also seen. No centreboards are used, but leeboards of considerable size are used. These raft kattumarams are known by different names which denoted the size of the craft as well as the type of fishing for which the craft is used.

From Nellore district towards north upto Srikakulam in Andhra Pradesh, and further north towards Orissa another distinct type of boat kattumaram is seen. These are well developed boat kattumarams, and, irrespective of their size, are constructed in a similar fashion, with minor regional variations. These craft are constructed by lashing together 4 or 5 (usually four) shaped logs. Two identical halves with a right and left half are lashed together to form the craft. Each half is made by joining together two shaped logs using wooden pegs, which will remain joined till the service life of the craft, and only repairs will be done. These craft are provided with one or two (usually one—two numbers regional variation) long centreboard/boards, rudder, balance board, stem and stern pieces and wash strakes. All the craft invariably use sail for propulsion. Under sail, these craft possess excellent sea-keeping qualities. The range in size from 4 m to 9.5 m OAL. They are comparatively beamier than the boat katumaram of the Tamil Nadu and Kerala coasts. The types seen towards the Orissa coast are also constructed more or less on the same principle, but more crude in shape, construction, and appearance. It is estimated that there are more than 47,000 units of kattumaram which included all the three types.

Dug outs

As the name implies, these draft are made from a single log of wood, which is hollowed out, by burning/charring, or scooping/digging the inside, and shaping the outside to form a boat and hence the name dug-out. The mid-ship section/shape is rounded or flattened and rounded, depending on the requirement as well as the size of the timber log used for making the craft. There is no keel for the craft, but the bottom is made ticker than the sides which are made thinner. The sides will be more or less straight without any flare, but sometimes flaring inwards. Thwarts laid across provides transverse strength and stiffness.

The art of making a dug-out can be compared to craving or sculpture, as these crafts are beatufully shaped and fashioned and possess excellent lines. The size of the dug-out depends on the size of the timber available, which will restrict the length, beam and depth of the craft. They range in size from a tiny "one boy" canoe of 2.0 m OAL to large odam of about 10 to 15 m OAL with a carrying capacity of 10 to 15 persons/crew and fishing gear.

The craft are constructed mostly in the locality where it is to be used. They are truly Indian in design and construction. The dug-outs are generally known as 'malabar dug-out', as this is the traditional craft very popular in Kerala. They used to be exported to Arab countries also. They are being made in Karnataka, Maharashtra and Gujarat also, but are still termed 'malabar dug-outs'.

Craft in various sizes are used for different types of sea fishing all around the Indian coast. They are used for fishing in rivers and lakes and for all general purposes also. Dug-outs are the most popular and predominant fishing craft in many areas in Kerala, Karnataka, Gujarat and Maharashtra also, eventhough these crafts can be seen in almost all fishing villages all around the coast. It is worth mentioning that the entire fishing craft in fishing villages like Jaleswar and Mangrol in Gujarat are dug-outs. In India, the first outboard engine was fitted to a dug-out canoe in Jaleswar during 1953, marking the beginning of the out-board mechanization programme in the country. Subsequently most of the craft in those areas were mechanized with outboard engines/motors. Attempts to mechanize the large types with inbard engines and inboard-outboard engines elsewhere met with varying degrees of success. They have not yet become popular or accepted by the fishermen. In these areas in Gujarat, the dug-out canoes are the typical beach landing craft at these regions are surf-beaten and sanday without any sheltered areas or harbours. The craft possess very good qualities of a beach landing craft, by virtue of its light weight and keel-less round bottom. Owing to its light weight as well as limited carrying capacity, there is a possibility of capsizing near shore and consequent damage to the outboard engines while negotiating surf and beaching the craft.

Attempts made to evolve and introduce a surf boat to replace these crafts by conducting trail demonstrations and using prototypes designed by FAO naval architects did not succeed very much as they were not accepted and adopted by the fishermen. As such the dug-outs will continue to be the preferred craft of the fishermen until a replacement craft becomes acceptable to them.

Dug-outs are known by different names - like odam and vallam in Kerala, toni in Bombay, nody in Gujarat. It is estimated that dug-outs number more than 47,000.

Built-up banoes/coats

Built-up canoes/boats cannot be grouped under regular plank built boats, as they are not of the carefully constructed type. They cannot be grouped under dug-outs also as they are not true dug-outs in the strict sense of the term. A typical example is the Hody of the Bombay coast, which is nothing, but a widened copy of the dug-out. The craft use an outrigger similar to that used by the Ratnagiri type of boat, which is also developed from an outrigger canoe. The base is a dug-out canoe and the sides are skillfully spread by means of wedges, till they attain the required flare. On the flared edges, a series of strakes flaring outwards are raised, till the dug-out is changed into a beamy and fairly roomy boat with good carrying capacity. The craft invariably use an outrigger canoe for stability and as a net tender. These are the smallest of the three types of Ratnagiri deep sea boats; the larger two types being the Ratnagiri Machuwa type. They range in size from 7.5 m to 10.5 m OAL.

The largest type of built-up canoe is the outrigger boat or "Padavu"; which are used exclusively for beach/shore seining. These are long, deep, and widely spread canoe shaped blank built boats, the planks being stitched without any frames. Transverse strength is provided by few thwarts. This craft does not carry a mast, as it rows only while paying the net. Another type of distinct outrigger conoe is the "Kilakarai" out-rigger canoe. The basic craft is a true dug-out canoe, to which a narrow wash strake is attached vertically on the sheer without any flare. The dug-out canoe is not spread and as such can be used without an outrigger in calm waters. Two types exist, one using a single pole outrigger and the other type using a double pole outrigger. Towards the Palk bay and the Strait, dug-out outrigger canoes with a different type of outrigger arrangement are used.

While the predominant traditional fishing craft in Kerala is the dug-out ranging in size from 6 m to 12 m OAL, a larger version of the Malabar sailing dug-outs is being used in the Kanara and Konkan coasts, and costs of a dug-out more than 8 m. long provided with one strake (rarely two also) planking for raising the freeboard. These are wider than the common paddling dug-outs and rigged to hoist sails.

In the Gulf of Mannar region, another type of plank built canoe called the "boat canoe" is used by the fishermen along with the predominant boat type kattumaram. These are dug-out canoes spread by wedges and heightened by flared wash strakes 20 cm to 30 cm high from the gunwale.

Masula boats are yet another type of built up canoe found along the Coromandel coast and the Andhra coast towards Vishakapatnam. These can be considered as the east coast counterparts of "padavu" of the Karnataka coast. These range in size from 8 m to 12 m OAL. Smaller types are found more towards Tamil Nadu along the Coromandel coast, and the larger ones are more popular towards Vishakapatnam. These are known as "Padahu"/"Padahu" and "Salangu" locally.

These are also constructed more or less on the same lines as a big canoe, both ends pointed, plant built on a flat base, without frames and the planks stitched. Transverse strength/ stiffness is obtained by thwarts laid across. Like its west coast counterparts, these are also used mainly for shore/beach seining, and hence no mast is carried. The craft is paddled with cars. It is found that these crafts were initially used along the Tamil Nadu coast only, and was adopted by the Andhra Pradesh fishermen much later, consequent to the development of beach seining in Andhra Pradesh.

The type of traditional fishing craft very popular towards the Bengal coast are the "Batchari type" and "Chot type". Both by virtue of their lines of construction and shape can be grouped under "Built up canoe". The Batchari boats are very narrow in beam to its length. A typical craft measuring 13 m to 14 m OAL will have a beam of only 1.5 m to 1.75 m, and a depth of approximately 75 cm to 80 cm and a low freeboard. The sheer line foreward and aft are curved upwards, which make the stem and stern very high, and the stern as high as the stem. The stem and stern are pointed with considerable rake and provide the craft with a considerable overhanging bow and stern which in turn reduces its water line elngth by more than 50 per cent of its OAL. The bottom is rounded and there is no keel. No frames are provided, but curved floor timbers, the ends of which raise to a small height are provided. The plank seams are rabetted and fastened with double pointed flat iron staple nails, and the planks are stapled from inside as well as from outside. The staple nail thickness is accommodated in a recess out on the planks. These are open boats and a longitudinal strengther-top stringer-provides transverse stiffness and londitudinal strengh respectively. A loose deck of split bamboo sticks is erected by the fishermen when required.

The 'chot type boat' has short overhangs and a high free-board with more beam to its length. A typical chot boat measuring approximately 10 m OAL will have a beam of approximately 2.5 m. These can carry heavier fishing gear than the Batchari boats. They are keelless and have found bottom. Planking is carvel and fastened to the frames using iron fastenings. No deck is provided, but a loose deck of split bamboo is provided.

Plank built boats

Under this category can be grouped all the innumerable types of craft used all along the coast of India, each type being very typical of the region or locality. Variations and overlaps in designs and constructions exist in the same region also. An attempt is made to desciibe some of the prominant important types and their salient featutes.

Malia flat bottomed boat ?

Probably, this craft can be considered as a primitive plank built boat and the most simplest from of its kind. The boats are double ended, flat bottomed with carvel type of planking, built up on a simple backbone assembly consisting of a keel, stem, and stern (stem post and stern post). Stem and stern are almost vertical without any rake. Few sawn frames are provided. Shese crafts range in size from 3 m to 6 m OAL with beams from 90 cm to 1.25 m and depth ranging from 50 cm to 75 cm. These have a very low draught approximately 8 to 16 cm as their bottom is absolutely flat, their midship section shape having the cross-sectional shape of an open rectangular box. Due to its low draught, the boat is used in very shallow waters of the inter-tidal zone around Malia and

Surbari in the Rann of Kutch. Small stake bag nets, called "Gunja nets", are being operated by these boats for catching prawns.

Machuwas ?

The term "Machuwa" means a fishing boat in the language of the Sind Sailor. In India also, the term Machuwa is used to refer certain types of fishing craft in different regions which may or may not have similarities in design or construction. As cush the name Machuwa is more a term used to designate certain fishing crafts in every region rather than due to any speciality in the design or construction of the craft itself.

(i) Towards the north-west coast of India, especially in Jamnagar, Porbunder and Veraval regions, one typical type of craft is termed as Machuwa, with regional designations like, Jamnagar/Halar Machuwa, Veraval Machuwa and so on. All these crafts are constructed more or less on the same principle on a regular backbone assembly, comprising a keel, stern, and stem posts, usually with a transom stern, wide beam, and a moderately raking stem. Planking is carvel type and are fastened to the frames using irion nails, clinched on to the inside. Frames are roughly out grown timber having natural curves, and hence no boat will be exactly similar in lines, eventhough it may generally appear to be so. A number of longitudinal stringers are spiked to the frames inside. These crafts range in size from 8 to 10 m OAL, the larger ones being more popular towards the Jamnagar region and are designated as "Halar machuwas". The smaller types are popular towards the Veraval region. There are two versions in this smaller type. Once is a longer and narrower version than the other with a pointed raking stern and is called "Veraval Lodhia". The other is a broader version with transom stern and is called "Veraval Machuwa."

All these crafts have the characteristics of the 'Great Kotia' of the northr-west coast, also known as 'Wahans' which are the age old sailing coasters ranging in size from 18 m to 24 m OAL of approximately 150 tonnes, engaged in coastal trade, as well as trade, with the Persian Gulf and East African countries since centuries. This trade relations would have certainly influenced the design and construction practices of these traditional crafts. This is quite evident from the Kotia, which has a great fore-reaching bow, with a raking stem, deep forefoot, raking stern and the hoisting of the universal 'lateen sail' which are sufficient proofs of Arab influence in traditional boat building. The craft is provided with a castellated deck poop at stern quarters and a properly laid main deck. The bow is low and unobtrusive.

All the above mentioned machuwa type fishing crafts are also constructed more or less on the same lines of the Kotia with minor variations and possess similar characteristics as that of the Kotia and as such an affinity towards Arab designs. While the Kotia is provided with a well-laid main deck, the machuwas are all undecked and sometimes provided with a short or long fore and aft decks only.

(ii) Another type of large machuwa seen in the Gulf of Cambay region is used for fishing as well as for coastal trading. The majority of these craft do fishing in the Gulf of Kutch during the Ghol-Dara season for about three months, as well as in other nearby places during Bombay duck season, and engage themselves in coastal trading during the time when fishing becomes uneconomical. The stem of these crafts is strongly ranked and sharp, stern is truncated with a slight rake. When the craft is used for carrying cargo, the freeboard is increased by attaching a temporary bamboo mat weatherboard.

The above type is the smallest of the three types available in this area, the larger two types being used exclusively for carrying cargo, their carrying capacity ranging from 40 to 100 tonnes. All these types of crafts show characteristics of both the north-west coast type Kotias as well as the "Pattemars" of the Konkan and Kanarase coats, which are also essentially coasters.

(iii) Another type of machuwa which is called 'Bombay Machuwa' is a modification of the Pattemar. These are long craft with comparatively broader beams. A typical craft measuring approximately 15 m OAL will have a beam of approximately 3.5 m and a depth of approximately 1 m. The bow is long and raked, with a great overhang and considerable sheer. It is a shallow and beamy craft with great buoyancy foreward and aft, and well adapted to the coast. A typical example is the "Satpati type boat" which is very common around the Versova, Bassein and Satpati coasts of Maharashtra. It posseses excellent sea-going qualities and is considered by naval architects as the best boat suitable for the Indian coast. It is worth mentioning that the FAO naval architects have designed a 'monsoon boat' based on the lines of these craft. They usually will have only an aft deck and sometimes a main low deck at a lower level than the aft deck. Freboard is comparatively low, as these boats are used for gill-netting mostly.

(iv) Another type of Machuwa is the "Ratnagiri Machuwa" evidently modelled from the built up canoe form. The craft is an open boat with very broad beam, long overhangnig bow, round stern, and raked stern post. These boats are employed exclusively for gill-netting and have comparatively low freeboards to facilitate easy handling of gear and use a "lateen rig" sail on a single mast. All the above types of Machuwas are found suitable for mechanization. It worth mentions that the Veraval Lodia and Machuwa as well as the Halar Machuwa and the Satpati type boats were successfully mechanized with inboard engines during the fifties.

Tuticorin type boat

In the Gulf of Mannar region, a typical type of craft is commonly known as the "Tuticorin type boat". These are relatively narrow in beam to its length. A typical craft of approximately 9 m OAL has a beam of approximately 1.75 to 2 m and a depth of approximately 1.5 m. These are double-ended with nearly vertical stem and stern without any rake. The sheer line is almost straight. Built of locally available timber, using frames of natural curves, the frames are not carried up to the gunwale, but cut away below the sheer plank. The top sheer plank is much broader than the hull planks and is framed separately with short prices of frames, not fastened to the sides of the regular frames but at a distance away from it. These are a locally developed type and hoist a different type of sail on a single mast, not found in other regions. Some of these crafts were mechanized.

Navas

Other than the plank built Masula boat used for beach saining in the Tamil Nadu and Andhra coasts, another type of plank built boat called 'Navas' are used for fishing along the Andhra coast, especially towards the Kakinada and Masulipattinam regions. Navas used in the Kakinada region are called "Kakinada Nava" and the Navas used in Masulipattinam area are called "Masulipattinam Nava". The crafts are constructed without much variation and is a locally developed shallow water craft suitable for beach landing as it can ride over the surf. These are double ended, keel-less, and round bottomed with a narrow beam. Planking is carvel type and heavy frames are used. Few longitudinal strengtheners are provided on both sides. Fastenings are of iron. Short fore and aft decks are provided. The craft hoists a lateen rig sail on a single mast. Removable leeboards are used while sailing. The Masulipattinam navas sometimes use two masts. The craft are used for drift netting, stake net, set net and long line operations. They are used for beach seining also and have replaced Masula boats in certain areas in Andhra Pradesh. In certain areas, they are used in place of kattumarams.

Diamond harbour type boat

Towards the West Bengal coast can be seen three distinct types of craft, which are not seen in any other part of the country. They are the Batchari, Chot and Diamond Harbour. The Batchari and Chot have already been mentioned under the built-up canoe group.

The Diamond harbour type boat is constructed more on the lines of the Tuticorin type boat, double ended with nearly vertical stem and stern post, and round bottom. Planking is carvel type, with long floor timbers and built up frames from gunwale extending to the floor timbers only. Unlike the Tuticorin type boats, these boats have considerable beam to its length. The boats vary in length from 7 m to 15 m OAL. The boat is provided with foredeck and an aft deck and a large cargo space extending from foredeck to aft deck, as these boats are used for carrying cargo also.

Apart from the traditional fishing crafts, there are over 12,300 mechanized fishing crafts, ranging in size from a 7.4 m wooden Pable boat to a 35 m steel vessel. Most of the small and medium sized crafts are wooden boats. Boats have 17.5 m OAL are steel vessels. A few small steel boats are also used for fishing. The smaller vessels are operating gill nets and trawl nets. Medium sized vessels are used for trawling and purse-seinnig. Large steel vessels are used for trawling, purse-seining, tuna long lining, and jig fishing.

GEAR

Fishing is the art of câtching aquatic living things and the implement/tool used for the capture of fish is termed fishing gear. Various types of fishing gear and techniques are being used for catching fish from time immemorial. Every gear and technique has been evolved through generations of trial and error, depending on various factors like the species of fish to be caught, size, shape and weight, its reaction to light colour, shape, sound, obstructions and so on its feeding habits, breeding habits, swimming habits, swimming speed and depth, and many other behavioural aspects like, seasonal migration, shoaling habits and so on. Based on all these factors, a wide variety of fishing gear and methods are used for catching fish throughout the world, and in India also, innumerable varieties of fishing gear and methods are used.

All the fishing gear and methods have been evolved on three basis principles :

(1) *Luring* : The fish is lured or attracted within reach and then captured/caught.

(2) *Trapping* : The fish is trapped unawares and then caught—the preference of fish is to be ascertained first.

(3) *Attacking*. To effect a direct injury on the fish, to prevent its escape and then catch it.

Combinations of the above principles are used for many fishing methods, for example lurning and snaring, lurning and attacking, sharing and attacking. All fishing gear and methods come under two broad groups namely, dynamic or active and static or passive.

While dynamic or active gear may appear to be more effective in catching efficiency, static or passive gear is also equally efficient. Large stake bag nets, which are stationary gears, account for a major portion of the total landings in certain areas. The gill net, which also is a passive gear, accounts for the maximum landings of quality fishes in many areas. Similarly large beach seines and purse-seines, which are the most important dynamic or active gear, account for the bulk landings of certain species of fish in certain seasons.

It is estimated that there are more than 30,00,000 units of fishing gear of different types and descriptions available in the country. They include the simplest type of gear like a simple handline or cast nets to the more complicated beach/shore seines and the modern purse-seines. In fact representatives of almost all type of fishing gear and methods found all around the world can be seen in India also, either in similar form or in a modified form.

An attempt is made to briefly indicate the different types of fishing gear used in the country and their relative importance. Following are the classification of Prof. Dr. Von Brandt.

Fishing without gear

Probably this is the most simplest known method of catching fish throughout the world and is one of the popular methods adopted in India in pearl eyster and chank fishing. A very good pearl oyster and chank fishing ground exists off Tuticorin in the east coast of India in depths of 10 to 12 fathoms. The method employed is hand picking of oysters and chanks by diving. Naked diving is done by experienced fishermen, who can remain underwater upto 2 to 3 minutes. Similarly in the Halar coast in the Gulf of Kutch chank and pearl oyster fisheries exist. In this area also the method employed is hand picking, but instead of dividing, the fishermen have the advantage of the low tide, which exposes a wide area of the seabed near shore for long distances.

Wounding gear

Spears, harpoons, bow and arrow, blow pipes, etc. are some of the important types of gear used for catching fish. The principle employed is to inflict an injury on the fish, thereby killing it instantaneously or making it unable to move or escape. These implements will usually have sharp and pointed ends with barbs, like a fish hook. Sometimes a line is attached to the other end with which the fish is lifted up. Some spears will be long with pointed and sharp ends, with or without barb, to pierce the fish.

The application of this method of fishing is very much limited even though it is being practised in areas where the coast is rocky for catching lobsters and crabs. Use of blow pipes, bow and arrow, etc. are very popular in inland areas. It requires great skill and experience to use this method.

Stupefying method

The principle employed in this fishing method is to paralyse the fish temporarily, thereby restricting its movements and preventing its escape. This method is not popular in the marine environment, but is used in inland areas. Poisoning and dynamiting are the methods practised, but these are banned by law. Electrical fishing is the most modern method of stupefying fish and is an important method in some developed countries. However this method has not yet been developed in India.

Line fishing

The principle involved in this method is to lure the fish to take a bait. Hooks are concealed in the bait and the fish gets hooked when it tries to vomit or spit out the bait. In principle, hooks are not required. Hooks are added to the bait and the fish is caught when it vomits or spits the bait, when the line is pulled. There are several types of line fishing, from a simple hand line to a much complicated long line which can either be set or drift and made to fish in any desired depth.

The simplest form of line fishing is the one which is very popular along the south west coast of India for catching lobsters, used without a hook. The baited line is dropped in water to the bottom and lifted up slowly and skillfully bringing up the lobster, which follows the bait. When the lobster nears the surface, hand scoop nets are used to take the lobster. The usual bait is mussel meat.

Another simple hand line is the one with a baited hook used either from the shore or from a boat. When the fish takes the bait, the line is suddenly pulled with a jerk and the fish gets caught in the hook.

Simple hand lines with baited hooks are used all around the Indian coast and the fishing activity is limited to a subsistance level. Multiple handlines with several baited hooks, depending on the depth of operation, are used in deeper water in the south west coast of India in rocky bottoms and also in many areas in Tamil Nadu and Andhra Pradesh in the east coast of India, mostly for catching perches. During good seasons very good catches are recorded by this type of gear.

Pole and line is only a variation of the simple hand line. Instead of the hand line being held in hand, the line is attached to a long pole. Hooks are baited and the principle of operation is the same as that of the simple hand line. But the pole and line gear is a very important and popular gear in many parts of the world for catching Tuna, and is slightly different from the simple hand line attached to a pole. The hooks are specially shaped and shining, and is without the barb, which is normally seen in all fishing hooks. These hooks are not baited like the common hook with barh. In India, pole and line is an important fishing gear for catching tuna around the Lakshadweep islands and Minicoy islands, and is responsible for the entire landings of tuna in the country. To some extent the economy of the islands also depends on tuna fishery. The principle of catching tuna is by using live bait. Instead of baiting the hooks, the live baits are carried onboard small boats and when the sheals appear, the baits are thrown overboard in small quantities. As the fish start eating the bait, the fishermen skillfully drop/dip the shining hook attached to the line fastened to the pole in the midst of the tuna shoal, and the fish swallows the bait mistaking it to be the bait. As the hooks are barbless the hooked fish can escape also. But the swift hand of the experienced fishermen fish taking the bait, that is, hook, pulls the line with the hooked fish and drops the fish into the boat. The hook comes out of the mouth of the fish immediately as it is barbless and the operation is repeated. During a good "eating spree" a considerable number of tuna can be landed within a short period. This operation is a very swift one and requires considerable skill and experience. This method and gear are very special and is found to be in use only around the Lakshadweep and Minicoy islands.

Long lines are yet another type of line fishing gear found to be very popular in almost all regions all around the coast and is considered as an important fishing gear. The principle of this gear is to suspend a number of hand lines or branch lines with baited hooks from a very long main line which is held in position in water with floats attached to it with float lines. The baited hooks can be allowed to fish in any desired depth, by adjusting the float line, depending on the depth and area of operation, as well as the species of fish to be caught. Most of the long line gear used around the country are either for sharks, rays and cat fishes etc. as well as for perches from rocky bottoms. Both set and drift long lines are used. For catching sharks a modified form of long lines made of hardware material like chain with the branch lines attached to the main line using swivels are used and are usually known as revolving chain hook for shark. This gear is very popular along the Tamil Nadu coast.

Long lines, being the popular lines fishing gear used all around the cost, is known by different local names: Kaichoonda and Aiyaram choonda in Kerala, Thundil in Tamil Nadu, Beppu in Karnataka etc. It is worth mentioning that in Tamil Nadu when a Kattumaran is used for line fishing, the craft is called "thundilmaram".

Troll line which is another type of line fishing gear is also used in India, but the use of this gear is limited to certain areas like the Gulf of Manner. The principle involved is to drag or pull a few numbers of artificially baited hook. The lines are attached either directly to the craft used for dragging the line, or attached to the outrigger poles erected on the craft. Outrigger poles are used to prevent the lines from getting entangled especially when few lines are dragged. In India this gear is used by the fishermen on traditional craft like a kattumaram or other types of sailing craft, the mechanized boats are also used for operating troll lines very rarely. Seer fish, tuna, caranx, and so on are the important species generally caught on troll lines. Fairly good catches are recorded during good seasons. Kattumaram fishermen from Kanyakumari district are seen moving towards north to the west coast following the fish and land their catches in the nearby shores.

Hand line fishing appears to have good prospects of being developed as a commercial feasibility in many areas of India where there are narrow patches or strips of uneven, rocky and rough bottoms. This is evident from the large quantities of Rock Cod (Kalava) and other types of perches caught on the hand lines operated in certain grounds in depth range of 70 to 100 m in the west coast of India during the studies conducted by the Integrated Fisheries Project on hand lines using hand reels from medium and large vessels.

Long line for tuna is yet another possibility in Indian waters especially in the exclusive economic zone. India could not embark on tuna long line fishing venture for want of proper vessels and technical skill. Steps have already been taken in this regard and a few vessels belonging to the Government of India have already started training personnel for developing the skill for tuna long line fishing.

Fish trips

In modern fishing, fish traps appears to be losing importance. The principle of catching is to lure fish to enter a trap, but prevent its escape. In India, even though trap fishing is being practised in many regions in varying intensity, it has not gained importance, as in the case of the large and complicated Japanese set nets—set trap nets—also known as "Fyke nets". Traps can be made in various shapes and sizes, using rigid hardware materials like wire mesh, welded mesh, or bamboo or netting materials. The opening or entrance to the trap is on the principle of one way valve either conical in shape or the inside of the opening is provided with flaps or flappers which will open inwards only, allowing the fish to enter the trap and prevent their escape.

Trap fishing also appears to have good prospects for development in the country, and has already been developed as a commercial feasibility at the Integrated Fisheries Project for catching rock cod (kalava) and other types of perches from the narrow strip or patches of rocky and rough grounds, where perches are abundant, and trawling operations cannot be conducted, within depth range of 70 to 100 m along the west coast of India.

Traps used in the country are mainly basket traps and those made with roots of palmyra trees. Lobster pots used in the south-west and south-east coast of India and in certain other areas in the west coast are the most popular and important fish traps.

Weirs and pounds, locally known as 'Waghas' in Gujarat and as 'Maljal' in Orissa are another type of fixed traps found in certain areas. Enclosures are made near the shore especially at the entrances to river mouths by piling up stones loosely, their heights reaching less than the high water level. During high water, fish will enter these enclosures for feeding, as the river entrances can contain food for the fish. As the water recedes during low tide, the water level will come down and the enclosures will be exposed, and the fish get trapped inside the enclosures. During the low tide period, the enclosures will be more or less completely exposed and the fish which are trapped inside can be caught. In certain areas, instead of using stones, the enclosure is formed by netting erected on poles in a similar way. During low tide water gets filtered through the net, and the area will be exposed from where the trapped fish can be caught. Use of these types of fixed fish traps are effective only in places where the tidal difference is high. Waghas and Maljal are popular towards the north west-coast in Gujarat as well as in the Orissa coast.

Traps for jumping fish

The principle employed in this method is to lay floating obstacles such as fish hedge, or net wall, so that certain fish, which have the habit of jumping or leaping or when frightened or encountering an obstacle, can be caught. A horizontal/flat floating trap or raft can be used to catch the fish as they jump or leap and fall back.

In India, traps for jumping fish are not popular. However, in inland areas such methods are in use. Changalapayikkal/ Changadampayikal is a popular fishing method practised in the Kerala backwaters for catching prawns. The principle is to drag a long chain jointly by two canoes, to disturb fish at the bottom, so that when it jumps/leaps it falls in the boat and can be caught.

Bag nets with fixed mouths

This is one of the important gears used in India, especially in the north-west coast for catching Bombay ducks. They are considerably large conical shaped bag nets, fixed/set either on stakes or with the help of anchor stones keeping the mouth of the net open facing the current. These are essentially tidal bagnets and are set facing the current. Fish which swim with the current or brought by the current are caught in the cod end of the net, from where it can be removed. "Dol nets" which are the important type of set bag nets found Bombay fall under this group. Bombay ducks, pomfrets, prawns and so on are caught generelly in this gear. These nets are considerably large, the length of the bag ranging from 150' to 180' or even more, and the mouth opening may be 60' × 60' or more. These nets are operated in depths ranging from 10 to 30 fathoms, and usually three nets will be set in one line. A large number of nets will be set in the fishing ground and fish are removed from the net during the change of tide.

In Gujarat, fixing of the net is very using anchor stones, while in Maharashtra, spikes are used to fix the net. Fixing the stakes as well as anchor stone and operation of the gear etc. are much complicated and are done using very ingenious methods. A smallar version called 'Bokshi' net is used in shallow waters and is operated in the same principle.

Stakes bag nets/bag nets with fixed mouths are used all around the coast in many areas, each having its own regional importance and known by their local names. These types of fishing gear are the traditional type used in India since generations, and will continue to retain their importance.

The smallest of the type is the one used in the inter-tidal zone in the Rann of Kutch called "Guoja nets" found in Malia and Subari area. The craft used for fishing is the popular Malia flat bottomed boat. Stake bag nets are very important in the inland sector also.

Dragged gear

The principle employed is to drag the gear through water either on the bottom, surface or midwater, and sweep the area, collecting all the fish which come in the way of the opening of the net.

All types of trawl nets for catching prawns, lobsters, and fish can be grouped under this category. Trawl nets are essentially conical shaped bag nets, with long or short wings; depending on the design of the gear; which can be dragged in water, with the help of a boat, either in the bottom, mid-water or surface, the mouth of the net being kept open by various devices, when the net is being dragged. The usual practice is to use a pair of otterboards/otterdoors, attached to the wings, which will effect horizontal opening for the net during dragging. Vertical opening is effected with the help of floats and sinkers attached to the head rope and foot rope respectively. These trawl nets are called otter trawls. Other devices and methods are also used to effect horizontal and vertical opening for the net. However, the trawl nets used in India are outer trawls.

Various designs and sizes of trawl nets are used in India by the mechanized fishing boats, the majority of them being engaged in bottom trawling only, especially for prawns. Bottom trawling is more popular than pelagic trawling or mid-water trawling, even though the latter two methods have good scope for development. Mid-water trawling operations were initiated in the west coast of India, but was discontinued owing to certain social reasons. Trawling gear, even though not a traditional Indian gear, has been well adapted in India and is found to be well suited to Indian conditions.

"Thuri valai" (or) 'Vella valai' of the Tamil Nadu coast, and 'Iraga valai' of the Andhra coast, which are being classified as 'Boat seines' can be considered as primitive trawls, as this gear is similar in shape to that of a trawl net with a conical shaped body and long wings. This net is also dragged in water, with the help of two craft, usually two kattumarams, and has a reasonably good catching efficiency.

Seine nets

The principle is to enclose by encircling a located shoal of fish with the help of a long wall of netting, equipped with floats on its upper margin on edge called the head rope and with weights or sinkers on its lower margin or edge called the foot rope, so that the netting remains stretched in water depth-wise. After the encircling operation is completed, the trapped or enclosed fish can be removed from the enclosure. The net can be shot or set from a point on the shore, and encircle the sheal of fish paying the net with the help of a boat, and return to a point on the shore away from the setting or starting point. The depth of the net will be more than the depth of operation and hence the float line floating on the surface and the foot rope touching or dragging the bottom will prevent the escape of the trapped or enclosed/encircled fish. The net can be hauled on the shore from both sides or wings, till the encircled fish are collected or concentrated in a smaller enclosure/area near the shore, from where the fish can be removed. In some cases, a small conical bag is also provided in the middle of the net, so that fish get collected in the bag from where they can be removed.

Such nets which are operated from the shore are known as shore seines or beach seines and are very popular along the west coast as well as the east coast of India, especially in regions where the coast have long stretches of sandy beaches. Sardine and mackerel are the most important species of fish caught in these nets. In fact prior to the introduction of modern methods like purse-seining, the entire landings of sardine and mackerel were by these nets. These are considerably large nets and are known by different regional names. These nets are called "Rampani" and "Kairampani" in Karnataka, "Kambavala", "Karamadi" in Kerala, "Peruvalai and Periavalai" in Tamil Nadu, "Peddavalai" in Andhra Pradesh and "Mahajal" in Orissa.

If the fish shoals are away from the shore it may not be possible to catch them with the help of beach seines. In such cases, two boats will carry the net and encircle the shoal of fish in the sea, and the net will be hauled on the boat itself. Such nets which are set/shot from a boat and hauled on to the boat are known as boat seines. In some cases only one boat will be used.

Boat seines are very popular along the west coast and east coast of India and are known by their regional names. "Thangu vala" and "Thattumadi" are important types of boat seines in Kerala. "Thuri valai" of the Tamil Nadu coast and "Iraga valai" of Andhra coast are the important boat seines of the east coast. Both the "Thuri valai" and "Iraga valai" are considered as primitive trawls, by virtue of their shape and method operation. "Thangu valai" of the west coast is more like a semi-circular bag, with the ends or wings formed by long lengths of rope, to which, gudgeon leaves are attached to form a scare line. "Thuri valai" and "Iraga valai" are conical shaped bag nets with very long wings resembling a modern trawl.

Surrounding nets

In principle, these nets are also similar to seine nets and fish are caught by encircling a shoal (surrounding a shoal). In fact both seine nets and surrounding nets can be combined to form a single group. Encircling or surrounding gill nets can be grouped under this classification. Instead of laying the net across in water like a wall, these nets are laid around a shoal of fish—that is a shoal of fish is surrounded by a gill net—encircling them and the fish get gilled as well as entangled in the netting. Under this category, the "Ring nets" and "Purse-seine" are grouped. The principle employed in the ring net and the purse-seine is to close the bottom of the net after encircling a shoal of fish, thereby preventing the escape of fish through the bottom, which will not be possible with the boat seine, as the depth of the net is usually less than the depth of operation. As far as beach/shore seines are concerned, the foot rope usually touches or drags along the bottom, thereby preventing the escape of fish through the bottom. Most of the boat seines are not deep enough to reach the bottom, and the foot rope of the net is hauled in first onboard the boat, quickly leaving the head rope with floats, and the net assumes the shape of a bowl with the encircled fish trapped inside, from where it cannot escape. Hauling of the foot rope is done very quickly within a minimum possible time, as otherwise the fish may escape. Hence boat seines will be smaller in size also.

The advantage of the ring net and the purse-seine is that they can be made of considerably large size, even upto 1200 m. Head rope, due to the possibility of getting the bottom of the net closed after completing operation. Another advantage is its size, which makes it possible to negotiate a large shoal of fish, as well as a fast swimming shoal like mackerel and tuna. Closing of the bottom is effected by attaching a series of rings to the foot rope through which a line is passed. By pulling this line, the rings get bunched up and the bottom gets closed. This is a very simple method used on a valet or purse and hence the name purse-seine. The rings are termed as purse-rings, and are almost the same with minor variations in design and operation. In fact purse-seine net originated from ring nets and other round hauls.

In India, purse-seining was introduced first by the earstwhile Indo-Norwegian project. Operation of purse-seine net was being done in Goa by the Portugese, but became popular as an efficient method to catch shoaling fish like sardine and mackerel only after the introduction of purse-seine fishing by the earstwhile Indo-Norwegian project. Since then the maritime states especially in the west coast of India, were attempting to popularize the gear among the traditional fishermen. Karnataka, Kerala and Goa could succeed in introducing purse-seining. Very good landings of sardine and mackerel were recorded in all the above places. Of the late operation of purse-seine has been restricted to fishing grounds beyond the area demarcated for the traditional fishermen using conventional fishing gear and methods.

There is a possibility of developing purse-seining for catching tune for which exploratory and experimental studies are necessary.

Dip or lift nets

The principle is to submerge in water a rectangular netting with or without a loose centre portion so as to give a bowl shape for the gear when hung by its four corners on suitable frames; and raise the net rapidly out of water periodically. Such nets can be termed as dip or lift nets, and can be operated either from the shore or from a boat. The types which are operated from shore are usually from river entrances or in backwaters, and cannot be strictly considered as marine fishing gear, even though many dip nets can be seen being operated from seashore also. "Chines dip nets" or "lift nets" ; as they are popularly known and found in Kerala and Karnataka are the important types of dip/lift nets used in India.

Use of dip/lift net in sea is not very popular in India, except in very limited areas like the Coromandel coast in Tamil Nadu, where a typical gear known as "Mada valai" and "Eda valai" is used. These nets are conical shaped bag nets with a square mouth opening. The net is submerged in water by four kattumarams holding the net by its four corners, and slowly lifting the net. Good catches are recorded in these type of dip/lift nets during good seasons. Both mada valai and eda valai are similar in shape and construction. Eda valai is smaller than Mada valai.

Falling nets

The principle is to cover the fish with a cover pot or a flat or conical netting, thereby enclosing the fish under the cover, from where it cannot escape. Cast nets are the best known gear in use in India in marine environments. Cast nets and plunge baskets are used in inland areas also.

Cast net is a circular netting more conical in shape, the edge of the circular netting being provided with lead weights. In some nets, the edges are folded inside to form pockets also. The centre of the net is provided with a small ring through which a series of lines are attached to the margin or edge of the net. These lines are known as "draw strings". The net is 'plaited' in one hand and with great skill is cast in water over the fish, when they are seen. The net spreads and falls over the fish and sinks down due to the weight at the edges, trapping the fish underneath. The draw strings held by the fishermen is slowly pulled, bringing the fish to the small enclosure formed from where the fish can be removed. Sometimes the fish gets trapped in the peripheral pockets of the net from where it can be caught. Cast nets are very popular all around the Indian coast, and is used since generations. Cast net fishing is done more on subsistance level only. They are known as "Veedu valai", "Veesu valai", "Beesubala", "Mani valai", and so on.

Gill nets and tangle nets

Gill nets are considered as universal gear, as it is used by the fishing community throughout the world in both marine and inland environment. Gill nets are the most important traditional fishing gear, used all around the Indian coast and is responsible for the landings of different types of priced fishes like promfrets, seer fish, hilsa, mullets, perches, lobsters, prawns, etc. In fact almost all types of fish can be caught on gill nets.

The gear is a long wall of netting, laid across in sea, either on the surface, mid-water or surface. The mesh size and spread depends on the species to be caught. When the fish tries to pass through the mesh opening, it gets caught at the gills. Hence the name "Gill nets". The upper margin/edge of the netting is mounted to a rope called the head rope, and the lower margin/edge is mounted to a rope called the foot rope. The head rope is provided with floats and the foot rope is provided with weights or sinkers. By adjusting the amount of floats and weights, the net can be made to fish in any desired depth. For certain surface drift nets, no weights are provided. The net can be allowed to drift with the current or can be set to remain in a fishing ground. Accordingly, gill nets can be "set or drift".

As mentioned earlier, gill net is the most popular traditional type of fishing gear found all around the coast; various types are in use, each type having its own regional importance and known by different regional designations. Generally, gill nets are known by the name of the species of fish intended to be caught with the gear e.g. Chala vala, Aila vala, Vala valai, Vanjra valai, Kavala valai, Eral valai, and so on.

Certain nets are specified, by their size, Chinna kavla valai, Motha valai, Pedda valai, and so on. Certain others indicate the depth of operation as well as condition of operation like set or draft and so on e.g. Kettu bale, Odu bale, Tharthi, Thagla and so on. Some of the small gill nets made of 1/2 number and 1 number nylon twines are called by the material specification like Ara valai, Oru valai, and so on.

As indicated earlier, the principle of catching fish by a gill net is that the fish gets caught in the mesh by their gills when it tries to pass through the mesh opening of the net. The mesh size, mesh opening, and the spread of the net depend on the species of fish to be caught. This being the principle, fish can be caught by getting them entangled in the meshes of a gill net also. Such nets will have a very loose hanging without much spread. Hence gill nets can be made to work as entangling nets also.

Gill nets are normally laid across like a wall. It can be laid around a shoal of fish, encircling them and are known as encircling gill nets.

Gill nets are usually single walled and in some cases, double walled, or triple walled. The latter types are not popular in India. Triple walled is more popular than double walled and is known as "Trammel net". Trammel nets are very effective where the current is not strong. The net is made of three layers of netting, the inner or middle layer of very small mesh size, with very good spread (tight hanging). Any type of fish which tries to pass through the netting gets pouched in the middle small meshed netting through the large meshed outer layer of netting. Trammel nets are being used only on experimental basis and have not yet become popular.

While the above classification gives a general idea about the different types of fishing gear used all around the Indian coast, there are a few age-old important fishing methods like, "Kola fishing" (flying fish fishing) practised since long in the east coast of India which does not find a place in the classification. The principle comployed is to induce the fish to collect around the bushes carried by the fishermen to the fishing ground so that the fish can be scooped out with a scoop net when they collect around the bush tolay eggs. This is an age-old method, practised by fishermen to catch flying fish during the breeding season. The gear used for inducing the fish is only few bunches of bushes of certain plants to make them collect around the bush for laying eggs, and a small scoop net for taking the fish from water. The fishing ground for the flying fish fishing is far away from the shore, and kattumarams are used for this fishing. Kattumarams when used for "Kola fishing", the kattumarams are termed as "Kolamarams".

7

DEVELOPMENT OF INFRASTRUCTURE
Fishery Harbours

N. P. BHAKTA

INTRODUCTION

FISHERY harbours are an important link between the actual operation of catching fish in the seas and its delivery in fresh condition to consumers. The fishermen would require to spend maximum amount of time on their fishing operations and minimum time on landing the catch. Therefore, every facility should be afforded to them to approach the harbour with the least possible delay. This would necessitate that the fishery harbour is situated close to several fishing grounds and that the fishermen do not have to wait for tides for entry or exit.

In the context of the energy crisis and import of diesel at high cost, fishery harbours located closest to fishing grounds would save fuel and time and reduce the cost of production of fish. It may be of interest to know that for a fishing vessel which makes daily trips, the cost of fish production would go up by Rs. 120 per tonne for every additional nautical mile it has to commute (Appendix I). On the other hand, transportation of fish by truck would cost hardly half a rupee per tonne and consume 1/100th of the fuel required in commuting the same distance. Thus there is no need to emphasize that fishery harbours should be located closest to the entrance of a harbour or an estuary or a river and not several kilometres inside.

Development of infrastructure such as landing quays, berthing jetties, fish handling, and auction sheds, and services like maintenance and repair facilities, adequate supply of fuel, ice, and water are of great importance for efficient fishing operations. Thus establishment of fishery harbours with the necessary infrastructure is essential if marine fish production is to be increased. Fishery harbours should contain the following facilities. (See Figs. 7.1 and 7.2):

(a) Landing quays for quick and hygienic unloading of fish with sufficient sheltered back space for landing, cleaning, sorting, weighing, and display of fish for auction;
(b) Berthing jetties for idle berthing of boats and to replenish provisions and fishing gear required for the next voyage;
(c) An outfitting quay for quick replenishment of fuel, water, and ice;
(d) Repair quay and service facilities for conducting necessary routine maintenance and repairs to the engine and boat;
(e) The depth alongside the quays and jetties at lower low water springs should be a minimum of 2 m. for small vessels and a maximum of 5 m. for vessels up to 30 m. in length;
(f) Slipways or sloping hards for hauling up boats with workshop facilities for conducting major repairs and annual maintenance;
(g) Fish auction halls close to the landing quay for cleaning, sorting, weighing, display, and auctioning of fish;
(h) Ice plants, chilled fish, and cold storages for supply of ice and storing chilled and frozen fish close to the landing and outfitting berths;
(i) Sufficient area for parking of vehicles, establishing processing plants, auxiliary industries and fishing hardware stores for buoys, anchors, sinkers, and so on with proper roads connecting these industries and other facilities;
(j) Sufficient area for mending nets, drying fish, and fish meal plants; and

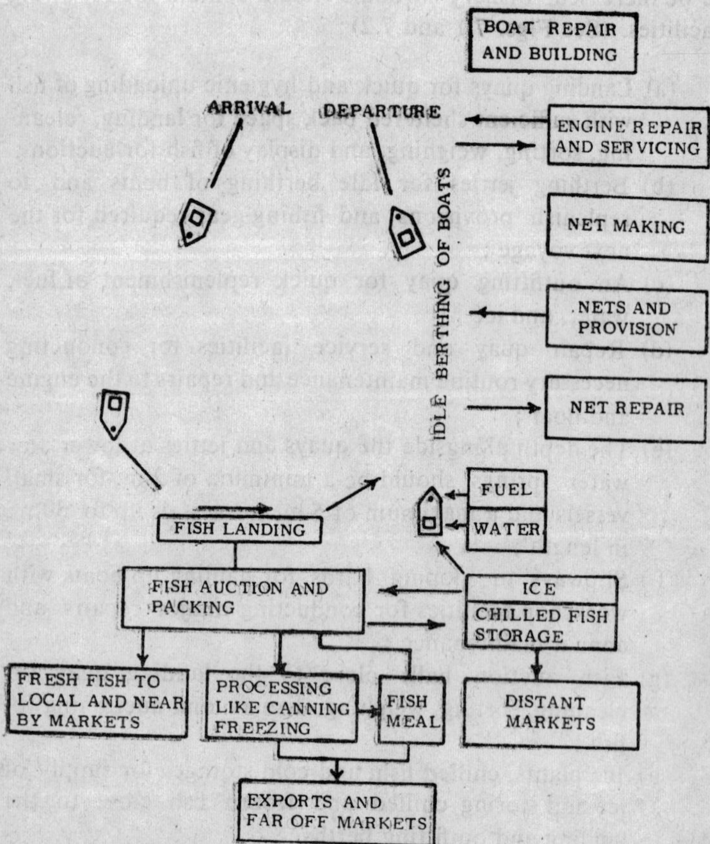

FIG. 7.1 : *Flow diagram*

LANDSIDE FACILITIES

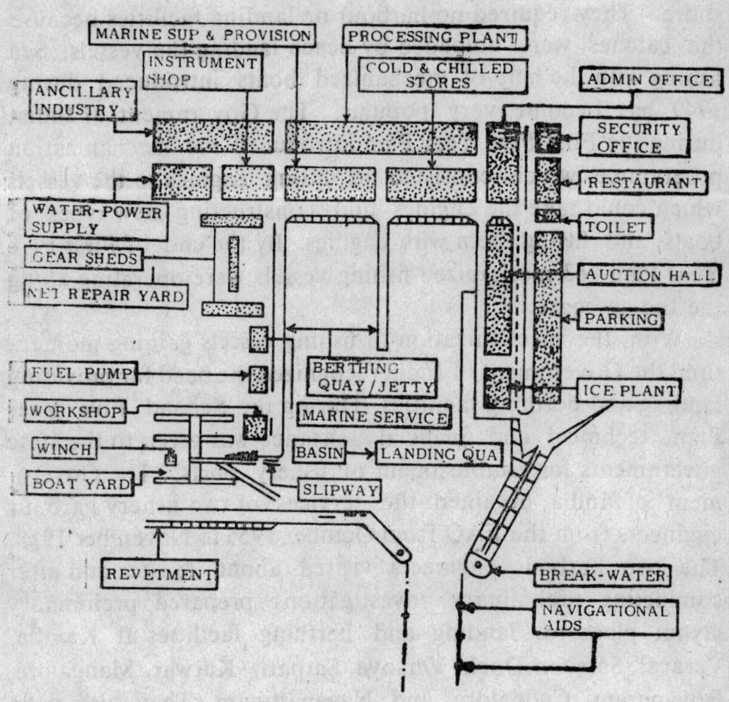

FIG. 7.2 : *Waterside facilities*

(k) Area for administrative buildings, shops, restaurants, dormitories, post and telegraph office, and security office.

FACILITIES AVAILABLE/UNDER CONSTRUCTION

Till the late forties sea fishing along the Indian coast was done with sailing craft or canoes which did not go far from the shore. They required no harbour or landing facilities because the catches were unloaded by beach landing the vessels. Sea fishing with the help of mechanized boats introduced during 1949 has become very popular. The Government of India, during the First Five Year Plan introduced the mechanization programme which consisted of fitting engines to the vessels which could take the engines and constructing new types of boats and fitting them with engines. By the end of First Five Year Plan 863 mechanized fishing vessels were operating along the Indian coast.

With the mechanization of fishing vessels gaining momentum, the Government of India recognized the need for providing landing and berthing facilities. During the Second Five Year Plan, technical and financial assistance was given to the state governments for establishment of fishery ports. The Government of India obtained the services of two fishery harbour engineers from the FAO from October 1955 to November 1958. The two harbour engineers visited about 28 sites and after conducting preliminary investigations prepared preliminary layout plans for landing and berthing facilities at Kandla, Veraval, Sassoon Dock, Versova, Satpati, Karwar, Mangalore, Royapuram, Cuddalore, and Nagapattinam. They also gave their assessment for the sites of Jaffrabad, Mangrol, Porbunder, Bassein, Dahanu, Malpe, Beypore, Thangasseri, Vizhinjam, Pulicat lake, Ennore, Adayar, Tuticorin, Punakayal, Periyathalai, Leepuram, Muttom, Collachel, and Manakudy. The report and recommendations of the experts were made available by the FAO in early 1960. However, based on the layout plans given by the experts the fishery harbours at Veraval in Gujarat and Cuddalore in Tamil Nadu were taken up for construction and development during 1957 and 1958 respectively.

In 1961, the assistance of one more fishery harbour engineer was obtained for a period of 12 months from the FAO. He visited 30 sites and suggested preliminary layouts for fishery harbours and landing centres at about 23 sites without conducting any investigations. His report was made available by the FAO by early 1963. During this plan construction of landing and berthing facilities at Kandla, Porbunder, Navabunder, Jaffrabad, Umbergaon, Karwar, Bhatkal, Mulky, Mangalore (jetty), Azhikkal, Cannanore, Beypore, Azhicode, Vizhinjom, Tuticorin, Nagapattinam, and Kakinada were taken up. Out of the two sites taken up during the Second Five Year Plan, Veraval was under construction whereas Cuddalore was completed. Of the landing and berthing facilities taken up for construction during the Third Five Year Plan itself, work at Kandla, Porbunder, Navabunder, Jaffrabad, Bhatkal, Mangalore (wooden jetty), Azhicode, and Nagapattinam was completed.

In the three annual plan period, work at Veraval was completed, landing and berthing facilities were provided at Mandapam (Palk Bay), Karaikal, Azhikkal, Beypore, and Ponnani, and construction was taken up at Umersadi, Honnavar, Coondapur, Mandapam (Mannar), Cuddalore (II stage), Rameswaram, and Namkhana.

With the phenomenal increase in mechanized fishing boats the Government of India was keen to provide infrastructure facilities for the operation of mechanized vessels at the earliest and, therefore, approached the UNDP (SF) for assistance in investigating and reporting about 15 to 20 fishery harbours during the Fourth Plan. The Government of India established the Pre-Investment Survey of Fishing Harbours at Bangalore for a period of five years with the technical assistance of UNDP. The assistance mainly consisted of provision of technical experts (engineers and economists) and equipment to give inservice training to the counterparts and prepare project reports for about 15 sites. The Project investigated 16 sites, reported on 15, and recommended 13 sites for development during that period. The aspects considered during the pre-investment studies were geographical, engineering, fishery resources, and present level of exploitation, economic, factors, fishing areas, and the potential background of siting of fishery harbours. From January 1975, the Swedish International Development Authority gave similar assistance as UNDP (SF) for 19 more months during which period four more sites were investigated and three were recommended for development. From August 1976 the Project continued as a subordinate office of the Ministry of Agriculture and conducted investigations at 16 more sites and recommended 12 for development. The sites investigated and recommended by the Pre-Investment Survery of Fishing Harbours from the date of its inception are given in Appendix II. During the Fourth Plan, the landing and berthing facilities at Karwar, Cannanore, Tuticorin, and Kakinada were completed. Provision of guiding lights and removal of rocks and sand in the entrance to the creeks were also completed at about 38 sites, mostly in Maharashtra. All pre-investment investigations such as surveys, sub-soil investigations, and model tests were taken up for siting, landing and berthing facilities at the major ports of Bombay, Mangalore, Cochin, Tuticorin, Madras, Vishakapatnam, Paradeep, and Roychowk. Detailed estimates were made and investment decisions were taken in respect of Bombay, Cochin, Madras, Vishakhapatnam, and Roychowk.

During the Fifth Plan (1974-78) and the subsequent two rolling plans construction of landing and berthing facilities for deep sea fishing vessels were taken up at the major ports of Sassoon Dock (Bombay), Cochin, Madras, Vishakapatnam, and Roychowk (Calcutta). While the construction of facilities at Cochin, Vizag, and Roychowk were completed those at Sassoon Dock and Madras were still in progress. At minor ports the landing facilities at Dhamra taken up in October 1975 were completed in addition to the facilities at Thal, Uttan, Karanja, Datiwara, Kulgaon, Alavakodi, Gangoli, and Chandipur taken up during the plan. In addition construction of fishing harbours were taken up at Jakhau, Mangrol, Veraval (II stage), Kolak, Ratnagiri, Honnavar (II stage), Malpe, Mallipatnam, Kodikkarai, and Nizampatnam. Landing and berthing facilities at Bavanapadu and second stage works at Porbunder, Mangalore, and Kakinada were sanctioned.

By the first year of the Sixth Five Year Plan the construction of jetty at Mallipatnam was completed and construction of facilities at Kakinada (II stage) was started and the construction of facilities at other places was in progress. Construction was yet to start at Bavanapadu and Mangalore (II stage).

The facilities at Kandla are not put to use because they are located far inside the Kandla creek in the gulf of Kutch and it is a very long cruise to the fishing grounds. The facilities at Cannanore are also not being used because the bay is getting silted and the quay is high and dry at low waters. However, mechanized vessels do anchor in the bay to take advantage of the protection afforded by the breakwater. Work at Umbergaon has come to a standstill as the contractor has deserted the work.

From the above, one can visualize that the progress of construction of landing and berthing facilities for fishing vessels has been very slow. It has to be appreciated that construction of ports and maritime works is a slow and time-taking process because the work has to be executed adjusting to the daily variation of tides and vagaries of weather and sea, and involves the hazard of working in water splashing areas. Procedural delays mainly account for the time taken for scrutiny of the projects by various agencies and the various formalities to be followed in getting clearances at both state and central levels. The procedure to get a project cleared takes two to four years. Physical causes are non-availability of small, experienced and properly equipped contractors to take up maritime works in remote places (no big contractor having the equipment would be interested in taking up small projects), delay in obtaining construction materials owing to remoteness of the site, non-availability of dredgers and right type of equipment for construction, and change in designs during construction due to change in site conditions and/or fresh oceanograpnic data. Financial causes are inadequate funds for the schemes or the project both at central and state levels and the financial limitations of the small contractors who take up these jobs. Natural causes are cyclones and storms affecting the work, prolongation of bad weather periods, unexpected calamities, and breakdown of communications during such calamities. Artificial causes are shortage of power, diesel, cement, steel, and skilled labour and the fact that many times due to bad planning of work by the contractor himself gets into difficulties. In addition, delays in land acquisition for construction of facilities and quarry sites and litigations by parties against the construction also contribute to slow progress. As such no cause or agency can be singled out for the delay in execution of projects but it is the combined effect of several cause and agencies. In spite of the fact that both central and state governments are very keen to have facilities constructed at a very early date, the factors described above have retarded the progress considerably.

The number of ports at present catering to many of the fishing vessels are about 33 which are designed to cater to about 4000 mechanized boats and 75 deep sea vessels. At present 17 more fishing harbours (including 6 II stage) are under construction and these would cater to about 4000 more boats and 175 deep sea vessels. These 44 ports would cater to about 8000 fishing boats and 250 deep sea vessels in all. Thus the landing facilities are far below the needs of 15,000 fishing boats now operating and more so for the 19,000 mechanized boats and 350 deep sea vessels that are likely to operate by the end of the Sixth Plan. Facilities available and under construction at fishing ports in different maritimes states along with ice plant, cold storage, freezing, and frozen capacities are given in Appendix III.

RECOMMENDATIONS FOR DEVELOPMENT OF INFRASTRUCTURE (FISHING HARBOUR)

From the above description it appears that future fishing harbours should be developed keeping in mind the available infrastructure and the norms of approach projected. Accordingly, the following strategy for future development would emerge :

(1) Wherever infrastructure is already available fishing harbours should be classified into small, medium and large

depending upon their location and engineering potential and take up second stage development to meet the optimum exploitation requirements, and

(2) Identify new sites for development.

Considering these aspects, fishing harbours recommended for development in each state are given below :

Gujarat

In Gujarat, out of 18 fishing ports required, two are to be large (Sivrajpur and Veraval), one medium (Porbunder) and the rest small. Out of the above, 4 small ports have been provided at Porbunder, Jaffrabad, and Veraval. Veraval is being expanded to cater as a large fishing harbour and Porbunder is being developed as a medium part. The small ports of Mangrol, Jakhau, and Umbergaon are under construction. Development of one more small port at Bulsar, in the near future, is recommended.

Maharashtra

Large ports, one at Agardanda and other at Ratnagiri, one medium port at Bombay, and 8 small ports at other centres have been proposed for Maharashtra. Out of these the large port at Ratnagiri and the medium port at Bombay are under construction. One more small port at Satpati is recommended for development in the near future.

Goa

Goa will have one large port at Karanjhalen and two small ports at Chapora and Betul. Goa has no fishing harbour at present and as such construction at Karanjhalen could be taken up early in a phased manner such that during the first phase it shall serve as a medium fishing port and later it could be enlarged into a large fishing port.

Karnataka

Karnataka needs one large port at Malpe, one medium port at Karwar and 6 small ports. Facilities are available at Karwar, Honnavar, Bharkal, Gangolli, Mulky, and Mangalore as small fishing harbours. The facilities available at ports other than Karwar and Mangalore are not very useful, but Mangalore is overcrowded. Additional facilities are under construction at Mangalore and Honnavar. A large fishing port is under construction at Malpe which is nearing completion. As such in the near future a small fishing harbour at Tadri would be necessary. Work is likely to be taken up in the near future with the assistance of foreign aid.

Kerala

One large port at Cochin, 3 medium ports at Cannanore, Beypore, Vizhinjom, and ten small ports are required for Kerala. Out of the above, the large port at Cochin, two medium ports at Cannanore and Beypore, and three small ports at Baliapatnam, Ponnani, and Azhicode are in existence. But Azhicode, Ponnani, and Cannanore are difficult to use due to siltation. One more medium size port at Vizhinjom and a small port at Neendakara are now under construction. One more small port at Puthiappa is recommended for development in the near future.

Tamil Nadu

The Tamil Nadu state requires 16 small ports, one medium port at Cuddalore and two large ports—one at Chinnamuttom and the other at Madras. The large port at Madras is under construction while the medium port at Cuddalore is in existence. In addition, small ports at Tuticorin, Mandapam, Mallipatnam Rameshwaram, and Nagapattinam are in existence and one at Kodikkarai is under construction. But port of Nagapattinam is not useful due to difficulties in navigation while Cuddalore needs improvement. One more small port at Valinokkam could be taken up for development in the near future.

Andhra Pradesh

About 12 small ports and four medium ports at Krishnapatnam, Machilipatnam, Kakinada, and Bavanapadu, and one large port at Vizag would be necessary for Andhra Pradesh. The large part at Vizag is nearing completion and the medium ports at Kakinada and Bavanapadu and a small port at Nizampatnam are under construction. Plans for the medium fishing port at Krishnapatnam are ready and will be taken up for construction in the near future.

Orissa

Orissa would require one large port at Paradeep, one medium port at Dhamra, and 9 small ports. Out of these the medium port at Dhamra and a small port at Chandipur are in existence. The large port at Paradeep is in the planning stage. A small port at Nuagar has been planned and is likely to be taken up for construction in the near future.

West Bengal

For West Begal one large port at Roychowk and two small ports at Digha and Frazergunj are necessary. Roychowk has already been completed. A small port at Digha could be provided in the near future.

Pondicherry

Two small ports at Pondicherry and Karaikal are required. One at Karaikal is already in operation and one more at Pondicherry could be provided in the near future.

Summarizing the above, recommendations on the proposed development of fishing harbours in the near future would be providing small fishing ports at Bulsar in Gujarat, Satpati in Maharashtra, Puthiappa in Kerala, Valinokkam in Tamil Nadu, Pondicherry in the Union Territory of Pondicherry and a medium port at Karanjhalen in the Union Territory of Goa, in addition to the small fishing harbours at Tadri in Karnataka, Nuagar in Orissa and Digha in West Bengal and a medium port at Krishnapatnam in Andhra Pradesh already contemplated for development with the assistance of aid giving agencies.

Plans and estimates are available for most of the sites mentioned above except for Bulsar in Gujarat which requires detailed investigations. The salient economic features of the proposals at the above fishing harbours, except for Bulsar, may be seen at Appendix IV. The abstract estimates for Bulsar may be seen at Appendix V.

MANAGEMENT OF FISHING HARBOURS

Fishery management has now acquired importance in our country with increase in mechanized fishing activity and fishing harbours. Management and running of a fishing harbour requires a suitable and efficient agency. Thus, activities such as allotment of land in the harbour for various industries, providing various supplies and services, conducting auction, maintenance of statistical information, and monitoring of the activities under one roof become imperative. From the experience gained from the advanced fishing countries, Fisheries Terminal Organization (FTO) as an agency came to be identified for fulfilling the above needs and to release the fishermen and the fishery industry from the clutches of tradition and customoriented influence of the middlemen.

The agency can be organised under the Indian Companies Act 1956 with diverse functions of which the following would be important :

(1) To allot land available within the fishery harbour complex for various fish processing and ancillary industries, net and craft repair, fish drying and storage and collect revenue.
(2) To organise fish landing, inspect quality and arrange them for auction, conduct auction, and collect fees for this purpose from the merchants.
(3) To arrange delivery of ice, fuel, and water to thc boats on payment of the actual cost plus a nominal fee for the service, and
(4) To meet the coast towards regular maintenance of the fishing harbours and its approaches with the assistance of the concerned engineering division of the ports department, out of the revenue earned from the first two activities.

Advantages of managing the above functions under one

agency are obvious as the arrangement besides aiding functional efficiency would avoid red tape and other delays. Labour unrest, strikes, and so on which are a common feature with port organizations could be completely avoided if they are managed by people interested in the fishing industry.

A draft Memorandum of Association for the FTO may be seen at Appendix V page 267. This can well be adopted to suit local needs without losing the essential features for which the agency is meant. The FTO could also be a fishermen organization like a co-operative society or association, or corporation.

To be effective the FTO has to be suitably staffed. The Table 7.1 illustrates the nature of staff needed for an FTO while the actual personnel required depend upon the number of vessels in operation and the quantum of fish landings at a particular port. The pay scales of the FTO personnel would also similarly depend upon those in vogue in the state government or other local bodies.

TABLE 7.1 : **The FTO staff members**

Sl. No.	Designation/category
1.	Managing Director
2.	General Manager
3.	Deputy Manager (for large ports)
4.	Accountant
5.	Market Superintendent
6.	Salesmen (Auctioneers)
7.	Sales Clerk
8.	Cashier
9.	Clerk/Typist
10.	Peon
11.	Foreman
12.	Watchman
13.	Driver
14.	Temporary Labour

Revenue—rates and mode of collection

A certain amount of revenue should be earned from the fishing harbour to run, maintain, and renew the harbour and other facilities and for the functioning of FTO. The required revenue can be earned by

(1) Charging rent on the land leased out to various fish processing and ancillary industries ;
(2) Collecting commission from the merchants on every kg. of fish that moves out of the harbour either for local consumption or for export ;
(3) Charging a nominal berthing charge on daily basis for the number of days the boats stay in the harbour depending upon the size of the boat ;
(4) Collecting a nominal service charge over the actual cost for supplying fuel, water, and ice at the outfitting quay ;
(5) Selling power to the various industries within the harbour complex by obtaining bulk power for the harbour complex from the State Electricity Board ; and
(6) Charging a nominal fee for using the repair facility in addition to other incidental expenses for hauling the boat and so on, or giving the whole repair complex on lease to a contractor and charge a lease amount.

Out of the charges mentioned above, the berthing charges for boats, charges for the repair facilities, and the service charges for supplying ice, fuel, and water at the quay should be very nominal as these are to be paid by the fishermen, boat owners or operators, while the other charges could be so calculated as to meet the following expenses :

(1) running the harbour and meeting the establishment costs of the Fishery Terminal Organisation ;
(2) to meet all the expenditure with regard to annual maintenance of the fishing harbours structures, the roads within the harbour complex ; and maintenance dredging along side the quays and approaches, if any ;
(3) to accumulate the depreciation fund at 2 per cent of

the cost of the fishing harbour complex for renewal and future expansion of the harbour ; and

(4) to establish a benevolent or welfare fund to assist fishermen families in case of any disaster or calamity or for conducting marriages, and so on.

The charges should be such that they would attract the boats to come and land within the harbour. By keeping the berthing charges nominal and not charging any fees on the fish landed the boats would be eager to avail the facilities within the harbour. When all the boats land at the fishing harbour the merchants would naturally come to the fishing harbour for purchase of fish who can be charged a commission for the purchase of fish anywhere from 5 paise per kg. for low quality fish to 50 paise a kg. for prawn which earn a very high price. On the other hand, if the fishing boats are charged a high rate for berthing and on the fish landed, the boats would prefer to land the fish on the beach outside the harbour and enable the middlemen and the merchants to have their stranglehold on the fishermen. Further the harbour would also lose the revenue because one cannot earn much by charging a few hundred of boats, whereas one can earn a lot by charging a nominal fees or commission for every kg. of fish moving out of the harbour.

The proposed Fishery Terminal Organization can be formed with people interested in the welfare and progress of the fishing industry. The FTO can prove a suitable agency for efficient operation and maintenance of the fishing part and fishing activities and collect the necessary revenue.

APPENDIX-I

INCREASE IN COST OF FISH PRODUCTION DUE TO COMMUTATION OF ONE NAUTICAL MILE

1. *Vessel data*

(a)	Vessel size	10 m
(b)	Horse power of the engine	60
(c)	Fishing trips/year	200 (daily trip of 10 hrs.)
(d)	Catch per trip	250 kg. (50 tonnes/year)

2. *Cost of fuel*

(a) Time taken to cover 2 n.m. (1 n.m. each way) at 5 knots = $\frac{2}{5} \times 60$ — 24 minutes

(b) Additional fuel consumed to cover this distance in a year $200 \times \frac{24}{60} \times 60 \times .15$ — 720 litres

(c) Cost of this additional fuel = 720×2.50 — Rs. 1800

(d) Cost of lubricants etc. to cover this additional distance — Rs. 200

Total cost on fuel and lubricants — Rs. 2000

3. *Catch lost*

(a) From 2 (a) it is seen each boat loses 24 minutes/day in commuting this distance.

Hence time lost in 200 days $= \frac{200 \times 24}{60}$ — 80 hrs

(b) Catch lost due to fishing hours $80 \times 250 \div 10$ — 2000 kg

(c) Cost of catch lost at Rs.2/- per kg. of fish $= 2 \times 2000$ — Rs. 4000

4. *Additional cost of fish production*

Cost of fish production $= \frac{\text{Rs. } 2000 + \text{Rs. } 4000}{50}$ — Rs. 120/t

Appendix-I (Contd.)

5. *Cost of road transportation of same 1 ton for 3.5 km (2 n.m.)*

(a) Truck capacity	5 tonnes
(b) At 5 km/litre it requires $\frac{3.5}{5} = 0.7$ litres to cover this distance	
(c) Cost of this fuel $= 0.7 \times 2.5$	Rs. 1.75
(d) Lubrication etc.	Re. 0.25
Total	Rs. 2.00
(e) Hence cost of transportation of fish for this additional distance $= \frac{2.00}{5}$	Rs. 0.40 or 40 paise/ton

6. Additional fuel burnt in conveying 50 tonnes of fish by road $= \frac{50 \times .7}{5}$ — 7 litres only as compared to the 720 litres per boat.

APPENDIX-II

SITES INVESTIGATED AND REPORTED UPON BY P.I.S.F.H. BANGALORE

Name of state	Name of sites investigated	Name of sites for which project reports prepared	Status
1	2	3	4
Gujarat	Shivarajpur	—	Report under preparation
	Porbnnder	Porbunder	Work being taken up
		Mangrol	Under construction
		Veraval	Under construction
Maharashtra	Dahanu	Dahanu	Dropped in favour of Satpati
	Satpati	Under preparation	Re-investigated due to increase in fishing activity
	Mora	—	Investigations completed
	Dighi	Dighi	Dropped in favour of Agardanda
	Agardanda	Agardanda	Proposal under revision
	Jaigarh	—	Not proposed
	Ratnagiri	Ratnagiri	Under construction
Goa	Karanjhalen	Karanjhalen	Under consideration
Karnataka	Karwar	Karwar	Sanction awaited
	Tadri	Tadri	Sanction awaited
	Honnavar	Honnavar	Under construction
	Malpe	Malpe	Under construction
	Mangalore	Mangalore	Work being taken up

1	2	3	4
Kerala	Puthiappa	—	Proposal under examination
	Neendakara	Neendakara	Sanction awaited
	Vizhinjam	Vizhinjam	Sanction awaited
Tamil Nadu	Chinnamuttom	Chinnamuttom	Sanction awaited
	Veerapandiapatnam	—	Report under preparation
	Valinokkam	Valinokkam	Sanction awaited
	Mallipatnam	Mallipatnam	Completed
	Kodiakkarai	Kodiakkarai	Under construction
	Pazhayar	Pazhayar	Sanction awaited
Pondicherry	Pondicherry	Pondicherry	Sanction awaited
Andhra Pradesh	Krishnapatnam	Krishnapatnam	Sanction awaited
	Ramayapatnam	Ramayapatnam	Dropped
	Nizampatnam	Nizampatnam	Under construction
	Narsapur	Narsapur	Dropped
	Kakinada	Kakinada	Under construction
	Bavanapadu	Bavanapadu	Sanctioned, work being taken up
Orissa	Rushikulya	—	Preparation of report pending for completion of model study
	Nuagar	Nuagar	Sanction awaited
	Dhamra	Dhamra	Completed
West Bengal	Digha	—	Report under preparation
	Pratappur	—	Site not feasible

APPENDIX-III

FACILITIES AVAILABLE/UNDER CONSTRUCTION AT FISHERY PORTS IN INDIA

Sl. No.	Name of the port	Range of tide in M	Depth at entrance in M	Depth alongside the quay in M	Length of quay in M	Number & size of boats to be catered in M^{18}	in M^{18}	Capacities in tonnes: Ice plant per day	Ice store	Freezing plant per day	Frozen store	Bunkering: Fuel	Water	Auction hall	Remarks
1	2	3	4	5	6	7	8	9	10	11	12	13	14	15	16
A.	*Gujarat*														
1.	Jakhau*	2.3	2	0.0	60 T Head jetty	60	—	10	100	nil	nil	yes	yes	yes	T head with 366 m approach well connected by road
2.	Porbunder* (II Stage)	2.6	3.0	2.1	800 (quay)	400	—	225	865	35	1025	under construction			A slipway is proposed. Well protected and connected to highway. A full-fledged fishing harbour is under construction.

1	2	3	4	5	6	7	8	9	10	11	12	13	14	15	16
3.	Mangrol*	2.2	3.0	2.5	380 (quay)	180	—	86	nil	nil	nil		-do-	)	Well protected with break waters and connected by road but no slip-way is proposed
4.	Veraval* (II Stage)	2.2	6.0	3 to 4	1680 (quay)	570	26	235	1640	115	1285		-do-	)	
5.	Navabunder	2.7	2.0	1.0	160	80	—	nil	nil	nil	nil		nil		Well protected and connected to highway.
6.	Jaffrabad	2.7	1.5	1.0	275	200	—	nil	nil	nii	nil		nil		Well protected and connected to high-way
7.	Ummarsadi	5.0	1.5	1.0	22	20	—	nil	nil	nil	nil		nil		-do-
8.	Kolak*	5.0	1.2	1.0	48	40	—	nil	nil	nil	nil	under cons-truction		nil	Well protected and connected by road but entry hazardous
B.	*Maharashtra*														
9.	Uttan	3.9	1.0	0.5	113	50	—	nil	nil	nil	nil	nil	nil	yes	Well connected by road
10.	Kasara	3.7	9.0	3.0	300	250	—	ice is brought from out-side and fish moved out for sale and processing				yes	yes	yes	Nerry wharf in Bombay well pro-tected

Appendix-III (Contd.)

1	2	3	4	5	6	7	8	9	10	11	12	13	14	15	16
11.	Sassoon Dock*	3.7	9.0	0.54 (3.0)	453 (350)	700	—	57	41	7	59	yes	yes	yes	Well protected & connected by road (Bracket figure show under construction)
12.	Ratnagiri*	2.7	4.0	3.0	300	390	—	160	320	12	360	under construction			Well protected with breakwater and connected by road. Slipway is under construction
13.	Karanja	3.7	2.0	1.0	33	30	—	nil	nil	nil	nil	nil	nil	yes	Well connected by road.
14.	Datiwara	3.7	0.5	0.6	33	30	—	nil	nil	nil	nil	nil	nil	yes	-do-
15.	Kulgaon	3.6	6.0	2.0	66	50	—	nil	nil	nil	nil	nil	nil	yes	-do-
16.	Thal	3.6	6.0	1.0	105	60	—	nil	nil	nil	nil	nil	nil	yes	Well connected by road
C.	*Goa*			nil				nil				nil			
D.	*Karnataka*														
17.	Karwar	2.1	6.0	1.5	160	150	—	60	110	10	50	yes	yes	yes	Well protected and connected by road
18.	Honnavar* (II Stage)	1.8	2.0	3.0	280	180	—	30	80	6.5	100	yes	yes	yes	-do- and slipway is under construction

1	2	3	4	5	6	7	8	9	10	11	12	13	14	15	16
19.	Alvakodi	1.4	1.0	0.5	33	30	—	3	nil	nil	nil	nil	nil	nil	Well protected but connected by Kutcha road
20.	Gangolli	1.3	1.5	1.5	66	50	—	3	nil	nil	nil	nil	nil	nil	-do-
21.	Malpe*	1.2	6.0	4.5	500	150	5	20	50	nil	300	yes	yes	yes	Well protected & connected by road. A slipway is under construction
22.	Mulky	1.1	1.0	1.0	33	30	—	3	nil	nil	nil	nil	nil	nil	Connected by Kutcha road
23.	Mangalore* (II Stage)	1.1	2.2	1.0	222	260	—	150	450	—	400	yes	yes	yes	Well connected by road. 225 m quay is being taken up for construction
E.	*Kerala*														
24.	Azhikkal	1.0	1.6	1.5	100	60	—	100	300	10	600	yes	yes	yes	Entry hazardous, well protected & connected by road.
25.	Beypore	1.4	1.4	1.5	130	140	—	25	130	5	175	yes	yes	yes	-do-
26.	Cochin	0.6	9.0	6.0	500	900	59	45	100	26	940	yes	yes	yes	-do- and slipway under construction

Appendix-III (Contd.)

1	2	3	4	5	6	7	8	9	10	11	12	13	14	15	16
27.	Vizhinjom*	0.90	12.0	48	240	60	40	550	1100	75	2250	under construction			Well protected with breakwater and connected by road. Slipway is proposed
F.	*Tamil Nadu*														
28.	Tuticorin	0.7	2.0	3.0	400	400	—	5	15	3	50	yes	yes.	yes	Well protected with breakwaters and connected by road. Slipway available
29.	Mandapam (Gulf of Mannar)	0.5	2.0	2.0	150	100	—	15	110	11.5	50	yes	yes	no	Well protected and connected by road
30.	Rameswaram	0.5	2.0	2.0	60	60	—	5	5	nil	nil	nil	nil	nil	Not protected and not connected by road, only rail connected
31.	Mandapam (Palk bay side)	0.5	1.0	1.0	110	100	—	nil	nil	nil	nil	nil	nil	nil	Not well protected but connected by road
32.	Mallipatnam	0.6	3.0	2.5	60	40	—	10	10	nil	nil	under construction			Unprotected but calm and connected by road

1	2	3	4	5	6	7	8	9	10	11	12	13	14	15	16
33.	Kodiakkarai*	0.6	2.0	2.0	60	40	—	10	10	nil	nil		-do-		-do-
34.	Nagapatnam	0.6	1.0	1.0	90	60	—	2	2	nil	nil	nil	nil	nil	Well protected & connected by road but entry hazardous
35.	Cuddalore	0.6	1.0	2.0	270	180	—	2	2	nil	nil	nil	nil	nil	-do-
36.	Madras*	1.1	6.0	6.0	490	500	50	not available			under construction			yes	Well protected with breakwater and connected by road. A slipway is under construction
G.	*Pondicherry*														
37.	Karaikal	0.6	1.0	1.0	20	10	—	1	2	nil	nil	nil	yes	no	Well protected & connected by road but entry hazardous
H.	*Andhra Pradesh*														
38.	Nizampatnam*	1.06	1.2	2.3	200	60	—	18	54	2	60	under construction			Entry hazardous but well protected by road
39.	Kakinada* (II Stage)	1.34	2.5	2.2	1640	475	115	92	90	19	600	under construction			Well protected with breakwater & connected by road

Appendix-III (Contd.)

1	2	3	4	5	6	7	8	9	10	11	12	13	14	15	16
40.	Bavanapadu*	1.16	2.28	2.08	245	200	—	70	210	4	120	under construction			Well protected with breakwaters but road is to be made
41.	Vishakha-patnam* (II Stage)	1.40	8.00	6.00	1220	300	50	205	250	42	1005		-do-		Well protected with breakwater & connected by road. A slipway is available
I.	*Orissa*														
42.	Dhamra	2.8	3.6	2.0	200	50	—	6	nil	nil	nil	yes	yes	yes	Well protected but not connected by road
43.	Chandipur	3.2	1.0	0.5	128 (T Head jetty)	50	—	10	10	nil	nil	no	no	no	Well protected and connected by road, entry hazardous
J.	*West Bengal*														
44.	Roychowk	6.0	8.0	6.0	120 (T Head jetty)	—	15	25	100	nil	nil	yes	yes	nil	Well protected & connected by road

Notes : (1) *ports under construction.

(2) Those ports where no separate facilities are available for fishing boats and such of those facilities which cannot be used or not being used are not included in this statement.

(3) Does not include private ice plants, cold storages, freezing plants and frozen storages.

APPENDIX-IV

SALIENT ECONOMIC FEATURES OF SATPATI FISHING HARBOUR

(a) *Fishing Fleet* (Nos.)

Existing	— 12 metres	65
	— 13.2 metres	170
New	— 12 metres	25
	— 13.2 metres	240
Total		500

(b) *Investment* (Rs. lakh)

(i) Fishing vessels	547.75
(ii) Fishery harbour	700.00
(iii) Shore establishments	78.46
(iv) Pre-development expenditure	3.00
Total	1329.21

(c) *Additional landings* (tonne)

(i) Crustaceans	—
(ii) Fish	11575
Total	11575

(d) *Project revenue* (Rs. lak)

(i) Export markets	259.20
(ii) Indian markets	613.30
Total	872.50

(e) *Return on vessel investment* (%)	*12 m*	*13.2 m*
(i) Before depreciation	78.5	54.8
(ii) After depreciation	69.6	46.2

(f) *Internal rate of return* (%)

Basic Statement	23—24
Sensitivity analysis (%)	
(i) 20% reduction in landings	13—14
(ii) 20% increase in investment	18—19

Appendix-IV (*Contd.*)

SALIENT ECONOMIC FEATURES OF KARANDHALEN FISHING HARBOUR

(a) *Fishing fleet* (Nos.)			
11 metres			150
14 metres			75
16 metres			25
Total			250
(b) *Investment* (Rs. lakh)			
(i) Fishing vessels			965.60
(ii) Fishery harbour			500.00
(iii) Shore establishments			406.30
(lv) Operating capital			157.73
Total			2029.63
(c) *Additional landings* (tonne)			
(i) Crustaceans			7350
(ii) Fish			22650
Total			30000
(d) *Project revenue* (Rs. lakh)			
(i) Export markets			1006.94
(ii) Indian markets			857.70
Total			1864.64
(e) *Return on vessel investment* (%)	*11 m*	*14 m*	*16 m*
(i) Before depreciation	27.3	33.4	46.2
(ii) After depreciation	18.8	26.5	37.5
(f) *Internal rate of return* (%)			
Basic statement			31—32
Sensitivity analysis (%)			
(i) A 20% reduction in landings			19—20
(ii) A 20% increase in investment			24—25

Appendix-IV (*Contd.*)

SALIENT ECONOMIC FEATURES OF VALINOKKAM FISHING HARBOUR

(a) *Fishing fleet* (Nos.)	
Existing —9.8 metres	20
New —9.8 metres	130
Total	150
(b) *Investment* (Rs. lakh)	
(i) Fishing vessels	209.30
(ii) Fishery harbour (revised on 10.4.81)	77.00
(iii) Shore establishments	42.30
(iv) Pre-development expenditure	3.00
Total	331.60
(c) *Additional landings* (tonnes)	
(i) Crustaceans	780
(ii) Fish	5720
Total	6500
(d) *Project revenue* (Rs. lakhs)	
(i) Export markets	283.91
(ii) Indian markets	112.95
Total	396.86
(e) *Return on vessel investment* (%)	*9.8 m*
(i) Before depreciation	52.1
(ii) After depreciation	42.5
(f) *Internal rate of return* (%)	
Basic statement	39—40
Sensitivity analysis (%)	
(i) 20% reduction in landings	29—30
(ii) 20% increase in total investment	32—33

Appendix-IV (Contd.)

SALIENT ECONOMIC FEATURES OF PONDICHERRY FISHING HARBOUR

(a) *Fishing Fleet* (Nos.)		
Existing	—9.1 m to 11 m	125
New	—9.1 m	175
	—11 m	50
Total		350
(b) *Investment* (Rs. lakh)		
(i) Fishing fleet		280.20
(ii) Fishing harbour		120.00
(iii) Shore establishments		61.26
Total		461.46
(c) *Additional landings* (tonnes)		
(i) Crustaceans		1352
(ii) Fish		9168
Total		10520
(d) *Project revenue* (Rs. lakh)		318.02
(i) Export markets		
(ii) Indian markets		216.25
Total		534.27
(e) *Return on vessel investment* (%)	*9.1 m*	*11.9 m*
(i) Before depreciation	42.6	47.7
(ii) After depreciation	33.6	38.4
(f) *Internal rate of return* (%)		
Basic statement		36—37
Sensitivity analysis		
(i) A 20% reduction in landings		25—26
(ii) A 20% increase in total investment		29—30

APPENDIX-V

COST ESTIMATE OF SATPATI FISHING HARBOUR (1981)

Sl. No.	Description	Unit	Quantity	Rate	Amount	Total
1	2	3	4	5	6	7
1.	*Earthwork*					
	(a) Dredging	m^3	3,34,100	30	1,00,23,000	
	(b) Cutting	m^3	42,000	5	2,10,000	
	(c) Surfacing of area reclaimed from dredged spoil	m^3	22,000	24	5,28,000	
						1,07,61,000
2.	*Break waters*					
	(a) North breakwater	m	1,150	23,000	2,64,50,000	
	(b) South breakwater	m	690	13,700	94,53,000	
	(c) Reclamation bund of landing quay	m	64	5,750	3,68,000	
	(d) Reclamation bund of repair quay	m	90	1,200	1,08,000	
	(e) Sand arrester	m	170	7,400	12,58,000	
						3,76,37,000
3.	*Quays*	m	340	29,600	1,00,64,000	1,00,64,000
4.	*Sloping hard*	m^2	2,250	60	1,35,000	1,35,000
5.	*Auction hall*	m^2	2,400	800	19,20,000	19,20,000

Appendix-V (Contd.)

1	2	3	4	5	6	7
6.	*Traffic areas and surfacing*					
	(a) Road pavement	m^2	21,200	55	11,66,000	
	(b) Hard surface	m^2	22,500	40	9,00,000	20,66,000
7.	*Navigational aids*	LS			45,000	45,000
8.	*Ancillary facilities*					
	(a) Water supply	LS			14,00,000	
	(b) Power and lighting	LS			10,00,000	
	(c) Administrative office	LS			8,00,000	
	(d) Canteen, shops and toilets	LS			4,00,000	
	(e) Drainage and sewerage	LS			3,00,000	
	(f) Fencing	LS			1,00,000	40,00,000
		Total				6,66,28,000
		Add contingencies at 3%				19,98,849
						6,86,26,840
		Add work charge estt. at 2%				13,72,537
		Grand total				6,99,99,377

Say Rs. 700 Lakh

Appendix-V

COST ESTIMATE OF KARANJHALEN FISHING HARBOUR (1981)

Sl. No.	Description	Unit	Quantity	Rate	Amount	Total
1	2	3	4	5	6	7
1.	*Breakwater*					
	(a) Bock 0-0.5 t	t	3,27,090	45	1,47,15,000	
	(b) Rock 1.6-2.4 t	t	86,000	65	55,90,000	
						2,03,05,000
2.	*Earthwork for reclamation*	m^3	3,80,000	18		68,40,000
3.	*Stone pitching*	t	26,000	48		12,48,000
4.	*Quays*	m	510	9,000		45,90,000
5.	*Slipway with transfer system*	LS				85,00,000
6.	*Auction hall*	m^2	3,000	600		18,00,000
7.	*Surfacing traffic areas*	m^2	20,000	90		18,00,000

Appendix-V (Contd.)

1	2	3	4	5	6	7
8.	*Ancillary falicities*					
	(a) Water supply	LS			8,00,000	
	(b) Drainage and sewerage	LS			5,00,000	
	(c) Electrification	LS			7,00,,000	
	(d) Port office	LS			3,00,000	
	(e) Fuel supply	LS			1,50,000	
						24,50,000
			Total			4,75,33,000
			Add contingencies at 3%			14,25,990
						4,89,58,990
			Add work charge establishment 2%			9,79,180
			Grand total			4,99,38,170
			Say Rs. 500 lakh			

APPENDIX V

COST ESTIMATE OF VALINOKKAM FISHING HARBOUR (1981)

Sl. No	Description	Unit	Quantity	Rate	Amount	Total
1	2	3	4	5	6	7
1.	*Dredging and reclamation*					
	(a) Dredging	m^3	12,500	25.00	3,12,500	
	(b) Reclamation	m^3	33,000	18.00	5,94,000	
						9,06,500
2.	*Breakwater*					
	(a) Stones 0.8 t to 1.0 t	m^3	2,900	78.00	2,26,200	
	(b) Stones 0.4 t to 0.5 t	m^3	1,900	78.00	1,48,200	
	(c) Stones 100 kgs. & below	m^3	10,800	70.00	7,56,000	
	(d) Concrete M 150 with 10% plums for breakwater wall	m^3	750	400.00	3,00,000	
	(e) Concrete M 150 for surfacing & grouting	m^3	330	354.00	1,16,820	
						15,47,220
3.	*Quays, jetties, revetment*					
	(a) Quay	m^3	141	6,820.00	9,61,620	
	(b) Berthing		302	8,150.00	16,46,300	

Appendix-V (Contd.)

1	2	3	4	5	6	7
	Revetment					
	(i) Stones 0.5 t	m^3	400	90.10	36.040	
	(ii) Stones 30 kg. to 50 kg.	m^3	950	85.70	81,415	
	(iii) Stones 10 kg. and below	m^3	600	85.70	51,420	
						27,76,795
4.	Repair facilities, slopping hard and boat parking repair concrete platform	LS				5,00,000
5.	*Auction hall*	m^2	975	500.00	4,87,500	4,87,500
6.	*Roads and surfaces*					
	(a) Approach road	m^2	1,500	39.38	59,070	
	(b) Internal roads	m^2	8,500	39.38	3,34,730	
						3,93,800
7.	*Ancillary facilities*					
	(a) Other surface like net dry	LS			1,11,000	
	(b) Other internal roads	LS			1,11,000	
	(c) Drainage & sewerage	LS			60,500	
	(d) Water supply	LS			1,81,500	
	(e) Offices & toilets	LS			1,11,000	
	(f) Power and lighting	LS			1,11,000	

Appendix-V (Contd.)

1	2	3	4	5	6	7
(g) Fencing		LS			30,250	7,16,250
			Total			73,28,065
			Add contingencies at 3%			2,19,842
						75,47,907
			Add work charged establishment at 2%			1,50,958
			Grand total			76,98,865
			Or Say 77.00 lakh			

Appendix-V (Contd.)

COST ESTIMATE OF PONDICHERRY FISHING HARBOUR (1981)

Sl. No.	Description	Unit	Quantity	Rate	Amount	Total
1	2	3	4	5	6	7
1.	*Dredging and reclamation*					
	(a) Dredging	m^3	75,000	20	15,00,000	
	(b) Reclamation	m^3	9,000	24	2,16,000	
						17,16,000
2.	*Quay*					
	(a) Quay	m^3	332	10,500	34,86,000	
	(b) Revetment	m^3	4,300	80	3,44,000	
						38,30,000
3.	*Auction hall*	m^2	2,625	600		15,75,000
4.	*Boat repair yard*	LS				7,00,000
5.	*Roads*	m^2	3,900	90		3,51,000

Appendix V (Contd.)

1	2	3	4	5	6	7
6.	*Ancillary facilities*					
	(a) Pavements					
	(*i*) Asphalt	m^2	11,000	90	9,90,000	
	(*ii*) Macadam		3,900	60	2,34,000	
	(b) Fuel station	LS			1,00,000	
	(c) Drainage & sewerage	LS			3,50,000	
	(d) Office toilets and canteen				4,50,000	
	(e) Water supply				6,00,000	
	(f) Power and lighting				4,50,000	
	(g) Fencing				70,000	
						32,44 000
			Total			1,14,26,000
			Add work contingencies at 3%			3,42,780
			Add work charge estabishment at 2%			1,17,68,780
			Grand total			2,35,376
						1,20,04,156
			Say Rs. 120 lakh			

APPENDIX VI

MODEL MEMORANDUM OF ASSOCIATION

I. The name of the Organization is Fisheries Terminal Management Organization.

II. The registered office of the organization will be situated at.........

III. The objectives for which the organization is established as under:

A. MAIN OBJECTIVES

1. To carry on the business of administering, managing, supervising, and protecting the fish auction hall, ice supply, ice plant, cold storage, freezing plant and frozen storages, servicing of engines and fishing gear, supply of spare parts, supply of fuel and lubricants, fish drying and curing yards located within the premises of fishing harbour at......
2. To carry on the business of manufacturing, servicing, repairing, marketing, transporting, selling, importers, exporters, dealers, hires of marine diesel engines, out-board motors, fishing nets and accessories, winches and accessories, warehouses and stores facilities, ice plant, cold storages, freezing plant, canning plant, transport, vehicles and so on.
3. To acquire, purchase or otherwise take over any of the industries or projects, falling within the ambit of paragraph III (A) 1 to 3 either from the Government or statutory bodies, co-operative societies, companies, firms or individuals on mutually agreed terms.
4. To promote the development of the fishing harbour.

B. SUBSIDIARY OBJECTIVES FOR ATTAINMENT OF MAIN OBJECTIVES

5. To acquire and take over industrial and import licences,

concessions and privileges on payment of actual out of pocket expenses incurred thereof.

6. To carry on business as experts, advisers and researchers in all matters relating to the field of business mentioned in III (A) 1 to 3.
7. To collect and maintain fishery statistics relating to fishing vessels in landings, fishing days, fish catches by species, boatside prices, vessel operational economics, resource analysis to check dangers of over-exploitation by vessels, market prices, export statistics, market disposition of fish and fish products, statistics relating to shore establishments covered in the fishing harbour complex and also in close proximity affecting the fishing industry through trained and qualified statistical staff under the guidance of a specialist with fishery economics background.
8. To enter into the contracts, agreements and arrangements with any other company or organization in India or abroad for carrying out by such other company or organizations on behalf of the organization and objectives for which the organization is formed.
9. To repair, alter, remodel, clear, renovate, convert, manipulate and prepare for resale and resell any goods belonging to the organization from time to time.
10. To employ experts to investigate into and examine the conditions, prospects, value, character and circumstances of any business carried out by the organization.
11. To carry on any business or branch of a business which the organization is authorised to carry on by means of or through any agency or company.
12. To carry on business as financiers, commercial agents.
13. To appoint directors or managers of any other company in which the corporation is or may be interested.
14. To take part in the management, supervision and control of business of any company or undertakings and for that purpose to appoint and remunerate any directors, trustees, experts or agencies.
15. To purchase, acquire, take on lease, hire any immovable or movable properties or any rights and privileges which

the organization may think necessary or convenient for the purpose of business and in particular any land, property, leasements, machinery plant and so on, and to retain the property so acquired for the purpose of the organization's business or to turn the same to account as may deem fit.

16. To let on lease or on hire purchase system or to lend or otherwise dispose of any property belonging to the organization and to finance the purchase of any article and the letting thereof on hire purchase system, or otherwise.

17. To plant, cultivate, utilize and turn into account any estates or lands for any industries.

18. To purchase, take on lease or otherwise acquire any lands for future development and to lease out any such lands and to sell or otherwise dispose the lands.

19. To acquire by concession, grant, purchase, barter, lease licence or otherwise any tracts of country, seabeds and other water sheets together with such rights as may be agreed upon by Government or owners thereof and to expand such sums of money as may be deemed, requisite and advisable in the exploration survey and development thereof.

20. To acquire, construct, purchase or take on lease any vehicles, boat, trawlers, ships, barges, launches and to maintain and develop the same for conveyance of persons, merchandise and goods for carrying out the business of the organization.

21. To establish, provide, maintain and conduct or otherwise subsidise experimental workshops, technical research, tests of all kinds and to promote research studies in science and technology, laboratories that may be considered likely to assist any of the businesses which the organization is authorized to carry on.

22. To erect, construct, purchase, enlarge, alter and maintain and sell buildings and structures of any kind necessary for the organization's business.

23. To aquire, construct, maintain, carry out, improve work, alter, control and manage fishing harbours, jetties, water

ways, docks, dry docks, slipways, warehouses, ice plants and cold storages, fish processing plants, workshops and other works which the organization may think conductive to any of its objects.

24. To let out or hire or sell all or any of the the property of the organization whether immovable or movable including all and every description of apparatus or appliances.

25. To purchase or buy any other means, acquire and protect, prolong and renew, whether in India or elsewhere any patents, rights, licences and concessions which may appear likely to be advantageous or useful to the organization.

26. To buy, sell, manufacture, refine, manipulate, import, export and deal both in wholesale and retail in commodities substance, apparatus, articles, and things of all kinds capable of being used by the organization for its business.

27. To carry out and transact all kinds of agency business except Managing Agency business.

28. To carry on any other trade or business whether manufacturing or otherwise which may seem to the organization capable of being carried on in connection with any of the organization's objects.

29. To amalgamate with any company or companies having objects altogether or in part similar to those of the organization.

30. To pay for any properties, rights, or privileges acquired by the organizations.

31. To pay all the costs, charges, and expenses of and incidental to the promotion, formation, registration and establishment of the organization and the issue of its capital including any underwriting or other commissions, brokers fees and charges in connection herewith and to remunerate or make donations to any person, firm or company for the service rendered or to be rendered in introducing any property or business to the organization.

32. To enter into any arrangement or agreement with any Government or authorities, municipal, local or otherwise that may seem conducive to the organization's

objects and to obtain from any such Government or authority, any rights, privileges, and concessions which the organization may think it desirable to obtain and to carry out, execute and comply with any such arrangements, rights, privileges and concessions.

33. To draw, accept and make and to endorse, discount, and negotiate promissory notes, hundies, bills of exchange, bills of lading and other negotiable or transferrable instruments.

34. To borrow or raise money or to receive money or deposit at interest, or otherwise in such manner as the organization may think fit, and in security of any such moneys so borrowed, raised or received to mortgage, pledge or charge the whole or any part of the property, assets or revenue of the organization, present or future including any uncalled capital by special assignment or otherwise or to transfer or convey the same absolutely or in trust and to give lenders the power of sales and other powers as may seem expendient and to purchase, redeem or pay off such securities.

35. To accumulate funds and lend, invest or otherwise employ moneys belonging to entrusted to the organization and to invest and deal with the moneys in any investment movable or immovable upon such terms and conditions as may seem proper and from time to time every such transactions in such manner as the organization may think fit.

36. To sell improve, manage, work develop, lease, mortgage abandon or otherwise deal with all or any part of the property, rights and concessions of the organization.

37. To create depreciation fund, reserve fund, sinking fund, insurance fund or any special or other funds and to utilize the funds for carrying out the business of organization and for other purpose whatsoever conductive to the interests of the organization.

38. To provide for the welfare of the employees of the corporation and the wives, widows and families or dependents by building or contributing to the building of houses or dwelling or quarters or by granting money

pensions, gratuities, allowances, bonuses or benefits of any other kinds or by creating, subscribing or contributing to provident and other funds.

39. To do all such things as are incidental or may be thought of conductive to the attainment of objects of the organization either alone or in conjunction with others so that the word "organization" in this Memorandum when applied to this organization shall be deemed to include any authority, partnership or other body of persons whether incorporated or not.

40. To carry on any of the business of engineers, mechanics, tool makers, moulders, metal workers to sink wells and to execute all works and things necessary for obtaining storing, selling delivering, merchandise.

41. To acquire the right to use all apparatus and equipments in connection with the generation, accumulation, distribution, supply and employment of electricity or any other power including all cables, wires and appliances for connecting.

42. To carry on the business of electrical, mechanical and civil engineers, suppliers of electricity for the purpose of light, heat, motive power or otherwise capable of being used in connection with the objects of the organization.

43. To indemnify members, officers, directors, agents and servants of the organization against proceedings, costs, damages, claim in respect of anything done or ordered to be done by them for and in interests of the organization or any loss, damage or misfortune whatever which shall happen in the execution of duties of their office or in relation thereof.

44. And generally to do whatever is necessary and conductive or incidental to the attainment of any of the objects and the purposes of the organization.

IV. Liability of the members is limited.

V. Share capital of the FTO is........divided in................... equity share of Rs.........each with rights, privileges and conditions attached thereto as provided by the Articles of Association of the company for the time being with powers to increase or reduce the capital of the corporation and to provide shares in the capital for the time being into several classes and to attach thereto respectively such preferential different qualified or special rights, privileges or connections as may be determined by or in accordance with the Articles of Association and to vary, modify or abrogate any such rights, privileges and conditions in such manner as may be for the time being provided in the Articles of Association of the company.

8

MANPOWER REQUIREMENTS
Review of the Present Marine Fisheries Education and Training in India

K. CHIDAMBARAM

INTRODUCTION

EDUCATION and training must be active processes by which capabilities of the personnel can be improved to meet the organizational needs. The development of the marine food industry needs development of education and training as it depends upon the national capability to understand, exploit, and utilize the resources of the seas and the marine environment rationally. Understanding the seas is the task of fisheries science, while exploitation and utilization are the responsibility of fisheries technology. Development of fisheries science requires an adequate system of education in the different segments of science at different levels, while development of fisheries technology needs an organized system of training at different levels.

COURSES IN MARINE FISHERIES AND RELATED SUBJECTS

Primary fishery schools

The states of Maharashtra, Karnataka, Kerala, and Tamil Nadu run primary fishery schools. They are so named by virtue of their location in fishing centres and catering mostly to fishermen's children. They are vocational institutions imparting, besides the normal educational curriculum, some basic knowledge of marine fisheries. Regional language is the medium of instruction in these schools. They number about 54 and the intake capacity in each primary school average to forty children in each standard. These schools are under the Education Department of the respective states.

The syllabus covers teaching in traditional fishing methods, traditional fishing crafts and gears, fish fauna of the area, local fish preservation methods, carpentary work relating to construction of traditional fishing crafts, and so on. However, the course does not lay the foundation for higher studies in fishery science and technology. Children undergoing this educational course, do not stand to progress in the profession they undertake. Most of the fisher children either during the curriculum or on completion of primary education, prefer to join their parents in their traditional occupation for economic reasons.

Fishery high schools

Fishery High Schools exist in Maharashtra and Kerala and number about 12 in Maharashtra and 3 in Kerala. Of these, 11 in Maharashtra are in the private sector and the rest under the control of the Education Department of the respective states. The average intake capacity of each of these schools is about 40 in each standard from VI to XI. These schools follow a vocational education pattern where the students are taught marine fisheries as a special subject in addition to the usual curriculum. These schools again are so named by virtue of their location in bigger fishing centres, catering mostly to the children of fishermen and fish traders. Some primary fishery schools in the two states form the feeder schools to these fishery high schools. Here too, most of the boys during the curriculum leave their studies and join their parents in the traditional occupation for economic reasons.

Polytechnic diploma course

The fisheries division of the *Central Polytechnic*, *Madras*, offers a professional post matriculate fishery diploma course. It is under the Board of Technical Education, Tamil Nadu.

The intake is about 30 annually. The course is organized on the semester system.

The diploma course at the Madras Polytechnic, cover studies of fundamentals of marine fisheries, inland fisheries, fisheries technology, navigation, and seamanship mostly in theoretical aspects. The course lacks intensive practical approach. Specialisation in any particular branch of fishery science is not the aim of this Institute and therefore the polytechnic candidates need specialized training further in specific fields to serve the marine fishery industry. The Staff Training Centre in Tamil Nadu state conducts, therefore, an inservice training course for these polytechnic candidates freshly recruited in the fisheries department to qualify them for specialized fisheries subjects. The National Committee on Science and Technology (NCST) has recommended a reorganisation of this Institute to make it more practical oriented.

Degree course in fishery science

The College of Fisheries, Mangalore, under the University of Agricultural Sciences, Karanataka, has been conducting since 1969 a four-year degree course in Fishery Science (B.F.Sc.) Forty students who have passed P.U.C. or equivalent with science subjects are admitted annually.

The Fisheries College, Tuticorin, was established in 1977 under the Tamil Nadu Agricultural University, Coimbatore, and is conducting a four-year degree course in Fishery Science (B.F.Sc.). The intake is 20 annually preferably science undergraduates.

The Fisheries College, Chalakudy under the Kerala Agricultural University also runs a four-year degree course in Fishery Science. The annual intake is 20.

The syllabus at the College of Fisheries, Mangalore, includes fishery biology, aquaculture fishery hydrography, fishery economics, fishery statistics, fish processing technology, fishery microbiology, fishery bio-chemistry, and fishery engineering. The other colleges have adopted the same syllabus. The syllabus is very comprehensive. Besides theoretical aspects, the course work includes practical aspects, research, and so on in the laboratories attached to the College, as well as guidance in the central fisheries research institutions.

However, it is noted that this degree course lacks orientation in intensive management training in every field of fishery science. This would mean that the candidates should be made to feel the significance of cost consciousness and the financial and social returns to various fisheries development aspects. Follow up studies of fisheries schemes financed by commercial banks are also very important to improve the financial and technical appraisal of fisheries projects. Such studies greatly help investment decisions in the fisheries sector. Financial institutions require personnel for monitoring and evaluation studies of fisheries schemes to obtain a very useful feedback. The course in fishery science at the degree level, if taken care of this aspect, would be useful to the industry. It is also considered necessary that following additions may be made to the syllabus to make the course more professional.

(1) Physio-chemical properties of the natural, artificial and synthetic fibres and their use in fishing industry.
(2) Outer forces exerting influence on fishing gears.
(3) Rational type of rigging of trawls with regard to the bottom condition.
(4) Rational type of otter boards and calculation on the optimum size and weight of otter boards.
(5) Tendencies of the trawl warp lengths and their influence on the catching capacity.
(6) Correlation between the vertical and horizontal opening for a given design of trawl.
(7) Hanging coefficient for head lines, foot ropes and side lines, methods of seizing, rigging, and so on.
(8) Deformations of fishing gears while in operation, their causes, and methods of prevention.
(9) Accidents during trawling and means of avoiding them.
(10) Relative correlations between mesh size and length and weight of fish in gill net operation.
(11) Technique of fishing with drift gill nets with warp above or below nets.
(12) Premature wear of fishing gears and measures for eliminating it.

(13) Net making machineries—single shuttle, multi-shuttle and knotless—working principles of primary methods—adjustments for depths and making of knots—securing the length in number of rows and so on—loom planning to effect economics in the various nets by the use of splitting devices between shuttle.

(14) Squid jigging and light fishing technology.

The fish processing technology course should also include studies on hygeine requirements for handling, transport, and distribution of fish for maintenance of quality. Greater emphasis must also be laid on the multifarious utilization methodologies for the low price fish reported to be available in abundance in the entire economic zone of the country. A few other important requirements are indicated below.

(1) *Requirements on board of the fishing vessel*
- (i) fishing vessel sanitary requirement
- (ii) treatment of fish on board

(2) *Requirements at the point on unloading*
- (i) unloading of fish
- (ii) transport practices of fresh or chilled fish
- (iii) temperature requirements
- (iv) methods of transport of frozen fish
- (v) transport practices of frozen fish
- (vi) general provisions relating to the transport of fresh, chilled and frozen fish
- (vii) sanitary provision for the transport of fresh, chilled, and frozen fish
- (viii) containers for fresh unprocessed fish

(3) *Requirements for processing and wholesale establishments*
- (i) receipt of fresh, chilled, and frozen fish into plant
- (ii) requirements for processing establishments
- (iii) yards outside working areas
- (iv) storage rooms or establishments producing fresh fish fillets and fish products
- (v) cold storage requirements

(vi) processing plant equipment
(vii) plant operation
(viii) vermin control
(ix) requirements for persons engaged in the preparation and processing of the products
(x) staff facilities in processing establishments

(4) *Requirements of retail sale establishments*
(i) fish preparation room or area
(ii) shop servicing area
(iii) storage requirements
(iv) yards and outside working areas
(v) dwelling accommodation
(vi) equipment and utensils
(vii) fish exhibited for sale
(viii) cleaning of premises, items of equipment and utensils, cleaning and disinfecting processes and procedures
(ix) vermin control
(x) requirements for staff
(xi) repairing methods
(xii) water quality in cleaning and processing

Education in fisheries co-operatives is also important at the graduate level. The function of fishries co-operative is to increase the economic power of fishermen through co-operative production and utilization. In order to perform this function and to make sound development in the management, co-operatives are required to have in their staff, excellent talents and expertise. The cultivation of such talents and expertise is one of the most important tasks of an educational institution. The curriculum should comprise the basic subjects necessary for the management of production and utilization besides business practices, financing, and accounting along with practical training in model fisheries co-operatives.

B. Tech. degree course (naval architecture & marine engineering)

The Indian Institute of Technology, Kharagpur, offers a four-year degree course (Bachelor of Technology) in naval architecture and marine engineering. The course includes designing and construction of large ships, but no specialized course in naval architecture of fishing craft. There is, however, a provision for study of naval architecture relating to small boats including fishing vessels as an elective subject for one semester.

The programme of the development of deep sea fishing in the country has been rather slow and defective and this is partly attributed to the lack of knowledge of most suitable types of designs and sizes of deep sea fishing vessels, fishing gears, and equipment. Lack of intimate knowledge and experience in the designing and construction of fishing vessels and lack of facilities for manufacture by large ship yards have been the causes for the poor interest in this field. It is, therefore, necessary to ensure that this is suitably organized in the interest of the development of deep sea fishing. Deep sea fishing has been recognized as one of the industries in which foreign capital and expertise may be required. This arrangement would help in evolving designs of deep sea fishing vessels for different regions of India for different functions. For this purpose, qualified graduates in naval architecture and marine engineering for designing and construction of fishing vessels are required. The educational programme on design and construction of fishing vessels should cover (1) the choice of size and type of vessels and essential features of their layout, (2) choice of material of construction, (3) scantlings and structural designs, (4) crew requirements and standard accommodation, (5) speed-power relationship, (6) criteria for stability for the nature of operating conditions, (7) nature of preservation of catch on board, (8) requirements of mechanical and electronic equipment for fishing, (9) choice of engines and installation, (10) model tests of prototype vessels and comparison of model test result factors, (11) full scale trials to determine the trawling pull and its correlation with propeller dimensions and engine power, (12) studies to determine minimum scantlings, (13) studies on economics of the designs over several years to select optimum size vessels, and (14) studies on the actual requirement of materials, wastage, percentage for different structural members and detailed manhour analysis in construction to enable assessment of accurate cost estimates and methods of reduction of costs in the construction process.

Long voyages bring the fishing vessel and crew on their own, with 24 hour duty, demand a high degree of operation, reliability and protection against the forces of nature. Besides the construction of fishing vessels aiming at simple handling, economic operation low capital investment, easy maintenance, appropriate living and working environment, should be based on fishing experience in regard to provision of functional facilities and should follow national and international regulations.

Studies in designing of fishing vessels will also depend on accurate information on the operational conditions like location of grounds and nature of fishing, the catch rates and the composition of catch and their variations, the type of handling and processing on board, fish hold capacity, nature of holds, duration of fishing trips and so on. Information from developed countries on fishing vessel types, layouts, sizes and operating conditions, developments in the fishing techniques and the items of equipment used for fishing, the trends in preservation of catch, its processing on board the vessel and their storage, design data for hull forms, propulsion, manoevarability and stability, propulsion units, auxiliary units, electrical and hydraulic systems and other items of equipment, standards of accommodation, electronic aids for navigation and fishing, centralized controls and communication systems, handling arrangements, and so on, will also be useful in the educational programme. It is necessary that the Indian Institute of Technology is suitably strengthened to provide a separate graduate course on fishing vessel designing and construction.

B.E. degree course (naval architecture and fishery engineering)

The College of Engineering, Waltair, runs a graduate course in mechanical with marine engineering and naval architecture as special subjects. The course includes maritime law, seamanship, navigation, marine machinery, power plants, and construction of small crafts. However, it is seen that this course lacks the intensive practical aspects. The college has no facilities of its own for practical studies and depends upon the port and naval establishments in Vishakhapatnam. This Educational Institution can also be strengthened to provide studies in fishing vessel designing and construction as a special. Fishery engineering is also assuming an increasingly important role both in exploitation and utilization of the fishing industry. In view of this, the NCST report recommends initiating a degree programme in fishery engineering at the Karnataka Regional Engineering College, Surathkal, with co-operation from the College of Fisheries, Mangalore.

M.F.Sc. degree course (fishery science)

The College of Fisheries, Mangalore, under the Karnataka Agricultural University has been offering two post-graduate courses with specialization either in industrial fishery technology or fish production and management.

The Industrial fishery technology course covers fishing and fish processing technology while the fish production and management course includes fishery biology, aquaculture and fishery hydrography. These two courses have also biochemistry, microbiology, statistics and economics as supporting subjects. Besides theoretical coaching, the study includes practical aspects, research work, and so on, in the laboratories attached to the college as well as guidance in the central fisheries research institutes. In addition to the course work, a thesis is to be submitted. These practical oriented courses are quite comprehensive and cover all aspects of fishery science to acquire sufficient professional skill.

However, additional subjects as pointed out above for the B.F.Sc. Courses are to be included to make the courses more useful. In addition, it will be a great asset to the fish production and management course, if the syllabus includes marine fishery management studies. Fisheries management with its associated problems is of importance to a developing country like India, particularly as we have to manage the resources in the extended jurisdiction coming under national control. Development of profitable fisheries in the extended jurisdiction may not be possible unless and until we develop technical expertise, managerial staff, and trained personnel. Therefore, need for education and training in fishery management covering stock assessment exploitation, utilization, marketing and economics.

Management study on fisheries resources should cover (1) Objectives, (2) Effects of extended jurisdiction, (3) Special needs of a developing country like India, (4) Past performance in management, (5) Communications of technical analysis of the biological and economic consequences of management actions to decisionmakers, (6) Management techniques and conservation such as limiting the size and quantity of fish exploited, closing of nursery areas, and fishing seasons, (7) Concepts and models used in fishery management, (8) Management of shared or trans-boundary fish stocks, in areas of jurisdiction of two adjacent coastal states, (9) Compilation of data on the timing and location of catches, associated fishing effort and biological data such as size composition, (10) Management policies, (11) Concept (scientific, economic, social and administrative) principles and definition of fishery management, and (12) Investment systems. It will also be useful if the fish production and management course includes the subject of marine pollution in relation to the protection of living resources. This is an important aspect on which marine fisheries development depends. The study should cover (1) Marine pollution in world fisheries, (2) Forest industry wastes, other industrial wastes, radio active wastes and so on, (3) Techniques for control of industrial wastes, (4) Sources of sea pollution by oil, (5) Microbiological pollutants, (6) Biological transfer of pollutants and their efiects, (7) Strategy for pollution control, (8) International & national legislation and regulatory institutions, (9) Ecological effects of marine pollutants, (10) Investigations of actue pollution problems affecting fisheries in coastal water and estuaries, (11) Monitoring of aquatic pollution, and (12) Regulations for control and prevention of pollution.

M. Sc. degree course (industrial fisheries)

The Faculty of Marine Sciences in Cochin University (FMSCU) Cochin, offers a post-graduate degree course in industrial fisheries. The annual intake is 15 students. The subjects covered are marine fisheries, fishing craft and gear technology, fish processing technology, fisheries economics and management. Though this course has been found useful, it lacks sound foundation, as it is not based on a related under graduate programme either in the same university or in any other Institution. Besides, the University does not have facilities to impact practical training. It depends on the central fisheries research institutes and the fish processing industries which may or may not be functioning on sound scientific lines. Practical work should be on sound and correct lines and not in plants which require improvements. Industrial fisheries education in other developed countries requires training of personnel on board factory fishing vessels which undertake 3-4 month long fishing voyages in hydrobiological research, fishing operations, fishing gears, handling of catch, processing of varied fish products on board, use of different processing machinery, fishing equipment and fishing aids, and so on. In this University not even a medium size fishing vessel is available to impart these aspects of training. The present course at the University will, therefore, be truely useful if these practical aspects are also taken into consideration in the educational curriculum. It will also be useful to include aspects like determination of the most economic size and horse power of mechanized boats to be used under varying onditions, use of cheaper material for boat construction, reduction in the cost of engines, reduction in operating costs through improved maintenance determination of the type and design of the most viable fishing gear for different fisheries in each region and so on.

M.Sc. degree course (mariculture)

The Central Marine Fisheries Research Institute (CMFRI), Cochin, offers an M.Sc. Degree in mariculture research. The intake is 10 candidates. The syllabus includes basic science, research methodology, marine biology, oceanography, physiology of marine animals, fishery biology, fish culture, culture of crustaceans, molluscs, seaweeds and so on, integrated farming, fish farm engineering, management of mariculture farms, and dissertation on selected subjects. These subjects of study are quite comprehensive but will have to be backed with practical orientation.

M. Tech. degree course (fishing harbour engineering)

The Karnataka Regional Engineering College, Surathkal, has a two-year post graduate industrially oriented course (M. Tech.) in marine structures, coastal engineering sedimentation and harbour planning. The basic studies cover wave hydrodynamics wind wages, marine structure analysis and designs, coastal sedimentation, and harbour planning. The college has its own workshop, laboratories, and machinery for practical training. This institution can be developed for imparting an educational course in fishing harbour engineering, its planning and maintenance and management.

With the development of marine fishing activities in the exclusive economic zone, requirements of fishing harbours, their running and maintenance are on the increase. At present, there are only about 20 ports with landing and berthing facilities for fishing boats on a long coastline of nearly 6,000 km. By and large, the progress of construction of fishing harbours in India has been rather slow mainly because of scarcity of trained engineers to undertake marine works and lack of suitable equipment. The solution would lie in training more and more civil and mechanical engineers in fishing harbour engineering at post-graduate level.

A fishing harbour offers shelter for vessels and services for vessels and crew as in commercial ports. There are significant differences in the way of operations, characteristics of the vessels, and fish and other products to be handled, and even differences in the service needs of vessels and crew while in harbour.

The theory and practice of commercial harbour design is comparatively well developed and experience has been gained while observing the achieved results in the already constructed harbours. These results can generally not be directly applied in fishing harbour research, planning, and design because of significant differences. The only exception was the rules of design which are identical in the main marine structures design (breakwaters, piers, quays, and so on) as they are dictated by the forces of nature.

Planning a fishing harbour would require an assessment of the needs of the consumer (demand) including the forecast on the processing to be performed in the harbour and storing capacities required, fish to be handled in the harbour both quantity and kind, fishing vessels to be allocated and serviced in the harbour, and workshop and repair facilities. Any other services to be rendered in the harbour are derivatives from the three basic assumptions based on biological, technical and economical forecasts.

Fishing harbour planning and designing require studies on :

1. Appraisal of the existing situation
2. Estimating planning horizon and intermediate steps
3. Population and regions to be served
4. Total demand for fish, based on the direct assumption
5. Processing forecast
6. Study of the distribution and consumption in time
7. Assessment of the fishing grounds, kind and quantity of fish to be harvested
8. Quantity and quality of fish to be landed
9. Technology of fishing, dimension and equipment of the fishing vessels on the different fishing grounds
10. Fishing cycles of the fishing vessels
11. Traffic pattern in the fishing harbour
12. Distribution of the quantities of fish landed
13. Berthing needs in the fishing harbour
14. Site survey of the region in which the fishing harbour is to be constructed
15. Depth requirements
16. Spatial requirements
17. Dimension of the main marine
18. Handling technology, characteristics of the landed fish as a cargo, applied handling equipment, scheme of handling the landed fish before despatch or sorting
19. Storing technology and capacity needed
20. Despatch facilities
21. Installations needed to supply to the fishing vessels before departure from the harbour

22. Processing plants requirement
23. Maintenance and repairing requirements of fishing vessels
24. Facilities for servicing the crew, and
25. Administration of the fishing harbour and connected services

M.Sc. degree course (marine sciences)

The Andhra University, Waltair, has two year post-graduate academic courses (M.Sc.) in marine geology, physical oceanography and marine biology.

Annamalai University, Porto Novo, has a two year post-graduate academic course (M.Sc.) in marine biology and the faculty of Marine Science.

University of Kerala, Trivandrum, has a post-graduate course in fisheries and aquatic biology research.

The universities of Madras, Madurai and Bombay offer M.Sc. (Zoology) courses with fisheries as a special subject.

The Tata Institute of Fundamental Research Bombay, conducts a post-graduate course in marine geo-chemistry.

Though the post-graduate courses in the marine sciences are all of academic nature, they have been useful in providing personnel for marine fisheries research.

M. Tech. degree course (ship designing and construction)

The Institute of Technology, Madras, has facilities for post graduate course in coastal engineering, designing and testing of ships, fishing crafts, marine structures, and so on. The vast facilities at the I.I.T., Madras are not being availed for training engineering graduates in designing and construction of fishing vessels. This and I.I.T., Kharagpur can be developed for an intensive course on this subject.

Post-graduate diploma courses in fish processing technology and fish culture technology

The College of Fisheries, Mangalore, provides two post-graduate diploma courses in fish culture technology and fish processing technology.

Studies for both courses are comprehensive and practical oriented. The syllabus for the fish processing technology course includes theory and practicals in canning and freezing technology, ham and sausage technology, refrigeration and food processing machinery, bio-chemistry, microbiology, and so on. This course will be more useful if the subject of refrigeration on board fishing vessels is also included. Refrigeration on fishing vessels had not been paid any attention in the country till recently. Now that the country has to take greater efforts towards exploitation of the deeper waters of the economic zone with large fishing vessels which can remain at sea for longer periods, persons trained in most suitable refrigeration techniques and the operation of machinery are required to serve on board the fishing vessels. The following subjects are recommended :

1. Spoilage and refrigeration—to cover preservation of fish chilling, freezing and cold storage, thermal properties, fish temperature and heat content and resistance to heat flow.
2. Icing—to include storage in ice, temperature, cleanliness labour crushed ice, flake ice, tube ice, cooling capacity, fish hold conditions in vessels, heat gains, treatment of fish before storage, cutting, heading, bleeding, bulk storage without ice, shelfing, boxing at sea, transfer at sea, amount of ice, storage rate, standard of icing, supplements to ice, like antibiotic ice, salt water ice and gas storage.
3. Fish hold-to cover cleanliness, drainage, fish room linings, heat gains from fish, bacterial action, electrical equipment details of types of pipe and stanchions, bottom, sides, bulkheads and so on.
4. Fish hold insulation—to include methods and materials, presence of water, properties, varied requirements of insulation, and so on.
5. Mechanical refrigeration with ice—(*a*) pipe grids, their operation, cooling capacity, deposit, temperature control, (*b*) forced connection cooling—heat gains, boxing, cooling capacity, deforest temperature control (*c*) jacketed fish hold-semi-jacket system and conduction

jacket, and (*d*) supperchilling—quality factors, refrigeration plant and supperchilling with bulk storage.

6. Refrigerated Sea Water (RSW)—the RSW system, storage tanks, pumps and piping, mechanical refrigeration, water chillers, super-chilling and cleaning in the RSW system.
7. Refrigeration Plant—vapour compression, compressors, condensors and receivers, primary and secondary refrigerants, pumps, piping, accessories and controls.
8. Freezers—temperature measurement, rate of freezing, low temperature, quick freezing, output and freezing time. Airblast freezers, plate freezers, immersion and spray freezers.
9. Cold Storage—design and operation, heat gain and moisture migration, dehydration, temperature, linings, seals, insulation, cooling system, pipe grinds, forced circulation of air and so on.
10. Freezing at sea—processing before freezing, storage rate, freezing of whole fish, refrigeration capacity, quality factors like bleeding, gutting, delay before freezing, quality control, freezing time and so on.

Another aspect to be considered is the subject of radiation processing of shrimp products. Perishability is a cost increasing factor common in the marketing of seafood products. Modern preservation techniques, particularly the various methods of freezing, have been highly effective means of extending storage/shelf life and have paved the way for universal distribution of the frozen products in many fisheries. Nonetheless, problems of quality maintenance persist in the seafood industry and there is ample justification for continued efforts to improve preservation methods. This is especially true for the shrimp industry which is confronted by a proportionately small but costly spoilage problem. Irradiation preservation is one of the methods which has been found suitable for seafood products. Considerable work has been done on the commercial feasibility of using irradiation as a preservation technique for shrimp products. Ionizing radiation, which is a relatively low cost technique, can effectively eliminate spoilage organisms, as well as bacterial pathogens and animals parasites without compromising on the qualities on taste and texture. Commercial investments in shrimp irradiation processing is reported to be highly attractive.

Post-graduate diploma course (fishery science)

The Central Institute of Fisheries Education (CIFF), Bombay, formerly under the Government of India and presently under the ICAR, offers a two year post-graduate diploma course in fishery science.

The subjects taught at the Institute are covered under three major divisions, the fishery biology division, the fishery technology division and the fishery administration and economic division. The fishery biology division includes studies on marine fisheries, oceanography, limnology and inland fisheries. Besides lectures and laboratory work, the course provides for practical experience on board the Institute's training vessel in fishing and oceanographic studies as well as various aspects of fish culture at the fresh and brackishwater fish farms of the Institute.

The fishery technology division includes studies on fishing craft, fishing gears, and fish processing technologies with lectures and laboratory work besides practical work on board the Institute's training vessel and the pilot commercial fish processing plants of the Institute. The fishery administration and economics division includes studies in fishery economics, fish marketing, co-operation, and fishery statistics as related to fisheries.

Post graduate diploma course (coastal aquaculture)

The University of Madras conducts a post-graduate diploma course in coastal aquaculture.

Post-graduate diploma course (harbour engineering)

The Indian Institute of Technology, Bombay, provides inservice training and conducts a post-graduate diploma course in dock and harbour engineering to candidates sponsored by the port authorities and other government departments. Studies include investigations, planning, and designing of harbours, including fish harbours.

Post-graduate diploma course in international trade

The Indian Institute of Foreign Trade (IIFT), New Delhi, under the Government of India, Ministry of Commerce, New Delhi conducts a professional one year post-graduate diploma course in International Trade for the benefit of fresh graduates to take up careers in export marketing establishments including seafood industry.

Ph. D. programme in fishery sciences

The College of Fisheries, Mangalore, has started Ph. D. courses in fishery biology, aquaculture, fishery hydrography, and fish processing technology. Facilities for Ph. D. course in mariculture are also available at the Centre of Advanced Studies in the Central Marine Fisheries Research Institute (CMFRI), Cochin. The syllabus in fishery biology at the College of fisheries, Mangalore, includes systematic ichthyology, biology of fish, crustaceans and molluscs, behaviour of fish, physiology of fish, pathology and parasitology of fish, food and feeding habits of fish, spawning of fish, osteology and taxonomy of fish, diseases of fish, and control methods. The syllabus for fishery hydrography covers oceanography, planktonology, limnology, marine meteorology, marine geology, pollution, primary production, and so on. The syllabus for aquaculture includes fresh water aquaculture, coastal aquaculture, fish nutrition, management of farms and hatcheries, culture of food organisms, breeding of food fishes, and so on. The syllabus for fish processing technology includes freezing techniques, packaging technology, operation of processing plants, fishery by-products, canned foods, technology of sausages, other fish paste products, quality control, spoilage of processed foods, fermented marine products, marine oils, fish mean and F.P.C. dried fish products, nutritive value and so on. These courses are very comprehensive and quite useful.

At Ph.D. level, it will be very useful to introduce the scientific discipline of marine fishery resources assessment which is a pre-requisite for the development of the marine fishery industry. There is considerable gap in the ground to be covered with reference to bottom trawling. The investigations on purse seine fisheries have been taken only with reference to oil sardine and mackerel, leaving all other pelagic fishery resources to be still surveyed and assessed for increased production. Hardly any effort has been expended on the gill-net fishery for extension of operations beyond the present range. Hardly any attention has been laid on the introduction of midwater trawling as a new fishing method. The gill-netting and midwater trawling would constitute important operations as most of the quality fish inhabit midwaters.

The resources survey and assessment work consist of two aspects, namely prospecting of new or underutilized stocks of fish and the monitoring of assessment so as to maintain the stocks at the optimum sustainable yield. Prospecting aspect includes determination of commercial accumulation of different fishes in single or multispecies fisheries, their distribution and densities, correlation of these features with environmental factors, behaviour of different stocks towards various types of fishing methods, and a preliminary economic assessment of exploitation. The monitoring aspect is a continuous process of investigations for assessing different stocks of fisheries in relation to fishing pressure and changes in environment with a view to forecasting the magnitude of the fisheries. It is thus obvious that fishery resources survey and assessment constitutes a multi-disciplinary activity involving research in biological, oceanographical, technological and economic aspects. Such an integrated approach needs to be developed and this should form the pre-requisite to further expansion of marine fisheries. The marine fishing industry in India has been repeatedly emphasizing the need for essential assessment data projected in terms of economic considerations to formulate projects, as only such data will enable investment of capital for expanded marine fishing on commercial lines. Exploratory survey organizations, therefore will have to get personnel trained in the assessment methodology of the resources potential. It is significant to mention in this connection that the Asian Development Bank has recently approved technical assistance grant for a training programme in fisheries stock assessment and statistical data collection, to train fisheries personnel from the countries bordering the Bay of Bengal.

It will also be useful to introduce at Ph.D. level courses on Management of resources, industrial fish processing at sea, fish distribution and storage system, fish marketing, and mariculture, as indicated.

(*a*) Management of fisheries resources should be an integral factor in fisheries development. The application of sound management principles cannot wait for the period of heavy exploitation biological factors important to management decisions can be described by the relation of catch to (1) total amount of fishing mortality co-efficient or the proportion of stock within is caught per unit of time, and (2) the sizes of fish caught. Effective management decisions are the results of clear ideas of the objectives of management action. The objectives of management are to maximize production from a particular fishery or from the fishing industry in general and to maximize the net economic returns. A wide range of methods of management are available including limits on seasons, fishing grounds, fish sizes, fishing gears, number of fishing vessels, catches, extent and intensity of fishing, and so on. Management would also involve enforcement of suitable regulations and measures of conservation.

(*b*) Management of industrial fish processing at sea will include, fishing time, quality of fish caught in each haul, gutting rates between hauls, capacity of processing machinery required on board, constraints on processing the catch immediately, storage space requirement, yield at each stage of the processes, economic and technical advantages and disadvantages of different methods of processing for a variety of products, and so on.

(*c*) Fish marketing management may include the following subjects : (1) Developments in fish marketing in India and developed countries ; (2) Analysis of market demands for fish, covering trends in fish consumption and consumer attitudes ; (3) Techniques for fish marketing, (4) Consumer tastes and preferences and development of new products and modification of old ones ; (5) Appropriate standards in relation to biological and chemical contamination ; (6) Quality requirements of products for different markets ; (7) Evaluation of the costs of quality control in manufacture and the implications of these costs for the choice of alternative markets for end products ; (8) Possibilities of increasing the value in manufacturing by improved handling, additional processing, and development of new end products, (9) Evaluation of the markets within the country and the standards and preferences within those markets (Analysis of barriers to product acceptability and use such as duties, tariffs, and so on.) ; (10) Markets outside the country including dimensions of important markets for principal products ; (11) Role of MPEDA to assist in production problems, finding new markets or expanding old ones, development of new products, instituting advertising campaigns and so on ; and (12) Fish marketing management involves studies on the survey of developments in the application of quantitative methods to marketing problems in the fishing industry, studies on demand analysis, business gains, sales functions, market demands, price of fish, fish quality specification, seasonal changes in demand, consumer income, prices of substitute products, market research, market promotion, advertising, marketing tactics, and so on.

(*d*) Management of fish distribution and storage system involves encountering of unique and peculiar problems. The distribution system is characterized by day-to-day variation of quantities to be delivered, destinations, transhipment points, transport by road or rail, routing, costing, number of vehicles required each day, container system, inventory control, and so on. Hygiene requirements of handling, transport, and distribution of fish for the maintenance of quality are also important. These requirements on board fishing vessels, at the point of unloading, at the processsing and wholesale establishments, retail establishments, and so on vary.

(*e*) Mariculture management covers economic aspects of sea farming, legal aspects of sea farming, site selection and analysis, problem of fouling, control of wave and tide motions, sea farm construction techniques, sea bed farming techniques, floating cages, rafts, and so on.

Edible oysters, Mussels and Clams, though commercially attractive in many countries, one consumed in India in very much limited quantities. In other parts of the world where they are in great demand, they are cultured on a commercial scale to augment these resources. In India, the CMFRI has been engaged in the studies and investigations in the culture of not only oysters, mussels, and clams but also on the culture of prawns, lobsters, crabs, molluscs, and fishes in the sea. Edible system's are under scientific culture in countries like USA, Canada, Holland, France, Japan, Philippines, and Australia. Improved techniques of off-bottom culture are being increasingly adopted in these countries and it has been observed that this method yields much higher production than the old method of bottom culture. The most common species of edible oysters inhabiting the creeks along the east and west coasts of India are *Crassostrea gryphoides*, *C. discoides*, *C. madrasensis* and *C. culcullata*. Except for a very limited exploitation in natural beds near Bombay and Madras, no need has been felt in the country in the past to undertake production beyond the quantities collected from the natural beds, though oyster culture practices were adopted in Madras some decades ago. The potential for oyster culture would, however, need consideration from the view point of export of this commodity in canned or deep frozen form. In this context programmes have now been undertaken for surveys assess the productive areas and for development of the requisite expertise in the advanced techniques of oyster culture. It is also necessary that training of manpower-technical, mangerial, and operative—will have to be organized.

Edible mussels (Mytilus sp) occur all along the east and west coasts. Fishing for mussels as at present is undertaken by the coastal population. The techniques adopted for mussel culture in European countries are very similar to those of oyster culture. Mussel culture with the application of advanced techniques would be one of the most productive forms of mariculture, Kovelong, and Vizainjam, and has great prospects for expansion. In this context, people will have to be trained and educated on the economic feasibility of mussel culture for export and domestic consumption.

Edible clams are represented in India by *Meretrix*, *Katalysia*, *Villorita*, *Gafrarium* and *Papita* species found in greater abundance than oysters and mussels on both coasts of India in brackish waters, estuaries, and inter tidal regions. They are harvested by hand picking. Considerable investigations have been carried out on the areas of availability, present mode of harvesting, their replenishment by natural recruitment, their consumption, culture techniques for increasing production, and so on. The development of this marine food will also require adoption of proper culture techniques which involve transplantation of clam seeds from densely populated beds where extensive spawning occurs, to thinly populated beds or new areas, and production of seed clams in hatcheries. There is a vast export potential for this marine food and prospects of expansion of this industry will depend on training of man-power in these techniques. Other important mariculture activities are the culture of fish, lobsters and prawns in sea water. These are not practised in India. There are possibilities of intensive culture of some of our marine fisheries chiefly threadfin (*Polynemus indicus*) and sand whitings (*Sillage sihama*) as they are highly priced fish and their landings appear to be declining. They can be cultured in enclosed areas of sea in floating cages kept in the sea. Investigation and training of personnel especially towards the types of net cage enclosures in the sea, breeding them under captivity or collection of adequate quantities of seed fish from wild stock without affecting the natural fisheries, suitable feeds to make the culture economically feasible, and so on, will enable an increase in marine fish production of the country for export and domestic markets.

Marine algae is another important sea food whose production requires to be considered by culture methods. Indian seaweeds are available in considerable quantities in Gulf of Mannar, Gulf of Kutch, Chilka lake, and around the Andamans and Lakshadweep Islands. Commercial utilization of seaweeds as raw material began by about 1940 and today there are quite a few industrial units utilizing marine algae in the manufacture of agar-agar and sodium alginate. But it is reported that the supply of seaweeds is hardly sufficient to maintain the production capacity of the existing industrial units. This situation, therefore, calls for the necessity for increased production of seaweeds by culture methods. This is an industry of considerable importance and yet is least developed. It is a subject of considerable complexity, biologically, technically and commercially. There are variation in seaweed species, habitats, accessibility and topography, chemical properties, availability and utilization, and methods and costs of harvesting and processing. Training in this science should cover (1) Principal groups and species of seaweeds, resources and potential output ; (2) Harvesting methodologies of seaweeds ; (3) Trends in exploitation ; (4) Drying of seaweeds, (5) Seaweed products and production technology ; (6) Seaweed as food ; (7) International trade in seaweeds ; (8) Demand for processed seaweed products ; (9) Demand for seaweeds as food and for other uses; (10) Development prospectives ; (11) Management and conservation ; and (12) Seaweed cultivation and harvesting.

Ph. D. programme in marine sciences

Universities at Madras, Annamalai, Madurai, Kerala, Cochin, Andhra, Bombay, Baroda and Calcutta have courses for Ph. D. in selected fields of biological sciences and marine sciences. Some of these Universities offer fisheries as a special subject.

REVIEW OF THE TRAINING COURSES IN MARINE FISHERIES AND RELATED SUBJECTS AT DIFFERENT LEVELS

Training courses for fishermen

Mechanised fishing boat training certificate course

A number of Fishermen Training Centres were established in the maritime states and Union territories under the Departments of Fisheries for training fishermen in the operation and maintenance of mechanized fishing boats and marine engines up to 60 HP, as well as in the fabrication, operation, and maintenance of fishing gears. They number 2 in Gujarat, 4 in Maharashtra, 1 in Goa, 2 in Karnataka, 5 in Kerala, 6 in Tamil Nadu, 1 in Andhra, 3 in Orissa, 1 in Andaman, and 1 in Lakshadweep. The duration of the course varies from 6 to 10 months. The candidates are paid a stipend ranging from Rs. 50 to Rs. 125 per month. The intake capacity also varies from 22-60 annually, according to the states. The success of the mechanised fishing programmes of the maritime states has been contributed to a large extent by these fishermen training centres. The subjects cover fishing methods, fishing gears, elementary principles of navigation, and running and maintenance of marine diesel engines. The following aspects of this course require consideration for their improvement.

The training imparted relates mostly to bottom trawling for prawns. The fishermen at most of the centres are neither trained nor motivated for other methods of fishing which can be undertaken with the same fishing craft. The training in bottom trawling also appears to be concentrated more on the theoretical aspect than on the practical aspect, since at many of the training centres the training boats are either not available or under repairs for long periods. The need for effective practical training in different methods of fishing is important for attracting fishermen on a continuous basis.

Further, the method of theoretical coaching at these centres is not centered around giving more importance in the introduction, development, and application of different teaching aids. Experience has shown that the use of visual aids in such institutions is more effective to trainees to mould their career, inasmuch as these aids stimulate interest in learning, keep to economic time and effort, help to reduce verbalism in teaching methods, and provide variety in the class room procedures. Visual aids especially flip charts, posters, wall sheets, display boards, models, exhibits, and projection aids relating to fishing boats, engines, fishing equipment, fishing gears and operations are, therefore, very essential.

One of the subjects in which the fishermen are trained is engine maintenance. However, considering the educational qualifications and mechanical aptitude of the fishermen, the variations in the design characteristics, and the maintenance schedules prescribed for different types of engines, the training imparted is not being oriented with any bias for a particular make of engine. This leaves a wide gap in the knowledge of the fishermen about the special features of their engines. It would, therefore, be desirable that the manufacturers of engines are associated with fishermen training centres for giving refresher courses to the instruction and fishermen in the proper operation and maintenance of their make of engines.

The National Commission on Agriculture had recommended that necessary rules for uniform application in all maritime states, with reference to the training of candidates for the manning of all mechanized fishing boats which are 25 tonnes gross or below should be framed including the recognition of the certificates issued by the State Directorate of Fisheries, as the necessary competency certificates for operating such boats outside the harbour limits. The commission had also recommended that the training imparted at the fishermen training centres in different maritime states should be based on a standard pattern of syllabus, equal duration, and uniform rules for testing proficiency, to be framed jointly by the fisheries organizations of the maritime states and the central government. The commission has recommended further that the fisheries organizations in the maritime states should take necessary steps to enable fishermen training centres to assume additional function of developing necessary liaison and building up effective extension service amongst the working fishermen in the region with a view to improving their working systems

(7) Instructions on maintenance of fishing logs and preparation of fishing charts;
(8) Fishing with light;
(9) Deck layout for different types of fishing;
(10) Otter board designs, construction, and performance;
(11) Squid fishing and purse seining;
(12) Measuring instruments necessary for fishing methods and application;
(13) Care of the catch;
(14) National legislation and treaties relating to the law of the seas;
(15) Operational aspects of the use of radar at sea, including principles of radar, adjustments of controls, using information provided by radar as an aid to navigation, limits of accuracy and performance, and so on;
(16) To act effectively and constantly with emergencies at sea, like fire, man overboard, transfering an injured man to another vessel, towing, damage repairs, small cracks, leakages, and so on;
(17) To be successful as Fishing Second Hands and ultimately as Fishing Skippers, the training, besides qualifying the candidates to become able navigators, must include important general aspects of oceanography, meteorology marine biology, marine geology, chemistry and physics of sea water, and so on to enable them to become efficient in fishing operation as well.

The syllabus at the CIFNET for the Fishing Vessel Engine Driver Course also needs inclusion of the additional subjects, as listed below for better orientation.

(1) Ship safety—fire course;
(2) Tanks cleaning and inspection from the aspect of safety precautions;
(3) Ship construction and stability;
(4) Centre of gravity, centre of buoyancy, metacentre and metacentric height;
(5) Stable, neutral and unstable equilibrium;
(6) Statical stability, stability curves and range

(7) The effect on the static stability by raising or lowering of weights and taking on board or discharging of weights such as fuel oil, fish, and so on;
(8) The effect of free board on the range of stability;
(9) The effect of free surface on the metacentric height;
(10) Knowledge of the stability information of a fishing vessel;
(11) Effect of water on fire fighting;
(12) Water-tight doors, latches, insulation plugs, double tanks, and so on;
(13) Running and maintenance of refrigeration machinery;
(14) Running and maintenance of electronic equipment;
(15) Running and maintenance of generators;
(16) A visit by the trainees to some of the manufacturers of plants on diesel engines and ancillary equipment;
(17) The total electrical loading calculations, battery care, generating equipment including calculation on its capacity, generator drive ratio, location control, precautions, and so on;
(18) Types of batteries and battery care;
(19) Running and maintenance of hydraulic machinery;
(20) Kurtz nozzles-advantages and basic principles.

Boat building foreman certificate course.

The 15 months training course at the CIFNET, Cochin, trains a cadre of technicians who will be to take up responsibilities as foremen of wooden fishing boat building yards and to be able to interpret fishing vessel drawings, prepare moulds and lofts and take part in actual building of boats. Subjects of study, both theory and practicals, include fishing for different motorisation and mechanisation, theoretical naval architecture, fishing boat terminology, carpentary work in boat building, lofting, preparing moulds, engine installation, steering arrangement, boat building yards, wood working machinery, workshop practice and drawing. Presently, the course concentrates on training in wooden boat building only and the evaluation committee of the Goverment of India on this Institute has rightly ... importance of expanding the course to include training in boat building practices, other than wood, like ferrocement, FRP, and so on.

Shore mechanic certificate course

This is a one year course at the CIFNET, Cochin and Madras. This course trains a cadre of mechanics who will be able to carry out repairs and maintenance of marine diesel engines as well as other fishing machinery and equipment. The subjects of study, both theory and practical, include fundamental principles of marine engines, types of marine engines, and their components, starting arrangements, transmission of propelling power, remote controls, preventive maintenance, installation, fault diagnosis and rectifications, maintenance schedule, workshop practices, workshop tools, basic knowledge of electricity, electro-magnetism, electric circuits and fishing boat wiring, smithy, turning, welding, and so on. The course has not been useful to the candidates in qualifying themselves in higher fields of specialization because of limitations in their academic qualifications. It, however, enables the candidates to qualify themselves as engineers of fishing vessels after gaining the required sea time on board seagoing fishing vessels.

Fishing gear technician certificate course

This is a 9 months course at the CIFNET, Cochin and Madras. This course enables candidates to acquire proficiency in designing and fabrication of fishing gears. The subjects of study for this course includes fishing gear classification, fishing gear materials, designing and fabrication of fishing gears and their accessories, fishing methods, fish behaviour, electronic fishing aids etc. This course has not been very popular course lately as the fishing Second Course at the CIFNET and the Mechanized Fishing Boat course at the Fishermen Training centres enables the candidates to acquire sufficient proficiency in fishing gear fabrication. Besides, the availability of machinemade webbings for nets enable them to fabricate the net quite easily. The Evaluation Committee of the Government of India on the CIFNET has therefore suggested the annual intake capacity of this course at the Institutes be reduced.

Radio telephone operator statutory certificate course

The Radio Telephone Operator's course is of nine months duration at the CIFNET, Cochin and Madras and this is a statutory requirement for operating the RT equipment on board fishing vessels. Though the actual course is for handling navigational and various fish finding electronic equipment, the candidates obtatin professional proficiency certificates as radio telephone operators. Most of them are employed on board large fishing vessels as deckhands-cum-radio telephone operators. After Institutional training, the candidates will have to qualify at the examination conducted by the Government of India, Ministry of Communication. The course trains the candidates in the operation and maintenance of RT equipment. Studies, both theory and practical include fundamentals of electricity and magnetism, electronic components in a RT set, propagation of N.M. waves, regulations and procedures for communication, and so on. The Evaluation Committee on CIFNET has recommended that this course be expanded to include a study of electronic fishing and navigation aids also in greater detail and duration of course to be increased to 12 months.

Refrigeration technician certificate course

This course of 6 months duration, with an intake capacity of 12 per course, is conducted by the IFP, Cochin, under the Government of India, Ministry of Agriculture, for the benefit of junior cadre candidates employed in state fisheries departments and private fish processing firms. Subjects of study and practicals include fundamentals of refrigeration, refrigeration machinery and components, refrigeration systems, hygienic standards in fish handling and storage. This course is not conducted regularly. The training is arranged when sufficient number of candidates are sponsored. The course has been found useful in developing the skills of the refrigeration technicians. The Department of Fisheries, Orissa, is reported to run a two-year apprenticeship training course for refrigeration mechanics. This is an inservice training meant to meet the shortage of technical personnel required for manning the ice plants in Orissa.

Fish processing technicians certificate course

This is a training course of 6 months duration at the Integrated Fisheries Project (IFP), Cochin, financed by the MPEDA, Cochin. The course is meant for the personnel deputed by the government departments, public sector organizations, and processing industry. The training includes practical work in the processing plant and machinery at shore and on board the fishing vessels of the Institute. Theoretical studies cover basic microbiology freezing techniques, canning techniques, fish sausage technique salting and trying of fish, smoking of fish, refrigeration engineering, and so on.

Purse sein master fishermen certificate course

This is an 8 months course with an intake capacity of 10 per course at the IFP, Cochin, for the benefit of fishermen and the candidates deputed by the government departments and industry. This course has enabled the introduction of purse seining for sardines and mackerels in coastal waters of Karnataka and Kerala. Theoretical and practical studies include purse seine designs, fabrication and preservation of purse seines, location and capture of .sardines and mackerel shoals etc. The training is both on shore and on board the institute vessels.

TRAINING COURSES FOR GRADUATES AND POST-GRADUATES

Certificate course for teachers of fishermen training centres

This is purely an inservice course of 6 months duration at the CIFNET, Cochin, for the benefit of candidates sponsored by the State Departments of Fisheries. The training covers various aspects of teaching methods, organisation of fishermen training centres etc. This course will have to be designed to meet the practical needs of the centres.

Training course for staff in fisheries departments

This is a inservice course varying from 6-10 months duration conducted at the Staff Training Centres of the respective state departments of Fisheries in Kerala, Tamil Nadu,

Andhra Pradesh, Gujarat and Orissa. The course is meant for the graduates and post-graduates newly recruited by the fisheries departments. Subjects of study include fisheries science, meteorology, marine biology, marine fisheries of India, coastal aquaculture and mariculture, marine pollution, preservation and processing, fishing craft and gear, navigation and seamanship, fishery statistics, marketing and extension, fishery co-operatives and so on.

This course is generally run on satisfactory lines, but a proper grounding in the basic fundamental aspects of integrated rural development and extension techniques of fishery science is felt essential. Besides, the programme is confined to the respective states and do not offer opportunities to the personnel to acquaint themselves with the developments in other states. Another feature which requires serious consideration is the need for posting of interested and knowledgeable staff as teachers at these centres, so as to lay a strong foundation among the newly recruited personnel undergoing training.

Training course for staff of Karnataka fisheries department

This is an inservice training course conducted at the College of Fisheries, Mangalore, for the benefit of the newly recruited technical staff deputed by the Karnataka Department of Fisheries from the level of Assistant Inspectors to Deputy Directors of Fisheries. Subjects for training are similar to those at the state staff training centres, with special courses in fish farm management and composite fish culture. The duration of the course varies from 3 to 45 days. This training enables the candidates to keep abreast of the activities of the fisheries department. The well equipped library at the college also enables them to improve their knowledge. However, it is felt that the duration of the training should be increased to make the course useful.

Training course in fish processing technology

This course is also an inservice course conducted at the Central Institute of Fisheries Technology (CIFT), Cochin, in fish processing techniques, inplant hygeine, and manufacture of fish products. This course is arranged only on specific requests. Similar courses are also arranged periodi cally by the institute at its summer institute for the benefit of research workers, and the development officers of the state fisheries departments and the industry.

A training course in fish processing, fishery by-products, quality control, raw material handling and so on, is also conducted by the CFTRI, Mysore, for the benefit of M.Sc. (Food Tech.) students for a period of 6 months and for the benefit of research workers for a period of 6-8 weeks.

Training course in coastal aquaculture

This is a summer institute course of 4-6 weeks duration conducted by the CMFRI, Cochin, in coastal aquaculture, more specifically in brackish water prawn culture for the benefit of teachers, research workers, fisheries department officers, and extension officers of the state departments of fisheries and the industry. Though this training course is useful for presenting a common forum for exchange of experiences and update the participants in the latest information in aquaculture technology, this subject requires greater thrust in training, mainly the areas covering seed production, induced breeding and reproductive physiology, nutritional requirements and culture of live food organisms, farm engineering, prawn pathology, prawn genetics, hatchery management, harvesting and post-harvesting technology, proven information on economic viability synergy and recycling in prawn culture, and integrated sea farming. Success of prawn culture depends largely on the efficiency with which it is carried out and the personnel involved in it. The development and operation of prawn culture on improved lines require trained personnel of different categories. In the accelerated programme, a large number of research personnel are required to carry out advanced research on different aspects of prawn culture. Managerial personnel with technical as well as administrative knowledge are also essential to manage the prawn farms. A large number of skilled operatives in survey and selection of suitable sites for prawn culture, seed procurement and production, culture operations, and fishing are also required. The training needs of the different categories of personnel are varied. At present there are very little facilities to import training for different aspects in different levels. Training in prawn farming is done at a few centres. These will not be sufficient and intensive training facilities will have to be developed in each state, so that the trained personnel at different levels are available when other infrastructure facilities are built up.

Training course in fishery research management

This is an inservice training course conducted by the Agricultural Scientist's Training College, Hyderabad, for the benefit of postgraduates recruited to the ICAR institutions. The training is in administration and management of research activities and includes institutional training followed by field training in ICAR institutions. A similar course on management of research programmes in agricultural sciences including fisheries is also provided by the IIM, Ahmedabad, since very recently. The course is of 2 years duration for graduates in different disciplines with experience in agriculture and allied subjects and working in public and private sector organizations, as well as in financial institutions. This course prepares the participants for rural development projects for public and private sector organizations.

Training course in pakaging of foods

This course of four weeks duration on packaging technology, management, distribution, transportation, testing, printing, standards, and environmental considerations is conducted by the Indian Institute of Packaging, Bombay. The training programmes have been quite useful to the manufacturers of packages for marine products and users to keep abreast of the technological changes in the methods of manufacture and choice of packaging materials, manufacturing machinery, quality control, and so on.

Training course in export marketing management

A variety of short term certificate training programmes are

conducted by the IIFT, New Delhi, in import policies, export marketing, export procedures and documentation, overseas markets, financial business operations, legal aspects of international marketing, and so on. A similar, but of 6 months diploma course is conducted by the Indian Institute of Export, Baroda. The syllabus for the course includes export management, business correspondence in export trade, technique of selecting products for export, pricing technique, principal exports and trade centres, market choosing technique, export market research, distribution system, export advertising, export promotion, shipping procedures, documentation, export finance, and so on.

Training course in oceanographic surveys

This is an inservice course conducted by the Naval Hydrographic Department, Bombay, for the benefit of graduates from marine and survey departments and marine research institutes. The subjects cover oceanographic surveys, sampling techniques, and hydrography.

Training course in salt manufacture and recovery and utilisation of marine chemicals from salt works, desalinazation of sea water and use of sea water for aquaculture

This inservice course is conducted by the CSMCRI, Bhavnagar, for the benefit of candidates sponsored by the state and central government departments. Salt, as a fish preservative, is important to the fish processing industry. The salt content in brackish water and coastal waters is also of importance in coastal aquaculture and mariculture and to this extent this short term training course is useful to the seafood industry.

Training course in fisheries extension

All the fisheries research institutions in the country are engaged in fisheries extension work in some form or other. The CIFT, Cochin, with its extension, Information and Statistics Division imparts to the industry, the technical know-how and assistance as part of the extension work on fishing and fish processing technology through various media like answering technical enquiries, personnel discussions, demonstrations, supply of designs and drawings, film shows, publications, exhibitions, open house discussions, technical pamphlets, handouts, bulletins, newsletters, and so on. In most cases, however, the information does not furnish the economic aspects.

The CMFRI, Cochin, conducts summer institutes as a scheme of extension education and transfer of technology developed at the institute for the benefit of the university teachers, research workers, and scholars to update and improve their knowledge in coastal aquaculture and mariculture. Besides, it publicize its results of investigation through popular articles, special bulletins, radio talks, seminars and discussions with fish farmers.

The EFP, Bombay, brings out periodically newsletters and bulletins highlighting the results obtained during the exploratory fishing operations covering the characteristics of the fishery resources for the benefit of the industry, including the potential of the fishing grounds, specifications of fishing vessels and fishing gears employed, economic features of exploitation, and so on.

The IFP, Cochin brings out newsletters on the latest developments and findings the practical fields of fishing operations, processing, and marketing of fish, sometimes with economic aspects.

The state fisheries departments also carry out extension service relating to their developmental activities in coastal fishing, fish seed production, fish cultural practices, various fishing methods and so on among the rural folk through film shows, exhibitions, seminars, and so on.

There is, however, no training centre in the country for imparting extension service covering all facts of the marine fishery industry. The work at the Central Fisheries Extension Training Centre (CFETC) at Hyderabad relates to inland fish culture. This Institute has to be strengthened or a new one established for training in all aspects of marine fisheries activities, the composite courses to cover the managerial personnel and the courses in specific areas to meet the needs of the lower and middle level extension workers. Marine Fisheries extension work has remained a weak link of marine fisheries development and, therefore, basic organizational changes will have to be made in this direction. This would include setting up of training courses for popularization of processing techniques, fleet operations, better techniques of trade statistics, fishery products and bye-products, and so on. Adequate testing facilities are also needed to become a part of extension programme in view of the importance in commercialization of operation.

SUMMARY AND RECOMMENDATIONS

While tracing the growth of marine fisheries education and training in India, it has been indicated that regular educational and training institutions at state and central levels came to be established during the early 1960s. However, they remained as inservice institutions only, in asmuch as they have been training matriculates, graduates and post-graduates in science who are already in the service of the various departments of fisheries and fisheries industrial establishments and sponsored by these establishments. It was only during the late 1960s that some serious thought was given to the organisation of professional education in fisheries on the lines of the facilities existing in the field of other Agricultural sciences such as agriculture, forestry and veterinary sciences and a concept was developed to initiate steps for establishing professional education and training facilities in fisheries science, under the agricultural universities. The Karnataka University of Agricultural Science was the first to establish professional fisheries education and training facilities at the university level through the establishment of the College of Fisheries at Mangalore in 1969. This University had an initial advantage of a well established MPPTC in collaboration with Japan for taking over practical training courses in fish processing. By the end of the 1970s, the Universities of Agricultural Sciences, Tamil Nadu and Kerala, had also established Fisheries colleges. Besides these agricultural universities, some universities in the country have also started fisheries courses in their marine sciences faculties and zoology departments. By the close of 1981, more agricultural universities, fisheries research institutes under the ICAR, and the marine sciences faculties of universities have planning to organize professional courses in fisheries science at graduate and post-graduate levels. With such a growth envisaged in the fisheries education at university level it becomes important to take suitable steps to ensure that the professional education and training required at the school level especially in rural areas are not ignored but built up.

In fisheries education and training, manual skills are of great importance. Demonstration on a black board is seldom impressive unless followed by a practical field demonstration. Professional courses at different levels in the marine fisheries sector will, therefore, have to be more practical oriented so that qualified hands after completion of their courses will gain sufficient professional confidence, apply their knowledge and the uptodate techniques they have acquired, and contribute to the progress and improvements in their specialized fields. The requirements of such qualified hands for the various fields of marine fishery science and technology will have to be met at different levels and not confined to university level alone. The different requirements may be categorized below :

(1) Those of primary cadre, professionally qualified with practical training, as skilled operatives, with certificates, in respective disciplines after their school education;

(2) Those of junior cadre, professionally qualified with practical training for the categories of field assistants, survey assistants, technical assistants, supervisors, technicians, and so on with diplomas in respective disciplines after matriculation or undergraduate education;

(3) Those of middle cadre professionally qualified for the categories of managers, development officers, and so on with graduate degrees or post-graduate diplomas in the respective disciplines ; and

(4) Those of a senior cadre, professionally qualified for the categories of regional development officers, research officers, teachers, and so on with post-gradute degrees

or diplomas in respective disciplines, for organizing and implementing fishery related programmes.

An analysis of the present educational and training courses in marine fisheries and related subjects in the context of the above requirements highlights fisheries education and training at the school level (primary cadre) in some states is only of nominal value with no practical approach, while at the matriculate level (primary and junior cadre) and graduate, post-graduate and Ph. D. levels (middle and higher cadres) there is very little practical approach. This pattern, in the context of the country's future developmental needs, has to improve upon its professional competence at all levels with more practical orientation and commercial management bias in every aspect. While reviewing the various courses at the different institutions in this paper, a few suggestions have been made to supplement and improve the existing syllabi for some of the courses. The following areas require greater thrust in education and training :

(1) Methodology of assessment of marine fisheries resources;
(2) Management of marine fisheries resources;
(3) Coastal aquaculture and mariculture technology and hatchery management;
(4) Fish marketing and management;
(5) Fish distribution, storage and transport management;
(6) Fishing harbour engineering and management of fishing harbours;
(7) Designing and construction of fishing vessels;
(8) Seed weed culture technology;
(9) Fishery extension techniques;
(10) Refrigeration and processing of fish at sea;
(11) Evaluation of pollution and control measures;
(12) Conservation and regulatory measures.

The NCST points out that education and training in marine fisheries and technology is provided by many institutions at different levels within the country with very little co-ordination between them. Another lacuna in the present system of education and training is the absence of adequate practical training for a minimum period owing to lack of specialized facilities, etc.

Another aspect of importance is fishery literature. Text books, manuals, and teacher's Guides are still to be brought out. Some efforts have been made by fisheries research institutions to publish comprehensive bibliographies periodically relating to several aspects of fisheries science and technology. FAO has been publishing fishing abstracts and guides to fishery education and training. Some organizations like the Kanagawa International Fisheries Training Centre, Japan, has published standard text books on fisheries. Popular publications prepared expressly for the benefit of fishermen, who are not literate or out barely literate, and featuring illustrations accompanied by minimum of text are lacking. Many excellent teaching materials, in English, French, Russian, German, Japanese and other languages have to be translated.

It is truism that fewer the pupils in a class, more time the teacher can devote to each individual. But some feel that the number of pupils should justify the total expenditure, but this does not produce the results one would expect. The educational and training institutions should normally fix the annual intake depending on the teaching laboratory, workshop, and other facilities. However, in some institutions where short term training courses are conducted, neither the intake capacity nor the periodicity of the courses has been fixed. Training in such institutions is arranged on adequate demand from the government departments or the industry. The intake capacity for a course in each of the Institutions will have to be reviewed periodically and planned after an assessment of the national requirements. The initial selection of trainees in any discipline is of paramount importance, yet it is difficult to establish criteria which make it possible to recruit satisfactory personnel. Intelligence and adaptability coupled with physical fitness appear to be much more important. At present, the educational and training institutions display a linkage with the government. This has the operational advantage of facilitating nature of training including possible integration of national training needs with institutional plans. But it has also the constraints in the day-to-day working, seeking procedural clearances, personnel appointments, and financial sanctions. As a result, there appear a dichotomy between the status and tasks in these institutions by which tasks are pushed down and authority rests with higher administrative levels. This linkage leads to a dominating influence of administrative machinery which will not be able to act in time and without full understanding of the situation and conditions obtaining in the institutions. The proximity of such institutions with government makes them prone to the dysfunctional features of administrative influence and, therefore, not conducive to the cause of education and training. A full fledged professional course in the Science and Technology of Marine Fisheries and connected subjects will have to integrate under the control of one authority different aspects of education, training, research, and extension. Besides lack of uniformity in the educational and training pattern and lack of co-ordination, there is considerable disparity in the standards.

The NCA is of opinion that conducting educational and training courses should not form part of the programme of the fisheries research institutions. It, however, feels that the productive results of investigations can best be communicated at different levels through the training programmes conducted by the research institutes only. Some feel that the coastal aquaculture technology developed at the CMFRI, CIFRI, CIFE, and so an can be utilized for training the primary sector and the junior technical cadre respectively through the existing fishermen training centres in the states and the CIFNET. The Evaluation Committee of the CIFNET has recommended that the processing training programme at the junior technical cadre now undertaken by the College of Fisheries, Mangalore, IFP, and CFTRI can be taken by the CIFNET at Cochin and Madras and that the teaching staff required for such courses at these centres can be trained at the central fisheries research institutes and the college of fisheries, Mangalore. Establishment of a fisheries technical university under the ICAR is another suggestion made by a few to meet the needs of higher education in fisheries. Another view is that fishery education at all levels be entrusted to agricultural universities suggesting that all higher education for training research scientists, teachers, managerial, and higher level technical personnel may be imparted in these universities and that the present training arrangements for middle and lower technical personnel which are of *ad hoc* nature and which are available at various centres under different agencies may be established as separate fisheries polytechnics under the agricultural universities. How far an agriculture university will be able to handle industrial fisheries required careful examination, since industrial marine fishery is distinct from inland fisheries. Though the latter may be more allied and complementary to agricultural operations, the industrial marine activity cannot be considered as an allied agricultural activity. The NCST has suggested the establishment of a Commission on Oceans and Ocean Resources (COOR), to help assure availability of educated and trained manpower adequate for all the national marine resources and development programmes, besides attending to planning, guiding, directing, and executing through the existing organizations, where they exist, a unified approach to the problems of the ocean, the atmosphere, and the marine resources. However, it will be desirable and effective if separate fisheries universities are established to meet the country's needs at different levels. These will remain as autonomous bodies with fisheries college and training institutes in each region for different levels, both existing as well as new ones, and affiliated to each regional university. The location, scope and areas of stress of such fisheries universities would have to be so planned that fewer centres of better quality are set up in different subjects in different regions covering a few states rather than proliferating centres in the same subject fields within each state. This would ensure uniformity in educational and training pattern and parity of standards at different professional levels in all the institutions of a region and would assist in avoiding duplication and overlapping.

In Japan, the school, college, and university education in fisheries are interlinked with practical training in all aspects. The Japanese School system makes it compulsory to finish 6 years of the primary school course and 3 years of the junior high school course. Those who finish this course enter the 3 year senior high schools. Some of the high schools have fisheries courses and some are called fisheries high schools with considerable number of courses on fisheries. These are established in major fisheries centres all over Japan. The aim of the fisheries education in the high schools is to train the students in the technical knowledge and practical skill as well as general education, so that they become independent entrepreneurs or technicians. The objectives include :

(1) To let the students understand correctly the role the fisheries play on the development of Japan's industrial economy.
(2) To let the students understand the geographical environment of Japan and the importance of fisheries in such conditions and to make them realize how important it is to understand and protect the fisheries resources.
(3) To let the students acquire basic knowledge and practical skill in all fields of fisheries industry.
(4) To let them understand the legislation concerning fisheries and cultivate in them the spirit of abiding by these laws.

The college courses are of four years duration and each college has its own unique curriculum under the fisheries faculty or department of fisheries of general universities. The entrants are selected from those who have finished the senior high school course. Graduates from these colleges enter separate fisheries universities for their master's or doctor's degree in fisheries.

REFERENCES

Abasiekong, E.A., The Role of Public Relations in Rural Development Programmes, *Journal of the Indian Institute of Public Administration.* Vol. XXVI, No. 2, 1980.

Choudhury, L.H., Training for Development, *Journal of the Indian Institute of Public Administration*, Vol, XXVI, No. 2, 1980.

Cole, R.C. & D.W.F. Hall, Guide to Fishery Education and Training, F.A.O., Fish, Pap (128), 1973.

Central Institute of Fisheries Operatives, Report of the Evaluation

Committee on the Central Institute of Fisheries Operatives, Cochin, 1973.

Central Institute of Fisheries Operatives, Report of the Syllabus Committee on the Central Institute of Fisheries Operatives, Cochin, 1974.

CMFRI, Marine Fisheries Information Service, Technical and Extension Series No. 6, Cochin, 1979.

Central Institute of Fisheries Education, Report of the Evaluation Committee on the Central Institute of Fisheries Education, Bombay.

Central Institute of Fisheries Education, Report of the Inflow Committee on the Central Institute of Fisheries Education, Bombay.

Government of India, Report of the National Commission on Agriculture, Part VIII : Fisheries, Ministry of Agriculture & Irrigation, New Delhi, 1976.

Government of India, Draft Five Year Plan 1978-1983, 1978.

Johnson, S., Report to the Government of India, Ministry of Agriculture, on the Central Institute of Fisheries Operatives, 1963.

Kyokai, Asia, Japanese Fisheries, Japan, 1960.

National Committee on Science and Technology, Marine Resources, NCST Sectoral Report, Govt. of India Press, Simla, 1975.

Saxena, A.P., Some Background Factors in the Choice of Training Methodologies, *Journal of Indian Institute of Public Administration*. Vol. XXVI, No. 1, 1980.

9

MANPOWER PLANNING
An Assessment for the Next Decade

K. CHIDAMBARAM

INTRODUCTION

OF THE many constraints and impediments in developing fisheries in India, the most important one is lack of well trained manpower. It may be seen from the Table 9.1 that India ranks next only to Japan, Indonesia and Philippines.

MANPOWER PLANNING IN MARINE FISHERIES DEVELOPMENT

Capture fisheries, culture fisheries and utilization of fisheries resources constitute the three main areas in the marine fisheries sector. The principal objectives of planning for the development of these three segments of the marine fisheries in the country, are, to step up the fish production in the capture and culture fisheries, both through the traditional and industrial sectors and to improve and diversify the systems of utilization of the fish catch for domestic and export markets. The achievement of the objectives, however, depends to a large extent on the availability of trained manpower and its useful deployment.

The main features of marine fisheries are :

(1) The capture fisheries is a hunting activity. The resources are invisible and mobile. Besides many resources are to be found in the international waters.

TABLE 9.1 : **Manpower planning in the o her countries**

Country	Estimated Employment	Structure of Industry		Source of Fish as % from		Utilization % for	
		Traditional	Industrial	Inland	Marine	Domestic	Export
East Africa							
Ethiopia	3700	—	—	4	96	15	85
Kenya	25000	—	—	66	34	95	5
Tanzania	40000	—	—	85	15	87	13
Malagasay	6000	—	Some	75	25	90	10
West Asia							
Kuwait	6000	—	40%	—	100	60	40
Iraq	4200	—	—	89	11	90	10
Pakistan	164000	50%	50%	10	90	33	67
Sri Lanka	65000	80%	—	5	95	100	—
India	400000	—	—	40	60	95	5
East Asia							
Malaysia	80000	—	—	1	99	67	33
Indonesia	883000	—	Some	33	77	99	1
Philippines	688000	—	Some	10	90	100	—
Hong Kong	45000	—	Some	2	98	90	10

Burma	142000	—	—	30	70	100	—
Thailand	75000	—	Some	10	90	95	5
Far East							
Korea	367000	60%	40%	—	100	87	13
Japan	570000	—	Most	2	98	90	10
Oceania							
Australia	18000	—	Most	1	99	76	24
New Zealand	4400	—	Most	2	98	65	35

Source : R.M. Lawson.

(2) The culture fisheries depend largely on the availability of fish seed, the biotic and abiotic conditions of the water areas and husbandry and management.
(3) The climatic, mateorological and biological conditions give rise to large fluctuations in the resources, both in the capture and culture fisheries, and
(4) Fishery products are highly perishable and demand different processing and preservation techniques resulting in different commodity terms and they have after carving marketing patterns.

These characteristics necessitate development of different kinds of skills. The marine fisheries sector in India may be divided into traditional and industrial segments. The traditional segment which comprises subsistance fisheries is characterized by a low income per head, a low capital labour ratio and a low level of technology and productivity. The industrial segment, on the other hand, is characterized by the existance of commercial markets for inputs and outputs—and a high per capital income, high capital labour ratio, and high level of technology and productivity. This distinction between the traditional and industrial segments has an important bearing on manpower planning in marine fisheries development.

Attempts in India to determine the future requirement of manpower for marine industries have encountered serious difficulties. There is also no one agency with the overall responsibility for assessing the requirement of manpower, although several agencies in the country operating with nominal co-ordination are supporting, initiating and planning programmes on marine education and training of manpower (NCST 1975).

MANPOWER REQUIREMENT ON CAPTURE FISHERIES

The relatively low production in capture fisheries is mainly attributed to the low level of fishing effort in deeper waters and the use of primitive fishing craft and gears employed in coastal waters. Increasing the fishing effort in the deeper waters of the economic zone by the industrial sector requires information on the economic viability of exploiting the deep water and distant water fish stocks, employment of large and complex fishing vessels with a corresponding high capital investment and an integrated infrastructure. This would require intensified research, resource surveys, expertise in designing and constructing large fishing vessels, designing and fabrication of fishing gears, fishing techniques, operation and maintenance of fishing, propulsion, refrigeration, hydraulic electronic and electrical equipment, and designing, construction and maintenance of fishing harbours, repair yard docks, and maintenance services. We will now examine each employment of capture fisheries and estimate manpower requirements.

Marine Fisheries Research is of special economic importance because of the large area available for exploitation and limitations imposed by fluctuations in fishery resources. Research in the country presently is mostly in coastal fisheries and comprises collection and compilation of production statistics, coastal survey on fishing villages, craft and gears, stock assessment, hydro-biological studies of the economically important food fishes, evaluation of the exploratory fishing data, environmental studies, primary and secondary production studies, culture of marine fishes, marine pollution, and so on. Considerable work remains to be carried out on determining the untapped fisheries resources in the deeper waters, assessing the maximum sustainable yield from the exploited fisheries and planning control and regulatory measures, methodology for rational exploitation of various fisheries resources, analytical methods in respect of production economics and management, social and economic setup of the fisheries in different areas and extension.

The existing research and field centres will have to be strengthened and upgraded and some of the existing centres will have to be shifted to other centres of greater developmental activity for undertaking investigations. It is necessary that 15 more research and field centres are established in West Bengal, Orissa, Andhra Pradesh, Karnataka, Maharashtra and Gujarat. It is also necessary that the CMFRI establishes another four divisions as below :

(1) A fishery economics and statistics division—This is an important field for development. A fishery economist must be will versed in the analytical methods with respect to production economics. He must also possess a fair technical knowledge of the way in which the fisheries work to enable him to apply the principles of economics efficiently.

(2) An extension division to look after all types of extension activities and consultancy services along with demonstration projects, pilot projects and sponsored projects for technology transfer.

(3) A separate division for investigation on interdisciplinary fields such as nutrition, physiology and pathology in fin fishes and shell fishes.

(4) A fishery conservation division for investigations on fishery acts and regulations.

The existing biology division also requires functional bifurcation into two divisions, namely, the pelagic fisheries division and demersal fisheries division for proper strengthening and coverage of the investigation on these groups. The fishery resources assessment division needs adoption of advanced methodology such as aerial surveys, acoustic methods, remote sensing and under water surveys for better stock assessment, preparation of fishery Atlases, fishery forecasting and formulating suitable management policies on the resources. Studies on hydrography, primary and secondary productivity, and other related aspects in the economic zone with the help of research vessels are also needed. Intensive studies on the base line observations and monitoring of pollutants in areas contaminated by industrial effluents are required. But the most important requirement of the Institute is research vessels. Taking the above facts into consideration, we would see that the requirement of additional personnel in the next 10 years for the Institute would be around 4000.

Marine Fisheries Technological Rerearch in capture fisheries is carried out at the Central Institute of Fisheries Training (CIFT), Cochin. Activities at the Institute, relating to capture fisheries in the marine sector are organized under crafts, fishing gear, engineering and extension, information and statistics divisions. The Institute has four research centres, three on the West Coast and only one on the East Coast. The crafts division undertakes investigations on evolving new and cheaper construction materials for fishing craft in place of conventional but costly timbers, suitability and efficiency of materials other than wood for construction of fishing craft, evolving efficient measure for protection of existing wooden fishing craft and components against marine deterioration and designing of small mechanised fishing boats. The gear division undertakes studies on comparing and establishing the relative merits and demerits of different natural and synthetic fibres for fabrication of fishing gears, evolving efficient methods of preservation of fishing gears against marine deterioration and working out quality standards of different types of gear materials. Investigations towards evolving improved and new designs of fishing gears, standardising the types and sizes of crafts for different types of fishes and evolving better techniques in fishing for maximum exploitation of a particular species are some of the other items of work undertaken by this division. The Engineering division undertakes studies towards working out quality standards for selection of marine engines of different sizes of boats and different methods of mechanised fishing, electric and electronic instruments for testing and measuring purposes both in research and investigations, as well as in commercial fishing and testing of indegenously manufactured marine for assessing the performance and suggesting improvements. The Extension division undertakes investigations on such of the problems of the industry which require collection, compilation, analysis and interpretation of statistical data towards economising production and improving efficiency.

These activities at four centres are mostly concentrated on coastal fisheries. The Institute has, therefore, to be strengthened by establishing five more research centres on the Esat Coast and 3 more on the West Coast and by including investigations on the development of capture fisheries in the deeper waters of the economic zone, covering the designing of the most suitable sizes and types of large deep sea fishing vessels, diversified fishing gears and fishing techniques, efficient fishing gear accessories and fishing equipment. Development of improved traditional fishing craft in materials like FRP, ferrocement and so on with suitable power drives, efficient fishing equipment and diversified fishing gears are also required to be taken up at the Institute. In addition, separate economic division, electric, electronic and fishing equipment development division and marine machinery maintenance and improvement division if established at the Institute would provide valuable information to the developing industry. Besides, two large research vessels and 6 medium size vessels for the Institute to carry investigations would also be necessary. Taking the obove facts into consideration, the requirement of additional personnel for the Institute would be around 400.

EXPLORATORY FISHING SURVEYS

The objectives of exploratory fishing surveys carried out presently by the Exploratory Fisheries Project, Bombay, and the Integrated Fisheries Project, Cochin are chartering of fishing grounds, determination of fishing seasons, examination of the types of fish available assessment of the suitability of the different types of fishing vessels for commercial exploitation, assessment of the availability of the different types of fishing gears and fishing equipment for various fisheries and making available data and information on the commercial possibilities of marine fishing operation. The exploratory surveys have been confined mostly in waters up to about 80 depth and this too, very much on the West coast than on the East coast and Andaman and Lakshadweep waters. The exploratory operations have been mostly restricted to demersal trawling only, while other fishing techniques have not been adequately employed. The area surveyed is reported to be 0.2 million (adequately) sq. km. mostly with trawl gear, which is about 10 per cent of the economic zone area. Considerable work, therefore, remains to be carried out to establish the economic feasibility of commercial exploitation of the demersal, midwater and pelagic resources potential of the deeper waters of the entire economic zone, to infuse confidence in the industry to venture in this field for increasing the country's marine fish production. In view of the specialised nature of fishing, tuna requires to be investigated separately.

The Government of India, has stressed the importance of exploratory surveys for the development of the deep sea fishing industry and have provided for the acquisition of thirty eight exploratory deep sea fishing vessels of different sizes during the Sixth Five Year Plan for exploratory purse seining, demersal trawling, squid jigging, long lining, tuna fishing, lobster fishing, midwater and pelagic trawling and so on. Considering the above facts, the requirement of additional personnel in the next ten years for the two exploratory organizations would be about 700.

PLANNING AND CONSTRUCTION OF FISHING HARBOURS

Infrastructure planning activity in capture fisheries is undertaken by the Pre-investment Survey Project on fishing harbour at Bangalore. Development of fishing harbours with infrastructure which is an essential prerequisite, if marine fish production is to be increased. Considerable work has been carried out in the past towards the selection of suitable sites, taking note of the geographical and engineering aspects, present level of fisheries exploitation, fish areas, economic factors and so on and plans drawn out to accommodate for a total of about 11,000 small mechanized boats and 160 large fishing vessels, but the actual construction of most of these harbours has not been completed. Construction of fishing harbours is carried out through Port Trusts, Marine Departments of the State Governments, and private and mechanical engineering construction firms in the different regions of the country. So far, fishing harbours at Veraval, Cochin, Tuticorin, Vizag, Roychuk and Port Blair have been completed. The fishing harbours at Malpe and Madras are under construction. A few more in other states are expected to be taken up soon. For some, feasibility studies have been undertaken and are in the process of being designed. All these developments may not be enough for the expansion of fleet in the next 10 years. In the context of the development indicated, the requirement of additional personnel in the next 10 years in this field would be about 200.

Commercial fishing is carried out in the country in the private sector and corporate sector by about 110,000 traditional fishing crafts, about 15,000 small mechanized fishing boats and nearly 75 medium and large fishing vessels. The traditional fishing craft are mainly catamarans, dugout canoes and plank built boats, and are all built with wood. They are not mechanized except for a few with outboard drives. They operate shore seines, boat seines, gill-nets, hooks, lines and so on. The small mechanized boats range in size from 5.5—13 m but the most popular are 9 m and 10 m boats. They are also built mostly of wood except for a few in FRP. These boats operate mostly trawl nets and a comparatively low number operate purse seine nets and gill-nets. Large steel fishing vessels in the commercial sector range in size from 16.5 m to 28 m and are employed by industrial houses, state government undertakings and paivate entrepreneurs purely for demersal trawling for prawns.

Introduction of at least 3,500 improved traditional fishing crafts in FRP with outboard drives for diversified fishing in the different regions of the country, 5,000 mechanized fishing boats in FRP ferrocement for diversified fishing, and 350 deep sea fishing vessels in steel, all for commercial operations would be necessary.

With this additional fleet strength in the next 10 years, annual marine fish production is estimated to increase by about 0.85 million tonnes from the present level of 1.4 million tonnes according to the report of the working group on fisheries for formulating the Sixth Five Year Plan. The scope for this increase of about 0.85 million tonnes will be particularly from low value fishes like white bait, small sciaenids, small carangids, lantern fish, and other miscellaneous small fish. Besides, there will be substantial additional landings of cat fish, perches, ribbon fish, sharks, mackerels, sardines, squids, cuttle fish, etc. The main emphasis, however, will be to produce high priced varieties in the fishing fleet like prawns, lobsters, pomfrets, seer, tuna, and so on. With this increase in the fishing fleet, the marine fish production will go up by about 1.13 tonnes. In the context of the development indicated the requirements of additional personnel for commercial fishing operations would be about 50,000.

CONSTRUCTION OF FISHING VESSELS

There is no organized industry for construction of traditional fishing craft. They are built and repaired in most of the fishing villages by builders who have learnt the art from their elders. Construction of small wooden mechanized fishing boats commenced in the 1960s after the initial efforts of the FAO and INP in designing and constructing the prototypes. Since then it has developed enormously and there are today about 112 wooden boat building yards, with a capacity to construct about 2,000 boats a year. Since wood is becoming scarce and costly, yards for construction of traditional crafts and mechanized boats in FRP have been established in Gujarat, Maharashtra, Karnataka, Tamil Nadu and Andhra Pradesh in the private sector. A yard for construction of mechanized boats in ferrocement was also established at Madras and a few small mechanized boats were constructed quite successfully with the available technology. This yard has since been closed. There are another 17 yards with a capacity to build 29 fishing vessels a year in steel in varying sizes. In view of the non-availablity of suitable timber, most of wooden boat building yards are likely to switch over to FRP, ferrocement, and so on.

Capacity for constructing large steel fishing vessels upto 40 metres exists in the public sectorship building yards at Bombay, Goa, Vizag and Calcutta. But the designing aspect has not been adequately developed at these yards. They mainly build ocean cargo carriers, naval crafts, harbour crafts, barges, dredgers, and so on. They also undertake construction of fishing vessels provided construction designs are made available to them. Though a private yard in Goa is concentrating exclusively on construction of steel fishing vessels of about 23m size with imported designs, the construction technology and the installation of machinery and equipment do require to be advanced further.

Demersal quality and low value fishes, mid-water and pelagic quality and low value fishes are unexplored and unexploited. A deep sea fishing fleet would comprise fishing vessels rigged up for demersal/midwater trawling, purse seining/pole lining and squid jigging/light fishing. Fishing vessels employed by developed countries for fishing in deeper shelf waters are in the range of 24-45 m and vessels beyond 45 metres in size are all factory vessels for long distance fishing.

Exploratory fishing operations conducted in the 1960s by the Exploratory Fisheries Project have highlighted that the most suitable vessels for commercial demersal trawling in the deeper shelf waters of the Bay of Bengal would be about 30-36 m in size with a designed main engine power of 450-500 HP. The Fisheries Technical Mission had identified stem trawlers of 32 m size with 450-560 HP engine for demersal fishing and trawler-cum-purse seiners of 23 metre size with 300 HP engine for demersal and pelagic fishing as suitable vessels for exploiting deep water fisheries of the country. The IIFT has indicated that fish vessels of 22-27 m with 350—450 HP engine would be suitable on the east and west coasts. Many other researchers have suggested other sizes.

Construction of improved traditional fishing craft and mechanized boats in wood, FRP and ferrocement will continue to be in the marine fisheries sector and manpower required for the yards will continue to be provided by the marine fisheries educational and training institutions.

However, construction of deep sea fishing vessels in steel will continue in the industrial sector. The existing large shipyards can meet this requirement for the fishing industry along with construction of cargo ships, naval craft, harbour crafts, tugs, dredgers, and so on. But these shipyards will require naval architects with special training in designing of fishing vessels for various functions and needs of the country. The Government of India has engaged the services of W.E. A for a detailed study of construction of fishing vessels in the country.

Education and training aim to create personnel at different levels to achieve technical and economic progress. In pursuance of this aim, the trainers have an important function. They should be well experienced in the technical skills and in the training techniques in terms of their content, application, and relevance. The education and the training aspects in capture fisheries at various levels have been presented elsewhere.

The greatest handicap is the lack of adequate number of fishing vessels for practical education and training. The Sixth Five Year Plan provided for an additional fleet of 9 training vessels for these institutes.

The Plan also provides for an increase in the intake of students for graduate course and post-graduate fisheries courses at CIFE, Bombay, to 80 and 120 per year. Short term courses for training management personnel for the fishing industry have been proposed at this Institute. Four additional centres for training fishermen in small mechanized boat operations in the West Bengal and Orissa as well as two additional CIFNET substations in the north-east and north-west coasts have also been proposed. The intake at CIFNET is also proposed to be increased to 1320. per year.

MANUFACTURE OF SYNTHETIC FISHING GEAR MATERIALS AND FISHING GEAR ACCESSORIES

Considerable progress has been made in the manufacture of synthetic fish net twine fibres, twines, ropes and machine made webbings during the last two decades. However, they are all in short supply and cost is prohibitive. Efforts will have to be made to increase their production capacity as well as to establish new plants to meet the demand in the next 10 years. Fishing accessories like steel wire ropes, floats, standard otter doors, butter flies, denlinees, purse rings, bobbins, shackles, blocks etc. are not readily available. However, the requirement of these materials for the fishing industry presently is not large enough as compared to that in the shipping industry and therefore does not warrant establishment of separate fisheries industrial estates. It would be enough if the existing industrial manufacturing units of these items are strengthened by indicating the special requirement of the fishing industry. Hence manpower requirement in this field specifically for the marine fisheries field is not indicated.

MANUFACTURE OF MARINE MACHINERY AND EQUIPMENT

Various types of marine engines up to 120 HP for small mechanized boats along with stem gears, reverse and reduction gear boxes, cooling water pumps, reduction motors, auxiliary generators, batteries, ISA and FFA, life rafts, navigational equipment and so on have been developed. However, their production capacity, supply of spares, and servicing facilities require not only to be strengthened in the next 10 years but also their performance need to be improved wherever necessary especially in the manufacture of winches, power blocks, and other hydraulic equipment. Efforts in the manufacture of marine engines of more than 350 HP and equipment for larger fishing vessels have been initiated recently and the development in this regard as well as that in the manufacture of fishing navigation and electronic equipment will have to move at a faster pace.

Units manufacturing these items are not exclusively for the fishing industry but are engaged in the manufacture of rallied machinery to meet the demand of multifarious indusrial needs. This activity will also have to continue in the industrial sector but geared to the needs and requirement of the fishing industry for both coastal and deep sea fishing. Manpower requirement in this field also has not, therefore, been indicated here. The additional technical manpower which will meet these requirements would be about 60,000.

MANPOWER REQUIREMENT IN CULTURE FISHERIES

Areas available for coastal acquaculture

Brackishwater for fish cultural purposes are estuarine basins, backwaters, tidal creeks, brackishwater lakes and coastal lagoons. Accurate estimate of the extent of brackishwater area available for culture in India are not available. While the Government of India has indicated about 1.42 million hectares of brackishwater are available, other estimates have ranged from as low as 0.8 million hectares to as high as 2.75 million hectares.

Current production

Area utilized for brackishwater fish and prawn culture is placed at about 15,000 hectares in 1973. The Government of India has indicated that about 12,000 hectares are being utilized for fish and prawn culture in West Bengal and Kerala. Another estimate is that nearly 0.61 million hectares are utilized for coastal aquaculture. Professor M.S. Swaminathan estimates the brackishwater areas which are being utilized for some sort of prawn culture as 0.02 million hectares.

Information on the total production of fish and prawn through brackishwater culture exclusively is not available. However, the embanked 'Bhasabada' fisheries of the Gangetic delta in West Bengal have been giving yields ranging between 350 and 2000 kg/ha a year, average being 500 kg. The paddy field fisheries of West Bengal have been giving an yield of 100-300 kg/ha a year. The prawn filtration of 'Pokkali' fields in Kerala is much better organized and yields from 800 to 2000 kg/ha a year.

Potential

Capture fisheries is becoming more and more capital intensive especially with the rising cost of fuel. Although culture fisheries cannot replace capture fisheries, they would certainly supplement the total marine fish production. Scientific coastal aquaculture and mariculture are profitable industries for augmenting marine fish production as large areas of estuarine swamps, mud flats, backwaters and coastal seas of the country offer tremendous potential. Aquaculture and mariculture in our coastal waters are still in their infancy, even though some of our brackishwaters have been used for traditional fish culture for centuries. Fast growing marine fish and prawns are plentiful in the Indian seas and the young ones of these species abound in the tidal creeks and shallow coastal areas during specific seasons. Several innovations in the cultural and engineering practices have been accomplished in the fisheries research institutes.

It is estimated that about 200 million hectares of cultivable brackishwater areas, if developed, can produce about 0.46 million tonnes of fish per annum at the minimum production rate of 225 kg/ha a year and that, per hectare production can be increased to about 100 kg/ha per year by adopting scientific management practices. In addition, it should be possible to reclaim more swampy and marshy estuarine areas after surveys and biological investigations. Professor Swaminathan estimates that by intensive prawn culture, a production rate of about 1,000-1,500 kg/ha a year could be obtained. P.U. Varghese estimates that, if only 20,000 hectares are brought under scientific prawn culture, the production can be raised to about five times the present estimated level of 4,000 tonnes per year.

Present level of activity

Considerable work has been carried out by the CMFRI, Cochin and the CIFRI, Calcutta, in coastal aquaculture research, extension and training. Technology for aquaculture systems of most of the marine organisms have been developed to some extent. The NIO, Goa, CIFE, Bombay, fisheries colleges of the agricultural universities, Karnataka, Tamil Nadu and some other universities have also taken up programmes in coastal aquaculture at the investigation and training levels. The MPEDA, Cochin, has formulated programmes in assisting the development of coastal aquaculture and for training the fishermen and farmers. Coastal aquaculture operations on a pilot commercial scale have also taken up and are planned through the departments of the fisheries and fisheries development corporations. These activities, however, are mostly concentrated on one item, namely prawn, because of the high unit value, it fetches in the export market.

The culture of brackishwater fish and prawns in India on a commercial scale has till recently been based only on traditional empirical methods. Such practices in essence relate to raising temporary bunds or barriers enclosing the tidal water, thus retaining the available fish and prawn for short periods until they grow to marketable size. This system is not fish culture in the real sense of the term but is generally known as "trapping-cum-holding". This system of culture prevalent in

West Bengal and Kerala are known as "Bashabada" fisheries in West Bengal and "Pokkali" in Kerala. Scientific culture of brackishwater fish and prawns has recently been taken up in the country by the central research institutes and also maritime state governments. Very recently due to effective extension work, quite a few enterprising entrepreneurs as well as large industrial houses shown interest in taking up coastal aquaculture on commercial lines. These activities in the private sector are also concentrated on the culture of commercially important prawn species only. There is, however, vast scope for taking up aquaculture systems for various other marine organisms like edible oysters, mussels, clams, crabs and fish and sea weeds. None of these exist presently as sizeable commercial activities.

Government policy

Coastal aquaculture is a means to recycling and upgrading low grade food to high grade protein rich food through scientific methods. Intensive culture is for developed countries where limited land, high labour costs, and high valued species of higher tropic level are obtained. In developing countries like India, there will have to be marked preference for the small scale sector and extensive aquaculture with low cost farming techniques because labour is cheap. Employment, improved nutrition and higher living standards of the rural poor are the objectives of the integrated rural development programme through aquaculture. The strategy of the government is to adopt a package of technical assistance, input supply, institutional finance, and so on in all the fishing villages where facilities for coastal aquaculture exist. A few pilot scale projects already established in the country for prawn culture have determined the feasibility of technology transfer. Yet it is necessary to establish more viable pilot projects for the culture of other marine organisms as well as create and activate a category of fish farmers and co-operative agencies in this field through soft loans, technical assistance and allotment of water areas. As an accelerated programme, intensive culture should also be encouraged through large industrial houses.

which have the capital, efficient management and marketing potential.

In addition, to give a fillip to the utilization of vast brackish-water resources, the government of India has been providing 100 per cent assistance to the state governments for the establishment of 50 hectare farms to enable them to adopt the techniques developed by the research institutions for producing about 2,000 kg. of fish and prawn per hectare per year as against the normal production of about 700 kg. The government observes that compared with paddy production in the estuarine areas, fish production can yield 10 times more yield and provide employment to over 2 million people, if all the estuarine areas are reserved for fish culture. The physical target for the development of coastal aquaculture during the Sixth Five Year Plan has envisaged an areas of 50,000 hectares of brackishwater areas to produce about 1,00,000 tonnes of fish at the end of the plan period with an employment potential of 2,50,000 personnel. The plan provides for training 10,000 fishermen in coastal aquaculture during this period.

REQUIREMENTS FOR INCREASED PRODUCTION THROUGH COASTAL AQUACULTURE

Tremendous potential exists for increasing brackishwater culture in the country provided scientific methods and techniques are followed. Capital requirement in the industry is not excessive and a minimum return of nearly 15 per cent is possible under average conditions. The requirement for development would be surveys of suitable areas, adoption of culture systems, availability of trained manpower and allotment of land on long term lease to entrepreneurs. Coastal aquaculture and mariculture are techniques of culture and/or farming of aquatic organisms and by feeding a crop in water, until it has grown to harvestable size and then harvesting and processing it for market.

Steps to increasing the prouductivity of culture/farming system can be classified into semi-closed and closed systems. The open system is the natural system where nature supplies all the management as long as harvesting pressure is not too heavy. But this system requires careful management measures relating to elimination of predators, fertilizing the water, control of diseases, and so on. The semi-closed system is characterized by the use of natural waters which are allowed to pass through the system. This character allows for improved management, since the location and facilities can be tailored to the needs of the system and controls can be exercised over variables such as water temperature, water volume, water velocity, predators and diseases. In a closed system, the working fluid is placed inside the system and it is seldom ever exchanged with sources outside the system. The fluid is circulated within the system by pumps or other devices. This system allow enviromental parameters to be closely controlled for faster growth. But this system needs high capital and operating cost.

Survey of areas requires investigations on the types of estuarine areas, land regulations and rights, tidal fluctuations, elevation and contour, water and soil characteristics, vegetation of fish farms, fish seed resources, economics of fish culture in the area etc. Site selection is the most critical part of the coastal aquaculture activity. Engineering aspects are also important in coastal aquaculture, including water supply to meet both quantity and quality, pumps to move water against energy gradient, construction of enclosed structure, filtration in aquatic cultural system, aeration of farms, and so on. Seed availability is a key factor in brackishwater culture. Until such time as the production of seed of culturable speccies of brackishwater fish and shell fish is achieved by induced breeding and hatchery techniques, collection of seed from natural resources has to be depended upon. Fortunately most of the brackishwater system in the country have been found to be dependable sources of fish and prawn seed. While natural seed abundance generally fluctuates from season to season and from centre to centre, the information presently available clearly indicates the possibilities for organizing systematic collection of fish and prawn seed from natural resources as an industry. However, for a large scale coastal aquaculture programme, natural collection will not be adequate. Breeding and batching of seed, therefore, should be given the highest priority. Prawn and fish hatcheries should be planned and established at suitable centres. Though capture of berried prawns and the subsequent release of eggs under controlled conditions have been nearly perfected, rearing prawn to the fry stage has not been quite successful in the country. Research on these aspects should be intensified. Equally important is the feed, especially in high density commercial culture. Suitable feeds which are economical to use and which give best conversions have to be evolved. Attempts must also be made to produce natural feed in the culture environment. Commercial culture activities for crabs, lobsters, clams, edible oysters, sea weeds, and so on are also required to be intensified.

DEVELOPING CULTURE FISHERIES FOR DEVELOPMENT AND MANPOWER REQUIREMENTS

The requirement of trained manpower to meet the needs of increased production in coastal aquaculture and mariculture would be in research and development, survey and designs of farm extension, training and commercial farming operations. This requirement can be grouped under five main categories.

(1) Those for research as research scientists (biologists, calturists, hatcherists, research assistants and so on.)
(2) Those for education and training as educationists and trainers (professors, readers, lecturers, teachers, demonstrators, and so on), qualified with graduate or post-graduate or doctorate degrees in aquaculture.
(3) Those for extension activities as extension workers.
(4) Those for commercial farming operations as managers of farms and hatcheries, as culturists, hatcherists, technical assistants, and so on.
(5) Those for commercial farming operations as skilled operators, field assistants, seed collection and production assistants and so on in farms and hatcheries.

COASTAL AQUACULTURE AND MARICULTURE RESEARCH AND DEVELOPMENT

Research activities are concentrated presently at a few centres only namely, Kakadwip, Mandapam, Tuticorin, Cochin, Mangalore, and Waltair and therefore require to be strengthened. More centres will have to be established to take up research work relating to biology, hydrography, culture technology, collection and transport of seed, induced spawning, techniques for rearing of larval stages, farming systems, artificial feeds, control of diseases and predaters, pollution etc. in respect of many species of prawns, lobsters, crabs, fin fishes, mussels, oysters, clams, cockles, seaweeds and so on. As a prerequisite for providing a strong research base, the research centres and institutions should establish demonstration farms close to the research centres. Hatchery techniques for large scale production of seed will have to be developed and hatchery centres established at selected centres. The research centres will also have to work out the economic feasibility of culturing the organisms for transfer of proven and viable technologies to prospective end users. Considering the scope for the above development activities in this field, it would be necessary to establish thirty-six additional research and development centres in the country.

Extension

The central research institutes as well as the maritime state governments have been conducting extension work relating to development of fin fish and shell fish culture. But this activity has been at a low level, and therefore, the extension activities require strengthening not only on the technical details but also on the economic aspects. It would be necesssary to have in each maritime district of a state an extension unit with adequate trained staff in acquiring the culture technology.

Training

The intake capacity of the institutes training personnels in aquaculture and mariculture will have to be increased in view of the anticipated demand for more personnel. Consequently the number of teaching personnel will also increase.

Commercial fish farming operations

Besides manpower and technical expertise, the main requirements of successful commercial farming operations could be progressively brought under culture and fish seed supply.

The area which could progressively be brought under culture in the next 10 years is estimated on the assumptions that the area available for culture is 2.6 million hectares, the area presently under culture is 0.05 million hectares, and that the annual increase in the cultured area is 3-4 per cent. The details, are given below and about 0.77 million hectares of brackishwater area could be brought under culture which amounts to an increase of 28 per cent. This area estimated to yield nearly 0.385 million tonnes in the next 10 years.

Year	Area remaining unutilized (million hectares)	Area under culture (million hectares)
1981	2.55	0.05
1982	2.45	0.15
1983	2.36	0.24
1984	2.27	0.33
1985	2.19	0.41
1986	2.11	0.57
1987	2.03	0.49
1988	1.96	0.64
1989	1.89	0.71
1990	1.83	0.77

The fish seed requirements are estimated on following assumptions : (1) Area under intensive and extensive culture at 50 per cent each ; (2) Stocking rate as 50,000 seed in the ratio of 7 : 3 for prawn : fish in intensive culture; (3) Stocking rate as 10,000 seed in the ration of 1 : 1 for prawn : fish in extensive culture ; and (4) Seed survival rate at 60 per cent.

Manpower for commercial farming

For intensive culture (in 50 per cent of the area of 0.77 million hectares which can be brought under acquaculture which is 0.385 million hectares) approximately 60,000.

For extensive culture (in 50 per cent of the area of 0.77 million hectares which can be brought under aquaculture which is 0.385 m. ha.) approximately 5,000.

For fish seed production and collection (seed requirement assumed as 84,000 million per year approximately 100,000.

Manpower for research and development (36 centres have been assumed, 9 for sea weed and pearl oyster culture, 9 for lobster and crab culture, 9 for prawn culture and 9 for cage/pen culture of sea fishes) approximately 5,000.

Manpower for extension work approximately 700.

Manpower for teaching aquaculture technology and systems approximately 200.

Thus the additional technical manpower requirements in the next ten years would amount to nearly 1,20,000.

MANPOWER REQUIREMENT IN MARINE FISHERIES RESOURCES UTILIZATION AND MARKETING

Current utilization and marketing of marine fish

Of the total current marine fish production of about 1.4 million tonnes in the country, about 70 per cent is marketed in fresh condition with or without ice, 19 per cent salted and sundried, 6 per cent processed mostly frozen and 5 per cent reduced to fish meal and manure. It is estimated that fish is mostly distributed around the production centres or the nearby interior markets and that only 40 per cent of the fresh fish requirement is met.

According to MPEDA registration, there are 321 cold storage plants, 268 freezing and 64 canning factories in the country with an installed capacity of 1176 tonnes for freezing and 246 tonnes per day for canning, mostly handling prawns for export. The installed capacity of cold storage is about 27,000 tonnes.

The problem of marketing of marine fish in India is rather complicated in view of the nature of fisheries, widely dispersed landings, and varied types of markets. Gujarat produces large quantities of fish but on account of the local food habits, most of the catches has to be marketed in other states. Orissa is an important production centre, but for economic reasons, the bulk of the catches have to be marketed in Calcutta. Though Bombay is a large producing and consuming centre and handles a considerable volume of fish coming into the city from the neighbouring states, the demand is greater than the supplies. West Bengal and the adjoining states do not produce adequate quantity of fish but the demand in these states is so high that the present supplies from the neighbouring states are not enough to meet the demand. Landings of fish in Kerala and Karnataka are large and of the large surplus after meeting the local consumption, a small quantity alone is transported to the neighbouring states while the rest are salted and dried, and sometimes turned into manure. Tamil Nadu and Andhra Pradesh are good marine fish producing states, but the production is not enough to meet the demand within the state. Bulk of interstate traffic in fish packed in ice is carried presently by rail or truck and it is the experience of the industry that considerable quantity is spoilt. Besides, in many places, fish markets are controlled by middlemen and their hold is so great on the producers that ultimately the producers and the consumers are the worst sufferers. They do perform certain functions, but their activities are not conducive to the development of healthy marketing practices.

Export of marine products from India to 88 countries in the world during 1979, accounted for nearly 92,000 tonnes valued at about Rs. 2,620 million. But this performance was based on the export of prawns mostly. Of the above quantity exported, export of fish and fish products in 1979, formed nearly 28,000 tonnes only, valued at about Rs. 135 million.

Scope for better utilization and marketing of marine fish

A production of about 2.635 million tonnes (1.4 million tonnes current production and 1.235 million tonnes additional production through capture and culture fisheries) is estimated in the next ten years as indicated earlier and on the advantageous utilization of this entire catch depends the successful development of the capture and culture fisheries. The composition of marine fish catch estimated for the next ten years will consist mainly of about 50 per cent quality fish, 30 per cent miscellaneous small fish and 20 per cent shell fish. There is vast scope for the development of domestic market for quality fish in fresh and frozen form and miscellaneous small fish as dried fish, frozen minced meat, F.P.C. and fish meal.

Dried fish falls within the economic reach of the vast masses of population and this will remain in vogue for a long time to come due to taste and difficulties in providing certain facilities. But the method of processing has to be improved, to command foreign markets besides satisfying the needs in the domestic market. In other developed countries, domestic fish marketing is conducted at central places through co-operative agencies or separate fish marketing organizations. Such agencies provide the necessary infrastructure required for handling, storage, transport and marketing of fish. In a country like India, there is a greater need for having centralized fish marketing systems to develop the domestic market through a cold chain scheme which links major production centres and interior marketing points. Such agencies in different regions will also be able to pay attention for improvement in the utilization of fish and for a significant reduction of waste, by the application of sound and recognised practices of hygeine and sanitation at all stages of handling, storage, transport, distribution and marketing—both from, for marketing fresh and for further processing in dried and frozen state and enforce quality control measure and rigorous inspection systems. Though this development requires a vast dynamic organization for each region, it would provide a training ground for export oriented industries and also a sufficient cushion to the industry, whenever there is setback in the export market.

The prawn export industry, has weak domestic base as there is not much of a developed internal market to fall back upon in case of any unfavourable trade trends. Dependence on the supply of raw material from one source for which there is limited scope of utilization and markets would have adverse effect on the processing industry, if there are fluctuating instabilities in the prawn fishing in the international market. Considerable development effort, therefore, is necessary not only to establish diversified markets and diversified products of prawns but also to improve the performance of the country's exports of fish and fish products.

As per estimates, the world demand for fish is expected to increase to nearly 70 million tonnes in the next five years. In USA, the consumption of fish and fish products averages to about 400,000 tonnes per year, as fillets, steaks, fish sticks, minced meat, etc. Imports of these items account for about 314,000 tonnes annually, chiefly from Canada, Norway, Denmark, Iceland and Japan. UK imports about 55,000 tonnes of fish annually from Norway, Iceland and Denmark and this is not enough to meet the demand. The imports into Canada of nearly 25,000 tonnes of fish per year from Netherlands and Japan do not meet their domestic demand. Likewise, imports of fish into Sweden, France, West Germany and Italy amounting to about 180,000 tonnes per year is not enough to meet the local demand. Japan imports about 250,000 tonnes of fish per year and India's contribution was only 237 tonnes both as frozen fish and dried fish in 1979. The annual demand for fish in Middle East countries is estimated as 50,000 tonnes currently, while India's export to these countries as frozen fish amonnted to about 2,500 tonnes only in 1979. South East Asian countries have also a vast market potential for fish but India's exports to these countries were only 200 tonnes as fresh and frozen fish in 1979. This situation is due to the fact that as the established world trade patterns and consumer preferences are changing in the context of the expanded territorial claims by coastal nations and, as the established producers search for additional supplies, the structure of the world market for fish in both composition and source is undergoing considerable change. India can take advantage of this situation through joint ventures with foreign collaboration in respect of processing techniques as well as the processing machinery for handling the Indian fish to suit the international markets, in as much as the whole concept of utilization of fish for export markets is undergoing a revolutionary change in the world.

The Sixth Five Year Plan provides for an export target of 150,000 tonnes valued at Rs. 330 crores, taking all the above factors into consideration and in view of the fact that the envisaged increase in the marine fish, production would come from the deep sea fishing operations, covering more fish varieties.

Present level of activity in the marine fish utilization and marketing

Considerable technological researches and investigations are being carried out at Central Institute of Fisheries Technology and Central Food Technological Research Institute, Fisheries College of the Agriculture University at Mangalore and some of the other universities in the country and the R & D wings of the industrial houses engaged in the fishery industry on the fundamental aspects of biochemistry and microbiology, on fish preservation, handling, storage and distribution, methods for processing different types of fishery products and by-products, standardization of quality of different processed fishery products, designing equipment and machinery for optimum utilization of fish catch and so on.

The education and training activity in marine resources utilization is presently carried out at the CIFT, Cochin, IFP, Cochin, Fisheries College Mangalore, CIFE, Bombay, Cochin University, CFTRI, Mysore and some other universities. The packaging and marketing aspects are looked after by the Indian Institute of Packaging, Indian Institute of Foreign Trade and a few private organizations. The Sixth Five Year Plan propose to establish a new centre for fish handling and processing with an intake capacity of 40 per year.

The commercial activity in marine resources utilization is mostly in the private sector, though a few are also engaged in this field. The resources handled are prawns, lobsters and cuttle fish which are all directed for export. A few fisheries corporations have also undertaken domestic marketing of fresh and processed fish and fish products within the state. The commercial activity also includes manufacture of refrigeration and freezing, canning and fish meal machinery, and accessories to a limited extent.

Government of India policy towards development of marine fish utilization and marketing

The main objectives of the policy of the Government of India in so far as they relate to the utilization of fish and marketing are : (1) enhance the quality of fish by providing infrastructure; (2) introduce better processing methods, including diversified processing ; (3) improve fish markets and distribution system ; (4) undertake market surveys on a countrywise basis so as to obtain an insight into market behaviour ; (5) establish an agency for continuous monitoring of market intelligence ; (6) introduce regulated fish marketing (7) develop a cold chain for linking up production centres with marketing centres ; and (8) rationalize exports by exporting high value varieties, items having little or no domestic demand, items on which production for domestic marketing would not be economical and improving quality packing and adopting market strategy.

Requirement for the development of marine fish utilization and marketing

Fish technology and marketing management have not been adequately developed and practised in the country. This is evident from the fact that the entire marine fish catch of the country is not fully and profitably utilized. In keeping with the objectives of the Government of India policy, the main fields in the marine fish utilization and marketing requiring development are : fishery technological research, infrastructure improvement, improvement of fish handling practices, introduction of better processing methods including diversified processing, improving market surveys and market intelligence, introduction of regulated fish marketing, establishment of cold chain and extension and training.

DIFFERENT FIELDS IN THE MARINE FISH UTILIZATION AND MARKETING SECTOR FOR DEVELOPMENT AND ESTIMATED MAN-POWER REQUIREMENT IN NEXT TEN YEARS

Fishery technological research

This activity is presently being carried out at the CIFT,

Cochin, under the ICAR, College of Fisheries, Mangalore, under the Agricultural University, Karnataka, CIFE, Bombay under the ICAR, CFTRI, Mysore, under the CSIR, IFP, Cochin, Cochin University and some other universities in the country. These institutions with a few sub-centres in the country are concentrating research activities on processing, packaging, bio-chemistry and microbiology of fishes, development of equipment and machinery for fish freezing and canning, fish handling, fish storage and operation of pilot plants, quality standards of production, avoiding wastages and improving quality of processed products. These activities also include transportation of fish over long distances, evolving effective methods of utilization of processing factory wastes and low value fishes, improvements of the methods of preparation and utilisation of different types of fish bye-products like fish oil, shark fins, fish maws and so on, efficient methods of preservation and processing fish by freezing, canning, dehydration, accelerated freeze drying, curing and smoking, assessment of the nature and extent of quality losses in fish products under different conditions of storage, methods for production of diverse products from fish, preparation of ready-to-serve convenient foods, methods for economising production, etc. other investigations are towards assessment of nutritive value and chemical composition of different types of fish, nature and extent of spoilage in fish and processed fish products under different conditions of preservation and storage, the nature and extent of postmortem changes in quality brought about by them, isolation of useful constituents of fish, the nature and extent of micro-organisms introduced into fish due to terrestrial contamination, changes brought about in quality of fish and fish products by the action of these micro-organisms, the extent of preservation of bacterial growth, methods of detection and enumeration of different types of bacteria encountered in fish and fish products, suitable culture media for specific types of organisms, micro-biological methods of determination of vitamins in fish and fish products, general guidelines on the preservation of fish on shore, on fishing vessels and in processing plants, maintenance of good sanitation in processing establishments, working out standards of quality for different types of processed fish products, etc.

But many priority areas for research and investigations, still remain to be carried out. Some of them are highlighted below :

(1) Study of the progressive bio-chemical and bacteriological changes occurring in different fishes when held in cold storage. to evolve objective tests for quality freshness of fish in question.

(2) Study of the chemical composition of different fish species to assess the amenability to different handling and processing techniques.

(3) Basic studies of the fibriller proteins of different fishes.

(4) Study of fish lipids in relation to the development of rancidity in processed and stored fish products.

(5) Study of the water soluble sarcoplasmic proteins of fish muscles.

(6) Study on using ionising radiation on commercial scale for preserving fish from spoilage.

(7) Study on improved methods of producing standard fish meal, fish oil, FPC, and so on.

(8) Study on the peeling of shrimps with the use of enzyme.

(9) Study on the frequent occurrence of vibrio parahaemolyticus in frozen fish.

(10) Use of liquid carbon-dioxide, nitrogen and air for freezing of fish.

(11) Study on overcoming oxidation and rancidity in frozen sardines and mackerels during long storage.

(12) Freezing of fish fillets and dressed fish.

(13) Use of chilled sea water and ascorbic acid for preservation of black spots on frozen prawns.

(14) Processing of clams, mussels and oysters as canned and frozen products.

(15) Use of aluminium cans in the canning industry.

(16) Use of alternative preservatives and synthetic casing for preparation of fish sausages.

(17) Production of low cost fish products of proven acceptability.
(18) Improvement in fish flour production.
(19) Utilisation of waste from fish processing industry.
(20) Design and development of machinery for handling and processing fish.

It is necessary that the research activities presently being carried out in different institutions are strengthened and suitably co-ordinated to avoid overlapping. It is also necessary that more field research centres at important fish landing and processing bases are organized to intensify the activities in applied research towards priority areas.

Infrastructure improvement

This aspect of development would cover development of fish landing centres, industrial estates for development of fish based industries, development of fish processing complexes, provision of ice plants, at fishing harbours, provision of covered fish landing platforms and provision of pre-processing sheds.

Development of fish landing centres

Infrastructure development and adopting a package of development activities with a view to improve the infrastructure for fish handling facilities in fishing villages are very essential for fuller utilization of all the marine fish catch landed at each fishing centre for domestic and export markets. The infrastructure will include provision of approach roads, water supply, ice plants, service stations, fish curing yards, insulated trailers, facilities for fish auction and storage, and so on. At least 40 fishing landing centres in each maritime state and 10 in each Union Territory with the above package approach will have to be developed.

Area development for fish based industries

It is necessary that separate areas are earmarked for fish based industries in the area development plans of corporations, municipalities, and local bodies. Wherever fishing harbours are established or proposed to be established, the areas immediately adjoining such fishing harbours should be allocated or at other convenient locations for fish-based industries. Keeping in view of the scope for further development of fish-based industries, additional areas should also be acquired and developed by providing adequate roads, supply of water, electricity and HSD, provision of auction halls, pre-processing sheds, processing factories, drains and repair yards, arrangements for disposal of factory effluents and so on. Besides the organization on pre-involvement and pre-investment survey of fishing harbours, it is necessary that a separate division in each maritime state is established to plan the requirements in this respect.

Development of fish processing complexes

These complexes in each state should be considered in public sector/co-operatives for assisting small entrepreneurs. The complexes may consist of large processing halls, ice plants, cold storages, frozen storages, water storages, waste disposal, processing machinery, standby generators, etc. to meet the requirement of small processors. Here individual processors may be allowed to make use of these facilities on a rental system. Such composite fish processing complexes are very popular in many developed countries. Each complex would require an independent agency to manage, run and maintain the complex on commercial lines.

Provision of ice plants at fishing harbours

In most harbours no provision for adequate supply of ice and storage exists. At fishing harbours, large ice plants of capacity ranging from 50-500 tonnes are necessary. They should preferably be located at the wharfs with automatic ice dispensing arrangements. This activity at the planning level may be entrusted to the existing organisation for the pre-investment survey of fishing harbours and at the construction stage by the Fisheries Terminal Organisation referred earlier.

Provision of covered fish landing platforms

The fishing harbours will mainly cater to the large fishing vessels and mechanized boats. However, bulk of the marine fish landing is in fishing villages which do not have proper facilities. Marine Products Exports Development Authority (MPEDA) has been assisting the state governments in providing small fish landing platforms. The minimum requirement of such platforms in the next ten years will be about 1000.

Improving fish markets

Fish marketing requires a great deal of development and improvement as regards quality, transportation and distribution. Supplies are not only uneven in the different parts of the year but there are also areas of glut side by side with large parts of the country with meagre supplies. Loss through spoilage is often heavy. This development field requires technical and economic skills for proper marketing systems covering transport, packaging, preservation, processing and production patterns to suit consumer tastes, organizing co-operatives or other marketing agencies.

There is not one organized fish market maintained in a hygienic state. It is, therefore, necessary to organize improved large fish markets and retail fish markets at all important places. The large fish markets should have facilities like ice plants, chilled fish storage and overhead fresh water tanks for continuous chlorinated water supply and facilities for disposal of waste. The retail fish markets will have, besides the above facilities on a small scale, display and fly proof stalls as well as insulated cabinets. It will also be necessary to improve the system of door to door sale of fish by providing powered three wheelers with insulated chests. In the next ten years, about 200 large markets and 1000 retail markets would have to be installed.

Introduction of regulated fish marketing

At present there is no national level fish marketing organisation. It is desirable to start a system of regulated fish marketing for which authorized areas should be notified and fish dealers registered. While such regulated fish marketing has the advantage of controlling malpractices, collection of production and price statistics, recovery of loans, and so on, the physical manageability of introducing regulated marketing has to be carefully studied in each state.

Provision of pre-processing sheds

Sanitation at peeling sheds is far from satisfactory. The sanitary requirement of these sheds should be similar to the processing halls. At least 1000 such sheds will have to be provided at important fish landing centres.

Improvement in fish handling practices

The need for marine fisheries extension is of importance in this field. Marine Products Exports Development Authority (MPEDA) may undertake this activity with a separate cell to co-ordinate extension work of at least 20 fields extension units to be established during the next ten years for bringing out publicity literature, films, etc. This field of activity would cover in-process quality control and self inspection, popularization of ice, insulated boxes, insulated and refrigerated rail and road vans, and so on.

INTRODUCTION OF BETTER PROCESSING METHODS INCLUDING DIVERSIFIED PROCESSING

The development of fish landing centres through adoption of a package programmes, described earlier, has a provision for establishment of yards for hygienic preparation of cured fish. These yards would work under the supervision of extension workers.

With the provision of area development for fish-based industries and development of fish processing complexes, capacities would be created to meet the future development mainly for fillet freezing, blast freezing, freeze drying, Carbon-dioxide, nitrogen freezing, and so on.

With the possibility of introducing aluminium as a packaging material for canned fish products, it would be possible to establish eight large canning units, two medium units and restructuring the twenty existing canning plants.

Establishments of "cold chain"

Preference for different varieties of fish varies from region to region. The demand and supplies also vary according to seasons. It is, therefore, essential that a system of procurement, transportation and distribution is effected taking into account the varying supply and demand. When regular supplies are available, fish could be marketed in a chilled condition. Any surplus could go for freezing and frozen products could be stored for release during the lean season. This would also help in stabilizing fish prices. It will ensure high quality for fish. However, this would require a chain of cold storages and refrigerated transport facilities. A cold chain scheme during the next ten years could be established covering Cochin, Mangalore, Visakhapatnam and Veraval as production centres, and Calcutta, Delhi, Bangalore, Bombay and Hyderabad as marketing centres.

Education and training

The existing facilities in the country for education and training personnel in marine fish utilization and marketing have been indicated. However, in the context of further development in the next 10 years, facilities for education and training at the existing institutes especially at the College of Fisheries, Mangalore, will have to be strengthened and the intake capacity increased to meet the demand for additional requirement of personnel. If this is not feasible, the establishment of a separate fish processing training institute has to be considered to train personnel connected not only with microbiological and analytical work relating to quality control and inspection, fish processing technology, extension work in fish handling, sanitation hygiene, processing and quality control, and product development, but also in the erection, maintenance, and repairs of plants and machinery.

Indigenous manufacture of processing equipment and machinery

At present, machinery for meat picking, shrimp grading, fish filleting, skinning, FPC manufacture, dehydration, aluminium can making and so on, are not fabricated in the country. It would, therefore, be necessary to encourage the industrial sector to take up this activity after assessing the specifications and requirement. A 50 per cent subsidy in the initial stage would enable the marine fish utilization industry to grow at a faster pace.

Based on these analysis, the requirement of additional personnel in the marine fish utilization and marketing sector would be around 16,000.

SUMMARY

The importance of manpower planning and assessment of the future additional requirement of manpower in the marine fisheries development in the country has been highlighted in this chapter. Information on the present level of activity in the three main fields of marine fisheries sector, namely, capture fisheries, culture fisheries and utilization of marine fish and marketing as well as the scope for their future and further development has been presented. Existing technical manpower in these fields of activity comprising mainly research, education and training, development and commercial aspects has been approximately assessed as over 6 lakh personnel. The additional technical manpower required in the next ten years has been estimated as about 182,000. The breakup figures of the additional manpower in different categories is summarised below :

A. Capture fisheries

(1) Marine Fisheries	320
(2) Marine Fisheries Technological Research Scientists	185
(3) Naval Architects	5
(4) Boat Building Foremen	360
(5) Statisticians and Economists	10
(6) Engineers (Marine, Harbour, Civil, Mechanical, Electric, Electronic, Hydraulic, Refrigeration and Production Engineers)	484
(7) Junior level Scientists (Gear Technicians, Technical Assistants, Supervisors)	200
(8) Junior level Engineers	80

(9) Skippers	460
(10) Engineers (Fish Vessel)	460
(11) Engine Drivers (Fishing Vessel)	850
(12) Fishing Second Hands	850
(13) Wireless Operators	446
(14) Draftsmen	35
(15) Deckhands, Oilmen, etc.	6269
(16) Moulders for FRP/Ferrecement Crafts	300
(17) Fleet Managers	70
(18) Trained Fishermen in outboard drives and driversified fishing	14,000
(19) Trained Fishermen in Mechanized Boat Fishing	25,00
(20) Technical staff for educational and training institutions	204
Total	54,540

B. Culture fisheries

(1) Fish Farm Managers	4,235
(2) Fishery Biologists	72
(3) Fish Culturists	72
(4) Hatcherists	4,672
(5) Lecturers	50
(6) Teachers	100
(7) Extension Workers	700
(8) Fish Farm Engineers	72
(9) Research Assistants & Technical Assistants	11,488
(10) Field Assistants	8,830
(11) Skilled Operators	80,950
(12) Replacement on account of retirement, resignation etc. (approx)	159
Total	1,12,400

C. Utilization of marine fish and marketing

(1) Technological Research Scientists	2,410
(2) Development Officers and Assistant Development Officer	650
(3) Technical staff for management for processing complexes	650
(4) Extension staff	2,032
(5) Processing Technologists	1,200
(6) Fish Marketing staff	1,650
(7) Education and Training staff	100
(8) Technical staff for quality control inspection	500
(9) Processing and Procurement supervisors	1,000
(10) Skilled operators	5,000
Total	15,192
Grand total (A+B+C)	181,142
or	182,000

An analysis of the total additional requirement of nearly 182,000 personnel in the three fields of marine fisheries sector during the next ten years, reveals that about 12 per cent would be graduates and post-graduates for the high level cadre, 15 per cent matriculates and post-matriculates for the junior level cadre and 73 per cent at the non-matriculate (fishermen) level as skilled operators. In each field of marine fisheries sector, however, the requirement would be as indicated below:

Field of activities	Additional requirement of personnel	Graduates & post-graduates	Matriculates & post-matriculates	Non-matriculates (fishermen)
Capture fisheries	54,550	4%	13%	83%
Culture fisheries	1,12,400	10%	18%	72%
Marine fish utilization & marketing	15,192	60%	5%	35%
Total		182,142 or	182,000	

The additional manpower, if provided, will enable to increase in landing from the deep and distant water area of the economic zone for exploitation and to bring nearly 0.77 hectares of additional brackishwater area under coastal aquaculture. This would raise the level of annual marine fish production of the country from the present level of 1.4 million tonnes to about 2.635 million tonnes. A fuller utilization pattern of the entire production of marine fish catch would also become possible for both export and domestic market.

REFERENCES

Alikunhi, K.H., Shrimp farming in India, Present status and future prospects, *Proceedings of the First National Symposium on Shrimp Farming*, Printed and published by the MPEDA, Cochin, 1980.

Anon, Brackishwater Fisheries Development in Tamil Nadu, Working Paper—unpublished, 1929.

Bapat S.V. & Kurian, A., Present status of small scale fisheries and Coastal aquaculture—Paper presented at the seminar at Madras on the role of Small Scale Fisheries and Coastal Aquaculture in rural development, organised by CMFRI, Cochin.

Chidambaram, K., Suitable Deep Sea Fishing Vessels for India, Report of the Fisheries Technical Mission to the Government of India, 1966.

Chidambaram K. Strategy for commercial shrimping—*Proceedings of the First National Symposium on Shrimp Farming*, Printed and published by MPEDA, Cochin, 1980.

Central Marine Fishery Research Institute (CMFRI), Cochin (ICFR)—1978, Special publications No. 1 *Pearl culture training*, special publication No. 2 *Mariculture Research and Development*, 1978.

CFTRI, *Proceedings of symposium*, Fish Processing Industry in India, organised by the association of food scientists and technologists (India) and CFTRI, Mysore.

Dutta N.P. Vice Admiral, Report of the sub-committee for development of fishing trawlers for the development of fishing council for shipbuilding, ship repairs and ancillaries, 1978.

Dwivedi S.N., Prospects and prospectives in Prawn Culture, *Proceedings of the First National symposium on shrimp farming*, Printed and published by MPEDA, Cochin, 1980.

Davis Foas C., *Manpower Planning*; *Managing Economic Development in Africa*, Cambridge, Mass., USA, M.I.T. Press, 1963.

Gerhardsen, G.M., Fisheries Education and Training in growth and development progromme, IPFC Proceedings, Section III, *Symposium on Fisheries Education and Training at Honolulu in 1966*—Published by IPFC Secretariat, Bangkok, 1968.

George, P.C. *et al*, Fishery Resources of the Indian Economic Zone. Souvenir issued on the oecasion of the Silver Jubiee celebrations of the IFP, Cochin, 1977.

FAO, Year Book of Fisnery Statistics, 1978.

Government of India, Draft Fourth, Fifth and Sixth Five Year Plans, Planning Commission.

Government of India, Report of the National Commission on Agriculture, Part VIII, Fisheries, Ministry of Agriculture and Irrigation, New Delhi, 1976.

Government of India, Report of the Committee on Fisheries Education, Printed by the Manager, Govt. of India Press, Ministry of Food and Agriculture (Department of Agriculture), Faridabad, 1960.

Government of India, Report of the working group on Fisheries for formulation of Sixth Five Year Plan, Ministry of Agriculture, 1978.

Government of India, Draft Five Year Plan, 1978—1983, Planning Commission.

Hamlisch, R., General consideration in Manpower Planning and their application in the construction of Fisheries Development Programmes, IPFC proceedings section III, *Symposium on Fisheries Education and Training at Honolulu in 1966*—Published by IPFC Secretariat, Bangkok, 1968.

Indian Institute of Foreign Trade (IIFT), Survey of India's Export Potential of Marine Products, Report of the US agency for International Development, for Govt. of India Ministry of Foreign Trade.

Irani, K.K. Time ripe for profitable fishing ventures, *Symposium on the need for a techno-economic survey of the deep sea fishing, resources*, published by AFC, Bombay.

Jhingran, V.G. and Gopalakrishnan, V., Prospects for development of Brackishwater fish and shrimp culture in India, *Journal of Fisheries Research Board of Canada*, Vol. 30, No. 12, PT 2, 2341—2343, 1973.

Jhingran, V.G., Some aspects of Brackishwater aquaculture in India, *Bulletin of the Department of Marine Sciences*, University of Cochin. Vol. VIII, I, pages 25—29, 1975.

Jhingran, V.G *et al.*, Methodology for survey of Brackishwater areas in India for coastal aquaculture, Indo-Pacific Fisheries Council, FAO-72/1, 1970.

Koh. Yoon, Ho, Korea: A case study in promotion development through Fishermen's Training, Paper presented at the Technical Conference on Fishery Management and Development, Vancouver, J. Fish, Res. Bd. Can., 9 p. 1973.

Lawson, R.M., Fisheries Development and Planning in the Indo-pacific Region, it's objectives and constraints—*procedings of IPFC*, 16th session, Jakarta, Indonesia, Section III, IPFC, Secretariat, FAO, Bangkok, 1974.

Mammen, T.A., Key note address delivered at the Seminar at Madras on the present status of the Small Scale Fisheries and coastal Aquaculture, organised by the CMFRI, Cochin, 1978.

MPEDA, *Statistics of Marine Products Exports*, Printed and published by the MPEDA, Cochin, 1979.

National, Committee on Science and Technology, Marine Resources, NSST Sectoral Report, Printed by the Manager, Government of India Press, Simla.

Poliakov, M.P., Exploratory Trawling the Bay of Bengal, Report to the Govt. of India, No. 1573, FAO, Rome, 1962.

Rowat, R, FAO Report to the Federal and Regional Government of Nigeria on the development of education and training in the field of Agriculture and related subjects, 1964.

Shetty, H.P.C., Evaluation of present technical training system in Fisheries and suggestions for modernisation, Paper presented at the seminar on the role of small fisheries and coastal aquaculture in integrated rural development at Madras, organised by the CMFRI, Cochin, 1978.

Swaminathan, M.S., Shrimp farming—A new dimension to the scientific utilisation of our aquatic wealth, *Proceedings of the First National Symposium on Shrimp Farming*, Printed and published by the MPEDA, Cochin, 1980.

Silas, E.G., Status of prawn culture in India and strategy for its future development, *Proceedings of the First National Symposium on shrimp farming*, Printed and published by MPEDA, Cochin, 1980.

Varghese, P.U., Potential of Brackishwater Prawn Culture in India, *Proceedings of the First National Symposium as shrimp farming*, Printed and published by MPEDA, Cochin, 1980.

White Fish Authority, Study of Fishing Vessel Building Requirements for Development of Heavy Industry, India—Project Report No. 436, 1980.

Exploratory Fisheries Project, Bombay, Indo-Polish Industrial Fisheries Survey along the North West Coast of India—Report No. 3, 1977.

Kutty, M.N., Technical and managerial manpower requirement for integrated coastal aquaculture and their training needs, paper presened at the seminar on the role of small scale fisheries and coastal aquaculture in integrated and rural development at Madras. organised by the CMFRI, Cochin, 1978.

10

EVOLUTION OF CHARTERING POLICY AND ITS IMPLEMENTATION

U.K. SRIVASTAVA
AND
RAJESHWARI MEHTA

INTRODUCTION

INDIA had been keen to enter deep sea fishing from the turn of the present century. However, the history of the programmes is rather dismal. At policy making level, the importance of deep sea was realized only twenty years ago. Foreign collaboration was accepted for priority industries of which deep sea fishing was one.

It has been estimated that the Exclusive Economic Zone (EEZ) with an area of about 2 million sq. km. can support an annual yield of about 4.5 million tonnes of fish. The present catch of about 1.5 million tonnes is only one-third of this potential. Even this quantity comes mainly from shallow coastal waters extending to about 70 metres depth. The present contribution of deeper waters is hardly one per cent of the total catch. It is estimated that about 99 per cent of the total marine catch is confined to 15 to 20 per cent of our EEZ. Much of the future additional landings will come from offshore and deep sea areas. if these areas are properly developed. Major constraints in the development of deep sea fishing are as follows :

1. Lack of reliable data on deep sea fishery resources and knowledge regarding the types of vessels and gears suitable for exploitation of these resources.
2. Lack of adequate infrastructure for harvest and post-

harvest technology.

3. Requirement of a massive capital investment with a high degree of risk.
4. Non availability of trained personnel.
5. Rising cost of fishing operations.
6. Low consumer preference for many varieties of deep sea fish.
7. Government policy is also one of the major constraints. Too many restrictions on import of fishing vessels prevent the entrepreneurs from entering deep sea fishing.
8. Lack of incentives and encouragement to fishermen as well as lack of proper marketing facilities are prime causes for the delay in development of deep sea fishing.
9. Deep sea fishing in India is totally export oriented. High value fish go for export but there is no remunerative domestic market developed for low value varieties.

Deep sea fishing is a highly capital intensive industry. Apart from actual fishing boats, fishing gears and other equipments, extensive shore based support facilities are required which also call for substantial capital investment. It also requires constant government support at appropriate stages. Deep sea fishing activity requires efficient management skills with a strong organization to take decision for a quick turnround of fishing vessels at ports, ensure immediate repairs, proper handling, and marketing the fish.

The earlier attempts to exploit deep sea resources were to introduce steam trawlers which were unsuccessful as the requirements of the craft and gears for deep sea fishing were not properly known. To overcome the constraints in exploiting the deep sea resources, the government introduced a new policy in June 1977 of chartering of vessels from foreign countries to operate in Indian waters.

ROLE OF CHARTER

The economic viability of fishing operations beyond present fishing areas and new untapped resources is not known. The industry was by and large hesitant to make large capital investment for deep sea fishing operations because the returns were not known. Therefore, the government permitted charter of foreign vessels keeping in mind the following objectives :

1. To establish abundance and distribution of commercially important fish resources in unexplored and under-explored areas of the deep sea.
2. To assess craft and gears suited for the operations.
3. Transfer of technology, training of required manpower for manning the vessels, processing, marketing, and management.
4. To enlarge deep sea fishing fleet on ownership basis.
5. To increase export of marine products.
6. To develop the marketing of those new species in domestic markets.

Adequate provisions have been made in the charter terms and conditions to achieve these objectives and to safeguard the national interest. Priority of charter is given to public sector undertakings, fishermen co-operatives, small and medium scale entrepreneurs, and large industrial houses.

Major advantages of the chartering policy are as follows :

(a) A chartered fleet, if performing well, can be assembled within a short period which permits the government to add in the current fishing fleet without waiting to build new vessels which takes many years.

(b) These are time-bound arrangements and can easily be cancelled at short notice if performance does not meet the expectations.

(c) In the initial experimental period no eventual investment is done, which is a real advantage in a capital shy country.

CHARTER POLICY

The terms and conditions for charter were finalized for the first time in September 1977. The conditions are listed below :

1. The Indian companies were to submit quarterly returns of fish landings.
2. The foreign company was to arrange training to the nominees of charterer or of the Central Government.
3. Area of operation was beyond the area of operation of small mechanized and non-mechanized boats.
4. Inspection of the equipment and machinery by the Government at times
5. Restriction on the use of wireless equipment, when at shore.
6. Restriction on research, that is, data collection not to be undertaken by the vessel.
7. Clearance under the Indian Merchant Shipping Act was also applicable to them.
8. No payment of technical or royalties or marketing commission was to be made to the foreign company.
9. Export of marine products should be made from Indian ports only.

It should be noted that there was no obligation on the Indian company for the acquisition of vessel, there was no condition on employment of Indian crew, there was no licence fee and no bank guarantee. Many deficiencies were left in the first policy which necessitated some modifications. As a result, the conditions were reviewed and certain improvements were made in the basic policy with effect from 1978 which were again reviewed and modified in January 1981. The terms and conditions of the latest charter policy are listed in Annexure-I. The salient features of the same are as follows :

(a) The basic objective of chartering defined as to establish the abundance and distribution of fish resources, to assess suitable craft and gears for economic operations, transfer of technology and to enlarge the deep sea fishing fleet on ownership basis.

(b) Priority of charter applications to go to public sector undertakings, fishermen co-operatives, small and medium scale entrepreneurs, and large industrial houses in that order of preference.

(c) Requirement of paid-up share capital of the charterer company fixed at Rs. 5 lakh.

(d) The initial charter agreement for 3 years, renewable by 2 years (total not exceeding 5 years).

(e) The maximum number of vessels allowed for charter to one applicant for one type of fishing limited to five. If fishing operations required pairing then five vessels would mean five pairs, that is, ten vessels.

(f) The Indian company was under financial obligation to purchase a stipulated number of vessels not exceeding the number of chartered vessels. For this, a bank guarantee of Rs. 2 lakhs (Rs. 1 lakh in bank guarantee and Rs. 1 lakh cost deposit) per chartered vessel was stipulated. The bank guarantee was for purchasing the vessels at the end of the stipulated period. Since January 1984, the security amount has been raised to Rs. 3 lakhs per vessel, half of which is to be paid in the form of fixed deposit receipt and half in the form of bank **guarantee.**

(g) Area of operation to be beyond 12 nautical miles from the shore.

(h) In the charter agreement, insistence that foreign company will not take away more than fixed percentage of the catch value (that is, 85 per cent).

(i) Provision for putting Indian scientists on board the vessels provided.

(j) For the first time a licence fee of Rs. 10,000 per vessel per annum was fixed. There continued to be a large number of conditions revolving around security/safety.

(k) The foreign company is required to open a letter of credit in favour of the Indian company to avoid litigation in respect of payment to the Indian company.

In November 1981 the Maritime Zones of India (Regulation of Fishing by Foreign Vessels) Act was proclaimed. The Act and the rules have been provided for a number of charter conditions. Major improvements introduced through the rules are as follows :

Obligatory purchases

The charterer shall give an undertaking in the form of bank guarantee before the commencement of the charter that he shall purchase the vessels as per the conditions given in the rules. The first vessel must be acquired and put into operation within 18 months, subsequent vessels must be acquired in a phased manner and the last (fifth) vessel (in case of five vessels) at the end of 51 months from the date of charter obligation.

Recently a notification has been issued that the chartered vessels shall fish beyond territorial waters or in deep sea areas beyond the depth of 40 fathoms whichever is further to protect the small fishermen who fish near the coast areas. (Some of the companies have found their operations uneconomical as the continental shelf of the peninsular India is very narrow and beyond 50 fathoms there is a reef and slope. As a result many vessels have started going back after completing their present voyage.)

EXPERIENCE GAINED IN IMPLEMENTATION OF CHARTER POLICY

As per the latest data available, 110 chartered vessels have been operating in Indian waters of which 24 are chartered by the public sector undertakings and the rest by the private sector. The datails of the same are presented in Annexure-II. It is found that the majority of chartered vessels are from Taiwan. The main reason for selection of Taiwanese vessels has been their immediate availability for commissioning and they have been found operating efficiently in the Indian waters.

Due to compulsions of poor fishing in their own home waters, loose talk on enormous fishable resources in Indian seas and absence of forethought, many foreign firms offered to charter fishing vessels. Most of the charters were undertaken by prospective deep sea fishing companies as their own fishing or joint venture in fishing. To them the proposal was found very attractive as they were making quick money without investing large capital or risk. In fact the government realized the advantages to these companies but due to their interest of exploiting deep sea resources the government became liberal and provided them enough infrastructure as well as financial assistance. Many charters from the western countries found the fish catch far less than anticipated and the catches having very little marketability in their own country. No wonder they foreclosed the charters. As a result the number of chartered vessels operating in Indian waters came down to 18 (1982) from 69 (1979) (Table 10.1). On the other hand fishing companies from South East Asian countries found that with their proximity to the fishing grounds, cheaper and functional fishing vessels, less paid and hard working crew and a ready market for fish varieties from this region, they would make a profit even after paying 15-20 per cent of the catch value to the Indian parties. Which again added to the number of chartered fishing vessels.

The charter policy has been reviewed from time to time and necessary changes/modifications have been introduced on trial and error basis to meet operational requirements. The experience of the implementation of charter policy is, however, not much encouraging. The major points are described below.

Acquisition of vessels

The basic objective of implementing the scheme of obligatory purchas was to enlarge the fishing fleet of deep sea which could not be fulfilled as the charterer companies were not purchasing the vessel within a fixed time. Hence, the government has to resort to penal actions like suspension/cancellation of charter permits, invocation of bank guarantees, and so on. The actual problems were : (a) late submission of proposals by the charterers did not give time to the government to examine the proposals ; (b) defective proposals (like import of very old vessels) were cancelled ; and (c) some times terms of payments not being acceptable to the charterer.

Accordingly, the time schedule for charters to commence the acquisition of vessels was fixed to 4-6 months from the date of commencement of the charter operation. Moreover, the government has stipulated that the second hand vessels more than five years old should not be allowed for charter.

As a result of these modifications the charterers have come forward with viable proposals. The government has issued letters of intent/permission to six companies for import of 14 vessels.

TABLE 10.1 : **Performance of chartered vessels**

	1979	1980	1981	1982	1983
1. No. of chartered vessels at the end of the year	69	33	4	18	74
2. No. of Indian cos. engaged in charter operation	4	3	1	5	13
3. No. of voyages performed in the year	205	43	4	27	92
4. Average value of total catch per voyage made by chartered vessels (Rs.)	9,194	3,239	22,066	105,255	124,517
5. Indian company's share/ voyage (Rs.)	1,379	486	3,310	15,788	18,708
6. Average price of fish catch (US$/ton)	433	212	294	1,000	879
7. Area of operation	Bay of Bengal East Coast Arabian Sea West Coast)	Bay of Bengal (East Coast)	Bay of Bengal (East Coast)	East and West Coast beyond 12 nautical miles	All along the Indian coast beyond 12 nautical miles from shore except prohibited areas.
8. Average duration of voyage	50 days	37 days	42 days	59 days	71 days

in the coming years. The details of the companies who already made obligatory purchase under the above conditions are presented in Annexure-III. For encouraging obligatory purchases, financial assistance at a concessional rate of interest for trawlers is given to promote the construction of trawlers in the country. A subsidy of 33 per cent of the cost of trawler is granted to the shipbuilders. Relaxation has been made to the companies in raising debt equity ratio to the level of 6:1 in stages corresponding to the stage payment of loan and subsidy.

In addition to the above, the Shipping Development Fund Committee (SDFC) soft loans for acquisition of deep sea fishing vessels are also made available as described below.

1. Soft loan to the extent of 90 per cent of the trawler value @ 7½ per cent interest is available which should be repaid in 15 annual instalments with one year moratorium.
2. For indigenously constructed vessels the buyer can avail loan up to 95 per cent of the price @6.75 per cent interest. The conditions of repayment of the loans are same as above.
3. For the import of second hand trawlers, loans are available to the extent of 75 per cent of the determined cost. Repayment period is limited to two-thirds of the residual economic life of the vessel with no moratorium. However, these soft loans were not available to large business houses. So far, 9 companies have availed SDFC soft loans for acquisition of 20 indigenously constructed vessels. Subsidy to two Indian shipyards for construction of vessels has been recommended by government.

Predominance of Taiwanese vessels

Most of the chartered vessels operating in Indian waters are from Taiwan, with Taiwanese registration and crew. Most of those were bull pair trawlers. To diversify the source of technology government restricted grant of charter permission to Taiwanese vessels and specially bull trawlers. As a result, an increase in the number of specialized vessels such as gill netters, and squid jiggers has taken place.

Depth zone

As such the area of operation prescribed for chartered vessels was beyond the territorial waters. However, in the west coast, the continental shelf being gentle in slope, the shallow waters extended beyond the territorial water limit where the smaller mechanized boats operate. Hence, the conflict between these two started as both operate in the same area. To resolve this the Government amended a rule that chartered vessels should operate only beyond the territorial waters or in the high sea beyond 40 fathoms whichever is further. This will result into the exploitation of unexploited deep sea waters and simultaneously protect small fishermen also.

Mesh size of Nets

So far, the Government has not specified any rule for the size of nets to be used by chartered vessels. However, Government has advised charterers to use mesh size of nets of 80 mm at the end, in order to prevent damage to juvenile fish by use of smaller mesh size of nets. Steps are being taken to determine the specific mesh size for the use of chartered vessels.

Disposal of fish

A serious problem in relation to chartered vessels is of disposal of trash fish by charterers. At present, the charterers throw trash fish back into the sea and do not bring them to the port as they fetch very low prices. As per the estimates, in the first 50 days of the voyage, each trawler throws about 2 to 3 tonnes of trash fish per day. It has been an intractable problem for the Government to ensure compliances by the chartered vessels.

Assessment of catch

The Government has appointed personnel to assess the catch of chartered vessels. However, rural assessment of specieswise catch of chartered vessel has not been possible because the fish is stored under temperature of —40°C which the personnel cannot verify. Hence, the reports of these officers are generally based on the logbooks of crews. However, various alternatives are being considered by the Government to plug this loophole.

The question may well be asked as to what we have gained by charters. Some Indian companies would have earned through charters, but as the charter did not run the full term, the earnings would have been minimal. Many might find it an excuse for not purchasing their vessels. We have trained some Indian crew, but they might get absorbed on on-fishing activities if Indian vessels are not acquired in the meanwhile. However, it has not resulted into expected transfer of technology as the secrets of operations of foreign vessels were not made known to Indian operators. At the same time, Indian entrepreneurs also did not bother to look into technology as they were satisfied with what they got in terms of profit and were not interested in technology development.

Our major limitation was surveying our resources, it costs Government of India about Rs. 85 lakhs to charter one large vessel for one year to collect resource information. It costs not less than Rs. 20,000 per day on each of the large vessels used for research and survey. Yet these organizations could not utilize the unprecedented opportunity provided in collecting resource data and the related biological and oceanographic data by posting a scientist on board for which the charter had special provisions. Again the chartered vessels had been supplying catch statistics. This data has not been processed so far and in the absence of spot checking, the data if now processed, cannot be taken as correct, particularly since the bulk of the by-catch was discarded in the sea.

ANNEXURE-I

TERMS AND CONDITIONS FOR CHARTER OF FOREIGN FISHING VESSELS

(As on 1st November, 1982)

1. If the charterer is a company, the paid up share capital of the company shall not be less than Rs. 5 lakhs during the charter period.

2. The charterer shall have the requisite managerial personnel who possess the necessary experience in fishing.

3. Charter will be permitted for a period of three years, renewable on satisfactory performance for another two years. The maximum number of vessels that may be chartered by one applicant for one type of fishing will be limited to five. This restriction shall not be applicable to Public Sector Undertakings, State Fisheries Corporations and Fishermen Co-operatives. Wherever pair trawling is involved, each pair will be treated as one vessel for determining the maximum number of vessels (20 M length and above) before the end of the stipulated period of time as per the following schedule :

No. of vessels or pair of vessels permitted	Number of months from the beginning of the charter operation when obligatory purchase and actual fishing operations become due				
	First vessel or first pair of vessels	Second vessel or 2nd pair of vessels	Third vessel or 3rd pair of vessels	Fourth vessel or 4th pair of vessels	Fifth vessel or 5th pair of vessels
One	18				
Two	18	30			
Three	18	24	33		
Four	18	24	33	42	
Five	18	24	33	42	51

4. The charterer will have to give before the commencement an undertaking in the form of a bank guarantee, before commencement of charter an amount of Rs. 2 lakhs (one lakh in bank guarantee and one lakh in cash) per fishing vessel to the central government that he shall purchase the required number of vessels and put them in operation as per clause 3 above.

5. The charterer shall ensure that at least 20 per cent of the crew are Indian citizens and are posted as understudies to foreign skipper, the engineer and to the other operational crew and they shall be kept in readiness to embark on the chartered vessels at the time of inspection of the vessel by the authorised officers and shall remain on board throughout the charter period.

6. The area of operation of the chartered fishing vessels shall be beyond the territorial waters, namely, 12 nautical miles from the shore, unless otherwise specifically permitted for any specialised type of fishing and subject to any other area restrictions and further these vessels shall operate beyond the area of operation of mechanised boats and shall be as per the direction of government from time to time.

7. There will be no payment of technical fees or royalties, over and above the charter hire. The charterer shall not pay any marketing commission without the prior approval of the government.

8. The charterer will make irrevocable arrangements for purchasing the prescribed number of vessels either by import or from an Indian shipyard before the expiry of the stipulated period.

9. The charter party shall be entered into on the basis of the model charter party appended. They will, however, have freedom to make modifications to suit their requirements, but shall in all cases obtain prior approval of the government to the final charter party before commencement of fishing operations. The charter party shall provide for settlement of disputes between the parties by arbitration in India.

10. The chartered vessels shall carry all documents, like Director General of Shipping licence, attested copy of permission letter, crew permit and so on at the time of naval inspection of vessels. Three documents shall be retrieved at the time of

customs clearance and redelivered to the vessel when she makes reentry in the Indian waters. The vessel shall also carry up to data valid permit.

11. The Central Government may post scientist/observer on board each of the chartered vessels ; the charterer shall ensure that the Indian scientists and observers, when so directed by the Central Government, are permitted on board the chartered vessel for collection and examination of such data and material as may be required by the government and see that such scientists and observers are provided proper food and accommodation on board the vessel by the master of the vessel.

12. Every application for charter shall be in the prescribed form and shall be accompanied by a fee of Rs. 500 which shall not be refundable. The charterer shall also pay to the Central Government an amount of Rs. 10,000 per vessel per year at the time of taking delivery of the permit.

13. The charterer shall furnish to the Central Government (Department of Agriculture and Co-operation, New Delhi) valuation and seaworthiness certificate for the chartered vessel from an appropriate authority of its flag state and also furnish a copy thereof to the Director General of Shipping, Bombay.

14. The operation of fishing vessels will be subject to provisions in the Merchant Shipping Act and permission of the Director General of Shipping shall be obtained for the movement of the chartered vessels in Indian waters. The charterer shall cause to be furnished to the Central Government the necessary certificates to the effect that the chartered vessel meets with the requirements in respect of safety of vessels and crew as per the provisions of the Merchant Shipping Act, 1958.

15. The entire equipment and machinery fitted on the fishing vessel shall be open for inspection by the representative of the Government of India. The foreign collaborator shall furnish in advance seven copies of the complete details of the equipment, namely, radio, radar, other sensors, scientific contrivances for biological oceanographic observations and its accessories and machinery, international call signs, range of radio frequencies/ channels and parameters of communication equipment on each vessel. Any change in the details given shall be communicated and specific approval of the Government obtained for their use.

No electronic intelligence gathering equipment shall be fitted on board. Equipment essentially required for fishing, however, may be allowed. The vessel shall operate only after obtaining all the necessary clearances from the Government in this respect.

16. Representatives of the Government may inspect the chartered fishing vessels at any time without prior notice. Skippers and others on the said fishing vessels shall furnish whatever information that is required by the representatives during such inspection.

17. The charterer shall give an undertaking (in duplicate) to the effect that :

(a) No oceanographic research surveys or exploration and so on shall be carried out within our territorial waters.

(b) No oceanographic research, surveys and other investigations shall be carried within our Exclusive Economic Zone (Zone extending up to 200 miles from our coast) without the prior express approval of the Government of India.

(c) No oceanographic research, surveys and other investigations shall be carried out beyond 200 miles from the coast, where part of the operations come within the zone extending upto 200 miles from the coast, without prior approval of the Government of India.

18. The foreign crew on the fishing vessels shall be employed only after obtaining necessary clearance from the Central Government in this regard. The crew of the chartered vessel shall be issued with laminated identity books/cards carrying their photographs and their personal data to facilitate identification. Such books/cards shall be issued by the Indian companies to the foreign crew at the time of naval inspection and retrived at the time of customs clearance. These shall be made available to the crew on the vessel's re-entry into Indian waters along with other documents. In case of new crew fresh books/cards shall be issued. Such documents shall be kept in the custody of the skipper and shall be accounted for. Every subsequent change in the foreign crew shall be made only after the clearance from the Central Government.

19. The charterer shall furnish 10 copies of the list of particulars of its employees both foreign and Indian and also ten copies of the list of particulars of foreign personnel employed in the chartered vessels. Any change in the personnel and equipment/ machinery on board the chartered vessels or in the shore establishments shall be reported to the Department of Agriculture and Co-operation.

20. The applicant shall be issued a letter of intent for preparing themselves for satisfactory compliance of pre-operational formalities, such as security aspects and training. Only when the Government are satisfied about the fulfilment of these formalities, a letter of permission shall be issued for commencement of operations.

21. Commencement of fishing operation—no foreign vessel fishing in the maritime zone of India under the licence of permit granted under these rules shall commence fishing operations without clearance from the Coast Guards.

22. The chartered vessels shall report its location and the quantum of catch in the hold to Coast Guard Station and P.C.S. signal (Position, Course, Speed Signal) to Naval Wireless Station daily as at 08.00 hours in accordance with the Admirality List of Radio Signals, Volume 1.

23. Details of arrival and departure of chartered vessels in the Indian ports shall be forwarded simultaneously to Naval Headquarters, New Delhi, Coast Guard Headquarters, New Delhi and the Department of Agriculture and Co-operation, New Delhi.

24. After the initial clearance by the authorised officer and after each re-entry at the port of operation, the chartered vessel shall return to her port of operation at least once during thirty days. This period, however, can be increased on merits, depending on the endurance of the vessels. The charterer shall ensure that the catch is correctly evaluated.

25. The charterer shall furnish to the Government of India voyage-wise statement of fish catch and exports from the chartered vessels with all the necessary details as required in the prescribed proforma.

26. The fishing vessels and their appurtenances, fish catches exports, fuel, lubricants, spare parts, packing materials, fishing

materials and so on will be subject to duties and taxes as may be applicable under the Indian laws. If the fuel charge is to be borne by the foreign collaborator, payment shall be made in foreign exchange by the foreign collaborator.

27. Prior to commencement of shipment the foreign collaborator shall produce revolving and confirmed letter of credit in favour of Indian company or make advance payments to the Indian party towards the value of the catch after deducting proportionate charter fee for each voyage.

28. Violation or non-fulfilment of any of the conditions stipulated above before commencement of fishing operations shall result in cancellation of the permission issued.

29. The charterer shall confirm to all the existing Government of India's Act/Orders requiring operators of vessels to obtain licences or permissions for various equipment/facilities/ radio frequencies individually or collectively.

30. Display of licence or permit on board the vessels—(i) Subject to sub-rule (ii) of Rules under the Maritime Zones of India Rules, 1982, a copy of the licence or permit duly attested by the issuing authority, shall be kept on board the foreign vessel described in the licence or permit while the vessel is in the Maritime Zones of India and shall be produced for examination by an authorised officer at his request. (iii) Every foreign vessel described in the licence or permit may enter in the maritime zones of India or proceed directly to an Indian port for obtaining a copy of a licence or permit if :

(a) all fishing gear on board the vessel is stowed in the manner specified in Rule 14 of Maritime Zones of India Rules 1982

(b) the master of the vessel complies with any direction given to him by an authorised officer.

31. Damage to Indian vessel prohibited. No foreign fishing vessel fishing in the maritime zones of India under the licence or permit granted under these rules shall cause any damage either wilfully or through gross negligence to any fishing vessel, fishing stakes, fishing gear, fishing net or other fishing application owned or in possession of an Indian citizen.

32. Prohibition to carry any explosives, poisonous or noxious substances.

(a) No foreign vessel or any person shall carry or have in its possession or control any explosives, poisonous or other noxious substances or apparatus fitted for or capable of utilising an electric current, with the intension of using such explosive, poisonous or other noxious substances or apparatus for killing, stunning, disabling or catching fish. Any explosives, poisonous or other noxious substance found on board any vessel or in possession of any person, shall be presumed, unless the contrary is proved, to be intended for the use specified above.

(b) No foreign vessel or any person shall attempt to destroy or abandon any fishing gear, fishing net or other fishing appliances, explosives, poisonous or other noxious substances or any other object or thing with the intention to avoid their detection or seizure.

33. No fishing is to be done for protected species which are covered under the Wild Life (Protection) Act, 1972 (53 of 1972). Such protected species if caught are immediately returned to water alive, if possible, if not they shall be retained and preserved on board the vessel and accounted for and shall be surrendered at such place as may be directed by the authorised officer.

34. Charterer shall not undertake shrimping operations for exploitation of coastal shrimp.

35. The charterer shall ensure that the chartered vessel reports to the authorised officer before and after every fishing voyage and delivers the copy of the permit in its possessions to the charterer before every departure to the foreign port.

36. The Government reserve the right to stipulate such additional conditions as may be considered necessary or to modify the conditions stipulated above.

37. The charterer shall be bound by all or any of the terms and conditions applicable to the licence except conditions applicable prescribed in clause (a) of sub-rule (1) of rule 5 of the Maritime Zones of India (Regulation of Fishing by Foreign

Vessels) Rules 1982 and shall be bound by such additional conditions or restrictions also as may be specified in the permit in the above mentioned rules.

ANNEXURE-II

PARTICULARS OF INDIAN COMPANIES WHO HAVE BEEN PERMITTED TO CHARTER FOREIGN FISHING VESSELS FOR OPERATION IN INDIAN EXCLUSIVE ECONOMIC ZONE

Sl. No.	Name of the company and address	No. of vessels for which letter of intent issued	No. of vessels for which letter of permission/permit issued	Allotted base of operation
1.	Metropolitan Trading Company, 10/76, Haines Road, Bombay	5	5	Cochin
2.	Bottle Glass Pvt. Ltd. 2E/22, Jhandewalan Extension, New Delhi	10	10	Goa
3.	Tropical Shipping Company, Visakhapatnam	10	10	Visakhapatnam
4.	Varuna Marine Products Pvt. Ltd., D-37, Panchsheel Enclave, New Delhi	10	10	Goa
5.	Orissa Maritime and Chilka Area Development Corporation, 103, Suryanagar, Bhubaneswar	17	10	Paradeep
6.	Golden Fisheries Pvt. Ltd., 8-81, Defence Colony, New Delhi	15	15	Tuticorin
7.	Nava Bharat Ferro Alloy Pvt. Ltd., Nava Bharat House, 6-3-654, Samajaguda, Hyderabad	8	8	Visakhapatnam

8. Srinivasa Seafood Pvt. Ltd., No. 12, Industrial Development Area, Visakhapatnam	4	4	Madras
9. Shrimp India Pvt. Ltd., Plot No 17, Kirlampudi Layout, Visakhapatnam	4	4	Madras
10. Gujarat Agro Marine Pvt. Ltd., Patel Building, Ellisbridge, Ahmedabad	10	10	Okha
11. Four Season Fisheries Pvt. Ltd., 15-10-3, Krishnanagar, Visakhapatnam	4	4	Madras
12. Akama Marine Pvt. Ltd., 8-3-7, Vijayanagar Palace Layout, Peda Waltair, Visakhapatnam	4	4	Madras
13. V.B.C. Exports (Pvt.) Ltd., 10-27-13, Waltair Upland, Visakhapatnam	4	4	Madras
14. Kerala Fisheries Corporation Ltd., Shanmugham Road, Box. No. 2617, Cochin	16	4	Cochin
15. Coastal Trawlers Pvt. Ltd., 42-1-13, Vallabhai Street, Kakinada	4	2	Madras
16. High Sea Foods Pvt. Ltd., New Delhi	2	—	Madras
17. G P. Marine Products (India) Pvt. Ltd., 4-5-3/2, Vijaya Vihar, Ring Road, Guntur	4	4	Madras
18. West Coast Lighterage Co., Pvt. Ltd., 91/92, Bajaj Bhavan, Nariman Point, Bombay	4	—	Cochin
19. Bali Cold Storage Pvt. Ltd., 79, Dr. C.P. Pamasami Iyer Road, Alwarpet, Madras	4	—	Madras

ANNEXURE II : (*Contd.*)

20. Appu International Pvt. Ltd., 109, Bhagat Singh Market, New Delhi	4	—	Madras
21. Maharashtra Fisheries Development Corporation, N.K M. International House, 3rd Floor, 178, Backbay Reclamation, Bombay	6	—	Goa
22. Kanchanaganoa Sea Foods Pvt. Ltd., D. No. 5-50, Gunadala, Vijayawada	4	2	Madras
23. Eilon Hinengo Ltd., 67, B.R.B. Basu Road, 1st Floor, Calcutta-1.	2	—	Yet to be decided
24. Blue Chrome Pvt. Ltd., 37, Golf Links, New Delhi.	4	—	Madras
25. Leo Sea Foods Pvt. Ltd., C-24, Green Park Extension, New Delhi.	4	—	Madras
	Public Sector	24	
	Private	86	
	Total	110	

Source : Ministry of Agriculture and Co-operation, Government of India, New Delhi.

ANNEXURE-III

POSITION REGARDING COMPLIANCE OF CHARTER TERMS AND CONDITIONS ON OBLIGATORY PURCHASE BY THE INDIAN COMPANIES

Sl. No.	Name of the company	No. of vessels permit-ted	No. of vessels brought for ope-ration	Starting date of operation in Indian EEZ	Acquisition of vessel due	Comments
1.	Metropolitan Trading Company, Bombay	5	5	24-12-81	Ist vessel 24-12-1982 IInd vessel 24-12-1983 IIIrd vessel 24-12-1984 (As per earlier schedule)	The company has not acquired the first vessel under charter obligation. The permit issued for one vessel (namely) Jiuh Long-No. 1 was suspended. Second vessel was due on 23-12-83. Since they have not made any firm arrangements to acquire the vessel indigenously, the bank guarantee of Rs. 2 lakhs furnished by them has been invoked. A show cause notice was also issued to the company on 15-2-84. The remaining four vessels of the company were also suspended on 16-3-84. It is reported that two of the chartered vessels of the company have gone back to their home port along with catch and Indian crew without customs clearance and so on and without giving 15% catch value due to the Indian company.

ANNEXURE III : (*Contd.*)

2.	Bottle Glass Pvt. Ltd., New Delhi	10	10	15-6-82	Ist vessel 15-6-1983 IInd vessel 15-6-1984 IIIrd vessel 15-6-1985 (As per earlier schedule)	Fresh proposal for import of vessels of less than five year old was submitted on 4-7-83 and it was considered by FVAC on 13-12-83 for one vessel only. (The delay was due to finalisation of policy on permitting second hand vessels). A letter of intent was issued to the Company on 4-1-84 for the acquisition of one second hand fishing vessel Chilung No. 1 from Singapore. Subsequently as per the request of the company, L/I was issued for import of two second hand vessels on 10-4-84 against the earlier L/I for one vessel. The company has now requested 90 days' time to convert the L/I into a letter of authorisation. Permission for two vessels was cancelled and it was also decided to invoke the bank guarantee of Rs. 2 lakhs furnished by the company. The company has now obtained stay order from Delhi High Court on the operation of Ministry's order of invoking bank guarantee and cancelling the permit of two vessels. The company has also submitted a proposal for indigenous construction of two vessels.

3.	Tropical Shipping Company, Visakhapatnam	10	10	14-4-82	Ist vessel 14-4-1983 IInd vessel 14-4-1984 IIIrd vessel 14-4-1985 (As per earlier schedule)	The company was issued a letter of intent during December, 1983 for the acquisition of a second hand vessel from Singapore. They did not fulfil the conditions to the letter of intent. Subsequently they represented to allow them to import one pair of second hand vessels. As the company failed to fulfil the conditions on obligatory purchase, the permit issued to four of their chartered vessels was cancelled and also invoked the bank guarantee of Rs. 2 lakhs. But the company obtained stay orders from Delhi High Court on the operation of Ministry's orders. The company also submitted a proposal for the import of two new vessels from Korea. This was considered by Fishing Vessels Acquisition Committee on 21-3-84 and 19-5-84. The Committee recommended to allow the company to import two vessels. A letter of permission has been issued to the company to import two vessels from Korea on 19-7-84. The company has also submitted proposals for indigenous construction of two vessels which is separately under examination.

ANNEXURE III : (*Contd.*)

4.	Varuna Marine Products Pvt. Ltd., New Delhi	10	6	16-5-82	Ist vessel 16-5-1983 IInd vessel 16-5-1984 (As per earlier schedule)	The company's proposal to import second hand vessels was considered by FVAC during which time the company withdrew their offer. Permission for one pair of vessels was cancelled. The proposal dated 7-1-84 submitted by the company for acquiring two new deep sea fishing trawlers from Australia was considered by the FVAC on 6-2-84. The company was issued an L/I for the import of two vessels from Australia on 2-5-84. The company has now represented to amend certain conditions in the L/I. Steps have been taken to invoke the bank guarantee of Rs. 2 lakhs furnished by the company. The above actions were taken as the company failed to make irrevocable arrangements to acquire vessels by the due date in May 1983. The company has also submitted a proposal for indigenous construction of two vessels.

5.	Orissa Maritime & C.A. Dev. Corporation, Bhubaneswar	10	10	14-2-83	Ist vessel 14-8-1984 (Schedule as per Maritime Zone rules)	The proposal received from the Corporation during January 1984 for the import of trawlers from Holland was considered by the FCAC on 21-3-1984. The Committee felt that the type of vessels proposed could be constructed indigenously and the Corporation was advised to submit proposal for indigenous construction of two vessels. The corporation has since submitted a proposal for indigenous construction of two vessels with M/s. East Coast Boat Builders and Engineers, Kakinda, which is separately under examination. Due to violation of charter terms and conditions regarding posting of Indian crew, two vessels of the corporation were suspended on 9-2-84.
6.	Golden Fisheries Pvt. Ltd., New Delhi	15	12	21-10-82	Ist vessel 20-4-84 (Schedule as per Maritime Zone rules)	The company first submitted a proposal for the acquisition of two new vessels from Australia. This proposal was withdrawn by the company and a subsequent proposal in January 84 was submitted for the acquisition of four vessels from Korea. This was considered by FVAC on 6-2-84. AL/I was issued for two vessels on 10-5-84. The company now

ANNEXURE III : (*Contd.*)

						wanted time upto middle of August 84. However, they are being given time upto 31st July, 84. The company has also submitted a proposal for indigenous construction of two vessels with M/s. East Coast Boat Builders and Engineers Ltd., Kakinada. The company's request for substituting five gill-netters stating that their operation was not economical was received in the Ministry after the optional period of three months. Also the company had indicated that they are not obliged to acquire vessels against these gill-netters. In view of this, permit for five gill-netters was cancelled and the bank guarantee of Rs. 2 lakhs invoked.
7.	Nava Bharat Ferro Alloys, Hyderabad	8	8	29-1-83	Ist vessel 28-7-1984	The company has submitted a proposal during December 83 for acquiring two second hand trawlers from Hong Kong with subsequent clarification. This was considered by FVAC on 6-2-84, 21-3-84 and 19-5-84. After the company had agreed to modify some of the specifications of the vessels, the committee agreed to allow the company to import two second hand vessels from Hong

						Kong. However, the Committee felt that as the company is an MRTP company from December 83, they are not eligible for SDFC loan. The company has been issued a letter of intent to import two second hand vessels from Hong Kong on 24-7-1984. The company has also submitted a proposal for indigenous construction of two vessels from East Coast Boat Builders and Engineers, Kakinada. The company's four vessels were suspended on 18-1-1984 due to violation of charter conditions on voyage duration.
8.	Srinivasa Sea Food Pvt. Ltd., Visakhapatnam	4	4	28-3-83	27-9-1984	The company submitted a proposal in December 1983 for the acquisition of two trawlers from Australia. This was considered by FVAC on 6-2-1984. Ministry issued import authorisation of two vessels to the company on 24-4-84. The company now stated that their Australian collaborator has entered into a licence contract with one Singapore firm who will be constructing their vessels. The company has therefore sought Ministry's approval for entering a contract with the Singapore

ANNEXURE III : (*Contd.*)

						firm. Ministry has not agreed to this and company has been informed. The company has also submitted proposal for two indigenous trawlers with M/s. Alcock Ashdown and Company, Bhavnagar.
9.	Shrimp India Pvt. Ltd., Visakhapatnam	4	4	9-3-83	8-9-1984	The company's proposal for acquiring two vessels from Korea was discussed by FVAC on 21-3-84. The FVAC has recommended to allow them to import two vessels. The company has been asked to place orders for indigenous construction of two vessels immediately and alternatively to furnish a bank guarantee of Rs. 5 lakhs. The company vide their latter dated 1-6-84 has submitted only two copies of contract and specification for the construction of two indigenous vessels with M/s. Bharti Shipyard (Pvt.) Ltd., Bombay. Further copies and other particulars are awaited.
10.	Four Season Fisheries Pvt. Ltd. Visakhapatnam	4	4	24-6-83	23-12-1984	The company has submitted a proposal for the indigenous construction of two fishing vessels of 23.5 M. from M/s. Alcock Ashdown & Co. Ltd., Bhavnagar for which SDFC loan application has

						also been received. The loan application is being processed separately.
11.	Gujarat Fisheries Dev. Corporation Ltd., Ahmedabad	10	10	27-7-83	26-1-1985	The Corporation has submitted a proposal for the construction of two indigenous trawlers from M/s. Alcock Ashdown Co Ltd., Bhavnagar on 31-3-1984. Loan application has also been received from the Corporation and is being processed separately.
12.	Akama Marine Pvt. Ltd. Visakhapatnam	4	4	6-9-83	6-3-1985	In March 1984, the company submitted a proposal for the import of two trawlers from Korea. This was considered by FVAC on 19-5-1984 and recommended to allow the company to import two vessels. The company has been asked to submit proposal for indigenous construction of two vessels immediately and alternativety furnish a bank guarantee of Rs. 5 lakhs. The company has since submitted copy of their indigenous construction proposal.
13.	V.B.C. Exports Pvt. Ltd., Visakhapatnam	4	4	14-10-83	14-4-1985	The Company submitted a proposal for indigenous construction of two trawlers from M/s. Alcock Ashdown & Co. Ltd., Bhavnagar, which is separately under examination.

Source : Ministry of Agriculture and Co-operation, Government of India, New Delhi.

11

JOINT VENTURE IN FISHERIES

R.D. PUSALKAR

AND

T.A. MAMMEN

BACKGROUND

THE WORLD demand for fish and fishery products has been steadily increasing in the post-war period. This is partly because of the increased production, better purchasing power, particularly in the affluent countries, and technological and infrastructural improvements in fishing, processing, storage, transportation, and distributing of fish and fishery products. Fish and fishery products have moved up from the position of poor man's food to the position of expensive and luxury food articles. Apart from palatability, low fat content, easy digestibility and preference to animal proteins led to increased demand by both undernourished and over-nourished, the convalescent and the figure conscious. The trade in fishery products trebled between 1970 and 1978, that is, from US $3,481 million—the average for 1970-72, to US $10,810 million in 1978. While a part of the value increase may be attributed to price increase and currency changes, there is no denying of the *per se* increased volume of fish trade. In fact the trade has increased at a faster rate, compared to the increase in fish production.

In the field of marine fisheries, the 25-year period after the Second World War witnessed rapid expansion of marine fishing by industrially advanced countries like Japan, USSR, USA, Norway and Canada. Some of the economically less advanced countries like Korea, Thailand and Taiwan have also developed their deep sea fishing to a very significant extent. The fishing companies in these countries, over a period of years, have built up a large fleet of fishing vessels, including a distant water fishing fleet, capable of remaining in the fishing grounds for long stretches with supporting boats that would keep them supplied with food, water, fuel and other necessities on the one hand and periodically remove the catches to the home port on the other.

In contrast to this rapid growth, world fish production has tended to stagnate due to a variety of reasons during the last five years. This is because in some areas the limits of maximum sustainable yield level have been reached and in a few cases even exceeded, necessitating conservation measures. In some areas pollution and scare of pollution were depressing marketing and hence production. Measures aimed at protection of mammals prevented certain types of fishing. The high cost of harvesting consequent upon high fuel costs, increasing wages and operating costs, high initial cost and so on tended to make fishing by using large vessels—an unworkable proposition for the low priced varieties. The enforcement of EEZ not having the economic means for their exploitation coupled with high stakes demanded for licensing of fishing by foreign vessels and restrictive approach to joint ventures are some of the important factors that led to the present stagnation in world fish production.

IMPACT OF DECLARATION OF EXCLUSIVE ECONOMIC ZONE

The most important development in the management of marine fisheries is the declaration of the Exclusive Economic Zone (EEZ), starting with the extension of territorial water and later fishing limits. The trend gained momentum in the early 1960s with the announcement of a 200-mile claim by the Latin American countries. Following the trend of discussions at the UN Conference of the Law of the Sea (UNCLOS), about one hundred countries declared EEZ, mostly upto 200 miles from the coast. This created a new situation in which the fishery-advanced countries were faced with the reality of EEZ in terms of which the resources they were exploiting suddenly became the property of littoral states. According to FAO, as much as 99 per cent of the world fishery would come within the scope of EEZs, if all littoral states were to declare EEZ, leaving only 1 per cent of the known fishery in areas of open access. As a result of this development, fishery developed nations were faced with the problem of surplus vessels on one hand and dwindling areas for operation on the other hand. In contrast to this, the fishery developing countries which came to possess large areas of the sea were unable to exploit the resources of their own. Many fishery management experts feared that the world fish production might plummet in the face of inaccessibility of the stocks to countries having the capability for exploiting the resources and inability of the littoral states in exploiting the resources themselves.

Declaration of EEZ came at a time when the distant water fishing was probably at its highest. The reaction of these countries to the declaration of EEZ varied. Some countries openly refused to accept the EEZ concept and wanted the old concept of 'common heritage' to continue ; while others conveniently ignored it, or at least their fishing companies ignored it. The fishing boats of these countries sneaked into EEZ of littoral states after making an assessment of the likely chance of detection. Where resources were good and the chances of detection remote, they increased their poaching efforts. This resulted in increased surveillance and legal enactment to inflict deterrent punishment for violation of the EEZ. In this context some countries negotiated for fishing rights under a licence or with payment of royalty fee. Proposals of chartering of foreign fishing vessels, and joint venture enterprises were found to be acceptable propositions to the contracting parties. The littoral states also found these attractive.

Joint ventures in industrial development

The term 'joint venture' is a familiar expression in industrial parlance. Basically 'joint venture' is taken to be an association of two or more parties in the execution of commercial projects, who share the risks and benefits. A 'joint venture' may be an 'equity joint venture', in which case the arrangement often entails setting up of a separate joint company where each of the parties holds a proportion of the capital shares ; or a 'contractural joint venture' in which the relationship between the two parties entering into joining ventures governed solely by contractural relations. When the partners are from two different countries, it becomes an 'international joint venture' or 'extra-regional joint venture', very often the developed partner providing the expertise, the equipment and marketing channels, while the host country partner providing the natural resources and supporting facilities. Joint ventures may also be 'intra-regional' following the principle of Technical/Economic Co-operation among Developing Countries (TCDC and ECDC). The Conference of Heads of States or Governments of Non-aligned countries visualized an Action Programme of Economic Co-operation. The various UN organizations are supporting this idea of joint ventures, recognizing their role in increasing fish production, meeting the legitimate aspirations of developing countries—their fishing as well as finding profitable alternate use for the excess fishing fleet from countries having vessels surplus to their own EEZ. Besides the UN, which brought out a 'Manual on the establishment of joint venture arrangements', the FAO issued a number of technical papers on joint ventures in fisheries, bilateral fishery arrangements, case studies and so on. FAO conducted a seminar on the subject at Colombo in January, 1980. FAO has also identified joint ventures as one of the medium term plans for quick exploitation of the resources of the EEZ. It was also one of the areas of interest of the now defunct Indian Ocean Fisheries Commission.

Joint venture in fisheries

Fishing is a subject particularly amenable for joint venture. Unlike land based industries, the fishing vessels can be moved very quickly from one place to another and the joint venture can start off almost immediately. While joint venture in fisheries got a special fillip in recent years due to compulsions of the new regime of the sea, joint ventures have been in vogue for a very long time. Initially when the sovereignty of nations was limited to territorial waters and that too limited to 3 to 6 miles, the main attraction in joint venture for distant water fishing nations was in getting shore support for drawal of fuel, water, provisions and repair facilities for their vessels, a local market for inexpensive varieties and processing and storage facilities for expensive varieties before shipment to their home markets. The host partner hoped,to gain through sharing of costs (equity participation), fisning vessels, fishing technicians and general assistance in building up the industry. The host countries, mostly in Asia, Africa and Latin America looked at development of fisheries with multiple goals of earning hard currency, meeting protein shortagc and bringing economic benefit through employment and income generation.

The progress of discussions at the UN Conference on the Law of the Sea (UNCLOS) had also its impact on the outlook of developing countries on joint ventures in fisheries. In accordance with the Information Composite Negotiating Text (ICNT) before UNCLOS III, while the littoral state is responsible for determining the total allowable catch of the living resources in the EEZ, where it cannot harvest the entire catch, other countries including landlocked countries and geographically disadvantageously placed countries could claim excess to this resource and there could be compulsory conciliation on this access to the surplus resource. The implied reference to ICNT was to factors such as significance of the living resources of the area to the economy of the coastal state concerned and its other national interests, the rights of the land-locked state and certain developing coastal states in the subregion or region ; the requirements of the developing countries, need to minimize economic dislocation in states whose nationals habitually fished in the zone or which have made substantial effort in research and identification of stocks. This turn of events made it obligatory that littoral states should either quickly develop their fishing capability or bear the threat of compulsory conciliation of agreeing to share their EEZ resources with other countries. The question of concluding joint ventures in that context became a matter of prudence, if the economic and political gains of EEZ declared were to be sustained. While this clause of compulsory conciliation stands inoperative now, the weakness of declaration of EEZ, without corresponding arrangements for saturation of the area with its fishing fleet, has been exposed.

Another point that emerged is the cost of surveillance. It is perhaps cheaper for the governments to saturate the EEZ with a fleet of fishing vessels, compared to the cost of protecting the resource from poaching through strengthening the machinery for surveillance. Some countries have even come to the conclusion that the cost of surveillance exceeds the value of resource it seeks to protect. The rationale of protecting a living resource has also been questioned. Here is a resource which is renewable, which grows, lives a life span (which in tropical regions has a short life span) and wasted to humanity, if it is not harvested before it dies a natural death. Hence mere denial of access to this resource on the strength of unilateral extension of sovereignity without measures to harvest the resource is only a dog in the manger policy.

Advantages of joint venture to the host company

It is well known that in several developing countries, fishing is and has been a way of life from very early times. The artisanal sector has over the years developed skills adopting low cost, labour intensive techniques. In many coastal areas the artisanal fishery, along with small mechanised boats, has reached a level beyond which prospects for increased fish production are limited, unless offshore and deep sea resources are tapped for which technology, equipment and expertise are generally lacking. While, in a way, the technology can be evolved and indigenous equipment and expertise developed, there is no need to adopt this expensive, and dilatory procedure, when technology can be borrowed along with equipment and expertise. Under joint venture, foreign technology is inducted as a package deal with vessels, equipment, personnel and marketing arrangements. Foreign collaboration would also give the advantage of preferential tariffs and use of foreign brand names. It also gives a great deal of stability in the competitive and quality conscious food markets, where marine products from developing countries have to pass through established market chains to gain acceptance. From all these considerations, it is advantageous to the host company to seek joint venture with suitable foreign company.

Besides, many fishery developing countries have tied up other economic gains and developmental activities in consideration to permission for foreign vessel operation. Charging a licence fee is one of the widely practised provisions. In some cases, the value of licence fee is a flat amount per annum per vessel. In an agreement concluded by Mauritania with Greece and Poland in 1977 the licence fee is reported to be fixed at US $ 200 per GRT. Several other agreements provide that the flag state will grant loans to the coastal state on favourable terms. Most joint ventures have a provision for training fishermen of the littoral state by owners of fishing vessels or they may send experts to the littoral state, or give fellowships for training in institutions located in the flag state. Research support is another form of assistance received from the flag ship country. There are a few agreeements which provide for the setting up of research centres or laboratories in the territory of coastal states (e.g. 1973 agreement between Mauritania and the Soviet Union). Indian Charter guidelines provide for a licence fee of Rs. 10,000 per annum, 20 per cent of the crew to be Indian and that too as understudies to important functionaries like skipper, engineer and so on and room for a scientist on board the vessel. The licence fee is nominal but still serves to establish ownership rights. The provision of 20 per cent Indian crew enables the crew to complete the prescribed sea-time to sit for competency certificate examinations and gain practical experience in commercial fishing. The presence of a scientist on board helps collection of a valuable fishing data, which would otherwise be difficult and costly to collect. It is also a built-in safeguard against unlawful activities.

Advantages of joint venture to the developed partner

Access to the fishery resources of another (host) country is today the foremost consideration of foreign companies in joint ventures in the fishery developing countries. Other advantages to the developed partner/foreign country are : (i) availability of a base in the proximity of area of fishing ; (ii) opportunity to engage less costly local labour ; (iii) long term gain on account of sale of fishing vessels, processing plants and their spare parts ; (iv) additional scientific and technical information consequence to the facility of observation under diverse conditions ; (v) export of know-how for profits ; (vi) prospect of new ventures in third world countries, using cheaper inputs by pooling of resources ; (vii) access to local markets for products not having an economic price in their country ; and (viii) shore support for fuel, water provisions, replacement of crew, and so on.

ROLE AND REACTIONS OF HOST COUNTRY

Role and reactions of the host country to joint venture depend on its economic and political structure. Countries like India with regulated economy have a selective approach to joint ventures, varying with industries, parties and partners. While fishing is not a licenced industry, fish processing is licenced. Foreign participation in the equity would require approval of the Foreign Investment Board (FIB), the import of goods by the Capital Goods (CG) Committee and clearance for large business houses by the Licensing-cum-MRTP Advisory Committee. These committees have representations from various economic ministries, subject matter ministries and so on. Screening by various ministries and organizations is understandable as it involves induction of foreign capital, foreign equipment and foreign personnel. Starting of large industrial activity with foreign assistance often goes counter to other national priorities like self-reliance, protection of interests of weaker sections, restrictions in the growth of monopolies, conservation of financial and other resources and so on.

Deep sea fishing with joint venture has security overtones also. Various fish detection devices are incidentally devices to collect data which are relevant for military operations, particularly submarine operations. Information on thermocline, thermal/stratification, sound reverberation, and so on are considered significant from defence angles. There is, therefore, risk of some sensitive data being collected by foreign vessels under the guise of innocent fishing operations. Joint venture in fishing implies foreign presence in our waters, which can be close to defence installations, oil rigs, and so on having strategic importance. It is in this context that many developing countries have restrictions on conduct of oceanographic surveys by joint venture companies, although viewed from the fishing company's point of view, collection of such oceanographic data is essential for adopting a scientific approach to fishing. Joint venture also carries the risk of violations of customs, immigration and quarantine restrictions. Joint venture tends to the growth of large houses and monopolistic tendencies, leading to concentration of wealth and economic power, which can give an unfair advantage over the smaller units.

Large scale fishing, spot purchases and related processing and marketing operations by large Indian companies in collaboration with large foreign companies can have a depressing effect on smaller units unaided by foreign collaboration and sophisticated technology. There can also be adverse impact from the conservation angle. Some fish species which spend part of the time in coastal waters and part of the time in offshore waters may be fished out in the offshore waters, leaving very little to migrate to the coastal waters for fishing by the artisanal group. Joint venture also facilitates the operation of poaching vessels under the guise of authorised vessels. It makes surveillance more difficult. The government has also to guard itself against possible under-invoicing and also ensure that the due share of the Indian party is fully reflected in the accounts and the amounts are repatriated. Important Indian regulations and concessions concerning joint ventures in deep sea fishing with foreign collaboration are presented in Appendix-I.

Until recently Indian joint ventures abroad were allowed only in the form of export of machinery and equipment. It is only recently that cash investment has been allowed, even though cash investment is still of a marginal character in view of the fact that India itself is an importer of capital. In contrast to the paucity of capital, India has a surplus of manpower, both trained and untrained. Most of the Indian joint ventures abroad have high manpower content. However, Indian participation in the field of fisheries has been limited to technical and scientific expertise and that too mostly in inland fish culture.

Experience in deep sea fishing and joint ventures

India has been keen to enter deep sea fishing from the turn of the present century. The earlier attempts to introduce steam trawlers were unsuccessful. The first deep sea fishing company to be established (1946) was the West Coast Fisheries Corporation by the then Government of Travancore, who brought three vessels of 19 metres length from U.K. While the vessels could carry out mother vessel fishing quite successfully, there were many operational problems and the corporation was wound up later. Around the same time Tata Co. (Fisheries Division) bought a couple of shrimp trawlers with Mexican crew, but this operation was also a failure. Based on the successful operation of TAIYO MARU 17, the New India Fisheries was registered in 1954 as a joint venture company and even now this is the only successful joint venture deep sea fishing experience in this country. In 1964 the Orissa Fisheries Corporation purchased a few Polish trawlers, but could not operate them economically. During the last two decades various other unsuccessful attempts were made to get vessels from G.D.R., Poland, Denmark, France, USSR, USA and so on. While negotiations dragged on for years, nothing concrete happened. During 1963-64 proposals were in an advanced stage to obtain 2 gift vessels from Sweden and acquire twenty fishing vessels of 17.5 metres length under Swedish credit. This proposal had to be shelved in the wake of opposition from the indegenous yards. Finally, instead of import, 40 vessels of 17.6 metre length were constructed indigenously to meet the demand of the various Government institutions. Since there were complaints about the quality of indigenous construction by the users, it was decided to import 50 vessels, against which 15 could be imported. Under another proposal a pooled order for 30 more vessels was made with a Mexican yard, against which 28 vessels have arrived. A proposal for import of 60 more vessels although initiated in 1977, could result in the acquisition of only 2 fibre glass vessels. Six more steel vessels are in advanced stages of construction in Holland and one expected to reach India during 1984.

Apart from import of fishing vessels, various proposals have been made from time to time to enter into joint venture with various fishing companies, including a proposal by Van Camp Fishing Company with TOMCO. Sun Harbour Co. with State Fisheries Corporations. Starikist with STC and Kerala Fisheries Corporations and so on, There was also an unsuccessful attempt to establish a joint sector Marine Diesel Engine Co. factory with technical collaboration with Yanmar Diesel Engine Co. The proposal got delayed on account of opposition from indigenous engine manufacturers. In order to avoid further delay, HMT was designated as Indian collaborator, but they failed to arrive at an agreement. While the proposal was picked out by another private company, this also failed to come off.

The first charter fishing was by New India Fisheries followed by a Polish factory vessel charter by the Government of India. Later, charters were negotiated and included by many private parties and a large number of chartered vessels were operated, but none of the latter chartered resulted in the establishment of joint ventures, which was the objective of most of the charters. In view of the failure of these charters, revised guidelines and terms and conditions for chartering foreign fishing vessels have been announced, according to which charters are obliged to purchase vessels In a phased manner. The experience of recent proposal for joint ventures, including charter, is summarised in the following paragraphs to facilitate a discussion on the subject.

New India Fisheries Limited (NIF)

New India Fisheries is the only fishing company in India to successfully develop out of a joint venture. At one time the company operated 13 fishing vessels with bases at Bombay, Cochin, Visakhapatnam and Paradeep. A study of the working of this company gives insight into the factors responsible for success and failure in deep sea fishing as well as in joint ventures.

In the first instance there was no haste in the choice of partners. The foreign partner Taiyo Fishing Company had occasion to operate fishing vessels in Bombay for sufficiently long time to assess the resources as well as economic viability. They came first in 1951 as consultants to give a technical opinion on 'Jala Ganga', a purse-seiner brought by a Bombay firm. They were then requested for advise on the operation of Jyoti, another private fishing vessel brought to Bombay. Here Taiyo's advice was to try it as a bull trawler along with another similar vessel. It is to the credit of Dr. Setna, the then Director of Fisheries, Bombay, to offer the state's vessel Tapase to try out bull trawling. Once the experiment was found successful, Taiyo Fishing Company applied for special fishing licence for one year trial with Taiyo Maru 17, a 250-GRT fishing trawler. Here also Dr. Setna was able to get them the licence. The operation of Taiyo Maru 17 gave the confidence to Dr. Setna to think of establishing the first Indian fishing company, and for the Taiyo Fishing Company to support the proposal. Dr. Setna who retired in 1953 as Director of Fisheries, Bombay, got the joint venture company registered in 1955 and continued till his death in November 1969 as its Managing Director. The organization of this fishing company and its successful working are glowing tributes to the entrepreneurship of Dr. Setna and the whole-hearted support by the Taiyo Fishing Company. The Taiyo Fishing Company was indulgent from the very beginning. At the time of formation of the company when they were asked by the Government to be a minority share holder with 49 per cent shares, they agreed. However, when it was found difficult for the Indian parties to raise that share capital, they offered to guarantee the safety of Indian capital and also payment of a minimum dividend of 6 per cent on the equity capital, a condition for which there was no occasion to invoke during the joint venture period. However, the Taiyo took over management responsibility and provided skippers and engineers and processing and other experts from time to time to see that vessel and processing operations were carried out properly. When the cost of operation increased and tended to be uneconomical with the highly paid foreign crew and low price of fish in Bombay, they diversified into shrimping, for which new sets of vessels and a base at Cochin were provided. In 1972 when the Company affairs deteriorated due to mismanagement, the parent company's assistance was of immense help in revamping the organization. In 1977 the parent company provided two freezer trawlers on charter with the option for the New India Fisheries (NIF) to purchase if found suitable. The operations were found satisfactory and the vessels were purchased at pre-determined price. While the company faired well under the stewardship of Dr. Setna, his death in 1969 led to deterioration in management and finally in 1972 Greaves Cotton and Company took over management, who with the help of the parent company could pull it out of the morass.

During 1976 when New India Fisheries Limited chartered two large vessels with on-board freezing facilities, they had serious difficulties in obtaining various clearances. This was a time when rules applicable to the chartering of fishing vessels were not clear. While fishing vessels are exempt from payment of excise duty, these vessels on arrival were assessed excise duty at penalty rates for importation without valid papers. New India Fisheries (NIF) had to go on appeal and in spite of an appellate tribunal's decision in their favour, it took several years for NIF to get reimbursement of excise duty paid under protest. Even when the excise duty was waived on the vessel proper, the authorities took a rather restricted view in charging excise duty on fishing gear, processing equipment, linen, crockery and so on, as if they were not part of a fishing vessel. The compliance to rules of Mercantile Marine Department in regard to safety, LSA and FFA also tended to be costly and time-consuming. Finally when the company decided to purchase the vessel at the end of charter, no loan was forthcoming from the Shipping Development Fund Committee. But the company was advised to take a bridging loan on the understanding that when Shipping Development Fund Committee (SDFC) loan becomes available, the bridging loan from commercial bank could be returned. This hope has not materialized so far. In the meanwhile, the company's management was taken over by Vaz Forwarding Company. In the meanwhile, Their finances deteriorated partly as a result of the losses enumerated above and partly due to their own mismanagement.

The experience of NIF clearly establishes that unless there was somebody like Dr. Setna with knowledge of fisheries and acquaintance with administration and a firm like Taiyo Fishing Co. to provide the back up, New India Fisheries would not have initially survived. The second part of their experience also speaks volumes on how a sound company can go into the verge of liquidation in the face of inordinate delays in the various government departments in translation of various accepted policies into action.

INDO-POLISH SURVEY UNDER BILATERAL ARRANGEMENT ALONG THE NORTH-WEST COAST

This was in the nature of a contractual joint venture between two countries. An Indo-Polish Marine Fisheries Agreement was signed in April, 1973, which provided for, among other things, cooperation between the two countries in the survey of marine fishery resources in India. Later in May, 1975, a team of Indian technical experts visited Poland and selected a 1005 GRT vessel and an agreement was concluded in August 1976 between the two governments to undertake an industrial survey of the fishery resources of the north west coast of India by Odra Deep Sea Fishing Company, Swinojscie, Poland at a cost of US $ 932,2000. Accordingly, 'M.T. Mauraena' conducted survey along the Gujarat and Maharashatra coasts from January 1977 to December, 1977. The objectives of the survey as enumerated in the agreement are as follows :

(a) To assess the nature, quality and quantity of commercially exploitable fish and other living resources (demersal, columnar and pelagic);
(b) To make data available for the preparation of feasibility reports for the fishing industry with special reference to obtaining assistance from financial institutions;
(c) To assess factors contributing to fluctuations in the availability of fish and other living resources mentioned above in time and space; and
(d) To raise national capability in fishing technology with reference to resources and area mentioned above.

The vessel carried out surveys in the continental shelf, off the Gujarat and Maharashtra coasts. Within 30 fathoms the survey was confined to the morphology of the sea bottom. In other areas surveys were carried out using bottom trawls and pelagic trawls. However, a good part of the area, particularly between 50—70, fathoms, was unfit for bottom trawling. The survey revealed that horse-mackerel and ribbon fish formed the bulk of resources. However, the survey did not throw much light on items (b) and (d). When the survey was industrial, the catches were below expectation and there were serious problems of disposing of bulk quantities of cheap fish landed by this vessel.

Kelbex International Limited, Delhi

When Indo-Polish survey was going on, Kelvinator of India Limited decided to enter deep sea fishing. They formed a joint venture company with Rybex of Poland for fishing and processing of marine products. The new joint venture company proposed chartering of 4 vessels over a period of 3 years from their collaborators in Poland and purchase of 4 other vessels from Holland. Of the four vessels proposed for charter, three were of 80 m. length and the fourth of 70 m. length. The vessels proposed for purchase were two of 23 m. length, one of 60 m. length and another of 90 m. length. The project operations started in 1978 with an 80 m. vessel. The vessel had to undertake idle voyage from Poland to India. By the time the vessel reached Bombay, the fishing crew arrived by air. During the short period of operation, the crew had to be replaced, for which the company engaged a chartered aircraft. The catches were of miscellaneous varieties having little or no local demand and was exported where also it could not have realised a renumerative price. At one time when a bumper catch of the cat-fish was netted, the company had serious problems of disposal of the catch. It had also problems in contacting the vessel in mid-sea. Even though the base of operation was shifted and mid-sea loading was permitted to avoid the loss of time and money in transferring the catch at port, the vessel owners incurred heavy losses and decided to terminate the operations.

Peejay Indo-Bulgarian Fisheries Limited, Delhi

This joint venture was between Kibno of Bulgaria with a newly formed Indian company Peejay Indo-Bulgarian Fisheries Limited. The foreign company had a fleet of 35 deep sea fishing trawlers of over 80 metres length, 40 trawlers of 35 metres length, 7 carrier vessels of over 35 metres length, a capital investment of over $ 250 million and an annual turnover of $ 120 million. They employed more than 7,500 people and handled more than 1,70,000 tonnes of fish annually. The main activity of the foreign company was in deep sea fishing, spread all over the world. They owned cold storages in Bulgaria as well as large fish meal and fish canning plants. They had specialization in fish farming, fish breeding and had under their control three research institutions in the field of processing and sea fisheries, apart from schools of fishermen. The foreign company had a joint venture in Nigeria. The Managing Director of the Indian company was associated with the foreign company in the founding of the Nigerian joint venture company. On an understanding reached between the two companies, it was proposed to charter two trawlers of 80 metres length, which were considered ideal for deep sea fishing operations in Indian waters. After successful operation of these two vessels, it was proposed to acquire a fleet of 12 trawlers and 2 carrier vessels to undertake fishing and processing, including freezing and conversion into fish meal. The joint venture company was to have a foreign equity of 40 per cent while the remaining 60 per cent was to be retained by the Indian company. The necessary permission for joint venture as well as chartering was issued by the government. The company thereafter commissioned the operation of an 82 metre chartered vessel by December 1978. According to the agreement with the hirers, the charterer was to pay $ 1.2 million per annum as hire charge. However, in case the catch value was less than the hire charge, the hire charge would be limited to 80 per cent of the catch value and remaining 20 per cent would remain with the Indian company. While the catch realization is reported to be far less than what was anticipated, the Indian party was interested in continuing the charter, as it still meant some profit and carried no obligation to purchase any vessel under the then prevailing charter permission. However, the foreign company finding the operations uneconomical terminated the charter.

Tata Oil Mills Company, Bombay (TOMCO)

TOMCO started diversifying into fishing from 1972, based on a prevalent talk about good business prospects in deep sea fishing. They were at that time already in processing relating to animal feed, protein isolates and shrimp. They had their own shrimp processing plants in Verval, Cochin, and Madras and hired plants at Bombay, Ratnagiri, and Mangalore. However, the company lost in 10 years out of the 12 year operations and finally decided to close down their processing activity in 1979-80.

At the time TOMCO was diversifying into deep sea fishing in 1972 the expectation was that the company could improve its business of processing and export of marine products by having captive production units. They had plans to invest on about 12 vessels, against which they got 2 vessels imported from Mexico and placed order with an indigenous yard for two 17 m. vessels. The Mexican vessels on their voyage to India were damaged when got stranded at Fiji while passing through cyclonic weather. While the vessels could be repaired and refloated, its refrigeration system failed completely and hence the vessel had to use ice in its operations in India. The order placed in 1973 with indigenous yard was executed only in 1979 at a cost of Rs. 19 lakh each, as against the cost of Rs. 12 lakh each for their imported 23 metres mexican vessel. The indigenously constructed vessel is said to be totally substandard and could not be put to use and the investment on these two vessels was a total loss.

When in 1977 Government announced their policy of import and chartering of vessels, the company decided to charter a large fleet of vessels from Thailand (Thailand vessels had been fishing in this area and knew our resources), select the best size and design and train Indian crew and get select the best size access to the export market in Thailand for fish varieties.

TOMCO proposed charter of 25 vessels of 42 metres length from Thailand. Being a large house, the proposal required the approval of LC and MRTP Advisory Committee. The sanction for charter was issued on February 1978. In their case a new condition was included, which was followed in all subsequent permissions also stating that non-exportable varieties should be marketed by them in up-country markets and not just dumped in the port markets. But this had no effect on TOMCO as the entire catch was being exported. However, a mistaken notion was created right from the beginning that a large house would not be permitted to charter any vessel less than 40 metres length. TOMCO found that their chartered vessels were functional, crew hard working and the provision of first charge of 20 per cent to the Indian party attractive. The arrangement worked well in the first year ; but in the second year the charter ran into difficulties. The fuel price in India went up to Rs. 1100/KL and it was even higher (Rs. 1700/KL) in Thailand. When the Thailand government controlled fish prices, the vessels had to stop fishing and in the meanwhile the validity of charter expired. As the arrangements for repatriation of the sale proceeds between the two parties were not quite satisfactory, TOMCO had to recover Rs. 40 lakh at the end of charter, for which the Thai company surrendred ed two vessels. But the vessels could not be purchased as permission was received only by December, 1981, while applications were filed in May 1979. To avoid loss of revenue, the company in the meanwhile applied for permission to operate these vessels with Indian crew. Here again approval was received only by the end of November 1980 permitting dry charter operations till the end of December 1980. Evidently the time was too short to avail of this permission. In the meantime, the two vessels remained at their moorings to deteriorate. Being wooden hulled vessels, there was apprehension that the vessels might spring leaks and go down into the sea. So the company carried out essential repairs at a cost of Rs. 9 lakhs. The loss due to non-operation of these two vessels during this two and a half years is computed at Rs. 1 crore. TOMCO's initial success on charter of Thai vessels was soon recognized as attractive and two more companies got permission for chartering 25 and 20 vessels, respectively, from Thailand. While a national charter fee was fixed for each vessel, the Indian parties were sure to make a handsome profit after meeting its overhead charges out of their share of 20 per cent. As the charter at that time carried no other obligation, by the end of 1979, as many as 26 applications were filed for chartering 418 vessels, mostly from Thailand and Taiwan, besides authorization already given to 9 parties for chartering 82 vessels, including 70 vessels from Thailand.

Golden Hind Shipping (India) Private Limited

This company was incorporated in July 1978 and operated 25 Thai vessels of 26 metre length and above from Port Blair at a charter fee of $ 266,000 per vessel. The Indian charter was required to pay all expenses on fuel, port dues and other running expenses. If the catches were less than the anticipated figure, then the charter amount would be limited to 80 per cent of the sale proceeds. According to their estimates each vessel would catch 700 tonnes per annum and this could be sold at $ 500 per tonne. The charter operations were economical for both parties and requests were made for grant of extensions, which were granted for a while.

Universal Food Private Limited, New Delhi

Following the successful charter of TOMCO and Golden Hind Shipping (India) Pvt. Ltd., a proposal was made by Universal

Foods Private Limited (at that time Golden Dragon restaurant) for chartering 20 vessels from Yuhong Company, Taipei (Taiwan). However, for reason of delay they shifted the source of charter to Seawest and Company of Thailand. According to the agreement, 20 vessels of 26-36 metre length would be chartered and the charter fee would be $ 16,000 per voyage. The Indian company also secured its interest by limiting the charter fee liability to 80 per cent of the sale proceeds. In the second phase, the company proposed to form a joint venture company with 60 per cent Indian equity shares and 40 per cent shares being held by the foreign company. For the major part of 1979 and 1980 the charter was continued when further extension was not granted pending introduction of a revised procedure of charters.

Britannia Industries, Bombay

Britannia Industries first entered the field of shrimp processing before entering into deep sea fishing. Being a FERA company, it had to take clearance from LC and MRTP Advisory Committee. They started the business in shrimp processing in 1971 with a letter of intent. But even after 10 years, they are still to get their letter of intent converted into industrial licence. While interviewing the General Manager, it appeared that the present hitch is about restricting processing to their own catch—a condition not indicated in the letter of intent. Their plant is in Thane (Bombay), whereas the operation of their vessels along the west coast was disastrous. Hence they had to move their vessels to Visakhapatnam and obviously they cannot feed their plant at Thane with their catch from Visakhapatnam. Besides, the plant capacity far exceeds the production by their own vessels. The company also feels that such a far-reaching condition cannot be imposed now as a pre-requisite for industrial licensing, when no such provision was prescribed in the letter of intent.

In 1973 the firm decided to enter into deep sea fishing. Asked as to what prompted them to enter this line, it was explained that it was a time the Britannia Industries was a foreign majority (51%) participation company and there were very few avenues of diversification. Since the general talk at that time was very much in favour of deep sea fishing, the company took this decision. It was also thought at that time that possession of captive unit, by way of its own fishing fleet, would be the answer for getting a regular, dependable supply of raw materials. They also felt that earning foreign exchange through exports would place them in a more advantageous position in the matter of foreign exchange release for their other activities.

While arrangements were being made for procuring large vessels, the company started fishing with small fibre-glass boats. Then came the two Mexican trawlers of 23 metres length costing Rs. 35 lakhs each. A locally made 17.5 metre vessel was also acquired, although it never worked. The Mexican trawlers were not able to break even at Visakhapatnam. Attempts to operate from west coast were, as already mentioned, disastrous.

The company filed an application in 1977 for chartering an 80 metres vessel from East Germany for a period of 3 years. Although they were keen about this charter and sent their delegation to East Germany, the collaborators lost interest and they have stopped chasing their case which is still pending disposal. The company has also apparently lost interest in both shrimp processing and deep sea fishing in the wake of accumulated loss, protracted labour problems, crew problems, steep rise in fuel costs and wages, and above all hurdles in getting the necessary clearances.

Trans-Continental Fisheries (India) Private Limited

Trans-Continental Fisheries Private Limited was incorporated in October 1979 with the object of initiating a joint venture in fishing with Canpex Corporation, London, but for some reason, the collaboration did not materialize. Earlier the promoter of this company had proposed the formation of a comany under the name Consolidated Fishing Corporation for a joint venture with Agro-Fisheries (West Africa) Limited, Lagos, Nigeria, with sponsorship from Dalmal and Sons Limited, London. According to this proposal, Consolidated Fishing Corporation proposed to have operational bases at Visakhapatnam, Madras, Bombay and Cochin. The company proposed to invest Rs. 6.5 crore on vessels and processing plants and Rs. 10 lakhs on land and buildings and a working capital of Rs. 35 lakhs. It was proposed that in the initial stages the company would charter 4 trawlers of 80/90 metre length for one year on a fixed cost time charter. It was also envisaged that the charter hire charges would be paid out of earnings and that there would be no net foreign exchange outgo. The payment of hire charges would be further restricted to 90 per cent of the value of exports. If 90 per cent of the value of exports exceeded the charter hire, then the payment was limited to fixed hire charge, and the rest will accrue to the Indian company. Although the necessary government sanction was received, the Indian company had to give up this proposal. Very soon an alternate proposal on similar lines was submitted with Canpex Corporation, London, and the Indian party changed its name to Trans-Continental Fisheries (India) Limited. The necessary sanction for change of collaboration was also granted by the government by May 1979, and the necessary agreement for collaboration was signed and other formalities completed. For the second time the collaboration failed to start. When the promoter of the company was contacted for the reason, his reply was "the information available about potential of the sea seems so uncertain. Reports of catches vary from source to source and nobody is able to pay anything categorically. The whole thing gives an impression of being a gamble . . . ."

International Sea Foods Private Limited, Hyderabad

This company was incorporated in May 1977 and was given permission to charter two shrimp trawlers of 67 ft. length from Well Aids International, Abu Dhabi, for a period of two years. Right from the biginning there was apprehension whether a vessel, which was 7 years old, would be suitable. But, the charterers got over the initial objection by giving a certificate of fitness. The necessary formalities were gone through and the two vessels started operating from Visakhapatnam. However, the vessel was mostly under repairs and did not fish most of the time. The total catch during the first year was only 3.655 tonnes for one vessel and 0.432 tonné for another vessel. The government did not issue permission for extension of this charter operation.

Asra Sea Foods (P) Limited, Bombay

Originally Asra Sea Foods Limited made a proposal for chartering 4 vessels, 2 from Holland and 2 from Spain. Subsequently, they changed their proposal to chartering one stern trawler of 37 metre length from Spain at a hire charge of Rs. 60 lakhs for 400 days and a 15-year-old vessel for a hire charge of Rs. 106.6 lakhs for the same period. The Indian company was registered with an authorised capital of Rs. 25 lakhs and a paid up capital of Rs. 12.5 lakhs. The company had proposals to establish a chain of processing and quick freeze plants at Goa, Bombay and Daman to create a storage capacity of 550 tonnes of frozen fish at a cost of Rs. 1 crore. The chief promoter of the company (also a Director) had previous experience of running a cold chain in Nigeria with a turn over of $ 33 million and extensive business connections with fishing firms all over the world. The proposal did not materialize as, according to the promoter, "the Spanish owners, to say the least, are disgusted with the way we have been dealing with this case. They say they have submitted their offer in July 1978 and expected it to be decided in either way within a month or two. They never expected the Indian Government would take four months to consider the case and then suggest some modifications. So long as they are concerned, the offer is no longer valid". The party also raised certain fundamental issues as to why the government should look into the rate of charter fee or profitability when the risk was entirely theirs.

Aquamarine Products Exports Private Limited, Kakinada (A.P.)

Aquamarine Products Exports Private Limited, Kakinada, made arrangements for importing two 23 metre shrimp trawlers from Mexico with financial arrangements through SDFC and State Bank of India and a joint venture with Nichiro Gyogyo Kaisha Limited, Nichiro Gyogyo Kaisha Limited was a very large company operating 122 fishing vessels, including five nuclear powered mother vessels. They had their fishing operations in North Pacific, Baring Sea, South Alaska Bay, North-Western Atlantic, seas off west Africa and Arabian Peninsula. They operated long-liners, purse-seiners and pole and line fishing vessels. The proposal included chartering of four fishing vessels of over 36 metres length for one year initially with option to purchase at the end of the charter. The charter hire was fixed at $ 1,200,000 per annum per trawler as an all inclusive fixed amount. This was to be paid out of earnings, limited to 80 per cent of the earnings. The foreign company was to have 25 per cent equity participation and one

Director on the Board of Directors. Although the Indian company executed the necessary arrangement with the Japanese company, confirmed compliance to various terms and conditions of charter, supplied statement regarding the capital structure of the company and the necessary legal document regarding export obligation, the sanction is still kept in abeyance by the government, pending an enquiry into the disappearance of their two Mexican vessels on their way to India from Mexico.

Sun Harbour Industries

A proposal for joint venture with Sun Harbour Industries, San Diego, California, was mooted in 1977 by the Indian Embassy in USA. Thereafter a five-member delegation led by its President and the influential Mr. William Simon, former US Secretary of Treasury, visited Delhi, Bombay, Cochin and Visakhapatnam, and held discussions with various fishing enterprises. At the conclusion of their visit, they expressed interest in taking up a joint venture in tuna fishing in collaboration with Andhra Pradesh Fisheries Corporation and Kerala Fisheries Corporation. They had proposed that the project should be developed in 3 stages. In the first phase, with duration of one year, the known tuna resources would be harvested with a fleet of purse-seiners and 3 bait vessels. During the second phase, work would be undertaken to determine the most effective fishing methods and most productive fish waters for a duration of 18 months. In the third phase, spread over a period of 5 years, collaboration would develop to establish a fully integrated fish harvesting, processing and marketing industry with a fleet of 10 to 25 vessels and onshore freezing facilities. The total investment was indicated as in the region of $ 18 million. Sun Harbour Industries proposed an equity participation of upto 50 per cent. It was at this time that it came to light that the parent company of Sun Harbour Industries, namely, Westgate (California) Corporation was in financial difficulties and had already filed a voluntary debt relief petition in 1974 under the Bankruptcy Act. It was also revealed that the company was themselves charterers and marketing agents rather than owners of fishing vessels. In this context, negotiations ended in a pell-mell.

Proposals from USA and USSR

One of the earliest proposals was from Van Camp Sea Foods of USA. While negotiations continued for some years, the exact reason for the breakdown of negotiations is not known. Similarly, proposals have been received by various parties for joint venture fishing, processing and marketing with well known US fishing companies like Star-kist Sea Foods. Bumble Bee Sea Foods and so on. Similarly it is understood that USSR had been offering joint venture and charter arrangements with Indian fishing companies. The reason why these proposals have failed to materialize lends substance to the government's approach to 'Indian Ocean as a zone of peace, free from power rivalry' even in the case of fishing.

Joint Venture in Tuna Fishing by the State Trading Corporation of India (STC)

Large deep swimming tunas are mostly caught on long lines, while the surface swimming tunas (skip-jack and yellow-fin tuna) are caught on pole and line and purse-seines. On a global basis there is little scope for increasing tuna long lining, as many areas are already overfished. In India there is no commercial tuna long lining as the hooking rate in exploratory long lining was not found to be sufficiently high to engage them. However, there has been appreciable improvement in the hooking rate with the deployment of experts from Japan in recent years. Long lining using mechanized boats has been tried and found to be economical mostly because of the large quantity of sharks caught. As for surface swimming tunas, there is a traditional pole and line fishing in vogue in the Lakshadweep and the adjoining Republic of Maldives. Both countries have gone in for mechanized boats for pole and line fishing and their operations are economical. Operation of large pole and fishing vessel, although not tried by India, is believed to be economical in the Great Nicobar Island area, in the light of a UNDP assisted project in Thailand. Stray trials in Sri Lanka were not very encouraging. A much bigger catch is possible with large, sophisticated tuna-seiners, with a helicopter on board for scouting, a large purse seine net for impounding shoals, and onboard freezing and canning facilities to remain fishing for long periods. Operation of such super-seiners has been on the cards. The only significant example is that of the

State Trading Corporation of India (STC).

The State Trading Corporation (STC) has been trying to form joint venture enterprise in tuna fishing since 1976 and held negotiations with 12 foreign companies before one was selected for a feasibility study and another for an experimental commercial fishing. The companies with whom negotiations were held were :

1. Cofrepeche of France
2. J.C. Martinez of Philippines
3. C. Itoh of Japan
4. Safool of Adilaide (Australia)
5. Atlas of Denmark
6. Newfoundlands Ocean Resource Development Corporation (NORDCO) of Canada
7. Fisheries Development Limited, London
8. Europesca of Spain
9. Swedfish of Sweden
10. Austrek of Sydney (Australia)
11. Star Kist of USA., and
12. Societa Esercizio Cantieri of Italy (SEC).

Based on these negotiations, STC decided to enter into tuna fishing in a phased manner. In the first phase, it was proposed to have a feasibility study. NORDCO of Canada funded and fielded this feasibility study during 1983. Their report indicated reasonably good prospect for undertaking tuna fishing in Indian waters. The report, however, recommended an experimental commercial fishing, before undertaking a commercial tuna fishing.

Societa Eserizio Cantcieri (SEC) was contracted for the second phase to undertake an experimental commercial fishing for a period of one year, which will cost $ 5.5 million of which 80 per cent would be contributed by the Government of Italy, 10 per cent by SEC and 10 per cent by STC. STC's contribution will be in Indian rupees. Under the agreement signed in July 1984, and awaiting government approval, SEC will supply and operate a 68 metre tuna super seiner for one year and the catch is expected to be in the region of 7,000 tonnes. The sale proceeds will be shared equally between SEC and STC, no share being paid to the Government of Italy as their contribution is by way of grant.

Monitoring of the experimental commercial fishing will be done by Indian National Fishery Institutes, for which working arrangements are being made. During this phase, market tie-ups will also be arranged. If the objectives of experimental commercial fishing are substantially achieved, STC will move into the third phase.

The third phase is a joint venture in tuna fishing. Under the rules, the Indian partner is required to contribute 63 per cent of the share capital, which may be waived in case of tuna fishing to one of the majority participation by STC in the equity of the joint venture company, which may amount to $ 25 miilion. If everything goes well the new company will start commercial fishing by October 1985. State Trading Corporation (STC) is also considering the possibility of associating one Indian fishing company as partner. However, no decision has been taken on the partners, both Indian and foreign.

AN INTROSPECT INTO THE INDIAN EXPERIENCE

While India welcomes joint venture and foreign capital, and deep sea fishing is identified as a priority sector, the poor performance of the deep sea fishing in general and joint ventures in deep sea fishing in particular comes as a surprise, especially since 80 per cent of the central government's plan provision for fisheries development is towards development of deep sea fishing. The questions often asked are : (1) Are there not sufficient fish resources ? (2) Is the Indian bureaucracy so strong or inefficient ? (3) Are there no good Indian entrepreneurs ? (4) Is the infrastructure absent or inadequate ? and (5) Is there no remedy at all to this morbid situation ? These issues are considered below.

Are there no sufficient fish resources ?

It is unfortunate that the Exploratory Fisheries Project and the Central Marine Fisheries Research Institute could not come out with a more precise resource picture of the deep sea fishery resources. Neverthless the Exploratory Fishery Project has given qualitative and quantitative assessment of the ground fish resources available for harvesting particularly from the west coast. Likewise information is available on the pelagic fishery resources along the south west coast based on surveys conducted by the

Pelagic Fisheries Project. As a result of these surveys, it is estimated that substantial additional resources of catfish, perches, red mullets, sharks, sciaenids, cephalopods, pomfrets, ribbon fish, anchovies, tunas, mackerel, sardines, miscellaneous species, and so on are now known to be available for exploitation. However, the economics of operation, as revealed by exploratory surveys, are far from stimulating.

The fact that foreign fishing vessels are often found fishing in our waters even at the risk of confiscation of vessels and imprisonment of crew is considered in some quarters as indicative of economically attractive resources. But it should be noted that in quite a number of cases, these are only seasonal migrants trying to explore new pastures. Vessels from some of the South East Asian countries have more precise information of the resources and they have found it possible to exploit them economically. The viability of their fishing is because of their cheaper and functional type of vessels, extremely hard working crew, various incentives and concessions given by their countries to encourage distant water fishing and a much higher price realization in their country for the miscellaneous varieties of fish. It would, therefore, appear that it is not the lack of fishable resources but an approach, encouragement and markets similar to that of these fishery developed countries that is required for the development of deep sea fishing in India.

Is Indian bureaucracy so strong or inefficient ?

There is general feeling that a great deal of avoidable delays take place in government offices, but in reality delays are due to different reasons. In the first instance, over years the bureaucracy has only weakened. The decision making responsibility is now getting shifted to higher echelons in the administration, partly due to lack of delegation of powers at appropriate levels and partly because of the prevailing climate where officers find it safe to spread the responsibility over a larger section of the administration, lest motives be attributed to decision taken.

Another reason for delay is the proliferation of organisations, departments and ministries, lengthening the consultation chain and surfacing contradictory views. In the case of development of deep sea fishing, there is no denying that one should get suitable vessels at competitive prices. In deep sea fishing industry where economic viability is only at a high level of efficiency, extraneous considerations can spell disaster. If instead of good proven fishing vessels, the fishing industry is made to accept indigenously constructed vessels, which are twice as costly, with poor performance, indefinite waiting and insufficient stability, then fishing industry is bound to lose heavily. At the same time Department of Heavy Industry and Defence Production try to block imports to get more orders for their yards. Similarly Ministry of Finance may be worried about initial outgo of foreign exchange on foreign technicians and so on. These stances affect the viability of proposals and lead to considerable delays in the final acceptance of the proposal. Many entrepreneurs gave up their proposals in exasperation. As pointed out in the case of studies, quite a number of fishing companies have lost heavily on account of the stance taken by the various government departments. The inordinate delay in getting clearances is also scaring away investments and collaboration opportunities.

Discussion on this item will not be complete without reference to government policies. As indicated elsewhere, we cannot place too many restrictions in the path of a nascent industry. Today there is a great scope for joint ventures and charters. While selecting partners for joint ventures and charters, one should go by professional expertise and adaptability of technology to local conditions. For miscellaneous species, which form the bulk of our resources, technology of the South East Asian countries appears to be the most appropriate although many of them have a bad reputation for poaching. By inducting their assistance from the so-called poaching countries and big powers in joint ventures and charter, we would be able to quickly develop our deep sea fishing. Similarly USA has expertise in large-scale tuna fishing, particularly using super-seiners. Japan, Korea, Taiwan, Thailand and USSR have a large fleet of distant water fishing vessels with experience of the region. If we induct fishing enterprise from these countries, we can quickly develop our fisheries, for which purpose objections on poaching history, big or small powers and so on should not come in the way. In fact, many of the developing countries in the region were technologically far behind India and have forged ahead simply because in the interest of development of fisheries, such considerations were given only a secondary place. A careful examination of the subject will reveal that many of the governmental objections on account of poaching, big powers, defence interests, foreign exchange out-go and economic viability are frivolous.

Poaching

Foreign fishing vessels sighted in our waters are from Japan (not nowadays), USSR, Korea, Thailand and Taiwan, which are the leading marine fishing countries of the world with a sizeable fleet of distant water fishing vessels. In the past also, they have been fishing in our waters, when our sovereignity extended only to territorial waters. The following statistics will reveal their position in the world fisheries :

TABLE 11.1 : **World fisheries**

Name of country	Marine fish production (millions of tonnes)	Rank in marine fish production	Per capita consumption fish (kg/annum)
Japan	9.97	1	66
USSR	8.30	2	N.A.
Taiwan	0.87	—	35
Korea (South and North)	3.38	5	40
Thailand	1.56	8	22
India	1.49	13	3
World	63.80	—	13

Source : FAO Fishery Statistics, 1979.

Big powers

The big powers are also fishery advanced countries, occupying the second and third positions in world fish production.

Defence interests

There is always a tendency to accommodate defence interests without an argument. In the first place, in these days of remote sensing, there is not much scope for keeping any such secret, as it is no longer necessary to take out a vessel for collecting any such data. Secondly even if such data is required to be collected or confirmed, the freedom of passage enjoyed by cargo and passenger vessels is sufficient for this purpose. Thirdly, one hears about joint oceanographic explorations and naval exercises by the very kind of vessels that are equipped for this purpose. If these have no risks, where is the risk with a fishing vessel ?

Foreign exchange

Marine products come seventh in the order of foreign exchange earnings commodities of India. A small amount advanced in foreign exchange is made good in a short time in foreign exchange through export of marine products. If charters and foreign collaborations are allowed, then there is no initial foreign exchange outgo either.

Economic viability

The entire risk is taken by the participating agencies, who are better placed to take an investment decision. Even if the project fails, there is no risk so far as government is concerned and in most cases for the Indian party also, as the entire risk is taken by the foreign collaborator. If Indian fishery is to develop, some risks have to be taken, but the present arrangements provide the best possible protection against economic risks. Here again, cost of delays is much more crucial, compared to operational risks, as is revealed by some of the case studies.

Is the infrastructure absent ?

The infrastructure required for successful deep sea fishing is many and varied. It includes fishing harbours with facilities for quick turnover at ports, adequate trained manpowers, fish handling and processing facilities, dependable markets, and so on. A large number of fishing harbours, capable of handling deep sea fishing vessels are under construction. But many port trusts and port departments have raised user charges to such levels that they work as a disincentive. Paradeep is an example of this. This applies to fuel, purchase tax, labour wages and so on.

Special mention must be made about labour. This country has the most progressive labour laws, which in essence would mean less work and more emoluments and facilities. Unless there is a change in the attitude of labour and a climate of disciplined and sustained work, deep sea fishing will be a non-starter. Many of the land based labour laws are clearly not applicable to sea jobs. After all the wages given are significantly higher to compensate for the rigorous nature of the work. Separate rules should be framed to cover work on board fishing vessels.

Deep sea fishing in India is export oriented. While high priced varieties should be exported, export of low priced varieties, besides being uneconomical, is denying fish to the local population. It is distressing to note that shrimp trawlers discard the major part of their catch and concentrate on shrimp which may be only 10-15 per cent of the catch. This is because a remunerative domestic market has not been built up for these varieties. Relatively simple procedures of processing can make these products quite acceptable in the domestic market.

Are there no good entrepreneurs ?

Deep sea fishing has attracted the major business houses in India. But many of them have turned back sustaining and incurring huge losses in the process. They can survive only if assured of a certain minimum volume of business, as their overheads are higher. While there is no restriction to big companies in the export trade, several restrictions are clamped on them in respect of export of marine products. For instance there is a condition that large business houses should not enter into the local market to purchase raw material for processing. Similarly when soft loans from SDFC are available to large business houses for the purchase of large ships, the SDFC loans for purchase of fishing vessels are not available. A sea-change in the approach to deep sea fishing is necessary before entrepreneurship can develop.

APPENDIX-I

IMPORTANT INDIAN REGULATIONS AND CONCESSIONS CONCERNING JOINT VENTURES IN DEEP SEA FISHING WITH FOREIGN COLLABORATION

The basic policy of the Government of India is to welcome foreign invesment on a selective basis in fields in which such investment would be of advantage to the Indian economy. One of the fields covered in the selected items is deep sea fishing. The Indian regulations concerning joint ventures with foreign collaboration are as follows.

Equity participation

Foreign equity participation up to 40 per cent is allowed either in cash or kind. In the case of export oriented industries and industries requiring sophisticated technology such as deep sea fishing, majority participation may be considered on merits. The foreign share capital should be by way of cash without being linked to tied imports of machinery and equipment or to payments for know-how, trade marks, brand names, and so on.

Technical collaboration

The collaboration agreements are approved normally for a period of five years from the date of agreement of five years from the commencement of production provided production is not delayed for a period of three years from the signing of agreement. Extension of the duration is agreed on merits and if the Government is satisfied that the technology transferred is not properly assimilated in an industry under consideration or the agreement relates to export oriented industry. There should be provision in the agreement that there would not be any restriction on the Indian company in the matter of procurement of capital goods, components, spares, raw materials pricing policy, selling arrangements and so on. The collaboration agreement should not also place any export restriction on the Indian party without valid reasons. The Indian party will be free to export to any countries except when the collaborator has sub-licensing arragements. There should be no provision for use of foreign brand names on products for internal sale, although there is objection to their use on products to be exported. In case any consultancy is also considered necessary, any Indian consultancy firm should nevertheless be the prime consultants.

Export oriented industries

Foreign investment and collaboration are liberally welcomed in industries which are predominantly export oriented and where the link with foreign collaborator will provide an avenue for export 100 per cent of all exportable marine products should be exported.

Procedure

Entrepreneurs desirous of setting up an industry with foreign collaboration have first to obtain a letter of intent. Entrepreneurs have to apply to the Foreign Investment Board (FIB) for the issue of a Letter of Intent.

Industrial licensing

Fishing as such is not a licenseable industry in India. However, the share establishments for processing of marine products have to be covered by an industrial licence to be issued by the Government of India. Small and medium entrepreneurs whose investment does not exceed Rs. 10 million in land, buildings, plant and machinery are generally exempted from licensing. In order to reduce the delay involved, government have decided that it will be sufficient to apply for capital goods and foreign collaboration clearances straightaway for schemes which are eligible for exemption from industrial licensing. Such units, will, however, require registration with the concerned authorities such as the Directorate General of Technical Development and so on.

Employment of foreign technicians by joint ventures

Employment of one fishing technician, and one engineer on each fishing vessel operated by the joint venture company is allowed. The employment of one fleet manager in case the number of vessels operated exceeds two is also permitted.

Flags to be flown on vessels operated by joint ventures

If the vessels are owned by the joint venture company they have to be registered in India and fly the Indian flag. If the vessels are chartered, they may fly the flag of the country of registration during the charter period.

Conditions governing the operation of the fishing vessels by joint ventures

(i) The vessels should operate beyond the range of operations of mechanised and non-mechanised fishing boats and as per the directions given by the Government from time to time;

(ii) The full list of the main items of equipment and machinery including acoustic equipment and communication equipments should be furnished to the Government;

(iii) The vessels should start operation only after they are inspected by the nominated officials of the Government of India and duly cleared by them;

(iv) The full list of the names, nationalities and qualifications of all the crew members should be furnished to the Government;

(v) The foreign personnel should be employed only after obtaining specific clearance of the Government. The Indian counterpart should make arrangements for the training of Indian counterparts personnel under the foreign technicians;

(vi) The joint venture company should furnish once in a quarter full particulars of the data of fishing operations gathered during the period;

(vii) Government will have the right to inspect the vessels at any time; and

(viii) The foreign collaborator should undertake to provide full technical and managerial know-how to the joint venture enterprise.

The position concerning concessions and incentives given to joint venture enterprises is broadly as under :

CONCESSIONS

1. No discrimination is made against foreign capital once it is admitted into the country.
2. Remittance of profits and dividends is freely allowed.
3. The repatriation of foreign capital investment is allowed freely together with profits ploughed back and any capital depreciation in the value of investments.
4. Fisheries techicians/engine drivers/fleet managers are exempt from income tax on remuneration up to Rs. 4,000 per month for an initial period of two years. The remuneration in excess of Rs. 4,000 per month will be liable to tax. If the employer pays the tax on such excess remuneration the perquisites represented by such payment of tax by the employer will also be exempt from further taxation in the hands of the technician. In the initial period of two years from the date of arrival in India the whole of the remuneration, the perquisities represented by such payment of tax by the employer will be exempt from further taxation in the hands of foreign technician for further period of two years.
5. The holiday is given for newly established industrial undertakings. The profits of a new industrial undertaking is exempted from tax upto 7½ per cent per annum on the capital employed as computed under the rules prescribed.

   The deduction from profits upto 7½ per cent is allowed from the year of commencement of the business in the next four years. If the profits are in excess of 7½ per cent such excess is taxed. Where there are no profits or where the profits fall short of the capital employed, such deficiency in profits is allowed to be carried forward and set off in the subsequent years upto the end of the eighth year, including the initial year of assessment. While the carry forward is permitted upto the end of the eighth year, the deduction up to 7½ per cent of the capital is limited to five years. These concessions will, however, be available only when the company is not formed by the split up or reconsideration of a business already in existence, it is not formed by the transfer to a new business or a building machinery or plant and employs 10 or more workers in a manufacturing process carried on with the aid of power (Section 80J of Income Tax Act, 1981).

6. Inter-corporate dividends received by the foreign company from the Indian Company are taxed at 25 per cent (Section 115A of Income Tax, 1961).
7. Depreciation allowance is granted to tax-payers on buildings, furniture, plant and machinery at prescribed rate. This varies from 2.5 per cent to 100 per cent depending on the nature of the item.
8. Under the existing provision of the Income Tax Act, interest payable by an industrial undertaking in India on moneys borrowed by it under a loan agreement entered into with any approved financial institution in a foreign country is exempt from income-tax. Interest payable by industrial undertakings in India on any money borrowed or debt incurred in a foreign country in respect of purchase outside India or raw materials or capital plant and machinery is also exempt from tax, to the extent to which such interest does not exceed the amount of interest calculated at the rate approved by the Central Government in this behalf. (Section 10 (15)/IV of the Income Tax Act, 1961).

12

MARKETING OF MARINE FISH*
Some Policy Issues

AMARJEET SINGH
AND
V.K. GUPTA

MARINE fish landings increased from 815 thousand MT in 1965 to 1394 thousand MT in 1978 showing an annual rate of growth at 5.1 per cent. More importantly, exports of marine products increased from 15.5 thousand MT in 1965 to 78 thousand MT in 1978 with an annual growth rate of 29 per cent (Table 12.1).

The nature and extent of growth of marine fish landing was influenced by changes in fishing fleet. Non-mechanized boats decreased in all the maritime states except in Tamil Nadu and Pondicherry. The highest average annual decline of 1780 was for Andhra Pradesh. On the other hand mechanised boats registered an average growth of 1130 boats per annum. This was typified mainly by growth in trawlers, with the exception of purse seiners in Karnataka. Maharashtra, Kerala and Gujarat were leading states in the use of mechanized boats (Table 12.2).

The landing and berthing infrastructure support for mechanized boats, however, remained poor. In 1978, there were only 42 jetties and 15 fishing harbours to accommodate more than 14 thousand mechanized boats. The maximum number of jetties were in Gujarat (17) and the maximum number of harbours in Kerala (6). Only 13 jetties and 10 harbours were under construction during 1978. The capacity was even smaller for larger boats (23 mts and above).

*The paper is taken from U.K. Srivastava and M.D. Reddy (Ed.) *Fisheries Development in India*, Concept Publishing Company, New Delhi, 1983, pp. 139-74. This has been reprinted here with the permission of the authors and editors.

TABLE 12.1 : **Coastwise production and exports of marine fish (1965-78)**

(Qty. in '000 MT)

Year	Production*			Exports**	
	East coast	West coast	Total	Quantity (product weight)	Value (Rs. '000)
1965	195	620	815	15.5	69.2
1966	238	702	940	19.2	135.2
1967	223	622	845	21.8	199.3
1968	240	644	884	24.8	220.2
1969	262	649	911	30.6	330.7
1970	272	809	1,081	37.2	355.4
1971	273	886	1,159	34.0	391.7
1972	264	705	969	38.3	581.3
1973	313	903	1,216	48.8	795.8
1974	368	912	1,280	46.6	763.1
1975	430	988	1,418	53.4	1049.1
1976	423	926	1,349	62.2	1798.6
1977	335	921	1,256	65.0	1797.4
1978	354	1,040	1,394	78.0	2121.6

Source : *Production data obtained from CMFRI publications.
**Export data obtained from Marine Products Export Development Authority, Cochin, 1978.

The rapid growth in mechanized boats, and the decline in non-mechanized boats led to several changes in the structure of the fishing industry. The industry experienced entry of a large number of entrepreneurs including large business houses in establishing export oriented processing facilities. However, in spite of the growth in the fish production, the price indices of fish increased at a faster pace than prices of all food articles as well as all commodities (Table 12.3). This raised questions in relation to the role of intermediaries, and about the adequacy of marketing infrastructure. This paper examines the prevailing marketing systems with a view to :

(a) analyse the fish marketing flows, both in terms of utilisation pattern, and physical flows,
(b) analyse costs, commissions, risks, profits, and structure

TABLE 12.2 : **Growth of fishing fleet in different states, India, (1972-77)**

	Non-mechanised crafts[a]			Mechanised crafts[b]		
	1972[a]	1977	Annual decline	1972	1977	Annual growth
Gujarat*	3,900	3,371	—106	1,237	2,368	226
Maharashtra	11,150	7,640	—702	2,431	3,108	135
Goa	N.A	2,889	—578	70[a]	408	68
Karnataka	8,600	8,140**	—77	1,123[a]	1,525	80
Kerala	30,600	27,559	—608	2,014*	2,936	243
Tamil Nadu	30,200	37,000	1,360	1,084	2,152	213
Pondicherry	1,900	2,350**	75	151*	211*	10
Andhra Pradesh	32,900	24,000	—1,780	400	809**	58
Orissa	N.A.	7,000	—1,400	122*	395(b)	55
West Bengal	N.A.	3,030	—606	5*	216	42
Total	1,19,250	1,22,979		8,637	14,178	1143

Note : *a* *Excluding Kutch Region.
[a]includes inland fish crafts figures in parentheses of column relating to 1973-77 are the per cent change in the total number of crafts between 1961-62 and 1973-77.
**figures relate to 1978-79.

Note : *b* [a]indicates data to 1972-73.
*relates to 1973-74.
**relates to 1979.
(b) 1977-78.

of various fish marketing organizations,

(c) estimate the price spread under different sceneries, and

(d) analyse the role of co-operatives and corporations in the domestic fish marketing system.

MARKETING FLOWS

Changes in the use flows

The estimated production in 1978-79 was 15 lakh* MT. It was used as below :

Fresh	—43.8%
Dry edible	—31.5%
Fish meal	—14.7%
Exports	—10.8%

It is important to note that there was a continuous decline in the share of production of domestic fresh fish in the total marine fish production. The share of domestic fresh fish consumption was 71.2 per cent in 1966. It declined to 43 per cent in 1978-79 (Table 12.4). As a result, the availability of the net domestic fresh fish virtually remained almost static between 1966 and 1978-79. This resulted in a steep rise in the fish price indices. Price indices of fish reached 1851.4 (base 1961-62) all commodities (Table 12.3). It is estimated that the demand pressure for domestic fresh fish consumption on marine fish is likely to increase considerably by 1985, due to rising population and incomes. Our estimates are that the demand supply gap will be of the order of one million tonnes by 1985.

The decline in the share of production of domestic fresh fish can be attributed mainly to the factors such as the nature of

*The fish production statistics are available from two sources : (a) State Government of the respective maritime states, and (b) Central Marine Fisheries Research Institute (CMFRI), Cochin. Further, the estimates used in this paper are compiled on the basis of the data obtained from the respective state governments. However, there are few states, such as Andhra Pradesh for which there are no estimates of fish landings available from State Governments. In such cases we have used the data from CMFRI.

mechanization, and lack of proper marketing infrastructure. As already stated the non-mechanized boats which mainly produce for domestic consumption were declining in numbers. Growth in the mechanized fleet had been dominated by trawlers which mainly catered to exportable species or dry fish varieties. adding very little to supplies for domestics fresh fish market. In case of purse seiners, the landings were usually in very large quantities, and the existing marketing systems and infrastructure could not cope with the landings resulting in large scale diversion to drying yards. There is an urgent need for overall policy for the required boat and gear mix, and the nature of marketing support.

TABLE 12.3 : **Annual average indices of wholesale prices of fish, food and all commodities**

(1961-62=100)

Year	Price indices of fish	Price indices of food articles	Price indices of all commodities
1970-71	—	203.9	181.1
1971-72	384.9	210.3	188.4
1972-73	484.7	239.5	207.1
1973-74	757.1	295.6	254.3
1974-75	1,021.3	364.0	313.9
1975-76	1,271.3	347.7	302.7
1976-77	1,397.4	330.1	310.7
1977-78	1,599.0	368.9	336.5
1978-79	1,851.6	366.4	366.5

Source : Compiled from various issues of *Monthly Wholesale Price Index*, New Delhi : (Economic Advisor, Ministry of Industrial Development, Government of India).

While the share of domestic fresh fish in the total landings decreased by half, between 1966 and 1978-79, the share of dry edible and fish meal virtually doubled (Table 12.4). It is interesting to note that the varieties used for dry edible fish are mostly those which do not have a ready market in fresh form in nearby places or which are landed in large quantities and the fresh fish marketing infrastructure cannot bear it (mackeral and sardines).

Over 76 per cent of the fish used for fish meal, or manure,

TABLE 12.4 : Utilisation pattern of marine fish in India for selected years

(*Qty. in '000 MT*)

Year	Fresh	Dry edible	Fish meal	Exportable	Total
1966	634.2	158.2	63.9	34.0	890.3
	(71.2)	(17.8)	(7.2)	(3.8)	(100)
1969	525.0	228.8	103.8	56.0	913.6
	(57.5)	(25.0)	(11.4)	(6.1)	(100)
1972	491.1	286.0	134.9	68.0	980.9
	(50.1)	(29.2)	(13.8)	(6.9)	(100)
1975	675.1	441.6	200.0	106.0	1,422.7
	(47.5)	(31.0)	(14.1)	(7.4)	(100)
1978-79	657.3	482.4	225.3	169.7	1,529.7
	(43.0)	(31.5)	(14.7)	(10.8)	(100)

Source : 1. For 1966, '69, '72 and '75, F.A.O. *Year Book of Fishery Statistics* used incorporating following :

(a) Cured fish, that is, sun dried and salted have been clubbed to indicate dry edible fish.

(b) Miscellaneous and reduction of fish has been treated as fish Meal.

(c) Exportable fish figures have been obtained from Fisheries Department, Ministry of Agriculture for 1969, '72 and '75.

(d) Frozen and canned fish for year 1966 have been treated as exportables.

(e) The utilisation figures as arrived at have been deducted from CMFRI landing data to arrive at fresh fish use.

2. For 1978-79 data, refer *Marine Fish Marketing in India*, Vol. VI, (Ahmedabad : Centre for Management in Agriculture, Indian Institute of Management).

came from demersal fishing operations, which expanded considerably due to rapid increase in the number of trawlers. Along the Gujarat coast, catch in the trawlers has a 'trash' component over 45 per cent.* It is also important to note that this composition has been reported to be on the increase. The low prices of fish caught as trash also influenced the boat economics. If a

*Fish which commands very low prices in fresh condition and is usually used for fish meal extraction is called as 'trash fish'. For further details about the catch composition of different types of boats along Gujarat Coast, see U.K. Srivastava, M.D. Reddy and V.K. Gupta, (1982).

large share of such varieties could be used for consumption by mankind in the form of fish products, such as fish keema, fish paste and fish protein concentrate, not only the domestic supplies could be improved but also the boat economics.

Bulk landings of pelagic varieties during peak season presently cause gluts in the market, and fish prices often reduce to uneconomic levels. Data collected for Karwar indicated that roughly 88 per cent of the landings were in three months, when the average price was less than half of other months. Further, our study revealed that such large fluctuations were not observed in the consumer markets specially those located far away from production centres. There is, therefore, a need for evening out the supplies over the year, which can be conveniently achieved, through freezing and storage operations when prices are low, and selling the same in the off season. The experiences of the Karnataka Fisheries Development Corporation in this regard are worth noting. It is important that similar operations are developed in other states and this operation is integrated on an all-India basis owing to the location of demand centres.

The utilization pattern, however, varied widely across the states, (Table 12.5). Share of fresh fish in total state landings was more in southern states than northern ones. Maharashtra, Kerala and Tamil Nadu produced about 68 per cent of dry edible fish, while Gujarat, Maharashtra and Karnataka accounted for over 77 per cent of the fish used for fish meal extraction. The five maritime states of Kerala, Maharashtra, Tamil Nadu, Gujarat and Karnataka contributed 91 per cent of the total exportable varieties landings. Production units for processed fish (fish products) would, therefore, have to be located in these states.

The coastal fisheries are already showing signs of over exploitation, specially on the west coast, and lower east cost. It is, therefore, necessary to develop deep sea fishing. This is even more important today in view of our sovereign rights over the renewable fishery resources of the 200 mile Exclusive Economic Zones (EEZ). In this zone fishery resources are estimated at 1.71 million tonnes for the off-shore continental shelf area. Survey results upto date indicate that about 70 per cent of the species mix, for the zone may not find domestic market without

TABLE 12.5 : Statewise use flow of marine fish, India 1978-79

(*Qty. in MT raw weight*)

States	Fresh fish		Dry edible		Fish meal		Exportable		Total	
	Quantity	Percentage	Quantity	Percentage	Quantity	Percentage	Quantity	Percentage	Quantity	Percentage
Gujarat	60,318 (26.2)	9.18	68,130 (29.6)	14.12	88,062 (39.3)	39.08	13,461 (5.8)	8.17	2,99,971 (100)	15.03
Maharashtra	1,50,052 (38.8)	22.83	1,29,714 (33.6)	29.89	54,122 (14.0)	24.02	52,383 (13.6)	31.79	3,86,271 (100)	25.25
Goa, Daman and Diu	14,385.5 (43.5)	2.19	8,955 (27.1)	1.86	7,743 (23.4)	3.44	1,986 (6.0)	1.20	33,077 (100)	2.16
Karnataka	68.400 (44.88)	10.41	42,100 (27.66)	8.73	32,100 (21.0)	14.25	10,200 (6.46)	6.19	1,52,800 (100)	9.99
Kerala	2,08,938 (56.0)	31.79	92,472 (24.8)	19.17	13,460 (3.6)	5.97	58,469 (15.7)	35.48	3,73,339 (100)	24.41
Tamil Nadu	89,734 (42.1)	13.65	90,177 (42.4)	18.69	17,626 (8.3)	7.82	15,362 (7.2)	9.32	2,12,899 (100)	13.92
Pondicherry	3,380 (49.5)	0.51	2,720 (39.8)	0.56	380 (5.6)	0.17	350 (5.1)	0.21	6,830 (100)	0.45
Andhra Pradesh	34,374 (41.9)	5.23	30,973 (37.7)	6.42	7,378 (9.0)	3.27	9,391 (11.4)	5.70	82,116 (100)	5.37
Orissa	23,783 (60.0)	3.62	10,840 (27.3)	2.25	2,500 (6.3)	1.11	2,547 (6.4)	1.55	39,670 (100)	2.59
West Bengal	3,902 (30.6)	0.59	6,286 (49.3)	1.30	1,943 (15.2)	0.86	623 (4.9)	0.38	12,754 (100)	0.83
Total	6,57,266.5 (42.97)	100.0	4,82,367 (31.53)	100.0	2,25,314 (14.73)	100.00	16,772 (10.77)	100.00	15,29,720 (100)	100.00

Note : Figures in parentheses represent percentage of total.
Production estimates of CMFRI have been used for all states except Maharashtra, Gujarat and Goa.

conversion into products. To make deep sea fishery economically attractive, and expanding supplies to the domestic market there is a need for developing an all-India cold chain starting with selected deep sea landing centres.

Physical flow of fresh fish

The consumption of frseh fish was highly concentrated in and around the producing centres. Consumption in producing centres and at other locations very near to producing centres and at other locations accounted for about 50 per cent of the fresh fish production. Demand centres located away from producing centres upto a distance of 200 km. from the coast presently consumed another 45 per cent. The balance about 5 per cent alone went to demand centres located beyond 200 km. from the coast (Table 12.6). Large consumption of fish was in the metropolitan cities accounting for 23.2 per cent of total fresh fish. Urban areas consumed 31.4 per cent and the remaining 45.4 per cent was consumed by rural households. The demand was also found to be concentrated around few selected varieties. Hardly any effort has been made to educate the consumers towards accepting lesser known but largely produced fish varieties. It is suggested that such education may be started, to begin with in the urban and metropolitan centres. However, this has to be taken up hand in hand with product development and market development efforts, in terms of the all-India cold chain as suggested earlier.

Given the above consumption pattern, most of the inter-state flows of fresh fish were only around the coast line. In any case the inter-state flows were not very high as they accounted for only 12.4 per cent (82.084 MT) of the production. Furthermore, importance of such movements also varied widely by states. Karnataka exported 48 per cent of its production, Gujarat 23.7 per cent and Orissa 33.6 per cent (Table 12.7). Maharashtra received 16.3 per cent of its consumption while West Bengal imported 78.4 per cent. Most of the states were importers as well as exporters for reasons of varieties and seasons (Table 12.8).

Means of transport

About 55 per cent of the inter-state flows of fresh and 97 per cent of the flows within the states were by road. Road transport was

TABLE 12.6 : **Statewise consumption pattern of marine fresh fish according to distance from coast, India (1978-79)**

State	Consumption at LC's LA's and LAC's	Consumption at CC's Located		Total consumption
		Within 200 kms. from coast	Beyond 200 kms. from coast	
Gujarat	10,600 (22.4)	35,818 (75.9)	800 (1.7)	47,218
Maharashtra	1,09,540 (62.1)	64,962 (36.8)	2,000 (1.1)	1,76,502
Goa, Daman & Diu	5,200 (35.9)	9,304 (64.1)	—	14,504
Karnataka	12,050 (33.7)	9,956 (27.8)	13,800 (38.5)	35,806
Kerala	1,25,728 (61.2)	79,710 (38.8)	—	2,05,438
Tamil Nadu	49,282 (46.7)	51,562 (49.9)	3,500 (3.4)	1,03,344
Pondicherry	1,380 (40.8)	2,000 (59.2)	—	3,380
Andhra Pradesh	10,088 (36.3)	13,261 (47.5)	4,565 (16.2)	27,914
Orissa	1,617 (10)	14,106 (87.2)	450 (2.8)	16,173
West Bengal	350 (1.9)	17,702 (98.1)	—	18,052
Non-coastal states	—	—	8,935 (100)	8,935
Grand total	3,24,835 (49.4)	2,98,381 (45.4)	34,050 (5.2)	6,57,266

Note : Figures in parentheses are percentages in state totals.

preferred as it saved on handling costs. For long distance transport, however, rail transport was the preferred one.

Estimates of average time taken between catch and purchase by the final consumer varied between 20 and 30 hours. The time taken for distant markets was the highest, and was more than 70 hours on some of the routes. About half of the time, the fish

TABLE 12.7 : **Statewise physical flow of fresh fish, India (1978-79)**

(Qty. in M. Tonnes)

State	Inflow	Inflow as percentage of State consumption	Outflow	Outflow as percentage of State landing	Fresh fish State landings	State consumption
Gujarat	1,200	2.54	14,300	23.70	60,318	47,218
Maharashtra	28,770	16.30	2,595	1.73	1,50,052	1,76,502
Goa, Daman & Diu	539	3.72	420	2.91	14,385	14,504
Karnataka	520	1.45	32,839	48.01	68,400	35,806
Kerala	8,900	4.33	12,400	5.93	2,38,938	2,05,436
Tamil Nadu	18,025	17.44	4,415	4.92	89,734	1,03,344
Andhra Pradesh	655	2.34	7,115	20.70	34,374	27,914
Orissa	390	2.41	8'000	33,63	23,783	16,173
West Bengal	14,150	78.38	—	—	3,902	18,052
Pondicherry	—	—	—	—	3,380	3,380
Non-coastal States	8,935	100.00	—	—	—	8,935
Total	82,084	12.49	82,084	12.49	6,57,266	6,57,266

TABLE 12.8 : **Inter-state flow of fresh domestic marine-fish, India (1978-79)**

(*Qty. in M. Tonnes*)

Despatch States	Receiving State Gujarat	Maha-rashtra	Goa	Karna-taka	Kerala	Pondi-cherry	Tamil Nadu	Andhra Pradesh	Orissa	West Bengal	Non-coastal	Total
Gujarat	—	6,800	—	—	—	—	—	—	—	—	7,500	14,300
Maharashtra	1,200	—	—	—	—	—	—	275	—	260	860	2,595
Goa	—	100	—	320	—	—	—	—	—	—	—	420
Karnataka	—	21,200	539	—	6,400	—	4,400	300	—	—	—	32,839
Kerala	—	—	—	100	—	—	12,300	—	—	—	—	12,400
Pondicherry	—	—	—	—	—	—	—	—	—	—	—	—
Tamil Nadu	—	—	—	100	2,500	—	—	80	—	1,735	—	4,415
Andhra Pradesh	—	670	—	—	—	—	1,325	—	390	4,155	575	7,115
Orissa	—	—	—	—	—	—	—	—	—	8,000	—	8,000
West Bengal	—	—	—	—	—	—	—	—	—	—	—	—
Non-coastal	—	—	—	—	—	—	—	—	—	—	—	—
Total	1,200	28,770	539	520	8,900	—	18,025	655	390	14,150	8,935	82,084

remained without ice. It was reported by many organoleptic tests that consumers got unwholesome fish. Research studies do not point out its harmful effects on consumers. In view of the fact that in future we may like to cover more and more distant markets for fresh fish as well as we might feel the necessity for developing cold chain system for the development of deep sea fisheries, it is important to consider investments for improving both road and rail transports which are more adept for perishables like fish.

Physical flow of dry edible fish

As indicated earlier, dry edible fish constituted the second largest use. About 4.82 lakh MT of fish was converted into 1.73 lakh MT of dry fish in 1978-79. The drying operation was usually carried out in open beaches under the sun. The process of drying had implications on quality, health and sanitation, as well as resulted into losses because of birds and animals.

The bulk of the consumption of the dry edible variety was in rural areas (69.6%) and the consumption in urban and metropolitan cities was only 27.2 per cent and 2.3 per cent, respectively. The high rural consumption may be due to its respectively longer shelf life, and case of transport. About 38.4 per cent of the dry edible fish moved across the states. The consumption in non-coastal states was only 10.3 per cent and most of it was consumed in north-east region of the country (Tables 12.9 and 12.10). Even if we diverted a part of these flows to the suggested fish products and the cold chain, it needs to be noted that the overall flows are not going to change substantially with the exploitation of the EEZ resources. It is, therefore, important to raise the issue of improving our drying yards, and the drying practices without changing the present source of energy for drying.

MARKET INTERMEDIARIES

There were six principal types of market intermediaries with different functions in the marine fish trade. These were auctioneers, commission agents (purchase), wholesalers, commission agents (sales), retailers and vendors. A few of these intermediaries undertook multiple functions ; wholesale-cum-retail was the predominant multiple function. Processing (sun drying or salt curing) was

TABLE 12.9 : **Physical flow of dry edible fish in different states, India (1978-79)**

(*Qty. in metric tonnes of dry weight*)

States	Inflow	Inflow as percentage of State's consumption	Outflow	Outflow as percentage of State's production	State's landing	Total consumption
Gujarat	—	—	14,100	70.5	20,000	5,900
Maharashtra	10,874	29.9	13,386	34.4	38,914	36,402
Goa, Diu and Damnan	—	—	1,700	38.0	4,477	2,777
Karnataka	3,010	81.4	16,150	95.9	16,840	3,700
Kerala	7,545	18.3	3,350	9.1	36,989	41,189
Tamil Nadu	6,800	16.8	2,410	0.1	36,071	40,461
Andhra Pradesh	10,520	141.4	15,454	124.7	12,389	7,455
Orissa	6,526	60.6	88	2.0	4,336	10,774
West Bengal	3,534	59.2	78	3.1	2,514	5,970
Pondicherry	—	—	—	—	1,088	1,088
Total non-coastal states	17,907	100.0	—	—	—	17,907
Total	66,716	38.4	66,716	38.43	1,73,618	1,73,618

TABLE 12.10 : Inter-state flow of dry edible marine fish, India (1978-79)

(Qty. in metric tonnes)

Despatching States	Gujarat	Maharashtra	Goa	Karnataka	Kerala	Pondicherry	Tamil Nadu	Andhra Pradesh	Orissa	West Bengal	Non-coastal	Total
Gujarat	—	6,400	—	1,500	—	—	—	2,500	1,000	200	2,500	14,100
Maharashtra	—	—	—	1,000	—	—	—	1,200	2,500	1,186	7,500	13,386
Goa	—	170	—	510	—	—	—	1,020	—	—	—	1,700
Karnataka	—	3,100	—	—	6,700	—	1,550	2,300	—	—	2,500	16,150
Kerala	—	—	—	—	—	—	750	2,600	—	—	—	3,350
Pondicherry	—	—	—	—	—	—	—	—	—	—	—	—
Tamil Nadu	—	—	—	—	845	—	—	900	—	665	—	2,410
Andhra Pradesh	—	1,204	—	—	—	—	4,500	—	3,000	1,400	5,350	15,454
Orissa	—	—	—	—	—	—	—	—	—	83	5	88
West Bengal	—	—	—	—	—	—	—	—	26	—	52	78
Non-coastal	—	—	—	—	—	—	—	—	—	—	—	—
Total	—	10,874	—	3,010	7,545	—	6,800	10,520	6,526	3,534	17,907	66,716

the additional function taken up by fishermen or by one of the intermediaries.

Channels in fresh fish

Fresh fish passed through one to eight hands before it reached the final consumers located at a multitude of places in rural, urban and metropolitan centres. As against the commonly held belief about the existence of large number of intermediaries in the fresh fish trade, our study revealed that bulk of fresh fish (70%) passed only from one to three hands (Table 12.11). As shown in Fig. 12.1 during 1978-79, 16.4 per cent (1.08 lakh MT) of fresh fish was sold by fishermen directly to retailers or vendors, at the production centres. Another 28.1 per cent (1.84 lakh MT) passed through two-member channel. Sales through longer channels (of more than three members) was only 30.2 per cent while very little (only 0.85%) went through channels having more than seven members. The general belief that there are many intermediaries in fish marketing, therefore, does not seem to be correct.

Bulk of the sale (43.5%) was through auctioneers. About 40.1 per cent of the fresh fish production was sold through commission agents (purchase and sale) and/or wholesalers at LAs and LACs. Transactions, by and large, between fishermen and commission agents, and wholesalers represented the absence of auction system. Mutual negotiations between the two were based on long-term relationships, which became the guiding factor in the determination of prices and terms of trade. This is also indicative of the extent to which such intermediaries bonded boats/fishermen through linking credit with marketing.

The direct sale by fishermen to retailers/vendors was usually only at LACs and often constituted the totality of family enterprise where women from the same families retailed the catch of their own boats.

While a large quantity of fish passed through only one to three hands, the extent and the nature of bonding by these channels often led to exploitation of fishermen. At some of the landing centres, it was observed that over 60 per cent of the trade was handled by just about 10 per cent of the traders leading to incompetitive market. These traders also influence the auction

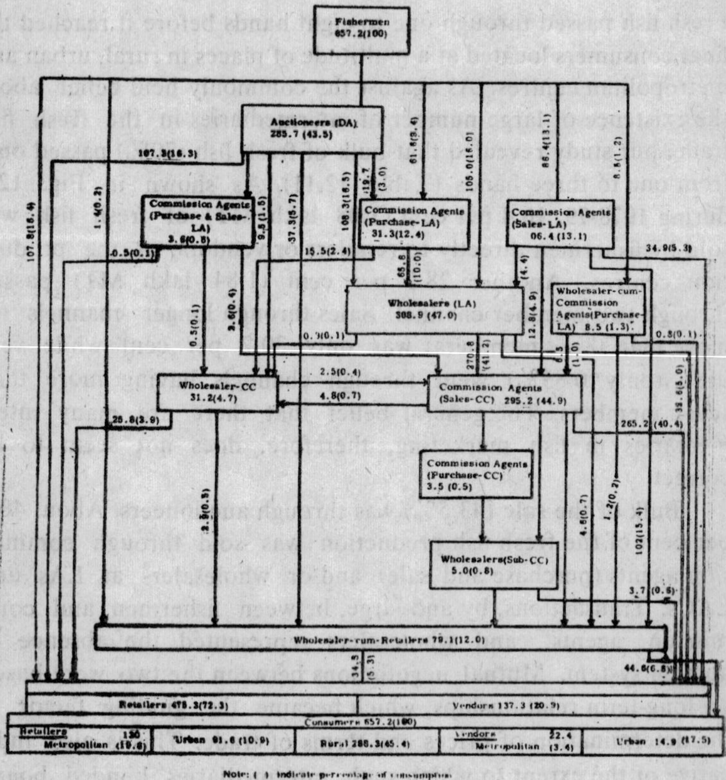

Note : Unit, M.T. in 000's.

FIG. 12.1 : *Fresh fish marketing channds in India (1978-79).*

TABLE 12.11 : **Zonewise fresh fish flow through channel intermediaries**

(*Qty. in '000 tonnns*)

No. of channel intermediaries	NWCR		SWCR		LECR		UECR		Total	
	Qty.	%	Qty.	%	Qty.	%	Qty.	%	Qty.	%
1	64.4	30.6	20.5	7.0	12.0	9.4	11.0	39.7	107.9	16.4
2	32.8	15.6	92.4	31.7	58.4	45.8	1.1	4.0	184.7	28.1
3	88.4	42.0	50.1	17.2	12.1	9.5	15.6	56.3	166.2	25.3
4	17.8	8.5	46.1	15.8	29.8	23.4	—	—	93.7	14.3
5 more than 4	6.9	3.3	82.6	28.3	15.2	11.2	—	—	104.7	15.9
Total production	210.3	100.0	291.7	100.0	127.5	100.0	27.7	100.0	657.2	100.0

Note : The outflows of zone, where only one intermediary of the zone was involved, have been included in three member channel intermediaries flow. And where two intermediaries were involved have been included in four member channel.

prices.* The observation indicated that the market for fish at most of the centres was oligopolistic. To make the trade practices fair and the market more competitive, the policies of the lending institutions will have to be reviewed to accommodate working capital needs. Simultaneously, development of regulated markets on the pattern of agricultural produce markets should be considered. This may include licensing of the market intermediaries, making auction compulsory, providing necessary infrastructure including marketing yards both for fresh and dry fish.

Channels given in Fig. 12.1 indicate that wholesalers at LAs mainly sold through commission agents (sale) at consuming centres ; 87 per cent of their purchases were through this channel.

The prices of fish at consuming centres (CCs) varied widely during a season depending upon arrivals from a multitude of locations. The wholesale intermediaries, therefore, need information, system, storage facilities, and risk bearing ability. In the absence of these, many of the wholesalers paid very low prices to fishermen or to commission agents to cover the risk of price fluctuations. Of late, fishermen themselves have started taking the above marketing risks, and resort to despatching directly to retailers at CCs under their title. In doing this they engaged one or two commission agents (sale) and they bore the risk of the trade. Also, the fishermen's co-operatives, specially in Maharashtra, followed this method successfully, and were able to give a better price to members. Linkage between producing centre's regulation and control with consuming centre's infrastructure will have to be built up. Co-operatives may be the vehicle to ensure the above. However, this needs to be investigated further.

The number and type of channel members varied widely by regions.** Out of the total production, it is important to note that

* The influence of the traders on the auction prices is both direct and indirect. In fact the traders/commission agents are found to have underhand practices to keep the auction prices at a low level.

**Following are the regions for studying fish production and marketing.

NWCR = North West Coast Region comprising Gujarat and Maharashtra.
SWCR = South West Coast Region comprising Goa, Karnataka and Kerala.
LECR = Lower East Coast Region comprising Tamil Nadu, Pondicherry and Andhra Pradesh.
UECR = Upper East Coast Region comprising Orissa and West Bengal.

west coast (SWCR and NWCR) accounted for more than 76 per cent of the production, the East Coast (LECR and UECR) produced only 24 per cent. In the West Coast, only about 34 per cent went through the auction system. The balance moved through different channels, mainly through commission agents and wholesalers. Absence of auction system is again indicative of the presence of bounding factor. It is also indicative of movement of fish to distant markets. Auction system operated more particularly where wholesalers and commission agents were catered to, while comparisons can be made in relation to fishermen's realisations between auction system and direct sales through agents, for want of information about real price paid by them to fishermen, several elements of marketing get determined through an auction sale. For instance, auction sale required some amount of grading, weighing/measuring and declaration of prices. Most of the fishermen were not aware of these factors. In view of the above, it is important to consider regulation of markets as indicated earlier.

Channels in dry edible fish

Processing (sun drying or salt curing) is an essential activity in case of dry edible fish. Fishermen themselves processed only 31.8 per cent of the production. Processors who like a trade handled 49.5 per cent and the wholesalers processed another 18.1 per cent (Table 12.12). As shown in Figure 12.2 dry edible fish also passed through one to nine hands before reaching the final consumer. Auction system was again used to a very limited extent, and it was similar to the fresh fish system. All the auction sales were in raw form.

There are also large transit markets in dry edible fish. In 1978-79 the turnover of TMs was 28 per cent (48.6 thousand MT) of the production. At TMs wholesalers handled 43.4 thousand MT and wholesaler-cum-commission agents handled 25.2 thousand MT. Within the TM, wholesalers bought from and sold to wholesaler-cum-commission agents (sale). As in the case of fresh fish there are regional variations in dry fish marketing practices also. Out of the total production of dry edible fish (173.6 thousand MT) the highest production was in the NWCR (33.9%), followed by SWCR (33.6%), UECR had the least production (4.0%). Fishermen of NWCR processed 80.6 per cent production of the region while in SWCR they processed only 1.9 per cent. Processors processing as percentage of regions production was highest in SWCR (98.1%) followed by UECR (61.5%). Wholesalers processed maximum in LECR (56.7%) while in SWCR they did not process at all (Table 12.11).

TABLE 12.12 : **Dry edible fish processing by different channel members (1978-79)**

(Qty. in '000 tonnes to dry weight)

Processing by	NWCR	SWCR	LECR	UECR	Total
Fishermen	47.5	1.1	5.1	1.6	55.3
	(80.6)	(1.9)	(10.5)	(23.6)	(31.8)
Processors	8.4	57.2	16.0	4.3	85.9
	(14.3)	(98.1)	(32.4)	(61.5)	(49.5)
Wholesalers	3.0	—	28.1	0.2	31.3
	(5.1)	—	(56.7)	(3.2)	(18.1)
Retailers	—	—	0.3	0.8	1.1
	—	—	(0.4)	(11.7)	(0.6)
Grand total	58.9	58.3	49.5	6.9	173.6

Note : Figures in parentheses are percentages of grand total.

Bulk of the dry edible fish (60.7%), as in the case of fresh fish, passed through a maximum of three intermediaries only. However, there were wide variations across the zone. Fishermen's direct sale to retailers was highest in NWCR (40.1%) ; the next highest (21.7%) in UECR. It was lowest in SWCR with only 0.3 per cent share (Table 12.13). It may be so because of the presence of auctioneers, and very low processing by fishermen's family. Flow through two-member channel accounted for one-fourth of the production and it was highest in UECR (42.1%), followed by LECR (33.7%). The overall share of three-member channel was 19.8 per cent and 39.3 per cent for more than three-member channel. SWCR had the highest (66.7%) share of more than three-member channel, maybe because of marketing systems and presence of transit markets (Table 12.13).

It must be noted that requirements of working capital are larger owing to the sun drying process and storage. That is also the area where costs can be high due to losses on account of

TALLE 12.13 : **Zonewise dry edible fish flow through channel intermediaries, India (1978-79)**

(Qty. in '000 tonnes of weight)

No. of intermediaries	NWCR		SWCR		LECR		UECR		Total	
	Qty.	%	Qty.	%	Qty.	%	Qty.	%	Qty.	%
1	23.6	40.1	0.2	0 3	1.6	3.2	1.5	21.7	26.9	15.5
2	14.9	25.3	9.6	16.5	16.7	33.7	2.9	42.1	44.1	25.5
3	12.6	21.4	9.6	16.5	10.5	21.3	1.7	24.6	34.4	19.8
More than 3	7.8	13.2	38.9	66.7	20.7	44.8	0.8	11.6	68.2	39.3
production	58.9	100.0	58.3	100.0	49.5	100.0	6.9	100.0	173.6	100.0

moisture, birds and weather conditions. We have already pointed out that only fishermen in NWCR are engaged in drying processing operation. This is not to say that they do not borrow money from the traders. It is, therefore, important to consider working capital finance in any small fisherman development programme.

Performance of channel members in fresh fish

Working results of four different types of channel members from our sample study across the states, namely, commission agents, wholesalers, retailers and vendors is given in Table 12.13. The average annual quantity handled by wholesaler was 394 MT, commission agent handled 222 MT, retailer 8.6 MT and vendor 4.2 MT. The gross margin as percentage of sale value was highest for vendors (24.7%) followed by wholesalers (22.4%), and retailers (19.6%). Commission agents had the lowest operating costs (1.5%) as they operate with little infrastructure and less personnel. Operating costs for vendors and retailers were higher (3.7% and 4.2%) as percentage of sale value. Annual profit as percentage of sale value for wholesalers and retailers was about 15 per cent. In net value terms, vendors on an average earned only Rs. 3,400 per annum, and the retailers earned Rs. 7,280. These earnings are no more than the amounts of wages which they could earn elsewhere. Wholesalers earned Rs. 1.43 lakhs, and commission agents about Rs. 0.4 lakh. The wholesalers had a better margin for the reasons of stipulated risks incurred both in transport and storage and absorbed all of price fluctuations in the distant markets. An average wholesaler had Rs. 87,780, while commission agents had Rs. 31,080 as total capital. The average amount of capital used by retailers was Rs. 150 and that of vendors only Rs. 30 (Table 12.14).

While the percentage of net profit of wholesalers and retailers was the same, it cannot be considered high for retailers as it did not include his wages. However, in case of wholesalers this may be justifiable, on grounds of risks in advancing credit mostly for working capital to fishermen which no institutional sources of finance were willing to undertake.

Performance of channel members : dry edible fish

Commission agents dealing in dry edible fish operated only in

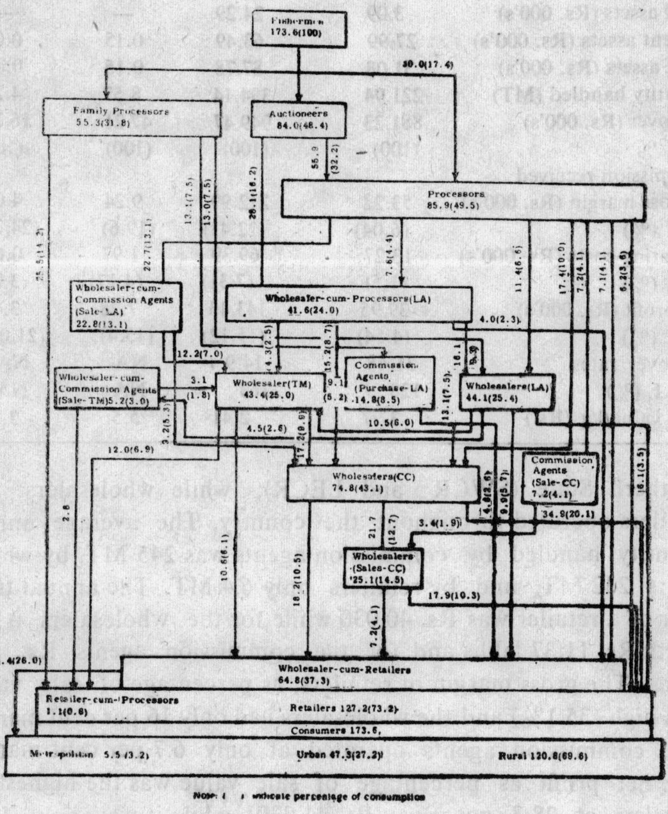

FIG. 12.2 : *Marketing channels of dry edible fish in India (1978-79)*

TABLE 12.14 : **Working results of fresh market intermediaries**

Particulars	Commission agents	Whole-salers	Retailers	Vendors
Fixed assets (Rs. 000's)	3.09	24.29	—	—
Current assets (Rs. 000's)	27.99	63.49	0.15	0.03
Total assets (Rs. 000's)	31.08	87.78	0.15	0.03
Quantity handled (MT)	221.94	394.14	8.57	4.23
Turnover (Rs. 000's)	881.23	949.47	47.21	16.2
%	(100)	(100)	(100)	(100)
Commission received				
Gross margin (Rs. 000's)	53.22	212.99	9.24	4.02
(%)	(6.04)	(22.43)	(19.6)	(24.7)
Operating costs (Rs. 000's)	13.27	69.39	1.97	0.6
(%)	(1.5)	(7.31)	(4.17)	(3.7)
Net profit (Rs. 000's)	39.95	143.46	7.28	3.4
(%)	(4.54)	(15.12)	(15.4)	(21.0)
Turnover rates	31.48	14.9	NA	NA
(R.O.I. (%)	128	163	NA	NA
Sales value/kg (Rs.)	3.97	2.41	5.5	3.8

Southern State (SWCR and LECR), while wholesalers and retailers operated throughout the country. The average annual quantity handled by commission agents was 245 MT, by wholesalers 232 MT, and by retailers only 6.4 MT. The annual turnover of a retailer was Rs. 40,030 while for the wholesalers it was worth Rs. 11.37 lakhs and for the commission agents Rs. 13.8 lakhs. The gross margin of retailers, as percentage of sale value, was high (35.1%) and the wholesalers had only 16 per cent margin. The commission agents operated at only 6.7 per cent margin. The net profit as percentage of sale value was the highest for retailers at 28.3 per cent (Rs. 11,330) while it was only 12.35 per cent (Rs. 114 lakhs) for wholesalers. The commission agents earned only 4.9 per cent (Rs. 0.68 lakhs). The average investment for wholesalers and commission agents was Rs. 81,200 and Rs. 62,750, respectively. The retailer, on an average, invested only Rs. 4,800. From the analysis it can be noted that there was more investment per retailer in dry fish business as compared to fresh fish. However, given the fact of high rate of return on investmests for all intermediaries, the trade cannot be said to be highly competitive (Table 12.15). The number of relailers of dry edible fish can be increased by providing working capital loans to more number of entrepreneurs. This would enhance competition among retailers on the one hand and demand on the other hand. It would also affect negatively on consumer prices and positively on fishermen's realisation.

Price spread of fresh fish

The price spread details of fresh fish for one to four-member marketing channels is given in Table 12.15. The consumer prices increased and share of fishermen in consumer rupee decreased, with the increase in the number of channel members. smaller channels operated for local sales, and larger channels for distant markets. Since the net cost of transport, packing, and so on, per kg of fish did not change by variety, low priced varieties find their way in the local markets, and only high priced varieties were despatched to distant CCs and Sub-CCs.

The fishermen's share in consumer rupee was the highest (80.6%) for the one-member channel, namely, direct sale to retailers/vendors. It was the least for four-member channel (27.9%) namely, auctioneer, wholesaler-commission agent and retailers/

TABLE 12.15 : **Working result of dry edible fish intermediaries**

Particulars	Commission agents	Whole-salers	Retailers
Fixed assets (Rs. 000's)	7.75	10.67	0.8
Current assets (Rs. 000's)	55.00	70.53	4.0
Total assets (Rs. 000's)	62.75	81.20	4.8
Quantity handled (MT)	244.90	231.81	6.4
Turnover (Rs. 000's)	1379.60	1137.07	40.03
(%)	(100)	(100)	(100)
Commission agents/gross margin (Rs. 000's)	92.79	182.93	14.07
(%)	(6.72)	(16.09)	(35.1)
Operating costs (Rs. 000's)	25.00	42.58	2.74
(%)	(1.81)	(3.74)	(6.8)
Net profit (Rs. 000's)	67.79	140.35	11.33
(%)	(4.91)	(12.35)	(28.3)
W.C. turnover ratio	25.00	16.1	9.98
R.O.I. (%)	10.8	173	236
Sales value/kg (Rs.)	5.63	4.90	6.25

vendors since total costs of marketing increased as the length of the channel increased. It was only 5.5 per cent of the consumer rupee for one-member channel while it was 30.9 per cent for the four-member channel. The important point is that the marketing channels are more profit intensive than that of cost intensive. The profits of the intermediary even in one member channel were 13.9 per cent which was far greater than the costs at 5.5 per cent. In the four member channel the profits are 41.2 per cent as compared to cost of 30.9 per cent (Table 12.16). It is, therefore, important to consider ways and means of reducing the length of channels on the one hand, and making the channels more competitive on the other. Marketing policies will have to be developed on this premise.

TABLE 12.16 : **Price spread analysis in fresh fish trade**

Particulars	Flow from			
	LAs to sub-CCs via CCs	LAs to CCs	At LCs	Direct sale to retailers
Consumer price	100 (69,197)	100 (6,055)	100 (3,837)	100 (3,445)
Retailers' profits	11.1	13.38	12.5	13.9
Costs	5.1	4.87	5.0	5.5
Wholesalers' (sub-CCs)				
Selling price	83.8			
Profits	15.8	NA	NA	NA
Costs	11.1			
Commission agents' (CC-LAC)				
Selling price	56.9	81.75	82.6	
Profits	1.9	5.52	8.9	NA
Costs	0.4	2.78	1.3	
Wholesalers' (LAs)				
Selling price	5.46	73.45		NA
Profits	12.4	11.59		
Costs	14.3	10.74		
Fishermen's price	27.9	51.22	72.3	80.6

Note : Figures in parentheses represent value in Rs. per MT.

Price spread : dry edible fish

It can be noted from Table 12.17 that the fishermen's average share in consumer rupee was 57.6 per cent. It did not vary substantially by the size of CCs. The total costs also remained similar. However, retailers in large CCs had higher profits (15%) than at medium (12.5%) and small ones (11.8%). Even though overall percentage of profits remained similar, wholesalers and retailers at large CCs had much higher turnover as compared to smaller CCs.

TABLE 12.17 : **Price spread percentage of marketing dry fish from landings to consumer by quantity of consuming centres (1978-79)**

Particulars	Large	Medium	Small	Overall
Consumer Price	100	100	100	100
	(6,019.5)	(5,096.3)	(4,866.3)	(5,394.9)
Retailers'				
Profits	15.0	12.5	11.8	13.29
Costs	9.1	11.3	7.0	9.90
Wholesalers' [CC (s)]				
Selling price	75.9	76.2	81.2	76.81
Profits	3.8	7.3	8.0	6.23
Costs	4.0	3.3	5.3	3.84
Wholesalers' (LA's)				
Selling price	68.1	65.6	67.9	66.74
Profits	5.7	3.8	4.9	4.64
Costs	4.4	4.2	4.8	4.46
Fishermen's price	58.0	55.6	58.2	57.64

Note : Figures in parentheses represent average consumer price per metric tonne in rupees.

Group	Annual consumption (MT)
Large CCs	More than 500 MT
Medium CCs	500—100 MT
Small CCs	Less than 100 MT

While discussing channels, it was explained that a large quantity of dry edible fish was directly sold by fishermen to retailers. This direct sale saved costs and margins of many intermediaries and was often done through weekly markets. For example, at the Marrole weekly market at Bombay, outstation retailers and wholesalers directly purchased dry edible fish from the fishermen of Bombay and Thane district. Dry edible fish had longer shelf life and, therefore, could be sold in such weekly markets leading to shorter channel lengths.

Role of co-operatives

Co-operatives were considered a suitable organizational intervention for not only increasing fishermen's share in the consumer rupee but also for looking after his other daily needs. However, the performance of co-operatives was poor in all the states of the country.

The share of co-operatives in the total domestic fish market was every small. The alarming feature was that the share of co-operatives had been declining over the years, in spite of larger allocations and efforts for the development of fisheries co-operatives (Table 12.18).

The co-operatives chiefly concentrated on providing term loans for mechanized boats. The mechanized boats, however, also required a large working capital loan for requisites and maintenance. Such finance was usually raised by the fishermen from the traders in the absence of alternative sources, and which led to the development of a 'bonding system'. This resulted not only in fishermen ignoring co-operatives for marketing, but also their inability to repay the loans from co-operatives. The fish marketing by co-operatives did not yield any price advantage usually over that of wholesalers. The co-operatives which operated as commission agents, however, did better in fish marketing. Needless to say, that a pre-requisite, for the efficient functioning was the adequacy of supply infrastructure like ice, packing materials and transport. Such societies who had these facilities and also acted as commission agents did better than others. By and large, fisheries co-operatives were not managed well and there was hardly any relationship with the co-operative structures upward wherever apex/district societies/unions operated.

Attempt should be made to develop adequate marketing infrastructure, and to meet fishermen's working capital needs, and market should be on commission basis. Vertical integration upto the retail market is necessary to make co-operatives effective. Additionally, trained manpower must be provided so that complex activities can be smoothly mangaged.

Role of corporations

Fisheries Development Corporations were set up in different maritime states to undertake diversification of fish products and marketing of fish in addition to deep-see fishery development.

The direction of development of corporations got somewhat predetermined as did their capital, in many ways as a large part of the capital was tied to assets like ice plants and cold storages, which were transferred to corporations from the department of fisheries. Karnataka, Orissa and Maharashtra, the only three states where co-operatives were relatively significant in the marketing of marine fish.

TABLE 12.18 : **Percentage estimate of marine catch handled by co-operatives in selected states**

States	Years				
	1972-73	1973-74	1974-75	1975-76	1976-77
Andhra Pradesh*	NA	NA	NA	NA	NA
Gujarat	2.12	1.66	0.78	0.79	0.33
Karnataka	3.77	3.54	1.74	1.08	2.08
Kerala**	1.6	1.04	0.8	0.76	0.28
Maharashtra	NA	NA	2.3	1.88	1.38
Orissa	1.27	1.5	1.25	1.05	1.23
West Bengal***	NA	NA	NA	NA	0.43
Goa	—	—	—	—	—
Pondicherry	—	—	—	—	—

Source : Estimates developed on the basis of RBI statement part II. The Co-operative Movement in India and Sales Value estimates developed by State Government of total marine fish.

* Andhra Pradesh figures were ignored as the RBI statements year by year repeat the same figures of sales by co-operatives and no figures were given for 1976-77. Our survey suggested that co-operatives in these years may have handled only very small quantities of catch.

** All primary co-operatives in Kerala were liquidated by state order in 1978-79 due to poor performance.

*** Catch and value data for West Bengal were not available, CMFRI statistics also combined West Bengal and Orissa until 1976. Further RBI estimates do not separate inland and marine fish.

The analysis of the data (1972-73 to 1976-77) showed that for most states the membership per fishermen's society declined or remained constant, but the number of societies grew. Qualitatively, the membership of the co-operatives could be assumed poor, because in almost all states the population of active fishermen was less than the membership of co-operative (Table 12.19). In other words, bogus or inactive fishermen could have been listed as members to boost the membership.

The overdue loans as a percentage to outstandings was as high as 80 per cent in Tamil Nadu (Table 12.20). In the absence of any data on distribution of the loans by type of loans, the analysis can be used to understand that the distribution of loans might be highly showed in favour of loans for boats and gears for mechanization, usually advanced to well-to-do members of the society.

About 58 per cent of the primary societies dealing in fish were in loss and only 24 per cent were in profit during 1972-73. This picture did not improve by 1976-77 (Table 12.21). The net loss of co-operatives in maritime states, for the five-year period under study amounted to 21.8 millions. Table 12.21 indicates that the greatest contributors to this net loss were Kerala and Tamil Nadu. No wonder that all co-operatives in Kerala were liquidated by 1978-79. The co-operatives are estimated to lose Rs. 1.00 million a year by 1981. The reasons for such large losses were many. One of the important reasons was the boat/gear financing schemes in the sector. These schemes need to be reviewed immediately. Fish handling, and supply of fishery requisites were the other loss-making activities. It was, however, observed that co-operatives which confined loans to gill-netters and outboard motors, did better in the marketing business than co-operatives which gave loans for trawlers.

Therefore, in a large measure the ability of the corporations towards raising additional resources from financial institutions was restricted (Table 12.22).

All the corporations were managed by senior employees of the state governments. Given the fact that the government employees were transferrable, the corporations lacked leadership and direction in management. Most of the corporations, as a result, ran into considerable losses.

Business activities of the corporations indicate that the

TABLE 12.19 : **Active fishermen population, coverage and growth in number of societies and membership in selected states**

States	Population covered by co-operatives*	Population of active fishermen**	1972-73		1976-77	
			No. of societies	Members per society	No. of societies	Members per society
Andhra Pradesh	N.A.	47,700	662	99	N.A.	N.A.
Gujarat	13,535	11,732	58	195	137	126
Karnataka	26,662	11,732	123	238	154	233
Kerala	75,856	74,241	1,026	109	738	101
Maharashtra	38,979	20,698	428	148	530	145
Orissa	9,321	8,828	156	133	190	128
Tamil Nadu	62,759	56,586	450	146	500	168
West Bengal	N.A.	606	577	66	714	68
Goa	3,720	N.A.	13	273	13	285
Pondicherry	5,374	N.A.	38	4,116	37	161

Source : *RBI Statements, Part II, The Co-operative Movement in India.

**Population figures are compiled from the data supplied by CMFRI, Cochin in Indian Fisheries 1947-77 issued on the occasion of the fiftieth session of the Indian Ocean Fisheries Commission held at Cochin from 19th to 26th October 1977.

TABLE 12.20 : **Change in advances and overdues**

(*Rs. '000*)

States	1972-73		1976-77	
	Out-standing	Over-dues	Out-standing	Over-dues
Andhra Pradesh	687	11 (2)	N.A.	N.A.
Gujarat	491	199 (40)	489	157 (32)
Karnataka	3,905	658 (16)	5,361	1,923 (35)
Kerala	1,267	964 (76)	1,214	689 (55)
Maharashtra	11,193	1,791 (16)	16,893	2,047 (12)
Orissa	1,863	1,696 (91)	1,803	1,562 (86)
Tamil Nadu	2,961	96 (0.01)	4,539	3,632 (80)
West Bengal	349	—	935	376 (40)
Goa	5	—	5	5
Pondicherry	229	48 (21)	453	27 (6)

Note : Figures in parentheses are percentage of overdues to outstandings.

Source : RBI Statements, Part-II, The Co-operative Movement in India.

marketing of fish domestically was undertaken only by two corporations, but again, it did not constitute a very significant part of their business. Diversification in marketing of fish products was attempted only by Karnataka and Kerala Corporations. Frozen fish keema and other products were sold locally and were also sold through their own sea-food restaurants. The products were also sold cheaper than fresh fish. Even though the sale of fish products was not large, an interest in the products has been evoked. Given the fact that the EEZ would be exploited sooner than later, product and market development would become all the more an important activity of the corporations.

TABLE 12.21 : **Changes in number of societies in profit and loss and actual figures of profit and loss**

(*Unit : in Thousands of Rupees*)

State	1972-73						1975-76					
	No. of societies in profit	No. of societies in loss	No. of societies without profit and loss	Total No. of societies	Profit	Loss	No. of societies in profit	No. of societies in loss	No. of societies without profit and loss	Total No. of societies	Profit	Loss
Andhra Pradesh	100	406	156	662	831	448	N.A.	N.A.	—	—	—	—
	(15)	(61)	(24)									
Gujarat	28	11	19	58	141	101	41	33	63	137	181	760
	(48)	(19)	(33)				(30)	(24)	(46)			
Karnataka	66	39	18	123	255	209	64	54	36	154	190	289
	(53)	(32)	(15)				(42)	(35)	(23)			
Kerala	83	941	2	1,026	104	4,563	24	716	8	748	114	17,895
	(8)	(92)	(Neg)				(3)	(96)	(1)			
Maharashtra	207	161	60	428	997	214	247	212	71	530	1,839	395
	(48)	(38)	(14)				(47)	(40)	(13)			
Orissa	39	21	96	156	258	11	63	52	75	190	210	69
	(25)	(13)	(62)				(33)	(27)	(39)			
Tamil Nadu	153	280	17	450	91	628	87	409	4	500	107	5,026
	(34)	(62)	(4)				(17)	(82)	(1)			

TABLE 12.21 : (*Contd.*)

West Bengal	146	158	273	577	185	210	226	256	232	714	414	381
	(25)	(27)	(42)				(32)	(36)	(32)			
Goa	3	10	—	13	6	42	2	3	8	13	13	31
	(23)	(77)	—				(15)	(23)	(62)			
Pondicherry	19	19	—	38	14	27	7	30	—	37	10	66
	(50)	(50)					(19)	(81)				
Total	844	2,046	641	3,531	2,081	6,453	761	1,765	497	3,023	3,078	24,910
	(23.9)	(57.9)	(18.2)				(24.3)	(58.3)	(16.4)			

Note : 1. Amount of profit/loss in both marine and inland fresh fish ;
2. Figures in brackets denote percentage to total.

Source : RBI statistical statements Part-II, The Co-operative Movement in India.

TABLE 12.22 : **Sources and extent of borrowing by corporations**

(Unit : In thousands of Rupees)

Name of corporation	Government loan	Commercial bank loan	Others	Total
A.P. Fisheries Corporation (1975-76)	—	912 (100)	—	912
Kerala Fisheries Corporation (1977-78)	33,454 (60)	4,311 (7.7)	17,991 (32.2)	55,756
Gujarat Agro-Marine Products Ltd. (1977-78)	1,938 (42.6)	— (57.4)	2,616	4,554
The Tamil Nadu Fisheries Development Corporation Ltd. (1977-78)	4,585 (23.4)	1,258 (6.4)	13,791 (70.2)	19,634
Karnataka Fisheries Development Corporation Ltd. (1977-78)	—	690	—	690

Note : Figures in brackets denote percentage to totals.
Source; Compiled on the basis of the balance sheets of the respective State Corporations.

The reasons of failure of the corporations in domestic fish marketing can be traced to unclear and vague objectives, lack of committed and professional management, and absence of proper organization to provide leadership. More autonomy and professional management are perhaps the key to their success.

13

LONG-TERM PERSPECTIVES OF FISH MARKETING IN INDIA*

T.A. MAMMEN

WHILE it is possible to analyse the past performance in fish marketing, projections on the future trends tend to be either mathematical or wishful. To be mathematical is a passive approach, while to be wishful may not be realistic. What is required is a dynamic approach, correcting the course as we go along. Hence a long term perspective can be taken only as indicative. Nevertheless, there should be a perspective planning to get a feel of the present and to have a foresight into the future. It will also serve to mould the thinking of the policy-makers and private and corporate enterprise.

India has done reasonably well in the field of agriculture and dairying through massive efforts in research, extension, and management fields. There is now a growing awareness that more attention should be paid to animal husbandry and fisheries, which are lagging behind. Consumption of meat and fish in India is one of the lowest, and these are the very two items that show rapid rise in price indices, indicating considerable supply gap.

DEMAND AND SUPPLY OF FISH : A REVIEW

In recent years, four studies have been carried out to analyse the present supply situation and to make demand projections of fish

* This paper was initially presented at the National Seminar on Fisheries Development in India, held at the Institute of Indian Management, Ahmedabad, on April 9-11, 1982.

in India.

The study by Indian Institute of Management, Ahmedabad (IIMA), is by far the most detailed one conducted so far and various analytical tools have been employed to make demand and supply projections. But the projections are of short term nature and that too only for marine fish.

Demand

IIMA's analysis of the present disposition of marine fish and demand projections are summarized in Table 13.1.

TABLE 13.1 : **Disposition of marine fish and demand projections**

(Qty, in million tonnes)

Component	1979 analysis		1985 projection	
	Qty.	Qty. in %	Qty.	Qty. in %
1. Human (domestic) consumption				
(a) in houses	0.912	65.8	1.900	65.9
(b) outside houses	0.045	3.2		
2. Industrial uses				
(a) feed manufacture	0.205	14.8	0.544	18.9
(b) other uses	0.030	2.2	0.050	1.7
3. Exports	0.194	14.0	0.390	13.5
Total	1.386	100.0	2.884	100.0

Source : V.K. Gupta *et al.*, *Marine Fish Marketing in India*, Indian Institute of Management, Ahmedabad, 1984.

If the 15 per cent compound growth rate estimated by IIMA is maintained, the demand for marine fish by AD 2000 would be about 20 million tonnes. Estimates of the National Commission on Agriculture for various time periods are shown in Table 13.2.

The demand projection by NCA is based on its assumptions of population growth and urbanization as shown in Table 13.3.

The provisional 1981 census figures would show that the population increase and decennial growth rates were different, and the trend is constant for population growth, while urbanization is increasing at the rate of 1.6 per cent decennially. These trends

TABLE 13.2 : **Demand projection of fish**

(*in million tonnes*)

Sector	1980		1985		2000	
	High	Low	High	Low	High	Low
Rural	1.50	1.34	1.85	1.48	2.39	1.89
Urban	0.85	0.76	1.16	0.93	3.14	1.70
Total	2.35	2.10	3.01	2.41	5.53	3.59

Source : Report of the National Commission on Agriculture (NCA) Part—III (1).

TABLE 13.3 : **Population growth and urbanization**

Year	Total Population (million)	Decennial growth percentage	Urban population (million)	Percentage of urban population to total
1961	442.21	—	79.61	18.00
1971	550.70	24.53	110.04	19.98
1980	659.54	19.76	146.96	22.28
1985	724.91	—	172.18	23.75
2000	935.35	19.11	272.86	29.17

Source : Report of the National Commission on Agriculture (NCA), Part—VIII (1).

may be projected as shown in Table 13.4.

It may be noted that in working out the demand it is assumed that population increases by 55.75 per cent between 1981 and 2001 and the total population will be over 1065 million by 2001.

Differential demand between urban and rural population

National Commission on Agriculture (NCA) has taken note of the differential demand between rural and urban populations, both in terms of higher growth rate and higher per capita consumption by the urban population. IIMA has further demarcated the demand from metropolitan cities* from the rest of the urban areas. Based

* However their definition of 2 million population for metropolitan cities would make comparisons difficult with other studies/classification.

TABLE 13.4 : **Population and urbanization trends passed on 1981 provisional census figures**

Year	Population (million)	Decennial growth (percentage)	Percentage of urban population
1901	238.4	—	10.9
1911	252.0	5.7	—
1921	241.2	—0.3	11.2
1931	278.9	11.0	12.0
1941	318.5	14.2	13.9
1951	361.0	13.3	17.3
1961	439.0	21.6	18.0
1971	548.0	24.8	19.9
1981	684.0	24.8	23.7
1991	843.6	24.8	25.3
2001	1065.3	24.8	26.9

Note : 1. Estimated on the basis of the assumption that the decennial growth during 1981-91 and 1991-2001 be same as during 1971-81 that is, 24.8 per cent.

2. Estimated on the basis of past trend.

on their survey, it was concluded that the total household and hotels', restaurants', and institutions', demand would be 19 lakh tonnes during 1984-85 ; rural areas accounting for the maximum with 10.78 lakh tonnes (56.7%) followed by urban and metropolitan locations with 5.94 lakh tonnes (31.35%) and 2.28 lakh tonnes (12%) respectively. The per-capita consumption figures for the metropolitan, urban and rural sectors, though vary a great deal among the survey rounds, indicate that the per-capita consumption in the metropolitan and urban locations* is about 33 per cent higher than the per-capita consumption of rural areas (Table 13.5).

Price linked demand and price elasticity

Like other consumer items, fish price has a very high impact on

* Per-capita consumption in the urban location including metropolitan cities has been estimated by the weighted average of per-capita consumption in metropolitan cities and urban locations. The weights were equal to the population.

TABLE 13.5 : **Per-capita consumption of marine fish during three all-India survey rounds**

(*Qty. in kgs.*)

Category	Survey round	Per-capita consumption observed during 4 weeks			Simple average
		Marine	Inland	Total	
1. Metropolitan cities	I	0.47	0.42	0.89	
	II	0.42	0.32	0.74	0.75
	III	0.33	0.28	0.61	
2. Urban	I	0.56	0.58	1.14	
	II	0.42	0.52	0.94	0.90
	III	0.45	0.18	0.63	
3. Rural	I	0.34	0.49	0.83	
	II	0.28	0.52	0.80	0.677
	III	0.11	0.32	0.40	

Source : V.K. Gupta *et al., Marine Fish Marketing in India*, Vol. III (2).

fish demand. In fact, it is the price that equalizes supply with demand. When demand is in excess of supplies, the price increases. In such a situation, the weaker demand drop out, majority of the consumers reduce quantity of purchase to suit the budget normally set apart for that purpose. However, in case of another segment of the population where fish is considered a staple diet, the purchase quantity is not very much affected. Hence the price elasticity of demand varies for different population segments, according to consumption habits.

Basket demand

A typical example of basket demand is the tuna. Tuna prices shadow the beef price in the international market, as they come in the same basket and one easily substitutes the other. When beef prices go up, the consumer switches over to tuna and vice-versa.

Prestige demand

By convention certain varieties of fish have a prestige attached to it : trout, salmon. It is a common experience in the Delhi market to see Indian halibut being called black pomfret and the red snapper as the pink pomfret and so on to entice the consumer to pay at a higher rate, capitalizing on the prestige attached to pomfret. Similarly, in certain countries what is sold as salmon is no salmon at all. The steak size of rohu in the Calcutta market is an example of prestige demand.

Supplies : Fish production has tripled during the last 30 years, but failed to make any significant impact either in terms of net availability, per-capita availability, or price stability. Table 13.6 gives a comparative statement of the price index for all

TABLE 13.6 : **Price indices**

	Price indices		base : 1970-71=100	
Year	All commodities	Food articles	Meat	Fish
1953	46.7	43.9	38.3	27.0
1954	44.0	39.8	37.1	25.2
1955	40.4	35.8	36.3	27.8
1956	45.3	40.7	35.8	28.1
1957	48.0	43.8	45.8	27.1
1958	49.0	45.8	38.9	30.4
1959	51.0	47.9	39.2	31.4
1960	54.2	48.3	44.3	34.4
1961	55.5	48.1	51.7	32.8
1962	57.5	52.0	57.6	45.2
1963	59.6	53.1	59.8	48.5
1964	68.8	62.8	65.6	58.5
1965	71.2	70.0	74.0	84.0
1966	79.7	78.8	81.0	96.2
1967	91.7	96.4	87.2	106.5
1968	91.3	93.8	87.2	110.5
1969	93.2	95.2	89.6	96.0
1970	99.0	100.4	98.1	97.7
1971	105.0	101.0	106.6	105.1
1972	113.0	107.9	114.7	115.6
1973	131.6	128.6	142.2	113.8
1974	169.2	165.2	182.2	159.3
1975	175.8	170.2	202.5	157.9
1976	172.4	152.2	191.7	172.7
1977	185.4	170.8	215.9	192.3
1978	184.9	173.4	225·9	228.9
1979	206.0	181.3	255.8	253.4
1980	248 0	207.3	306.4	267.0

Source : Compiled from various issues of the *Monthly Wholsale Price Index*.

commodities, food items, meat, and fish. While prices have been continuously rising, meat, and more especially fish prices have been rising at a faster rate. Fish prices have gone up by 10 times during the last 28 years. In comparison, the price index of all commodities has gone up by only 5.36 times, food items by 4.62 times, and meat by 8.00 times. The very high price rise for fish indicates that the demand for fish has far outstripped supplies. It is necessary to examine in this context the prospects for increased production in the coming years.

NCA supply projection

The National Commission on Agriculture (NCA) has made supply forecasts of fish and fish products as shown in Table 13.7.

TABLE 13.7 : **Supply forecast for fish and fishery products**

Source	1971	1985	2000
Fish catch from : inland	0.70	2.27*	4.50
marine	1.10	2.01	3.50
	1.80	4.28	8.00
Estimated exports	0.04	0.10	0.25
Fish meal and other industrial products	0.15	0.40	1.00
Balance available for human consumption	1.61	3.78	6.75

Souace : *Report* of the National Commission on Agriculture.
* includes production from culture fisheries.

IIMA forecast

In contrast to the highly optimistic supply position indicated by the NCA, IIMA has made four less optimistic supply projections ; the first set based on time series forecast using Box-Jenkins model ; the second set on the expectation of 100 per cent fulfilment of plan targets for the introduction of boats in the sixth plan, the third set based on attainment of 70 per cent of the plan targets for the introduction of boats and the fourth set based on resource constraints. A summary is given in Table 13.8.

IIMA, on the basis of time series projections, also considered that the present pattern of utilization as between fresh

TABLE 13.8 : **Supply forecast made by IIMA**

(Quantity in million tonnes)

States	Forecast by time-series	Forecast through estimation of boats		
	Set I	Set II	Set III	Set IV
All marine states excluding Lakshadweep and Andaman and Nicobar Islands	1.568	1.790	1.673	1.643

Source : *Marine Fish Marketing in India*, Vol. IV (2).

TABLE 13.9 : **Comparison of utilization pattern for 1979 and 1985**

(Quantity in '000 tonnes)

Utilization form	Year 1979	Year 1985 set III projections	Year 1985 time-series projections	Expected annual growth (%) III projection
Fresh domestic	597 (43.7)	738 (44.1)	683 (43.6)	3.94
Dry edible	426 (31.2)	524 (31.3)	488 (31.1)	3.83
Dry fish meal	197 (14.4)	232 (13.9)	228 (14.6)	2.96
Exportable	145 (10.7)	179 (10.7)	168 (10.7)	3.90
Total	1365	1673	1567	3.56

Source : *Marine Fish Marketing in India*, Vol. IV (2).

fish, dry fish, fish meal and export, would continue. Their projections have been presented while considering that at present marine fish production is stagnant, introduction of additional boats for conventional inshore fishing may not lead to a proportionate increase in production, hence even the conservative estimate of IIMA itself may be on the high side. While it could be argued that the IIMA projection is only in regard to marine fisheries and the scope for increased production is more on the inland side, it is disheartening to note that even inland fish production is not going up. Hence, if the present approach to fisheries development is to continue, it is likely that fish production by 1985 may not exceed 2.6 million tonnes (1.6 from marine and 1.0 from inland) and by AD 2000 3.4 million tonnes (1.8 from marine and 1.6 from inland).

PER CAPITA CONSUMPTION OF FISH IN INDIA

The conventional computation of per capita consumption by dividing fish production by the population is misleading, as India has a sizeable population of non-fish eaters. A good proportion of fish is going for fish meal and exports. Further, urban areas are better supplied with fish compared to rural areas. Hence an attempt is made here to work out the per capita availability of fish to the fish eating population separately for urban and rural areas for various census years (Table 13.10).

Table 13.10 would require some explanations, in regard to fish production statistics, and assumptions on fish eating population and weightage for urban population.

Fish production statistics

At the all India level, the first attempt in compiling fish production was made by the agricultural marketing adviser in 1946. Evolution of a proper methodology for the estimation of marine fish production in India was one of the early tasks of Central Marine Fisheries Research Institute (CMFRI). The multi-stage, stratified random sampling methodology developed by CMFRI for the estimation of marine fish landing is now being adopted by the states. From 1972 onwards the marine fish landing estimates computed by the states are being used in all official statistics. In regard to inland fish production, until 1964, estimates were arrived at as a percentage of marine fish production. From 1964 onwards the estimates of inland fish production computed by the states are being used for official statistics. While the method of estimating inland fish production is not satisfactory, the adoption of advanced technology in respect of marine fish production statistics has resulted in two divergent sets of

TABLE 13.10 : **Per-capita availability of fish for fish-eating population separately for urban and rural areas**

Year	Total population (million)	Urban population		Rural population		Urban fish-eaters	
		%	No. in million	%	No. in million	%	No. in million
1	2	3	4	5	6	7	8
1951	361	17.3	62	82.7	299	43.5	27
1961	439	18.0	79	82.0	360	46.0	36
1971	548	19.0	104	81.0	444	48.7	51
1981	684	23.7	162	76.3	522	51.8	84

Year	Rural fish eaters		Total fish eaters; with 33% weightage for urban population	Fish production (million tonnes)	Per-capita availability for fish eating population			
					Urban		Rural	
	%	No. in million			Gross	Net	Gross	Net
1	9	10	11	12	13	14	15	16
1951	46.7	142	178	0.752	4.22	3.17	5.61	4.20
1961	50.5	182	230	0.961	4.18	3.13	5.56	4.17
1971	53.6	238	306	1.852	6.08	4.57	8.09	6.07
1981	57.1	298	410	2.116*	5.16	3.87	6.86	4.80
				2.423**	5.91	4.43	7.86	5.89

* CMFRI estimate
** State estimate

figures. The fish production statistics are indicated in Table 13.11.

TABLE 13.11 : **Fish production statistics**

(Qty. in '000 tonnes)

Year	Marine landings as per		Inland landings***	Total with CMFRI estimate for marine	Total with state estimate for marine
	CMFRI estimates*	State estimates**			
1951	534.0	—	218.0	752.0	—
1956	718.8	—	293.5	1012.3	—
1961	683.6	—	277.4	961.0	—
1966	889.9	—	477.5	1367.4	—
1971	1161.4	—	690.2	1851.6	—
1972	980.4	974.4	665.8	1645.8	1640.2
1973	1220.4	1210.0	747.6	1968.0	1957.6
1974	1217.8	1472.0	783.9	2001.7	2255.9
1975	1422.7	1482.1	783.8	2206.5	2265.9
1976	1352.9	1374.7	799.2	2152.1	2173.9
1977	1259.8	1448.4	863.5	2123.3	2311.9
1978	1403.6	1489.7	816.4	2220.2	2306.1
1979	1388.4	1492.0	848.5	2236.9	2340.5
1980	1241.3	1548.0	875.0	2116.3	2423.0

*Published data of CMFRI, Cochin.

**Obtained from representative Directorates of Fisheries in different states and their aggregated.

***Published data of CMFRI, Barrackpore.

Fish eating population

There is no census data available on the extent of fish eating population. Hence this data is attempted based on incidental data.

(i) IIMA has concluded that, for the country as a whole, 53 per cent of the metropolitan population, 50 per cent of the urban population and 56 per cent of the rural population are fish eating. Considering that 23.7 per cent of the Indian population is urban, out of which 22.6 per cent (5.4% of the total) are in cities of over 2 million population ; the overall fish eating population may be taken as 54.5 per cent and in the urban (including metropolitan) 50.7 per cent may be taken as fish eating.

(ii) The rate of increase in fish eating habit is indicated by IIMA as a 3.5 per cent in 6 years, that is, a growth rate of 0.56 per cent per annum, compound.

(iii) Per capita consumption in urban areas is 33 per cent higher than in rural locations.

(iv) Of the total fish production only 75 per cent is available for human consumption (Table 13.9).

Computation of per capita availability over years

On the assumption that the present trend continues over years, per capita consumption for rural and urban population has been worked out for 1951, 1961, 1971 and 1981. The data presented in Table 13.10 show that even by the optimistic state estimates, the per capita availability figures are on the decline compared to 1971. Even going back to 1951, the present per capita availability is only 40 per cent higher according to state estimates and 22 per cent higher according to CMFRI estimates of marine fish production.

A comparison of Table 13.10 data with Table 13.12 data will show that the per capita availability of fish for consumption by human beings in India is about the lowest among south and south-east Asian countries.

IMPACT OF FISH SCARCITY

The rapid increase of fish prices, especially in the north-eastern regions is indicative of a supply gap. It is interesting to note that fish is already the favourite item for smuggling in tha region. If this trend is to continue, that is demand of marine fish alone going up to 20 million tonnes and total supplies only 3.4 million tonnes by AD 2000, fish prices would become several times the present level. The impact of this price increase will be :

(a) fish will move into the realm of luxury food and the poor people may have to give up eating quality fish.

(b) the quantity that is going for export and industrial

TABLE 13.12 : **Per capita availability of fish for human consumption in South East Asian countries (1974)**

Name of country	Per capita availability of fish for human consumption (kg/annum) for 1974
Hong Kong	44.5
South Korea	39.8
Indonesia	10.1
Malaysia	28.8
Philippines	31.5
Singapore	37.8
Thailand	21.5
Fiji	20.8
Gilbert and Ellice Islands	33.9
Papua New Guinea	10.2
Soloman Islands	14.8
Tonga	10.3
Bangladesh	10.0
Burma	12.2
India	3.3
Pakistan	1.3
Sri Lanka	10.7

Source : South Cina Sea Fisheries—fishery profiles.

purposes would get drastically reduced.

(c) wastage would be reduced, if not eliminated.

(d) more investments would take place for increasing fish production.

(e) popular demand would change government priorities and policies.

Impact on industrial uses and export

There is a basic difference in the utilization of primary foods between India and the developed world. In the developed world, much of the primary food passes through an extra food link, that is small and cheap varieties are converted into fish meal, fish meal fed to animals, and animal products form the human food. There is evidently a wastage in this process, as food conversion is always less than unity. On the other hand, in India, nearly the entire food consumption is at the primary food level itself and only fodder and agricultural wastage products (which are not acceptable as human food in that form) go for animal feeding. In India where fish is in short supply, obviously no fish can be spared for manufacture of animal feed, except fish offals.

The anticipated supply gap and consequent high price rise in India for fish and marine products would affect exports also. Only certain low-volume high-priced varieties will go for export, as the domestic market itself would be a major competitor for fish. Viewed against a background of huge unsatisfied demand in the domestic market, it would be unwise also to promote export of the less costly fish varieties. However, the pull between domestic and export market would be influenced by government policy based on the country's balance of payments position.

Avoiding wastages

Conversion of fish to fish manure and fish meal is a form of wastage. Besides, due to poor handling, partial wastage takes place right through the food chain. The practice of individual household trying to dress whole fish leads to wastage of fish offals. Instead, if nobbing, gutting and filleting are undertaken in processing factories, these offals would be available for fish meal. The more important savings will be through avoiding fish discards by shrimp trawlers and preservation of fish right from the point of capture to maintain highest quality.

More investment in increasing fish production

Fishery sector received scant attention in the past, and outlays for the fishery sector were meagre, ranging from 0.26 to 0.38 per cent of the overall Five Year Plan outlays (Table 13.13). Hence there is an urgent need for increasing investments in the fisheries sector.

Use of high cost technology

So far the low prevailing price of fish and clients from lower income brackets have prevented the adoption of high cost technology. However, when fish prices go up, there will be progressive adoption of high cost technology by way of deep sea fishing, culturing fish in fresh water, brackish water, and the open sea, and use of sophisticated methods of processing and marketing.

TABLE 13.13 : **Analysis of investments in various Five Year Plans**

(*Rs. in million*)

Five Year Plans	Total outlay	Total outlay for agriculture and allied sectors	Total outlay for fisheries	Percentage of fisheries outlay to Total outlay	Percentage of fisheries outlay to Total outlay for agricl. and allied sectors
First Plan	19600	2940	51.3	0.26	1.76
Second Plan	46000	5290	122.6	0.27	2.32
Third Plan	75000	10680	282.7	0.38	2.65
Fourth Plan	59020	27280	826.8	0.58	3.03
Fifth Plan	393220	43020	1512.4	0.38	3.51
Sixth Plan	975000	66090	3711.4	0.38	5.62

Source : Various draft Five Year Plan documents.

Changing government policies

While so far governmental agencies undertook research and development, the pressure of price rise would force these activities to move into the competitive fiield, where private companies will take up their own result-oriented research. The present restrictive approach and protectionism in respect of fish culture, fishing, processing, and marketing should be removed, and these activities should also enter the competitive field to obtain quick results.

FISH MARKETING

The foregoing analysis has revealed that fish supplies will be far short of demand leading to high price, and the consumption shifting to the higher income brackets, which would naturally expect prime quality, better hygiene, processing into convenience foods, attractive packaging and marketing through departmental stores, fast food outlets, pizza parlours, delicatessens, restaurants, cafes and so on. The habit of eating out, which has already made its begining in India, is likely to manifest itself more significantly, although fish marketing for domestic cooking would still account for the bulk of fish consumption in India by AD 2000.

Processed fish

The increasing quality consciousness, urbanization, larger proportion of working women, increased income, and general trend toward modernization would result in fish being marketed more and more in the processed form. According to the Ministry of Agriculture, currently (1979) 65.03 per cent of fish produced in India is marketed fresh, 5.63 per cent frozen, 22.17 per cent cured, 0.19 per cent canned, 5.37 per cent reduced to fish meal, 1.29 per cent used for miscellaneous purposes, and 0.3 per cent is accounted as fish offal. Once fish processing is undertaken, the quantity of fish offal would go up to about 10 per cent and this will form the raw material for fish meal. What goes now for fish meal extraction might go for curing and what now goes for curing is likely to go for consumption mostly in the form of minced meat preparation. A good proportion of the share that goes for fresh fish consumption will go in for frozen fish production, with the introduction of a cold chain for marketing frozen fish and fish products.

Value added processing

Several species are currently discarded or used for fish meal and curing. These are not likely to gain consumer acceptance, unless converted into value added processed food. The miscellaneous varieties caught in shrimp trawlers have such poor market appeal and demand. Therefore, fishing vessel owners prefer to throw them back into the sea. The meat from these species can be picked and products like fish outlets, sausage, ham, and so on can be prepared with this minced meat. Likewise white bait, which is currently being beach dried to produce a poor quality product, is an excellent raw material to produce fish tempura, fish paste, frozen curries, marinated products, sauce and so on.

Canning

Despite an initial good start, canning has not sustained in India, particularly because of the high excise duty and obsolete nature of cans and the need for importing tin plates and aluminium rolls. If India could produce proper grade tin plates and aluminum rolls for making deep drawn cans, then there is a tremendous potential for canning particularly for use in locations where infrastructure is lacking for frozen products. It is the shortage of electricity that has come in the way of making aluminium rolls for aluminium canning.

Preservation and fish handling at sea

The fisherman generally does not use ice at sea as he feels he would not recover this extra cost. The effect of not icing becomes manifest only after the fish has changed hands. But the general computation is that each hour spent without icing reduces the shelf life of iced fish by a day. Hence, use of ice on board fishing vessel/boats should be insisted to ensure landing of qualify fish. However, where best quality material is required, even on-board freezing may be necessary. The cryogenic group is separately working on producing cryogenic gas at a low price so that cryogenic freezing is done on board small fishing boats. But a cost-effective technology is yet to be evolved.

Fishing harbours

Apart from landing and berthing facilities, fishing harbours are essential for proper handling, storage, and processing of fish. The present practice of landing fish in about 2000 locations has to give way for landing at say 100 fishing harbours, where requisite facilities may be created.

Fish processing plants

The present facility for fish processing is geared for shrimp freezing. It is necessary to develop processing for domestic marketing, particularly blast freezers, horizontal and vertical plate freezers, individually quick frozen freezers, fillet freezers, battering and breading equipment, hygienic driers, aluminium canneries and equipment for making fish cakes, ham, sausage, and so on.

Insulated and refrigerated transports

In ulated and refrigerated, road, rail and water transport facilities are required to ensure proper preservation of fish in transport. Large road vans, including road trains, are economical for fish transport compared to rail vans particularly when used as stationary units also.

Large frozen storages

Frozen storages are economical when constructed as large composite storages meant for fish, meat, medicine, and so on for domestic and export marketing. The practice of individual companies owning small units should be replaced by large composite units with stand-by power and cooling units. Such units can be insured and banks will provide credit based on goods stored in such units.

Marketing outlets and routes

The Indian Standards Institution specifications for fish markets are inadequate. It is necessary to improve specifications and construct fish markets on a modular basis with built-in storages. Similar modules can be designed for mounting on trucks, pick-up vans, and cycle rickshaws.

While demand is not sufficient to justify fish marketing through full fledged markets, marketing may be done directly from vehicles playing on specified routes, halting at specified hours and places.

Marketing through cold chain

Fish processing, transport, storage, and release through retail outlets, departmental stores and so on may be carried out through cold chains, which may have a national grid, integrated with regional grids. Cold chain have a number of advantages. They are :

(i) They are the best form of ensuring supplies in prime condition,
(ii) They will absorb seasonal variations in supply and demand,
(iii) They would also serve for marketing of various value-added fishery products, which would inter-alia make catching cheap varieties an economic proposition,
(iv) They would avoid wastage of edible fish, while non-

edible fish would be used at processing plants for conversion to fish meal,

(v) They reduce the expenditure incurred on having to visit markets for buying fish every time fish is required to be purchased.

Quality control and brand names

While the system of export inspection by the Export Inspection Agency and self-inspection are prevalent, there is no such requirement for domestic marketing. The main difficulty with a highly perishable commodity like fish is because quality can deteriorate in the marketing chain. To protect the consumer from such risks, it is necessery to encourage emergence of brand names so that the consumer will associate quality products with certain brand names.

Market functionaries

The present market functionaries maintain an efficient organization, keeping the whole fishing industry moving. They mop up every bit of fish landed, effect supplies, maintain their own market intelligence, advance money to the producer, and meet the short term and long term credit requirements. The very fact that government owned corporations could not penetrate into this area shows their inefficiency. They, no doubt, make good profits, but there are two many intermediaries and some indulge in malpractices. But what is wrong if they make profit in a highly competitive field like fish marketing ? Similarly, each intermediary has a separate function, with his stake, his margin, and his well-defined functions. Even when large firms entered into the fishing business, they had to engage more persons, although it could be more vertically integrated. As regards malpractices, it is more a question of how far the fishermen, consumer, and others in the marketing chain are gullible. Wrong grading, under weight, under-invoicing, and so on are prevalent elsewhere also.

Role of public sector

Initially the government played only an administrative role ; then they took up development work. But very soon it was realized that government's style of working was not conducive to efficient management. This led to the creation of public sector undertakings. A number of fisheries corporations were formed, but none could make any significant impact on production, processing or marketing. This raises the question as to what should be the role of the public sector. It is well known that overhead costs are high in the public sector. In such a situation it is advantageous if the fisheries corporations undertake activities in certain critical areas and areas in which private industry is not taking adequate interest, and until such time that adequate interest is generated by the private sector.

Two such areas that may be operated by the fisheries corporations are :

(i) Management of fishing harbours, and
(ii) value added processing and marketing through cold chain.

REFERENCES

1. *Report of the National Commission on Agriculture,* Part III (Demand and Supply) and Part VIII (Fisheries), New Delhi : Ministry of Agriculture and Irrigation, Government of India), 1976.
2. V.K. Gupta *et al., Marine Fish Marketing in India,* Volumes I to VIII, New Delhi ; Concept Publishing Co., 1984.
3. *Demand of Fish and its Transportation and Storage in Selected Cities,* (New Delhi : National Council of Applied Economic Research), 1980.
4. Shambu Dayal, Projections for Demand of Fish in India, *Sea Food Export Journal,* 5 (5), May 1973.

14

EXPORT GROWTH OF MARINE PRODUCTS

KAMLA SURI

AMONGST the whole range of agricultural commodities, exports of marine products from India have shown a phenomenal growth during the past few years. Marine exports touched the Rs. 370 crore-mark during 1983, as against the target of Rs. 361 crore. The exports were higher by 8.2 per cent in terms of value and by 8.7 per cent in quantity over the previous year.

Total fish production in India touched 26 lakh tonnes during 1983-84. With this record output, the country now ranks as the largest producer of marine products in the Commonwealth. One significant aspect of this welcome development is the break-through in inland fish farming which has opened up possibilities of a manifold increase in fish production and export. As of now India tops in the inland sector of the world fish catch.

Heartening as it is, there is no room for complacency. Although India's performance in seafood exports has been impressive in recent years, its share in the global marine trade is only about 2 per cent. There are many constraints on account of which an optimum level of exploitation has been reached in various fishing areas which itself calls for concerted efforts.

The export of this non-traditional item remained more or less stagnant till the end of the seventies. Exports started rising from a modest amount of Rs. 35.5 crore during 1970 to as high as Rs. 79.6 crore in 1973 and to Rs. 104.9 crore during 1975. In the following years the export value of marine products continued to increase and was as high as Rs. 286.7 crore in 1981. It rose to Rs. 342.2 crore in 1982 and further to the peak of Rs. 370 crore in 1983 (Fig. 14.1).

Quantitywise exports also picked up gradually from the late sixties and reached the level of 53,412 tonnes in 1975. In the latter half of the seventies, the volume of marine exports continued to increase and touched an all-time high of 92,184 tonnes in 1979. There was a big fall of 19 per cent in the following year, but exports again picked up from 75,375 tonnes in 1981 to 78,175 tonnes in 1982 and have shown a steep rise of nearly 9 per cent to 85,000 tonnes in 1983 (Table 14.1 and Figure 14.2).

Some of the important factors which have contributed to the significant growth in export earnings during the past few years are : (1) favourable prices offered in the foreign markets for frozen shrimp and lobster ; (2) the rise in the U.S. dollar price in the international market which meant more rupees realized per U.S. dollar ; (3) good cuttle fish season in the west coast of India as a result of which the quantity exported almost doubled between 1981 and 1983 ; (4) improved landings of fish normally used for drying/curing ; and (5) increased fishing efforts by the introduction of deep sea fishing vessels under charter arrangements in recent years.

Amongst the items which contributed to higher export earnings in terms of quantity and value during 1981 and 1982 were frozen shrimp, fresh and frozen fish, frozen cuttle fish, and fillets and frozen squids. Dried shrimp showed some increase in 1981 and 1982 in quantity but fell in value in 1983.

A look at the structure of marine exports reveals that, out of the 30 main items exported, frozen shrimp continues to dominate the scene. This one item accounted for nearly 88 per cent of the total exports in terms of value and 70 per cent in terms of quantity in 1983. Its share was the same in terms of value in 1982 and nearly 73 per cent in terms of quantity (Table 14.3). The share of this item has always remained more than 55 per cent in terms of volume and more than 80 per cent in terms of value since 1978. This trend indicates its dominance in the composition of seafood exports in the past few years.

Some of the other items which have picked up recently are fresh/frozen fish which have emerged as the second largest export item in terms of both value and volume. Other items like frozen frog legs, frozen cuttle fish, frozen lobster tails have also improved

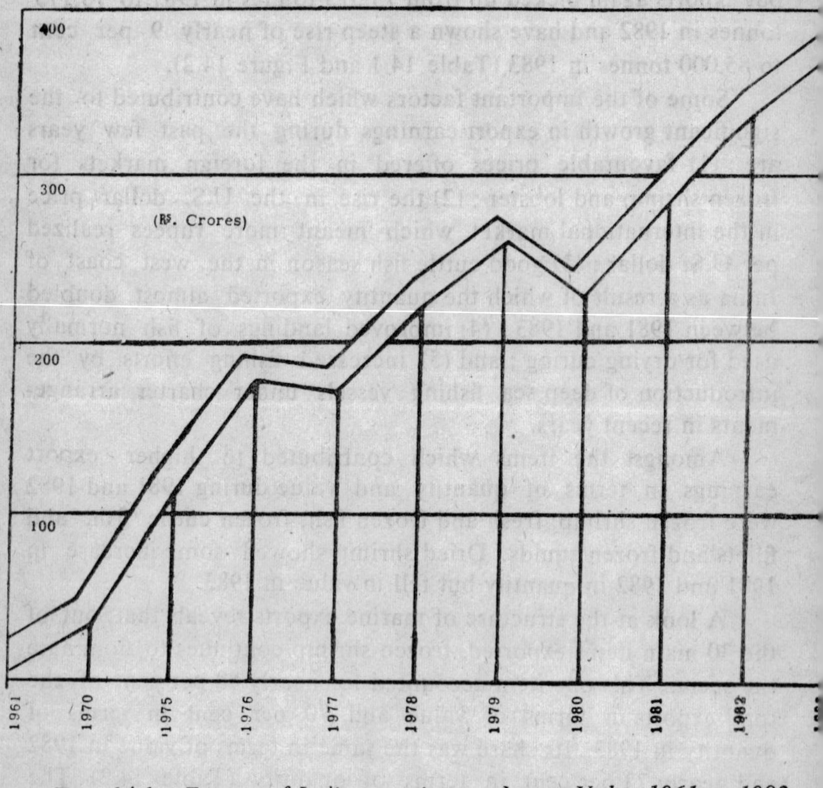

FIG. 14.1 : *Export of Indian marine products—Value 1961 to 1982*

TABLE 14.1 : **Export of Indian marine products (1961 to 1983)**

Year	Quantity (tonnes)	Value (Rs. crore)	Average (unit value) (Rs/kg)	Annual growth rates	
				Quantity in percentage	Value in percentage
1961	17,297	4.13	2.39	+ 5.9	+ 2.7
1962	11,619	3.75	3.23	—32.8	— 9.3
1963	17,908	5.86	3.27	+54.1	+56.5
1964	21,458	6.85	3.19	+19.8	+16.8
1965	15,457	6.92	4.48	—28.0	+11.1
1966	19,153	13.52	7.06	+23.9	+95.3
1967	21,764	19.93	9.16	+13.6	+47.4
1968	24,810	22.08	8.90	+14.0	+10.8
1969	30,584	33.07	10.81	+23.3	+49.8
1970	37,175	35.54	9.56	+21.6	+ 7.5
1971	34,032	39.17	11.51	— 8.5	+10.2
1972	38,271	58.13	15.19	+12.5	+48.4
1973	48,785	79.58	16.31	+27.5	+36.9
1974	46,629	76.31	16.37	— 4.4	— 4.1
1975	53,412	104.91	19.64	+14.6	+37.5
1976	62,151	179.86	28.94	+16.4	+71.4
1977	64,964	179.74	27.67	+ 4.5	— 0.7
1978	77,946	212.16	27.22	+20.0	+18.0
1979	92,184	262.03	28.43	+18.3	+23.2
1980	74,542	218.88	29.36	—19.1	—16.5
1981	75,375	286.71	38.04	+ 1.1	+41.0
1982	78,175	342.24	45.55	— 0.3	+19.4
1983	85,000	370.00	43.53	+ 8.7	+ 8.2

Source : Marine Products Export Development Authority.

their performance. However, the quantity and value of dried fish nosedived from 6311 tonnes in 1978 to 2597 tonnes in 1983 and from Rs. 3.2 crore to Rs. 2.1 crore respectively (Table 14.2).

The potential for increasing the exports of marine products other than shrimps is quite high, as Indian waters have good resources.

Frozen shrimp

Itemwise, frozen shrimp accounts for the bulk of the Indian marine products expected abroad. Out of the total exports of Rs. 370 crore in 1983, the share of this one item was Rs. 316 crore (88%). The rise was 11 per cent in 1983 and 21 per cent

TABLE 14.2 : **Pattern of marine products exports from**

Items		1973	1974	1975	1976
Frozen shrimps	Q	35,595	34,361	46,831	47,952
	V	5,58,122	6,37,326	9,43,386	16,06,499
Frozen froglegs	Q	2,698	1,454	1,317	3,170
	V	04,979	28,652	27,983	77,970
Frozen lobster tails	Q	380	456	402	513
	V	10,663	12,573	15,760	31,802
Fresh and frozen fish	Q	146	66	134	1,583
	V	731	767	1,884	16,383
Frozen cuttle fish and fillets	Q	14	141	1,017	648
	V	190	1,979	29,071	13,334
Frozen squid	Q	—	—	46	497
	V	—	—	305	6,162
Canned shrimp	Q	2,199	1,516	261	102
	V	52,369	47,842	5,999	3,935
Dried shrimp	Q	284	116	99	36
	V	3,230	1,426	1,132	385
Dried fish	Q	3,388	1,748	2,295	4,668
	V	10,955	6,658	9,061	17,341
Shark fins and fish maws	Q	252	259	307	268
	V	6,569	8,464	9,822	15,294
Other items	Q	3,530	6,512	703	2,714
	V	7,955	17,440	4,660	9,515
Total	Q	48,785	46,629	53,412	62,151
	V	7,95,763	7,62,127	10,49,063	17,98,620

Source : Compiled from various bulletins of CMFRI.
Q=Quantity in tonnes.
V=Value in Rs. 000.

India (1973—83)

1977	1978	1979	1980	1981	1982	1983
47,239	51,223	53,511	47,762	54,538	54,625	55,002
15,62,206	17,90,644	22,31,273	18,33,661	24,85,210	30,09,783	31,61,519
2,834	3,570	3,764	3,095	4,368	2,271	1,896
65,967	84,251	87,150	73,200	1,19,570	55,453	47,192
596	691	752	501	636	724	749
38,804	45,668	53,465	27,889	47,003	59,470	68,551
3,765	9,931	24,126	11,195	8,565	9,884	12,847
38,566	63,396	1,15,581	1,11,939	94,526	1,56,331	1,88,669
1,089	979	1,339	1,603	1,488	2,127	2,305
17,315	16,591	35,310	30,326	32,525	56,505	62,683
607	2,428	2,107	2,179	1,314	1,108	1,222
6,501	32,677	28,033	25,084	15,690	19,114	20,079
128	204	139	365	100	73	65
5,221	9,149	6,428	15,794	4,900	4,740	4,354
235	4	19	124	56	89	90
1,711	75	222	1,349	809	726	731
4,221	6,311	3,728	4,340	1,523	2,762	2,597
22,730	32,135	18,934	20,802	14,408	21,950	20,978
287	423	372	332	406	165	156
22,469	34,676	29,342	32,526	38,811	20,307	19,936
3,963	2,182	2,327	3,046	2,381	1,308	1,246
15,884	12,312	14,554	16,186	13,676	18,050	18,923
64,964	77,946	92,184	74,542	75,375	75,136	78,175
17,97,374	21,21,574	26,20,292	21,88,756	28,67,128	34,22,429	36,13,613

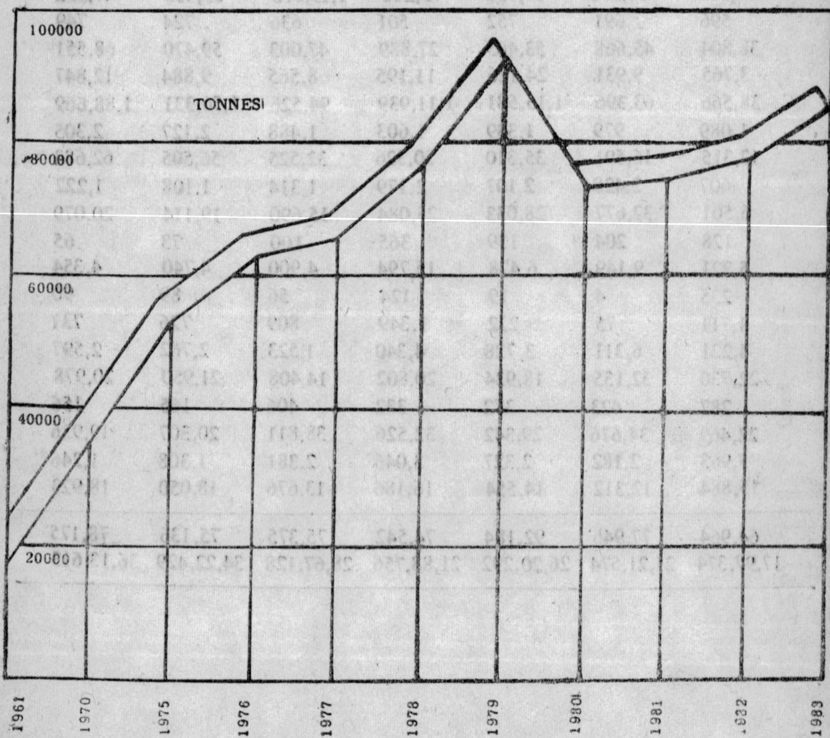

FIG. 14.2 : *Export of Indian marine products—Quantity 1961 to 1982*

TABLE 14.3 : **Structure of marine products exports from India (1973 to 1982)**

(*Share percentage*)

Items		1973 %	1974 %	1975 %	1976 %	1977 %	1978 %	1979 %	1980 %	1981 %	1982 %
1. Frozen shrimp	Q	73.58	73.69	87.68	77.15	72.72	65.73	58.05	64.07	72.36	72.70
	V	82.70	83.52	89.93	89.32	86.92	84.41	85.15	83.78	86.68	87.94
2. Frozen froglegs	Q	5.53	3.12	2.47	5.10	24.36	4.58	4.08	4.15	5.80	3.02
	V	5.65	3.75	2.67	4.33	3.67	3.97	3.33	3.34	4.17	1.62
3. Frozen lobster tails	Q	0.78	0.98	0.75	0.82	0.92	0.89	0.82	0.67	0.84	0.96
	V	1.34	1.65	1.50	1.77	2.16	2.15	2.04	1.27	1.64	1.74
4. Fresh/frozen fish	Q	0.30	0.14	0.25	2.55	5.80	12.74	26.17	15.02	11.36	13.15
	V	0.90	0.10	0.18	0.91	2.15	2.99	4.41	5.11	3.30	4.57
5. Frozen cuttle fish	Q	0.30	0.30	1.90	1.04	1.68	1.26	1.45	0.91	1.97	2.83
	V	0.02	0.26	2.77	0.74	0.96	0.78	1.35	0.57	1.13	1.65
6. Frozen squids	Q	—	—	0.09	0.80	0.92	3.12	2.29	2.92	1.74	1.47
	V	—	—	0.03	0.34	0.36	1.55	1.07	1.15	0.55	0.56
7. Canned shrimp	Q	4.51	3.25	0.49	0.17	0.20	0.26	0.15	0.49	0.13	0.10
	V	6.58	6.27	0.57	0.22	0.29	0.43	0.25	0.72	0.17	0.14
8. Dried fish	Q	6.94	3.75	4.30	7.51	6.50	8.10	4.04	5.82	2.03	3.68
	V	1.38	0.87	0.86	0.97	1.26	1.51	0.72	0.95	0.50	0.64

TABLE 14.3 : (*Contd.*)

9. Dried shrimp	Q	0.58	0.25	0.19	0,06	0.36	0.01	0.02	0.17	0.07	0.12
	V	0.41	0.19	0.11	0.02	0.10	Neg.	0.01	0.06	0.03	0.02
10. Shark fins and fish maws	Q	0.52	0.56	0.57	0.43	0.44	0.54	0.40	0.45	0.54	0.23
	V	0.83	1.11	0.94	0.85	1.25	1.63	1.12	1.49	1.35	0.59
11. Others	Q	7.23	13.96	1.31	4.37	6.10	2.77	2.53	5.33	3.16	1.74
	V	1.00	2.28	0.44	0.53	0.88	0.58	0.55	1.56	0.48	0.53
All	Q	100.00	100.00	100.00	100.00	100.00	100.00	100.00	100.00	100.00	100.00
	V	100.00	100.00	100.00	100.00	100.00	100.00	100.00	100.00	100.00	100.00

Note : Q=Quantity in tonnes.
V=Value in Rs. 000.

during 1982 in terms of value. In 1982, shrimp exports were the highest in terms of both quantity and value. Increased shrimp landings in Kerala and West Bengal as well as higher prices prevailing in export markets contributed to this rise.

Frozen froglegs

After reaching the all time peak in 1981, export of frozen froglegs suffered a setback during 1982 and further in 1983. The imposition of certain licensing procedures for the first time on frog catchers and processor adversely affected raw material supplies to processing plants. The frozen frogleg markets both in West Europe and the USA were rather depressed in 1982 and 1983 on account of the inventory build up during 1981. These adverse factors affected production as well as exports.

Frozen lobster tails

Export earnings of this item continued to increase in 1983 when it touched an all-time high of nearly Rs. 7 crore after the steep rise during 1982. The actual shipments effected in 1982 and 1983 were also higher from 636 tonnes in 1981 to 724 and 749 tonnes respectively. Japan is the main market for these but shipments improved to France and Netherlands as well.

Fresh/frozen fish

Exports of fresh/frozen fish touched a peak in 1983 both in terms of volume and value. Fish exports suffered a setback in 1980 and 1981 but have recovered both in terms of quantity and value. Export earnings reached Rs. 18.9 crore, while the volume touched 12,847 tonnes. The increase in export earnings was mainly because of the rise in the unit value which increased in both years, that is 1982 and 1983.

The central government is giving encouragement for catching more fish. Under the new charter policy, as many as 51 deep sea fishing vessels were licensed with effect from 1st April 1982. Larger supplies of high priced varieties like pomfrets, sole fish, and so on have also contributed significantly to the export boom. Moreover, UAE has emerged as a large buyer of Indian fish, replacing Kuwait. Exports to countries like Saudi Arabia, Singapore, Japan and Taiwan have also improved considerably.

Frozen cuttle fish

On account of the fairly good landings in India, exports of frozen cuttle fish (including fillets) too have shown a significant increase in terms of both quantity and value in 1982 and 1983. In 1983 the export of this item was the highest in terms of value and volume. Japan and France are the major markets for this item and the two countries together account for over 85 per cent in terms of quantity and 90 per cent in terms of value of this item. Exports to Japan have also increased by leaps and bounds in the past two years.

Frozen squids

Declining trend in the export of frozen squids both in terms of value and volume was halted in 1983, when it recovered to Rs. 2 crore and 1222 tonnes respectively. The shipments of this item had touched the peak of 2428 tonnes in 1978 but have been declining thereafter and reached the low of 1108 tonnes in 1982. During 1983, the recovery was mainly because of larger exports to France, Spain, Belgium, and Netherlands.

Dried fish and others

There has been a steep fall of dried fish exports since 1978. Though exports picked up in 1982 they have somewhat declined in 1983. Sri Lanka is the major buyer. Other major importers are Singapore, Mauritius and U.K. (Fig. 14.3).

Exports of other items like canned shrimp and canned crab meat are also looking up while those of shark fins and fish maws have declined sharply. As for canned shrimp and crabs, USSR is the leading buyer. On account of high cost of production and shortage, exports of shark fins and fish maws have not increased.

Among other items, there has been significant improvement in the export of frozen clams while there has been a fall in the export of sea shells.

Unit value realization

There has been a consistent increase in the unit value realization in recent years. It was as low as Rs. 2.39 per kg. in 1961, more than quardrupled by 1969. It continued to rise and was as high as Rs. 28.9 per kg. in 1976. It declined thereafter marginally in

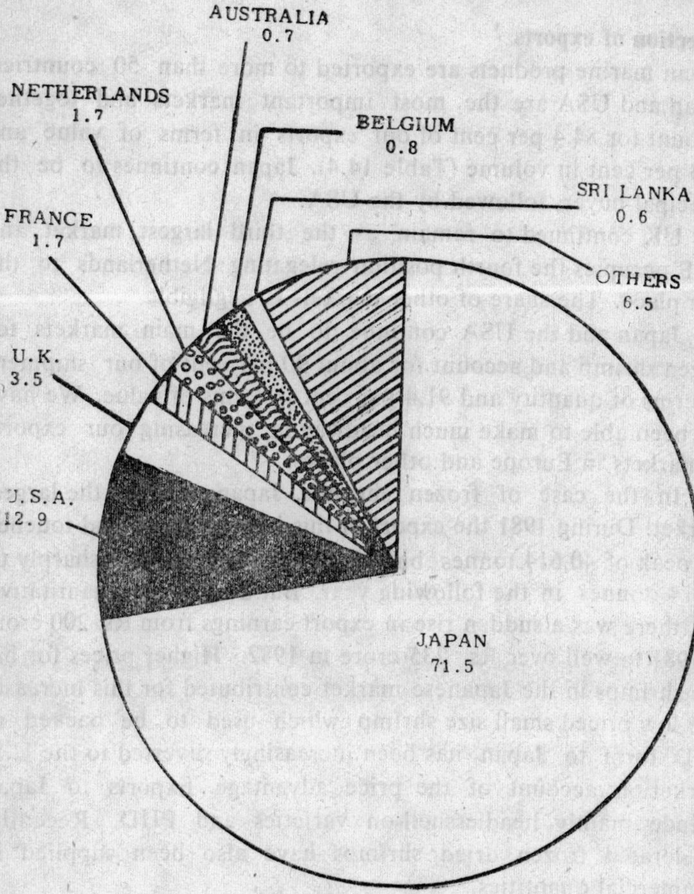

FIG. 14.3 : *Direction of Indian marine exports in 1982*
(percentage share in value)

the following two years to Rs. 27.7 and 27.2 per kg and picked up again and stood at Rs. 29.4 per kg in 1980. The unit value has spurted to Rs. 38 per kg in 1981 and further to Rs. 45.6 in 1982 but suffered a slight fall in 1983 at Rs. 43.5 per kg.

Direction of exports

Indian marine products are exported to more than 50 countries. Japan and USA are the most important markets and together account for 84.4 per cent of our exports in terms of value and 70.3 per cent in volume (Table 14.4). Japan continues to be the principal buyer, followed by the USA.

UK continued to remain as the third largest market and UAE occupies the fourth position relegating Netherlands to the fifth place. The share of other markets is negligible.

Japan and the USA continue to be the main markets for frozen shrimp and account for about 90 per cent of our shipment in terms of quantity and 91.4 per cent in terms of value. We have not been able to make much headway in increasing our exports to markets in Europe and other places.

In the case of frozen shrimps, Japan remains the largest market. During 1981 the export of this item to Japan had touched the peak of 40,614 tonnes but the supplies declined sharply to 37714 tonnes in the following year. But despite the quantitative fall, there was a sudden rise in export earnings from Rs. 200 crore in 1981 to well over Rs. 235 crore in 1982. Higher prices for big size shrimps in the Japanese market contributed for this increase. The low priced small size shrimp which used to be packed in PUD form to Japan has been increasingly diverted to the U.S. market on account of the price advantage. Exports to Japan include mainly headlesshell-on varieties and PUD. Recently, accelerated frozen dried shrimps have also been supplied in commercial quantities.

The Japanese market has been quite firm and steady for big size shrimps in 1982. Particularly, Calcutta Tiger and Vizag Pink prawn have been marketed at premium price. But the prices ruling for headless varieties were the highest on record in 1982. This significant price increase is mainly attributed to shortage of supplies from major sources.

Moreover, the exchange rate of Japanese yen to the US

TABLE 14.4 : **Major importers of Indian marine products and their share in our exports**

(Q—Quantity : V—Value) in %

Major importers		1973	1974	1975	1976	1977	1978	1979	1980	1981	1982
1. Japan	Q	47.8	42.1	58.6	44.9	42.1	43.5	41.4	50.0	55.5	53.6
	V	58.7	51.6	68.1	64.6	61.0	66.7	68.2	69.7	71.3	71.5
2. USA	Q	827.7	31.4	27.5	33.7	31.6	22.9	15.9	10.3	14.0	16.7
	V	25.2	32.1	21.7	25.8	25.8	18.2	15.3	9.3	11.7	12.9
Sub total	Q	75·5	72.5	86.1	78.6	73.7	66.4	57.3	60.3	69.5	70.3
	V	83.9	83.7	89.8	90.4	86.8	84.9	83.5	79.0	83.0	84.4
3. UK	Q	3.4	1.9	0.4	0.4	0.5	0.5	1.7	2.3	4.0	3.9
	V	4.2	3.6	0.3	0.4	0.6	0.6	2.2	2.6	3.5	3.5
4. France	Q	2.0	0.7	1.8	5.1	4.4	7.2	3.9	3.2	2,6	2.6
	V	2.1	1.0	1.9	4.1	3.9	5.5	3.2	2.7	1.7	1.7
5. Netherlands	Q	0.4	0.3	0.2	0.1	0.9	1.5	2.5	4.1	3.2	2.4
	V	0.4	3.6	0.2	0.1	0.8	1.2	2.6	3.8	2.5	1.7
6. Australia	Q	2.0	2.1	2.3	1.3	0.9	0.4	0.5	0.6	0.5	0.5
	V	2.3	2.5	2.4	1.2	1.2	0.5	0.9	0.9	0.7	0.7
6. Belgium	Q	1.6	2.0	1.0	0.7	1.1	0.5	0.6	1.6	1.1	1.1
	V	1.6	2.0	0.8	0.6	1.1	0.6	0.7	1.1	1.0	0.8
8. Sri Lanka	Q	7.4	4.5	3.7	6.7	6.2	7.6	3.7	5.5	1.1	3.3
	V	1.2	0.8	0.5	0.8	1.2	1.3	0.6	0.9	0.2	0.6
9. Others	Q	7.7	16.0	4.5	7.1	12.3	15.9	29.8	22.4	17.9	15.9
	V	4.3	2.9	3.9	2.4	4.4	5.4	6.3	9.0	7.4	6.6
Total exports	Q	100.0	100.0	100.0	100.0	100.0	100.0	100.0	100.0	100.0	100.0
	V	100.0	100.0	100.0	100.0	100.0	100.0	100.0	100.0	100.0	100.0

Source : Marine Products Export Development Authority.

dollar has also played an important role on the prices in recent years. Whenever the Japanese yen was weakening vis-a-vis the US dollar, the Japanese importers would clamp down the market and start quoting low prices. This process used to be reversed when the yen gained strength. But this pattern of price movements in relation to the exchange rate of yen has been completely changed during 1982 when the prices continued to rise to record levels in spite of the sharp drop in the value of the yen.

The USA is the next important market for frozen shrimp. Although exports have improved in the recent years, India has not been able to make much headway in capturing the vast US market potential. In fact, India lost to Ecuador in 1980 when India's exports were pushed down to the fourth rank among suppliers of shrimp to USA from second position which India occupied all along. In 1981, India moved into the third position and despite larger exports in 1982, it could not capture the second place.

West Europe

Exports of frozen shrimp to West European countries have been rising both in terms of quantity and value. The average unit value realization has also been quite high at Rs. 43 per tonne. But Western European prices are still not comparable to similar prices offered by Japan and the USA.

UK continues to be our principal market in Europe, followed by Netherlands, Belgium, France, and the Federal Republic of Germany. Some of the promising markets like Spain, Greece, and Sweden have not lifted any quantity in 1982. Except UK which has been a consistent market over the past five years exports to other countries in the region have been fluctuating.

We have also been losing in Australia where shrimp exports have been consisting of small size cooked and peeled variety. However, the exports have somewhat picked up in 1980 and 1982 and the unit value realization has also risen to Rs. 60.7 per kg. But exports continue to face tough competition in this market from Malaysia and Indonesia.

In the case of frogleg exports, West European countries continue to be the leading markets and accounted for a share of

68 per cent of our exports in terms of quantity and 62 per cent in value. Although, Netherlands, France and Belgium shared most of our supply to this region each one has been lifting only a smaller quantity particularly in 1982.

UAE is the principal buyer of fresh/frozen fish. Hitherto Kuwait to be the leading market for this item. Exports to countries like Saudi Arabia, Singapore, Japan, and Taiwan have improved considerably.

Japan and France are the major markets for frozen cuttle fish/fillets. In the case of dried fish, Sri Lanka is the principal buyer. Some supplies are also going to Mauritius and Singapore.

The countrywise analysis of marine exports given in the foregoing paragraphs bring to light some important points. Firstly, India is highly dependent on only two countries, Japan and the USA, for its exports and these countries are in a position to dictate terms and turn selective buyers. To quote an instance, in October 1979, USA resorted to blacklisting of Indian exporters of shrimps on health grounds. Though it was lifted in 1980 there has been a continuous fall in the exports.

Secondly, besides these two big buyers, not much efforts have been made to make inroads into other potential markets in the Far East Asia region including Sri Lanka and Australia where India can have the advantage of nearness.

Even in the European countries such as France, West Germany, UK and Belgium, there is big demand for Indian frozen fish and pomfret. Of late, demand is picking up in the Gulf countries.

Thirdly, the major item of exports is frozen shrimps. There is, however, a vast potential for increasing the export of other items such as lobsters, cuttle fish, squids, pomfrets, crabs and striplack.

In recent years, the operating costs have gone up considerably. Diesel accounts for 55 per cent of the operating costs. Poaching in the Indian waters by foreign vessels has increased in recent years, depriving the country of its precious marine wealth. The estimates made by the Association of Indian Fishery Industries reveal that India loses nearly Rs. 18 to Rs. 20 crore annually because of poaching. This can be prevented by stepping up the patrolling of the region. The need to evolve quality control measures is also important in view of the recent experiences.

The marine product exports target for the Sixth Plan was set at Rs. 555 crore by the end of 1984-85. Though the Rs. 370 crore mark was reached in 1983-84 this is way behind the plan target.

Concerted efforts are therefore needed to push up exports. Both quality and quantity of fish exports have been improved. Since 88 per cent of exports are directed to two sophisticated markets, Japan and the USA, all efforts should be made to improve the quality. Japan is the leading fishing nation in the world possessing the most diversified, extensive, and far-ranging fishing fleet. Indian exporters have a freight advantage in exporting to Japan. Utmost care therefore needs to be taken to ensure that the product is of high quality.

In the case of the US market, there have been complaints about quality and short-weight of frozen shrimps. Most of the fishery in India is carried out by country craft—particularly catamarans and dug-out canoes—which are not designed to carry adequate quantities of ice for preservation of catches. There is at least 8 to 10 hours time gap by the time raw material actually reaches the processing plants. Secondly, shrimp fishery is handled by thousands of small fishermen and their standards of handling of the raw material from catches to landing vary from craft to craft. Efforts should therefore be made to explain to the fishermen the importance of the use of ice right from the stage of fishery to the processing plants, so that the quality is maintained at the highest level.

Moreover, the fish catch, both inland and marine, needs to be improved in quantity as well as quality. At present, a certain amount of imbalance exists in certain areas where the optimum level of exploitation has been reached which itself calls for increased efforts. In states like West Bengal, Andhra Pradesh, Orissa and union territories of Lakshadweep, Andamans, and Pondicherry, there is vast scope for increasing marine catch. Kerala, Karnataka, Maharashtra, and Tamil Nadu need to make special efforts for enlarging their exploitation areas further into the shelf area as well as in the oceanic regime for pelagic resources (Table 14.5). Steps are also needed to exploit deep sea fishery

TABLE 14.5 : **State-wise annual marine fish landings in India 1977-81**

(Figures in tonnes)

States	1977	1978	1979	1980	1981
West Bengal	6,689	12,754	10,744	6,097	20,107
	(0.53)	(0.90)	(0.78)	(0.49)	(1.46)
Orissa	15,072	39,670	51,808	39,375	35,655
	(1.20)	(2.83)	(3.73)	(3.16)	(2.59)
Andhra Pradesh	1,00,756	82,116	91,426	1,16,013	1,16,143
	(8.00)	(5.85)	(6.59)	(9.29)	(8.43)
Tamil Nadu	2,06,046	2,35,008	2,17,394	2,17,394	2,21,296
	(16.39)	(15.17)	(16.93)	(17.39)	(16.05)
Pondicherry	6,462	6,828	10,068	9,390	10,755
	(0.51)	(0.49)	(0.73)	(0.75)	(0.78)
Kerala	3,45,037	3,73,339	3,30,509	2,79,543	2,74,395
	(27.37)	(26.60)	(23.80)	(22.36)	(19.90)
Karnataka	97,152	1,52,860	1,26,384	1,15,322	1,53,349
	(7.71)	(10.89)	(9.10)	(9.23)	(11.12)
Goa	24,731	27,111	25,388	24,490	34,498
	(1.96)	(1.93)	(1.83)	(1.96)	(2.51)
Maharashtra	2,64,452	2,84,244	2,93,326	2,31,763	2,78,587
	(20.99)	(20.25)	(21.12)	(18.54)	(19.77)
Gujarat	1,89.638	2,01,929	1,91,312	2,03,494	2,34,517
	(15.05)	(14.39)	(13.78)	(16.28)	(17.01)
Andamans	1,532	7,077	1,721	1,803	1,862
	(0.12)	(0.50)	(0.12)	(0.14)	(0.14)
Lakshadweep	2,215	2,780	3,846	2,909	3,300
	(0.18)	(0.20)	(0.28)	(0.23)	(0.24)
Private trawlers	—	—	16,840	2,244	—
	—	—	(1.21)	(0.18)	—
Total	12,59,782	14,03,607	13,88,380	12,49,837	13,78,457
	(100.00)	(100.00)	(100.00)	(100.00)	(100.00)

Note : Figures inside brackets represent percentage share of the state in the overall landings.

Source : Various bulletins of CMFRI.

resources, especially that of prawn and lobster. The southern states should also take the initiative to enter into oceanic 'Tuna'. (Table 14.6)

Chartered vessels have helped in increasing a larger catch and thus increasing exports. Yet this is only a pathfinder and the

TABLE 14.6 : **Item-wise of exports marine products and their average unit value realisation (1981 and 1982)**

Q : Quantity in Kgs.
V : Value in Rs.
Auv : Average Unit value Rs./Kg

Product		1982	AUV	1981	AUV
1. Frozen shrimp	Q	5,46,25,254		5,45,38,499	
	V	3,00,97,83,373	55.10	2,48,52,09,602	45.57
2. Frozen froglegs	Q	22,71,372		43,67,889	
	V	5,54,53,406	24.42	11,95,69,798	27.37
3. Frozen lobster tails	Q	7,23,911		6,35,746	
	V	5,94,70,465	82.14	4,70,02,995	73.93
4. Frozen cuttle fish	Q	6,39,475		2,42,803	
	V	1,51,90,281	23.77	46,16,809	19.03
5. Frozen cuttle fish fillets	Q	14,87,771		12,45,049	
	V	4,13,14,675	27.77	2,79,05,185	22.41
6. Frozen squids	Q	11,07,864		13,13,996	
	V	1,91,14,489	17.25	1,56,90,174	11.94
7. Fresh and frozen fish	Q	98,83,804		85,65,491	
	V	15,63,31,260	15.82	9,45,26,277	11.04
8. Frozen crab meat	Q	4,568		461	
	V	2,44,029	48.80	27,011	58.59
9. Frozen clams	Q	3,97,430		15,600	
	V	84,78,568	21.33	1,11,340	6.85

10. Canned shrimp	Q	73,297		1,00,459	
	V	47,40,466	64.68	49,00,347	48.78
11. Canned crab	Q	49,121		41,076	
	V	28,94,951	58.94	21,55,051	52.46
12. Canned clams	Q	—		10,070	
	V	—	—	1,85,794	18.45
13. Canned tuna	Q	—		10,176	
	V	—	—	3,73,015	36.66
14. Canned sardines	Q	—		2,880	
	V	—9	—	37,080	12.88
15. Dried shrimp	Q	89,477		56,069	
	V	7,25,978	8.11	8,09,377	14.44
16. Dried fish	Q	27,61,535		15,23,468	
	V	2,19,49,503	7.95	1,44,07,535	9.46
17. Sharm fins	Q	1,11,919		2,11,747	
	V	1,52,21,114	136.00	2,10,32,651	99.32
18. Fish maws	Q	53,495		1,94,013	
	V	50,86,277	95.08	1,77,78,625	91.64
19. Beche-de-mer	Q	37,143		47,841	
	V	17,23,558	46.40	26,28,757	54.95
20. Live fish	Q	309		—	
	V	2,392	7.74	—	—
21. Fish meal	Q	2,76,666		5,75,120	
	V	10,98,030	3.97	22,11,712	3.85

TABLE 14.6 : (*Contd.*)

22. Fish pickles	Q	270		502	
	V	378	1.40	13,590	27.07
23. Fish oil	Q	4,04,540		3,73,424	
	V	15,67,142	3.87	16,29,927	4.36
24. Cuttle fish bones	Q	24,802		28,581	
	V	4,70,276	18.96	3,86,881	13.54
25. Prawn pickles	Q	4,663		7,713	
	V	1,16,107	24.90	1,57,125	20.37
26. Sea fans	Q	1,612		719	
	V	94,909	58.37	31,714	44.10
27. Sea ferns	Q	1.425		4,202	
	V	90,028	63.18	86,060	20.48
28. Sea shells	Q	82,130		12,56,208	
	V	9,81,317	11.95	32,60,744	2.60
29. Sea dragon	Q	3,274		677	
	V	1,44,536	44.15	38,074	56.24
30. Oyster shell powder	Q	10,000		200	
	V	81,000	8.10	12,000	60.00
31, Clam meat pickles	Q	9,192		1,600	
	V	61,416	6.68	28,212	17.63
32. Aquarium fish	Q	—		1,415	
	V	—	—	13,997	9.8

33. Shrimp powder	Q	—		375	
	V	—	—	10,663	28.43
34. Sea horse	Q	—		9	
	V	—	—	8,910	990 00
35. Fish saw	Q	—		55	
	V	—	—	1,236	22.47
36. Fish nails	Q	—		670	
	V	—	—	2,66,920	398.39
Total	Q	7,51,36,319		7,53,74,803	
	V	3,42,24,29,105	45,55	2,86,71,28,187	38.04

Sourcc : Marine Products Export Development Authority.

experience needs to be adopted as a regular activity by the maritime states.

Sustained efforts are necessary for boosting the output from inland fishery resources. Steps should also be taken to conserve and develop the fish stock in rivers, develop and manage reservoir systems for higher fish output, and adopt more number of ponds and tanks for intensive aquaculture through adequate input mobilization.

15

FISHERY BY-PRODUCTS

H.P.C. SHETTY

INTRODUCTION

FISH production in India has trebled during the course of last three decades and this has placed India among the leading fish producing countries of the world. In spite of this, our present production falls far short of even our internal requirements, let alone having exportable surplus. In general, there has been an acute shortage of food in the developing countries, owing primarily to population growth outpacing food production. This has led to large scale nutritional inadequacies. According to a survey carried out sometime back by the Indian Institute of Public Opinion, about 79 per cent of India's population is suffering from acute malnurition and protein deficiency. It is in this context that fish as an item of food assumes significant importance. Fish is known to be by and large the cheapest and best source of animal protein which alone contains all the essential amino acids in right proportions. Fish is also rich in vitamins (A, D and B-Complex), minerals, and essential trace elements. Fish fat is rich in polyunsaturated fatty acids, which are known to be helpful in keeping down the cholesterol level in blood. The near absence of carbohydrate makes fish a safe item of food for diabetics too.

It is stated that consumption of 100 g of fish per day would meet 30 per cent of proteins, 10 per cent of fats, half of vitamins, and most of the minerals. But the present daily per capita consumption of fish in India is estimated to be only 7g, as against 104g, 82g and 60g respectively in Norway, Chile, and Japan.

This pathetic state of affairs is due mainly to inadequate quantity of fish produced, near non-availability of fish in remote interior places, diversion of sizable quantities of fishes for reduction, and poor purchasing power of a large section of India's population. Even in the world as a whole, the diversion of fishes for reduction has been showing an increasing trend. This is unfortunate in countries like India where fish production is inadequate to meet the nutritional demands of the population. It is, therefore, urgently necessary to bring in for direct human consumption as much of the presently produced fish as possible, in addition to going all out to produce substantially more fish from all sectors. A large number of attractive products for direct human consumption have already been developed in India from fishes which are generally utilized for reduction ; but most of them have remained largely within the confines of our research laboratories. In many cases, the economics of their commercial production even on a pilot scale is yet to be worked out, nor has their consumer acceptance been properly studied.

Apart from its value as a protein-rich food, fish has several other uses too such as for the preparation of fish meal, fish manure, fish oil, isinglass, shark fin, and a host of other by-products. These have arid uses in several diverse fields. There are a large number of conventional fish products, consisting of whole or cut pieces of fish in frozen or canned form. These are generally prepared from good quality table fish having a high consumer demand for consumption in fish condition. However, such products are excluded from the purview of this chapter, which would survey only by-products and unconventional products prepared from fish, which generally command only poor consumer demand on account of their small size, bony nature, poor taste; and so on and are often termed as "trash fishes".

RESOURCES

The present total annual fish production in India is around 2.4 million tonnes, of which about 1.4 million tonnes are contributed by marine waters. Species-wise total annual marine fish landings in India from 1969 to 1979 are given in Table 15.1, while similar species-wise landing figures in different states for the year 1979 are given in Table 15.2. State-wise distribution of pelagic and demersal fish during 1979 is depicted in Table 15.3. These tables give a fairly comprehensive picture of the range of India's total marine landings and the distribution of species-wise landings over space and time. These data would be useful for planning a meaningful utilization of our catches in different parts of the country.

It is estimated that about .5-30 per cent of our total marine landings and about 50-70 per cent of trawl catches consist of the so-called 'trash fish'. As mentioned earlier, these fish command only a poor consumer preference in fresh condition and hence are either subjected to non-sophisticated indigenous methods of preservation such as sun-drying, curing and so on or are diverted for reduction as fish meal or fish manure. While the former method makes these fish available for direct human consumption, the latter method removes from this scene altogether and will only contribute indirectly towards human food, through such products' utilization for meat production and raising agricultural crops. This makes it a longer circuitous food chain, involving the loss of a considerable quantum of valuable energy in the intermediate phases. In addition to the utilization generally of the trash fish for reduction purpose, quite often some prime food fishes, like the oil sardine, are also diverted for reduction. Because of the very heavy landings of oil sardine, the quantity thus diverted for reduction could indeed be quite considerable. This is an undesirable trend in view of the existing insufficiency of fish for meeting our minimum nutritional demands. Apart from the possibility of processing or preserving these fish by the age-old traditional methods for direct consumption, as is done quite often, it is now possible to prepare a variety of palatable products out of these fish for human consumption. The more prominent among this category are while baits, silver bellies, ribbon fishes, croakers, pink perch, smaller carangids, smaller clupeoids, saurida, and saurus.

The present total landing of about 1.4 million tonnes is essentially from only a narrow stretch of inshore waters (25-40 km from the shore), up to about 50 m depth. But the potential resources in the now declared Exclusive Economic Zone (EEZ)

TABLE 15.1 : **Composition of marine fish landings in India**

Sl. No.	Name of fish	1969	1970	1971	1972
1	Elasmobranchs	35,442	44,048	41.348	46,237
2.	Eels	3,052	6,983	4,056	4,509
3.	Catfishes	26,903	50,631	48,858	42,443
4.	Chirocentrus	9,337	9,158	9,366	9,532
5.	(a) Oil sardine	1,74,249	2,26,997	2,09,261	1,27,568
	(b) Lesser sardines	52,467	55,220	61,283	44,629
	(c) Hilsa ilisha	661	1,050	1,769	1,409
	(d) Other hilsa	7,873	9,492	10,361	12,229
	(e) Anchoviella	31,436	24,400	19,516	18,699
	(f) Thrissocles	9,009	14,087	10,801	11,130
	(g) Other clupelds	26,316	26,439	24,100	28,490
6.	(a) Harpodon nehcreus	76,276	78,443	71,508	51,570
	(b) Saurida and saurus	3,043	2,813	3,687	4,748
7.	Hemirhamphus and belone	981	1,814	1,018	687
8.	Flying fish	4,039	2,844	9,179	1,415
9.	Perches	12,865	13,913	12,993	15,247
10.	Red mullets	3,475	2,118	3,881	6,004
11.	Polynemids	3,480	7,168	7,252	7,100
12.	Sciaenids	35,041	41,903	36,903	40,159
13.	Ribbon fish	31,722	26,984	44,690	36,225
14.	(a) Caranx	21,415	18,412	20,592	27,009
	(b) Chorinemus	2,443	2,120	2,109	2,952
	(c) Trachynotus	149	143	17	2
	(d) Other carangids	7	966	304	308
	(e) Coryphaena	237	254	59	222
	(f) Elacate	309	518	347	403
15.	(a) Leiognathus	44,038	49,275	32,510	32,314
	(b) Gazza	102	154	156	78
16.	Lactarius	4,546	4,697	5,313	7,579
17.	Pomfrets	24,176	17,589	21,000	19,007
18.	Mackerel	91,837	1,39,206	204,575	108,971
19.	Seer fish	11,516	13,410	18,339	21,210
20.	Tunnies	3,445	3,015	6,032	5,760
21.	Sphyraena	1,996	1,530	1,271	2,367
22	Mugil	2,693	2,428	3,737	1,559
23.	Bregmaceros	1,684	2,196	4,345	5,488
24.	Soles	11,991	13,364	11,380	9,718
25.	(a) Peneaid prawns	72,133	89,857	72,109	78,361
	(b) Non-penaeid prawns	33,964	31,834	76734	85488
	(c) Lobsters	—	—	—	—

during 1969 to 1979

(*In tonnes*)

1973	1974	1975	1976	1977	1978	1979
44,917	66,054	65,230	54,605	62,216	61,621	52,843
3,869	4,011	51,710	8,296	12,997	8,781	7,155
52,642	76,196	68,689	43,540	53,504	39,231	48,817
11,090	9,026	11,813	10,358	11,909	10,990	10,274
1,44,395	1,26,676	1,59,240	169262	150130	168078	153971
1,08,523	83,921	1,12,117	100000	65,724	52,838	68,351
404	4,248	8,897	7,842	4,189	9,894	12,068
11,918	7,541	7,567	8,482	14,651	12,800	8,672
25,394	41,507	30,744	30,069	34,033	39,054	26,588
13,194	11,433	9,997	17,660	9,929	14,304	16,628
35.350	43,226	52,786	57,164	41,458	37,020	33,965
64,345	61,138	99,614	87,075	85,236	125481	126044
4,049	12,520	14,323	5,292	8,525	10,808	11,154
1,110	4,574	1,980	1,169	2,311	1,478	1,577
6,388	1,012	1,832	1,439	643	1,681	2,546
21,513	36 837	35,232	18,162	31,799	49,312	35,657
3,925	7,009	2,641	5,216	2,422	2,984	3,130
9,248	10,637	14,044	14,573	3,929	5,469	5,809
87,682	79,261	1,14,535	87,581	99,887	96,379	93,018
53,106	63,029	57,330	64,542	42,407	77,785	71,349
25,298	19,316	23,005	25,745	30,606	16,956	28,942
2,827	3,797	3,380	3,322	4,119	3,359	3,307
189	122	64	35	80	106	195
129	91	207	1,572	219	423	465
228	286	411	261	226	64	146
529	229	221	383	429	568	880
48127	50902	39813	42445	34,504	41,777	55266
41	338	424	966	61	104	197
13912	8913	11848	12045	10,961	7,906	4474
22052	22421	24987	37127	35127	41,434	40427
79423	37462	45947	65497	62136	85,233	71514
19700	19841	18897	20159	21119	20,779	29547
5678	10839	11285	19322	13005	13893	26595
3415	4862	2150	2388	2423	3709	2265
3138	4497	3515	2613	2269	2626	1400
4213	1872	1043	380	30	184	638
14642	18917	12044	10088	10810	13620	12203
136514	114934	141713	114640	96,472	129204	113665
66955	55244	79038	76787	73,992	50,652	63917
—	—	2991	2532	1,217	1,307	1135

TABLE 15.1 : (*Contd.*)

(d) Crabs and other crustaceans	5,670	10,832	9612	11599
26. Cephalopods	769	1,184	1505	1026
27. Miscellaneous	30,843	36,118	37513	48,598
Total	9,13,630	10,85,607	11,61,389	9,80,049

Source : CMFRI Marine Fisheries Information Service, No. 9, May-June-July, 1979.

TABLE 15.1 : (*Contd.*)

12508	16663	19893	19999	20,068	14,202	20304
1394	3677	7889	10,826	10,005	15,931	15032
56,226	72,718	97607	90,812	91,945	1,13,582	106250
1220240	1217797	1422693	1352855	1259782	1403607	1388380

TABLE 15.2 : **Estimated marine fish landings in India during 1979**

Sl. No.	Name of fish	West Bengal	Orissa	Andhra Pradesh	Tamil Nadu	Pondi-cherry
1.	Elasmobranches	244	4331	6994	12393	222
2.	Eels	—	2	245	119	88
3.	Cat fishes	140	1308	3799	5617	51
4.	Chitocentrus	407	1644	976	1839	167
5.	(a) Oil sardines	—	—	—	1011	—
	(b) Lesser sardines	—	2687	6180	33289	1998
	(c) Hilsa ilisha	660	9969	78	41	—
	(d) Other hilsa	38	359	1092	2761	12
	(e) Anchoviella	14	505	5888	11061	345
	(f) Thrissocles	270	295	3433	5542	429
	(g) Other clupeids	1517	1431	2518	3564	345
6.	(a) Harpodon nehereus	1211	449	717	1	—
	(b) Saurida and sourus	—	50	1379	1498	262
7.	Hemirhamphus and belone	—	28	100	624	6
8.	Flying fish	—	4	71	1599	854
9.	Perches	225	151	3095	5919	1004
10.	Red mullets	—	2	426	1448	203
11.	Polynemids	172	1491	1412	353	14
12.	Sciaenids	915	5351	8825	18948	306
13.	Ribbon fish	291	616	6337	21040	129
14.	(a) Carmax	71	326	3185	7022	537
	(b) Chorinemus	57	716	444	844	27
	(c) Trachynotus	—	—	—	182	—
	(d) Other carangids	—	—	56	23	—
	(e) Coryphaena	—	1	7	37	2
	(f) Elacate	—	1	—	535	—
15.	(a) Leiognathus	96	1108	3585	42866	746
	(b) Gazza	—	—	—	197	—
16.	Lactarius	—	5	945	1323	11
17.	Pomfrets	923	10109	2069	877	35
18.	Mackerel	—	306	2621	3521	424
19.	Seer fish	331	2444	5547	5228	105
20.	Tunnies	—	31	437	3211	1
21.	Sphyraena	—	5	62	1463	22
22.	Mugil	—	22	159	229	27
23.	Bregmaceros	—	—	—	—	—

(Figures in tonnes)

Kerala	Karnataka	Goa	Maha-rashtra	Gujarat	Anda-mans	Laksha-dweep	Pri-vate* traw-lers	Total
6954	2531	1280	12516	4926	88	364	—	52843
10	1	25	4033	2622	—	—	—	7155
11328	9920	846	10433	5320	55	—	—	48817
1125	258	122	1721	1970	45	—	—	10274
116834	33080	3030	16	—	—	—	—	153971
15814	4753	2471	927	—	132	—	—	68351
6	10	2	1071	231	—	—	—	12068
36	52	14	429	3837	42	—	—	8672
6552	1721	—	382	—	119	—	—	26588
1789	441	911	2832	686	—	—	—	16628
674	2278	378	15675	5552	33	—	—	33,965
1	5	9	59667	63984	—	—	—	126044
5326	155	104	2374	6	—	—	—	11154
257	49	13	126	185	88	101	—	1577
—	—	1	1	—	—	—16		2546
20239	181	203	3225	973	239	203	—	35657
127	30	—	859	8	—	27	—	3130
29	2	—	1600	736	—	—	—	5809
5237	2348	1492	21366	28230	—	—	—	93018
25,718	1193	548	10983	4491	3	—	—	71349
12339	1103	1343	2314	510	134	58	—	28942
128	59	140	416	466	—	—	—	3307
—	13	—	—	—	—	—	—	195
—	1	—	385	—	—	—	—	465
48	—	—	51	—	—	—	—	146
120	34	190	—	—	—	—	—	880
3597	1565	881	724	—	78	—	—	55266
—	—	—	—	—	—	—	—	197
253	433	291	430	783	—	—	—	4474
1737	250	138	14941	9319	29	—	—	40427
18585	40084	4391	1455	35	92	—	—	71514
6275	1645	1101	4027	2682	138	24	—	29547
15391	1717	742	1772	442	57	2794	—	26595
477	41	7	82	—	95	11	—	2265
39	—	14	38	751	121	—	—	1400
—	—	—	276	362	—	—	—	638

TABLE 15.2 : (*Contd.*)

24.	Soles	—	125	610	2337	162
25.	a. Penaeid prawns	410	2983	8697	10222	532
	b. Non-penaeid prawns	161	34	3117	897	72
	c. Lobsters	—	—	33	340	5
	d. Crabs and other Crustaceans	—	6	1109	5883	242
26.	Cephalopods	—	14	523	1903	50
27.	Miscellaneous	2581	2899	4655	17181	632
	Total	10744	51808	91426	235008	10068

Source : CMFRI, Marine Fisheries Information Service No. 9, May.

4487	874	893	2304	411	—	—	—	12203
29522	4654	1594	45638	8606	64	—	743	113665
75	6	—	56208	3347	—	—	—	63917
26	15	6	499	211	—	—	—	1135
7643	2740	1379	519	783	—	—	—	20304
2976	68	173	3959	5351	—	15	—	15032
8635	12074	646	7052	33496	69	233	16097	106250
330509	126384	25388	293326	191312	1721	3846	16840	1388380

June-July, 1979.

TABLE 15.3 : **Statewise distribution of pelagic and demersal groups of fishes during 1979**

(*in tonnes*)

Sl. No.	State	Pelagic	Demersal	Total
1.	West Bengal	6,419	4,325	10,744
2.	Orissa	23,133	28,675	51,808
3.	Andhra Pradesh	42,049	49,377	91,426
4.	Tamil Nadu	1,12,923	1,22,085	2,35,008
5.	Pondicherry	5,795	4,273	10,068
6.	Kerala	2,28,272	1,02,237	3,30,509
7.	Karnataka	97,889	28,495	1,26,384
8.	Goa	15,830	9,558	25,388
9.	Maharashtra	1,07,224	1,86,102	2,93,326
10.	Gujarat	1,04,476	86,836	1,91,312
11.	Andamans	1,145	576	1,721
12.	Lakshadweep	3,198	648	3,846
13.	Private trawlers	—	16,840	16,840
	Total	7,48,353	6,40,027	13,88,380

Source : CMFRI, Marine Fisheries Information Service, No. 22, August 1980.

are indeed vast and have been estimated to be in the order of 4.5 million tonnes, consisting of 1.4 million tonnes of demersal fish, 2.6 million tonnes of pelagic fish, 0.3 million tonnes of crustaceans, and 0.2 million tonnes of cephalopods. But this vast potential becoming available to us will depend on our ability to harvest the deeper waters, for which we are still ill-equipped.

POTENTIAL FISH DEMAND BY A.D. 2000

The aggregate demand will depend on population size and the purchasing power of the people at any given time. The quantity of fish required as per nutritional standards may not be the same that the economic condition permits people to buy. According to some estimates made by demographers, based on assumptions of future trends of fertility and mortality and the success or failure of family planning programmes, the likely range of population in India by A.D. 2000 would be 935.4 to 996.3 million. Based on the estimated per capita income at that time, the aggregate consumer demand for fish has been estimated to range from 3.59 to 4.53 million tonnes, with the per capita demand going up from the present 2.6 kg to nearly 5 kg per year.

While the above demand estimates may be realistic from the point of view of the purchasing power of people, it is also necessary to estimate the requirements based on the need to provide a balanced diet to the people. An average adult requires about 75 g of protein per day, of which at least 20 g must be of animal origin. Considering that 10 g of animal protein would be obtained from other sources like milk, meat, or eggs, an individual would require about 50 g of fish for getting the remaining 10 g of animal protein. This would amount to an average adult requiring 18.25 kg of fish per year. But since the requirements of the lower age groups up to 12 years are decidedly lesser, a factor of 0.6 could be applied which would make the average requirement of an individual to be 10.95 kg per year. If we assume that about 60 per cent of the population would be fish eating by A.D. 2000, the magnitude of fish requirement would range from 6.15 to 6.54 million tonnes. But it is very likely that the percentage of fish eating people might go up to 70 in which case the requirement would range from 7.17 to 7.63 million tonnes. The supply and demand projections for 1985 and A.D. 2000 are delineated in Table 15.4.

From the above projections made on the basis of nutritional requirements in which fish forms one of the main components of animal protein in the diet, the average per capita requirements of fish would be about 11 kg per year, as against the present consumption rate of only 2.6 kg per year. The projected total fish production in A.D. 2000 from both inland and marine fisheries is of the order of about 8.0 million tonnes. After deducting the quantities that are likely to be utilized for export and for the manufacture of fish meal and other industrial products, fish available for domestic consumption would be about 6.75 million tonnes, thereby raising the per capita availability to about 10.3 kg per annum, taking the total population to be around 935 million, with 70 per cent of them eating fish. This would just meet the nutritional requirements of the people. But this is fully dependent on our being able to achieve the projected target, for which it will be necessary to substantially increase our efforts in the relevant fields. Further, the quantity of fish left for domestic

TABLE 15.4 : **Supply and demand projections**

Year	Population (million)	Fish eating population (70% of col. 2) (millions)	Supply (million tonnes)			Export (million tonnes)	Quantity used for fishmeal and other industrial products (million tonnes)	Balance of fish for domestic consumption (million tonnes)	Per capita availability (kg/annum)	Demand as per nutritional standard @ 11 kg per capita per annum (million tonnes)
			Inland	Marine	Total					
1985	724.5	507.43	2.22	2.06	4 28	0.10	0.40	3.78	7.4	5.58
2000	935.4*	654.78	4.50	3.50	8.00	0.25	1.00	6.75	10.3	7.17

Note : *Minimum projections.

consumption would also depend on the quantities that might be drawn off for export or for industrial purposes for getting better returns.

FISH BY-PRODUCTS AND SPECIAL FISH PRODUCTS

A large number of fish by-products have been developed in different parts of the world. Some of them are being produced in India, even though only a few of them are produced on commercial scale. By-product means a subsidiary product produced incidentally while manufacturing some other major product, or a product made from some part or from out of the waste material resulting from the manufacture of a major product. Sometimes the entire fish is utilized for the production of what are normally known as by-products such as fish meal, fish oil, and fish manure. Of the various by-products, commercial production on a fairly good scale appears to be largely restricted to fish meal and fish oil.

Fish meal

In simplest terms, fish meal can be defined as dried and powdered fish that is generally utilized in the formulation of cattle feed and poultry feed. Fish meal varies greatly in quality and composition depending on the nature of raw material and the method of preparation, namely, whether from dried fish or through wet reduction process.

Methods of manufacture

Brief details of the various methods are given below :

(a) *From dried fish* : Miscellaneous small-sized fish are sun-dried on open prepared ground or on the beach. These are collected in centralized factories, where they are subjected to further sun-drying, sieved to exclude sand as much as possible, and finally pulverized. Sometimes salt-cured fishes which do not sell are also used as raw material. A couple of plants in the organized sector use dried fishes like Dhoma and Bombay dock which are pulverized and heat treated to reduce moisture content and destroy *Salmonella*.

(b) *Batch-type wet reduction process* : This is an indigenous method, which is a definite improvement over the method described above. This is employed generally for oil sardine, which is often landed in enormous quantities in Kerala and Karnataka. In this method the fish are cooked in mild steel cauldrons, pressed in manually operated presses, and after the separation of oil the press cake is dried and milled.

(c) *Continuous wet reduction process* : This method of factory production of fish meal is of recent origin. It is a composite process for producing both fish meal and oil, making use of oil sardine as the raw material. It consists of cooking the fish in horizontal steam jacketted continuous cookers having a screw conveyor and pressing the cooked fish in continuous expeller type screw presses, which discharge press cake and press liquor. The press cake is mechanically dried to obtain fish meal, while the oil is recovered from the press liquor by centrifuging.

(d) *Dry rendering process* : This method is suited for fish having only a low fat content (like the silver bullies) and, therefore, do not yield oil. This is not yet common in India. The process consists of cooking and drying the fish in one operation in steam jacketted, shaft stirred horizontal driers. A vacuum of 34—17KN/m^2 is applied to help water removal.

Specifications

There are two grades (A and B) of fish meal, for which the Indian Standards Institution has prescribed separate specifications. Grade A should have not less than 60 per cent crude protein and more than 10 per cent moisture and crude fat, and 3 per cent acid-insoluble ash. For Grade B, the specifications for moisture and crude fat are the same, while the minimum protein level is 50 per cent and the upper limit for acid-insoluble ash is 5 per cent. Trading in fish meal is mainly based on protein content. The sale value goes down if the sand content is high, while for export it is necessary to ensure that it is free from *Salmonella*.

Marketing

There is a good market for fish meal both within and outside the country. As it is, there appears to be a dearth of good quality fish meal for use within the country, primarily for incorporation into poultry feed. Some quantity of fish meal is also exported, but there appears to be good scope for considerably enlarging the export. To help increase fish meal production, prawn wastes from freezing plants and squilla, which is landed in considerable quantities by the trawlers, could be profitably utilized.

As on May 1979, there were 34 fish meal plants in India, with an installed capacity of 587 tonnes per day.

Fish oil

Fish oils are of two types, namely, body oil and liver oil. The former is extracted from oil sardines and the latter from elasmobranchs, mainly sharks.

Sardine oil

It is estimated that the quantity of sardine oil produced in India ranges from 3 to 10 kt. The heavy landings of oil sardines along the Karnataka and Kerala coasts are utilized for this purpose.

Methods of manufacture : The oil is extracted from the fish in different methods, ranging from crude to sophisticated.

(a) In the simplest and most crude method, the oil sardines are dumped into pits dug on the beach and are covered with sand. In course of time after the fish have rotted, the released oil oozes out over the top of the pit, from where it is scooped into tins. The residual matter in the pit goes as fish manure. The oil is boiled to remove the water. The oil obtained by this method is foul smelling and of inferior quality.

(b) The more scientific method consists of boiling the fish with a minimum quantity of water for about 30 minutes in large iron cauldroms and when pouring the cooked mass into strong gunny bags and pressing them in vertical batch type manually operated screw presses. The cooked liquor containing the pressed oil is allowed to stand for sometime in a cement cistern and the oil collecting at the top is collected through overflow into adjoining cisterns. This oil is boiled to remove water, before storage or sale. The press cake is sun-dried and used as either fish meal or manure.

The oil produced by both methods contains varying

amounts of physical impurities and free fatty acids, has poor stability, offensive odour and deep to dark brown or even black colour.

(c) The sophisticated and superior method of factory production of sardine oil through continuous wet reduction process has already been described earlier. There are a few plants of this kind along the Indian coast, with raw material capacity of 1-1.5 tonne/hour. The oil obtained by this method from fresh fish is almost bland, but develops fishy odour during storage. The colour of this oil varies from light yellow to light brown, depending on the freshness of raw material. The free fatty acid content is only 1-3 per cent. The oil content of oil sardine varies from 3-16 per cent depending on the season, with the higher fat contents coinciding with periods of the fish's peak landing. The fish on an average yields 7-8 per cent of its weight as oil in one season.

Uses : The crude fish oil produced by the first two methods is used as a preservative coating for country boats, in tanning of leather, and as a coating component for tiles before baking them. The superior quality obtained by the third method is preferred for leather tanning and is used in the manufacture of paints, surface coatings, printing inks, etc. This oil when refined and hydrogenated can be used in soap making. The refined oil can also be used as a packing medium for canned sardines and in oral therapy for lowering serum cholesterol levels.

Shark liver oil

This oil, rich in Vitamin A, compares well with the European cod liver oil. Sharks ranging in size from 0.3 to 6.0 m, with a liver size ranging from 250 g to 180 kg, are tapped for obtaining this oil. The oil yield ranges from 25-75 per cent of the liver by weight, with the Vitamin A potency ranging from 10,000 to 24,000 IU per gram. The manufacturing process is quite simple, consisting of heating the liver mass to free its oil, which is filtered through flannel and dehydrated with anhydrous sodium sulphate. A better method that is followed now consists of digesting chopped or minced livers with 2 per cent sodium hydroxide or 2-5 per cent (by weight) sodium bicarbonate, followed by steam cooking. The digested material is then centrifuged to obtain the oil.

This liver oil, because of its high Vitamin A potency, is generally blended with refined groundnut oil and Vitamin D is added. The levels of Vitamins A and D are so adjusted as to meet the requirements of Indian Pharmacopoeia before the oil is bottled or capsuled for medical use.

FISH SOLUBLES

Fish soluble is a by-product prepared from the stick water (press water) resulting from the manufacture of fish meal from whole cooked fish or cooked fish offal. It contains predominantly water soluble substances. The stick water contains minerals, vitamins, amino acids and many other nutritionally valuable substances. It is maintained at a temperature of 85°C to avoid spoilage till it is taken for concentration. To start with it is concentrated at 60-70°C for 30 minutes in an evaporator to coagulate proteins and precipitate enzymes. It is further concentrated in a vacuum evaporator till its total solid content goes upto approximately 50 per cent from approximately 5 per cent. The pH is adjusted to 4-4.5 and then it is stored in steel or red wood tanks or oak barrels. In use, it is mixed with dry animal feeds.

FISH ENSILAGE

Fish ensilage or liquid fish is produced from whole fish or fish offal generally by two different methods, one through autolysis and the other through microbial fermentation. The earlier attempts made in India at the Central Food Technological Research Institute were restricted to the latter method, while the former method where the liquefaction of fish is achieved through proteolytic enzymes of the fish itself was done for the first time in India at Mangalore at the College of Fisheries in 1978. In this type of autolytic degradation it is necessary to prevent micro-biological spoilage and this is achieved through the addition of sulphuric acid, formic acid, or some types of organic acids to keep the pH within acidic range. Formic acid was employed in the work conducted at Mangalore and pH was maintained at 4. In the other method, minced fish or fish offal is mixed with molasses and then inoculated with a strain of lactic acid bacteria.* The ensilage, obtained through any of the methods, forms a valuable food supplement and can be usefully mixed in the feed given to cattle, pigs and poultry. This product has both advantages and disadvantages. While fish meal plants would require a certain minimum quantity of raw material for economic running, ensilage has no such trappings ; even small quantities of fish or offal could be made use of as and when they become available. However, transportation poses a problem, since this liquid product would require water-tight containers.

FISH HYDROLYSATE

This is a type of protein-rich product prepared from hydrolysed fish meat. It can be used as a protein supplementing agent in biscuits, bread, beverages, and so on and also in the preparation of industrial and laboratory bacteriological culture media. Whole fish or fish fillets are dressed, minced and mixed with a little water. The pH is adjusted to five and the temperature is raised to 60-65°C. An enzyme (papain) is then added for achieving hydrolysis and the slurry is maintained at the same temperature till the completion of hydrolysis, after which it is quickly raised to boiling point and boiled for 15 minutes. It is then decanted, followed by centrifugation to remove bones and other larger pieces of undigested matter, clarification in a clarifier to remove most of the suspended matter and pressure filtration with hyflosupercel to obtain a clear hydrolysate. This hydrolysate is vacuum concentrated in a forced circulation evaporator from a solid content of about 8 per cent to about 30 per cent. This concentrate is then vacuum dried in a shelf drier at 8.5 KN/m^2 and 45-60°C. The cream yellow coloured powder obtained therefrom is stored in air-tight bottles.

Spray drying of a protein hydrolysate prepared from oil sardine has been successfully tried. Animal assay experiments

* Fermentation can also be achieved by adding papaya fruit's skin wastes (for the enzyme papain) on 5 per cent buttermilk.

carried out with this light cream spray dried powder have indicated it to be nutritionally comparable to skim milk powder.

FISH FLOUR

The term fish meal is used for the fish powder that is used in animal feed formulations. However, refined fish meal specially prepared in a hygienic way for human consumption is termed as fish flour. The process could be essentially the same as that for fish meal in the simplest method. However, since the fat and water contents and the odour have to be considerably reduced and the protein content increased, most of the methods of fish flour preparation are different. Such refined fish flours with very high protein content and low fat content are also known as Fish Protein Concentrates (FPC).

FAO has recognized three types of FPC :

Type A : A virtually odourless and tasteless powder having a maximum total fat content of 0.75 per cent.

Type B : Powder with a maximum fat content of 3 per cent, having a slight fishy flavour.

Type C : Normal fish meal produced under satisfactory hygienic conditions.

The commonest method of FPC preparation is by solvent extraction. The solvents are isopropanol, ethyl alcohol, hexane, acetone, methanol, ethanol, and so on.

Common method

The fish are minced after thorough washing and then fed to a series of three extractors by turn. The fish mince gets dehydrated in the first extractor, where it is agitated for about 50 minutes with the isopropanol containing liquid recovered from extractor-II. The contents of extractor-I are then fed to a continous centrifuge, where they separate into solid (wet-cake) and liquid. The wet-cake is fed into extractor-II having a temperature of about 75°C and is agitated for about 90 minutes with the liquid recovered from extractor-III. In this, the fat content goes down from 5 per cent to 1 per cent. These contents are then centrifuged and the resultant wet-cake conveyed to extractor-III, also having a temperature of 75°C. Fresh isopropanol is added here to the wet-cake and agitated for about 70 minutes. Here the fat content gets reduced to 0.3 per cent. The contents are again centrifuged and the resultant wet-cake repeatedly washed with pure isopropanol for about 50 minutes. The wet-cake is then heated in a rotating vacuum drier to evaporate the solvent. The dry matter is conveyed to a hammer mill, where it is ground to a fine powder and sieved and finally packed in suitable containers.

C.I.F.T. method

The C.I.F.T. has developed a slightly different method, where the minced fish is first subjected to glacial acetic acid and then to solvent extraction by an azeotropic mixture of n-Hexane and ethyl alcohol.

Partially hydrolysed and deodorized fish flour

This is prepared by a new method developed at the College of Fisheries, Mangalore, wherein no solvent extraction is resorted to. It is a simpler, safer, cheaper, and better method. There is no danger of residual effect of solvents and the product keeps well at room temperature for over a year without flavour reversion. This fish flour of creamy white colour contains 87-92 per cent protein and 7-8 per cent available lysine. This has been successfully prepared from a number of non-fatty trash fishes.

Dressed fish are deboned in a meat-picking machine and the picked meat is washed with a jet of cold water for 2-3 minutes. It is then boiled for 5-6 minutes in a steam jacketed kettle, after which it is washed alternately in cold and hot water for 4-5 minutes. The meat is then pressed lightly in a hydraulic press to remove the free water, after which it is minced in a powerdriven meat mincer. It is then partially hydrolysed overnight at room temperature by adding 1 N hydrochloric acid in the ratio of 1 : 1 (weight/volume). After completion of hydrolysis the next morning, the pH is adjusted to 7 by adding 1 N sodium hydroxide. The meat thereafter is again alternately washed in hot and cold water. The meat is then pressed in a hydraulic press and dried at 70°C in an electric drier to reduce the moisture level to 5-6 per cent. The dried material is ground to 0.5 mm particle size and treated with 1 per cent acetic acid. After drying again, it is stored in air-tight bottles or tin containers after cooling to room temperature.

The mild acid hydrolysis employed in this method is mainly for eliminating the coagulable and elastic properties of the proteins. However, it also helps in the removal of fat and residual bones. The fat content is mainly removed by repeated washing. The treatment of the final product with acetic acid is to prevent flavour reversion during storage. The yield is 4-6 per cent in relation to whole fish and 12-13 per cent to picked meat. The meat washings can be made use of for preparing 'fish extract' for use in microbiological media. The dressings of the fish can be converted into fish meal. The proximate composition of fish flour prepared from four types of fishes is shown in Table 15.5, while the nutritional quality of one of them is given in Table 15.6.

TABLE 15.5 : **Proximate composition of PHD fish flour from different species of fish**

	Fish flour from			
	Lactarius	Threadfin bream	Croaker	Ribbon fish
Protein %	91.87	92.85	87.48	87.24
Fat %	0.23	0.52	0.39	0.65
Ash %	0.89	0.52	0.89	0.23
Moisture %	5.98	5.36	5.98	8.50
Pepsin digestibility %	92.87	90.59	92.87	92.54
Available lysine (g/100 g protein)	8.02	7.98	7.08	7.63

TABLE 15.6 : **Nutritional quality of PHD fish flour prepared from threadfin bream**

Isocaloric diet containing	Protein content of the diet %	Initial body weight	Gain in wt. at the end of four weeks g	Total protein consumed during the period g	PER
Raw fish meat	15.63	37.75	115.50	43.06	2.68
PHD fish flour	15.51	41.00	83.24	35.93	2.32

P.H.D. MEAT AND ITS PRODUCTS

This was developed at the College of Fisheries, Mangalore, in 1974 as a precursor to the fish flour described above. The initial stages of preparation are more or less similar. The washed and dressed fish are cooked in boiling water for 15-20 minutes, after which meat is hand-picked. The picked meat is soaked in boiling water for 2-3 minutes and pressed in a basket press to remove water. This process of washing and pressing is repeated 5-6 times, after which the meat is minced in a power driven mincer. It is then left for overnight hydrolysis by adding 1 N hydrochloric acid in 1 : 1 proportion. The next morning pH of the meat is adjusted to 6.5 by adding 2 N sodium hydroxide solution. This is now ready for immediate use. It can also be preserved under frozen storage for 4 months and for about 15 days at room temperature by adding 1 or 2 per cent acetic acid.

It is now possible to partially hydrolyse the fish meat within a few hours, without having to wait overnight, by using enzymes like papain.

Destruction of elasticity and coagulability of the proteins through partial hydrolysis and deodorization through washings have enabled the easy incorporation of the PHD meat into a variety of products without affecting their odour, taste, flavour, texture, and consistency. The proximate composition of fish meat is not adversely affected by the hydrolysing and deodorizing processes, as is evident from Table 15.7.

TABLE 15.7 : **Proximate composition of meat of Lactarius lactarius and Otolithus sp. (croaker), before and after hydrolysis and deodorization**

	Lactarius lactarius		*Otolithus* sp.	
	Raw meat %	PHD meat %	Raw meat %	PHD meat %
Moisture	78.09	80.62	80.01	82.99
Total protein	18.11	15.06	16.25	11.94
Fat	1.65	0.33	2.07	0.55
Ash	0.83	0,23	1.37	0.40

About two dozen fish products have been developed by incorporating PHD meat prepared from trash fishes into the common vegetarian products. Most of these products have already been standardised. Among these products may be mentioned fish chakkuli, fish sevu, fish wafers, fish pappad, fish jam, fish biscuit, fish chapathi, and so on.

The development of PHD meat and PHD fish flour from trash fishes has opened a new vista for bringing trash fish for human consumption instead of permitting their reduction. Further, the technique of preparation of the various PHD meat/flour fortified products is so simple that they can easily be taken up on a cottage industry basis.

Details relating to proximate composition, shelf life, consumer acceptability and cost of production of some of the standardised products prepared with the incorporation of PHD meat are given in Table 15.8.

Canned fish paste

PHD meat made from trash fishes has also been successfully used at Mangalore for the preparation of canned fish paste by mixing it with various sub-materials at the following rates :

Ingredients	*Percentage*
PHD fish meat	70.80
Starch	12.00
Fat (Vanaspati)	4.00
Spices containing garlic	0.7
Pepper	0.5
Cinnamon	0.1
Lime juice	0.7
Onion	5.0
Salt	3.0
Green chillies	4.0

The above ingredients are mixed thoroughly and then packed into cleaned cans leaving sufficient head space, sealed, and sterilized at 250°F for 51 minutes. The sterilized cans are then cooled and stored at room temperature, in which they keep well for over a year. Panel tests have proved this product to be quite acceptable.

TABLE 15.8 : **Details of composition, shelf life and cost of production of the products prepared with incorporation of PHD meats**

Name of product	Proximate composition in percentage		Shelf life (at room temp.)	Acceptability	Cost of production
(i) Fish spirals (chakkuli)	Protein	23.76	6 weeks (in polythene bags)	97% families out of 1500 families tried	Rs. 8.26 per kg (subject to variation)
	Fat	25.57			
	Ash	0.94			
	Moisture	5.86			
(ii) Fish sevu	Protein	22.24	6 weeks (in polythene bags)	97% families out of 1500 families tried	Rs. 7.75 per kg (subject to variation)
	Fat	30.82			
	Ash	3.81			
	Moisture	6.31			
(iii) Fish pappad	Protein	28.30	6 months to 1 year (in polythene begs)	95% out of 1500 families tried	Rs. 5.00 per kg (subject to variation)
	Fat	1.52			
	Ash	2.56			
	Moisture	9.0			
(vi) Fish sandige (wafers)	Protein	17.18	6 months to 1 year (in polythene bags)	98% out of 1500 families tried	Rs. 4.70 per kg (subject to variation on small industry scale)
	Fat	2.67			
	Ash	1.84			
	Moisture	10.0			

(v) Fish jam	Protein	9.95	6 months to 1 year (in sealed bottles)	95% out of 1000 families tried	Rs. 3.20 per 1b. (on small industry scale)
	Fat	0.32			
	Ash	0.18			
	Moisture	31.05			
(vi) Fish diamond cut (salted/sweet)	Protein	19.15	4 weeks to 6 weeks	—	—
	Fat	31.45			
	Ash	0.32			
	Moisture	4.82			
(vii) Fish vermicelli	Protein	30.24	4 weeks to 6 months	—	—
	Fat	0.24			
	Ash	3.10			
	Moisture	7.13			

It can be used as bread spread and in sandwiches.

CANNED FISH FLAKES IN MASALA

A product made out of trash fish (croaker) at the College of Fisheries, Mangalore, it is prepared from a mixture of picked and minced fish meat (94%), starch (1%), fat (3%), and salt (2%). The mixture is ground well and pressed into flakes, which are then canned in a specially prepared masala medium. The proximate composition of this product is : protein 13.25 per cent, fat 9.21 per cent, ash 2.68 per cent and moisture 71.75 per cent. It has been adjudged as an acceptable product by panelists and keeps well for over a year at room temperature.

A similar product, but in dried form, has been developed by the C.I.F.T.

FISH SOUP POWDER

A readily acceptable trash fish product developed at C.I.F.T., the fish soup powder appears to have immense potentiality. While it can be prepared from any trash fish, best results have been obtained with threadfin bream, ribbon fish, catfish, and croaker. The various ingredients are put in the following proportion :

Ingredient	*Wt. in g*
Picked meat	750
Salt	170
Onion	750
Fat	125
Coriander	12
Starch	250
Milk powder	100
Sugar	15
Pepper powder	15
Ascorbic acid	1.5
Carboxy methyl cellulose	3
Monosodium glutamate	10
Garlic	5

The picked meat is cooked in water at 1 : 1 ratio or under pressure. The cooked meat is pressed into cakes in a canvas bag. The onion is fried in fat till it becomes brown, after which the cooked fish cake, coriander powder, salt, starch, sugar, pepper, monosodium glutamate and garlic are added to it and mixed thoroughly. This mixture is then ground thoroughly for about 2 hours in a wet food grinder until it becomes a fine paste, which is then spread into a thin layer in an aluminium tray and dried at 50-60°C in an artificial drier until the moisture content drops to about 6-7 per cent. This dried mass is pulverized in a blender, sieved and mixed well with ascorbic acid, carboxy methyl cellulose, and skim milk powder. This finished soup powder is packed in air-tight containers. The product has the following average analytical characteristics : protein 21.02 per cent, moisture 5.29 per cent, ash 18.09 per cent and fat 14.08 per cent. Sufficient precautions are taken to clean all the vessels used with chlorine water to ensure good bacteriological quality of the product. It keeps well in glass bottles and polythene coated aluminium bags for over 15 months. Trials have given an acceptability of over 95 per cent. Fish soup powder is also prepared in tablet form, by first converting the powder to granules by mixing the powder with gum acacia and edible gelatin to form a fine paste, which is then granulated to 40-60 mesh and thoroughly dried. The granules are then mixed with 5 per cent soluble starch and 0.5 per cent sodium stearate powders and tablets of suitable size (1 g) are made with the help of a machine.

PET FOOD

This is another product developed by C.I.F.T. in both canned form and powder form, suitable for cats and dogs. For the canned product, the trash fish is made into a paste after mixing with rice or wheat flour, vegetable (carrot), starch, shark liver oil, vitamins, and minerals in a wet food grinder for two hours. This paste is packed in a can, which is then sealed and sterilized in an autoclave for 70 minutes. For preparing the product in powder form, the ingredients are cooked under 15 lbs/square inch pressure for an hour, after which they are ground to a fine paste using just sufficient water. This paste is dried in a funnel drier (45-50°C) to a moisture level of less than 8 per cent and then powdered and packed in glass bottles or air-tight polythene bags or laminated aluminium bags. The canned product and the produce in powder form have protein contents of 23 per cent and 32 per cent respectively.

FISH FINGERS

These are prepared from the minced meat of trash fish. The fish meat, free from bones, skin, and adipose, is mixed with sufficient quantity of water to form a pasty mass of hard consistency. The paste is spread on an aluminium tray to a thickness of 3/4 cm and frozen at −40°C. After 2 hours it is taken out, cut into pieces of size 8 cm × 2.5 cm × 0.75 cm, packed in polythene paper and stored at −15°C to −20°C pending further processing. Before using, the fish fingers are taken out, dipped in egg batter, rolled over bread powder and fried in refined groundnut oil. The fish fingers can be kept in good condition at −15°C for one year.

FISH HYDROLYSATE INCORPORATED HIGH ENERGY FOOD

This is another trash fish product developed at C.I.F.T. Hydrolysate obtained from trash fish is concentrated, mixed with malt, cocoa, fat, and sugar, and the resultant slurry is vacuum dried. This gives a brown to golden yellow colour to the product. About 10-15 g of this product mixed with dilute milk or hot water will make a delicious beverage, free from bitterness and fish flavour. At 20-25 per cent level of fish hydrolysate, this product is completely free from fishy odour or flavour. At 35 per cent level of hydrolysate, the products' proximate composition will be as follows : protein 35.72 per cent, moisture 10.0 per cent, ash 3.2 per cent and fat 1.3 per cent. The product has good consumer acceptance.

FISH SAUSAGE

This is a speciality product of immense popularity prepared out of trash fishes, at present only at the College of Fisheries, Mangalore. The original product in synthetic casing is based on the Japanese type. But since this product has certain constraints in regard to its manufacture in India, the College of Fisheries has developed two more types, viz. fish sausage in natural casing and canned fish sausage.

Sausage in synthetic casing

Sausage can be prepared from a variety of trash fish (croaker, pink perch, ribbon fish, shark, catfish, *lactarius*, and so on), either taken singly or in combination. Both raw and frozen fish can be used. The advantage of the fish sausage in synthetic casing is that it can be kept at room temperature for about 1½ months by using the right type of chemical preservative. For preparing the sausage, the meat of the selected fish is machine-picked and minced. The minced fish meat is then ground thoroughly into a paste in a silent cutter (grinder) along with the various additives for about 15-20 minutes, maintaining the temperature of the paste below 15°C. The preparations of the various ingredients are as follows : minced fish meat 70 per cent, fat 4 per cent, starch 9.4 per cent, sugar 1.5 per cent, salt 2.25 per cent, spices 1.5 per cent, onion 1 per cent, sodium ascorbate 0.2 per cent, polyphosphate 0.17 per cent, monosodium glutamate 0.3 per cent, colour solution 0.13 per cent, ice water 9.25 per cent and preservative (permissible level). The time and temperature of processing of this semi-processed product are not sufficient to kill all the micro organisms and, therefore, chemical preservatives are required for ensuring a reasonable shelf life. Of the various preservatives tried so far, a combination of AF_2 (furyl-furamide) and potassium sorbate (0.1% and 0.2% respectively) gave the maximum shelf life of 50-60 days at room temperature, followed by AF_2 alone (0.1%) which gave a shelf life of 30-40 days. At 0.2 per cent level, glucone-lactone could preserve the sausage at room temperature for about 10 days, while fat coated ascorbic acid (FCSA) at 0.6 per cent could keep the sausage in good condition at room temperature for only 6 days, but for over 45 days at +10°C.

The ground paste is then packed into tabular 'saran' casings, sealed, pasteurized for 60 minutes at 88-90°C, cooled for 20 minutes at 20°C, reboiled at 100°C for 1-2 minutes, cooled, air-dried and stored. The proximate composition of the sausage preserved with AF_2 is: protein 15.12 per cent, fat 0.66 per cent, ash 2.20 per cent, and moisture 66 per cent. Depending on the type of fish used, the protein content could go up to 17-19 per cent.

The constraints in taking up commercial production of this type of sausage is that AF_2 is not yet a permitted food preservative in India and no suitable Indian substitute is available for the imported 'saran' casing. This, therefore, led to the developing of two other types of sausages.

Sausage in natural casing

This resembles the well-known meat sausage, in that the casing used is sheep intestine and it requires cooler storage. The intestine obtained from a slaughter house is thoroughly cleaned in running water to remove foreign objects, faecal matter, and so on and then washed in chlorinated water. It is then dipped in dilute salt solution for 1-2 minutes, after which it is pressed to remove extra water and stored in a cool place. In the alternative, intestines can be obtained from commercial manufacturers. At the time of sausage preparation, the stored intestine is taken out, desalted in fresh water, after which it is packed with the ground sausage paste.

The natural casing has a diameter of 14-18 mm. After stuffing, the casing is linked at 3″ intervals, which determines the size of the sausages. These sausages are then kept dipped in hot water or boiled 80°C for 20 minutes, which process gives the optimum jelly strength and elasticity formation, removes all pathogens, and causes minimum breakage. They can be stored in good condition up to 7 days in cooler storage at +2°C and for 6 months in frozen storage at −20°C. The only constraints with this product is that it cannot be kept at room temperature.

Canned sausage

This was developed to overcome the constraints encountered with the other two types of sausages, viz. casing, preservative and requirement of cooler storage. The canned product can safely be kept for over a year. However, this product would be comparatively costlier on account of the high cost of cans, but this aspect may be more than offset by the advantages it has over the other two types. The sausage paste is prepared as for the other two types and filled into processed sheep intestine, which is then linked to the required size depending on the size of the can to be used and boiled in water at 85°C for 20 minutes for obtaining adequate protein coagulation. It is then cut at the links and packed parallel to the can axis to give a fairly tight pack.

An alternative method to give shape to the sausage without the use of casing is to extrude the paste through a hand stuffer, boil the extruded cylindrical matter in water or fry in oil for 1 or 2 minutes, and then cut to required size and packed into cans. The packed cans are exhausted either mechanically or by steam, double seamed, and retorted at 115.6°C at 10 psi for varying durations depending on the type of packed and can size. The different packs tried are dry, brine and oil. Of these, the dry pack sausages were found to be the best from the point of view of quick heat penetration, reduced process time, retention of colour, flavour and resilient texture. These canned sausages are found to remain in good condition even after one year of storage.

FERMENTED FISH PRODUCTS

Trash fish can also be utilized for preparation of a number of fermented fish products.

Fish sauce

This is prepared from PHD fish meat, which is mixed with boiled onion and then added to tomato juice (extract). This mixture is slowly heated and stirred, during which period other ingredients are added one by one, till the required consistency of sauce is obtained. It is then cooled and packed in bottles for storing at room temperature. Its proximate composition is ; protein 3.98 per cent, fat 2.59 per cent, ash 1.69 per cent, and moisture 84.72 per cent. The product has been found to be fit for human consumption even after 24 weeks of storage at room temperature.

Fish pickle

Fish pickle without any fish flavour has been prepared from a number of trash fish by the traditional method of pickling. However, those prepared from pink perch and croaker with 10 per cent lime pieces and spiced as per the traditional practice in coastal Karnataka have provided to be the best. These products when kept packed in sterilized bottles remain in good condition for over six months.

FISH SHAVINGS

This is a new product developed from a trash fish (lizard fish-*Saurida thumbil*) at the College of Fisheries, Mangalore. This fish normally commands very poor consumer demand for fresh consumption on account of its taste and appearance. But it could be brought in for ready consumption by converting it into tasty smoked shavings.

After gutting, scaling, and washing, the fish is salted into the ratio of 1:10 (salt to fish) and left for curing overnight at room temperature. After discarding the self-brine liberated during the curing process, the cured fish is dipped in fresh water to get rid of excess salt and then loaded into the smoke chamber where it is smoked at about 75°C till the moisture level comes down to below 10 per cent. Dried sag wood and coconut husk in the ratio of 1:1 are used for generating smoke. The smoked fish, which develops golden yellow colour, is preserved at room temperature before further conversion into shavings. For this, the smoked fish is beheaded and the skin removed, after which it is chopped into thin shavings with the help of a carpenter's planning tool. These shavings will be in the form of thin leaf-like flakes of golden yellow colour, crisp texture, and smoke flavour. The yield is about 10-12 per cent. Its proximate composition is : protein 74.12 per cent, lipids 14.77 per cent, ash 6.71 per cent and moisture 4.34 per cent. The NaCl content is 5.61 per cent. It keeps in good condition for over six months at room temperature.

DRY SALTED SHARK CAKE

The shark is not generally relished for fresh consumption. It is mostly salt-cured. Dry shark cake, a new product, has been developed from shark meat. The shark meat is minced with simultaneous addition of common salt (2 : 1 fish to salt) and this mixture is left for an hour to allow salt penetration. This is then pressed to remove excess water and then moulded into cackes of $\frac{1}{2}''$ to $\frac{3}{4}''$ thickness and finally sun-dried. The product has the following approximate composition : moisture 19.1 per cent, crude protein 45.65 per cent, total ash 37.86 per cent, and NaCl 36.50 per cent. These cakes have a shelf life of over 3 months when kept in polythene bags at room temperature. The salt content of the cake can be reduced before use by boiling it in water for 5 minutes twice.

'FRICOLA'

Developed at the CFTRI, this product from lean fishes serves to give protein supplement at lesser cost than the usual de-fatted fish flour. Since the fat content is left as such in this product, the cost of production naturally comes down. Fricola is a fish-enriched farinanceous product of high protein content. It is prepared by blending the deboned and minced fish muscle with cooked rice in the ratio of 3 : 1 with requisite quantity of shredded coconut. The blend is flavoured with vanilla and fortified with minerals and vitamins. It is then dried in the form of thin flakes on a stainless steel roller dried at 30-40 lb/sq. in steam pressure. The product has white colour and is free from fishy odour. Its available lysine content is as much as 9.0 per cent of the total protein, which is about 35 per cent in the product. It keeps well for over six months at room temperature.

For consuming, milk or water is to be added to Fricola and heated to yield a porridge-like product. Sugar can also be added. It can also be used for preparation of curd by adding lime juice, salt and other condiments. The PER value of Fricola has been found to be superior to that of casein. Fricola has been found to be a satisfactory protein food in the treatment of children less seriously ill with kwashiorkor.

SHARK FINS

The caudal, dorsal, and pectoral fins of sharks have good export markets in South-East Asia, where they are used in the preparation of shark fin soup, a delicacy. The shark fin is only the raw material, while the finished product which is used for making soup consists of the translucent cartilaginous fin rays, which are rich in gelatin. However, India exports only the dried fins as such and they are further processed for use by the importing countries.

The fins are cut off at their base, washed thoroughly in sea water, and treated with a mixture of hot wood ash and slaked lime to remove the skin and meat. They are then dried for about 14 days. Either directly in the sun or in an oven till the moisture content comes down to about 7-8 per cent. The well dried product is crisp and brittle.

Drying of shark fins is yet to become an organized industry in India. However, it is done to some extent in Tamil Nadu, Maharashtra, and Gujarat from where they are invariably exported, since there is no domestic demand. The total annual production is estimated to be about 160 tonnes.

For taking out the fin rays from the shark fin, the dried fins are soaked in water, washed, and then again soaked in water acidified to a pH of 2.5 to 5 with glacial acetic acid for 6-7 days, by which time the fin gets softened. The softened muscle of the fin is then scraped off, exposing the fin rays, which are washed well in clean water and dried at 40°-50°C in an artificial dryer or in the sun, till the moisture content comes down to about 6-8 per cent. They are then packed in suitable moisture proof containers.

FISH MAWS

The product obtained by drying air-bladders found in some fishes (Indian salmon, catfishes, sciaenids, and eels) is known as fish maws. It is further processed into another product known as isinglass, which is used in the clarification of wines, beer and vinegar. But in India, only fish maws are generally prepared and exported. Only one concern, a part of an international organization, is known to manufacture isinglass in India.

Fish maws are prepared in three different ways : (1) The air bladders are thoroughly cleaned in fresh or sea water and dried in the sun till they become stone hard. (2) The bladders are cut open, the internal membranes removed, washed in fresh water to remove blood and membranes, beaten flat by a piece of wood and sun-dried. (3) The bladders are torn into shreds by hand, dusted with a little lime and sun dried. The annual production of fish maws in India is estimated to be about 155 tonnes and is mainly restricted to the coastal districts of Tamil Nadu, Kerala and Maharashtra.

ISINGLASS

Isinglass is high grade collagen produced from the air bladders of fishes. It can be prepared from both fresh air bladders and fish maws. The fish maws are soaked in water for several days. They are then cut into small pieces, which are compressed between hollow iron rollers and later on between ribbon rollers to produce isinglass in long ribbon form. The ribbons are quickly dried and then rolled on wooden spools into coils.

FISH GLUE, GELATIN AND PEARL ESSENCE

These are not produced on a commercial scale in India.

CHITOSAN

Huge quantities of head and shell of prawns are being thrown out from processing factories, amounting to as much as 40,000 tons per annum. These parts contain chitin, the structural material that holds together the shell. The chitin can be converted into chitosan, a product of varied industrial uses, such as sizing agent in textile industry, clarification of water, food thickener, adhesive, and as base for chromatography. Even by utilizing only 50 per cent of the prawn waste, we can produce about 1,000 tonnes of chitosan annually.

The waste is boiled with 0.5 per cent, followed twice with 3 per cent, aqueous sodium hydroxide solution. This removes the protein from the waste. Bleaching of the remaining material is accomplished by using hypochlorite solution containing 0.3-0.5 per cent available chlorine. It is then demineralized by immersing it in 1.25 N hydrochloric acid at room temperature. The resultant demineralized mass is washed free of acid and deacetylated at two different temperatures, (1) either immersing in 1 : 1 (W/W) aqueous NaOH solution for 2 hours at 100°C with occasional stirring, or (2) immersing in similar solution at room temperature (28-30°C) with occasional stirring, the samples being drawn at regular intervals for 15 days. The samples are washed free of alkali and dried in sun. The flakes of chitosan so obtained are coarsely milled. The chitosan is dissolved at 1 per cent level in 1 per cent acetic acid to form a viscous solution. Deacetylation at room temperature has been found to give a better product than the one produced when done at 100°C.

FISH MANURES

Fish manures are generally prepared by rather crude methods. The main types of fish manures that are traditionally prepared are of four kinds.

(i) *Fish guano* : This is the dried refuse left after the oil is pressed out from cooked sardines. It can also be used as fish meal after proper sieving.

(ii) *Prawn manure* : This is prepared from the prawn wastes (heads, tails, body shells) obtained from prawn processing plants. They are just sun-dried and packed in gunny bags.

(iii) *Dry fish manure* : Fishes such as sardines, mackerels, and horse mackerels which are spoilt and are unfit for use as food are spread on the beach and allowed to rot and eventually dry in the sun.

(iv) *Pit fish manure* : Fish wastes occurring during gutting operations are buried in pits for 1-2 months and allowed to ferment. The fermented material is then taken out and dried in the sun.

(The constraints, economic aspects, marketing and recommendations will be dealt with in the next report).

16

FINANCIAL REQUIREMENTS OF SMALL AND MEDIUM FISHERMEN AND THEIR CO-OPERATIVES

B.S. SAXENA

THE objective of this chapter is to assess the financial requirements of small and medium fishermen engaged in the Indian marine fishing industry, the extent to which they are met from indigenous and institutional sources, their terms and conditions and also their impact on the fishermen's return, working efficiency, and social and economic independence. This study is expected to help in progressively replacing the indigenous sources (particularly the middlemen) by institutional financing agencies such as the Integrated Rural Development Programme (IRDP), National Co-operative Development Corporation (NCDC), commercial banks, and state finance corporations techniques and locating new resources. This will not only make more financial assistance available to the fishermen and for infrastructure but will also go a long way in making the industry economically viable.

CONCEPT OF SMALL AND MEDIUM FISHERMEN

Of late the two terms—small and medium fishermen (specially small fishermen often pronounced as traditional or artisanal fishermen also) are frequently used in the context of fisheries development, especially in developing countries. However, very little attempt seems to have been made to define these concepts. The terms are highly relative and depend on the technological, economic and social development besides a few other factors. A small fisherman of today may become a medium fisherman of tomorrow with the improvement in technology and on account of changes in the developmental stage of the fishery of a country. Similarly, a small fisherman of a developed country may be more efficient, economically and socially more independent than a medium fisherman of a developing country.

The study of financial requirements of Indian small fishermen has added significance because they catch about 67 per cent of total Indian marine fish production, constitute about 90 per cent of total active fishermen population, and contribute about 0.5 per cent of the national income. But their living conditions are insecure which lead to unsocial habits and suffer from more inadequacy of investments, ice, transport, education, medical and other amenities of life. They are often compelled to arrange for their finances at more unfavourable terms than medium fishermen. In most cases, their economic and social conditions have hardly improved in the recent past and in some cases have even deteriorated in view of the competition from mechanized boat-owners. On the other hand, the number of medium fishermen as well as their production (which is estimated at about 32 per cent of total Indian marine fish production) are increasing rapidly. Moreover, they catch more prawns with greater ease and also command better economic, social and political influence.

FINANCIAL REQUIREMENTS OF SMALL AND MEDIUM FISHERMEN

Before analysing the nature, period, type, sources extent, and purposes of financial requirements of small and medium fishermen, it would be desirable to classify them as (i) Individual requirements and (ii) Infrastructural requirements. The individual requirements consist of hulls, engines, nets and fishery accessories owned either individually or by groups of individuals ; whereas infrastructural requirements may again be subdivided as those requirements which are essential for handling fish and fishing vessels and those required for social, cultural and literary uplift of the fishermen. The former consist of fishing ports, harbours, jetties, guidelights, roads, boat-building yards, net-making plants ; preservation and processing establishments such as ice, cold-storage, freezing, canning plants, peeling sheds power service-stations ; whereas schools, libraries and social clubs are required for the literary, social and cultural uplift of the fishermen. The infrastructure can be either state, co-operative, or individually owned, as follows :

Financial requirements of small and medium fishermen

1. Individual requirements
2. Infrastructural requirements
    1. Infrastructural requirements
        1. State owned
        2. Cooperatively owned
        3. Individually owned
    2. Social, literary and cultural requirements

Kinds of financial requirements

Like the financial requirements of Indian agriculturists, the financial requirements of fishermen also can be classified as long-term, medium-term, and short-term requirements depending upon their purpose, quantum, period of requirements, expected life of the assets so acquired, nature and size of the fishery concerned and so on. The long-term requirements are required normally for a period of more than 3 years for fixed assets such as hulls, engines, nets, fishery accessories, and so on ; whereas medium term loans are taken by fishermen both for productive as well as consumption purposes for a period say about 1 to 3 years. They consist of major repairs to their hulls, engines and nets, seasonal advances to crew, insurance charges, subsistence needs during the lay-off season ; social requirements for marriages, births, and deaths. Wages and expenditure on food for the crew, ice, water, minor repairs, traditional taxes and offerings, and kerosene oil constitute short-term requirements besides loading and marketing charges for the catch as follows :

Financial requirements of small and medium fishermen

Long-term requirements	Medium-term requirements	Short-term requirements
(a) Hull	(a) Major repairs for hulls and replacement of nets	(a) Minor repairs to boats and nets
(b) Net	(b) Subsistence requirements during lay-off season	(b) Traditional taxes and offerings
(c) Fishery accessories such as floats, sinker ropes, hooks and so on.	(c) Social requirements	(c) Expenditure on kerosene oil, ice water, food and so on
(d) Engines, winches, other boards and so on in case of medium fishermen	(d) Major repairs to engines, seasonal advances to crew-members, insurance charges etc. in case of medium fishermen	(d) Expenditure on diesel, petrol, lubricants, minor repairs of engines, wages to crew, harbour charges, loading and marketing charges and so on in case of medium fishermen

The various sectors of the fishing industry which require financial assistance can be classified as—(i) production, processing, operational, subsistence and price-support. Unlike developed countries, financial assistance in India for price-support is negligible and sporadic but significant for relief against natural calamities.

Assessment of long-term requirements

In view of the innumerable types of boats and nets, wide variations in their sizes, expected life, and above all varying combinations of craft and gears in different fishing seasons and for different fisheries, rapidly increasing price level, particularly timber costs, day to day technological developments, and above all inadequacy of reliable statistical data on the economics of the industry, it is extremely difficult to give even a rough idea of long term financial requirements of fishermen. However, a broad idea of long term financial requirements of small fishermen can be had from the different kinds and their respective numbers of non-mechanized boats as per appendixes 1, 2 and 3. According to the first survey

(1973-77), indigenous fishing boats of India were categorized into 31 kinds, with as many as 11 kinds in Orissa alone. The survey estimated the number of fishing boats at 98,192 all over India (except Maharashtra) ; whereas according to the second survey, the corresponding figure for 1980 was estimated at Rs. 1,34,741, that is, an increase of about 37 per cent over a period of 2 to 7 years. So far as the extent of variation in the sizes of boats is concerned, it can be imagined from the facts that the length of a catamaran varies from 4 to 8 metres, navas 6 to 11 metres, dug out from 8 to 10 metres, Salti 7 to 10 metres and so on. The expected life of a fishing boat varies from 5 to 15 years but some of the dug-out boats go even upto 50 years. Similarly, size of crew differs from 3 in case of a catamaran to about 20 on shore-seine plank-canoe.

The cost of a catamaran varies from Rs. 1000 to Rs. 12,000 and of a dug-out canoe from Rs. 25,000 to Rs. 50,000. The cost of an Ayilavala Unit (gill-netter) costed only Rs. 5,375 (1978). A fishing unit consisting of a catamaran, a cotton net, and a hook and line may be so small that it may cost as little as Rs. 2,000 but a financial requirement of Rs. 7,000 may be considered as ideal for being productive round the year.

The financial requirements of small fishermen for the purchase of their gears and other fishery equipments also vary widely on account of variations in their size, type, length, fabrication material (cotton/synthetic), mesh-size, ply and weight of nylon, ropes, floats and sinkers. Not only the shapes of different types of nets vary widely but the size of the same type of net also varies very much. For example, the length of a drift net may vary from 20 to 50 metres, of a boat-seine from 15 to 25 metres and encircling net from 6 to 10 metres. The average life of different types of nets also differs very much. The cheapest net is probably the hook and line for which a small fisherman may require an amount varying from Rs. 150 to Rs. 700 only but with heavy expenditure on account of operational losses. The cost of a prawn-net may vary from Rs. 1,200 to Rs. 1,500, share-seine from Rs. 3,000 to Rs. 8,000, drift net from Rs. 5,000 to Rs. 10,000, encircling net from Rs. 12,000 to Rs. 15,000 and a Rampani-net up to Rs. 1 lakh.

A broad idea of the long-term financial requirements of

medium fishermen can be had from Table 16.1.

TABLE 16.1 : **State-wise distribution of mechanized boats**

Sl. No.	State	Trawlers	Gill-netters	Purse-seiners	Dol-netters	Others	Total
1.	West Bengal	—	740	—	—	—	740
2.	Orissa	350	119	—	—	—	469
3.	Andhra Pradesh	580	—	—	—	—	580
4.	Tamil Nadu	2,614	143	—	—	—	2,757
5.	Pondicherry	160	3	—	—	—	163
6.	Kerala	2,630	362	37	—	9	3,038
7.	Karnataka	1,553	28	325	—	98	2,004
8.	Goa	494	274	66	—	74	908
9.	Gujarat	1,209	1,547	—	650	7	3,413
	Total (excluding Maharashtra, Andamans and Lakshadweep)	9,590	3,216	428	650	188	14,072
	Andamans*						10
	Lakshadweep*						213
	Maharashtra*						4,718
	All India						19,013

* Indian Fisheries—1947-77.

Source : Marine Fisheries Information Service, Central Marine Fisheries Research Institute, Cochin, *India*, Bull. No. 30, August, 1981 (ICAR), p. 30.

As can be seen from Table 16.1 that mechanized fishing vessels are also of different kinds leading to variations not only in size and design of the boats and horse-power of engine but fishery equipments as well. Therefore, their costs also vary widely (Table 16.2).

In view of the use of standard engines and designed boats for fishing, the variation in the costs of medium scale (mechanized) fishing units is not as wide as in the case of small scale fishing units. However, their requirements are more progressively increasing than those of the small fishermen.

TABLE 16.2 : **Item-wise cost for different types of boats at current prices, 1978 (Rupees)**

Sl. No.	Components	Investment			
		O.B.M. of length 9 m	Gill-netters of length 13 m	Trawler-cum-gill-netters of length 14.9 m	Trawler of length 14.9 m
1.	Hull	21,000	65,000	89,768	89,763
2.	Engine	6,000	84,000	94,554	94,554
3.	Winch	—	—	13,450	13,450
4.	Trawl-nets	—	—	7,000	7,000
5.	Gill-nets	12,250	21,000	21,000	—
	Total	39,250	1,70,000	2,25,773	2,04,767

Source : U.K. Srivastava, *et al.*

Assessment of medium term requirements

The medium term requirements of small fishermen normally consist of repairs to hulls, replacement of nets on production side and social requirements. The subsistence requirements consist of offseason need and those caused as a result of natural calamities like cyclones, famines and floods. In addition to the above, the medium fishermen required finance for repairs of engines, payment of insurance premium, seasonal advances to the crew, and so on. On an average these financial requirements can be repaid in about two years. The impact of medium-term financial requirements is in no way less serious than those of long-term requirements. If the long term-requirements are not available, the fishermen find it difficult to earn their livelihood but if medium term requirements are not met, both their existence as well as social prestige are at stake. Therefore, in the case of medium-term loans, it is not the period of requirements which is more important but consequences of their non-availability. The situation is further aggravated because the institutional financing agencies are unwilling to come forward to meet their medium-term financial requirements except in times of natural calamities that too, partly. The fishermen find no alternative except to fall an easy prey to the money-lender-cum-fish trader whose primary interest lies in their catches. With the progressive capitalization of the industry, there has been an appreciable increase in working capital requirements of the mechanized boat-owners. Besides works, an advance equivalent to 3 months' wages is normally paid to them. Recent increases in fuel prices have added to their misery.

Short-term requirements

The short-term requirements of small fishermen consist of wages for the crew and labour hired on shore, expenditure on food, water, ice, commission charges on the sale of fish, minor repairs to their boats and nets. In addition to the above, the medium fishermen have to incur expenditure on diesel, engine oil, maintenance and minor repairs to their engines. In the case vessels also of purse-seine fishing, expenditure is incurred on carrier vessels also. The availability of these working capital requirements is not a big problem because they are often met out of the sale-proceeds of the catch which has to be immediately disposed of due to its perishability. An idea of these costs, incurred by different types of fishing units, can be had from Table 16.3.

It may be observed that fuel and lubricants constitute important items of short-term requirements followed by expenditure on food for the crew. The percentage expenditure on fuel and lubricants in the case of an OBM boat amounts to more than 50 per cent of their total short-term requirements and also that they are highest in absolute terms in the case of a trawler as compared to other types of boats.

Total financial requirements of small and medium fishermen

It is very difficult to give even a broad idea of total financial requirements of small and medium fishermen in India. The absence of a National Fishery Policy is another constraint. For example, mechanization of fishing vessels has so far been one of the important aspects of fishery development programmes. However, in view of the progressive increase in energy costs, stagnation in shrimp production as well as quantity of their exports, and slow growth-rate of mechanization in the recent past, priority for mechanization programme needs to be reconsidered immediately. This need is also supported from a recent study

TABLE 16.3 : **Giving average variable costs per day for different types of boats**

(*in rupees*)

Sl. No.	Items of costs	Expenditure per			
		O.B.M. boat	Gill-netter	Trawler-cum-gill-netter	Trawler
1.	Fuel	38.28	53.67	103.84	144.67
2.	Mobile oil and other lubricants	9.07	14.38	17.16	17.94
3.	Wages to hired labour on the surface	2.91	4.60	6.15	6 55
4.	Food expenditure of the crew	13.46	22.81	16.96	15.26
5.	Expenditure on ice and water	1.54	6.02	6.18	10.86
6.	Cost of net repairs	5.59	12.50	11.52	3.58
	Total	70.85	113.98	161.81	193.81

Source : U.K. Srivastava *et al.*, Managing Marine Fishing Industry—An Analysis of Problems in Harvesting and Processing (A Micro Study in Gujarat State), 1979, p. 149.

Note : Salaries of persons employed on monthly basis are not included.

about the economics of artisanal and mechanized fisheries in Kerala.

Further, in assessing these requirements recent emerging trends regarding the availability of institutional financial assistance from agencies like NCDC, commercial banks, NABARD and the present rural development policy of the Government of India will also have to be taken into consideration. In 1976, the National Commission on Agriculture has envisaged total financial requirements of Rs. 500 crore over a period of 25 years on fishing vessels alone to increase the marine fish production to 3.5 million tonnes at an annual compound growth rate of 5.2 per cent. In view of the constraints, trends and conclusions stated above, it may not be unrealistic if we need a sum of Rs. 300 crore during the next 10 years for financial assistance to small and medium scale fishermen only, excluding infrastructural facilities and fishing vessels required for the exploitation of the resources of the Exclusive Economic Zone.

FISHERMEN'S INCOME

After an analysis of the financial requirements of fishermen, it is essential to examine their income and savings with a view to assess their investment generating capacity. Like their financial requirements their incomes also differ. Accidents resulting in damages to their nets, boats and sometimes even to their lives further tell heavily upon their incomes.

In 1961, the Indo-Norwegian Project estimated an average net annual income of Rs. 473 of a fisherman operating a Kochu-vallam (small canoe), Rs. 616 and Rs. 1,381 of 22-footer and 25-footer mechanized fishing vessel owners respectively.

In 1978, the per working day (for 311 days in a year) share of wages of a small fisherman was estimated at Rs. 14.22 and Rs. 26.57 in the case of Aylavala and Thanguvala unit respectively. An idea of their poverty can also be had from a recent socio-economic study of three fishing villages in Tamil Nadu, according to which, 61 per cent of the fisherwomen did not get any meals on some days in a year. Due to the subsistence and co-operative character of the industry and poverty of the fishermen most of the boats and also nets in a large number of cases are owned collectively. It is more so in case of small fishermen. They often engage non-owner fishermen either on share or wage-basis. These practices infuse a sense of collective ownership and lead to a more or less equal distribution of income. Still their incomes vary widely, as can be seen from Table 16.4.

It may be observed from the Table 16.4 that families in lower income-groups earn their living more from non-gainful activities than from gainful activities. Secondly, 70.2 per cent of the families earning through gainful activities are within the income group of Rs. 1,000 to Rs. 3,999 and account for 59.8 per cent of total income. According to a case study of Bassein Fishermen Sarvodaya Cooperative Society Ltd. (Maharashtra State) by the Vaikunthlal Mehta National Institute of Co-operative Management nearly 59 per cent of the households in 1960 had their income in the range of Rs. 1,500 to Rs. 4,000 per annum. In connection with the Ratnagiri Fisheries Project, the net profit of a trawler was estimated at Rs. 2,456 in 1976.

Fishermen's incomes are influenced by seasonal character of

TABLE 16.4 : **Percentage distribution of the household by income in Maharashtra State**

Sl. No.	Income ranges (Rs)	% Household by income from		Total income
		Gainful activity	Non-gainful activity	
1.	0-499	—	71.5	—
2.	500-999	5.6	14.3	5.6
3.	1000-1499	11.1	7.1	11.1
4.	1500-1999	20.4	7.1	19.9
5.	2000-2999	24.0	—	24.5
6.	3000-3999	14.7	—	14.3
7.	4000-4999	6.9	—	6.5
8.	5000-5999	6.5	—	7.3
9.	6000-6999	4.2	—	4.2
10.	7000-7999	1.9	—	1.9
11.	8000-8999	0.5	—	0.5
12.	9000-9999	2.3	—	2.3
13.	above 10,000	1.9	—	1.9
	Total	100	100	100

Source : A.G. Kalawar, *C.M.F.R.I.*, Bulletin No. 30-B Sept., 1981—Present Status of Small-Scale Fisheries in India and a few neighbouring countries, p. 16.

the industry, occurrence of fish-famines, type of fishing and even the nature of crews engaged as well as can be seen from the Table 16.5.

(2) To get the normalised value, the following assumptions have been made under the study.

(i) The catches of OBM boats were not affected much ;

(ii) The average daily catch (in value terms) during the year 1977-78 for gill-netters was less by 25 per cent than in a normal year ;

(iii) In case of trawlers and trawler-cum-gill-netters the catch during 1977-78 was less by 40 per cent than in a normal year ;

(iv) Trawlers and trawler-cum-gill-netters have more number of fishing days in a normal year when compared to current year.

TABLE 16.5 : **Showing total net income accruing for different types of boats in a season and its distribution between owner and crew members (Rupees)**

Type of boat	Net income when all the crew is hired	Net income when no crew is hired	Income of the owner in sharing				
			With one outside crew	With two outside crew	With three outside crew	With four outside crew	With five outside crew
1. *OBM*							
(Observed)	15850	27849	20529	13209	5889	—	—
2. *Gill-netters*							
(a) Observed	—2210	19760	14293	8813	3343	—2132	—7607
(b) Normalised	22155	42705	37230	31755	26280	20805	15330
3. *Trawler-cum-gill-netters*							
(a) Observed	—10896	9140	—	—	—	—	—
(b) Normalised	58894	78939	—	—	—	—	—
4. *Trawlers*							
(a) Observed	—20053	251	—	—	—	—	—
(b) Normalised	46620	66924	—	—	—	—	—

Source : U.K. Srivastava *et al.*, Managing Marine Fishing Industry—An Analysis of Problems in Harvesting and Processing (A Micro-study in Gujarat State), 1979, p. 163.

Note : The expected value of catch for the season as a whole is arrived at by taking weighted average of quarter-wise expected value of catch. The weights given are in proportion to number of fishing days in the respective quarters.

It will be observed from the Table 16.5 that all types of boats (gill-netters, trawler-cum-gill-netters and trawlers) except the OBM boats incurred losses on account of the reported bad season during the observation year (1977-78).

The study has made two more important observations—(1) the catch is more when the crew is not hired, and (2) the OBM boat-owners as compared to other boat-owners were not affected much by bad season. The former is understandable but the latter requires close study by fisheries biologists and technologists. On the basis of the normalized catches, the study has also concluded that all types of boats were able to break even and were able to get substantial income. The study further concludes (on the basis of normalized catch) that all kinds of boats are economically viable propositions. This observation requires attention of fisheries economists and administrators.

Another perceptible trend is the growing disparity between the income of small and medium fishermen, as can be seen from Table 16.6.

According to this study, the index of average real income of small scale fishermen has gone down from 132 to 128 and that of mechanized fishermen has gone up from 154 to 366 during the trinneal period 1969-71 and 1974-76. Another study also has supported this trend.

Another important as well as interesting trend emerging in the fishermen society is that the influence of fisherwomen in controlling the family expenditure as well as fishery requisites is more when family income is received by the fisherwomen specially when they (fisherwomen) sell the catches. "Of women taking part in financial decisions of a family, three-quarters take part in marketing the catch . . . . These women seem to play an important role in decision-making regarding the purchase of nets and fishing gear. A similar situation seems to exist regarding purchases of fishing craft".

INDEBTEDNESS—ITS MAGNITUDE AND CAUSES

In view of the low income and savings, added with uncongenial social, cultural and literary background, the savings and investment generating capacity of fishermen in general and of small

TABLE 16.6 : **Annual income accruing to the workers of non-mechanized and mechanized sectors during the period 1969-76**

Sl. No.	Year	Non-mechanized sector: Income* (current prices) (Rs)	Non-mechanized sector: Real income (Index)		Mechanized sector: Income** (current prices) (Rs)	Mechanized sector: Real income (Index)	
1.	1969	1536	100	132	871	100	154
2.	1970	2171	136		1772	195	
3.	1971	2617	162		1523	197	
4.	1972	1902	112		1252	103	
5.	1973	3118	151		4839	415	
6.	1974	3372	125	128	4848	316	366
7.	1975	3068	104		9197	547	
8.	1976	3900	105		3326	232	

Source : John Kurien Working Paper No. 68—Towards an understanding of the Fish Economy of Kerala State—A preliminary study of the current situation and trends in organisation, technology, production and distribution of income, June, 1978, p. 74.

* Income per worker calculated by taking 100 per cent of non-mechanized sector value of output.

** Income per worker calculated by taking only 30 per cent of mechanized sector value of output.

fishermen in particular is extremely low. The economic position of fishermen worsens during the off-season when, for their subsistence, they have to depend mainly upon the boat-owners who themselves require finances. The condition of the indigenous boat-owner also is not much better than the fishermen-labourers. However, the ownership of his boat helps him to get loans from the middlemen for self as well as for his dependent fishermen-labourers. This process establishes a chain of indebtedness from the fish merchant to the fishermen-labourers. In general, fishermen seldom have any savings. They often borrow money for occasional expenses both for productive as well as for unproductive purposes even during the fishing season.

This is so not only among our Indian fishermen but all over developing countries. "Insolvency has become the normal state of the majority of Aden Fisheries. It is a fact that a large part of the fishing population actually prefers to be in debt..., the more heavily a man is in debt, the more certainly will his creditor support him through hard times in order to exploit him in future". Unfortunately, fishermen have taken indebtedness as a part of their life, as is clear from the following verse :

The fishes are hard to net
Taxes are heavy and we are in debt.
From father to son—
Poor are the fishermen, every one.

(Free translation of a Chinese folk-song—"Song of the fishing lights").

The Indian fishermen community, whether it consists of Hindus, Christians, Muslims or others can be broadly divided into four economic groups : (i) Merchants and financiers. (ii) Owners of crafts and gears. (iii) Fishermen labourers. (iv) Other engaged in processing boat-building, net-making industry share-labour and so on.

Probably, the first published account regarding indebtedness is the Report of an Enquiry into the Socio-economic Survey in selected centres in Bomby area (Maharashtra State—1955). According to this flows report 75.3 per cent of the fishermen interviewed, revealed that they were indebted to the extent of Rs. 429 per (indebted) worker and the debt frequency of the indebted fishermen was reported as follows (worked out from Table 16.8).

Debt frequency	Indebted workers	
	Percentage	Number
(i) Up to Rs. 200	25.68	94
(ii) From Rs. 201 to Rs. 500	54.65	200
(iii) From Rs. 501 to Rs. 700	7.10	26
(iv) From Rs. 701 to Rs. 1,000	6.83	25
(v) Over Rs. 1,000	5.74	21
Total	100.00	366

According to an economic survey conducted by the Government of Kerala in 1957-58, the indebtedness among the fishermen of the State was estimated to the extent of Rs. 1.35 crore with 19.9 per cent families completely free from indebtedness, 42.6 per cent families indebted up to Rs. 250, 22.7 per cent between Rs. 251 and Rs. 500, 10.3 per cent between Rs. 501 and Rs. 1,000 and 4.5 per cent families indebted above Rs. 1,000 According to a study conducted by VMNICM, Pune, in 1968 of Bassein Fishermen Sarvodaya Co-operative Society, nearly 65 per cent of the households were indebted and their average indebtedness was Rs. 2,212.

An idea of indebtedness among small fishermen can be had from the fact that at least 95 per cent of the fishermen families borrowed money in the three fishing villages of Tamil Nadu surveyed.

TABLE 16.7 : **Showing debt position among the three fishing villages of Tamil Nadu State**

Level of indebtedness (Rs)		Fishing villages		
		Perianeclan karai	Chemmen cheri	Paltipulam
1—200	%	15	17	7
200—600	%	54	25	35
600—1000	%	5	3	7
1000—2500	%	18	41	31
2500—5000	%	5	12	11
5000—6000	%	3	1	7
6000—10,000	%	—	1	2
Total	%	100	100	100
	No	39	69	45

Out of 300 women interviewed, 273 reported that their families were in the habit of taking credit and 153 mentioned that they had borrowed last year. It was also observed that the borrowing capacity is very much influenced with the degree of the possession of fishery assets (boats and nets) and also that loans were taken not only by poor but by rich fishermen families as well. According to another survey in Maharashtra State, wedding was an important cause of indebtedness and 41.0 per cent of the loans were taken for the same, following by 26.5 per cent on account of low income, as can be seen from the following :

Sl. No.	Purpose	Extents of loan (Percentage)
1.	Low income	26.5
2.	Sickness	4.2
3.	Building and repairs	8.3
4.	Fishing business	5.0
5.	Wedding	41.0
6.	Miscellaneous	15.0
	Total	100.0

Source : Report of an enquiry into the socio-economic conditions of fishermen in selected centres in Bombay Area—Published by the Director, Government Printing Publications and Statistics, Bombay, 1955—Table No. 19 p. 28.

FINANCING AGENCIES

Fishermen arrange financial assistance from all and sundry sources which can be broadly classified into two types (1) Indigenous and (2) Institutional, as follows :

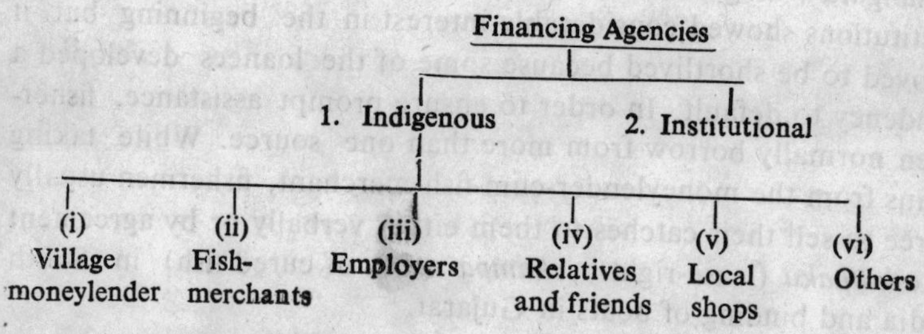

Indigenous financing agencies

Indigenous agencies financing fishermen are many moneylenders, pawnbrokers, fish-traders, employers, grocers, village-headman, boat and net owners, and so on. A moneylender may or may not be dealing in fish because he is primarily a moneylender whereas a fish merchant is first and foremost a market-functionary and has to lend money to village moneylender and commission to ensure his business. According to a 1955 survey, the village moneylender and commission agents-cum-traders accounted for 87.4 per cent loans in the Bombay area followed equally by employers and others that is, 6.3 per cent each. "Even now the bulk of credit (to finance fishing operations) is still provided by private individuals (that is, friends, traders, prawn-processors and professional moneylenders). The system is by tradition an integral part of the industry which caters for personal and business requirements. Apart from pawnbroking arrangements with moneylenders, loans are subject to personal credit-worthiness mostly without surety of fixed assets and consequently the interest-rates are higher than those charged by State Banks". According to another study on credit and indebtedness among the marine fishermen of south Kerala by FUCID--ISI, International Joint Project (1979) agencies is selected fishing villages of Kerala State, the unorganized financial resources still appear to be dominant—"The middlemen charged the fishermen usurious rates of interest and controlled the marketing of fish catches . . . . The unorganized sources accounted for 87.8 per cent of the loans and 82.7 per cent of the borrowings in Povar village, 90.7 per cent of the loans and 79.3 per cent of the borrowings in Purakkad village and 79.9 per cent of the loans and 38.2 per cent of the borrowings in Saktikulangara village". The report further states that the banking institutions showed considerable interest in the beginning but it proved to be shortlived because some of the loanees developed a tendency to default. In order to ensure prompt assistance, fishermen normally borrow from more than one source. While taking loans from the moneylender-cum-fish-merchant, fishermen usually agree to sell their catches to them either verbally or by agreement like *kuthaka* (lease-right), *champa* (sale of cured fish) in South India and binding of boats in Gujarat.

In a large number of cases, the middlemen-cum-moneylenders also approach the fishermen usually during the monsoon period and advance loans to them both for their subsistence and social requirements on the understanding that the catch of the coming season shall be sold to them usually on a pre-determined price—a practice which, with the commercialization of the fishing industry, is not declining. Of late even higher castes also are reported to have entered this business because of high and assured financial returns. On account of the lack of economic, social and political resources, competence to deal with institutional financial agencies and above all easy access to the middlemen, small fishermen are more under the clutches of middle-men-cum-money-lenders than medium fishermen. But the fish-merchants are equally important among medium-scale fishermen account of their special interest in processable and exportable varieties of fish.

The important reasons of borrowing money from fish-traders are that fishermen have often to sell their catches to them on account of transport difficulty, convenience, lack of time and sometimes even for better profits. For purposes of financing, even the fish merchants may be divided into (i) fish traders and (ii) raw material suppliers, that is, (prawn traders). Financing by fish merchants is more aggressive in the case of processable varieties of fish in order to ensure the procurement of raw-materials. The processors enter into contract with local traders to collect raw materials (specially prawns), normally against a fixed price and their margin of profit is generally higher. "Prawn traders, therefore, can and do give higher credit to fisherfolk (higher) than fish traders but at the same time demand a high rate of interest. The fisherfolk have to sell all their prawns to the trader as they are indebted to him ; most of them will have borrowed cash, others rice, during the lean season. The mode of repayment is exclusively by means of prawns. Most of the women reported that half the daily catch of prawns is taken by the trader to clear the debt ; for the other half they are paid in cash. The trader so manages affairs that the fisherfolk are still in debt at the end of the prawn season, and give him the prawn catch in the following year, rather than the fisherwomen selling it themselves in the city markets. As the mode of repayment is a fixed percentage of the daily catch and not a fixed amount of prawns or cash, the trader has to try and keep control over all the landings : he will be on the shore in good time so that no woman can go off unseen with a catch of prawns in order to sell it on her own for a better price. Many people seem to be aware of the fact that they are not paid a proper price for their prawns. Nevertheless they depend on the prawn traders as moneylenders.

The prawn trader is aware of the economic position of each fishing family and can easily judge how much money he can risk lending to them. Though the fisherwomen and men are aware of the fact that the prawn trader is making a great profit, they do not like the idea of reorganising the mode of marketing prawns by eliminating the trader because this would result in the loss of an important source of quick credit"—Bay of Bengal Programme Development of Small-Scale Fisheries, Bay of Bengal, $\frac{\text{BOBP/WP/14}}{\text{GCP/RAS/040/SWE}}$; Madras, India, Feb., 1982, p. 21.

In certain cases (South Kanara district), some of the mechanized boat-owners considered the sale of their catch through fish merchants quite competitive because they provide free ice on board, interest free working loans up to about Rs. 50,000 against which only shrimps are to be sold at a price lower than 7 to 8 per cent than the market price. In this process they save a commission of 5 per cent which they have to pay to co-operative societies. In Gujarat as late as 1979 it was observed that about 50 per cent of the sampled boat-owners had bonded their boats, as can be seen from Table 16.8.

TABLE 16.8 : **Pattern of binding boats by the sample fishermen**

Sl. No.	Types of boats	Number of boats		
		Bonded	Non-bonded	Total
1.	O.B.M.	3 (30%)	7 (70%)	10
2.	Gill-netter	4 (50%)	4 (50%)	8
3.	Trawler-cum-gill-netter	4 (66.67%)	2 (33.33%)	6
4.	Trawler	4 (66.67%)	2 (33.33%)	6

Source : U.K. Srivastava, *et al.*, Managing Marine Fishing Industry—An Analysis of Problems in Harvesting and Processing (A Micro Study in Gujarat State), 1979, p. 130.

Processors who bond boats advanced loans to fishermen as much as Rs. 1,61,333 out of their total investment of Rs. 2,25,000 according to a study by Srivastava *et al.* The practice is less important in the case of dry fish trade.

The interest rates at which finances are available to fishermen are not only high but vary widely as well as well on account of creditworthiness of individual borrowers who have been borrowing since generations. According to the 1955 survey,

> In a large number of cases, the interest rate was 37.5 per cent per annum. . . . About 67 per cent of the total indebted workers paid interest workers ranging from 10 to 37.5 per cent, while in the case of 63 workers or 17.2 per cent of the total, the interest rate ranged between 38 and 75 per cent of the total as most of them had taken loans from their relatives and employers.

According to a study conducted by CMFRI, moneylenders are alleged to charge 25 per cent or even more interest to the principal sum of rupees loaned till the entire amount is repaid in full.

The low and uncertain income of fishermen, their off-season subsistence requirements and above all non-availability of institutional finance for consumption requirements make them an easy prey of the middlemen-cum-fish merchants who often finance without security, irrespective of the fact whether the boat is insured or not. As stated earlier, there are instances where no interest is charged specially in case of an old and reputed fishermen who can be relied upon for delivering not only their own catch but for inducing others also to follow him. One of the important impacts of high rate of interest is that the development of a more capital-intensive fishery of deeper waters is adversely affected.

Institutional finance

The study of institutional finance can be divided into its types, objects, forms and sources.

History of institutional finance

Financial assistance has been available to Indian fishermen from times immemorial from State fisheries departments. To begin with, financial assistance was given in the form of tax-free salt and free water supplies to fish curing yards. Amenities like re-thatching of houses, scholarships to fishermen children and fishermen tours, construction of wells, houses, roads, setting up of gruel centres in times of distress and of cultural community centres, and so on, have also been provided more as upliftment of socio-economic conditions of the fishermen and to meet some calamities like fish-famine, flood, cyclones, and so on. But the era of planned development of the Indian economy has witnessed a more organized and systematic attempt in rendering financial assistance to fishermen in the form of subsidy and loans on various fishery inputs for augmenting both quantity and quality of fish production.

During the First Five Year Plan, financial assistance was passed on to fishermen mainly through co-operative societies in the form of cheaper fishery input supplies. This was followed by a system of subsidy and soft loans specially on boats and engines with the object of introducing mechanization. The cost of an engine was subsidized to the extent of even 50 per cent being shared equally between the State and Central governments. The balance was given as loan, repayable over a period of 7 to 8 years in easy instalments. This pattern continued till the end of Third Plan. In 1971, it was observed that the institutional finance (specially the government loans and subsidies) formed 95 per cent of total investments made on mechanized boats in the co-operative sector and 62 per cent in the private sector but the country boats were largely self-financed.

Types of financial assistance

Financial assistance can be classified into two broad categories : Direct and Indirect. Indirect financial assistance consists of expenditure on research, education, and training which helps the industry indirectly. Direct assistance can be subdivided into two :

(i) Assistance which leads to the collective benefit of the industry as a whole such as harbour development, refrigerated railwagon service, provision for landing and berthing facilities for fishing craft at minor ports, development of infrastructure for coastal fishing villages and so on. They are mainly in the form of grants-in-aid to meet capital cost of the projects and are often centrally sponsored schemes.

(ii) The other type of direct assistance is one which normally is received by individuals from institutional agencies such as government, commercial banks, co-operative societies or corporations etc. in the form of either subsidies or soft loans. They are mainly for increasing either the quantity or quality of production. The various types of fisheries financial assistances may be classified as follows :

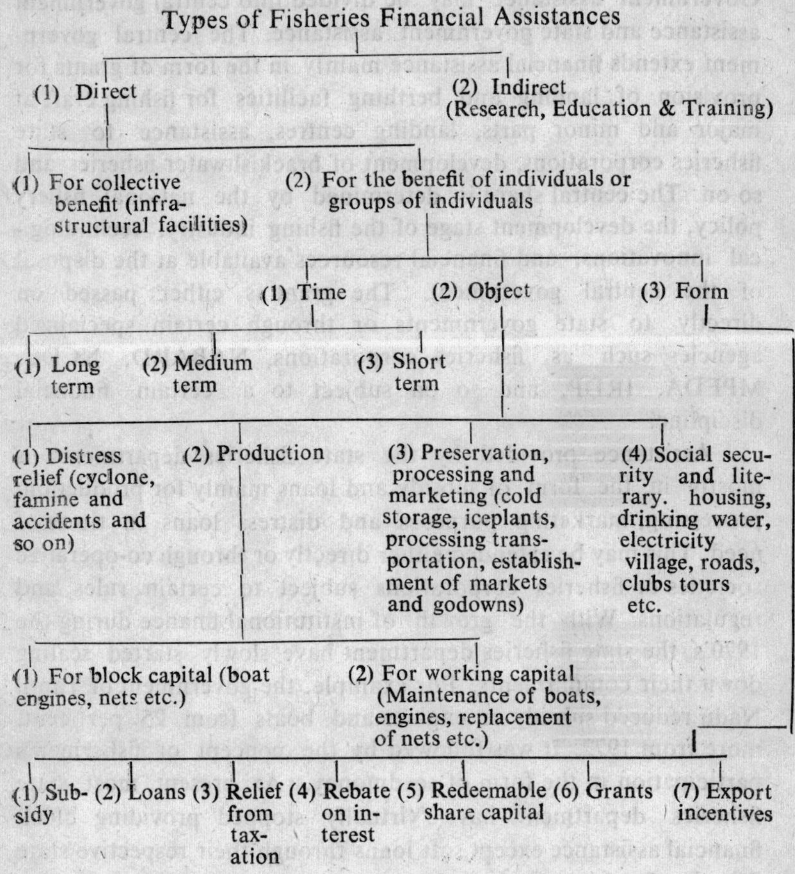

Institutional financing agencies

The various agencies through which these assistances are routed can be classified as follows :

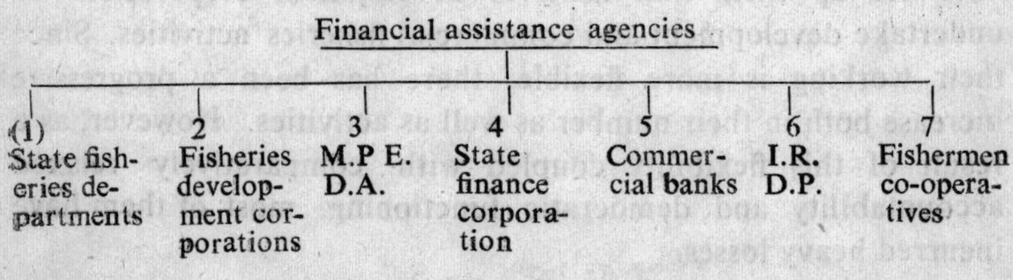

State fisheries departments

Government assistance may be divided into central government assistance and state government assistance. The central government extends financial assistance mainly in the form of grants for provision of landing and berthing facilities for fishing craft at major and minor parts, landing centres, assistance to state fisheries corporations, development of brackishwater fisheries and so on. The central share is determined by the national fishery policy, the development stage of the fishing industry, technological innovations, and financial resources available at the disposal of the central government. The grant is either passed on directly to state governments or through certain specialized agencies such as fisheries corporations, NABARD, NCDC, MPEDA, IRDP, and so on subject to a certain financial discipline.

Assistance provided by the state fisheries departments is mostly in the form of subsidy and loans mainly for production, processing, marketing purposes and distress loans in times of need. This may be extended either directly or through co-operative societies or fisheries corporations subject to certain rules and regulations. With the growth of institutional finance during the 1970's, the state fisheries department have slowly started scaling down their commitments. For example, the government of Tamil Nadu reduced subsidy on engines and boats from 25 per cent, more from 1972. It was followed by the concept of fishermen's participation in the form of seedmoney. At present most state fisheries department have virtually stopped providing block financial assistance except soft loans through their respective state fisheries development corporations.

Fisheries corporations

Besides the Central Fisheries Corporation, most of marine states have set up their own fisheries development corporations to undertake development and commercial fisheries activities. Since their working is more flexible, there has been a progressive increase both in their number as well as activities. However, as a result of this flexibility coupled with comparatively relaxed accountability and democratic functioning, most of them have incurred heavy losses.

Marine Products Export Development Authority (MPEDA)
The Marine Products Export Development Authority extends financial assistance to the registered beneficiaries mainly to improve the quality of exportable varieties of marine products and for export promotion. Some important features of MPEDA are as follows :

Insulated fish boxes : MPEDA provides insulated fish boxes at 50 per cent subsidy to the following types of beneficiaries :

(a) Boat-owners	=	2 boxes per boat
(b) Processing plant owners	=	4 boxes per plant
(c) Peeling shed owners	=	6 boxes per shed
(d) Bherry owners	=	1 box for every 50 acres Bherry subject to a maximum of 2 per registered owner.

From 1979-80 to 1981-82, MPEDA has provided 4.189 such boxes involving a subsidy of Rs. 12.188 lakh.

Fish-landing platforms : An initial subsidy of Rs. 57,500 is given by MPEDA for the construction of a fish landing platform at a site identified by the fisheries department and approved by MPEDA provided the land and subsequent by the State government. During the last 3 years (1979-80 to 1981-82), MPEDA has released a financial assistance of Rs. 14.69 lakh for the construction of such platforms. As soon as the demand for the same catches up, it would be desirable if the financial assistance is given against a matching grant from the State government.

Construction/improvement of peeling sheds : MPEDA grants a subsidy of 20 per cent for the construction/improvement costs of peeling sheds to a maximum limit of Rs. 10,000 per peeling shed. During the last 2 years (1980-81 and 1981-82), MPEDA has helped in the construction/improvement of 209 peeling sheds involving a financial assistance of Rs. 13.15 lakh. There is a scheme for the setting up of community peeling centres also in order to avoid peeling operations in unhygenic conditions by small fishermen/processors. In order to achieve this object, MPEDA has advanced a financial assistance of Rs. 6 lakh and Rs. 20 lakh to Kerala Fishermen Welfare Corporation and

Kerala State Fisheries Department respectively.

Setting up of mini-laboratories : Since 1979-80, MPEDA has started subsidizing the cost of setting up mini-laboratories in the processing plants to the extent of 50 per cent subject to a maximum limit of Rs. 30,000 per laboratory provided the equipments, chemicals, furniture and so on are as per the list supplied by MPEDA. During the last 3 years (1979-80 to 1981-82), 28 such laboratories have been set up involving a subsidy of Rs. 5.24 lakh.

Chlorine kits : Since 1981-82, MPEDA has started the distribution of chlorine kits to assess the chlorine levels in the water used by the processing industry.

Market promotion : In order to explore new markets or to introduce new items, MPEDA has been extending financial assistance since 1976-77 for the despatch of samples. Though the assistance is 100 per cent of the actual freight, it can be availed by a registered exporter only twice in a financial year. In order to avoid its misuse, the subsidy may be limited to about 50 per cent or so of the actual freight and the number of such samples to be despatched during the year may be increased.

These measures have improved the quality of the processed marine products and their consequent acceptability in the importing countries. It would be desirable if not only these schemes are followed more vigorously but a few more such schemes are implemented. However, recently (1981-82), MPEDA has started extending financial assistance for diversified fishing. Accordingly, during the year (1981-82), it has surveyed the fishery resources in the coastal belt of West Bengal for the production of sharks, anchoviella, labosters, and so on. In order to make an effective use of its financial resources, it would be desirable for MPEDA to confine its activities to the field of export promotion for the time being.

State finance corporations

Of late, state finance corporations have emerged as one of the important institutional agencies for financing the small borrowers in general and weaker sections of the community in particular on easy terms. During the 1970's, they have made good headway in fishing industry also, particularly in Orissa and Gujarat. For example, from 1974-75 to 1978-79 the State finance corporations of Orissa and Gujarat have respectively financed about 365 and 1025 boats with an average loan of about Rs. 2 lakh and Rs. 1.10 lakh amounting to about Rs. 7 and Rs. 11 crore. The repayment period is normally about 7 to 8 years with 8 monthly or half-yearly instalment. A gestation period of about 6 months is also provided. Provision of penal rate of interest up to 6 per cent of rebate up to 2 per cent and of 1/2 to 1 per cent commitment charges have also been provided to encourage prompt payment and utilization of the sanctioned term loans respectively. Like other institutional agencies provision is made for adequate securities, mortgage compulsory insurance, registration, hypothecation of the fishing boats and engines purchased out of these loans, margin of 20 to 30 per cent inspection by officers of State finance corporation, fisheries departments, co-operative departments, and so on. Loan is disbursed more in the form of direct payment to engines, fishery requisites and nylon suppliers rather than directly to the beneficiaries. It is also provided that partners/directors/proprietors shall not draw remunerations and interest on capital in any year till any sum due to corporation by way of instalment or interest fallen due in that year remains unpaid. They have also to raise capital deposits on matching disbursement basis of loan and corporation shall have first charge against the assets. An interesting feature of the loans in Gujarat is the guarantee for their repayment along with interest by Gujarat Fisheries Central Co-operatives Association (GFCCA), because the catch is supposed to be disposed off through it.

It is too early to comment upon the performance of State finance corporations in the fisheries sector. However, it can be safely concluded that it is not having a smooth sailing at least in Orissa where total outstanding dues were Rs. 7,67,83,435.82 (Rs. 5,18,98,835.82 as principal, Rs. 2,34,51,600.00 as interest and Rs. 14,33,000 as other charges) as on 30-10-1981 against total disbursement of Rs. 5,65,93,797.35. The recoveries are not adequate even to make up the outstanding interest. About 40 beneficiaries make up did not avail the term loan after its sanction. Out of 364 trawlers financed by the Corporation, about 25 trawlers are missing, 25 trawlers have not been released by the boat-builders, 5 trawlers are reported as capsized, engines have been removed from 28 trawlers, 23 trawlers have been abondoned, 5 seized by the Corporation, and only 157 trawlers were found plying at the end of 1981. Of them only 37 had upto date insurance coverage. In some cases, the insurance premium has been deposited by the Corporation but the cover notes have not been received. In many cases, OSFC number plates had not been affixed to the boats, hypothecation mark were either not inscribed or not legible, identical names were given and entrepreneurs had changed their addresses and names of trawlers without permission. Some of the reasons for the present state of affairs are that in a large number of cases the loans have been sanctioned to non-fishermen (such as doctors, lawyers, teachers etc.) and some beneficiaries have purchased more than one trawler. A large number of loans have been sanctioned more on the basis of personal influence of the beneficiaries than the securities offered by them or their fishing experience. Most of the beneficiaries get inflated quotations for fishery requisites and have thus evaded to pay even their seed money certain as well which also was reduced later from 20 per cent to 10 per cent in certain cases. The instalment is half-yearly and not monthly. Since there was no evaluation and monitoring, his experiment continued till 1979-80. Some of the beneficiaries have a feeling that O.S.F.C. cannot legally seize their trawlers and ultimately the loans shall be written off. Other reasons for poor recovery are rise in diesel and repair costs and decline in catch per boat due to increase in the number of boats operating mainly from Paradeep.

Recovery can improve if port facilities (such as unloading, refuelling, water, ice supplies) are allowed only to those beneficiaries who have cleared their dues, their other securities are attached and auctioned, and more harbours are constructed. Diesel and insurance facilities may be supplied at subsidized rates only to such boat-owners who have cleared their arrears and no more finance should be sanctioned till the economic viability ofthe whole project is re-examined.

Commercial bank

With the nationalization of commercial banks and progressive awakening for the welfare of weaker sections of society, commercial banks started advancing loans mainly for boats, engines, boat-building yards, and so on, in the early 1970's, provided these assets were hypothecated to them. In the initial stages, commercial bank finance made a good progress, particularly in Maharashtra and Karnataka, and slowly spread to other marine States. The Agricultural Finance Corporation (AFC) has also helped commercial bank financing by developing financing and appraisal norms for different types of viable fishery schemes.

Integrated rural development programme (IRDP)

Various rural development institutions such as Marginal Farmers Development Agency (MFDA), Marginal Labourers Development Agency (MLDA), Small Farmers Development Agency (SFDA), Self Employment Scheme (SES), Tribal Development Scheme (TDS), Economic Rehabilitation of the Rural Poor Scheme (ERRPS), Drought Prone Area Programme (DPAP), Command Area Development (CAD) and so on have been merged in the Integrated Rural Development Programme (IRDP) for effective uplift of the poorest of the poor rural families with an annual income of Rs. 3,5000 or so per family. The basic object of the programme is not only to extend financial assistance as a mere gesture but to generate capital assets and productivity also on continued basis in an integrated manner so that it leads to growth along with social justice. Working details differ from State to State but the basic objective of the scheme remain the same.

The programme is administered by an autonomous body under the chairmanship of the Collector with the assistance of the District Project Officer. The Block Development Officer (BDO) has to identify a prescribed number of beneficiaries in the ascending order from income point of view. The landless and marginal farmers that is with less than 2.5 acres of dry land get once in life a subsidy of 33.3 per cent and others 25 per cent of subject to a maximum limit normally of Rs. 3,000 and bank loan for the remaining cost of the project, provided the technical feasibility and economic viability of the project have been certified by the Assistant Project Officer (Fisheries). The subsidy is up to 50 per cent for transport vehicles if the scheme is sponsored through a co-operative society. In some States, the backward class beneficiaries get a margin-money of 20 per cent of the project cost from the backward classes corporation also as loan of 6½ per cent interest up to Rs. 5,000 and rest of the project cost from commercial banks as usual. The securities for these loans consist of the assets so purchased, huts of the fishermen, group-guarantee and so on. Normally the assistance, except the net fabrication charges, is either paid directly to the suppliers or through the Purchase Committee of the D.R.D.A. consisting of Assistant Director of Fisheries, Assistant Registrar of Cooperative Societies, President or Secretary of the concerned society, and bankers' representative. Sometimes credit camps are also organized to expedite the flow of financial assistance. Repayment is made normally in monthly instalments spread over a period of about four years depending upon the nature of the projects.

Since the scheme started with a new pattern only recently, it is too early to evaluate its progress. However, on the basis of the personal investigations of a few fishing villages in Andhra Pradesh and Orissa, it can be safely concluded that there is practically no recovery problem under IRDP unlike the commercial bank financing to medium fishermen (owning mechanized boats). The bankers' representatives visit the fishing villages at fixed intervals for collecting the dues. In a large number of cases, beneficiaries (particularly of Ramana Palem, Chinavacasala, Uppalanka, China Boddu, Venkatai Palem, Teda Boddu-Venkata Poleyam villages in Kakinada district) prefer to go regularly to their banks normally on market days and repay their loan-instalments themselves. Further the commercial banks also in these fishing villages prefer to deal with the beneficiaries directly rather than through co-operative societies.

According to present guidelines, the subsidy is released to financing institutions immediately after the loan is sanctioned so that the beneficiary has to bear interest only on the net amount. However, the beneficiary should be entitled to earn the subsidy only if he repays the loan in full. It will improve the recovery position very much. It is good that approval of the credit institution also is obtained while sanctioning the scheme for deserving households. The annual action and credit plans are prepared well before the financial year clearly specifying the unit-cost, physical targets for various sectors, demarcating the flow of funds through co-operative societies and commercial banks. The responsibility to execute the projects, support-guidance, completion time and so on are also very well defined. Since the IRDP is of recent origin and has various kinds of projects requiring different types of expertise, it is essential that its working should be evaluated and streamlined as an on-going function with regard to the norms for selecting beneficiaries, formulating project schemes, terms and conditions of the action plan, monitoring process, and so on.

Fishery co-operatives

As stated earlier, like other sector of Indian economy, fishermen co-operatives also have constituted a very important source of routing financial assistance to fishermen. The advent of NABARD and NCDC have further accelerated this process.

Fishermen co-operatives of India

As stated earlier, fishermen co-operative societies constitute one of the important agencies for financing the Indian fishing industry. In fact, the history of Indian fisheries development, financial assistance and fishery co-operatives is very much interlinked because the fishermen are poor and innumerable ; financial resources are scarce and above all fishing by nature itself needs more than one fisherman. Fishermen are financed directly as individuals, groups of individuals, through co-operatives, operating fishing boats on co-operative basis or fishing even through departmentally owned boats with fishermen working either on fixed or on share system of wages.

Historical appraisal of Indian fishermen co-operatives credit societies

Since it is often difficult to segregate the existing data into inland and marine fisheries co-operative societies and again their credit functions with production and marketing, the appraisal of fishery credit societies in isolation is very difficult. The first systematic attempt to examine the role of fishery co-operatives in India was made in 1962 when the Planning Commission set up a working group on fishery co-operatives which pointed out that production, storage, processing, and marketing are dealt in isolation. The societies are organizationally weak and need revitalization and adequate financial and technical support. In order to enable the co-operative societies play an effective role in the development programmes, the working group suggested the following measures :

(i) On the basis of adequate surveys, the existing fishermen co-operatives should be revitalized/regrouped and new societies should be formed according to actual needs ;
(ii) Credit facilities to primary societies should be linked to marketing through federations ;
(iii) Co-operative fisheries projects should be taken up in contiguous and viable areas served by fishing harbours ;
(iv) 50 per cent of fish production during the Fourth Plan may be achieved in the co-operative sector by channelizing proportionate share of funds from the plan outlays on various schemes through co-operatives ;
(v) The Reserve Bank of India Act may be amended to facilitate provision of credit facilities to fishermen co-operatives.

Again the Estimates Committee (Fourth Lok Sabha) examined the various aspects of fishermen co-operatives and recommended : "The Committee attach considerable importance to the development of co-operatives for undertaking distribution of fishery requisites, manufacture of nets, processing of fish and marketing. The co-operatives can also play a useful role in the field of boat-building. The Committee consider it imperative that efforts should be made to revitalise the primary societies and link them up with marketing federations. Maximum possible credit should be given to the primary societies through the marketing federations so that the co-operatives are not compelled to seek loan from merchants and middlemen to the detriment of the co-operative movement itself.

The Committee would like to stress in this connection the need for careful approach in the matter in order to ensure that the people genuinely engaged in fishing and fisheries are benefitted through the co-operatives and middlemen, profiteers and other foreign elements are kept out of such societies".

The Sub-Group on Fisheries of the Working Group on

Agriculture for Fourth Five Year Plan Draft (as revised on 1.8.1968), observed that the membership of fishermen co-operative societies announced 3.48 lakh comprising nearly one-third of the working fishermen of the country and at the end of 1965-66, their number increased from 200 in 1944 to 3328 fisheries co-operative societies and share capital of Rs. 94.11 lakh but the value of sales was only Rs. 516.48 lakh representing merely about 5 per cent of the total catches with 50 per cent of the co-operative sales in Mahrashtra alone. Only about 1197 (32.3%) societies showed profits. The eight maritime states accounted for the majority of fisheries co-operative societies and among them Andhra Pradesh, Kerala, Tamil Nadu, Maharashtra and West Bengal accounted for three-fourths of the total membership. In view of this state of affair the sub-group on Fisheries of the Working Group on Agriculture for Fourth Five Year Plan Draft (as revised on 1.8.1968) made the following recommendations :

(i) A comprehensive review should be made by the State government of the working of co-operatives and the fields in which they are competent to play a vital role in implementing the plan should be determined. The units, which can take up developmental work on the basis of their present organization or by strengthenig the organization, should be identified ;

(ii) As far as possible, all developmental efforts should be made through co-operative without affecting the production targets. Developmental assistance to co-operatives may be determined on the specific requirements of each organization within the framework of a broad pattern to be evolved according to the conditions prevalent in each state. The administration assisting the co-operatives in their development work should be suitably strengthened and should be in a position to give both technical guidance and help in business administration to the co-operatives ;

(iii) Special efforts should be made to initiate scheme to be financed by NABARD through co-operatives ;

(iv) As the level of competence of co-operative organisations varies from state to state, the role of co-operatives in implementing the various sectors of the (IV) Plan, should be determined in consultation with the state government.

(v) Fishery co-operative managerial staff may be trained.

An idea of the average membership can be had from the Report on Evaluation of the Programme of Mechanization of Fishing Boats, P.E.O., Planning Commission Government of India 1971 (p. 20). According to which the all-India average membership per society as on 30-6-1969 worked out to 287, highest being 473 in Mysore state followed by 456 in Orissa state. In Andhra Pradesh and Kerala, however, the average membership was 132 and 119 respectively. West Bengal reported the lowest membership of only 58 per society.

According to the National Commission on Agriculture (1976), developing the marine fishing industry through fisheries co-operatives has not met with any significant success. A broad idea of the performance of marine fisheries co-operatives can be had from Table 16.9.

TABLE 16.9 : **Performance of Primary Fishery Co-operatives in the maritime state (1976)**

State	Number of primary fishery societies	Societies showing profit	Societies showing loss	Societies with no profit no loss	Percentage societies showing profit
Andhra Pradesh	527	114	363	120	19.1
Gujarat	59	25	27	7	42.4
Kerala	985	130	780	75	13.2
Maharashtra	381	181	156	44	47.5
Karnataka	121	74	30	17	61.2
Orissa	154	48	63	43	31.2
Tamil Nadu	488	169	270	9	37.7
Goa, Daman and Diu	11	4	7	—	36.2
Lakshadweep	3	3	—	—	100.0
Total	2799	748	1,696	315	27.1

Source : National Commission on Agriculture, 1976, Part VIII, p. 160.

Since the statistical data given earlier by the Sub-group on

Fisheries (1968) covers both fresh water and marine fisheries societies and the data given above by National Commission on Agriculture (1976) is confined to marine fisheries, they are not strictly comparable. However, as against 32.3 per cent in 1968 only 27.1 per cent of co-operative societies were running on profit and 61.5 per cent were showing losses in 1976.

It is apparent that the number of viable societies has not shown any appreciable improvement during the last eight years (1968-76), specially in Kerala and Andhra Pradesh where percentage of societies showing profit was less than 20. Further the co-operative system has not been able to develop viable volume of business. According to the National Commission on Agriculture, this state of affairs is ascribed to several reasons such as vested interests of influential members, rising overdues, and poor management. According to a recent study, the total membership of marine fishermen co-operative societies in India during the period 1972-73 to 1976-77 has either declined or remained constant. There were only marginal changes in the paid-up capital and the reserve per society or per member. In most states, reserve funds and contribution of the government paid-up capital put together formed more than 50 per cent of the total funds of co-operative societies. The overdue loans as percentage to outstanding loans ranged between 86 per cent and 32 per cent in most cases except Maharashtra, where it was only 12 per cent in 1976-77.

Like agriculture, the fishery co-operative societies have by and large a three-tier system. In Gujarat, the movement started more from the system top when Gujarat Fisheries Central Co-operative Association was set up and then the primary societies came up. Of late, the district co-operative societies also are coming up. The need and urgency of co-operative movement in fisheries development can be imagined from the spontaneous response received by the Gujarat Fisheries Central Co-operative Association from the fishermen even without the primary and district co-operative societies. The numerical position of fishery co-operatives was as follows :

(*Rs. in lakh*)

Sl. No.	Type	No.	Membership	Share capital	Business turnover	Export
1.	Primaries	5331	5,97,000	587.50	2082.70	07.3
2.	Regional/district	72	27,914	147.20	668.20	39.5
3.	State level	9	4,834	77.50	471.50	98.6
4.	National level (year ending 30-6-1981)	1	32	5.06	—	—

Source : Agenda notes of first National Fisheries Co-operative Congress, Dated 26th June, 1982, p. 6.

The share capital of State, Central and Primary societies as on 30th June, 1978 was as follows :

		Paid up capital (*Rs. in lakhs*)	
		Government	*Individuals and others*
1.	State level	65.28	14.32
2.	Central level	98.08	41.97
3.	Primary level	114.56	151.90

It may be observed that the total paid-up capital of all fisheries co-operatives stood at Rs. 4.85 crore of which more than 50 per cent was distributed by the government. The average share capital at the primary level was less than Rs. 4,000 including government contribution.

As a result of various recommendations the Reserve Bank of India Act has been amended in order to include pisci-culture and marine fisheries along with other activities connected there-with or incidental thereto in agriculture and thus to provide adequate funds to fishermen co-operatives. The National Co-operative Development Corporation (NCDC) and the Agricultural Refinance Development Corporation (ARDC) now designated the National Bank for Agriculture and Rural Development (NABARD) are also found their best in this direction.

However, very few detailed economic surveys and appraisals, an important recommendation of most of the committees/commission, have been made to revitalize credit societies, linking them with marketing, determine their needs, structure, areas to determine potentialities of co-operative societies, extent and nature of financial assistance required according to specific conditions prevalent in different states. Adequate efforts are yet to be made for the elimination of non-fishermen, bringing 50 per cent of fish production objects, we may not only have to undertake surveys of the difficulties, limitations, and so on but also of the socio-economic conditions of the fishermen as recommended both by the Working Group on Fisheries Cooperatives of Planning Commission (1962) as well as the 1968 Plan Sub-Groups on Fisheries.

National Co-operative Development Corporation (NCDC)

The National Co-operative Development Corporation (NCDC) has been providing production Finance for mechanisation of boats, setting up of service centres, boat-building yards, and fishery requisites ; processing finance for preservation and processing plants such as freezing, canning, fish meal, oil extraction, ice-plants, cold storage and so on and also for transport vehicles including refrigerated and insulated vans, construction of godowns retail booths and so on since 1974-75. It also provides financial assistance for the establishment of technical and promotional cells, preparation of project reports, marketing surveys, and financial management studies.

For production and marketing purposes NCDC assistance towards share capital is provided as per requirements of individual cases on the condition that the society shall raise matching share capital from co-operative members to the extent of at least 5 per cent of earlier government share capital and also that the state government shall provide suitable subsidy to the society for managerial staff. For the purchase of surface transport vehicles (including refrigerated/insulated vans) by fisheries co-operative societies, it provides a subsidy and loan of 25 per cent and 50 per cent respectively to the state government which has to provide a loan and subsidy of 50 per cent each to the society. However, the NCDC assistance is released only after the proposal is approved, order is placed, and the state share of subsidy is released. For processing units, NCDC provides loan and subsidy upto 80 per cent and 20 per cent to the state government which extends a loan, share capital and subsidy upto 55 per cent, 25 per cent, and 20 per cent respectively, to the society. Twenty-five per cent of the loan/subsidy is released as ways and means advance after the society has acquired land, placed orders for machinery and the state government has released 20 per cent of cost (15 per cent in the form of share capital and 5 per cent as subsidy). The remaining release are made in relation to progress in expenditure. Similarly for storage purposes NCDC provides a loan of 50 per cent and subsidy of 25 per cent but in turn the state government has to extend a loan and subsidy of 50 per cent each. Fifty per cent of the financial assistance is released on the approval and acquisition of land and the balance 50 per cent after the government has provided full subsidy and the construction has reached plinth level.

By the end of March 1982 NCDC had sanctioned financial assistance to the tune of Rs. 974.419 lakh as below :

(*Rs. in lakh*)

	Purpose	No.	Amount
1.	Share capital	31	78.874
2.	Mechanized boats	366	696.925
3.	Country boats	512	17.456
4.	Ice plants/cold storages	9	65.091
5.	Godowns	26	8.268
6.	Transport vehicles	24	22.852
7.	Nets	2989	27.490
8.	Retail outlets	20	1.275
9.	Repair/service centres	1	2.800
10.	Processing units	5	11.956
11.	Margin money escalation cost	—	41.532
		Total	974.419

Out of Rs. 974.419 lakh, Maharashtra had been sanctioned Rs. 684 lakh followed by Tamil Nadu, Gujarat, Andhra Pradesh, Karnataka and Kerala States with Rs. 91.750 lakh Rs. 87.226 lakh, Rs. 28.625 lakh, Rs. 28.625 lakh and Rs. 6.725 lakh, respectively. In view of the fact that a large number of fishermen co-operative societies are dormant or ineffective NCDC has emphasized the need to undertake the survey of the working of fishery societies in order to identify the reasons for this state of affairs the State governments must also take necessary steps for the revitalization of potentially viable societies. Another important reason for non-functioning of fishery societies is the lack of definite schemes of business operations. Therefore, NCDC has required the directors of fisheries of all State governments to help the potentially viable societies to formulate suitable business programmes to be undertaken by these societies under the constant supervision of their field officers.

Agricultural Refinance Development Corporation (ARDC) now designated National Bank for Agricultural and Rural Development (NABARD)

ARDC is one of the State sponsored financial institutions which extends refinancing facilities through commercial banks, regional, rural and land development banks, or State co-operative banks for fishing vessels, and infrastructural and fish marketing facilities to the extent of 75 to 90 per cent of the loans advanced by the financing banks for period varying from 3 to 8 years depending upon the economics of the concerned schemes.

Till 31.3.1981, ARDC has sanctioned 647 fishery schemes involving an amount of Rs. 8,546 lakh. Ninety-three of them have been financed through the co-operative sector and the rest through commercial banks. The commitment of ARDC was Rs. 66.84 crore. Of which Rs. 39.29 crore had already been disbursed as on 31.3.1981. These schemes include the World Bank Projects of Gujarat and Andhra Pradesh amounting to US $ 38 million and US $ 36.5 million respectively in marine field and construction of fish-seed hatchery complexes in West Bengal, Bihar, Orissa, Madhya Pradesh and Uttar Pradesh amounting to US $ 40.8 million in the inland field. ARDC's perspective lending programmes for the fisheries sector consist of ARDC Credit Project III for the period 1979-81 for Rs. 20.97 crore and under ARDC. Credit Project IV for the period 1981-83 for Rs. 23.89 crore.

In view of the sensitive nature of operational economics particularly with regard to shrimp catches, migratory nature of fishermen, ARDC has emphasized upon the need of proper selection of beneficiaries and management of the project, role of follow-up studies, evaluation and monitoring arrangements, appointment of technical staff, besides formulation of exhaustive guidelines and check-lists for different types of fishery projects. The role of NABARD in financing fisheries has been analysed in details in previous chapter of this study.

Financial assistance in different states

As explained in earlier sections to encourage the small and medium fishermen, the State fisheries departments try to assist them financially to meet their infrastructural requirements. The position of availability of finance and the repayment conditions differ state to state. The fishermen get assistance in two ways : either in the form of loan as subsidy. The rate of interest of loan and the percentage of subsidy also changes from state to state.

Finance is provided for four sub-systems that is, (1) Production finance (2) Processing, Preservation and Marketing assistance (3) Operational assistance and (4) Miscellaneous finance.

Production finance

For fish production fishermen are provided loans as well as subsidy for the purchase of crafts and gears

(a) *For Craft and Engines* : In case of purchase at craft and engine, the financial assistance in form of subsidy is available from 15 per cent to 30 per cent in all the maritime states except Andhra Pradesh.

In case of Gujarat the fishermen get either a subsidy of 30 per cent or Rs. 20,000 (whichever is less) for purchase of in-board engine. In the case of Karnataka the amount is limited to 13,000 or subsidy of 25 per cent is provided and in exceptional cases, a subsidy of Rs. 30,000 is given on purchase of engine. The drawback of Karanataka is that subsidy for craft and engine is limited only for schedule caste fishermen. Likewise the Orissa fisheries department has reserved subsidy (25%) for artisinal/traditional marine fishermen. The system is little different in Kerala. Fishermen do not get direct subsidy or loan, instead. A group of 4 fishermen gets boat on hire-purchase for the period of 8 years.

Financial assistance in form of loan is available in all the states. In Andhra Pradesh 15 per cent margin money is provided for purchase of boats or nets if purchase is made through APFC. In case of Gujarat, fishermen get interest free loan upto Rs. 25,000 for big vessels and upto Rs. 5,000 for OBMS. Whereas in

Karnataka each punch-seine holder can get Rs. 30,000 as loan as @ 9 per cent interest. In Kerala and Orissa 75 per cent of the cost of fishing vessel is given as loan to fishermen. The only difference is that in the former the rate of interest is 4 per cent and the repayment period is fixed to 4 years and is available to to all the fishermen whereas in later it is restricted to traditional fishermen.

(b) *For gear and tackle* : For these inputs, there is no provision in Andhra Pradesh. In other states the rate of subsidy differs from 15 per cent to 33 per cent. In Gujarat a subsidy of 33 per cent is given for the purchase of fishing tackle and in Karnataka 25 per cent of the purchase money (which is limited to Rs. 12,500) is given for gill-nets. Tamil Nadu Fisheries Corporation has arranged 15 per cent subsidy on gears whereas in Kerala and Orissa 75 per cent of the gear cost of provided as loan @ 4 per cent and of the remaining 25 per cent, 15 per cent is given as subsidy in the former and full 25 per cent in the later. In Maharashtra it varies as the gear varies. Details of the same are presented in Appendix IV.

Processing, preservation and marketing assistance

Assistance for the above facilities is available only in 4 states namely, Gujarat, Karnataka, Kerala and Maharashtra. Gujarat state is very liberal in providing assistance for various infrastructure facilities like construction of boat building yards and net making plants ; ice plants, cold storages and so on. In Karnataka a loan-cum subsidy upto Rs. 15,000 at 7 per cent is available for construction of godown. If all the instalments are properly paid, 50 per cent of the amount is treated as subsidy. In Kerala the assistance in form of loan is provided only for fish vendors at 4 per cent. For processing plants, Maharashtra State government provides 25 per cent subsidy and 55 per cent amount as loan. Moreover, 20 per cent subsidy is available from NCDC. For transport also subsidy as well loans are available in Maharashtra (Appendix IV)

Operational assistance

This type of assistance is given in two states only. Gujarat Fisheries Department is providing managerial subsidy at 100 per cent, 75 per cent and 50 per cent in first, second, and third year respectively. Same type of arrangements are made in Karnataka. The difference is that in Karnataka the amount is limited to Rs. 1000 per year during the first 4 years in case of co-operative societies.

Miscellaneous assistance

Under this title financial assistance for housing, distress relief, and so on are provided to fishermen in some states. Andhra Pradesh Gujarat, Orissa and West Bengal have not made any provision for such relief. Karnataka and Maharashtra Governments have created Distress Relief Funds for fishermen. Tamil Nadu Supplies free houses or cheap houses (through PWD) to fishermen depending on their financial conditions.

CONCLUSIONS

Concept of small and medium fishermen

In view of the relativity of economic, technological, social and political parameters determining the distinction between small and medium fishermen and availability of statistical data, all non-mechanized boat-owners and operators may be broadly defined as small fishermen and all mechanized boat-owners and operators as medium fishermen.

Financial requirements

Taking into account the innumerable types of boats and nets, wide variations in their respective sizes, expected lives, combinations of crafts and gears, financial requirements of small fishermen consisting of a Catamaran, a cotton net and hooks may vary from Rs. 2,000 upto Rs. 1 lakh in case of Rampani fishing unit. The variations in the financial requirements of medium fishermen are less on account of standardization of boats, engines, nets etc. but may vary from about Rs. 50,000 in the case of an O.B.M. fishing unit to Rs. 5 lakh in the case of a 14-metre mechanized trawler.

Variations in fishermen's income

Like the financial requirements of fishermen, their incomes also vary widely not only between small and medium fishermen but amongst themselves as well depending upon the size of their boats, engines, nature of fishery, areas, fishing season and even personal skill and risk taken. Among the small fishermen, it may vary from Rs. 1,000 to Rs. 10,000 and among medium fishermen from Rs. 5,000 to Rs, 1,00,000 or more per family per year. An interesting feature is the better control over income when women-folk sell the catches.

Prevalance of indebtedness

Broadly speaking, about 75 per cent of the fishermen families can be easily taken as indebted. Even rich fishermen also borrow, probably because fishermen have reconciled with indebtedness as a way of life. Social and off-season requirements are important reasons for their indebtedness.

Interest rates

Interest rates differ from zero to about 75 per cent depending upon the surrendering of their as well as of other fishermen's catches and the extent by which they will be paid lower than the prevailing market price.

Declining role of state fisheries departments

With the emergence of financial assistance from different institutions such as commercial banks, NCDC, state finance corporations, fisheries corporations, MPEDA, DRDP, DRDS etc., there is a progressive decline in the departmental (state fisheries departments) financial assistance during the last decade. This trend is perceptible most in Tamil Nadu, Orissa and Andhra Pradesh but latest in Gujarat, Maharashtra and Karnataka (See Appendix IV).

More assistance to medium-scale fishermen

In view of the fact that mechanization of fishing boats has so far been considered to be the most important approach for developing the marine fishing industry, the various financial assistance programmes has benefited mostly the medium-scale fishermen who could furnish not only the securities required but exert influence as well. As a result, fish production by small-scale fishermen has declined. For example, according to a recent (1979) study by Syndicate Bank, production from traditional fisheries in Andhra Pradesh has declined from 1,49,289 tonnes in 1974 to 73,805 tonnes in 1977, resulting in reduced catch per unit of effort, per capita income and consequent sufferings.

Allotment of boats and "Benami" transactions

The system of restricted allotment of mechanized boats to a few selected fishermen and easy availability of institutional transactions. The prevalence of "Benami" mechanised boats is roughly estimated at about 25 per cent, 10 per cent, 8 per cent and 5 per cent in Kerala, Tamil Nadu, Andhra Pradesh and Orissa respectively.

Recovery of loans

The recovery of loans has on the whole been poor on account of several reasons such as high risks and uncertainties involved in the fishing industry, progressive increase in operational costs specially HSD, mobility of the beneficiary from one place to another in search of fish, insignificant stake of borrower in the boats and consequent "Benami" transactions, reduced catch hired and reported sale of fish specially prawns in open sea by hired crew, general feeling among the borrowers that government loans are normally waived off, diversification of incomes, and so on. However, recoveries from small fishermen have been more satisfactory. In some cases, they are reported to prefer to repay to banks personally rather than through co-operative societies.

Co-ordination between state fisheries departments and institutional financing agencies

Co-ordination between the state fisheries departments and state fisheries corporation on the one hand and the various institutional financing agencies on the other seems to be in adequate, probably on account of the recent entry of the latter into the industry and also indifference in a few cases. The reasons for the indifference appear to be in adequate availability of technical personnel for preparing feasibility reports and statistical data about the economics of the industry. Ad hoc relief in times of natural calamities: Almost all state fisheries departments provide *ad hoc* relief in times of natural calamities but this is yet to be systematized.

Emergence of institutional consumption finance

In view of the seasonal character of the fishing industry and consequent prevalance of middlemen-cum-traders, there is a thinking in a few states to provide institutional consumption finance also to fishermen especially during the off-season.

Progress of fishermen co-operative societies

By and large the performance of fishermen co-operative societies has not so far been impressive.

Membership of non-bonafide fishermen

Non-fishermen are still members of fishermen co-operative societies. Fish merchants can also become "B" class members of co-operative societies in a few cases. However, the state governments are aware of the problem and are taking steps to remove them. The recent efforts made by the Tamil Nadu government deserve a special mention.

Use of NCDC financial assistance

In spite of the fact that individual fishermen and co-operative societies can get upto 100 per cent financial assistance in the form of subsidy and loan from NCDC and state fisheries departments for acquiring fishing units and establishing preservation and processing plants adequate use of NCDC finance has not so far been made.

RECOMMENDATIONS

Identification of beneficiaries and objectives of financial assistance

It is often said that assistance goes to those who do not really need it. It is, therefore, necessary to identify for whom, why, how much in what form, when and under what terms and conditions financial assistance is required. Financial assistance to medium scale fishermen in future should be extended purely as a commercial proposition ; whereas it should be with commercial viability because financial requirements of small fishermen are low, yield higher internal rate of return, involve insignificant operational costs (specially HSD potentialities, allied industries and excellent recovery of loans). A recent advantage in the execution of financial assistance to small fishermen is the emergence of DRDS/DRDP under Integrated Rural Development Programme which provides a scientific procedure, financial discipline and an organization to take care of follow-up action, evaluation, feedback, and monitoring. Therefore, financial assistance to small fishermen is likely to yield more useful results especially in view of the recent enforcement of marine fisheries regulation of inshore waters by the states.

Demarcation of functions

In view of the emergence of various financing institutions besides the state fisheries departments, it is essential that their respective functions should be clearly defined and demarcated in order to avoid duplication. Probably, the state fisheries departments may confine themselves to developmental functions such as promotion of infrastructure, education and training, extension, socio-economic welfare etc. The commercial functions may be entrusted to state fisheries corporations which must be run at least on no-profit no-loss basis. There is absolutely no reason for them to incur losses. The co-operative societies should deal with local developmental problems relating to production, preservation, processing, pooling, marketing, transport and even exports of fish and fishery products besides socio-economic welfare of the fishermen. It may be surprising to note that the share of fishery co-operative societies in exports is negligible in spite of the fact that small and medium fishermen catch 99 per cent of total landings.

Need of greater co-ordination between state fisheries departments and financial institutions

Two specific fields in which the state fisheries departments can help the financial institutions are preparation of feasible project reports and recovery of loans. It will be desirable if liaison committees consisting of representatives of state fisheries departments, state fisheries corporations, concerned commercial banks, state finance corporations, DRDP/DRDS are set up at state and district levels to review periodically the overall economics of the industry, particularly the recovery position, in order to enable the concerned authorities to take appropriate action in time.

Introduction of revolving credit

As far as possible the fisheries financial institutions should be provided with a fixed amount of revolving credit. These institutions should review their own working annually so that the quantum of the fund may be adjusted accordingly.

Resources within industry

It is high time that the performance of MPEDA and its impact on the fishing industry in general and exports in particular is analysed critically in order to assess the percentage of exports cess which should be used for financing the fishermen, particularly the small fishermen on whose catches also the cess is being collected.

State stabilization fund

With the help of Reserve Bank of India, NABARD state governments, state and district co-operative banks, state stabilization funds should be created in each state in order to meet the situation arising as a result of bad and doubtful debts in the fisheries co-operative sector.

Formulation of state financial assistance rules, instructions, manuals etc. etc.

In order to avoid discrimination at administrative levels and to create awareness among fishermen about the fishery policy and details of financial assistance available in their respective states, it is essential that state financial assistance rules be formulated and implemented as to Maharashtra and Gujarat Manuals and instructions should be prepared in local languages for the guidance of officers and fishermen. It will enable all concerned to know the purpose, form, extent, procedure, terms, assistance and will also help and conditions regarding the availability of financial assistance and will also help in borrowing as well as in repayment. It will be desirable if model drafts for financial assistance rules, instructions and manuals are prepared by the

Government of India for adoption by states after necessary modifications to suit local requirements.

Payments in kind

As far as possible, all payments should be made direct to fishery in-put suppliers and not to the fishermen-borrowers. It would be all the more desirable if a "Purchase Committee" consisting of all concerned that is representatives of the state fisheries department, financing institutions, co-operative societies, fishermen's associations etc. is constituted.

Recovery of loans

Inadequate recovery of loans is reported to be the chief obstacle in the growth of institutional finance. The old concept of delivering the catch to co-operative societies for sale and recovery has proved to be ineffective. With proposed reduction of financial assistance to medium fishermen, reservation of inshore fishing grounds to small fishermen, progressively increasing operational expenditure and to exploit the offshore fishing grounds ; there is a clear case for adequate financial incentives in the form of subsidy on HSD oil and insurance premium. If this subsidy is paid only to such fishermen who have cleared off their loans as per schedule, the recovery problem will ease substantially. A progressively declining subsidy on interest rates during the early part of the loan say for 3 to 5 years, depending upon the economics of the fishery, may also be helpful in expediting the recovery. The proposed punitive measures for accelerating the recovery are conversion of subsidy into loan which should be recoverable as land revenue if the loan portion is not paid within the prescribed time-limit as is the practice in some states and denial of port-facilities to defaulters. The administrative measures proposed in this respect are intensive and uniform pattern of registration of fishing boats and prescription of a specific fishing base for each of them to be touched at least once in two months. Further, the loans should not be written off on any consideration except economic and that too in exceptionally extreme and hard cases.

Departmental social security system

As stated earlier almost each state helps the fishermen financially on *ad hoc* basis in times of natural calamities, but mostly without systematic approach. It will be desirable if a token premium is collected and substantial rates of compensation for different types of losses are prescribed like insurance companies. This will not only help in inculcating a sense of savings, investment, and social security but will also help in improving existing statistical data and also liaison with the state fisheries departments. It is hoped that the recently announced decision of the Government co-operative sector under group insurance scheme for getting an insurance policy of Rs. 15,000 by providing 50 per cent subsidy on the annual premium shall go a long way in achieving this object.

Discouragement of 'spoon-feed' approach

The spoon-feed approach of providing preservation and processing plants in the public sector instead of the co-operative and private sector, especially in fishery advanced states, deserves to be discouraged because the public sector is normally less efficient than the co-operative and private sector.

Abolition of selective allotment system

The system of selective allotment of boats, engines, and other fishery requisites needs to be discontinued. These assets may be supplied on the "first-come first-served principle" to those applicants who fulfil the prescribed administrative, financial and other conditions.

Allotment to co-operatives vs. individuals

Taking past performance in view, specially in Kerala and also in Andhra Pradesh to some extent, it may be more effective if financial assistance in the form of subsidized fishery requisites is granted to groups of individuals through co-operative societies as is done in Maharashtra.

Encouragement of project approach

In the interest of expeditious fisheries development with scarce financial resources, it would be more effective if a project approach as in Orissa state (i.e. Rajlaxmi, Kirtania, Dhamra and Astrang projects) is adopted by identifying selected production, preservation, and marketing projects on co-operative lines.

Periodical techno-economical evaluation

In order to ensure smooth functioning of each financial assistance scheme, it is essential that it should undergo a thorough techno-economic evaluation annually by the financing institution itself and by an independent professional agency after a period of at least three years. This will help in feedback, monitoring and timely action to modify the working of the scheme in order to achieve the desired goals more effectively.

Collection of statistical data

At present adequate statistical data about the economics of the industry are not available as a result of which, it is difficult to take timely and appropriate decisions—a fact which was emphasized by the National Commission on Agriculture. It is therefore, essential that efforts should be made in this connection in order to enable the industry to stand on its own.

Restriction of membership of co-operative societies

Only bona-fide fishermen who go for fishing into the sea for 100 days or so should be eligible to be members of co-operative societies.

Maximum utilisation of NCDC financial assistance

In view of the liberal as well as systematic financial assistance offered by NCDC all efforts should be made to make the maximum use in different sectors of the industry. It will ensure prompt assistance according to a certain procedure and financial discipline, effective utilization of the assistance and above all the timely recovery.

Setting up of fisherwomen co-operative societies

The experience of setting up of fisherwomen co-operative societies of Karnataka deserves to be adopted in all marine states. It is likely to accelerate not only the savings and investment but efficient marketing of catch as well.

Pygmy bank collections

Similarly, the recently introduced Pygmi bank collections in Karnataka deserves all encouragement. It is likely to be of immense help in providing off-season financial requirements of fishermen and keeping them free from the clutches of middlemen-cum-traders.

REFERENCES

1. CMFRI, Marine Fisheries Information Service No. 3, Cochin, 1978.
2. CMFRI, Marine Fisheries Information Service No. 3, Cochin, August 1981.
3. CMFRI, Economics of the indigenous fishing units at Cochin—A case study (Special Publication), Cochin 1978.
4. CMFRI Economics of the indigenous fishing units at Cochin—A case study, Cochin, 1970.
5. Government of India, Planning Commission Report on the Evaluation of Programme of Mechanization of Fishing Boats P.E.O., February 1971.
6. Government of India, Planning Evaluation Organization, Economics of Mechanized Boats, February 1971.
7. Gupta V.K. *et al.*, *Marine Fish Marketing in India* (Vol. VI), Centre for Management in Agriculture, Indian Institute of Management, Ahmedabad, 1982.
8. John Kurien and Rolf Willium, Econonics of Artisanal and Mechanised Fisheries in Kerala—A Study on Costs and Earnings, F.A.Os P.C.O. Trivandrum, July 1982.
9. Kalwar, A.G., present status of Small Scale Fisheries in Maharashtra, CMFRI, *Bulletin 30*, CMFRI, Cochin.
10. Krishnakumar, S., Strategy and Action Programme for a Massive Thrust in Fisheries Development and Fishermen Welfare in Kerala State (1980-83).
11. Mishra, S.N. and John Beyer, Cost Benefit Analysis—A Case Study of Ratnagiri Fisheries Project, Institute of Economic Growth, p. 4.
12. Srivastava, U.K. *et al.*, Managing Marine Fishing Industry—An Analysis of Problems in Harvesting and Processing (A micro/study of Gujarat State), Centre for Management in Agriculture, Indian Institute of Management, Ahmedabad, 1979.

APPENDIX-I

STATE-WISE NUMBER AND TYPE OF NON-MECHANIZED FISHING CRAFTS (1973-77)

Sail boats

Sl. No.	State	Nava	Catmanras	Padva	Palmryadhni	Big	Small	Dhoni	Dinghi	Plank Built Boats	Masula Boats	Cande	Vathal	Thoni	Vallam
1.	Andhra Pradesh	1,165	18,132	4,184	226	109	672	1,062	472	—	—	—	—	—	—
2.	Tamil Nadu	—	24,558	—	—	—	—	—	—	1,544	320	1,732	884	542	921
3.	Kerala	9,960	—	—	—	—	—	—	—	3,837	—	—	—	—	—
4.	Maharashtra	—	—	—	—	—	—	—	—	2,616	—	—	—	—	—
5.	Gujarat	—	—	—	—	—	—	—	—	2,420	—	—	—	—	—
6.	West Bengal and Orissa	522	4,342	—	—	—	—	—	60	—	—	—	—	—	—
7.	Pondicherry	—	1,670	—	—	—	—	—	—	—	—	—	—	—	—
8.	Karnataka	—	—	—	—	—	2,341	1,784	—	—	—	—	—	—	—
9.	Goa	—	—	—	—	—	—	—	—	—	—	—	—	—	—

Source : Compiled from Marine Fisheries Information Service, No. 3, Nov., 1970—CMFRI, Cochin (India) (1973-77 Census)

Sl. No.	State	Daugout Cans	Beach Seine Boats	Chal	Pankhaya	Carvel Built Boats	Patia	Masula Padava	Dinge	Padaga	Rampani Bendi	Kairampani	Pandi	Outrigger	Plank built hodi	Pande-vallem	Others	Total
1.	Andhra Pradesh	—	—	—	—	—	—	—	—	—	—	—	—	—	—	—	—	25,576
2.	Tamil Nadu	—	—	—	—	—	—	—	—	—	—	—	—	—	—	—	—	30,501
3.	Kerala	8,191	—	—	—	—	—	—	—	—	—	—	—	—	—	—	—	21,718
4.	Maharashtra	5,431	193	—	—	—	—	—	—	—	—	—	—	—	—	—	48	8,288
5.	Gujarat	1,777	—	—	—	—	—	—	—	—	—	—	—	—	—	—	—	4,197
6.	West Bengal and Orissa	—	—	100	371	45	162	345	517	—	—	—	—	—	—	—	—	6,667
7.	Pondicherry	44	—	—	—	—	—	—	—	53	—	—	—	—	—	—	—	1,767
8.	Karnataka	1,972	—	—	—	—	—	—	—	—	54	10	79	—	—	—	—	6,248
9.	Goa	—	—	—	—	—	—	—	—	—	—	—	—	820	258	40	—	1,118
	Grand Total																	106,480

Source : Compiled from Marine Fisheries Information Service, No. 3, Nov., 1978—CMFRI, Cochin (India) (1973-77 Census)

APPENDIX-II

DETAILS OF FISHING GEARS USED BY SMALL AND MEDIUM FISHERMEN IN INDIA (1973-1977)

Fishing gears	West Bengal and Orissa	Andhra Pradesh	Tamil Nadu	Pondi-cherry	Kerala	Karna-taka	Goa	Maha-rashtra	Gujarat	Total
Rampani	—	—	—	—	—	164	112	—	—	276
Shore seines	375	1,471	1,920	34	1,739	494	53	16,000	—	22,385
Nolon gillnet	1,427	16,676	3,232	—	3,044	4,478	—	1,36,596	10,491	1,75,944
Bottom set-gill-net	—	1,481	5,559	—	246	844	—	—	—	8,526
Gill-net	5,048	18,541	1,11,023	1,301	7,763	9,219	1,345	8,410	1,18,172	2,80,822
Drift-net	323	1,889	7,966	359	6,763	1,945	—	—	5,329	24,574
Drag-net	2,466	5,729	3,678	298	—	936	58	12,635	1,341	27,141
Bag-net	1,034	159	1,855	458	534	13	—	20,503	17,031	41,587
Purse-seines	—	—	—	—	—	124	22	—	—	146
Trawl-net	—	—	—	13	269	246	144	1,966	167	2,805
Boat seine	1,561	6,480	4,875	—	9,027	—	—	—	—	21,943
Encircline net	—	—	—	—	279	—	—	—	—	279
Books and line	48	2,587	6,107	43	2,887	996	177	—	1,598	14,143
Others	28,478	11,267	12,644	271	845	5,908	652	52,693	5,655	1,18,413
Total	40,760	66,280	1,59,255	2,777	33,396	25,066	2,563	2,49,103	1,59,784	7,38,984

Source : Marine Fisheries Information Service Centre, No. 3, Nov., 1978—CMFRI, Cochin (1973-77 Census)

APPENDIX-III

STATE-WISE FIGURES OF MARINE FISHING CRAFT AND GEARS IN INDIA—1980

Sl. No.	Items	STATES									
		West Bengal	Orissa	Andhra Pradesh	Tamil Nadu	Pondi-cherry Kariakal Mahe and Yenam	Kerala	Karna-taka	Goa, Daman and Diu	Gujarat	Total
1.	No. of fishing Crafts										
	(a) Mechanized										
	Trawlers	—	—	447	2,295	176	745	808	407	1,410	6,288
	Gill-netters	247	106	9	324	—	215	23	213	1,225	2,362
	Dol-netters	—	—	—	—	—	—	—	—	241	241
	Purse-seiners	—	—	—	—	—	7	173	39	—	221
	Others	63	—	—	8	—	14	74	—	18	177
	Total	310	106	456	2,627	176	983	1,078	659	2,894	9,289
	(b) Non-mechanized										
	Plankbuilt boats	3,972	3,262	11,359	8,957	83	4,376	1,747	1,108	3,040	37,904
	Dug-out canoes	89	186	1,781	2,210	72	10,415	4,454	1·397	1,080	21,634
	Catamarans	—	6,276	22,198	31,151	1,595	11,480	24	8	—	73,431
	Others	—	4	625	325	—	—	718	—	—	1,722
	Total	4,061	9,728	36,013	43,443	1,750	26,271	6,942	2,513	4,120	1,34,741

APPENDIX-III : (*Contd.*)

2. No. of fishing gears										
Trawl-nets	—	—	823	6,219	437	1,454	1,780	772	2,672	14,165
Purse-gill-nets	—	—	—	—	—	9	180	41	—	238
Drift/gill-nets	2,467	10,427	42,385	1,18,800	1,851	23,307	6,571	3,346	7,383	2,16,037
Boat seines	—	2,676	9,738	1,842	375	9,779	23	165	—	29,976
Fixed bag nets	6,200	2,770	14,617	1,842	152	—	941	430	21,057	40,017
Books and lines	869	15,265	10,752	22,111	720	2,949	1,587	127	2,376	56,776
Rampans	—	—	—	—	—	—	86	101	—	187
Share seines	436	2,093	3,042	4,549	84	2,926	3,924	987	—	18,841
Traps	61	515	130	8,919	9	2,239	—	—	86,952	98,825
Scoop-nets	345	37	2,925	1,840	362	1,371	—	—	—	6,080
Others	2,433	5,201	37,199	6,339	120	2,761	10,925	2,813	28,013	95,004

Source : Marine Fisheries Information Service, Central Marine Fisheries Research Institute, Cochin, INDIA. No. 30, August, 1981 (ICAR), p. 5.

17

COST OF PRODUCTION OF FISH

T.A. MAMMEN

BASICALLY the cost of production in a capture fishery is the cost of goods and services expended to get a unit of production. To this is added the margins retained by the various financing, supervisory, and marketing functionaries to arrive at the production price and the market price of the product. The production and market prices are greatly influenced by the competition among producers and purchasers, and between producers and purchasers.

BACKGROUND

Pre-mechanization era

The period prior to the initiation of the Five Year Plans (1951) may be called the pre-mechanization era in the Indian marine fisheries, when there were practically no mechanized boats in operation in India. This period was characterized by low fish production, low wages, and low price of fish. Only one-third of then Indian population of 361 million was fish-eating and most of the interior population could not get fresh fish owing to problems in preservation, transportation, storage, and distribution. Only 23 per cent of the marine fish production was consumed in fresh condition, as much as 68 per cent had to be cured before it could be sent for marketing while 9 per cent went into the production of fish meal and fish manure. The small quantity marketed fresh had to be hawked around for sales, as fish was then in the buyer's market. Only simple craft and gears were engaged, which again were largely constructed by their own effort. The fishermen, who belonged to a socially and economically weaker section of the community, had a low ranging for wages. Besides they had very little bargaining power, which was further reduced for a highly perishable commodity like fish. Hence, the cost of production of marine fish during the pre-mechanization era was in effect the low-rated wages for their labour.

Mechanization era

As a result of three decades of intensive effort, now about 11 per cent of the marine fishing craft in India is mechanized. But even this 11 per cent is exerting a tremendous influence on marine fish production as well as on the approach and reaction to the entire marine fishery. Largely due to the introduction of mechanized fishing boats, marine fish production is now close to 1.4 million tonnes, side by side with the increase in production, facilities for storage, transportation, and marketing have increased. Ice production and cold storage capacity, which were practically non-existent in 1950, increased by 1980 to 1,916 tonnes of ice production capacity per day and 35,943 tonnes of cold storage capacity. Similarly the number of processing (freezing) plants increased from 47 in 1969 to 276 in 1982. The fish-eating population increased three fold, that is from 33 per cent of 361 million population in 1951 to 55.5 per cent of 668 million population in 1981. New demand areas emerged in metropolitan cities and large industrial townships. Fish moved out of the buyer's market into the seller's market.

Marine fishery resources

Assessment of fishery resources is difficult. Firstly, unlike static resources, dynamic resources like fish are difficult to assess and that too in a vast expanse like the sea. Secondly, it is not just a question of assessing the standing stock, but a rational estimation of what is considered the level of maximum sustainable yield, taking note of the need to maintain a breeding stock, their breeding success, natural mortality, and so on. The problem is approached by studying their biology, monitoring the nature and extent of the present yield, and estimating the scope for fishing additional quantities.

Present marine fish production

Estimates of marine fish landings are made by the Central Marine Fisheries Research Institute as well as by various state governments. Table 17.1 gives a summary of these estimates.

TABLE 17.1 : **Marine fish landing statistics**

	CMFRI Estimates	Estimates by state governments
1951	534.0	—
1956	718.8	—
1961	683.6	—
1966	889.9	—
1971	1161.6	—
1972	980.0	974.4
1973	1220.4	1210.0
1974	1217.8	1472.0
1975	1422.7	1482.1
1976	1352.9	1374.7
1977	1259.8	1448.4
1978	1403.6	1489.7
1979	1388.4	1492.0
1980	1241.3	1555.0
1981	1378.5	1441.0
1982 (P)	—	1444.0
1983 (P)	—	1531.0

It is seen that despite the wide variations, both estimates indicates a near stagnation in production. From 1982 onwards fish landing figures reported by the states are reconciled with those maintained by the CMFRI. Table 17.2 gives details of species-wise fish landing as per estimates made by the CMFRI in terms of average for each major group along with the extent of variations recorded.

Scope for fishing additional quantities

In general, fish concentration decreases as one goes away from the shore. It is also relatively easy and more economical to fish in the near-shore areas. From these considerations, most of the fishing is concentrated fairly close to the coast. Barring the operation of a few deep sea fishing vessels the entire present

TABLE 17.2 : **Trend of marine fish production during 1971-81**

Sl. No.	Name of fish	Average	Minimum recorded		Maximum recorded	
			Qty. (T)	Year	Qty. (T)	Year
1.	Elasmobranchs	55,358	41,348	(1971)	66,054	(1974)
2.	Eels	6,954	4,056	(1971)	12,997	(1977)
3.	Cat fishes	52,460	39,231	(1978)	76,196	(1974)
4.	*Chirocentrus*	10,815	9,026	(1974)	12,805	(1980)
5.	(a) Oil sardine	158,668	115,744	(1980)	221,026	(1981)
	(b) Lesser sardines	75,129	44,629	(1972)	112,117	(1975)
	(c) *Hilsa ilisha*	5,738	404	(1973)	12,068	(1979)
	(d) Other *Hilsa*	11,056	7,541	(1974)	18,267	(1981)
	(e) *Anchoviella*	30,243	18,699	(1972)	41,507	(1974)
	(f) Thirssocles	13,460	9,929	(1977)	19,342	(1980)
	(g) Other clupeoids	39,712	24,100	(1971)	57,164	(1976)
6.	(a) *Harpodon nehereus*	91,391	51,570	(1972)	137,790	(1981)
	(b) *Saurida and saurus*	8,856	3,687	(1971)	14,323	(1975)
7.	*Hemirhamphus and belone*	1,760	687	(1972)	4,574	(1974)
8.	Flying fish	2,773	643	(1977)	9,179	(1971)
9.	Perches	29,693	12,993	(1971)	49,312	(1978)
10.	Red mullets	3,916	2,416	(1980)	7,009	(1974)
11.	Polynemids	8,033	3,929	(1977)	14,573	(1976)
12.	Sciaenids	82,496	36,903	(1971)	114,535	(1975)
13.	Ribbon fish	55,884	36,225	(1972)	77,785	(1978)

14.	(a) *Caranx*	22,815	9,166 (1981)	30,666	(1977)
	(b) *Chorinemus*	3,485	2,109 (1971)	4,985	(1981)
	(c) Other carangids	3,207	727 (1971)	23,194	(1981)
15.	Silver bellies	45,827	32,392 (1972)	69,449	(1981)
16.	*Lactarius*	8,962	4,474 (1979)	13,912	(1973)
17.	Pomfrets	31,920	19,007 (1972)	48,728	(1981)
18.	Mackerel	78,609	37,462 (1974)	204,575	(1971)
19.	Seer fish	22,102	18,339 (1971)	29,547	(1979)
20.	Tunies	13,689	5,678 (1973)	26,595	(1979)
21.	*Sphyraena*	2,614	1,271 (1971)	4,862	(1974)
22.	*Mugil*	2,685	1,400 (1979)	4,497	(1974)
23.	*Bregmaceros*	1,779	30 (1977)	5,488	(1972)
24.	Soles	12,993	9,718 (1972)	18,917	(1974)
25.	(a) Penaeid prawns	108,472	72,109 (1971)	141,713	(1975)
	(b) Non-penaeid prawns	68,085	55,244 (1973)	85,488	(1972)
	(c) Lobsters	11,620	679 (1980)	2,991	(1975)
	(d) Other crustaceans	19,470	9,612 (1971)	43,934	(1981)
26.	Cephalopods	8,015	1,026 (1972)	15,032	(1979)
27.	Miscellaneous	75,765	37,513 (1971)	113,582	(1978)
	Average (Total)	1,276,509			

Source : CMFRI

marine fishing is confined to areas well within the 50-metre depth contour.

The resources of the offshore and distant waters have been estimated based on trial fishing and/or on the productivity of these waters. Experts have also attempted to fit in mathematical models to relate observed data on a number of selected parameters to compute maximum sustainable yield levels. Two such estimates have been made with regard to the additional harvestable resources of the Indian Exclusive Economic Zone, one by George, *et al.* and another by Joseph. Their estimates are summarized in Table 17.3. While estimates vary, there is a broad similarity in the species available for exploitation and their overall magnitude. The most important reason for the current underutilization of these resources is the unsuitability of the craft and gear. Barring the government owned vessels intended for research, survey and training, all commercial fishing vessels are concentrating on the coastal shrimp. The industry is apprehensive of investing huge capital required for harvesting these resources, as the economic feasibility has not been established.

FISH PRODUCTION BY SECTORS

Introduction of mechanized boats has been the most important developmental activity, both for increasing production as well as to improve the quality of life of the fishermen. The programme, in spite of all attention bestowed by the government, the co-operatives, banks, and various social organizations could cover only 11 per cent of the fishing boats, with bleak prospect of providing the remaining with a mechanized boat. This has created a divison between those operating mechanized boats and those operating unmechanized boats. The emergence of the traditional fishermen as an important 'vote bank' has attracted attention of many political parties.

Lured by tax concessions on new industries and the scope for importing essential items for running their other industries as per import entitlement under the registered exporter's policy, many large houses were attracted into the fishing industry and this in turn focused public attention on the entry of big houses

TABLE 17.3 : **Additional harvestable resource as assessed by George *et al.** and Joseph****

Sl. No.	Name of fish	Additional harvestable resource as assessed by		Location of additional harvestable resource
		George *et al.*	Joseph	
	Pelagic species			
1.	Oil sardine	61	90	SW
2.	Other sardines	53	22	SE, NE, AN
3.	Anchoviella	203	123	SW, SE
4.	Other clupeids	80	45	NE
5.	Ribbon fish	213	214	NW, SW
6.	Carangids	239	132	All over
7.	Tunas & tuna-like fish	227	124	SW, NE, AN
8.	Mackerel	37	125	SW, NE
9.	Seer	21	5	All over
10.	Pelagic shark	—	70	All over
	Total	1,134	950	
	Demersal Species			
1.	Elasmobranchs	125	149	All over
2.	Cat fish	253	201	All over
3.	Sciaenids	140	151	All over
4.	Silver belies	52	44	All over
5.	Polynemids	30	—	NE
6.	Pel	—	29	NW, NE
7.	Perches	233	166	All over
8.	*Nemipterus*	—	129	All over
9.	Perch-like fish	—	51	NW
10.	Pomfret	52	86	NW, NE
11.	Penaeid prawn	53	36	All over
12.	Other crustaceans	45	12	All over
13.	Cephalopods	175	119	All over
	Total	1,602	1,171	
	Others	345	215	
	Oceanic	500	(not assessed)	
	Grand Total	3,137	2,336	

* George, P.C, B.T. Antony Raja and K.C. George, "Fishery Resources of the Indian Economic Zone", *Souvenir*, Integrated Fisheries Project, Cochin, October 1977.

** See Chapter 3 of this book.

into an area hitherto considered not respectable enough even for small and medium entrepreneurs.

Keen as were the new parties to enter fishing, quite a number of the parties that entered fishing withdrew after an initial stunt. The operators of non-mechanized boats complained that their dwindling catches were due to the ravages to the eco-system by mechanized boats, which mechanized boat operators complained about the operations of large vessels, including poaching vessels, as well as on high capital and operating costs. Recoveries of loans reached an all-time low and many wondered whether fishing had become uneconomical or whether it was only a reflection of the lack of financial discipline among the boat owners.

Growth of mechanized sector

Fishing is not a licensed industry. The state governments had a fairly accurate estimates of the number of boats introduced, so long as the scheme of mechanization of fishing boats was supported with government finance and government guaranteed finance. Official estimates of the number of mechanized boats in operation for the various Five Year Plans are as follows :

At the beginning of 1st Plan*	(1951)	9
At the end of 1st Plan**	(1955-56)	863
At the end of 2nd Plan**	(1960-61)	2,161
At the end of 3rd Plan**	(1965-66)	5,206
At the end of 3rd annual Plans**	(1968-69)	7,708
At the end of 4th Plan***	(1973-74)	10,613
At the end of 5th Plan†	(1977-78)	14,282
At the end of 6th Plan‡ (anticipated)	(1984-85)	19,282
Actual at the end of 1983-84$		20,052

* Souvenir, 20th Anniversary of CMFRI, 1967.

** Report of the Working Group on Fisheries, Fifth Five Year Plan, 1973.

*** Statistical Supplement to the 8th meeting of the Central Board of Fisheries, 23rd March 1976.

† Statistical supplement to the 10th meeting of the Central Board of Fisheries, 29th August 1981.

‡ Sixth Five Year Plan 1980-85, Government of India, Planning Commission.

‡ Agenda, National Workshop on Fisheries, 15th June 1984.

However, CMFRI census gave a lower number of mechanized boats in actual operation. They are :

Number in operation during 1973-77@	8,086
Number in operation in 1980†	9,289

@ Marine Fisheries Information Service, T and E Series, No. 30, 1981.
† Marine Fisheries Information Service, T and E Series, No. 3, 1978.

The latter figure does not include mechanized boats in operation in Maharashtra which, according to the state's census in 1977 is 3,108. Even in respect of others also the CMFRI census represents the number of boats which are owned or shared by the fishermen. Hence, the government's official estimates are adopted in this discussion.

Growth of non-mechanized sector

At the national level the data in regard to non-mechanized boats is scarce. These are :

1948-49*	73,343
1961-62**	98,318
1973-77***	106,480
1980†	134,741

* Handbook of Indian Fisheries, prepared for the 3rd meeting of the IPFC, 1951.
** Marine Fish Production in India, 1960-68, *Bulletin No. 13*, CMFRI, 1969.
*** Marine Fisheries Information Service, T and E Ser. No. 3, 1978.
† *Ibid.* No. 30, 1981.

The quinquennial live stock census reported a combined figure of boats for the inland and marine sectors and hence is not referred to here.

Although the planners have been hoping to progressively replace non-mechanized boats with mechanized boats, the introduction of mechanized boats could not keep pace with the introduction of non-mechanized boats. Table 17.4 gives the latest reported number of fishing craft in marine sector, one by the CMFRI and the other by the state and that too for different

TABLE 17.4 : **Fishing craft in India**

	Mechanized boats		Non-mechanized boats	
	CMFRI census 1980*	State estimate 1983@	CMFRI census 1980*	State estimate 1983@
1. West Bengal	310	577	4,061	3,100
2. Orissa	106	775	9,728	9,728
3. Andhra Pradesh	456	800	36,013	37,514
4. Tamil Nadu	2,627	3,641	43,343	43,343
5. Pondicherry	176	231	1,750	2,500
6. Kerala	983	2,961	26,271	34,660
7. Karnataka	1,078	2,100	6,942	6,942
8. Goa	659	996	2,513	2,513
9. Maharashtra	NA	4,167	NA	8,729
10. Gujarat	2,894	3,548	4,120	4,466
11. Lakshadweep	NA	231	NA	NA
12. Andamans	NA	25	NA	763
	9,289$	20,052	134,741$	154,258%

Sources : 1. Mar. Fish. Inf. Serv., T & E Ser. No. 30, 1981.
2. Agenda Notes, National Workshop on Fisheries, 15th June 1984—Ministry of Agriculture.

Note : * Refers to those owned/shared by fishermen.
@ As compiled by Ministry of Agriculture.
$ Excluding Maharashtra, Lakshadweep and Andamans.
% Excluding Lakshadweep.

years. The wide disparity in the number of mechanized boats by the two sources may be due to a large number of mechanized boats being owned by non-fishermen.

Impact of increasing number of mechanized and non-mechanized boats

Despite the unsatisfactory data base, an attempt has been made in Table 17.5 to work out the impact of the increase in the number of mechanized and non-mechanized boats. In Tables 17.6 and 17.7, fish production has been separately computed for mechanized and non-mechanized boats for each state. The information with regard to contribution by mechanized and non-mechanized sectors as well as for the more important species is given in Tables 17.8 to 17.10.

This comparative study leads to the following broad conclusions :

1. Mechanized boats have registered a steady increase in their number, horse-power, sophistication and fishing capacity. In spite of the keen competition among mechanized boats and between mechanized and non-mechanized boats, the catch per mechanized boat has more than doubled during the past 12 years.
2. The number of non-mechanized boats also registered an overall increase roughly at the same rate as the increase in population. But this increase in the number of non-mechanized boats was associated with a fall in fish production by about 39 per cent, during the past 12 years. This fall is apparent from 1977 onwards.
3. Mechanized boats and more especially small trawlers account for 80.6 per cent and 63.3 per cent of the panaeid prawn production, which is the backbone of the Indian export of marine products. In respect of other species also mechanized boats maintain a share ranging from 46.9 per cent to 80.6 per cent.

COST OF PRODUCTION

The cost of production of marine capture fisheries varies with various craft gear combinations and place and year of operation. Much of the operations with large vessels are mainly intended for research, survey and training and hence have no significance to the present study. In the absence of a system of voluntary reporting, regulated fish marketing, and so on, data for the present study are taken from various sample surveys, case studies, and well considered estimates. These are categorized as those relating to non-mechanized boats, small mechanized boats and larger vessels.

Cost of production of fish by non-mechanized boats

There are four important studies on the cost of production of fish in the non-mechanized (artisanal) sector, the first by the

TABLE 17.5 : **Impact of increasing the number**

	1969	1970	1971	1972	1973	1974
Production from mechanized boats (Tonnes)	178,027	245,766	238,020	322,785	392,575	373,832
No. of mechanized boats in operation (extrapolated)	7,850	8,650	9,450	10,250	11,050	11,850
Average catch per mechanized boat/year (Tonnes/boat)	22.68	28.41	25.19	31.49	35.53	31.55
Production from non-mechanized boats (Tonnes)	735,603	839,841	923,369	657,264	827,665	843,965
No. of non-mechanized boats in operation (extrapolated)	118,660	120,400	122,200	124,000	125,800	127,600
Average catch/non-mechanized boat/year (Tonnes/boat)	6.20	6.98	7.56	5.30	6.58	6.61
Total fish production from mechanized and non-mechanized boats for the year (Tonnes)	913,630	1,085,609	1,161,389	980,049	1,220,240	1,217,797
Total number of mechanized and non-mechanized boats in operation (Total of extra-polated number)	126,450	129,050	131,650	134,250	136,850	139,450
Average catch per boat (mechanized and non-mechanized included) for the year (Tonnes/boat)	7.23	8.41	8.82	7.30	8.92	8.73
Contribution of mechanized boats to overall marine fish production	14.49	22.64	20.49	32.94	32.17	30.70

of fishing boats

1975	1976	1977	1978	1979	1980	1981
538,000	549,000	610,000	—	—	—	839,288
12,650	13,450	14,250	15,050	15,850	15,650	17,450
42.53	40.82	43.15	—	—	—	48.10
854,000	803,000	648,000	—	—	—	534,007
129,400	131,200	133,000	134,800	136,600	138,400	140,200
6.60	6.12	4.87	—	—	—	3.81
1,422,693	1,352,855	1,259,782	1,403,607	1,388,380	1,249,837	1,373,295*
142,050	144,650	147,250	149,850	152,450	155,050	157,650
10.02	9.35	9.11	9.37	9.11	8.06	8.71
37.82	40.58	48.81	—	—	—	61.11

Note : * excludes production from Lakshadweep, and Andaman and Nicobar Islands.

Read off from graph in the absence of published data.

TABLE 17.6 : **Fish production from mechanized boats**

('000 *Tonnes*)

	1969	1970	1971	1972	1973	1974	1975	1976	1977	1981
West Bengal)	1	1	1	2	2	4	7	18	3	13
Orissa)										19
Andhra Pradesh	2	2	2	5	5	7	8	15	26	27
Tamil Nadu	28	37	29	26	33	31	53	82	47	107
Kerala	28	53	48	39	94	101	179	55	107	96
Karnataka	9	15	17	49	23	32	11	17	56	130
Maharashtra	74	98	111	164	183	126	146	235	213	241
Gujarat	36	44	31	37	51	71	124	100	145	173
Pondicherry	—	—	1	1	2	—	1	3	1	4
Goa	—	—	—	—	—	—	9	24	17	29
Total	178	246	238	323	393	373	538	549	615	839

Source : 1969-74—CMFRI Bulletin No. 27, 1976
1975-77—Proc. IPFC Sect. III 1980 (read from graph)
1981 —Marine Fisheries Information Service, T and E Ser. No. 41, 1982

Note : Difference in total due to rounding off.

TABLE 17.7 : Fish production from non-mechanized boats

('000 Tonnes)

	1969	1970	1971	1972	1973	1974	1975	1976	1977	1981
West Bengal)										7
Orissa)	22	31	17	13	20	22	36	36	18)	16
Andhra Pradesh	76	73	82	80	95	151	148	116	76	89
Tamil Nadu	124	119	132	129	149	144	168	163	157	115
Kerala	267	340	398	257	355	319	242	273	239	178
Karnataka	67	102	87	44	69	45	76	78	41	24
Maharashtra	95	94	105	56	44	59	108	50	52	31
Gujarat	46	48	51	38	71	74	68	68	47	61
Pondicherry	10	10	9	8	7	7	8	8	8	7
Goa	—	—	—	—	—	16	18	11	10	5
All India	736	840	923	657	828	844	854	803	648	533

Source : 1969-74—CMFRI Bulletin No. 27, 1976.
1975-77—Proc. IPFC Sect. III, 1980 (read from graph).
1981 —Marine Fisheries Information Service, T and E Ser. No. 41, 1982.

Note : Column total does not total to All India total for years 1969-74.

TABLE 17.8 : **Contribution of mechanized boats to the total marine fish production in India (1981)**

Sl. No.	Name of state/U.T.	Fish production (tonnes) By mechanized boats	By mechanized and non-mechanized boats	Percentage contributed by mechanized boats
1.	West Bengal	13,098	20,107	65.1
2.	Orissa	19,176	35,655	53.8
3.	Andhra Pradesh	26,507	116,143	22.8
4.	Tamil Nadu	106,664	221,296	48.2
5.	Kerala	96,321	274,395	35.1
6.	Pondicherry	3,781	10,755	35.2
7.	Karnataka	129,518	153,349	84.5
8.	Goa	29,513	34,498	85.5
9.	Maharashtra	241,260	272,587	88.5
10.	Gujarat	173,450	234,510	74.8
	Total*	839,288	1,373,295	61.1

*Excluding Lakshadweep, Andaman and Nicobar Islands.

Source : Marine Fisheries Information Service, T and E Ser. No. 41, 1982.

Programme Evaluation Organization (PEO) of the Planning Commission during 1968-69, the second by Messrs John Kurien and Rolf William, the third by Gulbrandsen and the fourth by Mr. R. Ravikumar, the last three from the Bay of Bengal Programme of the FAO during 1980-84.

PEO Study

The PEO took a sample of country boats in their study on "Evaluation of the Programme of Mechanization of Fishing Boats", for purpose of comparison. Their sample covered all the 8 maritime states, but no attempt was made to sub-divide country boats by the different gear-craft combinations. The survey is based on the operation of 67 country boats operating from 27 fishing centres. The all-India average investment on a country boat including gear, during 1968-69 came to Rs. 5,400, as against Rs. 39,000 for a mechanized boat. The average operational cost of a mechanized boat was about four times that of a country boat. It

TABLE 17.9 : **Role of mechanized fishing boats in the Indian marine fish production (1981)**

Sl. No.	Name of fish	1981 marine fish production (tonnes) By mechanized boats	By all boats	Percentage of mechanized production in total
1.	Oil Sardine	103,558	221,026	46.9
2.	Mackerel	23,295	48,503	48.0
3.	Bombay duck	98,673	173,790	71.6
4.	Sciaenids	66,664	82,686	80.6
5.	Perches	22,078	30,811	71.7
6.	Pomfrets	37,330	48,722	76.7
7.	Tunnies	7,419	15,525	47.8
8.	Penaeid prawns	67,277	83,513	80.6
9.	Non-Penaeid prawns	50,508	61,430	82.2
10.	Others	362,456	643,289	56.3
	Total*	839,288	1,373,295	61.1

*Excluding Lakshadweep, Andaman and Nicobar Islands.
Source : Marine Fisheries Information Service, T and E Ser. No. 41, 1982.

was found that an investment of Rs. 100 on a country boat yielded four times higher catch in quantity and two times in value compared to the mechanized boat. But, figures in respect of individual states varied quite considerably. (Tables 17.11 to 17.13).

While specific figures are nowhere indicated, it has been mentioned that the cost of equipment (net) accounts for the bulk of the capital cost, which is as high as 78 per cent in Andhra Pradesh.

On the operational size, salaries and wages accounted for an average of 76.9 per cent of the total operating costs, PEO has given the break-up of operating costs for the different states during 1968-69. (See Table 17.12).

Based on the data furnished by the PEO, the cost of production of fish using non-mechanized boats during 1968-69 for the various states is calculated in Table 17.13.

While the country boats caught less and earned even lesser, they showed a better return for investment in terms of value, fish production, and generating of employment. In terms of production

TABLE 17.10 : **Penaeid prawn catch as between trawler type mechanized boats and others (1981)**

Sl. No.	Name of state/U.T.	Penaeid prawn catch of 1981: By trawler-type mechanized boats (tonnes)	Total catch (tonnes)	Percentage contribution by trawler-type mechanized boats
1.	West Bengal	—	244	—
2.	Orissa	1,118	1,328	89.5
3.	Andhra Pradesh	4,658	6,728	69.2
4.	Tamil Nadu	11,612	13,548	85.7
5.	Kerala	16,305	22,268	73.2
6.	Pondicherry	290	336	86.3
7.	Karnataka	3,231	4,122	78.4
8.	Goa	2,025	2,237	96.6
9.	Maharashtra	13,737	21,717	63.3
10.	Gujarat	7,949	10,985	72.4
	Total*	60,995	83,513	73.0

*Excluding Lakshadweep and Andaman and Nicobar Islands.

Source : Marine Fisheries Information Service, T and E Ser. No. 41, 1982.

TABLE 17.11 : **Average investment per non-mechanized boat during 1968-69**

States	Average investment (Rs)
Andhra Pradesh	6,778
Gujarat	2,758
Kerala	3,864
Maharashtra	8,150
Karnataka	2,995
Orissa	2,079
Tamil Nadu	8,052
West Bengal	4,819
All India	5,419

per day these non-mechanized boats produced only 36.2 per cent as much as mechanized boats. This comparison is brought out in Table 17.14.

TABLE 17.12 : **Average operational cost of country boat in 1968-69**

States	Average operational cost (Rs.)	Repairs (%)	Salary and wages (%)	Others (%)
Andhra Pradesh	10,204	14.5	85.5	—
Gujarat	1,204	16.0	81.3	2.7
Kerala	3,124	10.1	89.9	—
Karnataka	591	100.0	—	—
Maharashtra	4,970	8.4	69.0	22.6
Orissa	202	37.0	—	62.1
Tamil Nadu	7,547	22.6	66.4	11.0
West Bengal	15,348	4.7	94.0	1.3
All India	4,608	14.7	76.9	8.4

TABLE 17.13 : **Cost of production of fish during 1968-69 using non-mechanized boats**

States	Gross return per boat		Cost of production Rs./kg.
	Weight (kg)	Value (Rs.)	
Andhra Pradesh	15,530	13,940	0.90
Gujarat	5,050	4,834	0.96
Kerala	11,380	4,241	0.37
Karnataka	59,429	12,583	0.21
Maharashtra	6,250	8,300	1.33
Orissa	1,670	1,115	0.67
Tamil Nadu	29,310	9,769	0.33
West Bengal	7,750	28,865	3.72
All India	17,675	8,931	0.51

BOBP study on economics of artisanal and mechanized fisheries in Kerala

The FAO Bay of Bengal Programme (BOBP) for the development of small scale fisheries carried out a detailed study on the economics of artisanal and mechanized fisheries in Kerala. Although the study did not attempt a cost of production analysis, there is sufficient data available to attempt a cost of production

TABLE 17.14 : **Percentage of gross returns on investment, opera- generated and gross returns per mandays during mechanized boats**

Name of states	Mechanized boats						
	Percentage of gross return on Rs. 100				Mandays of employment per Rs. 100 invested	Gross return per manday	
	Investment		Operational cost			Weight	Value
	Weight (kg.)	Value (Rs.)	Weight (kg.)	Value (Rs.)		(kg.)	(Rs.)
Andhra Pradesh	69.2	62.8	110.4	100.6	2.3	30.6	27.8
Gujarat	113.8	109.1	224.2	214.2	6.0	19.0	18.1
Kerala	45.1	50.3	106.8	119.1	2.1	21.6	24.1
Maharashtra	56.1	89.6	94.7	151.3	5.8	14.7	23.4
Mysore	75.7	58.1	183.7	141.1	2.0	36.9	28.4
Orissa	52.4	39.4	160.9	120.9	1.2	41.9	31.5
Tamil Nadu	146.8	75.3	188.0	96.5	2.1	71.6	36.7
West Bengal	4.6	7.3	13.8	22.0	1.1	4.3	6.9
	74.9	68.6	137.6	126.0	2.7	28.1	25.7

tional cost including depreciation, employment 1968-69 in the operation of mechanized and non-

Non-mechanized boats						
Percentage of gross return on Rs. 100				Mandays of employment per Rs. 100 invested	Gross return per manday	
Investment		Operational cost				
Weight (kg.)	Value (Rs.)	Weight (kg.)	Value (Rs.)		Weight (kg.)	Value (Rs.)
229.0	205.6	138.9	124.7	21.4	10.7	9.6
183.2	175.3	396.5	379.3	15.5	11.8	11.3
294.4	109.7	330.5	123.2	28.4	10.4	3.9
76.7	101.8	120.3	159.6	8.9	8.6	11.4
984.3	420.1	8010.5	1696.1	54.0	36.7	7.8
80.3	53.6	428.5	286.1	4.0	20.1	13.4
64.0	121.3	308.4	102.8	11.8	30.8	10.3
160.8	599.0	49.1	182.9	17.7	9.0	33.8
326.1	164.8	344.9	174.3	17.7	18.4	9.3

analysis. The following conclusions can be drawn.

1. Although the traditional non-mechanized sector in Kerala account for 64.9 per cent of the marine fish production of the state, operation of these non-mechanized boats is either at a loss or at a break even point. The operation of mechanized boats is found to be a losing proposition in Kerala.
2. The concepts of investment and return have very little significance in the artisanal sector, where the major cost is the wage, which is generally a share of the value of the catch. The craft and gear are generally collectively owned and in any case the investment is not much. In many cases, the owners of the craft and gear are themselves participants in the fishing activity and in some cases the owner's share of the divisible earning is less than his share as an owner, once allowance is made for various operating costs and allocations made for capital replacement and interest charges. Hence, 'livelihood and survival', rather than 'profits' is the prime motive for fishermen investing in craft and gear.
3. The average income of an artisanal fisherman is less than that of an average trawlerman. The income would have been much more, if only he had the facility to operate throughout the year. As it is, the number of days of operation of each craft-gear combination varies from 13 to 149 a year. No doubt in certain cases, the fishermen could fish with another craft-gear combination when the season for combination is over. It is the inclement weather particularly the monsoon that forces him to stay at home, although monsoon fishing is more productive and remunerative than fair weather fishing. One method of improving the income and economics of artisanal fishermen will be to provide monsoon launching and landing facilities to enable him to continue fishing during the major part of the monsoon period.
4. Of the gross earnings, 49 to 84 per cent was paid as wages to the fishermen, the percentage will be higher

if the value of food and other expenses are also taken into account.

BOBP evaluation on fishing craft development in Kerala

Motorization of the large canoe, the 'thanguvallam' is one of the most significant developments in the traditional fishing sector. This is a problem on which the Indo-Norwegian Project after preliminary trials in 1952-53 came to the conclusion that the thanguvallam is unfit for motorization with inboard and outboard engine. Now after 30 years the same boat has been motorized by merely clamping the outboard engine on a bracket costing Rs. 25 on the starboard side. Interestingly enough the 'thanguvallam' which is 15 metres long and carries a crew of 15, is propelled by a 5 HP outboard engine. Limited studies have shown that a motorized 'thanguvallam' operating an encircling net catches on an average 70 per cent more fish compared to the non-motorized version. Motorization also enabled making more trips, so that the value of the catch is 128 per cent higher in comparison with the non-motorized thanguvallam. John Kurien and Rolf William have reported that the encircling net is the only fishing technique in Kerala which has attained a return on investment, which is higher than the minimum interest of 36 per cent that prevails in the informal credit market in the artisanal fishing villages of southern Kerala.

Use of outboard engines on BOBP designed boats intended for gill netting did not result in any significant increase in income. But, the data presented would show as if the motorization has made the fishermen lazy. Once used to the outboard engine, the crew did not go out for fishing by rowing, if the outboard engine was out of order or kerosene was not available. On the positive side, credit should be given for eliminating the strenuous effort of rowing for 2-3 hours a day.

The experimental introduction of 100 outboard engines at Muttom in the sixties showed a general tendency for the fishermen to stop fishing when a good catch was obtained, and to go on searching for fish during the poor season for fishing. A similar trend is seen in Kerala also. But an intelligent use of the outboard engine is to use the engine to the maximum extent when the catches are good and stop using it when fishing is poor.

All outboard engines currently in use are operating on kerosene, which is not an efficient fuel. Hence BOBP tried a 5 HP industrial type aircooled diesel engine with direct drive as a propulsion unit. The engine is housed in a watertight box, which in turn is pivoted to enable the propeller and the shaft to be raised to avoid damage during beaching. While the idea is good, there are still defects with the engine and the transmission. The fishermen are also not showing much interest in this innovation, as motorization of the thanguvallam with outboard engine has caught their attention.

The BOBP also introduced small sailing boats as replacement of smaller canoes. But in actual operation it was found that fishermen could use sails only for 14 per cent of the total travelling time, mainly due to absence of favourable winds. Under optimum conditions they could probably use the sails for about 25 per cent of the travelling time. This would mean that the changes effected to make the craft suitable for sailing should be scaled down keeping in view the need for rowing most of the time.

Among other important findings of BOBP, mention must be made of the following :

1. The BOBP fishing gear specialist found that the large mesh gill nets in use in Kerala were of optimum twine, mesh size and well mounted. There was little that could be done to improve the fishing gear.
2. Most canoes did not carry sufficient quantity of small mesh gill net to utilize the full capacity.
3. The gill-netters currently in use were found to be overpowered. It is essential that engine horse power of gill-netters should be drastically scaled down to effect economy and to make gill-netting with mechanized boats a viable proposition in Kerala.

It must be mentioned in this connection that fishermen from Colachel are fishing very successfully with fairly high powered gill-netters. These fishermen, besides being experts in gill-netting, also shift their fishing from place to place depending on the availability of fish. While shifting if they are to operate from bar mouths, it is necessary to have sufficient power to negotiate against currents. Taking all these aspects, it would appear that motorizing the small canoe with low horse power outboard engine would be more acceptable. Such a craft will not require harbour for landing, as the canoe is easily beach landed. There is also no need to keep a watch over the engine, as the outboard engine is easily removed and kept with the owner when not in use.

BOBP commercial evaluation of beach landing craft IND-13

IND-13 is a beach landing craft designed by BOBP and built in marine plywood, which all seams taped with FRP and powered with Lombardini 5 HP engine. The engine is located in a water-tight metal box and the whole power plant along with propeller shaft can be titled so that the propeller will not get damaged during beach landing. However, the hull and the engine required improvements and IND-20 is the modified version. BOBP has given an estimate of relative economics of IND-20 and the local Nava boat, based on data collected on three IND-13 and three Nava boats (See Table 17.15).

If an interest at 12 per cent is charged on capital, both IND-20 and Nava are seen working at a loss, a loss of Rs. 3,718 in the case of IND-20 and Rs. 1,244 in the case of Nava. The calculation of BOBP require some refinement. In the first instance there is no need to set apart 40 per cent of the net income after deducting the cost of fuel, oil and food, as 5 crew members only are engaged on IND, as against 6 on Nava. A $33\frac{1}{3}$ per cent provision seems a more reasonable figure. If credit for $6\frac{2}{3}$ per cent is given the loss after making allowance for interest at 12 per cent would come down to Rs. 1,239, which is almost the same as Nava. In any case with this level of technological improvement, even the master-fishermen who were engaged on this boat were not prepared to purchase them and only one of them volunteered to pay even part of the income derived by operating these boats.

Cost of production of fish by mechanized boats

The cost of production as well as economics of mechanized fishing have been subjects of detailed study by various agencies and individuals, the notable ones being studied by :

TABLE 17.15 : **Estimate of costs and earnings of IND-20 beachcraft and Nava**

	IND-20	Nava
Number of crew	5	6
Number of fishing days	220	206
Catch per annum :		
Quantity (tonnes)	12.8	7.7
Value (Rs)	48,000	29,600
Investment (Rs)		
Craft hull	30,000	12,500
Engine	12,000	—
Sail-rig	1,500	—
Nets	20,000	20,000
Total	63,500	32,500
Operating costs (Rs) :		
Fuel and oil	5,316	—
Food Rs. 5/crew member/day	5,500	6,180
Crew share at 40% of gross income minus fuel oil and food	14,874	11,714
Gear repair and replacement	6,667	6,667
Engine repair and replacement	1,540	—
Hull repair	770	615
Insurance at 2%	1,270	650
Janata insurance for crew	60	72
Total	35,997	25,794
Surplus before depreciation and interest (Rs)	12,003	3,806
Depreciation (Rs) :		
Hull (15 years)	2,000	1,250 (10 years)
Engine (7 years)	1,714	—
Sail-rig	188	—
	3,902	1,250
Surplus after depreciation	8,101	2,556
Rate of return (%)	12.8	7.9

1. Prof. G.M. Gerhardsen, Senior Fisheries Adviser from the FAO.
2. Programme Evaluation Organization of the Planning Commission.
3. Commercial Banks.
4. Bay of Bengal Programme (in Kerala).
5. Indian Institute of Management, Ahmedabad.

Study by Prof. Gerhardsen

During his 2 years of work in India (1966-68) as Senior Fisheries Adviser from the FAO, Prof. Gerhardsen collected a mass of information on the working of mechanized boats in the various maritime states and came to the conclusion that mechanized fishing operations were viable and that subsidies could be withdrawn. These findings were communicated to the state governments in the form of guidelines for the preparation of the Fourth Five Year Plan.

PEO Study

The study by the Programme Evaluation Organization of the Planning Commission was on 'Evaluation of the performance of mechanization of fishing boats, from the point of fish production, income generation, employment, modernization, and so on. While the PEO did not attempt an analysis of the cost of production, adequate data are available to attempt a macro-analysis of the cost of production. In all, the PEO studied the working of 382 mechanized boats, spread over the 8 maritime states. As by then the mechanized boats had not clearly diversified into trawlers, gill-netters, long-liners, purse-seiners, and so on the analysis was on size difference and ownership difference. Mechanized boats were categorized as those below 10 metres and those of 10 metres and above. An analysis of the comparative performance of boats in the public, private and co-operative sectors, further categorized by size is given in Table 17.16. The data available in the PEO study has been made use of to work out cost of production in Table 17.17. Details of operational cost are given in Table 17.18. The salient observations of this analysis are as follows :

1. While private sector mechanized boats could operate on

TABLE 17.16 : **Comparative performance of public, co-operative and private sectors in the operation of mechanized boats during 1968-69**

Name of state	Category	Average no. of days at sea per boat per annum			Average gross earning per boat per annum (Rs. '000)			Average operational cost per boat per annum (Rs. '000)			Net earning per boat per annum (excluding interest and depreciation (Rs. '000)		
		Public	Co-op.	Private	Public	Co-op.	Private	Public	Co-op.	Private	Public	Co-op.	Private
Andhra Pradesh	A	131	184	212	15.7	27.5	49.0	21.1	25.4	35.9	−5.4	2.1	13.2
	B	—	—	211	—	—	29.9	—	—	22.9	—	—	7.0
Gujarat	A	—	—	207.1	—	—	20.3	—	—	9.3	—	—	11.0
	B	—	—	199.0	—	—	10.5	—	—	4.3	—	—	6.2
Kerala	A	—	109	160	—	18.6	34.5	—	20.4	26.7	—	−1.8	7.8
	B	—	152	159	—	17.8	22.1	—	17.0	14.4	—	0.8	7.7
Maharashtra	A	—	196	179	—	43.1	36.5	—	65.6	23.4	—	−22.5	13.1
	B	—	—	188	—	—	20.9	—	—	12.7	—	—	8.2
Mysore	A	—	—	150	—	—	27.9	—	—	17.5	—	—	11.4
	B	—	—	149	—	—	22.5	—	—	12.9	—	—	9.6
Orissa	A	110	—	—	23.0	—	—	15.3	—	—	7.7	—	—
	B	122	—	—	13.8	—	—	5.5	—	—	8.3	—	—
Tamil Nadu	A	87.0	—	220.2	1.9	—	48.5	9.6	—	39.7	−7.7	—	39.8
	B	176.5	—	180.2	5.1	—	40.2	12.2	—	33.0	−7.1	—	37.3
West Bengal	A	67	—	—	2.0	—	—	7.2	—	—	−5.1	—	—
	B	62	—	—	2.4	—	—	6.8	—	—	−4.4	—	—
All India	A	94.6	152.7	184.7	18.7	25.0	36.2	14.4	23.4	22.6	4.3	1.6	13.6
	B	96.6	152.4	177.6	8.9	17.8	22.6	6.8	14.6	14.5	1.1	3.2	8.1

Note : A=Mechanized boats of length 10 metres and above.
B=Mechanized boats of length less than 10 metres.

TABLE 17.17 : **Cost of production of fish using mechanized boats during 1968-69 (Rs.)**

Name of state	Capital	Depreciation	Interest on capital	Operating cost	Total cost of production	Total catch	Cost of production	Actual earning	Net income
	(Rs.)	(Rs.)	(Rs.)	(Rs.)	(Rs.)	(Kg.)	(Rs./Kg.)	(Rs.)	(Rs.)
Andhra Pradesh	46,762	4,672	5,845	27,133	37,650	36,940	1.02	33,531	4,119
Gujarat	20,068	2,007	2,509	5,535	10,051	13,390	0.75	12,838	+2,787
Kerala	56,411	5,641	7,051	14,740	27,432	19,570	1.40	21,825	−5,607
Maharashtra	30,688	3,069	3,836	20,781	27,686	21,930	1.26	35,054	+7,368
Mysore	50,938	5,094	6,367	13,689	25,150	30,821	0.82	23,669	−1,483
Orissa	48,789	4,879	6,099	11,603	22,580	26,140	0.86	19,639	−2,941
Tamil Nadu	60,091	6,009	7,511	32,950	46,470	76,540	0.61	31,291	−7,179
West Bengal	14,011	1,401	1,751	6,874	10,026	1,496	6.70	2,396	−4,478
All India	33,809	3,281	4,226	17,684	25,291	29,366	0.86	26,899	−1,608

TABLE 17.18 : **Operational cost of mechanized boats in 1968-69**

Sl. No.	State	Average operational cost (Rs.)	Average expenditure (Rs.) on			
			Repairs and replace-ments	Fuel and lubricants	Salary and wages	Others
1.	Andhra Pradesh	27,133	6,531	10,500	9,120	982
2.	Gujarat	5,535	735	1,694	2,955	151
3.	Kerala	14,740	3,276	6,910	3,581	973
4.	Karnataka	13,689	4,140	5,095	2,757	1,697
5.	Maharashtra	20,781	2,203	6,309	9,531	2,738
6.	Orissa	11,603	1,630	3,551	5,111	1,311
7.	Tamil Nadu	32,950	6,022	12,677	11,844	2,408
8.	West Bengal	6,874	596	130	6,009	139
	All India	17,684	3,216	6,355	6,549	1,564

an average for 184.7 days with mechanized boats of 10 metres length and above, and 177.6 days with mechanized boats of less than 10 metres, the public sector performance was 64.6 days and 96.6 days respectively; and the co-operative sector performance was 152.7 days and 152.4 days respectively. Naturally boats in the private sector could make a reasonable income over the operational expenses, while the other two sectors could only break even.

2. These operations when assessed on a purely commercial plane were found to uneconomical the average loss being about 6.4 per cent except in Maharashtra where it was economical. Since the capital was heavily subsidized and interest rates were much lower, the allottees of mechanized boats were naturally quite happy with the returns.
3. On an average 70 per cent of the income was spent on operational expenses, comprising 18 per cent on repair and replacement, 36 per cent on fuel and lubricants, 37 per cent on salary and wages, and 9 per cent on other operating costs. With 54 per cent of the operating costs relating to the machinery, it is essential that the

fishermen should use his machinery judiciously. It has been mentioned elsewhere that fishermen used his engine for short trips and fewer occasions when fishing was good, while unnecessarily went on searching for fish when fishing was poor.

Study by commercial banks

Commercial banks, NABARD, and so on have been closely monitoring the cost of production and economics of mechanized boat operations. While banks were generally happy with repayment position in making timely repayments in other states. Repayments were generally satisfactory in the cases of advance against full security or collateral provided by the loanee or when loanee himself had raised substantial capital. The maximum incidence of default was where the loan was secured by government guarantee. While the contract provided for seizure of boats on continued default, both government and banks were unwilling to invoke this provision as there could be deterioration in the condition of boat as well as theft of parts while in their custody.

Study by BOBP

The BOBP studies the economics of artisanal and mechanized fisheries of Kerala; based on which cost of production has been worked out in Table 17.19. During 1980-81, mechanized fishing operations were at a loss in Kerala, the percentage of loss being 20 per cent in respect of mechanized boats operating trawl nets and 35 per cent in respect of mechanized boats operating gill nets. According to the authors the year was an exceptionally bad one owing to poor fishing and steep increase in fuel price.

The crew remuneration on mechanized boat worked out to only 15 per cent in respect of trawlers and 26 per cent in respect of gill-netters. Yet in actual terms they were better paid than their fellow fishermen working on non-mechanized boats and that too under more strenuous conditions. The average remuneration per day of operation of a fisherman working on a mechanized boat in Kerala during 1980-81 came to Rs. 21.69 in respect of trawlers, and Rs. 20.45 in respect of gill-netters.

Non-operational expenses, namely, depreciation, interest on capital and insurance, came to 25.5 per cent of the capital cost;

TABLE 17.19 : **Cost of production of fish by mechanized boats in Kerala during 1980-81**

	Trawl net with mechanized boats	Large mesh gill-net with mechanized boats
Number of unit monitored	30	15
Capital investment on craft (Rs.)	128,500	24,733
Capital investment on gear (Rs.)	3,973	14,367
Expected life of craft (years)	10	10
Expected life of gear (years)	1	6
Depreciation on craft (Rs.)	12,850	2,473
Depreciation on gear (Rs.)	3,973	2,394
Interest on capital at 12.5% (Rs.)	16,559	4,888
Insurance at 3% (Rs.)	3,855	742
Total operating cost/trip (Rs.)	387	126.50
Average number of trips/year	157	98
Total operating cost per annum (Rs.)	60,539	12,397
Per capital remuneration to each crew member for the year (Rs.)	3,406	2,004
Average number of crew members	5	4
Total remuneration to the crew for the whole year (Rs.)	17,030	8,016
Interest on working capital (Rs.)	633	129
Total cost of production/year (Rs.)	115,659	31,039
Catch landed per annum (kg)	19,397	6,581
Cost of production (Rs./kg)	5.96	4.72
Price realized (Rs./kg)	4.79	3.05
Profit (+) or loss (—) (Rs.)	—1.17	—1.67
Percentage of loss	20	35

and 33 per cent of the cost of production in the case of trawlers and 34 per cent in the case of gill-netters. This is based on the usual norm of allowing 10 per cent on depreciation, 12.5 per cent on interest on capital, and 3 per cent on insurance. As the average life of a mechanized boat is well over 20 years, depreciation at a lower percentage is indicated. Similarly the interest payable is on the outstanding balance and would work out to annual interest payment of 8-9 per cent only. However, in an inflationary economy a higher percentage as depreciation is justified as the capital requirement of acquiring a new boat at the end of 20 years could be four times higher.

Operational costs account for 52 per cent in the case of trawlers and 40 per cent in the case of gill-netters of the total cost of production. The frequent upward revisions of fuel price were perhaps the single largest element that adversely affected the economics of mechanized boat operation. To some extent this fuel price increase has been compensated by increased price realization. This will be discussed in detail later.

Study by Indian Institute of Management, Ahmedabad

The Indian Institute of Management, Ahmedabad, carried out in 1977-78 a micro-study in Gujarat analysing the problems in harvesting and processing in the management of marine fisheries. Their study is based on a sample of 30 boats, which included outboard motors (OBM), gill-netters, trawler-cum-gill-netters and trawlers, all operating from Veraval. The study worked out the breakeven point in terms of number of operational days in the year of observation as well as for a normal year. A summary is given in Table 17.20.

The study reveals that the least sensitive and most viable fishing unit in Gujarat is the OBM, which breaks even by 95 days, where as it takes 138 days in the case of gill-netter, 114 days in respect of trawler-cum-gill-netter, and 115 days in respect of trawler. In the bad year like 1977-78, it takes 204 days for gill-netters, 230 days for trawler-cum-gill-netter, and 251 days for trawlers to breakeven. The latter two propositions are incapable of attainment.

At the breakeven level the fixed cost represents 65 per cent to 78 per cent of the total cost of production. In such a situation the burden of the fixed cost is almost crushing.

Of the variable cost, fuel and lubricants account for 66 per cent in case of OBM, 62 per cent in case of gill-netter, 75 per cent in respect of trawler-cum-gill-netter and 84 per cent in respect of trawler. With the further revision of fuel cost since then this percentage must have gone up.

Table 17.21 gives variety-wise composition and their value for the different craft-gear combinations. During 1977-78, OBM in Gujarat caught on an average 17 tonnes, as against 30 tonnes by gill-netter, 47 tonnes by trawler-cum-gill-netter and 64 tonnes by trawler. The unit value realized was Rs. 3.21 for OBM, Rs. 2.71 for

TABLE 17.20 : Breakeven point of mechanized boat operation in Gujarat during 1977-78

Items	OBM boats	Gill-netter	Trawler cum-gill-netter	Trawler
Annual fixed costs				
Boat repair and maintenance	600	1,716	2,032	2,340
Engine repair and maintenance	1,120	2,458	2,646	3,524
Others	1,026	4,122	4,678	5,864
Crew salaries*	6,000	13,500	16,704	16,704
Depreciation	8,125	20,750	22,597	17,212
Interest on borrowed capital	. .	13,687	19,124	19,124
Total	10,871 (16,871)	42,733 (56,233)	50,751 (7,445)	47,204 (63,908)
Variable cost/day				
Fuel	38.28	53.67	103.84	144.67
Lubricant	9.07	14.38	17.16	17.94
Wages to hired labour**	2.91	4.60	6.15	6.55
Food expenses of crew	13.46	22.81	16.96	15.26
Expenditure on ice and water	1.54	6.20	6.18	10.86
Cost of net repairs	5.59	12.50	11.52	3.58
Total	70.85	113.98	161.81	193.83
Calculation of breakeven point				
Expected value of catch/day	247	389	454	447
Normalised expected catch/day	. .	518	752	742
Average variable cost per day	71	114	162	199
Net contribution to fixed cost/day	176	275	292	248
Net contribution to normalised	225	405	590	543
Breakeven (no. of days)	61	155	173	190
Break when crew salaries are taken into account	95	204	230	251
Breakeven (days) with normalised catches	61	105	85	87
Break when crew salaries are taken into account	95	138	114	115

Note : *It is assmued that all except 1 is hired crew
**Salaries of persons employed on monthly basis excluded figures in brackets are total expenditure with crew salary, others are without crew salary.

Source : After U.K. Srivastava *et al.*, 1979.

TABLE 17.21 : Variety-wise composition of fish catch by different types of fishing boats along the Gujarat coast (1977-78)

Varieties	OBM catch (%)		Gill-netter catch (%)		Trawler-cum-gill netter catch (%)		Trawler catch (%)	
	Qty.	Value	Qty.	Value	Qty.	Value	Qty.	Value
Exportable Varieties								
(a) High priced	0.1	1.7	—	—	0.3	9.0	1.3	16.9
(b) Low priced	—	—	—	—	13.5	31.7	8.9	26.0
Sub-total	0.1	1.7	—	—	14.1	40.7	10.2	42.9
Table Variety								
(a) High priced	61.8	79.9	47.8	70.9	10.7	26.2	2.6	10.1
(b) Medium priced	7.6	5.3	9.6	7.4	8.7	8.4	5.9	11.1
(c) Low priced	30.3	13.0	41.9	21.0	23.4	14.2	19.6	17.7
Sub-total	99.7	98.2	99.3	99.5	42.8	48.8	28.1	38.9
Small schooling								
Fish	0.2	0.1	0.7	0.5	43.1	10.5	61.7	18.2
Total	100	100	100	100	100	100	100	100
Actual values	16891	54263	30257	82119	49117	93100	63926	85663
Unit	kg.	Rs.	kg.	Rs.	kg.	Rs.	kg.	Rs.

gill-netters, Rs. 1.90 for trawler-cum-gill-netter, and Rs. 1.34 for trawler per kg. of fish caught. In the case of OBM and gill-netter, practically the entire catch and value realized came from table fish, where as miscellaneous fish (referred to as small schooling fish by IIMMA) formed the main bulk of catch. The main income of trawlers came from exportable varieties, while table fish and exportable varieties accounted for the main income of trawler-cum-gill-netters. In Gujarat trawlers landed 28.1 per cent of table fish realizing 38.9 per cent of the gross income.

Table 17.22 gives an analysis of the number of fishing days and the value of catch on a quarterly basis. The best fishing season is the post monsoon period, accounting for the maximum number of fishing days and returns. While the production during the monsoon period is also good, the gross earning is drastically reduced as boats are not able to operate during the major part of the monsoon months. The least productive part of the year is the pre-monsoon period. This observation corroborates with the finding of the BOBP in respect of Kerala. But unlike Kattumarams, which can fish during the monsoon, mechanized boats suspend fishing during the monsoon months. Since mechanized boats are taking out of water during monsoon for annual repairs and also for want of space in the fishing harbour, there is no chance of their going fishing during the short spells of calm weather during the monsoon period.

Study by various state governments

Even though many state governments have undertaken close monitoring of the working of their mechanized boats to assess justification of any waver/rephasing of loan repayment, published information is lacking to attempt a cost of production analysis. Hence as a part of the present study a simple questionnaire was circulated and an analysis of the information received from various state governments is given in Table 17.23.

It is seen that the fishing operations are economical in all states except Karnataka.

In Karnataka, the gill net operations could just breakeven, the purse-seine operations could not earn sufficient to set apart 10 per cent on boat depreciation, and 20 per cent on net depreciation, while trawlers could not earn much beyond the operational

TABLE 17.22 : **Quarter-wise expected value of catch (catch terms) for different types of boats in Gujarat—1977-78**

Quarters	OBM boats			Gill-netters			Trawler-cum-gill-netter			Trawlers		
	Expected value of catch/day (Rs.)	No. of fishing days	Total value of catch (Rs.)	Expected value of catch/day (Rs.)	No. of fishing days	Total value of catch (Rs.)	Expected value of catch/day (Rs.)	No. of fishing days	Total value of catch (Rs.)	Expected value of catch/day (Rs.)	No. of fishing days	Total value of catch (Rs.)
Quarter I	340	12	4,080	465	12	5,580	338	12	4,056	618	12	7,416
July-Sept.				(620)	(12)	(7,440)	(563)	(15)	(8,445)	(1,030)	(15)	(15,450)
Quarter II	368	74	27,232	513	75	39,475	657	72	47,304	542	73	39,566
Oct.-Dec.				(684)	(75)	(51,300)	(1,095)	(75)	(82,125)	(903)	(73)	(65,919)
Quarter III	177	75	13,275	312	72	22,464	364	73	26,572	329	70	23,030
Jan.-March				(416)	(72)	(29,952)	(607)	(78)	(47,340)	(548)	(73)	(40,000)
Quarter IV	100	59	9,676	300	52	15,600	316	48	15,168	423	37	15,651
				(400)	(52)	(20,800)	(527)	(52)	(27,404)	(705)	(49)	(34,545)
Season as	247	220	54,263	389	211	82,119	454	205	93,104	447	192	85,663
a whole				(518)	(211)	(109,492)	(752)	(220)	(165,320)	(742)	(210)	(155,918)

Note : Figures in parentheses are the normalized, expected value of catches, number of fishing days and total value of catches respectively. To get the normalized value of different columns the following assumptions are made. (i) Catches of OBM boats are not affected much, (ii) the average daily catch (in value terms) during the year 1977-78 for the gill-netter boats was less by 25% than in a normal year, (iii) in case of trawlers and trawler-cum-gill-netters the catch during 1977-78 was less by 40% than in a normal year, and (iv) Trawlers and trawlers-cum-gill-netters have more number of fishing days in a normal year.

expenses. The trawler and purse-seine operations were economical in Karnataka until a few years back, showing that their number has increased to a level where it ceases to be economical. While it may be argued that the provision for depreciation is excessive as the life of a purse-seiner is about 20-30 years, but considering the replacement value, a higher replacement provision is desirable. Nevertheless in an inflationary economy such marginally losing propositions automatically become economical over a period of years with the fish prices increasing, while the capital invested remains unchanged. It has also to be appreciated that in Karnataka the purse-seine fishery depends on oil sardine and mackerel which are high fluctuating fisheries. Hence it is necessary to diversify. In fact the Karnataka purse-seiners have already started diversifying into fishing for cat fish and to some extent anchoviella. It is also very important to point out that use of high efficiency gear should always be associated with built-in safeguards against over-exploitation. Another area of useful diversification will be use of these purse-seiners for trawling, so that fishing can continue during the off-season for purse-seining.

It is the high percentage of quality food fish that sustains trawling and gill-netting along the Gujarat and Maharashtra coasts, and the shrimps along the Orissa and Andhra coasts. One of the reasons for the low returns of Karnataka mechanized fishing is the poor representation of quality food fish as well as large sized shrimp. Here the emphasis should be to resort to value-added processing to realize a better market value.

The labour content of purse-seine operations is very high, because the purse-seiners are not equipped with power blocks and has to depend on a number of other boats to ferry the catch. Hence a new design of purse-seine boats equipped with power blocks/triplex, large fish holds and fish pumps for discharge of fish would considerably reduce the labour cost. Such a move, although economical from the operator's point of view, may not be desirable under conditions prevailing in India.

Study by Krishna Iyer, *et al.*, 1983

This study is limited to the effect of increase in the number of fishing trips on the economic efficiency of 9.82 metres and 11 metres mechanized fishing boats along the Kerala coast. The study is based on the results collected from 50 boats of each category. The cost and earning tables are given in Tables 17.24 and 17.25.

TABLE 17.24 : **Cost and earning of a 9.82 m fishing trawler during 1980-81 for varying number of fishing trips**

No. of trips	Receipts (Rs.)	Average recepit per trip (Rs.)	Fixed cost (Rs.)	Variable cost (Rs.)	Percentage of profit to total cost
180	1,30,283	724	56,700	76,650	− 2.45
185	1,36,540	738	56,700	79,852	0
200	1,56,169	781	56,700	89,159	+ 7.09
225	1,91,735	852	56,700	105,670	+18.08
250	2,30,867	923	56,700	123,428	+28.17

TABLE 17.25 : **Cost and earning of a 11 m fishing trawler during 1980-81 for varying number of fishing trips**

No. of trips	Receipts (Rs.)	Average receipt per trip (Rs.)	Fixed cost (Rs.)	Variable cost (Rs.)	Percentage of profit over total cost
180	1,46,389	813	77,150	90,228	−12.54
200	1,73,960	870	77,150	1,03,966	− 3.95
210	1,88,593	898	77,150	1,11,142	+ 0.16
215	1,96,121	912	77,150	1,14,003	+ 2.60
225	2,11,602	940	77,150	1,22,275	+ 6.10
250	2,52,777	1011	77,150	1,41,822	+15.43

As is expected, the data shows a positive correlation between the number of fishing trips and net earning. Since the fixed cost remains unchanged, operation beyond a limit, the breakeven point, is a profit reduced to the extent of variable cost. The breakeven point is 185 days in respect of the 9.82 metres boat and 210 days for the 11 metres boat. The authors then proceeded to work out varying levels of prawn and fish in the catch to breakeven as well as to arrive a different slabs of profitability.

This study also confirms that ultimately it is the quantum of prawn catch that sustains fishing by mechanized boats, at least along the Kerala coast, where the percentage of quality fish in the trawl catches is poor.

Cost of production of fish by deep sea fishing vessels

The commercial fishing fleet in India is at present constituted by about 60 shrimp trawlers, mostly owned by private fishing companies, but some owned by state fisheries corporations. Among the private companies come the category of large houses. A comparative table based on the response received from fishing companies and corporations is presented in Table 17.26.

It is seen that shrimp trawling is profitable in the private sector. The public sector operated for fewer number of days had they also operated for the same number of days, the state corporations would have also earned profit. However, in recent years their operarions have considerably improved and are likely to breakeven in the near future.

The fixed cost in deep sea fishing is as high as 35 to 40 per cent, in spite of the fact that this sector has received concessional finance, which no other fishing sector has received. It is evident that at commercial rates of interest all these operations will be uneconomical.

Fuel accounts for a high percentage of the cost of production. During a full year a 365-380 HP trawler engine consumes about 350 kilolitres of fuel, whose price has gone up three times between 1978 and 1983. As a result during 1981, as much as 55 per cent of the operational cost was on fuel. Wages to floating staff account for 10 to 15 per cent of the operating cost, besides almost an equal expense on food expenses. While life on board fishing vessels is hard, their emoluments are also attractive as they get regular pay, an incentive allowance equal to or more than the pay, free food, and free accommodation. The income of fishing skippers is now one of the highest in the country.

Case studies on economics of boats

Surprisingly there are very few published case studies, although each boat owner must be making his own balance-sheet on the economics of operation. The extensive migration of mechanized

TABLE 17.26 : **Economics of operation of 23 metre shrimp outrigger trawlers of 104 to 154 CRT and 365 to 380 HP (Rs.)**

Ownership of vessel	Public sector	Private sector	
		Large house	Medium entrepreneur
Year of report	1980-81	1980-81	1978
Fixed cost			
Depreciation	123,000	150,000	225,000
Interest on capital	213,000	375,000	315,005
Insurance	51,250	37,500	45,000
Salary and wages to floating staff	96,764	185,000	120,000
Salary to shore staff	31,564	30,000	36,000
Office expenses	37,606	70,000	12,000
Others	33,530	25,000	90,000
Total	586,616	872,500	843,000
Variable cost			
Bonus, incentive allowance	155,450	100,000	120,600
Fuel and lubricants	375,955	825,000	390,000
Port dues	10,853	40,000	24,000
Repair and maintenance	123,733	200,000	180,000
Food items	148,844	170,000	—
Consumable stores	278,837	100,000	192,000
Processing expenses	—	—	300,000
Others	—	80,000	—
Total	1093,672	1515,000	1206,600
Income			
Fish	2,857	12,000	—
Shrimp	1433,503	2500,000	2400,000
Others	6,047	—	—
Total	1442,407	2500,000	2400,000
Net earning	(–) 237.881	112,500	350,400

boats and country boats following a fairly regular pattern is an indication of the better batch and income realization characteristic of that region for that part of the year.

Experience of Indo-Norwegian Project, Cochin

Thankappan Achari made an assessment of the impact of the

mechanization programme undertaken between 1956 and 1963 by the Indo-Norwegian Project. The mechanized boats used during those years were small, low powered and low prices, and supported by liberal subsidies Table (17.27).

TABLE 17.27 : **Capital cost of mechanized fishing boats under the Indo-Norwegian project during 1956-1963**

Type of boat	No. of boats issued	With or without gear	Total capital cost (Rs. '000)	Sub-sidised cost (Rs. '000)	Cost per boat Actual (Rs.)	Cost per boat Subsidised (Rs.)
1. 22 ft. (4.5 hp)	67	with gear	407	148	2,883	1,442
2. 23.5 ft. (8-10 hp)	23	without gear	151	96	6,748	4,322
3. 25 ft. (8-10 hp)	39	without gear	312	202	7,220	4,637
4. 25 ft. (16 hp)	9	with gear	159	101	16,400	10,425
	138		1,029	547		

Table 17.28 gives the economics of mechanized fishing, compared with that of traditional canoes, both big and small. This shows that, while the cost of production is highest in the case of mechanized boats, higher production and more especially the saving on the number of crew members has resulted in a higher *per capita* earning.

Pair trawling

Gopinatha Pillai and Sathiadhas of CMFRI have given an account of pair trawling under the guidance of BOBP in Palk Bag (Tamil Nadu). From February to April 1982, 1,069 units were operated catching 1,166.70 tonnes of fish, using mechanized boats of 9.14m to 9.75m length and having engine horse power ranging from 45 to 70. This works out to 1,093.5 kg. of fish per unit of operation. Apart from very high catch, the composition was very much in favour of high priced varieties namely, 29.66 per cent of silver pomfret, 29.96 per cent of rainbow sardine, 9.32 per cent cat fish, 5.75 per cent silver bellies, 4.79 per cent rays and, 2.98 per cent of miscellaneous fishes. The unit price realization was comparatively low in the absence of suitable marketing arrange-

TABLE 17.28 : **Economic results of fishing operations by small craft (Average for 1959-62)**

Items	Traditional canoes		Mechanized boats		
	Small	Big	22 ft. 4-5 hp	25 ft. 8-10 hp*	23.5 ft. 8-10 hp**
1. Annual catch per boat (kg.)	8,603	8,010	8,841	14,563	11,652
2. Annual gross fishing income per boat (Rs.)	2,389	3,667	3,643	7,248	8,156
3. Annual net income per boat (Rs.)	2,032	3,148	1,883	4,559	5,244
4. Size of crew per boat	5	10	3-4	4	4
5. Annual net income per crew member (Rs.)	406	315	538	1,140	1,311

Notes : * Reference year 1960-62.
** Reference year 1962 only.
In working out net income the actual capital cost of the boats was taken into consideration and deduction made at 10% for both engine and hull.

Source : SOUVENIR, Indo-Norwegian Project, 1972.

ments; yet the gross income worked out to Rs. 2,800 per trip (per day) as against an operating cost of Rs. 1,202; 70 per cent of the operating cost was on fuel and lubricants and the rest on crew wages. Kartha and Sadanandan reported a catch of 52,835 kg. from two-boat trawling during 30 days in 108 hours of actual fishing off Cochin using two mechanized boats of 9.6m length, realizing Rs. 74,803 or Rs. 2,493 per day. Cat fish, squid, white bait, and silver bellies dominated the catch. Similar high catches have been reported from Gujarat, when 14.3m trawlers undertook pair trawling. Here also pomfrets were the dominant species. It is also interesting to note that the large Taiwanese trawlers on charter with Indian companies are also concentrating on two boat trawling and high opening bottom trawls.

Long lining for sharks from mechanized boats

Mohan Rajan recorded "a success story of deployment of

mechanized boats for shark long lining" along the Kanyakumari coast. Experience shows that long liners are catching more sharks than tunas and tunalike fishes. Further the shark prices have improved and long lining for sharks has become attractive. The expenditure and receipts per fishing trip from a 32 feet boat operating 200 hooks is given in Table 17.29.

TABLE 17.29 : **Expenditure and receipts per fishing trip from a 32 feet boat operating 200 hooks (Rs.)**

Operational Expenditure	
(a) Cost of 100 litres of diesel oil per trip at Rs. 3.50 per litre	350
(b) Cost of 2 litres of engine oil	25
(c) Expenditure towards grease	5
(d) Total expenditure per trip	380
Receipts	
(1) Number of sharks landed by a boat operating 200 hooks at 5% hooking rate	10 Nos
(2) Weight of 10 sharks on an average of 25 kg/fish	250 kg
(3) Gross receipts from sale proceeds of 250 kg of fish at Rs. 5 per kg (Rs.)	1,250
(4) Net receipts after deducting operational expenditure (Rs.)	870
(5) Share set apart for the boat at 30% of the net receipt (Rs.)	261
(6) Share set apart for gear at 15% of the net receipt (Rs.)	130
(7) Share of the crew towards wages (Rs.)	478
(8) Receipt per head per trip of 3 days (Rs.)	79.90

OTHER ESTIMATES

Purse-seining with 13.25m boats along the Kerala coast

Pannikkar has estimated an internal rate of return of 24 per cent on basis assumptions for a 13.25m purse-seiner operating along the Kerala coast. The economics are sensitive as the availability of oil sardine and mackerel, on which the purse-seining is largely based, is subject to wide fluctuations. The price of oil-sardine, which is normally Rs. 1,250 to 1,500 per tonne, may drop to Rs. 100 per tonne in the case of unusually heavy landings. On the other hand, mackerel maintains a fairly steady price around Rs. 6000 per tonne, in view of its good curing qualities. The data furnished in this paper have been made use of for computing economics of purse-seine operation along the Kerala coast (vide Table 17.28). This works out to 35.7 per cent on investment, as against a losing proposition in Karnataka (Table 17.23). This explains the migration of Karnataka purse-seiners to Kerala. Perhaps the low density of purse-seiners and the higher price realization in Kerala explain better catches and more income.

Operation of encircling net from thanguvallam along Kerala coast

Pannikkar has contended that the pelagic fishery resources off the Kerala coast can support a maximum of 250 to 260 purse-seiners of the type currently in operation, while the scope for such purse-seiners in addition to the existing artisanal boats is

TABLE 17.30 : **Computed economics of operation of 13.25 m purse seiner along Kerala coast**

('000 Rs.)

I. *Capital invested*	
1. Vessel with engine and accessories	450
2. Purse-seine	225
Total	675
II. *Fixed Costs*	
1. Depreciation at 8.33% on vessel and engine	37.5
2. Depreciation at 33.3% on purse-seine	75.0
3. Interest on capital	20.2
Total	216.1
III. *Variable Costs*	
1. Carrier vessel rental at Rs. 250 per day	50.4
2. Running expenditure at Rs. 750 per day	150.0
3. Maintenance of vessel, engine and accessories	15.0
4. Maintenance of purse-seine	6.7
5. Share of crew at 32.5% of total revenue	206.6
6. Other charges	20.00
Total	537.3
IV. *Total of fixed and variable costs*	753.4
V. *Total revenue*	912.5
VI. *Net earning*	240.9
VII. *Net earning on capital invested*	35.69%

placed at 50-60 units only. He has, therefore, suggested that instead of regular purse-seiners, about 300 mini purse-seines may be introduced. Each mini purse-seine will requires 3 large canoes (thanguvallams), two for catching and a third for transporting. The one intended for transporting will be provided with an out board motor. The investments and returns are worked in Table 17.31.

TABLE 17.31 : **Economics of purse-seining from two thungu-vallams along the Kerala coast**

('000 *Rs*)

I. *Capital cost*	
1. Cost of 3 thunguvallams	75
2. Cost of one outboard motor of 10 HP	15
3. Cost of one 225 × 33 m two-boat purse-seine net	100
Total	190
II. *Fixed operating cost*	
1. Depreciation of vallams at 6.33%	6.25
2. Depreciation of OBM at	5.00
3. Depreciation of purse-seine net at 33.33%	33.33
4. Interest on capital at 12.5%	23.75
5. Insurance at 3%	5.75
Total	74.03
III. *Variable cost*	
1. Running expenditure @ Rs 150 per day for 250 days	37.50
2- Maintenance of vallam, OBM and net	10.00
3. Crew share at 60%	318.00
4. Other charges	10.00
Total	375.50
IV. *Total fixed and variable cost*	449.53
V. *Net Earning*	118.47
VI. *Earning as percentage of capital invested*	62.1%

The author has also observed that the proposal has an IRR of 36.5 per cent, but economically feasible only when one of three thungavallams is motorized. When all of them are motorized, the project IRR drops to an uneconomic level of 7 per cent.

Study by tropical fisheries consultancy services (unpublished) 1984
The TFCS in their project report on rehabilitation of fishermen affected by the National Range Areas in Balasore district has recommended adoption of low cost technology already in vogue in the private sector. The government sponsored introduction of mechanized boats has come to a halt, while private parties are active in introducing mechanized boats adopting the low cost technology. This trial, started 4 or 5 years back, is found to be working quite satisfactorily. The cost saving is through adoption of cheaper substitutes, which bring down the cost quite substantially, as will be revealed from Table 17.32.

TABLE 17.32 : **Comparative cost of conventional government supplied boats and boats introduced by the private sector (Rupees)**

Sl. No.	Components	Capital cost of mechanized boat (gill-netter)	
		Government introduced boats	Private boats
1.	Hull	105,000 (teak wood)	25,000 (saal wood)
2.	Engine	105,000 (new)	24,000 (reconditioned)
3.	Gear box	12,500 (standard)	2,500 (local make)
4.	Propeller shaft	3,500 (bronze)	200 (cast iron)
5.	Propeller	5,000 (bronze)	200 (Cast aluminium)
6.	Copper sheathing	15,000	—
7.	Gill net	15,000	15,000
	Total	261,000	67,050

No doubt the saal wood hull has a shorter life span compared to that of the teak wood. But there is nothing to be alarmed about it as the 10,000 non-mechanized boats in operation in Orissa are all built in saal wood. In the absence of copper sheathing, it is necessary to periodically haul up the boat and apply a fresh coat of coal tar. But with this hauling up, scrapping

TABLE 17.33 : **Comparative economics of operation of standard type and cheap type mechanized boats of Balasore coast**

Sl. No.	Item	Annual costing (Rs.)	
		Standard type boat	Cheap type boat
1.	Interest on capital @ 12%	31,320	8,046
2.	Depreciation :		
	(a) Engine and stern assembly	8,019 (at 6.6%)	2,505 (at 10%)
	(b) Hull	4,800 (at 4%)	1,650 (at 6.6%)
	(c) Net @ 50%	3,750	3,750
3.	Repair and maintenance :		
	(a) Engine and stern assembly	10,080 (at 8%)	10,820 (at 20%)
	(b) Hull at 8%	8,400	2,000
	(c) Net @ 20%	3,000	3,000
	Total fixed costs	69,369	31,771
4.	Fuel for 200 days	32,000	32,000
5.	Lubricants	6,400	6,400
6.	Food and provisions	7,500	7,500
7.	Miscellaneous	3,000	3,000
	Total variable costs	48,900	48,900
	Total of fixed and variable costs	1,18,269	80,671
	say	1,18,300	80,700
8.	Earnings :		
	(a) 20 tonnes of first class fish at Rs. 6/kg.	1,20,000	1,20,000
	(b) 20 tonnes of second class fish at Rs. 2/kg.	40,000	40,000
	(c) 10 tonnes of third class fish at Re. 1/kg.	10,000	10,000
	Total earnings	1,70,000	1,70,000
	Reduction for breakdown	—	17,000
	Net gross earning	1,70,000	1,53,000
	Disposable income after deducting fixed and variable costs	52,700	72,300
	Return on investment after setting aside 50% of disposable income as share for crew	10.1%	54.3%
	Share for each crew member	3,764	5,521

of hull, and application of coal tar, the hull has a very smooth finish and this in turn helps to maintain adequate speed. Similarly the reconditioned engine would carry on easily for 10 years, even though there could be some extra cost on maintenance. The relative annual operating cost of the two has been worked out by the TFCs in Table 17.33.

The TFCS has suggested certain improvements to the low cost mechanized boat, to make it fit for trawling also besides gill netting. This has the effect of pushing up the cost by Rs. 28,500, but increases the economics of operation as may be seen in Tables 17.34 and 17.35.

TABLE 17.34 : **Additional cost on improving the private sector boats of Balasore district**

Sl. No.	Item	Cost (Rs.)
1.	Improving the hull form	Nil
2.	Extra cost on standard gear box (high reduction)	10,000
3.	Large diameter, high pitch Koplan propeller in cast aluminium	2,000
4.	Kort nozzle	2,000
5.	Gantry	4,500
6.	Tiltable drum winch	6,500
7.	High opening bottom trawl	3,500
	Total	29,500

The given projection is indicative of the use of appropriate technology adopting a selective use of low cost technology blended with standard equipment for certain critical parts and a combination of trawling and gill-netting.

Economics of anchoviella fishing

The TFCs has suggested a two pronged strategy on anchoviella fishing :

1. To operate a specially designed 26m mid-water trawler in the Gulk of Mannar to undertake monsoon fishing (this vessel at other times will be deployed for cat fish,

Table 17.35 : Economics of operation of an improved low cost mechanized boat

Sl. No.	Item	Amount (Rs.)
1.	Interest in capital (Rs. 67,050 + Rs. 28,500) @ 12%	11,466
2.	Depreciation :	
	(a) Engine @ 10%	2,400
	(b) Hull @ 6.6%	1,650
	(c) Other standard items @ 6.6%	1,851
	(d) Gill net @ 15% (being used for a reduced period)	2,250
	(e) Trawl net @ 50%	1,750
3.	Repair and maintenance :	
	(a) Engine @ 33%	8,000
	(b) Hull @ 8%	2,000
	(c) Standard fittings at 8%	2,444
	(d) Nets @ 20%	3,700
	Total fixed costs	37,311
4.	Fuel, with higher provision for trawling—220 days	40,000
5.	Lubricants	8,000
6.	Food and provisions for 220 days	8,000
7.	Miscellaneous :	3,500
	Total of variable costs	59,500
	Total of fixed and variable costs	96,811
8.	Earnings :	
	(a) 2 tonnes of prawn @ Rs. 40/kg.	80,000
	(b) 15 tonnes of first class fish @ Rs. 6/kg.	90,000
	(c) 10 tonnes of second class fish @ Rs. 2/kg.	20,000
	(d) 30 tonnes of third class fish @ Re. 1/kg	30,000
	Total gross earning	2,20,000
	Disposable income after deducting fixed and variable costs (Rs. 2,20,000—96,811)	1,23,189
	Return on investment (after setting apart 50% of disposable income as share for the crew)	61,595
	Share as percentage of investment	63.6%
	Share for each crew member	8,788

ribbon fish, horse mackerel, deep water prawn, and deep water lobster and fishing).

2. To operate a fine mesh purse-seine for anchoviella along the Malabar-Karnataka coast using the presently popular 13.3m purse-seine boats.

The economics of fishing using the above craft-gear combinations are given in Table 17.36 and 17.37.

TABLE 17.36 : **Economics of operation of 26 metres trawler for anchoviella, cat fish, ribbon fish, horse mackerel, deep water prawn and deep water lobster along the south-west coast of India**

('000 Rs.)

I. *Fixed operation cost*	
1. Repair and maintenance	275
2. Insurance	109
3. Wages to floating staff	167
4. Interest on working capital	275
5. Overhead charges	220
6. Interest on capital at 75% (SDFC rate)	812
7. Depreciation	475
	2333
II. *Variable operating cost*	
1. Refrigeration expenses	20
2. Food allowance	94
3. Harbour dues	13
4. Unloading charges	130
5. Water, ice, miscellaneous	629
6. Fuel and lubricants	2331
	3217
III. *Total of fixed and variable operating cost*	5550
IV. *Anticipated income*	8400
V. *Net earnings*	2850

Tax and tax concessions

Under Income Tax Rules there is no exemption or special consideration to fishing. Most non-mechanized boats do not earn enough to attract income tax. Besides wooden boats are eligible for 10 per cent depreciation. This is available for mechanized boats made of wood. But once the original capital cost is fully depreciated, that is after 10 years, there is no more deduction

TABLE 17.37 : **Economics of operation of 13.3 metres purse-seiners along with modified canoes for anchoviella fishing**

('000 *Rs.*)

I. *Fixed operating cost*	
1. Repair and maintenance	108
2. Depreciation	75
3. Interest on working capital	18
4. Insurance	12
5. Repair and maintenance	75
6. Wages to permanent crew	24
7. Other fixed cost	119
Total	431
II. *Variable operating cost*	
1. Food allowance	23
2. Harbour dues	18
3. Ice, water, miscellaneous	74
4. Fuel and lubricants	209
Total	324
III. *Total of fixed and variable cost*	755
IV. *Gross income*	1240
V. *Less crew share*	313
VI. *New income*	927
VII. *Net profit*	172

on this account. Similarly a deduction of 7.5 per cent on newly established industry is also over with the fifth year. The relief also covers the interest on loan, but not the loan repayment. It would therefore be apparent that the tax concessions are less as years pass by, and mechanized boats owned by individuals and companies would come for taxation, while mechanized boats jointly owned would come within the exemption limit.

Tax and tax concessions are very important for the companies where who are required to make a flat tax payment of 60 per cent on the profits and a further surcharge of 5 per cent. The payment of surcharge can be saved if an amount equal one and half times the surcharge is credited to Industrial Development Bank. Considering that the loans taken for acquisition of fishing vessels have to be paid back with interest, repayment of capital after paying the tax would become a difficult problem unless full benefits of the tax concessions are availed of. These are :

1.	Interest on loan [section 18 (ii)]	100%
2.	Depreciation (Appendix 1 of Part I)	5% on capital until capital is fully depreciated.
3.	Export turnover of previous year (section 80 HHC)	1% on exports
4.	Export turnover in excess of the year previous to the previous year (section 80 HHC)	5% on the excess
5.	Profits and gains on newly established industry (section 80J)	7½% for 5 years on capital
6.	Amortization of preliminary expenses (section 80J)	10% for 10 years on preliminary expenses

Of these, the most significant deduction is under Section 80J. But in the normal course profits after various permissible deductions may not be sufficient to avail of this tax relief in full. In this context the provision of charter is quite helpful. Since the charter is permitted for a period of 5 years, 7½ per cent of investment on acquisition of fishing vessels can be set against income from charter for the full period of 5 years. If there is no charter there may not enough profits to claim this relief. Similarly, if there is no investment on the purchase of vessels there would not be any capital investment to claim this concession. The amount thus saved from taxation may be used for repayment of capital borrowed. It must be mentioned that without fully availing of these tax concessions, it would be very difficult to service loans after paying income tax at a flat rate of 62½ per cent. In other words, the present scheme of chartering of foreign fishing vessels, which provides for a share of 15 per cent on the value of fish caught, fits in very well with the income tax relief.

Apart from these concessions, there are other special incentives applicable to deep see fishing vessels. These include :

1. 50 per cent duty drawback on diesel oil, as this category

of fishing vessel is treated on par with ocean-going vessels.

2. The balance of 50 per cent on excise duty on diesel oil is also eligible remission linked with export of shrimps.
3. There is provision for soft loan for acquisition of deep sea fishing vessels. This is to the extent of 95 per cent carrying an interest rate of 6.75 per cent in the case of indigenously constructed vessels and up to 90 per cent at the rate of 7½ per cent in the case of imported vessels. Large houses are, however, not eligible for this soft finance.
4. A 33 per cent capital subsidy is admissible on the cost of indigenously built deep sea fishing vessels. This is by way of a price equalizer and is paid directly to the yard.
5. Import of fishing vessels does not attract excise duty. But any extra fittings and spares would attract excise duty.
10. Motorization of canoes using outboard engines is a promising area particularly to help reducing physical strain. But the use of such labour saving devices should not lead to laziness and reduction in real income.
11. There is scope for significant improvement in the economics of mechanized fishing, by going for cheaper substitutes wherever possible, standard equipment for critical parts, new deck arrangement and equipment, adequate fishing gear, and so on.
12. In the case of deep sea fishing efficient vessel design, fuel saving devices, popularization of certain varieties having low market demand, production of value-added items, and so on would considerably improve the economic viability. Judicious use of tax concessions, incentives, charter provisions, and so on would help better servicing of loans.

CONCLUSIONS

1. India has been following the principle of open entry into

fishing. Over years the number of both non-mechanized and mechanized fishing craft have increased and a stage has come when entry into fishing has to be limited with conventional craft and gear, both non-mechanized and mechanized, except for fishing new resources, or resources that are lightly fished at present.

2. There is need for effective demarcation of zones so that mechanized boats do not fish in areas where non-mechanized boats could effectively fish.

3. Mechanization of boats should be encouraged to increase production on one hand and to improve the quality of life of fishermen. But should be ensured that mechanized boats fish to increase production, rather than in getting a higher share of the catch caught even otherwise. This is particularly relevant in respect of high efficiency gear, whose operation has to be carefully monitored and necessary conservation measures taken to avoid hardships to those operating the less efficient gear and to prevent over-exploitation of stocks.

4. It is necessary to see that the returns of high investment fishing operations are maintained at economic levels by licensing units and closely monitoring their performance. Unrestricted entry of too many units, as for example trawlers in many states, and purse-seiners in Karnataka, have been the reason for uneconomic operations. There are several other potentially promising areas of diversification in fishing, for example use of high opening trawls, two boat trawls, mid water trawls, anchoviella fishing, shark fishing, tuna fishing, and so on. The usual pattern is that no sooner the viability of a method of fishing is established, there is an unrestricted rush and very soon that type of fishing also becomes uneconomical due to entry of too many units.

5. Fixed costs by way of interest, depreciation, and insurance present a major component of production, while fuel represents the single large variable cost. In an inflationary economy the pressure of fixed costs gets reduced in the overall cost of production as price of fish caught increases, while fixed costs remain unchanged.

Hence even marginally losing propositions become viable over a period of time.

6. In respect of variable cost, fuel price has been steadily increasing. The recent fuel hike sets in motion a vicious cycle of increasing prices. There is also need to introduce various fuel saving devices.

7. Wages to crew represent the major cost in the non-mechanized sector, a sizable cost in the small mechanized sector, and a relatively small cost in the larger vessel operations. At the same time, the economics of operation, particularly the larger vessels, depends entirely on the dedication for hard work by the crew.

8. Going by individual earnings, the crew of the non-mechanized boats get the least wages and their working conditions are more hazardous. The crew on mechanized boats have less hazardous existence and get better paid. The best paid are the crew of the larger vessels and their working conditions are also the best. Nevertheless their dedication to work is comparatively less as they are all hired labour, as against partners sharing the sale proceeds in the smaller boats. On large vessels also it has already been appreciated that a system of productivity linked payment of emoluments to the crew is essential to maximize production and earning to make investments on large vessels a viable proposition.

REFERENCES

Anon, *Handbook of Indian Fisheries*, Prepared for the Third Meeting of Indo-Pacific Fisheries Council, Madras, 1951.

Anon, Souvenir, 20th Anniversary, Central Marine Fisheries Research Institute, Government of India, Recreation Club, Mandapam Camp, 1967.

Anon, Marine Fish Production in India, 1950-1968, *Bulletin 13*, Central Marine Fisheries Research Institute, 1969.

Anon, Evaluation of the Programme of Mechanization of Fishing Boats, Programme Evaluation Organization, Planning Commission, Government of India, 1971.

Anon, Compounding and Discounting Tables for Project Evaluation, World Bank, 1973.

Anon, Report of Working Group on Fifth Five Year Plan (1974-79) Fisheries, Ministry of Agriculture, (Department of Agriculture and Co-operation), New Delhi, 1973.

Anon, *Statistical Supplement*, 10th Meeting of the Central Board of Fisheries, Mimeo, 1976.

Anon, Marine Fisheries Information Service (T and E), Series No. 3, 1978.

Anon, Marine Fisheries Information Service (T and E), Series No. 30, 1981.

Anon, *Handbook of Fisheries Statistics*, Mimeo, Department of Agriculture and Co-operation, Ministry of Agriculture, New Delhi, 1981.

Anon, Feasibility Report on Anchoviella Fishing, Mimeo, Tropical Fisheries Consultancy Services, Delhi, 1982.

Anon, Marine Fisheries Information Service (T and E), Series No. 41, 1982.

Anon, Agenda, National Workshop, 15th June 1984, New Delhi, Ministry of Agriculture (Department of Agriculture and Co-operation), New Delhi, 1984.

Anon, Proceedings, Seminar on Fuel Economy in Deep Sea Fishing, 11-12, November, 1983, Visakhapatnam, Association of Indian Fishery Industries, 1984.

Anon, Rehabilitation for National Range Areas in Balasore district—Fisheries Project, MS. Tropical Fisheries Consultancy Service, Delhi, 1984.

Gulbrandsen, Fishing Craft Development in Kerala, Evaluation Report, BOBP/WP/25, Bay of Bengal Programme, Madras, 1984.

George, P.C., B.T. Antony Raja and K.C. George, *Fishery Resources of the Indian Economic Zone*, Souvenir, Integrated Fisheries Project, Cochin.

Krishna Iyer, H., G.R. Unnithan, P.S. Rao, C.C. Panduranga Rao and G.R. Nair, The Effect of Increase in the Number of Fishing Trips on the Economic Efficiency of Fishing Trawlers along Kerala Coast, *Fisheries Technology*, 20 (1), 1983.

John Kurien and Rolf William, Economics of Artisanal and Mechanized Fisheries in Kerala, *Working Paper 34*, Small Scale Fisheries Promotion, South Asia, 1982.

Mohan Rajan, K.V., A Success Story of Development of Mechanized Boats for Shark Long Lining, *Sea Food Export Journal*, Vol. XIV (8) : 9-18, 1982.

Nair, K.M.V. and K.M. Joseph, Important Observations on Deep Sea Fish Resources made during 1983-84, FSI/Bull-13/84, *Fishery Survey of India*, Bombay, 1984.

Pillai, M., Gopala Krishna, and R. Sathiadhas, Pair Trawling Strikes Good Grounds for White Pomfret in the Palk Bay, Tamil Nadu, *Marine Information Services* (T and E), Series No. 39, 1982.

Ravikumar, R., Commercial Evaluation of IND-13 Beach Craft at Uppada, India, BOBPOWP/26, *Ibid*, 1984.

Silas, E.G., and K. Alagarswami, Country Status Report on India, Proc. Indo-Pacific Fisheries Commission, 19th Session, Kyoto, Japan, Sec. III, Symposium on Fisheries Development and Management of Small Scale

Fisheries, 1980.

Srivastava, U.K., M. Dharma Reddy, and V.K. Gupta, Management of Marine Fisheries : An Analysis of Problems in Harvesting and Processing (A micro study in Gujarat State), Centre for Management in Agriculture, Indian Institute of Management, Ahmedabad, 1979.

18

ROLE OF COMMERCIAL BANKS IN FINANCING THE MARINE FOODS INDUSTRY

N.K. THINGALAYA, P.G.P. RAMA RAO

AND

B. LAXMAN

THE entry of commercial banks into the field of fisheries is of very recent origin. Only after the advent of the mechanization of marine fishing did banks start to recognize the fishing industry as a credit worthy enterprise. Bank finance to the marine industry started flowing sometime during the late fifties. The process of mechanization of fishing vessels caught up slowly in the maritime states especially on the west coast. The mechanized boats were introduced by the Fisheries Department in some of the states without seeking any bank finance. The demonstration effect of mechanized fishing attracted a few entrepreneurs who sought financial assistance of banks which also became receptive to developments taking place on the marine front. They willingly accepted, as an experiment, a part of the risk which the entrepreneur was himself taking by making a huge investment in fishing. In the initial years when there was no empirical data or credit norms available to the bankers to judge the financial viability of the fishing operations, they were not in a position to fathom the risks involved in this venture. Realizing the importance of financing the developmental activities in this sphere, some of the banks have indeed boldly taken up financing of mechanized fishing. To them, it was perhaps like an entry into the vast unchartered ocean with the only hope that the finance given for this purpose would generate additional income as well as employment. Conditions were fortunately favourable in the early stages and this enabled quite a few commercial banks to go in a fairly big way for financing mechanized fishing as well as establishment of ice, cold storage, and freezing plants.

The maritime states in India abound in banking facilities unlike the industrially backward states. All the port-towns have branches of nationalized banks. In coastal Karnataka and Kerala, a few banks in the private sector also have established an extensive branch net work. According to information available, almost all banks in both public and private sectors are lending to the marine industry. From the data furnished by 16 banks (see Appendix I) it is observed that over 350 branches of banks in the maritime states entertain credit proposals from the fishing industry. This number is a gross underestimate as most of the banks have not furnished the data.

BANK CREDIT TO FISHING INDUSTRY

The banks' involvement in providing credit for mechanization has increased during the last two decades both on account of the increase in the number of boats and the increase in the cost of boats. The details regarding the total credit lent by banks for the earlier years are not available. According to the information specially obtained from the Reserve Bank of India at the end of June 1974, total advance made by the commercial banks in India to mechanized fishing amounted to Rs. 7.06 crore. The advances made to fish-canning, ice plants, freezing and preservation units have totalled Rs. 21.29 crore. On the basis of the data collected from the banks which have responded to the questionnaire sent by us, it is observed that the total advances made by 16 banks for mechanized fishing boats are of Rs. 22.17 crore at the end of December 1980. Details are given in Table 18.1. As the data pertains to only the responding banks in India this cannot be said to be total advances made by the banks in India for mechanized boats. The total for the banking industry can be roughly estimated around Rs. 35 to Rs. 40 crore. The state-wise details of the advances made by the responding banks are furnished in Appendix I.

Advances to allied fishing activities have been collected separately from the Reserve Bank of India. Figures relating to

TABLE 18.1 : **Bank advance for fishing boats (mechanized and country crafts)**

(*Rs. lakh*)

Name of the bank	Amount outstanding as on December 1980
State Bank Group	
State Bank of India	n.a.
State Bank of Mysore	18.08
State Bank of Saurashtra	135.99
Nationalized Banks	
Syndicate Bank	895.25
Canara Bank	294.72
Union Bank of India	177.41
United Commercial Bank	141.26
Indian Overseas Bank	170.41
Corporation Bank	150.66
Oriental Bank of Commerce	6.20
Bank of Maharashtra	33.01
Andhra Pradesh	33.81
Vijaya Bank	n.a.
Private Sector Banks	
Karnataka Bank Ltd.	143.75
Dhanalakshmi Bank Ltd.	11.44
Bank of Cochin Ltd.	5.22

advances made by the banking industry to fish processing, canning, freezing and preservation units in maritime states are given in Table 18.2.

During the last 3 years, the total advances have increased by nearly Rs. 20 crore. Nearly 40 per cent of the additional credit for fish processing and allied activities have been made in one state alone, Kerala. Other states where there has been considerable expansion in bank credit are—Andhra Pradesh, Maharashtra, and Orissa where the amount outstanding has been doubled during this period.

A conservative estimate of the advances to the fishing industry at the end of December 1980 would be about Rs. 100 to Rs. 110 crore. Advances to mechanized fishing would be around Rs. 50 crore and advances to allied activities would be about Rs. 60 crore. This estimate, however, does not include advances made

TABLE 18.2 : Bank advances to fish processing, canning, freezing and preservation

(*Rupees in lakh*)

States/Union Territories	As on the last Friday of June 1977			As on the last Friday of June 1980		
	No. of accounts	Credit limit	Amount outstanding	No. of accounts	Credit limit	Amount outstanding
1. West Bengal	36	142	157	66	409	258
2. Orissa	24	280	135	47	360	301
3. Andhra Pradesh	37	122	113	52	311	242
4. Tamil Nadu	103	616	497	125	999	751
5. Kerala	604	2662	1772	618	3586	2560
6. Karnataka	210	616	365	192	615	401
7. Maharashtra	88	671	326	140	1114	697
8. Gujarat	21	79	47	38	208	140
9. Dadra, Nagar Haveli	—	—	—	—	—	—
10. Goa, Daman and Diu	45	119	78	52	198	104
11. Lakshadweep	—	—	—	—	—	—
12. Pondicherry	4	3	3	5	5	5
13. Andaman and Nicobar Islands	—	—	—	—	—	—
Total	1172	5210	3493	1335	7805	5459

Source : Reserve Bank of India, Bombay.

to manufacturers of marine diesel engines or nylon nets. As the manufacturers of these crucial fishing equipments are multi-product companies having a wide range of products, it is not possible to assess the bank credit utilized for the production of marine diesel engines or nylon nets exclusively. Advances made by the banks to such cases may be estimated at about Rs. 10 crore on a rough and ready basis. Thus the stake of the banking industry in the marine industry may be estimated at Rs. 120 to Rs. 150 crore. When this is compared with the total advances, it accounts for less than 0.5 per cent. "Fishermen represent another sector of small borrowers who do not get sufficient institutional credit," opined a study group* of the National Credit Council in 1969. Though there has been some improvement in the availability of credit to the fishermen since then, the involvement of the banks in extending credit to fishing industry is not very significant as the above figures indicates.

TYPES OF BANK ADVANCES

Banks usually entertain loan proposals relating to purchase of mechanized boats, gears and nets, setting up cold storages and freezing plants for canning and freezing sea food, and refrigerated vans for transportation and export. These are the direct advances made by the banks. There are also certain types of indirect advances which the banks made to the units connected with the fishing industry. Advances are made, for example, for the setting up of mechanized boat building yards. This is the first step in the process of mechanization of fishing operations. Banks also finance large industries manufacturing marine engines and refrigeration plants and equipments. Of late, fibreglass boats are also being built by indigenous boat building yards backed by bank finance. For fish processing units, credit is extended on terms and conditions similar to those applicable to small scale industries. Working capital needs of these units are met by banks. Export credit is given to exporters at concessional rates. Besides fund-based credit limits like pre-shipment credit and post-shipment credit and non-fund-based credit facilities like letter of credit are also provided.

Credit is also extended to fisherwomen who handle fish processing, especially salting and drying. A large number of fisherwomen depend upon the trading of salted dry fish.

Traditional fishing boats are financed by institutional credit agencies to some extent. The traditional fishermen are given bank finance on a group guarantee basis to enable them to shift from traditional fishing to mechanized fishing. Recently in Karnataka, the District Rural Development Society of the state government has come forward to provide huge subsidy to groups of small

*"Organizational Framework for the Implementation of Social Objectives", Reserve Bank of India, Bombay, October 1969, p. 84.

fishermen to acquire purse-seine boats, through bank finance under the Integrated Rural Development Programme. Banks have been associated with this programme on a selective basis. The transition from traditional fishing to mechanized fishing has created a situation of growing conflicts between the small traditional fishermen and others using mechanized boats. This conflict is being resolved through the programmes like that above to some extent.

During the early stages of mechanization, the credit requirement for a 30-footer mechanized boat was roughly ranging between Rs. 40,000 and Rs. 65,000. The banks were financing up to 75 per cent of the cost. There has been a shift in favour of bigger boats, purse-seine boats, and trawlers. The credit needs of a purse-seine boat, comply with all gears, now range between Rs. 6 and Rs. 6.5 lakh.

Liberal subsidy offered by some of the state governments has enabled even small fishermen to approach banks to obtain loans for mechanized fishing, either collectively or individually. The increase in the number of fishing boats in certain fishings centres has created demand for ancillary activities. Taking advantage of the market for facilities like cold storage, transportation, and retail trading, banks are being approached for new lines of credit.

As most of these activities come under the purview of the small scale industries, banks reveal greater acceptance of the credit needs of these ancillary units. In the credit portfolios of banks, thus a variety of financing schemes meant for the fishing industry has emerged.

VIABILITY OF FISHERIES PROJECTS

Being commercial institutions, banks have set up certain standard norms to assess the economic and technical viability of all loan proposals. Exceptions are made in lowering the norms in special cases where the banking industry is convinced about the need for extending financial support to an upcoming enterprise. In the case of fisheries, banks have largely diluted the standard norms in view of the seasonality of fishing operations and the vast developmental potentialities. The economy viability of loan proposals is considered usually on a different footing. Broadly the following aspects are analysed.

Technical feasibility

The technical feasibility of a loan proposal from a branch for the purchase or construction of a mechanized boat is judged on the following factors relating to the area where the mechanized boat is proposed to be used.

Potential of the fishing groups

The coastal area must have the potential for mechanized fishing operations as observed in any of the official publications of the state government. Reference would be normally made to the State Fisheries Department to confirm the potential.

Infrastructure

Availability of facilities like berthing, ice and cold storages, freezing plants, and other marketing facilities is a must for the viability of the loan proposal. In the absence of these facilities, the boat cannot be economically used. The catches may have to be unremuneratively marketed, if the basic facilities are not available.

Availability of technical guidance

Accessibility to technical guidance from the fisheries department and fisheries research stations would largely enhance the stability of the fishing operations. Similarly, easy accessibility to technical services for repair and overhauling gears and engines would contribute to the lowering of the idle days.

Availability of skilled labour

Since mechanized fishing is a skilled job, it requires skilled labourers to operate the boat. Easy availability of skilled labourers locally is a highly desirable condition.

Experience of the borrower

The borrower's experience in fishing operations is another factor to be looked into. A trained fisherman (trained by the Fisheries Department) or one who has experience in working in a mechanized fishing boat is preferable to one who can just bring the margin money to obtain the loan.

Suitability of the boat

The technical feasibility of the loan proposal would be very much enhanced if the boat and gears to be used are capable of exploiting different species of fish rather than suited to one type of fish, usually shrimp. After satisfying the technical feasibility, the economic viability would be considered.

Economic viability

The test of economic viability is to assess whether the project would generate enough cash to pay off itself during a reasonable period of operations. The factors considered are the following :

Cost of the project

The total cost of the project is a crucial factor in the whole exercise. Under inflationary conditions, the cost of the project is likely to go up substantially, thereby lowering the repaying capacity by raising the financial outgo, including the interest component.

Subsidy available

The subsidy available from the state government is a positive factor reducing the debt burden of the borrower and also reducing the loan component of the proposal. Timely availability of subsidy is a great help in some cases.

Margin money

The borrower's stake in the project goes a long way in improving the economic viability of the project. The margin money varies from 10 to 25 per cent of the total project after deducting the subsidy component.

Number of fishing days

The number of fishing days the boat can operate largely determines the viability of the project. The volume of compulsory fishing holidays during the monsoon is one aspect which is examined to assess the viability.

The fixed and recurring expenditure

The wages and fuel expenses constitute the bulk of the operational expenditure of mechanized boats. Port dues, interest on borrowings, rent, and salary of permanent labourers are some of the overheads. An assessment of the gross annual expenditure is made using certain norms for the expenditure items.

Income generation

The income generating capacity is assessed based on certain assumptions of the number of days the boat would be working and likely quantity, and value of the catch. Very optimistic estimates of the fish catches are juxtaposed with the data available with the bank relating to the actual operating results of the earlier borrowers. An awareness of the periodicity of fish famines or price cycles is also very helpful in making the necessary adjustments in the cashflow analysis. This also enables the bank to determine the repayment schedule. To be viable, the project must generate sufficient income to pay off the instalments and interest after making available to the borrower a reasonable amount of money for his own maintenance.

In the case of other loan proposals relating to allied activities, their economic viability is judged like that of any proposal relating to small scale industries. For establishment of cold storages, ice plants, freezing, or canning units, the technical feasibility is determined by availability of fish demand for canned or frozen and storage capacity needed for preservation. The technical feasibility of a boat building yard is usually based on the demand for new boats over a period of time, the raw materials available, and the technical competence of the boat builders.

Acceptance or rejection of proposals

The loan proposals are usually discussed with the technical personnel of the banks at the branch level before a formal application is made. The branch level discussion itself can filter the proposals emanating from the prospective borrowers. Proposals of dubious viability or from speculative novices are discouraged at their level itself.

After the loan proposal is formalized and sent to the higher level work station for processing with the recommendation of the branch manager. It is thoroughly examined by the technical officers. The rejection ratio at that level is usually not more than 10 to 15 per cent. The controlling office which can scrutinize the proposals more objectively, free from local influence, would be rejecting the proposals only if they are found to be not in tune with the national policy.

The details collected from the banks regarding the number of loan applications received and the number of loan applications rejected during the last five years reveal that the rejection ratio is almost negligible. The available details are given in Appendix IV. Major grounds for rejection are usually the tendency on the part of the borrowers to concentrate on particular areas or on specific projects. Shipping facilities to countries having demand for canned fish are not available. Faster depletion of fisheries resources is feared and this apprehension has been held by the fisheries departments in many cases. When certain fishing centres are saturated with a fleet of mechanized boats, banks tend to discourage further addition to the fleet.

Imitating a successful entrepreneur is a known feature among small entrepreneurs. When a few ice plants start functioning profitability, a number of new entrants venture to put up ice plants through bank finance. In such cases, banks use their discretion to reject loan proposals. In Karnataka, the haphazard growth of new ice plants have endangered the functioning of the ice plants of the state fisheries development corporation. A surfeit of ice plants have come up in coastal Karnataka and Kerala, some of which are financed through non-banking agencies.

The fish canning industry perhaps has not yet developed a domestic market for its products. The performance of quite a few existing units is not very satisfactory. Lack of demand for these products is one of the factors which compels banks to discourage fish canning units in general. It is also reported that non-availability of regular shipping facilities to countries where there is demand for canned food is another problem faced by these units.

Paucity of funds with banks under conditions of credit stringency also could be one of the grounds for rejecting loan applications. However, this is a rare phenomenon as refinance facilities from the NABARD are usually available to banks.

Some of the common deficiencies noted in the proposals received by banks relate to an unrealistic assessment of the proposed venture. Sometimes it is a deliberate attempt to get through the project hurriedly while in some cases it is due to unrealistic optimism. Inflating the total financial outlay of the project is one of the most common means of providing for the margin money, specially where the margin stipulated is somewhat high. This tendency is common to all types of proposals relating to the marine industry as in the case of other proposal.

Over-rating the earning capacity of the project is done (boat loan) by estimating a very high quantity of fish catches and higher volume of gross earnings. This would make the proposal appear as viable. Such a proposal, if accepted, is likely to run into difficulties very soon, failing to ensure the return flow of funds.

Lack of proper planning and timing in launching of the project is another notable deficiency. This is more prominent in the case of mechanized boats. The construction of the hull and launching the boat for fishing, is, in many cases, not synchronized with the fishing season. The interest burden increases if the boat gets ready for launching at the fag end of the fishing season.

TECHNICAL PERSONNEL

The fishing industry is yet to receive the recognition from commercial banks as a specialized field requiring the services of technically qualified persons. This is largely due to the fact that the volume of advances made by the banks at present does not warrant the need for a special cadre of officers to supervise credit proposals. It took the banks a long time to appoint agricultural graduates and post-graduates were drafted into the banking fold.

With vast changes in the lending pattern of banks, both functionally and geographically, the staff recruitment pattern also has undergone certain changes. Now specialists from many fields like dairying poultry, piggery sheep rearing, and fisheries are being recruited. It is estimated that their number may be between 25 and 40. Details of this as furnished by the responding banks are given in Appendix V.

Officers handling fisheries projects are given special training through the active support of the National Bank for Agriculture and Rural Development (NABARD). A few training programmes on fisheries have been organized by NABARD. Many of the banks have reported to have taken advantage of this training programme.

There is certainly a case for building up the expertise to deal with fisheries projects to fully exploit the marine potential. Nationalized banks which have a large network of branches may have to bestow their attention on this aspect in their future recruitment programme.

SANCTION OF LOANS—TERMS AND CONDITIONS

The terms and conditions of loans granted to the fishing industry do not basically differ from other types of credit proposals. The additional risk involved in fisheries finance does not get transferred to the borrowers in terms of higher rate of interest or high margin stipulations. The risk premium is absorbed by banks. Since NABARD provides re-finance to the tune of 75-90 per cent for loans sanctioned and disbursed to fishery development schemes, there is an element of uniformity in terms and conditions governing these loans given by different banks. This facility has helped the commercial banks to finance fishing industry in a larger measure from 1970 onwards. Though refinance assistance from NABARD covers the entire gamut of the fishing industry, nearly 85 per cent of fishery projects formulated and implemented by commercial banks with NABARD refinance assistance accounted for financing the mechanized boats only. The terms and conditions followed by commercial banks while extending loans for purchase of mechanized boats under the NABARD scheme are given below :

Quantum of loan

The amount of loan to be advanced depends upon the size of the boat, material used for hull construction, and other equipments which the entrepreneur proposes to purchase. It varies roughly from Rs. 1.20 lakh in the case of a 30-footer wooden boat to Rs. 6.25 lakh for a purse-seine boat. A fibre glass boat of 32 feet size costs about Rs. 2.50 lakh.

Subsidy

Subsidies are given by the central and state governments to give a boost to mechanization, help the traditional fishermen to switch over to mechanized fishing and encourage deep sea fishing. However, the amount varies from purpose to purpose and from state to state. Banks stipulate that the subsidy should be paid to banks to adjust the amount borrowed or towards the margin requirements in the case of small fishermen.

Margin

Based on the financial status of the entrepreneur, the margin ranges from 5 per cent to 25 per cent of the total cost of the project. In the case of groups of smaller fishermen, a lower margin is prescribed.

Rate of interest

National Bank for Agriculture and Rural Development (NABARD) provides refinance to the banks at 6.5 to 7.5 per cent interest per annum and in turn banks are allowed to charge 10.25 to 12.50 per cent per annum from the borrowers. These rates compare very favourably with interest rate on other loans ranging from 16 to 18 per cent.

Rebate

A rebate varying from ½ to 1 per cent is allowed for prompt repayment of loan instalments. This incentive encourages the interest-conscious borrowers to repay the loan promptly.

Security

Loans are secured by hypothecation of boat, net, and other accessories proposed to be purchased by the entrepreneur.

Release schedule

Loan meant for engine, net, and other equipments is paid directly to the suppliers. Loan for hull is released directly to the boat builder depending upon the progress of the work. Generally the following pattern is being followed in the disbursement of loan for hull construction :

1.	Advance payment	10%
2.	Keel laying	15%
3.	Planking	20%
4.	Installation of engine	25%
5.	Launching	25%
6.	After trial	5%

The release is made after verification of the work by the bank personnel.

Repayment schedule
Loan has to be repaid in five years from the date of commencement of the first fishing operation. There are instances when the repayment schedule was relaxed when fish famines occurred in certain coastal areas.

Moratorium
No amount need to be paid till one month after launching the boat and during the off-season period of four months commencing from June.

Insurance
Insurance of boat against marine risks is mandatory. General insurance companies provide partial or complete insurance cover during the fishing season and the laid-off period.

Registration of boat
Boats have to be registered either with the Marine Export Development Authority or port authorities in the area where they operate.

Books of accounts
The borrowers are expected to maintain a register wherein the following details have to be entered daily: (1) Fish catches effected (species-wise); (2) Gross income derived by sale of fish; (3) Expenditure incurred on diesel oil, wages to crew and so on and (4) Net surplus available. However in actual practice, it is observed that most of the borrowers were not maintaining this register. Banks have been constantly impressing upon the

beneficiaries the need to maintain such details as the books will help the banker to follow the trend in fish catches, net surplus available to rephase the repayment schedule if need be, and take necessary corrective steps while formulating and implementing similar schemes elsewhere.

Details regarding the rate of interest charged by banks for various types of loans and details regarding the marginal stipulation and the type of security needed are given in Table 18.3.

TABLE 18.3 : **Terms and conditions of fishery advances**

Sl. No.	Purpose of loan	Margin percentage	Period of loan (years)	Rate of interest (percentage)	Security, general
1.	Country craft	4-15 20-40	3 5	10.75 12.50	Assets acquired out of loan
2	Mechanized boats	25-40	3-5	13.5 16	Hypothecation of boats and any other collateral securities
2.1	Mechanized boats through NABARD refinance	15-25	5	10.25 12.50	Hypothecation of boats
3.	Processing plant	25-30	5-10	11.85 17.00	Assets acquired out of loans
4.	Ice plant	25-30	5-10	13.5 17.0	Assets acquired out of loans
5.	Transport vehicle	25-30	5-10	13.5 17.0	Assets acquired out of loans
6.	Fish export (Packing credit)	25-40	3-6 (month)	12.5 15.0	Hypothecation of stocks, plant and machinery and premises and collateral securities

UTILIZATION OF LOANS

Utilization of the loan amount is ensured through a system of post-sanction supervision and physical verification through the branch staff. As the loan amount is released directly to suppliers of engine, net, and equipments, no misutilization of funds is noticed in this regard. However, in respect of hull construction, it is observed that some borrowers submit inflated quotations to make up the margin money. Efforts are being made to check this by constantly watching and verifying the expenditure incurred, keeping the specification for hull and materials used in view while the boat is under construction.

In the case of advances made for ice plants and cold storages, there are instances of the amount being diverted for other purposes especially when the borrower undertakes multifarious activities. Diversion is also possible in the case of lendings to fish freezers and exporters. The current sickness of some of the exporting units may be attributed to misutilization of borrowed funds.

There are hundreds of success stories of borrowers abreviated into mere figures in the accounting books of banks. An enterprising fisherman who ventured into mechanized fishing, by employing the trained young fishermen as crew, was remarkably successful from the beginning and gradually increased his fleet of boats through bank finance. Even a small non-nationalized bank in coastal Karnataka which financed a successful mechanized boat operator was willing to take up the risk of financing more boats, emboldened by its happy experience. There are quite a few large operators owning fleets of boats whose credit rating by banks is very high.

"Capitalist fishermen"—non-fishermen entrepreneurs who have entered mechanized fishing purely as a commercial preposition—have been successful where their overall supervision was adequate. They employ fishermen on daily wages and manage the financial transactions very carefully, by handling the marketing of the fish through their own fish vans. Some of the integrated fishing enterprises which operate a fleet of boats have cold storage and freezing facilities, and undertake exports have been very successful. They have been instrumental in increasing the employment opportunities in the coastal areas.

The cases of failures are large in number as far as the small mechanized boats are concerned. The absence of the borrower's financial stake in the mechanized boat is one of the most common reasons. Under certain state-sponsored programmes, the entire credit needs of the small fishermen for acquiring mechanized boats are met by banks. In a number of cases, of due to differences of opinion among the partners, boats remain idle. The promoters care very little to resume fishing operations.

The concentration of a large number of boats in particular areas has resulted in a glut in the local fish markets leading to a sudden fall in prices. The fishing operations in such cases become very uneconomical. The hostility of the local fishermen is another factor which tends to reduce the mobility of fishing vessels into different places, especially when they cross the state limits.

Frequent breakdown of the engine due to poor maintenance is another contributing factor. Exhorbitant repair charges and increase in the diesel price also add to the financial hardships.

One of the causes for the sickness of frozen fish exporting units is the excessive dependence upon one item of export shrimps, whose catches have fluctuated too wildly. Vagaries of the external markets' demand for frozen shrimp and the strict quality control measures imposed by the United States of America have caused great hardships to shrimp exporters. The sickness of these units has been aggravated by competition from other exporting countries.

The sickness of some of the fish canning units may be attributed to their failure to dispose off stocks accumulated after a bumper fishing season. A domestic market for these products is non-existent while the defence depots are the only buyers. The rigid stand of banks in assessing the credit needs of such units would diminish the chances of their survival.

MONITORING THE BORROWER'S PERFORMANCE

Monitoring the performance of borrowers is an important aspect of post-lending supervision which banks normally do in all their lending programmes. The efficiency of any lending programme depends to a large extent on the effectiveness of the monitoring system and the receptivity of the banks to attune their action programme according to the needs of the situation. As fisheries advances do not constitute a sizeable portion of bank advances, banks do not have a proper monitoring system at present. No.

systematic attempt seems to have been made by banks in this direction so far. As noted earlier only a few banks have appointed specialized officers to supervise fisheries advances. These officials are charged with the responsibility of appraising loan proposals, attending to recovery of loans, helping the prospective borrowers in drawing up suitable projects, and providing necessary guidance to entrepreneurs in making their venture a success. Officials stationed at the branch level constantly visit the landing centres during the fishing season, watch the movement of boats, and extend the necessary help and assistance to the financed boats. These officials also record the catches, value realized, expenditure incurred, and the net surplus available in the case of boats financed by banks. The movement of boats are also recorded. But this type of work is being done in a very small number of cases.

From the bank's point of view it would be uneconomical to employ specialized staff for monitoring the fisheries finance because of the very low volume. A few banks have taken up evaluation studies largely at the insistence of the NABARD. Available studies throw some light on the nature of funds utilization, improvement in fish catches, increase in income, and repayment performance. There is very little information to judge how far these evaluation studies have been taken cognisance by banks themselves and implemented in their lending programmes.

Monitoring the performance of borrowers on actual operating results would be very helpful. An attempt in this regard has been made by one of the banks to document the daily operational results by providing to the borrowers a 'record book'. But the follow up work does not appear to be very effective. It would be very helpful if banks can build up an information system for monitoring the performance. Judging the performance of the borrowers on the basis of the payment of instalments vis-a-vis the amount alone would be very short-sighted policy. This would be narrowly limiting the bank's capacity to play a positive role in the development of the fishing industry.

RECOVERY OF LOANS

The experience of banks vary very widely as far as recovery of the loans is concerned. The element of uncertainty introduced by the cyclical fluctuations in the fortunes of the fishing industry cannot be underestimated in any analysis of the recovery of advances made to this industry. Usually, years of very poor catches follow in succession years of bountiful fish catches. The repayment schedule of the banks get altered under such circumstances, much beyond the expectations of both borrower and lender. It has been observed that as in the case of agricultural advances, the recovery performance is fairly better in the years of good fish catches coupled with better prices. In years of fish famine, there is a more precipitous fall in repayment. According to available information, the overdue position in the case of advances made to the fishing industry vary very widely from less than 10 per cent in the case of a private sector bank to as high as 86 per cent in the case of a big nationalized bank. (See Appendix VI) Because of the inadequacy of data, it is not possible to pass judgement on the nature of the defaulters. Secondly, since data are available only for one year, it may not be advisable to draw inferences.

Among the factor which contribute to an increase in the default ratio, mention may be made of huge expenditure on repairs and maintenance, increase in the fuel cost, increase in the number of idle boats, and sometimes low prices for the varieties of fish caught. It has been observed that the cost of maintenance of the craft and gears is increasing with the age of the mechanized boat. Servicing charges for repairs are assuming greater proportion of the total operating cost in the case of older boats. The recent increase in the price of diesel oil has also contributed largely in lowering the earnings of mechanized fishing boats. On a number of days, the total value of the fish caught is much lower than the cost of the fuel consumed.

Wilful defaulters among the borrowers are certainly not non-existent. Banks have discovered in some cases that borrowers have deliberately defaulted to divert the income for investment elsewhere. However, wilful defaulters constitute a very small percentage of the total number of borrowers. The factors contributing to poor recovery performances may be now analysed in detail.

Cycle in fish catches

Fish famine is a periodical and biological problem inseparable from the marine enterprise. This issue deserves proper scrutiny by marine scientists and fisheries authorities. This phenomenon has created an apprehension in the financing circles which is likely to deter from financing further mechanized boats. Which is of utmost importance here is the need to analyse factors which result in cyclical fluctuations. If it could be scientifically analysed and the periodicity of fish production cycle is determined, then perhaps banks could readjust the period of loan and the repayment schedule. Alternatively if it could be proved that fluctuations in fish catches are more on account of the operation of the infalliable law of diminishing marginal returns, the implications would be altogether different. It is quite likely that intensive fishing operations by a large number of mechanized boats in the same fishing grounds may be resulting in diminishing marginal returns of fish catches of individual fishing units. Reckless fishing by many boats in a particular fishing ground may adversely affect the earnings of a majority of them.

Concentration on prawn fish

One major offshoot of mechanized fishing has been that the entire fishing operation is geared towards catching of only shrimps which has eventually emerged as a dollar earner. As a result very little effort has been made to capture other species of fish which are in abundance in the exclusive economic zone. Because of the increase in the cost of hauling, mechanized fishing operations become profitable only when shrimp which has a high premium is caught in large quantities. The increase in the number of mechanized boats operating in the same ground resulted in some sort of uncertainty in the total catches of individual boats. The phenomenon coupled with the increased demand for prawns by exporters has created a number of problems for all those who have a stake in fishing and allied activities.

Variation in the catches of different mechanized boats

One seemingly paradoxical situation is that even in a lean period there would be some boats which get relatively higher catches compared to others. This happens because of different timings of fishing operations or the depth at which trawlers operate. The differences in the knowledge of fishermen regarding fishery biology and oceanography also contribute to this.

Hike in the price of diesel oil and other spare parts

Frequent rise in the cost of diesel oil and other spare parts has made a deep dent in the earnings of mechanized boats. Acute scarcity of diesel during the peak fishing season has caused considerable damage to the earning capacity of fishing boats. The high fuel cost has considerably reduced the number of fishing days. There are many instances of boats remaining idle as the operators find it extremely costly to operate the boat using the costlier fuel.

Increase in the wages of skilled labourers

The phenomenal increase in the number of mechanized boats has created acute shortage of skilled and experienced labourers. This has resulted in a stiff competition among the boat owners to engage skilled and experienced labourers by offering higher wages and higher profit incentives.

Fall in fish catches

In normal times, boats do not hesitate to go deep into the sea in search of bigger fish catches. But in times of scarcity, as experienced in 1979-80 and 1980-81, they are restricting their fishing operations to familiar grounds leading to overfishing and this results in sharp decline in per boat fish catches.

BANKS EXPERIENCE WITH DIFFERENT BORROWERS

The bankers experiences regarding the utilization and repayment of loans for vary. There are a large number of factors which are common to different types of borrowers and hence their impact would be again different on these borrowers depending upon their location. It has been observed that small borrowers are more prompt repaying the loan. It has been consistently the experience of banks that the small fishermen who borrow for investment on country crafts or mechanized boats take care to adhere to the repayment schedule. Except during periods of poor catches or fish famine, there are not many cases of default or mis-utilization of borrowings. The bank experience with co-operative societies or co-operative ventures of fishermen operating fishing vessels or having freezing units vary from state to state. One problem about the co-operative enterprise is the lack of managerial skill as has been noted in many of the co-operative enterprises in various fields of activities in the Indian economy. The co-operatives largely draw from the District Central Co-operative Bank and the NABARD to meet the financial requirements. By and large, their dependence on commercial banks for their financial needs is very less. There are a few instances of some progressive fish marketing federations venturing into fish catches and export of frozen fish. They seek banks' assistance to meet their credit needs for export and provide them to guidance regarding foreign markets. Repayment is made more or less according to schedule in these cases. Where management of co-operative federations is in good hands, there have been very few instances of mis-utilization of borrowed funds.

In the case of large scale units, the experience has been that vagaries of the monsoon sometimes prompt the borrowers to divert borrowed funds for other purposes, especially when they have multifarious activities. Instances are not wanting in number where fish processing is one of the activities of the big borrowers, who divert borrowed funds more frequently.

Of late, a large number of big industrial undertakings including some of the FERA companies have ventured into the fishing industry for utilizing the concessions available from various sources including banks. The financial requirements of these big companies however are not of a large magnitude and only in exceptional cases they have borrowed from banks for a specific purpose. Largely they have invested the internal resources generated from their other business enterprises while entering into the fishing export business. As the financial management of these industrial giants are done on a more scientific basis, repayment schedules are carefully adhered to.

ENTREPRENEURS' VIEW ON MARINE INDUSTRY

The 'entrepreneurs' in the case of an industry like the marine industry needs to be analysed before we enumerate their viewpoints. The entrepreneurs can be divided roughly into three groups :

1. The small fishermen, who are largely unorganized and work on an individual basis,
2. The co-operative venture of fishermen or marketing federation supported by the state government, and
3. The capitalist fishermen or the business entrepreneurs having abundant business experience in other fields of economic activities.

The views and expectations of the entrepreneurs from the above three groups vary widely. In the case of a small fisherman, whose expectations not go beyond improving his economic conditions, he has in general very limited view about future of the fishing industry. He is more worried about the socio-economic conflicts that are emerging between small fishermen who are using the country crafts and the others who have adopted mechanized fishing. A feeling perhaps is getting stronger in the minds of these smaller fishermen that, unless they opt for mechanized fishing, their very survival is in danger. The second group of entrepreneurs appears to have some blind faith in the co-operative institutions and hope to cling to it despite the problems of stiff competition they have to face while competing with the established entrepreneurs of the third group. The capitalist fishermen are the new entrants into the fishing industry who are planning to reap a rich harvest by venturing into modern fishing operations. This group is interested in modernizing the industry by giving it a professional bent through capitalization.

The small fishermen

The small fishermen seek more financial assistance and concessions from banks. They look forward to the following liberal terms in the banks' landing programmes.

Reduction in the rate of interest

In coastal areas, the advent of mechanized fishing has brought about certain socio-economic changes. Where the country crafts were in large number, introduction of mechanized boats has resulted in a decline in the earnings of the traditional fishermen. They aspire now therefore to acquire mechanized boats. In order to enable them to go in for mechanization which is necessary for their very survival, they seek financial assistance from commercial banks. The plea made by them is that the rate of interest charged by commercial banks is very high compared to the normal return expected from an uncertain industry. The present rate of interest is very high and a reduction will be very helpful.

Reduction in the margin money

The persent cost of a purse-seine boat, complete with engine and other gears, is anything over Rs. 6.00 lakh. To provide a margin of 20 per cent of the total investment, the fishermen find it extremely difficult. Because of their meagre savings, they are compelled to borrow from moneylenders or fish traders who later on exploit them by bargaining for a lower price for their catches. It would be desirable therefore to reduce the percentage of margin insisted upon in these cases.

Extension of the repayment period

Advances obtained for purchasing purse-seine boats are to be repaid within a period of five years. This is too short a period especially because of the seasonality of the industry. A longer repayment period could tide over the problems arising out of cyclical fluctuations. Very often a regular periodicity of three or five years in fish production is noted. If the repayment period is fairly longer it can evenout the fluctuations. In the case of agriculture, the land development banks offer loans for land improvement for a fairly longer period at very concessional rates of interest. Since investment in mechanized fishing is very large, a longer period of repayment may be considered.

Reduction in insurance premium

The premium on marine insurance account for 12 per cent of net operating income. The interest on borrowings and the insurance premium together account for over 25 per cent of the net earnings of mechanized boats. Since there has been a huge expansion in the number of mechanized boats and since the accident ratio is almost negligible, the insurance companies may consider a lowering of the insurance premium.

Reducing port duties

In some of the minor ports and fishing harbours, the fees charged for providing berthing and landing facilites for mechanized boats is arbitrary and exhorbitant. In some of the smaller ports where the facilities are very meagre, there has been a tendency among the port authorities to raise the port revenues by raising the fees charged for fish landing.

Supply of diesel at concessional rate

The substitution of diesel power for manpower has rendered fishing a fairly costlier operation. With the recent hike in the price of diesel oil, the fishermen are finding it extremely difficult to penetrate into the ocean in search of new fishing grounds. It is, therefore, pleaded that diesel for fishing operations may be supplied at a concessional rate and exempt it from the central excise duty. It is already reported that this is under the consideration of the Government of India.

Expansion of the marketing facilities

The shifting fortunes of the fishing industry are affected by either over catches or lower price. At lending sites in the developing fishing centres, it is desirable to have marketing facilities including cold storage and freezing facilities. Availability of fish vans with cold storage facilities will be helpful in transporting the excess fish catches to the consuming centres away from the coastal area.

Co-operatives

There are co-operative fish marketing federations functioning in the coastal states. Some of them have ventured into integrated fishing operations ranging from mechanized fishing to freezing and exporting. Some of them are doing extremely good while a few others are just surviving. The views expressed by some of the members of the fish marketing societies regarding the future of the marine fishing industry may be briefly reviewed.

Though the co-operative ventures obtain financial requirements from the land development banks or apex co-operative banks refinanced by NABARD, at a concessional rate of interest, these agencies are not in a position to meet their requirements completely. When these co-operative units undertake the export of frozen shrimp, their credit needs have to be met by commercial banks. Again, though the packing credit limits are available at a concessional rate of interest, the working capital needs of these units have to be obtained at rates which they consider are fairly higher. A plea is made for lowering the margin, reducing the rate of interest, and extending the period of repayment.

The state fisheries development corporations also are institutional entrepreneurs engaged in the fishing industry. The views expressed by the representatives of some of these also relate to the need for extending cheaper credit facilities. One common complaint is that banks do not appreciate the peculiarities of the fishing industry and hence do not automatically readjust the repayment schedule in times of fish famines. The attitude of the banks in treating the fishing industry purely on commercial considerations is hindrance to its growth.

The capitalist fishermen

This section of entrepreneurs in the fishing industry are perhaps more vociferous and better organized than the other two groups of entrepreneurs. They have ventured into this industry, as they want to exploit the untapped resources. They are insisting that fiscal and monetary incentives may be given to the fishing industry. This group is also more organized and hence is well-versed about the various concessions and facilities offered by both central and state governments.

Exporters of prawns and other processed fish products plead that the burden of payment of the premium under the export credit guarantee scheme may be reduced or waived by the government. At present, this premium is borne by exporters themselves. It is also pleaded that cash incentives for the export of shrimps which is now reduced may be revised upwards to the original level of 10 per cent. As shrimp export has been fluctuating largely in the recent years, the cash incentives may help the exporters to a large extent financially. One of the very often repeated arguments is that banks do not view the fishing industry as one with immense development prospects. Banks are accused of having a very limited horizon in the development of fishing industry. It is argued that in the case of agricultural advances, though the default ratio was high in the initial stages, the policy envisaged a greater flow of institutional credit for developing the agricultural economy. The present prosperity of the agricultural economy is largely on account of the huge investment made by big farmers through financial support provided by co-operatives as well as commercial banks. If these institutions are deterred by the initial problems of organization and recovery, they would not have contributed largely to agricultural prosperity. In the case of the development of marine industry also, banks may have to take calculated risk when extending their lending operations. From the point of view of employment generation, the fishing industry has very high development potentialities. Banks may have to formulate schemes keeping in view the long term perspectives.

Activizing the role of banks

It is evident that commercial banks are yet to play an effective role in bringing about remarkable changes in the marine industry. In the case of agriculture, the green revolution has been brought about through various developmental programmes implemented by state governments, ably supported by institutional credit agencies. Some stray references are often made to the "white revolution" in the case of expansion of the dairy industry and "blue revolution" in the case of development of the marine industry. The so-called blue revolution however has not yet reached Indian shores.

Considering the extensive coastal area, huge capital investment is necessary for providing the basic facilities for initiation of the "blue revolution". Both central and state governments may have to find resources for developing the infrastructure for an increasing fleet of mechanized boats. Unless, these facilities are available entrepreneurs also may not be enthused in investing in this industry. In the case of small scale industries, state governments have adopted a number of programmes for the industrialization of backward districts in the country by offering a variety of fiscal and monetary incentives. Such facilities are not available generally for the development of the marine industry. The state fisheries development corporations also rely upon banks for their financial needs and not on budgetory provisions. They have not been able to play an effective role so far.

The banking industry has its own difficulties in enlarging its involvement in the development of the fishing industry. Banks are not willing to enter into this field on a large scale as they feel that they are entering into an unchartered ocean without any navigational support. They tend to become overcautious especially when their experience in the initial years are of a mixed nature due to the vagaries of the fish catches. The credit pattern of commercial banks in India is such that they cannot go in for fairly long term investments in the fishing industry. Even with the assistance of refinance facilities offered by the NABARD, banks do not have lending schemes which extend beyond 3-5 years. Special schemes have to be formulated to enable banks to take up lending programmes on a long term basis.

Fisheries development branch

To improve the effectiveness of the banks' lending to the fishing industry, banks can set up fisheries development branches in coastal areas on the pattern of Agricultural Development Branches (ADB) of the State Bank of India. Technical personnel can be posted at these branches to handle effectively pre-sanction processing and post-sanction supervision. Adequate expertise and also a reliable data base on fishing operations can be built up in such branches. The recovery of loans also can be improved by encouraging the borrowers to put their savings in the branch.

Fisheries development bank

The element of uncertainty compels bankers to be overcautious in lending. There is a need for exploring the feasibility of establishing a separate bank for financing fishery projects on all-India basis. The public sector banks and the Reserve Bank of India may contribute to the capital of the proposed bank. The insurance companies who collect a fairly large amount of premium from mechanized boats can also contribute to the share capital of the new bank. The NABARD can also be partner in the establishment of this bank. NABARD personnel who have been handling fisheries project may form the nucleous of staff of this bank.

Other financial agencies

Other all-India level financial institutions may also have to play a greater role in the development of the fishing industry. The general insurance companies, for example, have only a one-way relationship with the fishing industry, providing insurance facilities by collecting the premium. It can explore the fields for investing the premia collected in those sectors which may directly contribute to the development of the fishing industry. At present, investments are made in the share capital of various industrial undertakings including those industries which are manufacturing the gears necessary for the fishing industry. It is perhaps necessary to earmark a larger portion of the premia collected from the fishing industry for investment in such industries. The insurance companies perhaps can help the port authorities to augment their financial position. The port authorities can improve the facilities in fishing harbours by borrowing from general insurance companies at a lower rate of interest, as insurance companies have a stake in the life of the fishing boats.

National Fisheries Development Board

The feasibility of establishing, a National Fisheries Development Board on the pattern of the National Dairy Development Board may be examined. The NFDB may be entrusted with the responsibility of formulating national fisheries development policies, preparing blueprint for expansion, co-ordinating the activities of various fisheries development corporations, and guiding the programmes of financing the National Fisheries Development Bank. At present, the contribution of the fishing industry to the gross national product is very small. But this industry, if properly exploited, can contribute substantially to the national income. Outlays are determined largely by the limitation of the total resources than by the actual needs of this industry. The establishment of the Board may be helpful in formulating policies for an integrated development of the marine industry.

PROJECTION OF CREDIT REQUIREMENTS

Assessing the capital requirements of a risk-prone industry like the marine industry is indeed very difficult. This is made difficult because of the absence of a comprehensive development plan. No bank has made any attempt to assess the future credit needs of the fishing industry. The credit budget estimates of commercial banks have a limited time horizon. Hence, in the credit budget estimates of commercial banks, on estimate of the credit needs of the fishing industry available.

The district credit plans are prepared by lead banks for all districts in India also do not provide details regarding the credit estimates of this industry document.

Public sector outlay

Estimates of total investment made by the private sector and the public sector undertakings in the marine industry are not available. The plan documents provide the details regarding the outlays envisaged in the Five Year Plans during the last 30 years. Since private investment in any industry has a strong co-relation with investment in that industry as envisaged in the plan programmes, a review of the plan outlays meant for the fisheries projects may be made. Outlays in the last six plans are given in Table 18.4.

TABLE 18.4 : **Investment in various Five Year Plans**

(Rs. in crore)

	Plan outlay	Outlay for agriculture and allied sectors	Outlay for fisheries	Percentage of fisheries outlay to	
				Plan outlay	Outlay for agriculture and allied sectors
First Plan	1960	294	5	0.26	1.76
Second Plan	4600	529	12	0.27	2.32
Third Plan	7500	1068	28	0.38	2.65
Fourth Plan	15902	2728	83	0.58	3.05
Fifth Plan	39322	4302	151	0.38	3.51
Sixth Plan	97500	6609	371	0.38	5.62

As is evident, investment in fisheries continues to be less than 0.5 per cent of the total plan investment in India. Considering the employment potentialities and capabilities of this industry in mitigating the food scarcity, the investment is too meagre. There is a need for enhancing the total investment in the subsequent plans to create an atmosphere which will be conducive for greater investment by the private sector. During the next two plan periods a minimum of Rs. 1000 crore may be earmarked for fishery development.

Private sector investment

A large part of the marine business is handled by the private sector. The public sector undertakings account for an insignificant percentage of the total fishing operations. Though no estimate of the total financial needs of the private sector is available, it may be noted that total demand for credit may not be met completely by institutional credit agencies. In these circumstances, it will be very difficult task to assess the credit needs of this industry. If the national planners can find the necessary resources for investment as mentioned above, it may not be wrong to presume that the private sector would be making a matching investment. In that case, the total credit needs of the private sector for investment may be estimated at Rs. 1000 crore over a period of next 10 years. Based on available details regarding the investment made in various activities, the total amount necessary for investment in augmenting the fleet of mechanized boats, improving storage facilities, expanding the freezing capacity and enlarging the export of processed foods are given in Appendix VII.

The financial requirements are estimated on a rough and ready manner as a preliminary estimate based on certain assumptions of linear relationships between the estimates of the projected fish catches as available in the published sources and the use of fishing gears and crafts. The time horizon of the estimates is limited to a decade, as it would be very difficult to hazard any guess of the future pattern of development in the absence of the definite fisheries development policy. The estimates therefore could be considered as the first approximates. Efforts would be made later to refine the estimation, if the details of the projected expansion in the fleet of boats and other fishing gears and ancillary activities are available.

The financial requirements for the replacement of the traditional boats are estimated at Rs. 6.15 crore up to 1990. Assuming an annual growth of 5 per cent in the increase in the fleet of mechanized boats of all types, the number of boats which could be launched during the decade 1980-1990 is estimated at 1440. A state-wise assessment of the requirement of additional boats of different sizes is not attempted at this stage. The financial requirement works out to be Rs. 288.00 crore or about Rs. 28.8 crore per annum. The estimates are based on the 1980 price level. This estimate could be a gross underestimation, if large size trawlers are to be included.

It is estimated that about 37 new processing units could be established mostly outside Kerala and Karnataka. With the expansion in the fleet of mechanized boats, the need for establishing freezing plants in some of the states could be felt during the later half of the 80s. The financial requirements of these units are estimated to be around Rs. 2.00 crore. It may be noted here that there is considerable under-utilization of the installed capacity. Quite number of these units are already sick for one reason or other. A carefully drawn out nursing programme with a more judicious injection of finance is necessary to revive most of these units. The financial agencies which have already sunk their money in such units have to take steps to nurse them back to life. It is however not possible to estimate the financial needs of these units.

Considering the expected growth in marine fish catches during the sixth Plan period, there is a need for assessing the likely demand for cold storage facilities as well as demand for ice. The available figures relating to ice plants and installed capacity are gross underestimates. The figures published by the Marine Products Export Development Authority (MPEDA) relate to only the ice plants registered with MPEDA. There is a large number of unregistered ice plants in all the coastal districts. Hence, it is somewhat difficult to judge the scope for establishing additional ice plants. A conservative estimate of 60 new ice plants (of the average size) is assumed to be feasible during the next 10 years. Their financial requirements would be less than Rs. 1.50 crore.

As for canning units and fish meal plants, there is enough scope in some states if the state governments could provide the infrastructure. The credit needs of such units are estimated at not more than Rs. 1 crore.

The total financial requirements are estimated to be around Rs. 300.00 crore till 1990. The annual credit need is thus around Rs. 30.00 crore. The estimate of the credit requirements made by the National Commission on Agriculture compares favourably with the present estimate. Considering the cost structure of fishing vessels in 1973, the capital investment has been estimated to be Rs. 20.00 crore per annum. The methodology is not, however, elaborated in the report of the National Commission on Agriculture. A more systematic approach to the estimation of credit needs has to be adopted.

OTHER ISSUES

Marketing of fish and economic conditions of the large number of small fishermen who remain beyond the reach of mechanization are two issues which are of great importance. By recognizing their specific needs and by designing the developmental programmes suitably, greater contribution to their living conditions can be made with a little financial investment.

Preservation of fish by salting and drying is an age old subsidiary occupation of the fishing population. This job is mostly handled by fisher women. Nearly 30 to 40 per cent of the trash sea fish is preserved through this process. The volume of dried fish marketed varies from state to state. Bank finance is availed by them to a small extent. The whole process is carried out in less hygenic conditions for want of necessary facilities. Even the storage and transportation is done with makeshift arrangements. There is a need for organizing this business on more scientific grounds.

There is perhaps a case for organizing the Fishermen's Service Societies, on the pattern of the Farmers' Service Societies as recommended by the National Commission on Agriculture. The Farmers' Service Society is distinctly different from the primary co-operative society. The concept of Farmers' Service Society is such that under one roof besides the required credit, the other inputs required by the farmers are also marketed by the same agency. There are a large number of farmers' service societies functioning today in the country organized on co-operative basis either by commercial banks or by co-operative banks. On the same line, the Fishermen's Service Societies can be set up either by commercial banks or by co-operative banks. They could cater to the financial requirements of the small fishermen and fisherwomen who undertake fish processing and marketing. Simple equipments like baskets, drying mats and salt could be provided by the Fishermen's Service Society to their members besides extending required short term credit. This type of a society is entirely different from the Fish Farmers' Development Societies which are in vogue in some parts of the country. Emulating the excellent work done by the Farmers' Service Society set up by a few banks it should be possible for the banks to set up the Fishermen's Service Society of the same line. The State Fisheries Department can provide the necessary technical guidance as is done by the Department of Agriculture, Department of Animal Husbandry, and the Department of Co-operation in the case of Farmers' Service Societies. A few of the commercial banks which have lead bank responsibilities in coastal states may be sounded by the state governments to explore the possibilities of setting up such Fishermen's Service Societies. An initiative on the part of the state government is necessary in this sphere. Given the necessary support, commercial banks may come forward to establish such societies on a selective basis. It may be added here that in the case of the agricultural economy, the benefits of the development activities have been derived mostly by bigger farmers. It was therefore decided to formulate special programmes for ameliorating the economic conditions of the marginal and small farmers. The programmes like the Small Farmers' Development Agency and the Marginal Farmers' Development Agency were introduced. The Farmers' Service Societies have been established with a view to helping the marginal farmers, agricultural labourers, and village artisans. Similarly, in the case of rapid development of the fishing industry, the benefits of mechanization and the capital intensive operations are likely to accrue to only a section of the fishing community. A large percentage of the fishing population who have very little assets would certainly remain much beyond the reach of the new prosperity generated by mechanized fishing. This section of the fishing community can be certainly helped through the Fishermen's Service Societies.

REFERENCES

Annual Reports of the Tamil Nadu Fisheries Development Corporation Ltd. 1976-1977, 1977-78.

Bhatt, Tushar, Sea Fish—1. Big Rise in Demand Forecast—*Business Standard*, February 2, 1982.

Bhatt, Tushar, Sea Fish—2, Big Rise in Prices—*Business Standard*, February 3, 1982.

Bhatt, Tushar, Sea Fish—3. Investment and Returns—*Business Standard*, February 4, 1982.

Bhatt, Tushar, Sea Fish—4. Meeting the Million Tonne Shortfail, *Business Standard*, February 5, 1982.

Bhatt, Tushar, Sea Fish—5. Breaking the Monopoly of Traders, *Business Standard*, February 6, 1982.

Chidambaram, K., 'Fishing Industry—Special Features for Financing, *Financial Express*, April 13, 1978.

Gokhale, S.V., "The Manila Called Deep Ssea Fishing" *Science Today*, August 1982, Bombay.

Goyal, R.P., "Fisheries—The Financial Hurdles", *Economic Times*, February 28, Bombay, 1981.

Nakra, R.S. "Development of Fisheries and Indegenous Capacity", *Economic Times*, April 5, Bombay, 1978.

Papers presented at the Symposium on Development of Deep Sea Fishing held at Central Institute of Fisheries Technology, Cochin : February 1970.

Reserve Bank of India "Credit Needs and Problems of Fishermen in Tuticorin—A Case Study" Report of a Study Group of the National Credit Council at Organisational Framework for the Implementation of Social Objectives, Bombay, October 1969.

Report on the Evaluation Study of Mechanized Fishing Boats in South Kanara District—1973—1975. By Evaluation Cell, Agricultural Refinance and Development Corporation, Evaluation Study Series No. 9, Bombay—1976.

Report of the National Commission on Agriculture, Part VIII, Fisheries, Government of India, New Delhi 1976.

Report of Ministry of Agriculture 1980-81, Chapter VI, Fisheries, Government of India, New Delhi 1982.

Sahetiya Srichand : "Deep Sea Fishing still a Far Cry", *Economic Times*, February 28, Bombay, 1981.

Srivastava, U.K., *et al. Management of Marine Fishing Industry*, Oxford and IBH Publishing Co., New Delhi, 1982.

Thingalaya, N.K., "The Vicissitudes of the Fishing Industry : An Economic Analysis", *Pigmy Economic Review*, April—1973.

Unninayar, Seetha, "Indian Fishing in Deep Waters", *Business World*, August 16-29, Bombay, 1982.

Wagle, S.N., "Marine Fisheries Plan Unrealistic", *Economic Times*, May 23, Bombay, 1978.

APPENDIX-I

NUMBER OF BRANCHES INVOLVED IN FINANCING FISHING INDUSTRY

Name of the bank	Andhra Pradesh	Karna- taka	Kerala	Tamil Nadu	West Bengal	Mahara- shtra	Orissa	Guja- rat	Goa	Total
State Bank Group										
State Bank of India										
State Bank of Mysore	—	2	—	—	—	—	—	—	—	2
State Bank of Saurashtra	—	—	—	—	—	—	—	16	2	18
Nationalized Banks										
Syndicate Bank	9	49	28	4	—	7	4	—	11	112
Canara Bank	—	29	3	13	—	—	—	—	—	45
Union Bank of India	—	—	5	—	—	—	—	—	—	5
United Commercial Bank	—	—	—	—	—	—	—	—	4	4
Indian Overseas Bank	4	2	10	8	—	2	1	1	2	30
Corporation Bank	1	23	5	—	—	3	—	—	6	38
Oriental Bank of Commerce	—	—	—	—	—	—	—	—	1	1
Bank of Maharashtra	1	1	1	1	1	7	—	3	4	19
Andhra Bank	38	—	2	3	—	—	3	—	—	46
Vijaya Bank					—n.a.—					
United Bank of India	—	1	—	—	3	1	8	2	—	15
Private Sector Banks										
Karnataka Bank Ltd.	—	30	1	—	—	—	—	—	—	31
Dhanalakshmi Bank Ltd.	—	—	7	1	—	—	—	—	—	8
Bank of Cochin Ltd.	—	—	12	—	—	—	—	—	—	12
	53	136	75	30	4	20	16	22	30	386

APPENDIX-II

LOANS DISBURSED BY BANKS TO FISHING INDUSTRY

(1976-80)

Bank/State	Country craft and equipments		Mechanized boats and equipments	
	Account (No.)	Amount (Rs. in lakh)	Account (No.)	Amount (Rs. in lakh)
State Bank of Mysore State : Karnataka			15	18.10
State Bank of Saurashtra State : Gujarat	1402	41.38	47	32.16

APPENDIX-II : (*Contd.*)

(*Rs. in lakh*)

Bank/state	Country craft and equipments	Mechanized boats and equipments	Freezing and cold storage plants, processing, marketing, fish transport, export and other purposes
Syndicate Bank			
1. Andhra Pradesh	—	—	* 17.75
2. Tamil Nadu	—	—	* 39.01
3. Karnataka	—	*701.79	*188.13
4. Kerala	—	*135.84	* 36.72
5. Maharashtra	1.96	6.13	* 8.32
6. Orissa	0.93	27.00	—
7. West Bengal	—	—	* 0.41
8. Union Territory of Goa, Diu, Daman	—	* 57.62	* 39.01
	2.89	928.38	329.35

* Amount outstanding as on 31-12-1980, included loans sanctioned and disbursed under NABARD schemes.

APPENDIX-II : (Contd.)

(Rs, in lakh)

Bank/state	Country craft & equipments		Mechanized boats & equipments		Freezing & cold storage plants		Marketing		Fish transport		Other purposes	
	Account (No.)	Amount	Account (No.)	Amount	Account (No.)	Amount	Account (No.)	Amount	Account (No.)	Amount	Account (No.)	Amount
Canara Bank												
(i) Karnataka, Andhra Pradesh and Union Territory of Goa	65	2.15	44	46.70	1	3.72	39	0.15	—	—	19	3.62
(ii) Kerala	7	0.63	—	—	2	2.00	—	—	1	1.00	—	—
Total	72	2.78	44	46.70	3	5.72	39	0.15	1	1.00	19	3.62

APPENDIX-II : (*Contd.*)

(*Rs. in lakh*)

	Country craft and equipments		Mechanized boat and equipments		Freezing & cold storage plants	Processing Marketing		Fish transport	Export
	Account (No.)	Amount	Account (No.)	Amount		Account (No.)	Amount		
Union Bank of India									
(i) Kerala	204	1.56	—	—		17	103.90		
(ii) Tamil Nadu	130	3.08	5	0.30		—	—		
Total	334	4.64	5	0.30		17	103.90		
United Commercial Bank	49	1.04	8	4.00		—	—		

APPENDIX-II : (*Contd.*)

(*Rs. in lakh*)

Bank/state	1976		1977		1978		1979		1980	
	Account (No.)	Amount	Account (No.)	Amount	Account (No.)	Amount	Account (No.)	Amount	Account (No.)	Amount
Indian Overseas Bank										
1. Andhra Pradesh	10	3.83	150	5.95	332	3.86	369	6.98	336	14.36
2. Goa	—	—	3	0.05	10	5.07	25	2.94	56	1.64
3. Gujarat	—	—	—	—	37	3.70	12	0.06	—	—
4. Karnataka	—	—	—	—	—	—	27	0.29	44	1.15
5. Kerala	8	0.05	66	0.54	9	1.93	280	5.42	1065	15.28
6. Orissa	10	0.03	—	—	—	—	9	0.05	26	0.41
7. West Bengal	—	—	—	—	—	—	1	0.02	—	—
8. Tamil Nadu	66	0.42	34	2.70	39	2.53	944	21.29	368	11.07
9. Pondicherry	40	0.96	—	—	38	0.76	10	0.30	76	2.12
	134	5.29	253	9.24	465	17.85	1677	37.35	1971	46.03

N.B. 1. Purpose-wise details not available.

2. Data includes loans sanctioned and amount disbursed under NABARD schemes also.

APPENDIX-II : (*Contd.*)

(*Rs. in lakh*)

Bank/state	Country craft and equipments		Mechanized boats and equipments		Freezing and cold storage		Processing		Other purposes	
	Account (No.)	Amount	Account (No.)	Amount	Account (No.)	Amount	Account (No.)	Amount	Account (No.)	Amount
Corporation Bank										
1. Andhra Pradesh	—	—	1	0.25	—	—	—	—	—	—
2. Karnataka	53	8.44	36	28.89	5	7.75	98	132.27	28	532.34
3. Kerala	—	—	2	1.38	—	—	—	—	17	23.48
4. Maharashtra	—	—	—	—	1	6.16	—	—	72	328.76
5. Goa	1	0.02	25	4.83	1	0.10	—	—	5	25.98
6. All other states and Union Territories	—	—	1	0.25	—	—	—	—	—	—
Total	54	8.46	65	35.60	7	14.01	98	132.27	122	910.56

APPENDIX-II : (*Contd.*)

(*Rs. in lakh*)

Bank/state	Country craft and equipments		Mechanized boats and equipments		Freezing and cold storage plants		Export	
	Account (No.)	Amount	Account (No.)	Amount	Account (No.)	Amount	Account (No.)	Amount
Bank of Maharashtra								
1. Andhra Pradesh	—	—	9	7.90	—	—	—	—
2. Kerala-1980	50	1.50	—	—	—	—	—	—
3. Tamil Nadu-1980	—	—	1	0.90	—	—	—	—
Total	50	1.50	10	8.80				
Andhra Bank								
1. Andhra Pradesh	—	—	2	34.50	1	15.00	—	—
2. Maharashtra	—	—	—	—	1	15.00	—	—
3. Orissa	—	—	1	12.50	—	—	—	—
4. Kerala	—	—	1	22.00	—	—	—	—
Total	—	—	4	69.00	2	30.00	—	—
United Bank of India								
1. Maharashtra	85	1.42	—	—	—	—	2	144.26
2. Kerala	—	—	7	4.62	—	—	—	—
Total	85	1.42	7	4.62	—	—	2	144.26

APPENDIX-II : (*Contd.*)

(*Rs. in lakh*)

Bank/state	Country craft and equipments		Mechanized boat and equipments		Other purposes	
	Account (No.)	Amount	Account (No.)	Amount	Account (No.)	Amount
Karnataka Bank Ltd.						
1. Karnataka	21	1.58	52	45.52	—	—
2. Kerala	—	—	1	1.08	—	—
Total	21	1.58	53	46.60	—	—
Dhanalakshmi Bank Ltd.						
1. Kerala	—	—	—	—	—	—
2. Tamil Nadu	80	0.52	—	—	—	—
Total	80	0.52	—	—	—	—

APPENDIX-II :*(*Contd.*)

(*Rs. in lakh*)

Bank/state	Country craft and equipments		Mechanized boats and equipments		Freezing and cold storage plants		Processing		Fish transport		Export		Other purposes	
	A/c (No.)	Amount	A/c (No.)	Amount	A/c (No.)	Amount	A/c (No.)	Amount	A/c (No.)	Amount	A/c (No.)	Amount	A/c (No.)	Amount
Bank of Cochin Ltd.														
Kelala	—	0.10	—	0.72	—	0.10	—	0.35	—	0.24	—	12.65	—	—

N.B. Data relates to number of accounts and loans sanctioned only.

* The details of the credit disbursements made by the bank during the five-year period are based on the replies received from the responding banks. The data relating to various types of fishing advances in different states have been called for. However, they are not available on uniform basis. These data relate to the disbursements made by the banks under their own schemes.

APPENDIX-III

ADVANCES MADE BY BANKS THROUGH NABARD ASSISTANCE

(*Up to February 1981*)

State	Fisheries projects (Number)	Financial assistance (Rs. in lakh)	NABARD commitment (Rs. in lakh)	Total disbursement (Rs. in lakh)
West Bengal	4	29	23	2
Orissa	17	307	285	160
Andhra Pradesh	41	220	156	22
Pondicherry	1	26	21	—
Tamil Nadu	71	665	505	483
Kerala	100	645	476	341
Karnataka	97	1517	1097	956
Goa	57	546	436	322
Maharashtra	55	379	297	157
Gujarat	24	452	753	427
Total	467	5286	4049	2870

Source : National Bank for Agricultural and Rural Development, Bombay.

APPENDIX-IV

DISPOSAL OF CREDIT PROPOSALS OF FISHING INDUSTRY

(*1976 to 1980*)

Name of the Bank	Proposals received	Proposals accepted	Proposals rejected
State Bank Group	1555	1535	20
State Bank of India	—	-n.a.-	—
State Bank of Mysore	18	18	—
State Bank of Saurashtra	1537	1517	20
Nationalized Banks	841	800	41
Syndicate Bank	178	164	14
Canara Bank	163	159	4
Union Bank of India	135	127	8
United Commercial Bank	67	62	5
Indian Overseas Bank	—	-n.a.-	—
Corporation Bank	82	76	6
Oriental Bank of Commerce	4	4	—
Bank of Maharashtra	104	104	—
Andhra Bank	108	104	4
Vijaya Bank	—	-n.a.-	—
Private Sector Banks	583	458	125
Karnataka Bank Limited	274	185	89
Dhanalakshmi Bank Limited	154	153	1
Bank of Cochin Limited	155	120	35
Total	2979	2793	186

APPENDIX-V

TECHNICAL PERSONNEL EMPLOYED BY BANKS

Name of the Bank	No. of Officers
State Bank Group	
State Bank of Saurashtra	1
Nationalized Banks	
Syndicate Bank	2
Canara Bank	1
United Commercial Bank	1
Corporation Bank	3
Private Sector Banks	
Karnataka Bank Ltd.	1
Total	9

APPENDIX-VI

RECOVERY PERFORMANCE OF BANKS

(as on December 1980)

(Rs. in lakhs)

Name of the Bank	Amount demanded	Amount overdue	Default ratio (percentage)
State Bank Group			
State Bank of India	—	n.a.	—
State Bank of Mysore	4.50	3.43	76.22
State Bank of Saurashtra	49.27	33.54	68.07
Nationalized Banks			
Syndicate Bank	708.63	280.57	40.00
Canara Bank	112.40	52.76	46.49
Union Bank of India	—	26.52	—
United Commercial Bank	22.76	19.72	86.64
Indian Overseas Bank	—	n.a.	—
Corporation Bank	122.98	91.79	74.63
Oriental Bank of Commerce	0.48	0.39	81.25
Bank of Maharashtra	16.84	12.93	76.78
Andhra Bank	15.41	11.34	73.59
Vijaya Bank	—	n.a.	—
Private Sector Banks			
Karnataka Bank Limited	—	59.99	—
Dhanalakshmi Bank	2.85	0.15	5.26
Bank of Cochin Limited	2.65	1.25	47.17

APPENDIX-VII

FINANCIAL REQUIREMENTS OF THE MARINE FOOD INDUSTRY

Types of Fishing gears and plants	Existing size of the Fishing gears and plants	Estimated Increase in the size			Estimated Financial Requirements		
		1985	1990	Total	1985	1990	Total
	Number	Number			(Rs. in lakh)		
1. Non-mechanized boats	120000	6000	6300	12300	300	315	615
2. Mechanized boats (all types)	14000	700	740	1440	14000	14800	28800
3. Processing units	322	17	20	37	68	80	148
4. Ice plants	156	8	11	19	80	110	190
5. Cold storages	378	20	24	44	60	72	132
6. Fish Meal Plants	34	3	5	8	12	20	32
7. Canning plants	69	3	5	8	15	25	40
Total					14535	15422	29957

19

ROLE OF NABARD IN THE DEVELOPMENT OF MARINE FISHERIES

R.G. DANDEKAR

INTRODUCTION

It is now recognized that fisheries is one of the important allied activities of the agricultural sector. Planned development of the fisheries sector however started only with the launching of the First Five Year Plan in 1951-52. Through successive five year plans, the fisheries sector, particularly marine fisheries sector, has registered significant growth in fish production, improvement of infrastructure, and export trade of marine products. While during the initial period of development the industry to a large extent depended upon the financial resources of the government of India and various state governments, during the last 7-8 years the industry is availing more and more financial assistance from Commercial and State Co-operative Banks, with refinance facilities from NABARD (ARDC earlier).

Increase in production is mainly on account of the mechanization programme of the fishing craft. The mechanization programme was launched with a sizeable government subsidy towards the cost of marine engines, fishing boats, and fishing equipment. As the programme became popular with the fishermen the state governments gradually reduced the quantum of subsidy. During the last 10 years the mechanization programme on the east coast has gathered tremendous momentum on account of lucrative export markets for frozen shrimp. Even on the south-west coast the export potential of frozen shrimp was mainly responsible in the rapid progress of the mechanization programme.

NABARD'S OBJECTIVES

The main objective of NABARD is to extend financial support to the development of marine fishing industry to enable the industry to register over a period of years, substantial increase in marine fish production. National Bank for Agriculture and Rural Development (NABARD) also attaches great importance to support necessary infrastructure. Lack of facilities for handling perishable commodity like fish will render the efforts for augmenting fish production unrewarded because if shore facilities do not exist the producer would not get financial benefit of increased fish production. NABARD, therefore, extends financial support for creation of infrastructure to take care of fish production. With these objectives in view, NABARD believes that the fishing industry as a whole will be placed on sound footing and there will be a significant improvement in the socio-economic standards of the fishermen community.

SCOPE OF REFINANCE

Under the purview of NABARD refinance, the following components of the industry are considered eligible:

Fishing boats

The majority of schemes submitted by financing banks to NABARD are for financing purchase of mechanized fishing boats along with necessary deck equipment and fishing nets. While the majority of fishing boats are wooden boats ranging from 8.0 to 15.0 metres in length and equipped with 30 HP to 150 HP engines, recently NABARD has also supported financing of medium size steel fishing vessels of about 13.6 metres in length. Similarly on experimental basis, NABARD has also supported scheme for financing 23 meters deep sea fishing vessels equipped with 380 HP engines. These vessels, however, were built indegenously.

Along with mechanized boats, the traditional fishing craft

like catamarans, navas, and dug-out canoes are also eligible for refinance. This category of crafts is likely to benefit the traditional sector of the fishermen community who mainly depend on fishing in inshore waters.

Infrastructure

Establishment of ice plants, cold storages, freezing plants, fish canning plants, fish-meal plants, fish auction halls, service stations and workshops, bunkering facilities, and so on, are all eligible for refinance, provided the scheme includes the production-oriented items, namely fishing boats.

Refinance facilities are also available for transport, distribution, and marketing of fish. For this purpose refrigerated trucks or insulated trucks, fish stalls, and deep freezers can be financed.

GENERAL TERMS AND CONDITIONS OF REFINANCE

Schemes for development of marine fisheries are formulated by financing banks normally in consultation with the state fisheries department and submitted to NABARD whenever banks seek refinance facility. In order to enable the banks to formulate the schemes on proper lines, NABARD has prepared checklists for use of financing banks so that by following the checklists the banks may know whether necessary information required by NABARD for technical and financial scheme has been included in the scheme.

The scheme is scrutinized by NABARD financial and technical feasibility. If necessary, field studies are conducted by NABARD to assess the technical and financial viability of the schemes. It may be stated that with the circulation of checklists for the formulation of fishery schemes, the financing institutions have been submitted the fishery schemes which include necessary information so that the schemes can be scrutinized and cleared expeditiously. National Bank for Agriculture and Rural Development (NABARD) checklists for formulation of marine fishery schemes are given in Appendices I and II.

The state co-operative banks, commercial banks, including regional rural banks, and land development banks are considered eligible financing institutions for availing refinance facilities from NABARD. Depending upon the scheme, NABARD refinance is available to the extent of 75 to 90 per cent of the loans given by financing banks. The repayment period of loan is determined on the basis of surplus available in the unit economics of the schemes. For fisheries loans, the repayment period varies from 3 to 8 years.

As far as borrowers are concerned, NABARD accepts individuals, group fishermen, fishery co-operative society, partnership firms, and registered companies as beneficiaries of fisheries schemes. However, in all such cases the schemes have to be forwarded to NABARD through scheduled banks.

Regarding interest rates NABARD charges 7.5 per cent interest from financing banks and are permitted to lend money to the ultimate borrower at 11.35 per cent according to the prevailing practice.

State-wise and agency-wise distribution of marine fishery schemes sanctioned upto 31 December, 1983

NABARD has so far sanctioned 466 marine fishery schemes in all the maritime states of the country including Union Territories of Goa, Daman, Diu and Pondicherry. The total financial outlay on the above schemes is Rs. 93.45 crore out of which NABARD commitments is Rs. 73.68 crore. As on 3 December 1983 the actual disbursement made by NABARD in the marine fishery sector is Rs. 45.66 crore. A statement indicating agency-wise and area-wise distribution of marine fishery schemes is given in Appendix III. It will be observed from the statement that the majority of the schemes have been sponsored by commercial banks although a few integrated fishery schemes are being implemented in the co-operative sector. These schemes are sponsored by the state co-operative banks. The integrated schemes generally provide for financing of fishing boats to the fishermen members of the primary fishermen's co-operative societies and establishment of shore facilities such as ice plants, cold storages, processing plants, service stations, and so on. The schemes also include facilities for distribution and marketing of the catch. As regards schemes sponsored by commercial banks, they are largely related to financing of various types of fishing boats depending upon the scheme area and the nature of fishery to be exploited. The boats financed by commercial banks include small and medium sized (25' to 50') mechanized wooden trawlers, gill-netters, and purse-seiners for exploitation of mackerel and sardine fishery resources particularly off the Goa and Karnataka coast. It may be stated that recently some of the land development banks, after modifying their bye-laws to cover the marine fishery sector, are also sponsoring schemes for financing of fishing boats. The fishery schemes sanctioned also cover traditional sectors such as financing of catamarans, canoes, and supply of nylon gill nets to the traditional fishermen for exploitation of inshore fishery resources. Details of the boats sanctioned under the refinance scheme is given in the Appendix IV.

WORLD BANK ASSISTED FISHERY PROJECTS

In the marine fishery sector, the World Bank has sanctioned two projects, one each in Gujarat and Andhra Pradesh. The project covers improvement of fishery harbours, provision of shore facilities, and provision of credit for purchase of mechanized fishing boats.

Gujarat fisheries project

The total cost of the Gujarat Fishery Project sanctioned by the World Bank is around US $ 38 million. Some of the salient features of the project are as under:

(1) Improvement of fishery harbours at Mangrol and Veraval;

(2) Shore facilities at Mangrol and Veraval to provide necessary support for the existing fishing fleet and its expansion contemplated under the project;

(3) Credit facilities to individual entrepreneurs for establishment of fish processing plants such as freezing, and canning plants at Mangrol and Veraval harbours;

(4) Construction and supply of 270 14.8-metre long wooden mechanized boats;

(5) Assistance to traditional fisheries by providing 350 9-metre dug-out canoes and installing out-board motors

on them. Similarly supply of credit for purchase of 1050 out-board motors to the existing canoes is also contemplated in the project.

The World Bank Fisheries Project in Gujarat is expected to make a significant contribution to the fishery production of the state. At full development fish production would increase by approximately 44000 metric tonnes per year out of which about 3700 tonnes would be exportable quality shrimp.

World bank fisheries project in Andhra Pradesh

The total cost of the Andhra Pradesh Fisheries Project is approximately US $ 35 million. The salient features of the project are as under :

(1) Improvement of harbour facilities at Kakinada, Vishakapatnam, and Nizampatnam;

(2) Construction and supply of 300 numbers of 10 metre mechanized fishing boats for Kakinada and Vishakapatnam, 60 of 9-metre mechanized fishing boats for Nizampatnam, and 60 of non-mechanized 12-metre sail craft also for Nizampatnam. As in the case of Gujarat Project, this project also contemplates establishment of necessary infrastructural facilities near the fishing harbours. Funds for financing, purchase of fishing boats and provision of shore and infrastructural facilities in both projects would be channelized through NABARD.

OBSERVATIONS OF NABARD IN THE IMPLEMENTATION OF FISHERY SCHEMES

As indicated earlier NABARD has financed fishery schemes in co-operative and private sectors. Whereas the schemes in the co-operative sector are of integrated nature, the schemes in the private sector by and large are generally restricted to financing of fishing boats in the areas where adequate infrastructure exists.

Follow-up studies of some of the co-operative fishery schemes have revealed certain shortcomings in implementation. Often it sufficient care is not exercised while selecting the beneficiaries to whom fishing boats are allotted. In case the beneficiaries are not conversant with the operation of fishing boats, the performance is unsatisfactory. Another shortcoming is inefficient management of the project. The project officers who are generally deputed from the state fisheries departments are frequently shifted for administrative reasons. Such frequent changes adversely affect the success of the project. Because there is no continuity in the management personnel, the tendency of the beneficiaries is to become indifferent to project management and this results, many times, in pilferage of fish catches and ultimately affecting recovery performance of the project. Unless the beneficiaries are very sincere and loyal members of the co-operative societies there is every possibility of their fish catches being diverted to fish traders operating in the scheme area who are more than willing to purchase fish from such borrowers of the co-operative scheme on cash payment. This practice obviously affects the loan recovery of the co-operative project. It is the considered view of NABARD that the state governments may have to take necessary steps so as to remove the above drawbacks inherent in the co-operative fishery projects if such projects are to succeed.

It is generally observed in some of the follow-up studies of fishery schemes financed by commercial banks that the borrowers are mostly individuals who are required to contribute anything between 15 and 25 per cent of the cost of fishing boat as margin money. Considering the investment required for a mechanized fishing boat, the quantum of margin money is quite substantial and the borrowers have always a substantial financial stake in the scheme. This factor is largely responsible in NABARD's view, for better success of the fishery schemes in the private sector.

Another peculiarity of the fishing operations is the migration of boats from the scheme area to another in search of larger fish catch. It is quite common that the oprational area of fishing boats not only cuts across district boundaries but in many cases even state boundaries. Migration of fishing boats although create considerable difficulties in the proper monitoring of their operations cannot be avoided taking into consideration the nature of the industry. It may be pointed out that the operational economics for a majority of mechanised fishing boats are very sensitive to shrimp catches which account in the case of trawel fishing, anything between 60 to 75 per cent of the income. It is, therefore, felt that in order to ensure timely recovery of loans, the financing institutions may have to make arrangements for necessary supervisory staff. In many cases it is observed that the financing institutions except the fishermen borrowers to remit their loan instalments on their own. However, in many cases bacause of such undue expectations from the borrowers, the overdues of fishing loans go on increasing where there is not proper monitoring arrangements and the borrower has always a ready excuse for the default poor catch. There is lot of uncertainty and fluctuations in fish catches either from season to season or from year to year, unless banks make their own enquiries about the nature of fishing season, they may not be able to show satisfactory recovery performance of their fisheries loans. There is, therefore, an urgent need for the financing institutions to appoint technical fishery staff for monitoring the operations and supervising the recovery from fishing boats. It is heartening to note that some of the commercial banks have already appointed fisheries technical staff for loan recovery. However a lot needs to be done in this respect. Monitoring and Evaluation Cells at central and regional offices of NABARD conduct periodical monitoring and evaluation studies of fishery schemes. These studies give a very useful feedback. However financing institutions should also conduct similar studies.

Development of brackish water fish culture

In the marine fishery sector NABARD has recently included a development programme for the culture of brackish water fish. It is well-known that the country has a very extensive brackish water area which can be utilised with advantage either for monoculture or polyculture of brackish water varieties of fish such as mullet, channos, and shrimps. Brackish water fisheries development will have a great future, particularly for the culture of white and tiger prawns which are greatly priced in export market. National Bank for Agriculture and Rural Development (NABARD) would be willing to support development of brackish water fisheries by extending refinance facilities to eligible financing institutions.

Deep sea fishing

Declaration by the Government of India of the exclusive economic zone has made available a vast area for the fishing industry. The Government expects that private entrepreneurs and the corporate sector take full advantage by availing loan facilities which were offered till very recently through the Shipping Development Fund Committee under the Ministry of Transport and Shipping. For quite some time a dialogue is going on between the Government of India and NABARD to find out whether financing of deep sea fishing vessels can be routed through NABARD. In the interest of the industry, it is very necessary that the decision in this respect is taken as quickly as possible. Considering the cost of deep sea vessels and the number of vessels required, it may be stated that the credit requirement to finance deep sea fisheries programme will be very large. Even if another 200 vessels are to be in operation by the end of Sixth Five Year plan, the credit requirement may be anything between Rs. 120 to Rs. 140 crore.

PERSPECTIVE LENDING PROGRAMME FOR FISHERY SECTOR

NABARD has formulated perspective lending programmes to support small and medium sized fishing boats, creation of infrastructure for promotion of the marine fishery sector. NABARD has provided under the general line of credit popularly known as the ARDC credit project III for the period 1979-81 Rs. 20.97 crore and under ARDC Credit Project IV for the period 1981-83 Rs. 2389 crore for the development of the marine fishery. In line with the Government of India policy it has been emphasized in the aforesaid perspective lending programme the need for diversification of fishing methods as well as diversification of fishery products. This emphasis will imply that in future the credit requirement should be directed more towards mechanized fishing boats for operation of gill-nets, purse-seine nets, long lines,mid-water, and pelagic trawls. The reason for such emphasis is to avoid over exploitation of coastal fishery resources because by and large the level of exploitation of fishery resources from the coastal area barring certain areas is not likely to yield more fish. On the contrary it will result in reduction of catch per unit effort and will make the operations uneconomic. Therefore, as far as coastal fishery is concerned it is desirable to finance only such number of fishing units which are required to replace those which may be going out of commission.

The level of harvestable fishery potential can be achieved only if the fishery resources of the offshore and the deep sea regions can be economically exploited. This is possible not merely by employing big sized fishing vessels but by adhering to better utilization of low priced fish reported to be available in abundance in offshore and deep sea fishery regions. If these varieties of fish are processed into various fishery bye-products, it may be possible to diversify export markets. It is hoped that in the very near future the fish processing technology will be sufficiently developed so that it is possible to promote marine product export to a large number of countries. The success of economic exploitation of the fishery resources of the exclusive economic zone very much depending upon this factor.

APPENDIX-I

CHECK LIST OF TECHNICAL INFORMATION TO BE SUPPLIED WHILE FORWARDING TO NABARD MARINE FISHERIES SCHEMES

General

Name of the Scheme/Project

Sponsoring Bank

Scheme implementing Agency

Individual/Fishery Co-operative/Partnership firm

Registered Company

Proposed period

Financial outlay

Brief description about the existing activities concerning Marine Fisheries in the Scheme

(1) No. of Mechanized Boats in Operation

(2) No. of Non-Mechanized Boats in operation

(3) Estimated Annual Fish Landing by Mechanized/Non-Mechanized Boats

(4) Infrastructural Facilities available in the Scheme Area.

- (a) Landing, Berthing and Bunkering Facilities
- (b) Ice and Cold Storage Plants, production and storage capacities of the plants should be mentioned (in Metric Tonnes)
- (c) Freezing plants and Frozen storage capacities (Metric Tonnes)
- (d) Workshop facilities for the repairs of Marine Engine, Repairs to Boats
- (e) Stores supplying Fishery Requisites like Fishing Nets, Fishing Twine, Ropes, Anchores, Marine Paints, etc.
- (f) Arrangements for marketing of Fish Catch

The following information regarding Mechanized Boats to be proposed in the Scheme is essential for determining cost estimates of hull and engine.

(a) Size of boat
Overall length
Keel length
Breadth
Depth
(b) Type of timber to be used
(c) Source of supply of boats
(d) H.P. and make of the engine
(e) Details about deck equipment such as winch, gallows, Net hauler, etc.
(f) Type of nets to be used such as Trawl-Nets, Gill-Nets, and so on while proposing Gill-Nets, Specifications of Nets may be given. The specifications will include information on Length of Net, Depth of Net, Mesh size, Type of Netting Twine, Floats, Sinkers, etc.
In case of Trawl Net, Length of Head rope and Net Material should be specified. The above information is used to decide whether the nets are suitable to the Fishing Boats and the Area of their operation proposed in the Scheme.

Estimates of annual operational costs of mechanized boats

The estimates should include the following items of expenditures :

(a) Cost of fuel and lubricants
(b) Repairs to engine and hull
(c) Crew wages/share
(d) Insurance
(e) Replacement of fishing nets
(f) Marketing
(g) Port dues

Estimates of annual income

The estimates should indicate composition of prawn and fish catch such as white prawn, brown (large, medium and small). Prime varieties of fish and miscellaneous varieties. The sale price for different varieties of prawns and fish should be indicated.

Fisheries potential in the scheme areas

If possible, the scope for introducing additional fishing fleet in the area should be indicated. For this purpose, year-wise fish landings in the scheme area for a period of 3-5 years may be mentioned. This will indicate general trend of fisheries in the area. The information can be obtained from the State Department of Fisheries. The information may prove useful to determine whether there is sufficient scope to introduce additional boats in the scheme area.

Ice plant, freezing plant, canning plants

Information on the following points is considered essential :

(1) Location;
(2) Whether required quantity of water and power supply available;
(3) Whether type of quantity of fish catch in the area will justify capacities of processing plants proposed in the scheme;
(4) Whether the required machinery is available indigeneously or requires to be imported;
(5) Arrangements envisaged for shipment of processed fish for domestic/export market.

APPENDIX-IA

CHECK LIST

Scheme for development of marine fisheries

(To be completed by the Senior Executive/Officer forwarding the scheme)

Note : Ticks in boxes to signify that the details of relevant information as per guidelines circulated by NABARD furnished in the scheme on the following aspects :

(1) Objectives/nature of development;

(2) Whether the scheme area, that is villages or area from where the beneficiaries will be identified, location of processing units—retail marketing outlets, and so on, if any, has been specified?

(3) Whether the financing bank and its branches have been specified?

(4) Whether the scheme has been approved by the competent authority?

(5) Whether state government's clearance is given in case of schemes through LDBs?

(6) Background information : Traditional fishermen population, fishermen co-operative societies, if any, in the scheme area—status of development of the marine fisheries in the area—number of fishing crafts operating in the area, shore facilities, approach roads from the fishing villages, and so on.

(7) Implementing agency :

(a) In case of implementation through individual/groups of individuals criteria for identification and whether they are traditional fishermen, and so on.

(b) In case of implementation through a co-operative/firm/company/corporation, financial status of the agency, its organisational capabilities, nature of functions, and so on.

(8) Detailed cost estimates of different components of development separately for each item;
(9) Year-wise physical programme and financial outlay;
(10) Availability of material such as fishing nets, equipment, marine engines, machinery/refrigeration equipment for processing complex and so on, procedures for procurement and contracting procedures wherever relevant;
(11) Organizational arrangement for construction of processing units, and so on, arrangement for technical supervision of construction, if such items are included in the scheme;
(12) Financial returns:

(a) Estimated financial returns for each component of the investment namely fishing craft, ice plant, processing units, service station and so on for a period of 10 to 15 years;
(b) Cashflow statement of the firm/company/corporation/co-operative wherever relevant, for a period of 10 to 15 years; and
(c) Estimated financial rate of return.

(13) Lending terms : rate of interest loan maturity, down payment, nature of security, extent of subsidy, if any, available;
(14) Supervision and monitoring arrangements;
(15) Mode of providing risk cover;
(16) Arrangements for meeting the working capital requirements ;
(17) Infrastructure facilities:

(a) Arrangements for construction of boats, supply of engines, nets, and so on,
(b) Repair and service facilities,
(c) Arrangements for supply of ice, diesel, etc.
(d) Storage and processing facilities, and
(e) Marketing arrangements and retail outlets.

(18) Government support

(a) Supply of inputs such as quality timber from Forest

Department, material for manufacture of nets, and so on,

(b) Technical guidance and extension support,

(c) Whether necessary budgetary provision has been made/ proposed, if any, required ?

(19) Technical aspects:

(a) Fish resource data, present stage of exploitation, potential available and the scope for additional catch; whether the introduction of new boats is within the safe limits.

(b) Design and specifications of fishing crafts, marine engines, desk equipment, fishing nets etc. for processing and refrigeration complex, marketing outlet network.

(c) Quality of timber.

(d) Fishing in the area, that is, gill-netting, purse-seining trawling, and quantity and composition of catch per boat.

(e) Availability of offshore facilities and adequacy.

APPENDIX-II

CHECK LIST FOR FORMULATION OF FISHERIES SCHEMES TO DEVELOP BRACKISH WATER SHRIMP/FISH CULTURE

General

1. Name of the scheme/project
2. Sponsoring bank
3. Scheme implementing agency
   Individual/fishery co-operative/partnership firm/registered company
4. Proposed period
5. Financial outlay
6. Description of scheme area and fishery potential

Technical details :

1. Water area proposed for development
2. Type of development
   Excavation of ponds/reclamation of swamps into ponds/ paddy field shrimp culture/shrimp culture in Bheries
3. Whether nursery included in the scheme
4. Size of tanks/swamps/paddy fields/Bheries/nurseries
5. Elevation of land
6. Whether tidal water inundate the area/if so duration
7. Flood and drainage details of the area
8. Soil composition of the land
9. Possibilities of erosion by tidal action
10. Distance of tank/swamps/and so on from sea/estuary/other source of tidal water
11. Details of source of tidal water :

    (a) Extent of estuary
    (b) Total amplitude
    (c) Extent of monsoon flood
    (d) Water salinity—maximum and minimum

12. Details of excavation/reclamation
13. Depth of water after excavation/reclamation
14. Water supply to pond-gravitational flow/pumping
15. Level of feeder canal in relation to pond depth
16. Level of feeder canal in relation to source of tidal water
17. Details of inlet sluice
18. Detail of marginal dyke, intermediate bunds ;
    Height, width, free board, slope
19. Estimation should be given for the following items of work:

    (a) Excavation/desilting
    (b) Deweeding
    (c) Construction of bunds, sluices, and so on
    (d) Cost of motor with pump and other accessories
    (e) Pump shed, watchman shed

20. Type of culture, monoculture of prawns/polyculture
21. Species of fish/prawn seed
22. Whether required seed available in the scheme area ? If not what arrangements are envisaged for the same
23. Recurring expenditure may include following items :

    (a) Cost of fish seed
    (b) Cost of feed and manures
    (c) Cost of fishing operation
    (d) Cost of fuel charges to operate water pump
    (e) Maintenance of tanks
    (f) Lease/rental of tanks

24. Marketing arrangements—consuming centres, distance from production centre, transport arrangement, freezing and storing arrangement
25. In case of scheme implementing agency is FFDA detailed information on the working of FFDA
26. Estimates of annual income :
    Estimate should indicate per unit fish/prawn production and sale price per unit weight (unit may be considered as hectare or acre).

APPENDIX-III

STATE-WISE AND BANK-WISE INFORMATION OF MARINE FISHERIES SCHEMES SANCTIONED UPTO 31ST DECEMBER 1983

(*Rs in lakh*)

Sl. No.	State	State co-operative banks				Commercial banks				Total			
		No. of schemes	Financial assistance	NABARD's commitment	Disbursement of refinance	No. of schemes	Financial assistance	NABARD's commitment	Disbursement of refinance	No. of schemes	Financial assistance	NABARD's commitment	Total Disbursement
1.	Andhra Pradesh	17	454	354	118	96	1186	932	378	103	1640	1286	496
2.	Goa	1	40	30	30	69	593	472	369	70	633	502	399
3.	Gujarat	—	—	—	—	43	972	774	618	43	972	774	618
4.	Karnataka	2	207	143	137	155	2045	1544	1290	157	2252	1687	1427
5.	Kerala	4	171	169	56	111	712	523	414	115	883	692	470
6.	Lakshadweep	—	—	—	—	1	11	10	—	1	11	10	—
7.	Maharashtra	5	180	84	82	61	303	237	176	66	483	321	258
8.	Orissa	19	247	222	15	45	1090	982	291	64	1337	1204	306
9.	Pondicherry	2	46	34	15	1	26	21	—	3	72	55	15
10.	Tamil Nadu	2	100	69	64	84	792	608	513	86	892	677	577
11.	West Bengal	—	—	—	—	2	170	160	—	2	170	160	—
	Total	42	1445	1105	517	668	7900	6263	4049	710	9345	7368	4566

A SELECT BIBLIOGRAPHY

Systems

Churchman, Carles West, *The Design of Inquiring Systems : Basic Concepts of Systems and Organization*, Basic Books, New York.

Churchman, Carles West, *The Systems Approach*, Delacorte, New York, 1968.

Cleland Devid, I. and William R. Kind, *Systems Analysis and Project Management*, McGraw-Hill, New York, 1975.

Churchman, Carles West, *Management : A System Approach*, New York : McGraw Hill, 1972.

Churchman, Carles West, *Systems, Organisation, Analysis, Management : A Book of Reading*, McGraw Hill Book Co. ; USA ; 1969.

Condon, R.J., *Data Processing, Systems Analysis and Design*, Reston Pub. Co., Reston, Virginia, 1975.

Dent, J.B. and Anderson, J.R., *Systems Analysis in Agricultural Management*, Wiley, Sydney, 1971.

Fisher, G.R., *Cost Considerations in systems Analysis*, Americal Elsevier, New York, 1971.

Gane, G.P., and Trish Sarson, *Structured Systems Analysis : Tools and Techniques*, Prentice Hall, Englewood Cliffs, 1979.

King, William R, *The Systems Concept in Management, Journal of Industrial Engineering*, May 1967.

Nagrath, I.J., Gopal, M., *Systems Modelling and Analysis*, Tata-McGraw Hill Publishing Co.

National Systems Conference, *Proceedings of National Systems Conference*, Electrical Engineering Department, University of Roorkee, Roorkee, 1976.

Race, John, *Case Studies in Systems Analysis*, Macmillan, London, 1979.

Rothery, Brian, *et al*, *The Art of Systems Analysis*, Business Book, London, 1969.

Sivazliam, B.D., and L.E. Stanfed, *Analysis of Systems in Operations Research*, Prentice Hall, Englewood Cliffs N.J., 1975.

Van Gigch, John, P., *Applied General Systems Theory*, Harper &

Row, New York, 1974.

General fishery

Anon, Indian Fisheries 1947-1977, Fisheries Research, CMFRI, Cochin, 7, 21, 1977.

Anon, Statistical Supplement, 11th Meeting of the Central Board of Fisheries, Ministry of Agriculture, Government of India, New Delhi, 1979.

Christy, F.T., and Scott, A., *The Commonwealth in Ocean Fisheries : Some Problems of Growth and Economic Allocation*, John Hopkins Press, Baltimore, 1965.

D'Monte, Darry, I., Fishing in Troubled Waters, *The Times of India*, p. 11, May 14, 1978.

F.A.O., Statistics of Fish Catches of the World.

Food and Agriculture Organization, "Marine Fisheries in the New Era of National Jurisdiction" in the State of Food and Agriculture, 1980 (Rome, FAO), pp. 113, 1981.

George, K.C., Salt Water Fish Farming, *Sea Food Export Journal*, Vol. 3, No.11, November 1971, pp. 7-14.

George, M.J., Status of Coastal Aquaculture in India, Aquaculture in Countried Bordering Indian Ocean, *Mar. Bio. Association of India*, 1980, pp. 28-53.

George, P.C. and V.R.P. Sinha, Ten Years Aquaculture Development Plan for India 1974-84, *2nd Regional Workshop*, Aquaculture Development and Planning, Oct 1-15, Bangkok, Thailand, 1975.

Gokhle, S.V., The Indian Fishing Industry, Facts and Fiction, *Sea Food Export Journal*, Vol. 3, No. 8, August 1971, pp. 9-15.

Gokhle, S.V., Poor Nations and 200 Mile Zone : Few Fishing Benefits, *Economic Times*, Oct. 17, 1977, p. 5.

Gulland, J.A., *The Management of Marine Fisheries*, University of Washington Press, Scattle, 1974.

Gulland, J.A. "The Concept of the Maximum Substainable Yield and Fishery Management", FAO Fishery Technical Paper 70, 1968.

Jhingran, V.G., *Fish and Fisheries of India*, Hindustan Publishing Co., New Delhi, 1982.

Marr, John C., *et al.*, "A Plan for Fisheries Development in the Indian Ocean, FAO-IOFC/Dev/71/1, 1976.

Patel, A.R., "Fishing Industry—Problems and Prospects", *Eastern Economist*, Vol. 16, 1977, pp. 57-61.

Pillay, T.V.R., "Why Aquaculture : An Aquaculture Engineering", ed. F.W. Wheatan, John Wiley & Sons, New York, 1977.

Prasad, N.K., Marine Fisheries in India, *Sea Food Export Journal*, Vol. 4, No. 1, January 1972, pp. 165-70.

Prasad, R.R., Fisheries Development in India, *Sea Food Export Journal*, Vol. 4, No. 1, January 1972, p. 20.

Raghu, R., Fisheries Development in India, *Sea Food Export Journal*, Vol. 4, No. 1, January 1972, pp. 19-24.

Raghu Prasad, Prospects of Coastal Aquaculture. *Sea Food Export Journal*, Vol. XII, No. 2, February 1980, pp. 9-12.

Rao, K.V.R., Some Suggestions for the Betterment of Indian Fishing Industry and Fishermen, *Sea Food Export Journal*, Vol. 3, No. 9, September 1971, pp. 31-34.

Rao, P.S., Fish Production—Vast Scope for Research and Co-ordination, *Economic Times*, Vol. 4, December 4, 1967.

Reddy, M.P.M., and V. Hariharan, Problems of Coastal Erosion in India, *Sea Food Export Journal*, Vol. XI, No. 3, March 1979.

Scott, A.D., The Fishery : The Objective of Sole Ownership, *Journal of Political Economy*, Vol. 63, 1955, pp. 116-24.

Shapiro, S., *Our Changing Fisheries*, National Marine Fisheries Services, Washington, U.S. Government of Printing Office, 1971.

Shinde, A.P., India's Marine Fishing Industry, *Sea Food Export Journal*, No. 7, Vol. 3, July 1971, pp. 37-9.

Smith, V., On Models of Commercial Fishing, *Journal of Political Economy*, Vol. 77, No. 2, April 1969, pp. 181-98.

Srivastava, U.K. & *et al.*, "Management of Marine Fishing Industry", Oxford & IBH Publishing Co., New Delhi, 1982.

Srivastava, U.K. & M.D. Reddy, *Fisheries Development in India—Some Aspects of Policy Management*, Concept Publishing Co., New Delhi, 1983.

Thomas, V.M., Fish and Fisheries, *Farmer and Parliament*, Vol. 1, p. 13, November 1966.

Turvey, R., Optimization in Fishery Regulations, *American Economic Review*, Vol. 54, No. 2, March 1964, pp. 64-76.

Wagle, S.N., Marine Fisheries Plan Unrealistic, *Economic Times*,

Bombay, May 23, 1978.

Government policy

Govindan, T.K., "Government Policies and Their Effect on the Development of Fishing and Fish Processing Industries in India, "Seminar on Food Industries held at New Delhi by CIFT, 1966.

Marine fishery resources

Anon, Results of Exploratory Survey of Fisheries Resources of Wadge Bank Progress, Report No. 1, 1982.

Antony Raja, B.T., Our Pelagic Fishery Resources—Present and Potential Harvest, *Sea Food Export Journal*, Vol. 6, No. 1, 1974, pp. 79-85.

Banerji, S.K., An Assessment of the Exploited Pelagic Fisheries of the Indian Seas, *Proceedings of the Symposium on Living Resources of the Seas Around India*, Special Publication, CMFRI, 1973, pp. 114-36.

Cassidy, P.A., Commonality, Fishery Resources—Potential and Policy : Comment, *American Journal of Agricultural Economics*, Vol. 55, 1973, pp. 526-9.

Crushing, D., *Fisheries Resources of the Sea and Their Management*, Oxford University Press, 1975, p. 105.

Francis, T., New Dimensions for Transitional Marine Resources, *American Economic Review*, Vol. 60, No. 1, May 1970, pp. 109-13.

George, P.C., Antony, Raja, B.T., and George, K.C., "Fishery Resources of the Indian Economic Zone", in Souvenir issued on the occasion of Silver Jubilee Celebration of the Integrated Fisheries Project, Cochin, Oct. 1977.

George, P.C., *et al.*, "Fishery Resources of the Indian Economic Zone", in Souvenir issued on the occasion of Silver Jubilee Celebration of the Integrated Fisheries Project, Cochin, 1977.

George, P.C., Some Thoughts on Maximum Utilization of Coastal Fishery Resources of India, *Journal of the Indian Fishery Association*, Vol. 5, 1975.

Gidwani, Ineha, Fish Wealth Unexploited, *Economic Times*, 5, October 24, 1977.

Gulland, J.A., "The Fish Resources of the Oceans", *FAO*

Technical Paper 97, 1976.

Gulland, J.A., *The Fish Resources of the Ocean*, Fishing News (Books) Ltd., England, 1971.

Isbimine, T., The Law of the Sea and Ocean Resources, *The American Journal of Economics of Sociology*, Vol. 37, No. 2, April 1978, pp. 129-43.

Jones, S., and S.K. Banerji, A Review of the Living Resources of the Seas around India, Special Publication, CMFRI, 1973.

Joseph, K.M., "Comparative Study of the Demersal Fishery Resources of the Indian Waters as assessed by the 17.5 m. Trawlers", *Bulletin Expl. Fish Project*, 10, 1980.

Padki, M.B., "Resources and Productivity in Indian Fisheries", *Artha Vignana*, Vol. 13, No. 2, June 1971, pp. 181-204.

Panikkar, N.K., "Fishery Resources of the Indian Ocean", Paper presented to the Working Party on the Rational Utilization of the Fishery Resources of Indian Ocean, FAO, Rome, January 1967, pp. 23-5.

Prasad, R.R., "A Quantitative Assessment of the Potential of Fishery Resources of the Indian Ocean and Adjoining Seas", *Indian Journal of Marine Sciences*, Vol. 40, No. 1, 1970, pp. 73-90.

Rao, K.V., "Distribution Pattern of the Major Exploited Marine Fishery Resources of India", *Central Marine Fisheries Research Institute* (CMFRI) Bulletin Vol. 9, 1969, p. 69.

Rao, K. Virabhadra, "Distribution Pattern of the Major Exploited Marine Fishery Resources of India", *CMFRI, Bulletin*, 6 : 1-69, 1973.

Silal, *et al*, Exploited Marine Fishery Resources of India, *CMFRI, Bulletin*, No. 27, 1976, p. 25.

Silas, E.G., *et al.*, Exploit Marine Fishery Resources of India : A Synoptic Survey with Comments on Potential Resources, *CMFRI Bulletin*, 27, March 1976.

Shanbhogue, S.L., "Demersal Fishery Resources of India", *Sea Food Export Journal*, Vol. XI, No. 8, August 1979, pp. 9-16.

Results of Exploratory Survey of Fisheries Resources of Wadge Bank, Project Report No. 1, Exploratory Fisheries Project, Bombay, 1982.

Infrastructure

Anonymous (Government of India), "Guidelines, Terms and Conditions for Charter of Foreign Fishing Vessels, Ministry of Agriculture, New Delhi, 1981.

Balan, R., "Investment Reduction and Increase in Service Life of Kattumaram Logs, Bay of Bengal Programme, Development of Small Scale Fisheries, FAO, 1980.

Balasubramanyan, R., "A Wider Choice of Construction Materials for the Modern Fishing Boats", *Fishery Technology*, XII (2) : 87, 1975.

Balasubramanyan, R. "Fishing Crafts of India and the Different Timbers for Their Constructions", IPFC Occasional Paper 64/9, 1964.

Balasubramanyan, R. "A Review of Fishing Boat Types and Their Design Aspects", *Journal of Naval Architecture and Marine Engineering*, Dec., 22, 1960.

Bhakta, N.P., "Development of Infrastructure Facilities for the Optimal Exploitation of the Exclusive Economic Zone", *Fisheries Development in India*, Concept Publishing Co., New Delhi, 1983.

Burruugh, J.L., "Two Years Reports of the Fishing Gear", *Advisor to the Ministry of Food and Agriculture*, Government of India, Bombay, 1959.

Chidambaram, K., "Suitable Deep Sea Fishing Vessels for India", Report of the Fisheries Technical Mission to the Government of India.

FAO, *Fishing Ports and Markets*, Fishing News (Books) Ltd., London, 1970.

Krishnamoorthy, B., "Some Problems Relating to Mechanized Fishing", Seminar on Mariculture and Mechanized Fishing, Government Press, Madras.

Kuriyan, G.K., "New Fishing Gear and Methods Required", *Indian Farming*, Vol. XIX, No. 2, pp. 97, 1969.

Kuriyan, G.K. & S. Gopalan Nayar, "Common Indian Fishing Gear Preservatives—A General Account", *Journal of Asiatic Society*, 111 (1) : 21, 1961.

Mohan Rajan, K.V., "A Success Story of Development of Mechanized Boats for Shark Long Living *Sea Food Export Journal*, Vol. XIV, No. 8, August 1982, pp. 9-18.

Menon, K.G.R., "Maritime Rules, Regulations and Procedures Applicable to Fishing Vessel in India" *Sea Food Export Journal* Vol. 9, No. 11, November 1977, p. 27.

Rajan Abraham, A., "Estimation of Engine Power for Fishing Vessels", *Sea Food Export Journal,* Vol. XIII, No. 7, July 1981, pp. 17-26.

Sivadas, T.K., "Instrumentation in Fishing Gear Research". *Fishery Technology,* Vol. VII, No. 2, 1977.

Swaminath M., *et al.*, "Preliminary Report of the 5th Cruise of M.T. Murena and Supporting Vessels for the Period from 28th October to 14th December 1977", Report No. 5, *Exploratory Fisheries Project,* Bombay, 1978.

William H.D., and Sundstrom G.T., "Commercial Fishing Gear of the United States", U.S. Fish and Wildlife Services, Washington, Fish and Wildlife Circular No. 109, 1961.

White Fish Authority, "Study of Fishing Vessel Building Requirements for Department of Heavy Industry", *Project Report No. 436,* 1980.

George C.S., "Design of Ships in General and its Application in the Design of Fishing Vessels", *Sea Food Export Journal,* Vol. XII. No. 6, June 1981, pp. 21-26.

George, C.S. "Selection of Engines for Small and Medium Size Fishing Vessels" *Sea Food Export Journal,* Vol. XIV, No. 1, January 1982, pp. 21-6.

Rao, P.S., and A. Anorase, "Mechanized Fishing—Costs and Earnings from Boats," *Economic Times,* May 18, 1983, p. 9.

Mariculture

Alikunhi, K.H., "Brackish Water Aquaculture Development : Technical, Economic and Policy Issues", *Fisheries Development of India,* Concept Publishing Company, New Delhi, 1983.

George, M.J., "A Brief Review on the Progress of Prawn Mariculture", *Proceeding Seminar on Mariculture and Mechanized Fishing,* Government of Tamil Nadu, 1973, pp. 77-83.

Mohmed, K.H., "Marine Prawn Culture in India : An Appraisal of the Present Status and Future Prospects", *Proceedings Seminar on Mariculture and Hatchery Fishing,* Government of Tamil Nadu, 1973.

Qusim, S.Z., "Sea Farming : An Appropriate Technology for

Generating Sea Food", *Appropriate Technology*, No. 6, 1979, pp. 26-8.

Verghese, P.V., "Potential for Brackish Water Prawn Culture in India", *Proceedings on Symposium on Shrimp Farming*, Bombay, 1980.

"Mariculture Research and Development", *Special Publication No. 2*, CMFRI, Cochin, 1978.

Fisheries economics

Anderson, L.G., *The Economics of Fisheries Management*, Johns Hopkins Press, Baltimare, 1977, p. 214.

Chesnokor, M.I., *The Subject of the Economics of Fishery*, 1961.

Rao, P.S., "Price Policy for Marine Fish", *Sea Food Export Journal*, Vol. 3, No. 5, May 1971, pp. 17-26.

Rao, P.S. "Some Economic Aspects of Marine Fish Production", *Agricultural Situation in India*, Vol. 22, No. 8, November 1967, pp. 875-9.

Rees, R., "The Economies of Investment Analysis", Civil Service College Occasional Paper 17, HMSO, London, 1973.

Scott, A.D., "The Economies of Regulating Fisheries", in *The Economic Effects of Fishery Regulation*, (ed). R. Hamliseh, FAO Fishery Report 5, 1962.

Smith, J.E., "The Economist and Seafood Produce", *American Journal of Agricultural Economics*, Vol. 56, No. 5, December 1977, pp. 1038-46.

Stephen Cunningham, "The Increasing Importance of Economics in Fisheries Regulations", *Journal of Agricultural Economics*, Vol. XXXIV, No. 1, January 1983, pp. 69-78.

Srivastava U.K. and M.D. Reddy, "Investment in Harvesting, Processing, and Marketing Sectors of Marine Fisheries Required to Attain and Utilize the Projected (1985) Fish Landings", *Fisheries Development in India*, Concept Publishing Co., New Delhi, 1983.

Tonkin, J.M., "A Theoretical and Empirical Approach to Fisheries Economics", *Journal of Agricultural Economics*, Vol. 26, No. 1, 1975, p. 105.

"The Vicissitudes of Fishing Industry—An Economic Analysis", Research Department, Syndicate Bank, *Integrated Management*, Vol. 88, pp. 42-52.

Education & Training

Cole, R.C., and D.W.F. Hall, "Guide to Fishery Education and Training", FAO, *Fish*, Paper (128), 1973.

Choudhury, L.H., "Training for Development", *Journal of the Indian Institute of Public Administration*, Vol. XXVI, No. 2, 1980.

Davis Fogy, C., "*Manpower Planning, Managing Economic Development in Africa*", Cambridge, Mass, U.S.A., MIT Press, 1963.

Government of India, "Report of the Committee on Fisheries Education", Department of Agriculture, Ministry of Food and Agriculture, Delhi, 1960.

Gurhardsen,G.M., "Fisheries Education and Training in Growth and Development Programme", *IPFC Proceedings, Section* III, Symposium on Fisheries Education and Training at Honolulu in 1966, Published by IPFC Secretariat, Bangkok, 1968.

Hamliseh, R., "General Consideration in Manpower Planning and Their Application in the Construction of Fisheries Development Programmes", *IPFC Proceedings*, Section III, Symposium on Fisheries Education and Training at Honolulu in 1966, Published by IPFC Secretariat, Bangkok, 1968.

Kutty, M.N., "Technical and Managerial Manpower Requirement for Integrated Coastal Aquaculture and Their Training Needs", A Paper presented at the Seminar on the Role of Small Scale Fisheries and Coastal Aquaculture in Integrated Rural Development at Madras, organized by the CMFRI, Cochin, 1978.

Saxana, A.P., "Some Background Factors in the Choice of Training Methodologies", *Journal of Indian Institute of Public Administration*, Vol. XXVI, No. 1, 1980.

Sekharan, K.V., "Why a Professional Degree Course in Fisheries ?" *Sea Food Export Journal*, 4 : 1, January 1972, pp. 79-83.

Shetty, H.P.C., "Evaluation of Present Technical Training System in Fisheries and suggestions for Modernization". A paper presented at the *Seminar on the Role of Small Scale Fisheries and Coastal Aquaculture in Integrated Rural Development at Madras*, organized by CMFRI, Cochin, 1978.

Swaminath, M., "Fisheries Education and Training in India",

Fisheries Development in India, Concept Publishing Co., New Delhi, 1983.

Y. Ho. Koh, "Korea : A Case Study in Promoting Development Through Fishermen's Training", *Journal of the Fisheries Research Board of Canada*. 30 (12), Part 2, 1973.

"Report of the Evaluation Committee on the Central Institute of Fisheries Education", Central Institute of Fisheries Education, Bombay.

"Report of the Inflow Committee on the Central Institute of Fisheries Education", Central Institute of Fisheries Education, Bombay.

Deep sea fishing

Agricultural Finance Corporation Limited, *Symposium on the need for a Techno-Economic Survey of the Deep Sea Fishing Resources*," Bombay, 1973.

Das, S.K., "Joint Ventures—Problems and Prospects in Indian Marine Fisheries", in *Management of the Living Resources of the India's* EEL, CIFE, Bombay, December, 1981.

Gokhle, S.V., "Deep Sea Fishing—Foreign Collaboration a Necessity", *Sea Food Export Journal*, Vol. 4. No. 4, April 1972, pp. 13-9.

Gokhle, S.V. "The Maria Called Deep Sea Fishing," *Science Today*, Bombay, August 1982.

Gupta, V.K., Exclusive Economic Zone and New Opportunities : Policy Structure and Organisations : A Commentary and Major Issues", *Fisheries Development in India*, Concept Publishing Co., New Delhi, 1983.

Government of India, "Guidelines, Terms and Conditions for Joint Ventures and Import/Charter of Deep Sea Fishing Vessels", Ministry of Agriculture, New Delhi, 1977.

Irani, K.K., "Time Ripe for Profitable Fishing Venture," *Symposium on the Need for a Techno-Economic Survey of the Deep Sea Fishing Resources*, published by AFC, Bombay, 1973.

Khan, R., *The 200-Mile Economic Zone : Indian Ocean Fisheries*, Ankur Publishing House, New Delhi, 1977.

Kuriyan, G.K., "Fishing in the Deep", Souvenir—Fish Exporter's Chamber, July 1971.

Madhavan Nair, paper presented at the *Deep Sea Fishing Sympo-*

sium, Cochin, February, 1970.

Mammen, T.A., "Joint Ventures in Fisheries : The Indian Experience", *Fisheries Development in India*, Concept Publishing Co., New Delhi, 1983.

Menon, D. "Investigation on Off-shore and Deep Sea Fisheries Resources in Indian Waters", *Sea Food Export Journal*, Vol. 3, No. 12, December 1971, pp. 7-12,

Reddy, M.N., "Deep Sea Fishing—A Languishing Industry", *Economic Times*, 4, June 23, 1980.

Shyam Manjula, "Strategy for Developing Offshore Fisheries in the Exclusive Economic Zone (EEZ), *Fisheries Development in India*, Concept Publishing Co., New Delhi, 1983.

Silas, E.G., Investigations on the Deep Scattering Layers in the Laccadive Sea", *Proceedings of Symposium on Corals and Coral Reefs*, Marine Biological Association of India, 1972, pp. 257-74.

Singh, N.P., "Chartering : Its Role in the Development of the Indian EEZ", *Fisheries Development in India*, Concept Publishing Co., New Delhi, 1983.

Srichand Sahetiya, "Deep Sea Fishing Still a Far Cry", *The Economic Times*, Bombay, February 28, 1981.

Unninayar Seetha, 'Indian Fishing in Deep Waters", *Business World*, Bombay, August 16-29, 1982.

Marketing

Annakesavan, K., "Development of Fish Production and Marketing Through Co-operatives", *The Co-operators*, 19 : 1, 3-4, July 1, 1981.

Chako N.J., "Marketing Strategy Needed for India's Marine Products", *Sea Food Export Journal*, Vol. 9, No. 3, March 1977.

Dutt, B.C., "Vast Foreign Market Exists for our Marine Products", *Economic Times*, p. 3, May 13, 1967.

Government of India, *Marketing of Fish in India*, Directorate of Marketing and Inspection, 3rd Edition, 1971.

Gupta V.K. *et al. Marine Fish Marketing in India*, Volumes I to VI, Centre for Management in Agriculture, Indian Institute of Management, Ahmedabad, 1982.

Kurien, V.A., "Entry of Big business into Fishing : Its Impact on Fish Economy", *Economic and Political Weekly*, Vol. 13,

No. 30, p. 1559, September 1978.

Marsoo, R., "Food from the Sea : An Economic Perspective of the Sea Food Market", *American Journal of Agricultural Economics*, Vol. 56, No. 5, pp. 1030-7, December 1977.

Methew, K.J., and Others, Collection and Transport of Prawn and Fish Seed, *Symposium on Coastal Aquaculture*, Cochin, 1980.

Perigreen P.A., and Govindan, T.K., "General Transportation of Fish in India : Problems and Prospects", *Fishery Technology*, Vol. 15, No. 6, 1974, p. 114.

——and——, "Transportation of Fish in India : Problems and Prospects". *Fishery Technology*, Vol. VI, No. 2, 1969, p. 74.

——, and Nair M.R., "Handling and Transporting of Fish in India," The Tropical Products Institute Conference, London, July 1976.

Rao, B.S. "Problems of Marketing Fish", *Agriculture situation in India*", Vol, 24, No. 10, pp. 907-12, January 1970.

Singh, Amar Jeet and Gupta, V.K., "Marketing of Marine Fish : Some Policy Issues", *Fisheries Development in India*, Concept Publishing Co., New Delhi, 1983.

Venkataraman, R., and M.K. Kandeeran, "Marketing Potentialities of some New Fishery Products" *Sea Food Export Journal*, Vol. II, No. 5, 1970.

Demand Forecast

Bhatt Tushar

(1) Sea Fish—Big rise in demand Forecast
(2) Sea Fish—Big rise in Prices
(3) Sea Fish—Investment and returns
(4) Sea Fish—Meeting the Million Tonne Shortfall
(5) Sea Fish—Breaking the Monopoly of Trade,

Business Standard, Feb. 2-6, 1982.

Dayal, Shambu, "Projections for Production of Fish in India", *Sea Food Export Journal*, 5 (5), May 1973, pp. 23-7.

——"Projections for Demand of Fish in India", *Sea Food Export Journal*, 5 (4), April 1973, pp. 13-4.

Anonymous (Government of India), "Report of the National

Commission on Agriculture, Part III, Demand and Supply", Ministry of Agriculture and Irrigation, New Delhi.

M. Raghavachari, "Marine Fish Supplies : Trends and Projections", *Fisheries Development in India*, Concept Publishing Co., New Delhi, 1983.

Gupta, G.S., *et al.*, Marine Fish : Consumer Behaviour and Demand Forecast", *Fisheries Development in India*, Concept Publishing Co., New Delhi, 1983.

Demand for Fish and its Transportation and Storage in Selected Cities, National Council of Aoplied Economic Research, New Delhi, 1980.

Export

Cherian, C., Export Outlook for Indian Marine Products, *Sea Food Export Journal*, Vol. 4, No. 1, January 1972, pp. 1-4.

Haran, M.P., Export of Marine Products Facing the Seventies Financial Express, *Special Supplements* XXXV, 19 July 1971.

Nair, R.V., "On the Export Potential of Elvers and Cultured Eelsform India", *Ind. J. Fish*, 20 : 610-616, 1973.

Rao, S.N., "Product Development for Export," *Fisheries Development in India*, Concept Publishing Co., New Delhi, 1983.

Sri Kumaran, N.V.M., "See food Industry : An Assessment of its Development and Export Potential", *Financial Express, Export Supplement*, p. 8, 1967.

Brackish Water

Alikunhi, K.H., "Shrimp Farming in India—Present Status and Future Prospects" *First National Symposium on Shrimp Farming* Bombay, 1978.

——"Role of Hatcheries in Commercial Farming of Penacid Shrimps", *First National Symposium on Shrimps Farming*, Bombay, 1978.

Anonymous, Proposals for the Development of Fresh and Brackish Water Capture and Culture Fisheries Including Mariculture in Kerala during the VIth Plan Period 1978-83, Report of the Tash Force on Inland and Estuarine Fisheries including Culture Programme.

Chidambaram, K., "Strategy for Commercial Shrimp Farming", *Proceedings of First National Symposium on Shrimp Farming*,

Bombay, 1978, pp. 219-25.

Dwivedi, S.N., "Prospects and Perspectives in Prawn Culture", *Proceedings of First National Symposium on Shrimp Farming*, Published by MPEDA, Ministry of Commerce, Cochin, 1980.

Gopalakrishnan, V., "Potential for Intensive Cultivation of Estuarine Prawns in India", *Proceedings on Mariculture and Mechanized Fishing*, Government of Tamil Nadu, 1973.

Gopinath, K., "Prawn Culture in the Rice Fields", Travancore, Cochin, *Proceedings of Indo Pac. Fish Council*, 6, pp. 419-24.

Jhingran, V.G., *A Note on the Progress of Work under Considerated Project on Brackish Water Fish Farming*, ICAR, Published by Central Inland Fisheries Research Institute, Cochin.

Hameed Ali, K. and S.N. Dwivedi, "Semi Commercial Hatchery for Large Scale Rearing of Penacid Prawn Larvae", *Proceedings of First National Symposium on Shrimp Farming*, Bombay, 1978.

——, "Preliminary Experiments in Mass Rearing of Penacid Larve on Cheap Artificial Feeds", *Proceedings of 1st National Symposium on Shrimp Farming*, Bombay, 1978.

Kurien, C.V., and V.O. Sebastian, *Prawns and Prawn Fisheries of India*, Hindustan Publishing Corporation, New Delhi, 1976.

Patel M.J., and Others, "A Proposed Project on Brackish Water Fish Farm at Iodiya", *Proceedings of 1st National Symposium on Shrimp Farming*, MPEDA, Cochin, 1980.

Silas, E.G., "Research and Development Programme in the Culture and Propogation of Penacid Prawns", CMFRI, Special Publication No. 3, Summer Institute in Breeding and Rearing of Marine Prawns.

——, "Status of Prawn Culture in India and Strategy for the Future Development, *Proceedings of 1st National Symposium on Shrimp Farming*, Bombay, 1980.

Processing

Badonia Rajendra, "Cooked and Frozen Lobster", *Sea Food Export Journal*, Vol. XIII, No. 7, July 1981, pp. 27-8.

Bhatt, H.S., "Impact of Quality Control on Indian Sea Food Products", *Sea Food Export Journal*, Vol. 3, No. 5, May 1971, pp. 31-4.

Chakraborty, P.K., "Dehydration of Fish and its Scope of Commercial Exploitation in India", *Sea Food Export Journal*,

Vol. XII, No. 6, June 1981, pp. 9-20.

Cyriac Mathen, "Quality Control in the Indian Fish Processing Industry", *Fishery Technology*, XI (1) : 1.

George Joseph, K., "Indian Fish Curing Industry : Present Status and Some Suggestions for Improvement", *Sea Food Export Journal*, Vol. XII, No. 12, December 1980, pp. 15-26.

Gopakumar, K., *et al.*, "Fish Processing Industry in India", *Proceedings, Symposium on Fish Processing Industry in India*, CFTRI, 13-16 February, Mysore, 1975.

Govindan, T.K., "Convenience Foods from Fish", *Sea Food Export Journal*, IV (1) : 157, 1972.

———, "Packaging for Frozen Prawn Products Part-I", *Sea Food Export Journal*, Vol. XIV. No. 8, August 1982, pp. 21-4.

———, "Fish Processings Industry in India—A Retrospect, Present Status and Future Prospects", *Sea Food Export Journal*, VII (1) : 143, 1975.

———, "Our Fish Curing Industry", *Indian Food Packer*, XXIII (1) : 33, 1969.

Jagadeesh, K., "Keeping the Freshness of Sea Foods", *Sea Food Export Jaurnal*, Vol. XII, No. 1, January 1980, pp. 25-34.

James, M., Arul, *et al.*, Proceedings, Conference on "Handling, Processing and Marketing of Tropical Fish", 5-9 July, Tropical Products Institute, London, 1976.

Kaimal, P.N.R., "Fish Processing Industry in India—Highlights of its Future Development", *Indian Sea Foods*, IX (2) : 7, 1974.

Malathi Rangaswami, "Fish to Feed Millions" *Indian Review of Management and Future*, 1, 34-34, 1979.

Pillai V.K., *et al.*, "Fish Processing Industry—The Potential for Its Expansion and Diversification is Immense", *The Food Industries Journal*, Vol. III, No. 4, 1969.

Ramadhas, V., *et al.*, "Instant Live Food", *Sea Food Export Journal*, Vol. XII, No. 9, September 1980, pp. 17-20.

Santhanakrishnan, G., "Prospects for Diversification of Indian Marine Products", *Sea Food Export Journal*, Vol. XIV, No. 2, February 1982, pp. 9-14.

Saralaya, K.V., "Fish Processing and Diversification", *Sea Food Export Journal*, Vol. XI, No. 3, March 1979, pp. 9-14.

Sivaramakrishnan, A.S., "Fish Meal and Fish Oil Plants in India",

Sea Food Export Journal, Vol. XIII, No. 4, April 1981, pp. 15-8.

Sripathy, N.V., "Non-traditional Fish By-products : An Approach to Utilization of Low Price Marine Fish", *Sea Food Export Journal*, Vol. XIV, No. 6, June 1982, pp. 23-6.

Srivastava, Shri Prakash, "Fish Flesh—A Nutritious Food for Man", *Farmer and Parliament*, 6 : 10, 7—8, 27, October 1971.

"Marine Products—Feature", *Commerce*, 131 : 3371, 8, December 27, 1975.

FINANCE

Albin, F.V., Responsive Credit Policy for the Seafood Industry", *Sea Food Export Journal*, Vol. 3, No. 6, pp. 19-21, June 1971.

Anonymous, *Problems of Finance in Fishing Industry*, in the Symposium of Need for a Techno-Economic Survey of the Deep Sea Fishing Resources, A.F.C. Ltd., Bombay, May 1973.

Bhullar, K.S., "Credit for Fishing Industry", *Sea Food Export Journal*, Vol. 4, No. 1, January 1972, pp. 51-55.

Chidambaram, K., "Fishing Industry—Special Features of Financing", *Financial Express*, Bombay, April 13, 1978.

—— "Finances for Deep Sea Fishing Industry in India and Abroad", *Financing Agriculture* (4), 1971.

Goyal, R.P., "Fisheries—The Financial Hurdles", *Economic Times*, Bombay, February 28, 1981.

Kurien, V.A., "Financial Planning and Control in Fishing Industry", *Financing Agriculture*, 2-4, 31-34, January 1971.

——, "Financing the Fishing Industry", *Economic Times*, 5, 8, November 24, 1978.

——, "Availability of Finance for the Fishing Industry", *Sea Food Export Journal*, Vol. 2, No. 9, September 1970, pp. 9-18.

——, "Financial Planning and Control in Fishing Industry", *Financing Agriculture*, Vol. 2, No. 4, January 1971, pp. 31-4.

——, "Financing the Fishing Industry", *Economic Times*, p. 6, November 24, 1978.

Murickan, S.J., "Interlinkages of Credit, Labour and Marketing Relations in Traditional Fishing : The Case of Purakkad", *Fisheries Development in India*, Concept Publishing Co., New Delhi, 1983.

Saxena, B.S., "Prospects of Institutional Finance in the Indian

Fishing Industry", *Financing Agriculture*, Vol. 2, No. 4, January 1971, pp. 22-7.

Singh, V.D. and Sampath, V., "Role of Financial Institutions in Development of Integrated Fish Farming", *Fisheries Development in India*, Concept Publishing Co., New Delhi, 1983.

Steinar Olsen, "Fisheries Financing in Norway", *Symposium on the Need for a Techno-Economic Survey of the Deep Sea Fishing Resources*, A.F.C., 1973.

Sundaresan, R., "Financing Small Fishermen—A Challenging Task", CMFRI Bulletin 30-A, *Proceedings of the Seminar on Role of Small Scale Fisheries and Coastal Aquaculture in Integrated Rural Development*, December 6-9, 1978.

Financial Support to the Fishing Industry, Organisation for Economic Development and Co-operation, Paris, 1965.

ABOUT VISVESVARAYA CENTRE, BOMBAY

M. Visvesvaraya Industrial Research and Development Centre is a company incorporated on June 26, 1970, under Section 25 of the Indian Companies Act, with the object to organize, sponsor, promote, establish, conduct, or undertake scientific research in any way or by any means whatsoever and in any area or field. The Centre perpetuates the memory of Dr. M. Visvesvaraya, one of the architects of modern India, and spitomizes his conviction that India's prosperity depended on scientific research and its application for industrial development.

The activities of the Centre are principally directed towards increasing the export potential of the country by application of research in solving the day-to-day problems faced by Indian industry, agriculture, and trade and so increasing their productivity and competitiveness especially in foreign markets, and by undertaking activities like the establishment of an organization like the World Trade Centre, which would assist in this endeavour. In fact, the rationale for establishing the World Trade Centre as part of the Visvesvaraya Industrial Research and Development Centre is that it would, apart from directly helping the development of our trade and industry form over the years a very valuable asset, yielding year after year, large sums of money to be utilized in extending the Centre's research activities which in turn would improve the competitiveness of the country's products, small, medium, and large.

The concept of the World Trade Centre implies bringing together under one roof all the agencies, sources of imformation and business know-how connected with international trade and providing centralized facilities for the transaction of commercial deals. With this end in view, the trade centres the world over accommodate offices of governmental agencies, export promotion organizations, importers, exporters, forwarders, banks, conference rooms and hotels and restaurants as also exhibition space, showrooms, shops and consumer services. They also provide information and consultancy services to tenants and visitors. Essentially, a World Trade Centre is intended to enable a foreign businessman visiting the country to get all his transactions tied up without taking a step outside its premises. The World Trade Centre's movement is spreading rapidly and the Visvesvaraya Centre is a regular member of the parent body, the World Trade Centres Association, New York. The World Trade Centre, Bombay, is being developed by stages and the first phase, the Trade Centre Arcade, has been completed. The second phase consisting of a Commerce Centre and an Exhibition Centre is expected to be completed in next three years.

The Centre is managed by a Council of Management, consisting of prominent leaders in business and government nominees. Membership of the Centre is open to all persons and organizations interested directly or indirectly in scientific research for the development of Indian industry, agriculture, and trade.

INDEX